EIGHTEEN CENTURIES

OF THE

ORTHODOX GREEK CHURCH.

EIGHTEEN CENTURIES

OF THE

ORTHODOX GREEK CHURCH.

BY THE

REV. A. H. HORE, M.A.,

TRINITY COLLEGE, OXFORD;

AUTHOR OF "EIGHTEEN CENTURIES OF THE CHURCH IN ENGLAND,"
"HISTORY OF THE CHURCH CATHOLIC," ETC

WIPF & STOCK · Eugene, Oregon

Wipf and Stock Publishers
199 W 8th Ave, Suite 3
Eugene, OR 97401

Eighteen Centuries of the Orthodox Greek Church
By Hore, A. H.
Softcover ISBN-13: 978-1-6667-3352-5
Publication date 8/5/2021
Previously published by James Parker and Co., 1899

This edition is a scanned facsimile of the original edition published in 1899.

PREFACE.

THE present Work is an attempt to supply an acknowledged want, and to give, in a popular form, a history of the oldest Church in Christendom; the Church of the land hallowed by the sacred memories of our Saviour. To write a history of the Greek Church, says John Mason Neale, whose own valuable work was cut short, through his early death at the age of forty-six, is a difficult and a dangerous task. It seems, therefore, a presumptuous undertaking; my plea for indulgence must go for its worth; but that I am the owner of the house where Hymns Ancient and Modern, to which Dr. Neale was so valuable a contributor, saw their birth; where the first Committee meetings were held, and the chief contributors, he probably in the number, frequently met; is the excuse I plead, to be, in my humbler endeavour, his successor.

Dr. Neale might have added, that to write a history of the down-trodden Greek Church is also, in one sense, an unwelcome task; for it necessitates controversy; to me religious controversy is distasteful; and, as the lengthening shadows of the evening of life warn me that this may be the last which I shall write, I should have preferred a work of a different character. The conflicts for supremacy between Constantinople and Rome, and the arrogance and injustice of the latter were, in only a less degree than the Saracens and Ottomans, the cause of the fall of the Greek Church. The two Sees were placed by the great Œcumenical Councils on an equality; it is, therefore, necessary to point out the process and the causes, through which the downfall of the one and the victory of the other were effected. If it is shown that I have overstated my case; or if, in order to prove it, I have gone out of my way to introduce unnecessary or irrelevant matter, I shall be willing to acknowledge my error. I can only say that I have endeavoured not to do so.

My thanks for valuable assistance are due, amongst others, to the Very Reverend Eustathius Metallinos, Archimandrite, of the Greek Church at Manchester, and to my old schoolfellow, Mr. Morfill, Reader in Russian and the other Slavonic Languages at Oxford; but I must add the proviso that, for whatever of good may be found in the Book, I am indebted to my friends, whilst all errors (and I cannot but fear that there may be some) are my own.

HORKESLEY HOUSE,
   MONKLAND,
      January 1, 1899

CONTENTS.

			PAGE
INTRODUCTION		GENERAL VIEW OF THE ORTHODOX GREEK CHURCH .	1
CHAPTER	I.	THE CONFLICT BETWEEN THE FOURTH AND FIFTH EMPIRES	43
,,	II.	THE VICTORY OF CHRIST'S KINGDOM .	93
,,	III.	THE FIRST ŒCUMENICAL COUNCIL	111
,,	IV	THE STRUGGLE FOR THE HOMOOUSION .	132
,,	V.	THE SECOND ŒCUMENICAL COUNCIL .	167
,,	VI	THE THIRD AND FOURTH ŒCUMENICAL COUNCILS .	204
,,	VII	THE SEPARATIST CHURCHES OF THE EAST .	242
,,	VIII.	THE FIFTH AND SIXTH ŒCUMENICAL COUNCILS .	279
,,	IX.	THE SARACENIC CONQUESTS .	320
,,	X.	THE SEVENTH ŒCUMENICAL COUNCIL .	335
,,	XI.	THE CULMINATING SCHISM OF THE GREEK AND ROMAN CHURCHES .	364
,,	XII.	THE SCHISM WIDENED BY THE CRUSADES	408
,,	XIII.	INTRIGUES OF THE PALÆOLOGI WITH ROME, AND FALL OF CONSTANTINOPLE	442
,,	XIV	THE MAKING OF RUSSIA	486
,,	XV.	THE THREE ROMES	532
,,	XVI.	THE HOLY GOVERNING SYNOD	580
,,	XVII.	PARTIAL RECOVERY OF THE GREEK CHURCH	621
,,	XVIII.	THE GREEK CHURCH IN ITS PRESENT RELATION TO WESTERN CHRISTENDOM	659
INDEX	.	. . . .	695

INTRODUCTION.

General View of the Orthodox Greek Church.

THE Orthodox Greek or Eastern Church is the most ancient of the Christian Churches. Jerusalem was the mother-Church of Christianity; in Antioch the believers were first called Christians There is no certain proof that St. Peter was ever in Rome; there is certain proof that his mission was in Syria; and, if the words of his First Epistle (1 Pet. v. 13) are to be taken in their ordinary sense, that he proceeded as far as Babylon. St. Paul was a native of Tarsus in Cilicia. From the East the Gospel was brought into the West; the Church of Rome is a Greek Church; "a colony," says Dean Stanley, "of Greek Christians and Grecized Jews."

The original language of the Church, not only in the East but also in the West, was Greek. Of the Churches of the West, says Dean Milman, "the language was Greek, their organization Greek, their writers Greek, their Scriptures Greek, and many traditions show that their Liturgy was Greek."

The old Hebrew language became extinct during the Babylonian and Persian conquests, or was supplanted by the Chaldaic and Aramaic dialects. After the conquests of Alexander the Great, Greek became the prevalent language of Egypt and Syria, and for the sake of the Jews in his new colony of Alexandria, who had lost their own language and spoke Greek, the Scriptures were translated into the Greek language, and the translation, known as the Septuagint, had its place in the famous library of the Ptolemies. To quote Dean Stanley once more—" The humblest peasant who reads his Septuagint and New

Testament on the hills of Bœotia may proudly feel that he has an access to the original oracles of divine truth which Pope or Cardinal reaches by a barbarous and imperfect translation."

Rome, B.C. 148, subdued Macedon, and Greece became a Roman province under the name of Achaia. But Greece moulded the minds of its conquerors, and though the lands became politically Roman, they remained intellectually and socially Greek, and Greek was the language of the civilized world at the time of our Saviour's coming, those who spoke another language being called barbarians [a]. Greek, says Kurtz, was like a temporary suspension of the confusion of tongues (Gen. xi.) which had accompanied the rise of heathendom. And as Greek accompanied the rise, so was it the language of the growth, of Christianity. The earliest Fathers came from the East, and, with the exception of Tertullian (he too a native of Carthage), wrote in Greek. The earliest principal writers of Ecclesiastical history were Greeks; Eusebius, Socrates, Sozomen, Theodoret, Evagrius. All the Œcumenical Councils were held in the East, and their decrees and canons and the Nicene Creed were written in Greek. A Synod of the Greek Church, that of Laodicea, A.D. 367, determined the Canon of Scripture, and so "made the Bible."

Thus Greek Christianity is the parent of Latin Christianity, and the Churches of Rome and England are really, in the present divided state of Christendom, separated limbs of the Greek Church. To the Greek Church the Armenians, Transylvanians, Slavonians including the Bulgarians and Russians, and many other, once heathen, nations, owe their conversion. Uninterrupted successions of Metropolitans and Bishops of the Greek Church stretch themselves back to Apostolic times; venerable Liturgies exhibit doctrines unchanged and discipline uncorrupted. The same Eucharist is offered now, the same hymns are chanted by the Eastern

---

[a] Hence the Greek words. Church, Bishop, Priest, Deacon, Ecclesiastic, Paraclete, Epiphany, Liturgy, Litany, Hermit, Monk, &c.

General View of the Orthodox Greek Church.

Christians of to-day, as those of the Churches of SS. Athanasius, Basil, and Chrysostom. Fixing her Patriarchal thrones in the city of Antioch, where the disciples were first called Christians; in Jerusalem, where James the brother of our Lord was the first Bishop; in Alexandria, where St. Mark founded the Episcopate; in Constantinople, where the victory of Christianity was consummated; in the splendour of Byzantine glory; through the tempests of the Oriental Middle Ages; in the desolation and tyranny of the Turkish Empire; she is now, as she was at the beginning, immutable in faith, or, as she delights to call herself, One, Holy, Catholic and Apostolic [b].

Until the Fourth Century, and the foundation of Constantinople, Christianity continued to be, both in the East and West, a Greek religion. But after Constantine settled his capital in the old Greek City of Byzantium, whilst Greek Christianity continued to be the religion of the East, Latin by degrees supplanted it at Rome, and part of the Church services began to be said or sung there, and gradually in other parts of the West, in Latin. But it was not till the Pontificate of Pope Damasus (366—384) and the Translation, at his bidding, of the Vulgate edition of the Bible by St. Jerome, that the Roman Church became completely Latinized and turned from a Greek into a Latin Church. Not long afterwards we find a Pope, Cœlestine I. (422—432), excusing to Nestorius, Patriarch of Constantinople, his delay in answering a Letter, on the ground that he could not find any one able to translate it from Greek into Latin. And it is well known that Pope Gregory the Great (590—604), the first Pope to whom the title of Theologian can be applied, was completely ignorant of the Greek Language.

If one Church therefore more than another has a right to impose its language on Christendom, it is the Greek Church, for Greek is the language of the Septuagint, of the New Testament, and of the early Church.

[b] Neale's Introduction to the Holy Eastern Church.

In the earliest days of the Christian Church, the ecclesiastical divisions corresponded with the civil arrangement of the Roman Empire, of which Rome was at that time the capital. Consequently Alexandria and Antioch were the Metropolitan Sees of the Eastern, as Rome was of the Western, Church. Egypt had for its Metropolitan the Bishop of Alexandria, whose See extended over the whole of Africa, except that part which belonged to the European Præfecture, and acknowledged the supremacy of the Roman See; but that also was afterwards transferred to the Eastern part of the Empire, and consequently to the See of Alexandria. Jerusalem was dependent on the See of Cæsarea, Byzantium on that of Heraclea.

Subsequently to the foundation of Constantinople, but at what exact date is uncertain, Rome, Constantinople, Alexandria and Antioch were raised to the dignity of Patriarchal Sees, the four Patriarchates corresponding with the four Prætorian Prefectures created by Constantine. An ecclesiastical ascendency over the Churches of the East, which was afterwards confirmed by the Councils, was accorded to Constantinople, the New Rome as it was called, on the same ground that it had been accorded to the Old Rome, viz., that it was the seat of the Imperial government. By the Council of Chalcedon, Jerusalem was raised into a Fifth Patriarchate Contests for superiority soon arose between the Patriarchs of Old and New Rome. But the circumstances between East and West were widely different, and the contest was an unequal one. New Rome, being the See of the Imperial residence, was from the first hampered by the despotic interference of the Emperors, whilst at the same time it enjoyed only a barren precedence over the three other Eastern Patriarchates. The See of Old Rome on the contrary was the only Patriarchate in the West; and, being situated at a convenient distance from the civil government, enjoyed freedom of action; whilst to a certain extent it succeeded to the dignity vacated at Rome by the transference of the Imperial throne to

Constantinople. And, although after the suppression of the Western Empire it was subject to a Gothic King at Ravenna, acting under an Emperor resident at Constantinople, yet both Emperor and King resided at too great a distance to exact obedience, and the Popes of Rome became generally mere nominal subjects. Thus the Popes gradually acquired notions of temporal as well as of spiritual dominion; they put forth claims which it was impossible they could have done, had there been an Emperor or King resident in Rome; and those claims went on increasing, till in time the Popes magnified the Primacy, which they had originally enjoyed as Bishops of the Imperial city, into a divine authority handed down by St Peter, who, there is some reason for believing, may have been bishop of Antioch, but who was certainly never bishop of, if indeed he ever went to, Rome.

It was impossible for the Patriarchs of Constantinople, though recognized as the œcumenical Patriarchs by the Emperors, to assume the same power in the East as the Patriarchs of Rome did in the West, or to play the same conspicuous part in the world's history. Rome, freed from restraint, was able to become, in the Middle Ages, the barrier against the wickedness and injustice of Emperors and Kings, and the Christian world owes to the Church of Rome a deep debt of gratitude. But, instead of the gentle spirit of the Gospel, the Heads of the Latin Church resorted to carnal weapons, and to the abuse of the fearful engine of *excommunication,* the foulest contrivance since the creation of the world, whereby a minister of Christ claimed the power and right to deprive of the means of Grace, not only the guilty but innocent souls for whom Christ died From such a temptation the Heads of the Greek Church were, through local circumstances, free, and any defect, if defect there was, had its corresponding advantage, for the same circumstances which prevented them from rising to such a height of grandeur as that to which the Popes of Rome attained, secured them against falling into the abyss of moral degradation which often, especially in the Tenth Century, overwhelmed their Western brothers.

* * * * * * * *

For long ages past the existence of the Greek Church has been one continued martyrdom, and under the grinding oppression of its successive conquerors, Arabs, Mongols, Turks, it has indeed fallen low. Yet at the time when Constantinople was overwhelmed by the Crusaders and the Latin kingdom established, the Patriarchs of Constantinople and Rome were well-nigh on an equality. From that time the fate of Constantinople was certain. It was the Fourth Crusade and the action of Pope Innocent III. that led to its sacking by the Turks in 1453, the destruction of the Eastern Empire, and the downfall of the Greek Church. And since the days of Mahomet II., not the Turks alone, but, shame to say, Western Christendom also, have been its persistent enemies.

The existence of the Greek Church to the present day is alone a proof of its divine origin. The wonder is, not that it should have fallen so low, but that, afflicted on every side, oppressed by schism from within and cruel persecution from without, it should so nobly have struggled on; many of its members no doubt succumbed in the unequal contest; but the way in which the Orthodox Church has weathered the storm and adhered to its faith and Liturgy is little short of a miracle. "The Greek rite," says the Rev. W. Palmer[c], who afterwards joined the Church of Rome, "is like a plant which though covered with dust, and somewhat shrunk, has preserved its original shape and proportions, whereas the Latin is so changed that it is like a new building constructed in part out of the ruins of the old." "The Holy and Orthodox Eastern Church glories in the Lord over the long and terrible persecutions and conflicts of martyrdom; the Heavenly Bridegroom having pitied and loved, did not deprive it of the bright mystic candlestick and of all the

[c] Dissertations on the Orthodox Communion.

perfect and unsullied treasure of the Apostolic and God-delivered faith [d]."

The conversion of Russia by the Greek Church is the mightiest conquest the Christian Church has ever made since the time of the Apostles, and the future of that Church is a problem which it would be difficult to solve. Now that the dissolution of the Ottoman Empire in Europe, or at any rate the end of its tyranny over the Christians, is only a matter of time, will the Third Rome inherit the succession of the Second Rome on the Bosphorus? And what are to be the relations of the Church of England to that of Russia, and to the Greek Church generally? There are many points of contact; a national Church, an open Bible, the recognition of the principle of the vernacular language in the Church services [e], an unmutilated Eucharist, a married clergy, the acknowledgment of Christ as the alone Head of the Church; these points create a chord of sympathy between the Greek and English Churches. British Orders were probably derived from France, and French Orders from Smyrna, where Polycarp, the disciple of St. John, was Bishop; so that the Church of Britain was founded when the Church of Rome was still a Greek Church; and whatever debt of gratitude England owes to SS. Gregory and Augustine, it owes a more ancient and important one to the Greek Church.

The Orthodox Greek Church was, as before stated, in early time under the Four Patriarchs, of Constantinople, Alexandria, Antioch, and Jerusalem. In the Sixteenth Century a new Patriarchate, that of Moscow, was constituted for Russia, to complete the number of five Patriarchates, in the place of "Old Rome which had fallen

---

[d] Letter of the Patriarch of Constantinople to the Archbishop of Canterbury in 1870.

[e] Mr. Birkbeck, in a Lecture at Brighton on February 10, 1898, instances a tribe in Siberia possessing a language of only two hundred words, who in order that the services might be performed in their own language had to be educated before the Lord's Prayer could be fully translated

away," but it was supplanted in the reign of Peter the Great by the "*Holy Governing Synod of All the Russias.*" In 1833 the *Sacred Synod of the Church of Greece*, in imitation of the Holy Synod of Russia, was established for the Kingdom of Greece, as soon as it gained its independence; within his own Patriarchate, each Patriarch, and in Russia and Greece their Synods, which have Patriarchal rank, have full jurisdiction. There are also other independent Orthodox Greek Churches, three in Austro-Hungary, and those of Cyprus, Georgia, Servia, Montenegro, and Roumania. But all branches of the Orthodox Church own, theoretically, the supremacy of the Patriarch of Constantinople, as the Anglican Church throughout the world owns that of the Archbishop of Canterbury, and the Roman Church that of the Pope of Rome.

Besides the Orthodox Church there are several separate Greek Communities, under their own Patriarchs, of which mention will be made in a future chapter. They are in reality national churches which co-exist with, and sometimes have supplanted, the Orthodox Church; but they are, some of them heretical, and, so far as they are out of communion with the Orthodox Church, all of them schismatical.

As the higher clergy are forbidden, and the lower clergy are almost always, and at one time were even obliged, to be married men, the Bishops are taken from the monasteries, the superiors of which are styled Archimandrites (μάνδρα, a fold), and Hegumens (ἡγουμένοι), the monasteries following the Rule of St. Basil. The lower clergy are of two classes, the Regular, who live in monasteries, and the Secular, or Parish Priests; or, as the two classes are called in Russia, the Black and White Clergy. The monastic clergy are styled Kaloirs (καλογέροι), a title originally given, as the name implies, to *old men*, but now to all alike. The Clergy are not allowed to marry after they have taken Priest's Orders, and on the death of their wives may return into a monastery and are then eligible for Bishoprics. In Russia the Parish Priests are styled Popes, chief amongst whom are the Protopopes.

The time of the Parish Priests is so taken up in the daily routine of the services, and in mastering the interminable length of the Office-books, that they have little or no time to devote to study. The Office-books are contained in twenty folio volumes, in a language, vernacular indeed, but generally out of date, scarcely understood at all by the people, and little more by the clergy; besides an extra folio directing how they are to be used, and the manner in which the services are to be performed. There are different services for every day and for different parts of the day.

The services being said in Russia in the Old Slavic language, and in other countries in an idiom equally unintelligible, the people are not expected to take part in them. Their great length, sometimes extending to five hours, obliges the Priest to hurry over them in a manner which to our Western feelings seems scarcely reverent; and their length explains the great predominance in Russian congregations of the stronger over the weaker sex, women not being ordinarily able to endure the fatigue which they entail. Reverence for their office and an implicit confidence in their Priests is almost an article of faith, and the people are contented with the belief that they are praying for them.

Nearly every day in the week has its appropriate Saint, sometimes more than one, and on the observance of those days the people lay great stress. Sunday they call the Lord's Day (ἡ Κυριακή); the five following days they name numerically; Saturday, besides the Seventh Day, they style the Sabbath (σάββατον), and on that day, except in Holy Week, they consider it unlawful to fast.

The Fasts are very numerous (226 days out of the 365 in the year), and very rigorously observed, not only meat but nearly every kind of fish, as well as eggs, cheese, butter, and milk, being prohibited. Besides the Western Lent, there are three other Lents ; one lasting from Whitsuntide to St. Peter's Day, a second, for *the dormition of the Virgin* (κοίμησις τῆς παναγίας), (August 1 to August 15), a third, corresponding with our Advent, during the 40 days before Christmas. In monasteries another Fast is observed during the first fourteen days of September, to commemorate the Exaltation (ὕψωσις) of the Holy Cross. To compensate for the rigorous observance of these Fasts, an opposite license, which the Priests too often connive at, is practised on their Festivals.

The Greek Church bases its belief (1) on Holy Scripture ; (2) On the Nicene, or Constantinopolitan, Creed ; (3) On Seven Œcumenical Councils , (4) On Seven Mysteries or Sacraments. Beyond the Creed, no authoritative exposition of faith was promulgated till the XVIth Century, the *Treatise on the Orthodox Faith*[f] of St. John Damascene being considered a sufficient guide. The Greek Church holds that the writings of the Fathers are of great use, and to be consulted, but all doctrine must be brought to the test of the Bible. "Neither the writings of the Holy Fathers nor the traditions of the Church are to be confounded or equalled with the Word of God and His commandments, for the Word of God is one thing, but the writings of the Holy Fathers and Traditions ecclesiastical are another [g]."

"As regards the questions of doctrinal authority generally," writes Mr. Blackmore [h], "the members of the Eastern Church are neither bound in conscience, on the one hand, to every word of any modern documents, nor left free, on the other hand, to indulge in an unlimited license of criticism. Beyond the Creed itself, the Eastern Church has no general doctrinal tests .... no XXXIX Articles, like that subscribed in England."

The principal authoritative standards are the following :—

(1) The *Answers of the Patriarch Jeremias*, in 1576, to the Letters of the Wittenberg Divines, who wished to

---

[f] Ἔκδοσις ἀκριβὴς τῆς Ὀρθοδόξου Πίστεως.
[g] Duty of Parish Priests   [h] Doctrine of the Russian Church

General View of the Orthodox Greek Church. 11

strengthen the Lutheran cause by an alliance with the Eastern Church; this document was afterwards approved by the Council of Jassy, A.D. 1642, under Parthenius, Patriarch of Constantinople, and that of Bethlehem, A.D. 1672, under Dositheus, Patriarch of Jerusalem; and is entirely free from Latinism.

Between this and the two next expositions, says Mr. Smith, a Fellow of Magdalen College, Oxford, who was Chaplain at Constantinople in the latter part of the XVIIth Century[1], there is so great a difference "as shows the subtle designs of Rome, which took advantage of its poverty and distress to bring the Greek Church to a compliance with its doctrines in order to bring it into subjection." The two expositions to which he alludes are the *Confession of Peter Mogila*, and the *XVIII Articles of the Synod of Bethlehem*. "The success of Roman intrigues in the East may," says Mr. Masson[k], "be estimated from the fact that of the Greek Ecclesiastics who from the fall of the Eastern Empire to the beginning of the XVIIth Century (a space of 150 years) successively filled the Patriarchal throne of Constantinople, thirteen were the tools of Rome. The fate of the Patriarch Cyril Lucar is well known; from his firm resistance to papal domination he was for many years unremittingly persecuted by the agents of Rome, who at last accomplished his murder in 1638."

(2) The *Orthodox Confession of Faith* was the work of Peter Mogila, Metropolitan of Kiev in the Ukraine (1632—1647). It was written at a time when the Church of Western Russia was infected not only with Roman but Calvinistic doctrines, with both of which Mogila himself became unconsciously tainted. It was submitted to the Council of Jassy of 1642, which found in it *many strange and unorthodox doctrines*. After alterations made in the Council, and having been translated from Russian into Greek by Meletius Syriga, Exarch of the Patriarch of Constantinople, it was approved and confirmed by the four Eastern Patriarchs, and put forth

---
[1] Account of the Greek Church   [k] Apology for Greek Church, p 87

in 1662 (fifteen years after the death of Mogila), prefaced by a Letter from Nectarius, Patriarch of Jerusalem, as "*The Orthodox Confession of the Faith of the Catholic and Apostolic Church of the East*" It is in the form of Question and Answer, and consists of three parts; Faith, Hope, and Charity. It was approved in 1696 by Adrian, the last Patriarch of Moscow, and was acknowledged in the Spiritual Regulation of the Russian Church of 1720, and " all Russian theologians have rested very much on this book [1]."

(3) The next exposition is *The XVIII Articles of the Synod of Bethlehem* of 1672, which is a counter Confession to the "*Confession*" attributed to Cyril Lucar, the latter of which was of a decidedly Calvinistic character. They seem to have been for the first time communicated to the Russian Church in 1721 by the Eastern Patriarchs, to be sent on to England as their ultimatum to the Non-juring Bishops [m] who were seeking Communion with the Greek Church. Of these XVIII Articles, XVII., which treats of Transubstantiation, and XVIII., on Prayers for the Dead, have a strong tinge of Latinism, and in many points are modified in the Russian translation authorized in 1838

(4) Another exposition is *The Orthodox Doctrine* of Plato, Metropolitan of Moscow, which appeared in 1772 with the same threefold division as the *Orthodox Confession* of Mogila; but it never received Synodical authority. It is however an authorized text-book in the Greek Church, and, says Mr. Pinkerton, "has been introduced into almost every place of religious instruction in Russia." "The *Orthodox Doctrine*" is "scriptural and evangelical to a degree that must astonish those who are accustomed to regard the Eastern Church as in her standards and tendency merely on a level with the Western [n]."

(5) *The Longer* and *Shorter Catechisms* of the Russian Church are the work of Philaret, Metropolitan of Moscow. The former received the sanction, although not synodically,

---

[1] Blackmore's Russian Church, XXV.   [m] See Chap. XVI.
[n] Masson's Apology

of the Patriarchs, and, says Dr. Neale, makes good its title, "*A Full Catechism of the Orthodox Catholic Church of the East.*" Both Catechisms were in 1838 promulgated by the Holy Governing Synod, as "the Catechism of the Church herself," and have since then been in use in all the Churches and Schools of Russia.

(6) The last authoritative work is "*The Treatise on the Duty of Parish Priests,*" the work in 1776 of George Konissky, Bishop of Mogilev, with the assistance of Parthenius Sopkovsky, Bishop of Smolensk, which " has been adopted by the whole Russian Church (and even beyond its limit wherever the Slavic language is understood °);" and all candidates for Holy Orders are expected to be acquainted with its contents.

As to the structure and ornaments of the Churches. In the miserable state of oppression to which the Greek Christians have so long been subjected, it cannot be expected that in their sacred buildings splendour or anything that deserves the name of architecture can ordinarily be found ; in fact till recently, their churches were for the most part mean and ill-furnished, often almost subterraneous, as a necessary precaution against the avarice and rapacity of the Turks. " I have seen churches," says Sir Paul Ricaut, for some time at the end of XVIIth century Consul at Smyrna, " which are more like caverns or sepulchres than places set apart for divine worship, the top thereof being scarcely level with the ground . . . . . for fear that they should be suspected, if they raised them to any considerable height, of an evil intention to rival the Turkish mosques." But in this respect a better state of things has set in since the last century ; decent Churches have been erected, and there is no reason to doubt that, when the Greek Church has been emancipated from its fast-vanishing thraldom, its Churches will be, if not as sumptuous, yet as well adapted to God's service, as our own in England.

Where there is any architecture at all, it is of the By-

° Blackmore.

zantine style, the Cathedral of St. Sophia at Constantinople being the general model, although in Armenia there is another style, which is termed Armenian.

A Byzantine Church may, says Dr. Neale [p], be fitly described as a gabled Greek Cross, with domes, five and sometimes even seven in number, which in Cathedrals and even in some Parish Churches are gilded, and have an imposing outward appearance. An inexperienced eye might pronounce a Greek Church to be a mosque, except that "whatever is beautiful in the mosque of the Mahometans is derived from the Christians, whatever is unsightly is their own."

On some Russian Churches the Crescent still remains under the Cross; when the Grand Duke Ivan III. delivered his country from the Tartar yoke, he left the Crescent remaining and put the Cross on it as a mark of the victory of the Orthodox Church [q].

In a Greek Church no seats (except in Cathedrals and some larger Churches the stalls (στασίδια) for the Bishops) are provided for the Clergy or people, it being considered as an act of irreverence for any one of a lower dignity than a Bishop to sit in the House of God. The congregation, following the ancient practice, stand; they do not kneel in church, and only incline their bodies in receiving the Holy Communion; but they express their reverence by prostrating themselves, even touching the ground with their foreheads; especially is this the case with the lower classes.

Orientation of the Churches is more scrupulously observed in the East than in the West, and the practice of praying towards the East is almost universal amongst them. In their Churches there is a fourfold division;—

(1) The Narthex (νάρθηξ, πρόναος), the derivation of which is uncertain, some thinking it is so called as being νέρθε (*below the nave*), forms the western end, immediately inside which is the Font (κολυμβήθρα). The Narthex was origin-

[p] Holy Eastern Church, I. 169
[q] King's Rites and Ceremonies of the Greek Church in Russia

General View of the Orthodox Greek Church 15

ally set aside for catechumens, penitents, and the possessed (ἐνεργουμένοι), but is now the part occupied by women, the former women's gallery having fallen into disuse.

(2) The Nave (ναός), so called from the symbolical significance of a ship as a figure of our salvation (Gen. vii. 23); or *Trapeza*; where, in the case of cathedrals, are the stalls, one higher than the rest for the Patriarch, the others for the Metropolitans and Bishops.

(3) The Choir (χόρος) under the Trullus or Dome.

(4) The Bema (ἅγιον βῆμα), or Altar (θυσιαστήριον).

At the entrance of the Church there is usually a Porch (προαύλιον), extending along the whole Western width.

There are several sets of gates, as to the position of which accounts are so confusing, that it is difficult to determine their position; but perhaps the following description may be given. (1) The Beautiful Gates (πύλαι ὡραῖαι, so named from the Beautiful Gate of the Temple) leading from the Porch into the Narthex; (2) The Royal gates (πύλαι βασιλικαί), or Silver gates, in imitation of the Silver gates in St. Sophia's at Constantinople, dividing the Narthex from the Nave; (3) The Holy Gates (ἅγιαι θυραί), three in number with veils before them, leading from the Choir through the Iconostasis; the middle one into the Bema, which corresponds with the Chancel of Latin Churches[r], that on the North side to the Prothesis, that on the South to the Diakonikon. In the centre of the Bema, which is raised above the other part of the Church by steps[s], is the Holy Table (Ἅγια Τράπεζα), with four columns supporting a canopy (κιβώριον). The name of Altar is not commonly applied to the Holy Table, but includes the whole space between it and the Iconostasis[t].

This last is a high screen corresponding with our Altar rails, but higher and solid, so that the congregation is prevented from seeing the Consecration of the Elements

---

[r] Hence the Clergy were sometimes called οἱ τοῦ Βήματος, Bingham, Bk. viii. Ch. vi.

[s] Schann's Euchology.   [t] King's Rites and Ceremonies, p. 27.

and the Communion of the Clergy. On it are many Icons; one of the Saviour on the North, another of the Virgin Mary on the South side, others to different Saints, one being the Patron Saint of the Church[u]. Between the Iconostasis and the Choir is the part called the *Soleas* (σωλέας). On the North of the Choir in the Church of St. Sophia at Constantinople, but frequently in other Churches on the North of the Trapeza, is the Ambon (ἀναβαίνω), a stone, raised by one, two, or three steps, where the Deacon says the Ectænias, reads the Gospel, gives out the Church notices and the diptychs, and from which the sermon, when there is one (which till lately except in Russia was rarely, but now, especially in Constantinople and Greece, is frequently, the case), is preached. Before the Iconostasis, lamps, sometimes perpetually burning, are generally hung. The Epistle is read by the Reader.

At the back of the Holy Table is a representation of the Crucifixion, before which stands a lamp with seven branches. A Pyx (ἀρτοφόριον) containing the Reserved Sacrament stands on the Holy Table, a lighted lamp being suspended before it, and on the Table lies a Book of the Gospels and a Cross. The Antiminsia, or Consecrated Corporal, is spread upon the Holy Table over the usual covering, and forms an important feature in the Celebration.

The East end of Greek Churches is generally tri-apsidal. The centre apse is the Bema (Ἅγιον Βῆμα); the northern apse the Prothesis (Πρόθεσις), the southern the Sacristy (διακονικόν, σκευοφυλάκιον, μινσατώριον), these two last are generally divided, but sometimes not, from the Bema by walls (παραβήματα). The Sacristy is the Vestry for the Clergy. There is usually only one Holy Table and one Chapel; where there are more than one, it is generally in places which have been under Latin influences, as in Russia where the Russians have been brought into contact with the Latins of Poland and Lithuania.

Greek Churches contain no stoups for holy water. The

[u] King's Rites and Ceremonies

General View of the Orthodox Greek Church. 17

Piscina (θάλασσα), now commonly called χωνευτήριον, is in the Prothesis, near the Table of Preparation ; Church Bells are forbidden by the Turks, and consequently, except in Russia and in countries not subject to Turkey, are not used. Organs and musical instruments are rigidly prohibited by their own laws, and the singing, except in Russia, where it is of a very beautiful description, is generally of an indifferent character; totally different notes are used to those which we use, but their hymns, as may be judged from the hymns which have been translated by Dr. Neale, are very pleasing and melodious.

The only Creed which the Greeks recite in their services is the Nicene or Constantinopolitan ; which being an exposition and enlargement of the Apostles' Creed accounts for the omission of the latter. The Athanasian, which is probably a Western, Creed was palmed off on them in the XIIIth Century as having been composed by St. Athanasius, the great Champion of their Faith, when he was an exile in Rome , but if they were for a time deceived, they never accepted it without the omission of the Filioque clause.

A few words may be said as to the vestments worn by the clergy. The full canonical vestments of a Bishop are :—

(1) The Sticharion or Stoicharion, signifying purity, and corresponding with the Latin *alb*. It was originally made of white linen, but now, especially in Russia, it is of the richest silk or velvet, and on the ordinary days of Lent, of a purple colour.

(2) Epitrachelion, *stole*, but differing from the Latin stole, in that it has a hole at the upper extremity for the head to pass through. It represents the easy yoke of Christ. It and the Sticharion are attached to the body by the Zone (ζώνη).

(3) Epimanikia (a word compounded of the Greek ἐπί and Latin *manus*), wristbands, signifying the bands with which our Saviour was bound. They somewhat correspond with

the Latin *maniple*, but not altogether; as they are worn on both hands, and differ from it in shape.

(4) Phælonion, *chasuble* (or Phænolion, Latin *pænula*). This is by way of excellency the *vestment*, and none of the Clergy of an inferior Order to a Priest can wear it. It signifies the purple robe which the soldiers put on Christ, and is supposed to be the vestment, translated *cloak*, which St Paul left at Troas (2 Tim. iv. 13).

(5) Omophorion, *pall*, signifying the wandering sheep whom Christ brings home on His shoulder.

(6) Saccos, *dalmatic*, signifying Christ's coat without seam, woven from top to bottom.

(7) Epigonation, *kerchief*, so called because it reaches to the knee, representing the towel wherewith our Saviour girded Himself and washed the feet of the disciples.

The sacramental vestments of the Priest are the same as the above, omitting the Omophorion, the Saccos, and the Zone. The Deacon wears only two robes, the Sticharion, and, over his left shoulder, instead of the Epitrachelion, the Orarion (perhaps from $\omega\rho a$[1]), called also $\sigma\tau o\lambda\acute{\eta}$, and which exactly corresponds to the Latin *stole*, except that the word $\ddot{a}\gamma\iota os$ is embroidered on it.

The ordinary daily dress of an ecclesiastic is a tall flat cap, and a cassock of any sober colour that he chooses, over which is thrown a loose black cloak. A beard also is a matter of obligation.

The Greek Church recognizes seven Sacraments or Mysteries. This limitation or definition of the number of Sacraments was not known to the undivided Church, but was first defined by Peter Lombard, teacher of Theology at Paris (1159—1164), and the Latin Schoolmen. Scholasticism, it must be remarked, plays absolutely no part

---

[1] So called because the officiating Clergyman thus wears it in announcing the time for prayer Mouraviev, Letters on the Ritual of the Divine Offices, derives it from *orare*, to pray. Neale, Littledale, and Bulgaris give other derivations.

General View of the Orthodox Greek Church. 19

in the history of the Eastern Church, and the authority of the Schoolmen is disregarded. Yet, contrary to the usual conservatism of the Greeks, the exact number of seven Sacraments was probably imported into the Greek from the Latin Church. The Greek word μυστήριον is more comprehensive than the Latin *Sacramentum*, and in the Greek Church it is used in a wider sense. But, like the English, the Greek Church insists that two Sacraments only are generally necessary to salvation (τὰ κυριώτερα τῶν μυστηρίων ὧν δίχα σωθῆναι ἀδύνατον).

A mystery is defined to be "a ceremony or act appointed by God in which God giveth or sanctifieth to us His grace." From *The Orthodox Doctrine* of the Russian Church we learn ; "The two chief and most eminent Mysteries in the New Testament are Baptism and the Eucharist or Communion. Of the rest the Chrism and Penance belong to every Christian, but Ordination, Marriage, and the Sanctified Oil are not binding on all."

The Seven Mysteries or Sacraments are :—

1. Baptism (τὸ Βάπτισμα), whereby a person is mysteriously born to a spiritual life.

2. Unction with Chrism (τὸ Μύρον τοῦ χρίσματος), by which he receives grace, or spiritual growth and strength.

3. The Eucharist (ἡ Εὐχαριστία), by which he is spiritually fed.

4. Penance (ἡ Μετάνοια), whereby he is healed of spiritual disease, i.e. sin.

5. Holy Orders (ἡ Ἱερωσύνη), in which he receives power to spiritually regenerate, feed and nurture others by doctrine and Sacraments.

. 6. Marriage (ὁ Γάμος), in which he receives Grace, sanctifying the married life, and the natural procuration and nurture of children.

7. Unction with Oil (τὸ Εὐχέλαιον), in which he has medicine even for bodily diseases, in that he is healed of spiritual.

We must confine ourselves to a brief description of the

Sacraments, touching mostly on such points as are peculiar to the Greek Church.

(1) Baptism in the ordinary acceptation of the word *washing*, was during the first two centuries the universal rule of the Church. To the ancient rule the Eastern Church, with its capacious Baptisteries, still adheres, whilst the Western Church allows, as a necessity arising from climate, affusion, but it does not disallow immersion. Trine immersion is held by the Greeks to be of equal importance with the water in Baptism, it being the custom prevailing from the earliest ages, in order to signify the distinction of the Three Persons in the Trinity[y]. The Arian Eunomius[z] was the first to introduce single immersion into the Eastern Church.

The custom of rebaptizing converts from the Western Church, Roman Catholics not excepted, has only been abandoned by the Patriarch of Constantinople within the last 25 years. The Russian was the first of the Greek Churches to break through this long standing rule; in order to receive Western Christians without re-baptizing them, they in 1718 consulted Jeremias III., the Patriarch of Constantinople, who gave his consent. By the *Longer Catechism*, Baptism cannot be repeated, for "as a child is born but once, there can only be one spiritual birth." If a nurse or any other lay person of either sex, in the absence of a Priest or in case of necessity (εἰs καιρὸν τινὸs ἀνάγκηs), baptize an infant, the Priest, if it recovers, gives the Sacrament of Unction with Chrism. The *Duty of Parish Priests* says, "there are some ignorant persons who would re-baptize Romans as well as Lutherans and Calvinists when they come over to the Eastern Church. . . . But the Seventh Canon of the Second Œcumenical Council . . . . forbids to re-baptize not only such as are Romans

---

[y] For precisely the opposite reason single immersion was introduced into Spain by the Fourth Council of Toledo, A.D 633, against the Arians, who practised trine immersion to signify the different degrees in the Trinity.

[z] See Chap IV

Lutherans, and Calvinists (who all clearly confess the Holy Trinity, and admit the work of our salvation accomplished by the Incarnation of the Son of God), but even the Arians themselves and the Macedonians and Pneumatomachi and other heretics . . . . and orders that they should only be made to renounce and anathematize their own and all other heresies, and to be received by Unction with the Holy Chrism." Notwithstanding this, many Russians in the present day hold that Baptism performed by heretics is invalid.

Baptism is valid, so long as the proper form (*in the name of the Trinity*) and matter (*water*) are observed. The Sacrament may be performed either in a Church or in a house, but clinical Baptism, unless afterwards completed, is a bar to Holy Orders.

On the day of the birth of a child, or the day after, the Priest goes to the house, and uses a form of prayer for the mother and the child. On the eighth day the child (according to the strict rule) is taken to Church to receive a name, in accordance with Christ's receiving a Name on that day, but the rule, though frequently, is not generally observed. Forty days after the birth the mother goes with the child and sponsors to be churched in imitation of the Purification of the Virgin and Christ's Presentation in the Temple. It was at that time the infant was formerly baptized, but now Baptism, which takes the place of Circumcision, is generally performed on the eighth day [a].

At the entrance of the Church stands the font, which the Priest incenses for the Baptism. First takes place the Exorcism, or driving away the evil spirit with which an unbaptized person is supposed to be infected, and it is held to be in accordance with Christ's words, " In My name they shall cast out devils." The Priest having made the child a Catechumen by the Exorcism, turns it, as held by the nurse, towards the West (the region of darkness and sin),

[a] Georgia was an exception, where children were not brought to Church to be baptized till their eighth year, but this there is reason to believe is changed.

and blows three times (upon the mouth, the breast, and the forehead), with the thrice-repeated prayer that "every unclean thing hidden and lurking in the heart" may be driven out. The child is first anointed with oil blessed by the Priest, and then signed with the sign of the Cross, as a seal of divine Grace.

Next follows the Baptism proper. The child having been anointed is immersed three times, the first in the Name of the Father, the second in that of the Son, the third in that of the Holy Ghost, the Priest saying after each immersion, *Amen*. The form of the words used in Baptism differs from that of the Western Church, being instead of "I baptize thee," &c., "Such an one is baptized," a form which Romanists cavil at, because the person of the Priest is not brought into prominence. The child is then washed with a sponge, moistened with water; after which the Priest says, "Thou hast been baptized, enlightened, anointed, sanctified, washed, in the name of the Father, and of the Son, and of the Holy Ghost; now and for ever, even unto ages of ages. Amen [b]." The service concludes with the tonsure, or cutting off the hair, a practice which is ordered by the rubric to be done crosswise [c].

In the present day, says King, the prayer for the mother's delivery and the giving a name to the child are joined together and used the day of the birth or the day after; and if the Baptism is performed in Church, the Presentation is commonly added at the end of the tonsure.

(2) Unction with Chrism corresponds with and takes the place of Confirmation in the Western Church, confirming the Grace given in Baptism; but unlike Confirmation is conferred by a Priest, with ointment consecrated by the Patriarch or Bishop on the Thursday in Holy Week. In Russia it can only be consecrated in Moscow for Great, and in Kiev for Little, Russia. In the early Church laying on

---

[b] Smith's Account.

[c] This ceremony is perhaps in reference to that at Cenchræa (Acts xviii. 18) to signify that the new Christian is, like St. Paul, under a vow.

of hands immediately followed Baptism, whilst in the Latin Church, Baptism and Confirmation are now dissociated. In the Greek Church the Sacrament of Unction with Chrism follows immediately after Baptism, and is conferred without imposition of hands. "It is certain," says *the Longer Catechism*, "that the Apostles, for imparting to Baptism the gift of the Holy Ghost, used imposition of hands, but it may be supposed that the words of St. John refer to a visible as well as an inward Unction. The successors of the Apostles therefore introduced Unction with Chrism, drawing perhaps their precedent from the unction used in the Old Testament." It is grounded on 1 John ii. 20, "Ye have an unction from the Holy Ghost," and on 2 Cor. i. 21, 22, "he which stablisheth us with you in Christ and hath anointed us is God, who hath also sealed us;" whence the Sacrament is called "the Seal of the Holy Ghost[d]."

The baptized person is anointed with the sign, made with ointment, of the Cross, severally on the different parts of the body[e]—on the forehead, to signify the sanctification of the mind; on the chest, that of the heart; on the eyes, ears, and lips, that of the senses; on the hands and feet, of the works and whole walk of the Christian; at each sign of the Cross, the words σφράγις δωρεᾶς Πνεύματος Ἁγίου, Ἀμήν being repeated.

This sacrament is always administered on the admission of a Christian convert, and is not repeated except in the case of heretics and apostates on their re-admission into the Church. The only exception in the present day is with regard to the Tsar, who, like the Eastern Emperors in former times, is anointed for a second time at his coronation, which generally takes place in the Cathedral of the Assumption at Moscow. Immediately after the Communion of the Clergy, the Holy Gates are opened, the Tsar descending from his throne, proceeds to them, and after

---

[d] σφράγις δωρεᾶς Πνεύματος Ἁγίου.

[e] This is ordered to be done in the reception of heretics by the 7th Canon of the First Council of Constantinople.

being anointed by the Metropolitan, he is conducted to the Holy Table, where he receives the Eucharist in both Kinds separately, as no longer an ordinary layman, but the Lord's Anointed and temporal Head on earth of the Russian Church [f].

(3) The Eucharist. This Sacrament the Greeks sometimes call (as well as by its usual title, Εὐχαριστία) Εὐλογία, in reference to 1 Cor. x. 16, "the cup of blessing" (τὸ ποτήριον τῆς εὐλογίας). They also call it σύναξις or *union*, the Sacrament, that is, by which we are made one with Christ. Sometimes the Sacrament itself is called Liturgy (λειτουργία), but that word is generally applied to the Service. The matter of the Eucharist is leavened bread (ἄρτος, *raised*), for which the best wheaten flour is required, i.e. bread not impregnated with any foreign substance such as yeast. Communion in both Kinds is the express command and practice of the Orthodox Church, in accordance with the command of Christ, the practice of the Apostles, the Institution of the Sacrament as narrated by St. Paul, and the universal custom, previously to the separation, of both the Eastern and Western Churches. On June 14th, 1415, at the Council of Constance, the uncatholic decree was passed, ordering that the Eucharist should be administered to the laity in one Kind only, that of Bread. It was a time when there was an interregnum in the Papacy, Pope John XXIII. having been deposed in May, and his successor, Martin V., not appointed until November. The practice, which originated in the truism "Totus Christus sub utrâque specie," was adopted in the Western Church from a feeling of reverence, lest any of the consecrated Wine should be spilt; a similar feeling of reverence in the Greek Church shows itself in the mode of administering the Bread soaked in the Wine [g]. This latter precautionary expedient was recognized at the Council of Clermont-by

---

[f] Romanov's Sketches of the Rise and Customs of the Græco-Russian Church.

[g] "It should be most carefully guarded," says St. Cyril, "lest a crumb fall of that which is more precious than gold or precious stones."

Pope Urban II., who ordered it to be so administered to the sick, and in other cases of necessity, lest any of the Wine should be spilt. But the withholding of the Cup from the Laity was opposed to the strongest declaration of the Popes themselves. Pope Gelasius declared that the Sacrament should be either received in its entirety or not at all, and that the separation could not be effected without great sacrilege [h]. Leo the Great declared Communion in One Kind to be a Manichæan heresy, and a sacrilegious deceit, and those who practised it to be expelled from the fellowship of the saints [i]. In the famous Council of Clermont, A.D. 1095, under Pope Urban II., one of the Canons enacted that no one should communicate unless he received the Body and Blood of Christ separately and alike. The English Church at the Reformation returned to the Catholic practice; but the Roman Church in the Council of Trent confirmed the innovation, and it remains in the present day one of the great differences between the Roman and Eastern Churches.

The Roman Church uses unleavened bread (whence Romanists are called by the Greeks Azymites ('Αζυμῖται), and this is another of the principal causes of the schism between the two Churches. Says the *Orthodox Confession*: " What answer will the superstitious Pope be able to give at the dreadful day of Judgement, for having, in evident opposition to the Lord, taken away the Cup of Communion from the common people and for giving them the Communion only in unleavened wafers [j] ? "

The service in which the Eucharist is celebrated, which in the Latin Church is called Mass, is called in the Greek Church Liturgy (λειτουργία), and the celebrant (λειτουργός). The Liturgy ascribed to St. James is used in Jerusalem on the festival of that Saint. With that exception the Litur-

[h] Divisio unius ejusdemque mysterii sine grandi sacrilegio non potest provenire.
Notati et prohibiti a sanctorum societate, sacerdotali auctoritate pellantur.
The English Rubric directs, "*It shall suffice* that it (i.e. the bread) be such as is usual to be eaten, but the best and purest wheat bread that may conveniently be gotten."

gical offices of the Orthodox Church are three in number, those of SS. Basil, Chrysostom, and Gregory Dialogus (the Great), to the last of whom the Liturgy of the Pre-sanctified (ἡ λειτουργία τῶν προηγιασμένων) is generally ascribed [k]; all other Liturgies the Orthodox Church rejects as spurious [l]. The Liturgy of St James, though ascribed to the first Bishop of Jerusalem, is probably so called because it represents his teaching; its actual date being somewhere about A.D. 200. Dr. Neale describes St. Basil's Liturgy as "a recast of that of St. James," and St. Chrysostom's as "an abbreviation" and new edition of St. Basil's.

The Liturgy of St. Chrysostom is that in ordinary daily use; that of St. Basil is used on all the Sundays of the Great Lent, except Palm Sunday; on Holy Thursday and Holy Saturday, on the Vigils of Christmas Day and the Epiphany, and on St. Basil's Day. The Liturgy of the Pre-sanctified is that in general use during the Great Lent, except on Saturdays and Sundays and the Feast of the Annunciation, which are exempt from fasting; it is celebrated with the elements (hence called *Pre-sanctified*) consecrated on the preceding Sunday, the Priest communicating and exhibiting to the people, who may also communicate [m], the previously consecrated elements.

In the Liturgical office there is generally at least one Deacon attendant on the Priest. We will confine ourselves to the Liturgy of St. Chrysostom, that being the one most frequently in use. It consists of two parts, the Pro-Anaphora, corresponding with the Missa Catechuminorum, and the Anaphora with the Missa Fidelium, of the Western Church. It is preceded by a preparatory service, which is pre-eminently called the Oblation [n]. This service com-

---

[k] It is by some, however, attributed to Germanus, Patriarch of Constantinople.

[l] When a Liturgy is called by the name of any Father, all that is implied is that he made some alteration and improvements in the Liturgy which he found existing in the Church in his time.—Dict. of Christian Biog., under Chrysostom.

[m] This statement is from the highest authority, made to the Writer.

[n] Bulgaris' Catechism

General View of the Orthodox Greek Church. 27

mences with the προσκομιδή (προσκομίζω), the bringing in to the Prothesis by the Priest and Deacon of the Prosphers (προσφέρω), or Offerings (so called from the ancient custom of the people to bring to the church their offerings of bread and wine), from which the bread and wine for the Eucharist are taken. The Priest and Deacon entering the holy Bema say, "I will enter into Thine House;" robe themselves in the sacred vestments; go to the Χωνευτήριον, and washing their hands say, "I will wash my hands in innocency, and so will I go to thine Altar;" after this they go to the Prothesis; and the preparatory service commences.

The Prosphers, besides the wine, consist of five loaves, in allusion to the five loaves with which our Saviour fed the 5,000. They must be made, as has been before said, of the purest wheat flour, and leavened, and are round, and in shape like our cottage loaves. From the top part of one Prospher the Priest cuts a square piece bearing the fourfold inscription $IΣ \parallel XΣ \parallel NI \parallel KA$, or in Russian, $IC \parallel XC \parallel NI \parallel KA$ ('Ιησοῦs Χριστὸς νικᾷ). This is called the Seal. Into one part of the Seal he thrusts a lance (ἁγία λόγχη), saying, "He was led as a lamb to the slaughter;" into a second, saying, "and as a sheep before her shearers, so he shall not open (οὐκ ἀνοίξει) his mouth;" into a third, "in his humiliation, his judgment (ἡ κρίσις αὐτοῦ) was taken away;" into a fourth, "but who shall declare His generation." He then elevates the Seal, saying, "for His life is taken from the earth," and places it on the Paten (δίσκος), with the words, "The Lamb of God which taketh away the sin of the world, and on behalf of the sin of the world," and thrusts into it the Lance, saying, "And one of the soldiers pierced His side with a lance, and straightway there issued forth blood and water." This is the "Ἅγιος Ἀμνός (Holy Lamb), and is the part for Consecration.

The Deacon mixes wine and water in the Chalice which the Priest blesses; the practice of mixing water with wine (κρᾶμα) was universal in the early Church. Particles are then in like manner cut from the first and the four other

Prosphers, and placed with the Holy Lamb on the Paten. One portion is in honour of the Virgin Mary; another in honour of St. John the Baptist, the Prophets, Apostles, Martyrs and Saints; another commemorates living members of the Church, whose names are designated; another is in remembrance, as well as for the remission of sins, of certain deceased members whose names are also designated[o]. The Priest then censes the various ornaments in the Prothesis. The Holy Lamb alone is for consecration; the remainder of the Prosphers form the Antidoron[p], which corresponds to the Panis benedictus (*pain benit*) of the Latin Church.

There are three Oblations[q], the first being that at the Service of the Prothesis. The Paten is covered with a veil, usually of linen or silk, beneath it being placed a bent Cross, termed the Asterisk ($\dot{a}\sigma\tau\epsilon\rho\iota\sigma\kappa o\varsigma$), to prevent it falling on the Bread, the Priest saying the words, "And the star came and stood over where the young child was." The Chalice is covered with another veil, whilst a third veil called the Aer ($\dot{a}\eta\rho$) covers both together. The Bread and Wine are blessed with a solemn prayer ($\dot{\eta}$ $\epsilon\dot{v}\chi\dot{\eta}$ $\tau\hat{\eta}\varsigma$ $\pi\rho o\theta\acute{\epsilon}\sigma\epsilon\omega\varsigma$). The Paten and Chalice are then left in the Prothesis. The second Oblation is when they are taken from the Prothesis to the Holy Table; the third and solemn Oblation is made at the Prayer of Consecration.

After the service of the Prothesis is ended, the Proanaphora commences. There are two entrances, the Little ($\dot{\eta}$ $\pi\rho\acute{\omega}\tau\eta$ $\kappa a\grave{\iota}$ $\mu\iota\kappa\rho\grave{a}$ $\epsilon\ddot{\iota}\sigma o\delta o\varsigma$) and the Great ($\dot{\eta}$ $\mu\epsilon\gamma\acute{a}\lambda\eta$ $\epsilon\ddot{\iota}\sigma o\delta o\varsigma$). The former, preceded by several prayers, one of which is the Prayer of St. Chrysostom[r] which we have in our Prayer Books, and by a hymn corresponding to the Introit of the Western Church, is when the Deacon, having received the Book, often magnificently bound, of

---

[o] But see a Letter in *Church Times*, Aug 15, 1868, by W. Palmer.
[p] See below. [q] Comber, p. 84.
[r] The Prayer of St. Chrysostom, as is usual in the Greek Church, does not end in the Name of our Saviour

the Gospel from the Priest, taper-bearers going before, and the Priest after him, holding it on high so that the people may see, enters the Bema through the Middle Door, and deposits it on the Holy Table. Then follows the Trisagion, "Ἅγιος ὁ Θεὸς, ἅγιος ἰσχυρὸς, ἅγιος ἀθάνατος, ἐλέησον ἡμᾶς (" Holy God, holy and powerful, holy and immortal, have mercy upon us "). The Deacon reads from the Ambon the Gospel, and the Proanaphora concludes with the dismissal of the Catechumens by the Deacon ; ὅσοι κατηχούμενοι προέλθετε. Unction with Chrism, which in the Greek Church corresponds with Confirmation, is administered at once after Baptism. Catechumens therefore are those who have not been baptized, and are being instructed in the faith, and as there are not ordinarily such present in the Church, there are no Catechumens to depart.

The Great Entrance is then made commencing with the Ter Sanctus or Triumphal Hymn, (" Holy, holy, holy, Lord God of Hosts ").

The Priest advancing to the Prothesis, takes from under the Aer the Paten and Chalice, and, preceded by the Deacon who carries the Paten (probably on his shoulder, but according to the Rubric on his head), and the censer, and by taper and incense-bearers, himself carrying the Chalice, passes into the Nave of the Church, the people showing their reverence by crossing themselves, bowing their heads, prostrating themselves on the ground, and kissing the hem of his stole. If there is no Deacon, and only one Priest, the latter takes the Paten in his left hand, and "bears it on the nape of his neck, and carries the Chalice in his right hand before his breast," the censer being suspended from the fingers of one hand [s]. The Priest enters the Bema through the Middle Door, and first places the Chalice on the Holy Table, and then taking the Paten from the Deacon, places it there also [t].

[s] Covel, Account of the Greek Church, p 34.
[t] Dr. Covel comments severely on the ritual of the Great Entrance, and on the Deacon carrying the paten on his head or shoulder, and says the practice was evidently derived from the worship and sacrifices of the heathen.

Having entered into a more lengthened detail of the ceremonial than our space can well afford, we can only briefly touch on the remaining part of the service.

The completeness of the mystery is held by the Greek Church to be consummated by the Invocation of the Holy Ghost, following the words of Institution by our Saviour. The Deacon fans the Holy Table and the holy things upon it with the ῥιπίδιον (fan), and covers the Paten and Chalice with veils. Dr. King says [n], that a common fan (ῥιπίδιον) was originally used for the purpose of preventing flies from falling into the Chalice, but that it was afterwards changed into silver, and used in winter as well as in summer as a processional ornament. The fan is also used in other processions; in the account of the funeral procession of Philaret, the great Metropolitan of Moscow, we read of the superiors of all the monasteries of Moscow, and the Bishops of the adjacent Dioceses, being headed by the Metropolitan of Kiev, whilst the Arch-Priest carried "a perfect cloud of fans." The Kiss of Peace is then given, and the Priest inclining his body and placing his hand first upon the Bread, and then taking the Chalice in his hands, repeats the words of Institution: "Take eat . . . . drink ye all of this." He then offers the prayer of Invocation, "Send Thy Holy Spirit upon us, and upon these gifts which lie before us." Next, after some short prayers and adorations, the Priest, standing upright, and thrice signing the elements with the sign of the Cross, pronounces the words, "Make this Bread the precious Body of Thy Christ, and that which is in the cup the Blood of Thy Christ, changing them (μεταβαλών) by Thy Holy Spirit." After the Consecration just enough warm water is added as is sufficient to represent the temperature of our Lord's Blood.

The change, says *The Confession of Faith*, "is made by the operation (διὰ τῆς ἐνεργείας) of the Holy Spirit Whom the Priest invokes at that time, consummating the Mys-

[n] Rites and Ceremonies, p. 168.

tery by praying and saying, 'Send Thy Holy Spirit upon us, and upon these gifts that lie before us.' For after those words the μετουσίωσις immediately (παρευθύς) follows." The Priest then advancing to the middle of the Bema elevates the Paten, and returning, places it on the Holy Table. The Priests and Deacons then communicate.

During the Consecration the Bema is obscured from the people either by the gate from the Iconostasis being shut, or by a veil being drawn across it. This is meant to signify the mystical nature of the Supper of Christ with His Apostles, His sufferings, Death and Burial. After the Priests and Deacons have received the Bread and Wine separately, the gate is opened, or the veil withdrawn, to signify the appearance of the Saviour after His Resurrection. The Deacon standing at the gate with the Chalice, containing the Wine and the Bread sopped in it, lifted up in his hands, invites the communicants to draw near; the Priest takes it from the hands of the Deacon, and gives the Communion; a spoon (λαβίς) is dipped into the Chalice, and from it some of the consecrated Bread is extracted and put to the mouths of the communicants (who receive, according to the practice of the Early Church, standing), with the words, "The Servant of God N. receiveth the precious and holy Body and Blood of our Lord and Saviour Jesus Christ, for the remission of his sins and for everlasting life" (τὸ τίμιον καὶ ἅγιον σῶμα καὶ αἷμα τοῦ Κυρίου καὶ Σωτῆρος ἡμῶν Ἰησοῦ Χριστοῦ εἰς ἄφεσιν τῶν ἁμαρτιῶν καὶ εἰς ζωήν αἰώνιον).

"The Deacon wipes the mouths of the communicants with one of the veils covering the Holy Gifts [x]."

The Communion ended, the Holy Bread which remains unconsecrated (ἀντίδωρον, ἀντὶ τοῦ δώρου, *instead of the gift*), but which has been blessed by the Priest, is distributed amongst the people present, who take it home for the sick and such others as had been unable to attend at Church. The absent ones receive it with fasting and

[x] Neale's Holy Eastern Church, I. 524.

reverence, as a representation of the Holy Eucharist which was in the early Church received daily [y]. The rubric directs that the Deacon is to dispose of whatever of the consecrated elements remains " with the greatest circumspection, so that not the smallest particle may fall or be neglected, pouring wine and water into the cup, the better to drink it all, and then he must wipe the cup quite dry." This Service concluded, the Priest dismisses the congregation with the blessing.

The Greeks, it need scarcely be said, communicate fasting, not the slightest refection being allowed before communicating.

The Greek Μετουσίωσις in the Sacrament connotes the Roman *Transubstantiatio;* but there is between them the same difference as there is between the Greek οὐσία and the Latin *Substantia*, and the English *essence* and *substance*, the former not implying the materialistic sense of the latter. Neither word is primitive. In doctrine both Churches long followed the ancient Liturgies and Fathers, but subsequently to the separation between East and West the Latins adopted both the name and full doctrine of Transubstantiation. This was at the famous Lateran Council, A.D. 1215, under Innocent III. That Council declared that " Christ's Body and Blood are really contained under the species of bread and wine, the bread being transubstantiated into His Body and the wine into His Blood." The College *de Propagandâ Fide*, founded in Rome, A.D. 1622, by Pope Gregory XV., was influential in Latinizing the Church of Western Russia, many Russians being educated in it who returned to their own country imbued with Roman principles. In 1642 the word Μετουσίωσις found its way into the *Orthodox Confession* of Peter Mogila; Christ is said in it to be present in the Sacrament, κατὰ μυστηριώδη τρόπον, but also κατὰ μετουσίωσιν. In 1672 the word was imported into the XVIII Articles of the Synod of Bethlehem. Christ "is present on earth," it says, "in a mysterious manner by

[y] Ricaut's Present State of Greek Church, 1678.

Metousiosis, for the substance [z] of the bread is changed into the substance of His holy Body, and the substance of the wine into His precious Blood." "After Consecration" it says that "the bread and wine are transmuted ($\mu\epsilon\tau\alpha\beta\acute{\alpha}\lambda\lambda\epsilon\sigma\theta\alpha\iota$), trans-substantiated ($\mu\epsilon\tau\text{ουσιο}\hat{\upsilon}\sigma\theta\alpha\iota$), converted ($\mu\epsilon\tau\alpha\pi\text{οιε}\hat{\iota}\sigma\theta\alpha\iota$), remodelled ($\mu\epsilon\tau\alpha\dot{\rho}\dot{\rho}\upsilon\theta\mu\acute{\iota}\zeta\epsilon\sigma\theta\alpha\iota$), the bread into the Lord's body which was born in Bethlehem and ascended into Heaven, and the wine into the Blood which flowed from His Side on the Cross; and the bread and wine no longer remain after Consecration, but only the very Body and Blood of the Lord ($\alpha\grave{\upsilon}\tau\grave{o}$ $\tau\grave{o}$ $\sigma\hat{\omega}\mu\alpha$ $\kappa\alpha\grave{\iota}$ $\alpha\hat{\iota}\mu\alpha$) under the appearance ($\epsilon\check{\iota}\delta\epsilon\iota$) and form ($\tau\acute{\upsilon}\pi\omega$), that is to say under the accidents ($\sigma\upsilon\mu\beta\epsilon\beta\eta\kappa\acute{o}\sigma\iota\nu$) "By the word Metousiosis," it adds, "we cannot explain the mode of the conversion of the elements, for this is known to God alone; but they truly, really, and substantially become the Body and Blood of Christ."

The chief difference between the Greek and Roman Churches is with regard to definition, which the Eastern Church strives as much as possible to avoid. The Eastern Church does not argue for victory, it searches for truth. "The Roman Church is always trying to define the manner of change in the Sacraments; the Eastern Church says it is a mystery." In the Russian Church some alterations were made from the words of the Council. Instead of the words "the substance of bread and wine no longer remain," it says, "the bread and wine no longer remain;" instead of "under the accidents of bread and wine," "under the appearance and form of bread and wine."

From the time of the Council many Russian theologians adopted the Roman doctrine of Transubstantiation, whilst others strongly disapproved of it. After the reformation of the Russian Church in the last century, in the reign of Peter the Great, more evangelical principles prevailed, and a return to primitive truth manifested itself in Russia. Dr. King, who wrote in 1772, says that "the Confession" of Peter Mogila was at that time held in

---

[z] We follow the usual translation of οὐσία.

slight reputation. Since then, evangelical principles have found expression in the writings of Plato and Philaret, the latter of whom died in 1867, both Metropolitans of Moscow, and two of the most learned and revered Prelates who ever presided over the Russian Church. Plato says : " We must ever bear in mind, first, that the Gospel requires us to worship God in spirit and in truth ; secondly, that the only safe rule of worship is the Word of God, whereunto, says St. Peter, ye do well that ye take heed as unto a light that shineth in darkness." The views that those Prelates held now find favour with the more cultivated portion of the Russian people. A materialized sense of the Eucharist, Philaret disallowed. " The manner of our Lord's Presence in the Eucharist," he says [a], " is a mystery to be apprehended by faith, not a matter to be speculated or dogmatized upon, or to be reasoned about."

The *Longer Catechism*, the work of Philaret, says ; " As to the *manner* in which the Bread and Wine are changed into the Body and Blood of our Lord, none but God can understand ; only thus much is signified, that the Bread *truly*, *really*, and *substantially* becomes the very true Body of the Lord, and the Wine the very Blood of the Lord." The Catechism refers to the words of St. John Damascene ; " It is truly that Body united with the Godhead which had its origin from the Holy Virgin ; not as though that Body which ascended came down from heaven, but because the Bread and Wine are changed themselves into the Body and Blood of God. But if thou seekest after the manner how this is, let it suffice thee to be told that it is by the Holy Ghost, in like manner as by the same Holy Ghost Christ formed Flesh to Himself from the Mother of God." " The Russian Church," says Dr. Neale, " has evidently determined to decline the use of the distinction of the οὐσία and συμβεβηκότα in the Bread and Wine which the Council of Bethlehem brought prominently forward [b].

[a] Quoted by Headlam, Teaching of the Russian Church, p. 8.
[b] Introduction to the History of the Eastern Church.

General View of the Orthodox Greek Church. 35

In the *Longer Catechism* the question is asked, "Ought we to communicate often in the holy mysteries?" and the answer is; "Our mother the Church calls on all to confess before their ghostly Fathers and to communicate four times yearly, or even every month." The *Orthodox Confession* requires all to receive once a year, and, as a rule, the laity seldom partake of the Communion more than once, although some more serious people receive oftener. It is the practice in the Greek Church for the Priests to communicate every day. As to non-communicating attendance, the *Longer Catechism* prescribes that those who do not intend to communicate may and should take part in the Liturgy by prayer and faith, and specially by a continual remembrance of our Lord Jesus Christ. The laity claim and observe the right of attendance without communicating at the Sacrament, and the practice of "hearing Mass" is considered the principal service of the Church. The Holy Eucharist is administered to children after Baptism. This was the custom in the Primitive Church, but was discontinued in the Latin about the Thirteenth Century.

(4) Penance in the Greek Church is a mystery by which the Penitent, after fasting and prayer, and oral Confession, and the outward Absolution pronounced by the Priest, is inwardly loosed from his sins by Christ Himself. A man, says the *Orthodox Confession*, discloses his repentance (μετάνοια) or affliction of heart for sin committed "with a firm intention of mind to amend his life and readiness to fulfil that which the Priest, his spiritual adviser, may enjoin." Confession to a Priest is considered necessary for all persons, Clergy and lay persons alike. The Church prescribes that it is to be made four times a year; once a year, at Easter, is, however, the general rule, and there is reason to believe that even this is often commuted for a pecuniary fine. The degree of Penance is left to the Priest, but it must be proportionate to the circumstances and ability of the penitent. In Russia the law of the land prescribes Confession once a year. In

the *Spiritual Regulation* it is expressly enjoined that the Monks should confess and receive the Eucharist four times a year; and it requires all other persons to make their Confession at Easter.

Not every Priest in the Greek Church is a Confessor; Confessors are especially licensed for the purpose by the Bishops, and are styled πνευματικοί (spiritual persons). Confession, says *The Orthodox Doctrine*, ought not to be made generally, but with regard to particular sins, for "it is impossible that the hidden wounds can be cured." But ordinarily a general confession is made in answer to the Priest who recites the Ten Commandments, and then asks the penitent which of them he has broken.

It is sometimes contended that in the Greek Church the declaratory form of Absolution is not employed. Dr. Covel says, "The Confessors pretend to do no more than abate or remit the penance, declaring the pardon from God alone." It may be well on this point to quote the exact words of the Priest in the "*Order of Confession*";—"May Jesus Christ our Lord, through His grace, bounty, and love to mankind, forgive thee, my child, all thy sins; and I, an unworthy Priest, by the power committed unto me, do pardon and absolve thee from all thy sins, in the name of the Father, and of the Son, and of the Holy Ghost, Amen." But, says Dr. King, "it is evident that this sentence has been foisted into the Greek Church from the Latin" "The Priest," says *The Orthodox Confession* of Peter Mogila, which we have before seen is tinged with Latinism, "rightly and canonically forgives sins; as soon as any one receives Absolution his sins are immediately forgiven him by God through the ministry of the Priest."

"What is Confession?" asks *the Shorter Catechism*;— "The person who has sinned after Baptism confesses his sin to the Priest, and through him receives Absolution from Christ Himself."

(5) Holy Orders (ἡ Ἱερωσύνη, with which χειροτονία, laying on of hands, is synonymous), comprehend two higher classes;

General View of the Orthodox Greek Church. 37

the highest is the Episcopate, of which there are the grades of Patriarch, Metropolitan, Archbishop, and Bishop, who not only hallow the Sacrament themselves but transmit the power by the laying on of hands to others. The next Order is that of Priests, whose office consists of three principal parts, Confirming, i.e. administering, the Sacrament of Unction with Chrism, Consecrating the Eucharist in dependence on the Bishops, instructing and absolving the people. A lower Order is that of Deacons, whose duty is to assist the Priest and serve at the Sacraments. A still lower Order is that of the Sexton and doorkeeper (θυρωρός); the reader (ἀναγνώστης), who reads in church the Epistle and Gospel when the latter is not read by the Deacon; the choirman (ψάλτης ὑμνῳδός), whose duty is to sing the prayers and lead the hymns, the subdeacon, who has charge of the vestments and ornaments of the Church.

(6) Marriage is considered, agreeably to the words of St. Paul (Eph. v. 32), a mystery. The service consists of two parts, the Espousals and the Coronation. A preliminary condition of marriage is that either by certificate or subsequently to banns published in Church after Mass in three several services, no impediment is found to exist, on the ground,—(1) of consanguinity which extends to the sixth degree, (2) of natural affinity to the fifth degree; (3) of Spiritual or Baptismal affinity to the third degree. The presence of at least one paranymph (παράνυμφος, σύντεκνος) as sponsor, is required; this is "the friend of the bridegroom" (John iii. 29), whose presence is agreeable to a canon of the Council of Carthage, A.D. 398 [c].

Crowns are used to remind the parties that they will be crowned in Heaven, if they properly fulfil their duties. The Espousals ended, crowns made of flowers, or of vine or olive-twigs, one wrapped in gold, the other in silver paper, after being blessed by the Priest, are placed upon the heads of the bride and bridegroom; in Russia the crowns are often of very costly material, and are kept in churches for

[c] "Sponsus et sponsa ... a parentibus suis vel paranymphis offerantur."

the purpose. Eight days after the marriage there is a special service, performed either in church or at home, for dissolving the crowns, with a prayer blessing the union, and entreating that it may be unbroken, and that they may live in lawful marriage [d].

No marriages are celebrated in Lent; a second marriage (διγαμία) is disapproved of; a third marriage (τριαμία) is contrary to the Canons; whilst a fourth constitutes polygamy (πολυγαμία). The Greek Church declares the indissolubility of marriage except by death; the practice of the Greeks however is opposed to the rule of the Church; divorces are easily obtained, and for other causes besides unfaithfulness. We need only allude to the case of the Grand Duke Constantine of Russia, who in April, 1820, was by Imperial Ukase divorced from his wife, a Princess of Saxe-Coburg, without any plea of unfaithfulness being charged against her, and a few days afterwards contracted a second marriage which was performed by a Priest of the Orthodox Church. This teaches the lesson that the Russian Church must not cast stones at the Church of England, which has so many things in common with her.

Marriage of Secular Priests before Ordination was at one time compulsory, but the rule is now somewhat relaxed. The Emperor Justinian forbade the election of a married man to the Episcopate; the Council in Trullo, A.D. 691, confirmed the decree, and it remains unaltered in the present day; (hence arises the necessity of the Bishops being chosen from the monasteries). That Council also forbade, what still remains in force, the second marriage of the Clergy.

(7) Unction with oil. This mystery corresponds with that of Extreme Unction in the Roman Church; with the difference that, whereas in the Roman Church it is only administered when recovery seems hopeless (*in articulo*

---

[d] The above account is derived from a work, Ἀκολουθία τοῦ γάμου ἤτοι Ἀρραβῶνος καὶ Στεφανώματος τῆς Ἑλληνικῆς Ἐκκλησιάs, kindly sent to the writer by the Very Reverend Eustathius Metallinos, Archimandrite of the Greek Church at Manchester.

mortis), in the Greek Church it is administered in the hope that, whilst the *body* is anointed with oil, the sick person may be cured of his bodily as well as spiritual infirmities. It is sometimes objected that, as the Sacrament in the Greek Church is usually administered in case of extreme illness, the practice of the two Churches is virtually the same, and that in the Greek Church the Sacrament has degenerated into Extreme Unction. But such is not the case. The people consider that the Oil (blessed by the Bishop) has a particular virtue in curing *bodily infirmities;* and they are inclined to regard it as a specific in their ailments; whilst it at the same time enables them to resist the temptations of the devil.

The Sacrament was originally connected with the miraculous power of healing possessed in the primitive Church. Our Saviour sent forth His disciples and gave them power to "heal the sick." It was adopted by the Greek Church in agreement with the words of St. James (v. 14, 15): "Is any sick among you; let him send for the Elders of the Church, and let them pray over him, anointing him in the Name of the Lord; and the prayer of faith shall save the sick, and the Lord shall raise him up, and if he have committed sins, they shall be forgiven him."

As St. James uses the plural number, the Greek Church concludes that more than one Priest is required for the Sacrament. The number of *seven* Priests was adopted in allusion to the Seven Gifts of the Holy Spirit spoken of by Isaiah, and the Sacrament is not generally considered valid unless administered by at least three. But even that number is not rigidly adhered to, especially in country places, where so many as three Priests cannot be obtained.

The Priest anoints the sick person on the forehead, nostrils, mouth, breast, and both sides of the hands, and offers a prayer that God, "the Physician of the soul and body, would heal His servant of his infirmity." After this the Holy Communion is given him.

Before concluding this chapter some of the points of

difference between the Greek and Roman Churches may be mentioned.

The difference with regard to the Filioque Clause in the Creed between the Greek Church on the one hand, and the Roman and Anglican Churches on the other, is familiar to all, and as we shall have occasion to speak of it further on in this work, we need not dwell on it now.

The Greek Church utterly rejects Works of Supererogation, Indulgences, Dispensations, Intention, Purgatory, and the Immaculate Conception. Infallibility it neither claims for itself nor allows in others. With regard to Intention, it is evident that a Roman Catholic can never be certain whether he has received the Sacraments or not, and a wicked Pope or Priest can vitiate them. The Greeks do not believe in Purgatory; "there is no such thing" as Purgatory, says Philaret, "there is no need of any other kind of Purification, for the Blood of Jesus Christ cleanseth from all sin."

As to the Invocation and Intercession of Saints. From the earliest ages the Greek Church has held that there are two separate abodes, places of expectancy, for the souls of the departed, until the Resurrection; that the wicked are confined in regions of darkness and that the Saints enjoy a certain state of bliss, not to be consummated and perfected till the Resurrection[e]. *The Longer Catechism* teaches. "The Saints who belong to the Church in Heaven . . . . by their prayers and intercession, purify, strengthen, and offer before God the prayers of the faithful living upon earth, and by the will of God work graciously and effectually upon them." "The Greek Church," says Dr. King, "allows prayers for the dead, and even prayers for the remission of their sins, and pays regard to the relics of Saints and Martyrs, of which often superstitious use is made." The Invocation of Saints, *The Orthodox Confession* says, "is not repugnant to the First Commandment . . . . it is a uniting of our prayers with theirs. The Saints

---

[e] Stourdza, " Sur la doctrine et l'esprit de l'Eglise Orthodoxe "

when alive on earth prayed for others, and entreated others to pray for them, much more after death, when they are nearer God, and continually enjoy His presence, must they feel an ardent desire for the salvation of believers known to God."

They have never held the modern doctrine of the Immaculate Conception. Yet "the Greeks of all Christians in the world," says Dr. Covel, " seem to be φιλοθεοτοκωτάτοι, the most zealous admirers of the Mother of God. The Latins in this matter are extravagant enough, but truly the Greeks far outdo them.... they ascribe to her almost as great a precedence as to God Himself .... more prayers are made to her than to Christ."

A few words must be said as to their reverence for Icons. The Iconostasis or Iconstand, with the lighted tapers in front of it, is the most prominent object in their churches. On it Icons of our Saviour, the Virgin, the Apostles, and Saints are always painted [f]; in some Cathedrals it is resplendent with gold and precious stones of immense value. Icons are to be found everywhere. In every house the place of honour is assigned to them; in every room they are to be found in the right-hand corner, and the first salutation on entering is made to them. It is said that "when a person is about to commit a sinful act which might shock them, he or she is careful to draw a curtain before them [g]"

Strongly objectionable as this excessive veneration of Icons is, we must give some weight to their authoritative expositions and explanations. The Second Council of Nice determined the character of the veneration held to be due to Icons in the Eastern Church. Under Icons sanctioned by that Council, says Schaff, were understood the sign of the Cross, and pictures of Christ, of the Virgin Mary, of Angels and Saints. They may be drawn in colours, or composed of mosaics, or formed of other suitable materials; be placed in churches, and in houses, and

---

[f] Pinkerton's Present State of the Greek Church.
[g] Stepniak's Russian Peasantry.

in the streets, or made on walls or tablets, sacred vessels and vestments. Homage may be paid to them by kissing, bowing, burning lights and saying prayers before them, such objects being intended for the living objects in Heaven which the Icon represents.

Such homage to Western minds seems little short of a violation of the Second Commandment. But it must be borne in mind that the Greek word, προσκύνησις, translated *kissing*, is an ambiguous expression; a word including the worship of God, and extending to the ordinary salutation and respect paid to a friend [h]. By the educated classes the practice is carried to an extravagant height, and by the ignorant it is no doubt sadly abused, but the Greek Church condemns the abuse as superstitious. Images it strictly forbids, all *worship* of Icons it expressly declares to be idolatry. "I do solemnly protest," says Dr. Covel, by no means an ardent admirer of the Greek Church, "that I never saw in all my stay up and down Turkey, amongst the Greeks, any other statue or Crucifix than this" (namely one in Prusa, where the Pope (πάπας) had, he says, been brought from Rome), "neither did I ever meet with any other religious brass, relieve, sculpture, or carved work in any of the Christian Churches or Oratories."

We will conclude this chapter with a summary of the chief points on which the Greek Church differs from the Roman Church. It holds (1) that Christ is the alone Head of the Church; (2) That Œcumenical Councils can alone determine the doctrine and discipline of Christ's Church; (3) That the Holy Ghost proceeds from the Father alone, *through* the Son; (4) The free and unrestrained use of the Bible; (5) The marriage of the Clergy; (6) Communion in Both Kinds, and the mixing of a little warm water with the wine in the Liturgy; (7) Leavened bread in the Holy Communion; (8) Services performed in the vulgar tongue; (9) It does not allow instrumental music in the services.

[h] It corresponds with the now ambiguous words in our own language, *worship*, *worshipful*, and which we retain in our Marriage Service, "With my body I thee worship."

CHAPTER I.

The Conflict between the Fourth and Fifth Empires.

THE first four Empires—The Roman Empire—The Birth of Christ—The Wise Men from the East—Importance of the Septuagint Translation—Fulfilment of Prophecy—The misconception of the nature of Christ's Kingdom—The Day of Pentecost—Jerusalem the Mother Church of Christianity—Consequences of the Martyrdom of St Stephen—Saul the Persecutor—St. Philip the Deacon—Conversion of Saul—Antioch the centre of Greek Christianity—Paul's First Apostolical journey—Council of Jerusalem—Paul's Second Apostolical journey—Paul at Athens, Corinth, Ephesus—Paul's Third Apostolical journey—Paul again at Ephesus, in Macedonia, Jerusalem—Paul sent from Cæsarea to Rome—Foundation of the See of Alexandria—Peter could not have been at Rome before A.D. 67—First Persecution under Nero—Martyrdom of SS Paul and Peter—Foundation of the See of Rome—Fall of Jerusalem—Second Persecution under Domitian—St John at Patmos—Reason of the Persecutions—Third Persecution—The Christian Apologies—The Foundation of Ælia Capitolina—Second Fall of Jerusalem—Fourth Persecution—Conference of Polycarp and Anicetus as to Easter—Victor, Bishop of Rome, excommunicates the Eastern Bishops—The Forged Clementines—The Fifth Persecution—The Sixth Persecution—The Seventh Persecution—The *lapsed*—St Cyprian of Carthage and Stephen of Rome—The Eighth Persecution—Paul of Samosata—The so-called Ninth Persecution

THERE has always been one Church, although under two dispensations, the Jewish and the Christian; " Judaism was the husk in which the kernel of Christianity ripened." But contemporaneously with it four great Kingdoms (βασιλεῖαι) or Empires (*imperia*) passed along the stage of the world's history—the Assyrian, Persian, Grecian, Roman—all performing the work appointed them by God till "the fulness of time" should come; all preparing the way for the " fifth Kingdom," " not made with hands," which should last for ever.

Before the long promised Messiah came, the first three had run their allotted course, had misused their greatness, and having been "weighed by God in the balance and found wanting" (Dan. v. 27) had been succeeded by one still greater, " whose brightness was excellent, and the form thereof terrible" (Ibid. ii. 31). This was the Roman, the fourth great Empire of the world. The Prophet Daniel describes it as "bright and excellent," but "terrible;" bright and excellent, that is, in the majesty lent it by God, but "terrible" in the abuse of the gifts entrusted to it.

Only words expressive of extreme terror can be found by the Prophet to characterize the great Roman Empire. "Strong as iron .... as iron breaketh in pieces and subdueth all things," it was to "crush and break;" "dreadful and terrible and strong exceedingly" to "stamp the residue under its feet" and "devour the whole earth." But it too, like the Empires which went before it, was to be broken in pieces and become "like the chaff of the summer threshing floor" under "the great mountain that filled the whole earth" (Ibid. ii. 35).

The eras which we classify as B C. and A.D. are not an arbitrary distinction, but the one planned by God. At the time of Christ's Coming, the Kingdom of Brass, in the Prophet Daniel's language, had given way to the Kingdom of Iron, and for nearly a century and a half Greece had been a province of Rome. The physical might of Rome had subdued Greece, but the mind of Greece mastered Rome; the Romans gave up much of their old beliefs, and the Greek Deities were incorporated into the Roman faith. Rome governed almost the whole world, but the world under the Roman Empire, instead of becoming better had become worse. The epoch which witnessed the early growth of Christianity was, says Dean Farrar [a], an epoch of which the horror and the degradation have rarely been equalled, and perhaps never exceeded, in the annals of mankind."

In B.C. 63 Jerusalem was taken by Pompey; Hyrcanus, the last of the Maccabees, was made a tributary Prince, and Judæa became a Roman province. The sceptre having thus departed from Judah "the fulness of time" had come, and the Roman Emperor himself was made the unwitting instrument for carrying out God's decrees. "There went out

[a] Early Days of Christianity.

a decree from Cæsar Augustus that all the world should be taxed." Thus was brought about the fulfilment of Micah's prophecy (v. 2) that from Bethlehem He should come forth that was to be "the Ruler in Israel." "All went to be taxed, every one to his own city," and Joseph went from Nazareth to Bethlehem, the city of David, "because he was of the house and lineage of David." Women were not obliged by the edict to accompany their husbands, and the journey was long, some seventy miles; yet the Virgin Mary, by divine guidance, went with him, thus fulfilling the prophecy of Isaiah (vii. 14), "a Virgin shall conceive and bear a Son."

Immediately after the Saviour's Birth, Angelic messengers conveyed to humble shepherds, tending their flocks by night, the good tidings of great joy that on that day was born in the city of David a Saviour which was Christ the Lord. Twelve days afterwards occurred the event which we in the West commemorate as the Epiphany and the Greek Church as the Θεοφάνεια, the Manifestation of Christ to the Gentiles. Wise men (Μάγοι, as the Priests of Persia were called), recognizing in the Star which they saw in the East, the Star of Jacob predicted by Balaam (Numbers xxiv. 17), went to Jerusalem to enquire the birthplace of Him that was born King of the Jews. At Jerusalem the Star again appeared and went before them (προῆγεν αὐτούς) to Bethlehem, till it came and stood over (ἐπάνω) the place where the Child lay—whether it was in the φάτνη, or whether His parents had removed to a house in Bethlehem, we are not told;—but when they saw Him they fell down and worshipped Him, presenting Him with gifts, gold as to the King of Kings, frankincense to represent His eternal Priesthood, and myrrh to typify the Burial of the Man Christ.

We may rest contented with the simple statement given by St. Matthew, and by him alone of the four Evangelists, without troubling ourselves about astronomical calculations. It may, however, be mentioned in passing, that an astronomical phenomenon, viz. the conjunction of the three planets of Jupiter, Mars and Saturn in one constellation, a conjunction which occurs only once in 794 years, has been established without doubt to have occurred at the epoch of our Saviour's Birth. But two questions naturally arise, Why did the Star appear to Wise Men *in the East?* and How did they know that it was the Star predicted by Balaam? SS. Chrysostom and Jerome answer the first question. It was, says the former, "to penetrate the insensibility of the Jews, and to take all excuse from them if they would not receive Christ." "The Star," says St. Jerome, "arose in the East according to the prophecy of Balaam, and it was ordained to be a rebuke to the Jews, that they learnt Christ's Nativity from the Gentiles; and the Wise Men were led by it to Judæa that the Priests, being interrogated by them where Christ was to be born, might be left without excuse for ignorance of the event."

But how did the Wise Men know that the Star which they saw was the Star predicted by Balaam? in other words, that "the fulness of time" had come?

The translation of the Septuagint and the wide diffusion of the Greek language, consequent on the universal extension of the Roman Empire (ἡ οἰκουμένη), had rendered many of the prophecies of Scripture familiar to heathen nations. That some great event was about to happen, some extraordinary Person to appear, by whom deliverance from the tyranny of evil under which the world groaned was to be effected; a reign of peace to be inaugurated; was the belief, and more especially was this the case in the East, of Jews and Gentiles. The expectation was fostered by Roman writers. Only forty years before the Birth of Christ, the poet Virgil [b], "as if inspired," says Gibbon [c], "by the celestial muse of Isaiah, had celebrated the return of the virgin, the

[b] "Magnus ab integro sæclorum nascitur ordo.
    Jam redit et Virgo . . . .
    Jam nova progenies cœlo demittitur alto." (Ecl. iv.)
[c] Decline and Fall, III. 270.

The Conflict between the Fourth and Fifth Empires. 47

fall of the serpent, the approaching birth of the God-like child .... who should expiate the guilt of human kind;" and the Temple of Janus was, almost for the first time since the foundation of Rome, closed [d].

When Herod learnt, through the Magi, that a King of the Jews had been born, "he was troubled" for the security of his throne. So he enquired of the Chief Priests and Scribes where Christ should be born. They had no doubt, but at once told him in Bethlehem of Judæa, for it was written by the Prophet that out of Bethlehem "shall come a Governor who shall rule My people Israel."

The Magi were Persians, and to them the prophecy of Daniel would be familiar. Balaam was a Prophet of Pethor in Mesopotamia, and the Magi, being Priests, were, as St. Jerome says, "the successors of Balaam." Being also astrologers, when they saw the wonderful apparition of the Star, they would have no difficulty in construing the prophecy of Daniel, and that of Balaam. They would probably be less familiar with the prophecy of Micah as to the *place* of the Saviour's Birth; so they went to Jerusalem to enquire where He was born; of the Birth they had no doubt, and being led by the same Star, they at once recognized the predicted "Ruler in Israel" (Micah v. 2) in the Infant at Bethlehem

The Chief Priests and the Scribes knew that in the time and the Birth of Christ at Bethlehem their own Scriptures had been fulfilled, yet the Jews wilfully shut their eyes and refused to acknowledge or receive Him as the Messiah. That the Greeks or Gentiles in general, who lived under a polytheistic system, should fail to recognize in the lowly Birth of the Saviour the fulfilment of the Jewish Scriptures and cavil at the divine authority of the Gospels, is intelligible, but that the Jews who believed in One God with their own Scriptures should refuse to acknowledge the long-expected Redeemer is at first sight incomprehensible;

---

[d] The Temple was always kept open in time of war.

that which was to the Greeks (ἔθνεσιν) foolishness was to the Jews a stumbling-block (1 Cor. i. 23).

In order to understand the opposition of the Jews to the Gospel, we must look into the history of the Jewish nation. The Jews were impatient of the Roman yoke. The day on which Pompey took Jerusalem was the Sabbath, on which the Jews did not think it right to fight, and after the victory he penetrated into the very Holy of Holies. This profanation of the Temple the Jews never forgave, and in the civil war between him and Cæsar they took the side of the latter. The Maccabees made several unsuccessful attempts to re-assert their rights; Jerusalem was a constant scene of bloodshed; and at the time of the Saviour's Birth the Jewish nation groaned under the tyranny of Herod the Great, who, although a Jew and the husband of Hyrcanus' daughter Mariamne, was a vassal of the Roman Emperor.

The Jews expected a Messiah, but a temporal, not a suffering, Messiah, a powerful King of Judæa who would deliver their nation from the hated thraldom of Rome. John the Baptist was sent to "prepare the way of the Lord and to make His paths straight." This the fore-runner of the Messiah did in two ways —(1) by preaching repentance, for the wickedness of the people was immense, and without repentance it was impossible to receive the Gospel; (2) by teaching the application of prophecy to a *Spiritual* Messiah. The Chief Priests and Scribes (the teachers of the Law) knew and confessed to Herod that their Scriptures had been fulfilled in the Birth at Bethlehem; but Daniel had described the Son of Man as "coming in the clouds of Heaven;" whilst their Scriptures spoke in one sense they interpreted them in another, and the prophecy of Daniel they ascribed to His First, instead of to His Second, Advent.

Disappointed in their expectation, they forced themselves into the disbelief that He was the real Messiah. And this is the less remarkable when it is borne in mind that His own Apostles misunderstood the character of His Kingdom.

They too, as Jews, hoped that He would set up a temporal kingdom and deliver them from the Romans. When He told them how He must suffer many things of the Elders and Chief Priests, and be put to death, and the third day rise again, He rebuked Peter for misunderstanding Him; "Get thee behind Me, Satan, thou art an offence unto Me;" he, whose faith was before "a rock" ($\pi\acute{\epsilon}\tau\rho a$) was now a stumbling-block ($\sigma\kappa\acute{a}\nu\delta a\lambda o\nu$). Again and again we are told in the Gospels that they understood not His sayings; and on His very last day on earth they asked Him, "Lord, wilt Thou at this time restore again the Kingdom to Israel?"

So that if the Apostles misunderstood the character of Christ's Kingdom, it is less remarkable that the Jewish nation at large misunderstood it. They "demanded of Him a sign from Heaven" (Matt. xii. 38; Mark viii. 11; Luke xi. 16), "Master, we would see a sign from Thee;" some sign that He would be a King of the Jews, such as they wanted. They were ready to accept Him, if He would reign as their temporal monarch, and on more than one occasion He was forced to elude their intention of making Him a King. As He would not accept a temporal kingdom, they rejected Him; and though He was able to call to His aid "more than ten thousand angels" (Matt. xxvi. 53), they crucified Him; yet over the Cross Pilate wrote this superscription: "This is the King of the Jews."

Death was to Him the first-fruits of victory and the gate of life. His last act before His death was to pray for His murderers and for the penitent thief. But one work more had to be accomplished. They laid indeed His human body in the new grave, in the garden of Joseph of Arimathea; but, quickened in His human Spirit[e], He descended into the lower parts of the earth and preached there to the spirits in prison ($\dot{\epsilon}\nu$ $\phi v\lambda a\kappa\hat{\eta}$), which had been disobedient more than 2,000 years before. We must be contented to receive with reverence what has been so briefly revealed to us without

---

[e] $\theta a\nu a\tau\omega\theta\epsilon\grave{\imath}s$ $\mu\grave{\epsilon}\nu$ $\sigma a\rho\kappa\grave{\imath}$, $\zeta\omega o\pi o\iota\eta\theta\epsilon\grave{\imath}s$ $\delta\grave{\epsilon}$ $\tau\hat{\omega}$ $\pi\nu\epsilon\acute{\nu}\mu a\tau\iota$, 1 Peter iii 18.

striving to "be wise above what is written." After three days He gained the victory over death by rising from the dead, and after forty days longer on the earth, He ascended into Heaven. He led captivity captive (Eph. iv. 9), the captives that graced His triumph being Satan, sin, and death. He sat down at the right Hand of God, Angels, principalities and powers being made subject to Him. "He was clothed with a vesture dipped in blood," as a record of His own sufferings, and of the conflict of His Kingdom on earth before the final victory could be won; but "on His Head were placed many crowns," and His Father gave Him a Name which is above every name, "King of Kings and Lord of Lords" (Rev. xix. 12, 13, 16); "that at the Name of Jesus every knee should bow, of things in Heaven and things on earth, and things under the earth."

Thus He laid the foundation of the Christian Church. Not for Himself alone was the victory won, but by His victory the victory was foreshadowed for His Kingdom on earth. By His death He consecrated death, and by His Resurrection and Ascension He deprived death of its terrors. By depriving death and the grave of its sting He animated His Church to fight manfully against sin, the world, and the devil. If the General is in the forefront of the battle, we know with what courage it inspires his soldiers. So it was the unseen Presence of their Lord and Master in Heaven which encouraged the early martyrs in their long conflict with the Roman Empire, and nerved delicate women to endure not only death but sufferings worse than death, and tortures such as to us who read of them it seems impossible that flesh and blood could have endured.

During the forty days which He spent on earth after His Resurrection, Christ spoke of "the things pertaining to the Kingdom of God," i.e. His Church, and doubtless prescribed the plan of its government. St. Paul tells us (Eph. iv. 8) that "when He ascended up on high ... He gave *gifts* (δόματα) to men," and, 1 Cor. xii., he speaks of diversities of *gifts* (χαρισμάτων). It was believed in the early Church that these gifts were the gifts of the Holy Spirit bestowed on the Day of Pentecost. The first step which the Apostles took after the Ascension was to elect a twelfth Apostle to take the place of the traitor Judas; and Matthias was numbered with the eleven Apostles. Ten days after the Ascension, on the first great Festival, that of Pentecost, the χαρίσματα, or *gifts* of the Holy Spirit, were sent down from Heaven on the Apostles; a miracle, counteracting the confusion of tongues at Babel, was wrought; the Apostles were gifted with the tongues of all nations, because Christ had commissioned them to preach to all nations, and they were thus prepared for their mission to preach the Gospel, first in Jerusalem and all Judæa, and in Samaria, and then unto the uttermost parts of the earth. Other gifts were also bestowed on them; the power of healing the sick and casting out devils.

Thus Jerusalem was the mother-Church of Christianity, and St. James the brother, or more accurately the cousin, of our Lord, was appointed (and perhaps at this time) its first overseer (ἐπίσκοπος) or Bishop [f]. It is generally believed that the Apostles, in obedience to the Saviour's command, abode in Jerusalem for twelve years, only leaving it for short missionary tours in Judæa, and that they did not leave the Holy Land till A.D. 42. During their life-time they held the general supervision of the Church in their own hands, although here and there they appointed others as Bishops, to whom they gave power to ordain other Bishops as their successors, so that the office might never fail.

Our Lord having in His life-time appointed a second Order of the Ministry (Luke x. 1), that of πρεσβύτεροι, or Priests, the infant Church soon instituted a third Order of Deacons (διάκονοι), at first seven in number, on whom the Apostles "when they had prayed, laid their hands." Chief amongst the Deacons were SS. Stephen, "a man full of faith and the Holy Ghost," and Philip. Stephen "did great wonders and

[f] Eus. H. E, II 1.

miracles amongst the people;" and when "they were not able to resist the wisdom and the Spirit in which he spake," the Elders and the Scribes set up false witnesses and brought him before the Sanhedrim; and the holy Stephen died (A.D. 33) the Proto-martyr of the Christian Church.

The first effect of the persecution which ensued after St. Stephen's martyrdom was the spread of the Gospel by believers who were scattered abroad and sought refuge in the regions of Judæa and Samaria. Philip the Deacon escaped to Samaria, where he preached and worked miracles with such success that the people with one accord gave heed to him and were baptized, both men and women. But as he was a Deacon, he could only confer the Sacrament of Baptism; the Church in Jerusalem therefore sent over Peter and John, who "laid their hands on them and they received the Holy Ghost." This is the first notice we have of Confirmation.

Philip, under instruction of an Angel, next proceeded to the country of the Philistines, where he converted and baptized the Chamberlain of the Queen of Ethiopia, who was on his homeward journey from Jerusalem. Thus by means of Philip the words of prophecy were fulfilled; "Upon Philistia will I triumph" (Psalm viii. 9); "Ethiopia shall soon stretch out her hands unto God" (Psalm lxviii. 31).

Witnesses who had been suborned to give false evidence against Stephen "laid down their clothes at a young man's feet named Saul," and in the persecution of the Church which followed Stephen's martyrdom he bore a prominent part. Saul continuing to "make havoc of the Church;" "breathing out threatenings and slaughter against the disciples of the Lord," obtained (A.D. 34) from the High Priests a commission to proceed to Damascus, a city 133 miles from Jerusalem, and to seize and bring bound to Jerusalem any Christians who had fled for refuge to that city. On his road thither his intention was miraculously arrested;

the persecutor Saul was converted and baptized, and "straightway preached Christ in the Synagogues that He is the Son of God."

For some years a modified form of Judaism was combined with the two Sacraments which Christ Himself had ordained in His Church, Baptism and the Holy Eucharist. Like their Master, Who was born and lived and died a Jew, the first Christians observed the ceremonies of the Mosaic Law; they frequented the services of the Temple, and the rite of Circumcision was retained. The Apostles at first believed that the Kingdom of Christ was to be limited to the Jews; but the barrier between Jews and Gentiles was broken down through the conversion and Baptism (A.D. 41) by St. Peter, acting under divine inspiration, of Cornelius, a member of a noble family, and a Centurion of the Roman forces at Cæsarea.

For a few years "the Churches had rest throughout all Judæa, Galilee and Samaria." But, A.D. 44, a terrible calamity from the Jews visited the Church; Herod Agrippa "stretched forth his hand to vex certain of the Church, and killed James" the Apostle, son of Zebedee and brother of St. John, "with the sword." Thus St. James was the Proto-martyr of the Apostles.

St. Luke tells us that disciples flying from Jerusalem after the martyrdom of St. Stephen found their way to Antioch. Antioch, although it had fallen from the powerful position which it held under the Seleucidæ, was still, under the Roman Empire, regarded as the capital of the East, and was, next to Rome and Alexandria, the greatest city in the world. A great number of people at Antioch, we are told (Acts xi. 21), now "believed and turned to the Lord." When tidings of this success was reported to the Church in Jerusalem, they commissioned Barnabas to proceed to Antioch. Barnabas first went to Tarsus, the native city of Saul, where the latter was then residing, and together with Saul proceeded to Antioch, and at Antioch the two continued to preach for a whole year. There

Christianity took deep root, and "the disciples were first called Christians at Antioch."

Thenceforward Antioch became the centre of Greek Christianity, and was to the Greek converts what Jerusalem was to the Jewish converts of Judæa, Galilee, and Samaria. Over the Church of Antioch, according to ecclesiastical tradition, Peter presided as Bishop for seven years. Whether he was so or not, it is useless to enquire, for the reason that it is impossible to decide with certainty. It is probable that the Apostles did not, except in the case of St. James at Jerusalem, become Bishops of individual Sees, but that they exercised a general supervision, entrusting the newly-founded Churches to some Presbyter whom they consecrated to the higher rank of Bishop. There is reason to believe that Evodius was the first Bishop of Antioch, and, although he is not mentioned by St. Luke amongst the Prophets and Teachers of Antioch, that he was appointed at this time. Antioch was the first in date of the afterwards great Patriarchal Sees of the Church; to the Bishop of the See the exclusive title of Patriarch originally belonged, and Innocent I., Pope of Rome, claimed for it a special dignity on the ground of its having been the See of St. Peter.

Before proceeding further, it may be as well to draw attention to the fact that in estimating the value of ecclesiastical tradition it must be borne in mind that the nearer the source the purer is the stream. When we have St. Irenæus telling us that he could point to the very spot where he used to sit and talk with Polycarp, Bishop of Smyrna, and disciple of St. John, and that Polycarp would tell him of the frequent conversations which he had held with the beloved Apostle and others who had seen our Lord, tradition derived from such a source is second only to sacred Scripture. But when in the Third and Fourth centuries we receive statements recording events which are supposed to have happened in the First Century, with no trustworthy connecting link, their value, in destroying testimony which would otherwise be conclusive, is absolutely nil.

Barnabas and Saul had as yet only received the spiritual gifts (χαρίσματα) which fitted them for the office of Prophets and Teachers. Whilst the Prophets and Teachers of Antioch (Acts xiii. 1) ministered to the Lord and fasted, "the Holy Ghost commanded them to separate Barnabas and Saul" for the work to which they were called, that is, to the Apostleship of the Gentiles They were consequently ordained, and we soon find them reckoned amongst the Apostles (Acts xiv. 14). Immediately afterwards Saul, in company with Barnabas, started from Antioch on his First Apostolical journey.

The "Acts of the Apostles" is mostly confined to the missionary labours of the great Apostle of the Gentiles; we must presume a knowledge of that Book on the part of readers and confine ourselves to little more than touching on the countries through which he was the instrument of extending Christ's Kingdom.

The First Apostolical journey. Barnabas and Saul, in company of John Mark, cousin (ἀνέψιος) of Barnabas, left Antioch in Syria, A.D. 45 [g], and taking ship at Seleucia, the Port of Antioch, landed in the Island of Cyprus, the native country of Barnabas. From Salamis they traversed the Island, a distance of 100 miles, to Paphos the capital, and after the conversion of Sergius Paulus the Proconsul, Saul took the name of Paul. From Paphos they crossed to Asia Minor, landing at Perga in Pamphilia, where John Mark left them to return to Jerusalem. They then went to Antioch in Pisidia. There Paul preached in the Synagogue on the Sabbath day, and so long as he spoke to the Jews of the promised Messiah, they listened to him attentively. But when on the following Sabbath the Greeks flocked to hear him, the Jews were filled with envy and "spake against those things which were spoken by him, contradicting and blaspheming." "Seeing ye put it from you,

---

[g] This cannot be St. Mark the Evangelist, who died A.D. 62, whereas John Mark lived beyond that date.

and judge yourselves unworthy of everlasting life," he said, "lo! we turn to the Gentiles." The Greeks gladly heard him, and many of them were converted. Thereupon the Jews "raised a persecution" and expelled Paul and Barnabas from their coasts.

They next went to Iconium, the capital of Lycaonia, where a great multitude of both Jews and Greeks believed, but they were forced to fly from the city in consequence of a conspiracy to kill them. At Lystra, another city of Lycaonia, they for the first time came in contact with a thoroughly Pagan population, which, excited by Jews from Antioch and Iconium, stoned Paul, and dragged him out of the city, supposing him to be dead; but he contrived to escape to Derbe, also a city in Lycaonia, where many disciples were made, and Presbyters were ordained in every city; this is the first mention we have in the Acts of the Apostles of the second Order in the Ministry. Returning by the same route through Lystra, Iconium, and Pisidian Antioch, they arrived, after an absence of two years, at Antioch in Syria, where they remained a considerable time.

At Antioch they related how God had opened the door of Faith to the Gentiles. The Jewish converts now resolved that heathen converts must conform to the Jewish Law. A question of such importance, on which the very existence of the Christian Church depended, seemed to require reference to the parent Church at Jerusalem. Paul and Barnabas, therefore, and "certain others," amongst whom was Titus, an uncircumcised convert, went to Jerusalem, where the Apostles, and amongst them Peter, whose presence in the Council is the last mention of him made in the Acts, and John, assembled in a Council held under St. James (A.D. 50). SS. Peter, Barnabas, and Paul were the principal speakers, the deliberations being summed up by St. James, who, himself a strict adherent of the Jewish rites, proposed certain restrictions in that direction, whilst in his sentence a compromise in the spirit of Christian charity was adopted; the Gentiles were not to be troubled with unnecessary burdens, whilst they on their part should observe a respect for Jewish susceptibilities. The Council enacted; "It seemed good to the Holy Ghost and to us, that converts should abstain from meats polluted through being offered to idols, from the flesh of animals which had been strangled and contained blood, and from fornication."

St. Paul's Second Apostolical journey. After the Council, Paul and Barnabas, carrying with them its decrees, returned to Antioch, whence Paul started, this time accompanied by Silas, on his Second Apostolic journey (52—54). Paul was unwilling that Mark, who had left them on their first journey, should now accompany them, and so sharp was the contention ($\pi\alpha\rho o\xi\upsilon\sigma\mu\acute{o}s$) between him and Barnabas, that they parted, Barnabas and Mark going to Cyprus. There Barnabas, after having appointed Heraclides, who fixed his See at Salamis, as its first Bishop, is supposed to have suffered martyrdom. Paul and Silas, travelling through Syria and Cilicia, confirming the Churches and leaving the decrees of the Council of Jerusalem, passed through Derbe and Lystra. At the latter place they met Timothy, who is called a disciple, from which we may infer that he had been baptized by Paul in his previous visit. Though Timothy's father was a Greek, yet his grandmother Lois and his mother Eunice were Jewesses (2 Tim. i. 5), and by them Timothy had been from his childhood instructed in the Holy Scriptures. In the matter of circumcision or uncircumcision Paul himself was indifferent, but he now "took and circumcised him because of the Jews which were in those quarters."

Taking Timothy with them and founding Churches in Phrygia and Galatia, where Paul fell sick, and being forbidden by the Spirit to go into the province of Asia, they passed through Mysia, and were divinely guided to Troas, where they met with Luke "the beloved physician." Here Paul had a vision inviting him to go into Greece. Touching at Samothracia they arrived at Philippi, where Lydia, a sorceress, was converted, and also the gaoler of the prison in which the Apostles were, in consequence of their conversion of Lydia, confined, and from which they were miraculously released. Here Luke and Timothy were left; Paul and Silas, passing through Amphipolis and Apollonia, arrived at Thessalonica, the capital of Macedonia. There Paul preached for three Sabbaths in the Synagogue, and a great multitude of "devout Greeks, and of the chief women not a few," embraced the Gospel. But being assailed by a Jewish mob, Paul and Silas escaped to Beræa. There their preaching was blessed by the conversion of many, both Jews and Greeks. But Jews from Thessalonica stirring up a sedition, Paul left for Athens, Silas and Timothy (the latter of whom had rejoined them) continuing at Beræa.

Athens Paul found "wholly given to idolatry." Of the two philosophical schools in that centre of Greek learning, the Epicureans and the Stoics, the former were Atheists and the latter Pantheists, and the people signified their complete ignorance of the true God in an inscription on their altars, *To the unknown God.*

Standing in the midst of Mars' hill, the seat of their Council, the Areopagus, he preached to them of the God whom they "ignorantly worshipped." Thus was Christ's Kingdom set to oppose the city which with Alexandria was the most cultivated and philosophical in the world. Many of the people, when they heard of the Resurrection, ridiculed, but some, and amongst them was Dionysius the Areopagite, to whom tradition assigns the first Bishopric of Athens, believed.

From Athens Paul went to Corinth, the mercantile metropolis of Achaia. Here he was rejoined by Timothy and Silas. The opposition which he met with from the Jews was so violent that shaking off the dust from his feet, he told them that thenceforward he would go to the Gentiles. But when Gallio, the Proconsul of Achaia, treated the complaints of the Jews and questions of mere Jewish ceremonial with indifference, Paul remained a year and a half at Corinth, where he probably met and converted Aquila and Priscilla; and at Corinth a flourishing Church was established.

Paul now determined to leave Greece in order to attend the great Feast of Pentecost at Jerusalem. Touching at Ephesus, where the Jews requested him to prolong his stay, promising to return to them and leaving there Aquila and Priscilla, he landed at Cæsarea and went up and saluted the Church at Jerusalem. This is all we are told of his visit; he speedily went on to Antioch in Syria, where he arrived in the Summer, A D. 54. In that year Nero succeeded Claudius as Roman Emperor.

St. Paul's Third Apostolical journey. Quitting Antioch in company of Timothy, Paul first visited Galatia and Phrygia, confirming all the disciples; and passing by the "upper regions" of Asia Minor, he visited Ephesus for the second time, where he re-baptized certain converts who had received an imperfect form of Baptism from Apollos. At Ephesus he spent three years (54—57), and at that time probably appointed Titus Bishop of Crete (Titus i. 5).

For the space of three months he spoke boldly in the Synagogues of the Jews, but meeting with much opposition, he taught for the rest of the time in the school of one Tyrannus, as well as from house to house, preaching repentance and faith both to Jews and Greeks. St. Luke says (Acts xix. 10) that at this time "all they which dwelt in Asia heard the word of the Lord Jesus, both Jews and Greeks." As he had before made Corinth the Metropolitan See of Greece, so he now made Ephesus the Metropolis of Asia, and soon appointed Timothy as its Bishop.

From Ephesus he crossed to Macedonia, all the information St. Luke gives us is, "he departed to go into Macedonia," and "when he had gone over those parts and had given them much exhortation, he came into Greece," where he spent three months. From Corinth he at this time (A.D. 58) wrote his Epistles to the Romans, in which he announced his intention of visiting them on his road from Jerusalem to Spain. He then returned to Macedonia in the Spring and arrived at Philippi, where he was joined by Luke, for Easter (Acts xx. 6). Leaving Europe on his way to Jerusalem, he stopped seven days at Troas, where he raised Eutychus to life, and then visited the Islands of the Ægean Sea. From Miletus he sent to Ephesus, which was only a few miles distant, asking the Presbyters to meet him, and there he held a visitation of the Church of Ephesus, which included the Churches of the neighbouring towns. In a solemn charge he told them that they would see his face no more; that he was going "bound in the spirit to Jerusalem, not knowing what would befall him there," except that in every city the same testimony was given that bonds and afflictions awaited him. Launching thence, they sailed past Coos and Rhodes to Patara, where they changed their vessel for another bound to Phœnicia, and landed at Tyre, where they remained seven days. In vain the disciples implored Paul not to go to Jerusalem. Passing on they landed at Ptolemais (Acre), where they remained one day, and the next day landed at Cæsarea. There they abode "many days" in the house of Philip the Evangelist, one of the Seven Deacons, and the Prophet Agabus foretold Paul's imprisonment at Jerusalem. After an absence of several years (Acts xxiv. 17), Paul arrived at Jerusalem shortly before the Passover of A.D. 58.

The city was at the time crowded with Jews who had come from all countries to attend the Passover. The Judaizing Christians "zealous of the Law of Moses" he pacified by taking upon himself the vow of a Nazarite (Numbers vi. 2—5). But a greater difficulty arose from the Asiatic Jews, who had been acquainted with him during his long sojourn at Ephesus. Incensed against him not only as an apostate Jew, but because of the great success with which he had preached Christianity, they were with difficulty prevented from tearing him in pieces. He was brought before the Sanhedrim, but his announcement that he was a Pharisee and the son of a Pharisee, and that it was the doctrine of the Resurrection that was called in question, created such a tumult between the Pharisees who believed, and the Sad-

The Conflict between the Fourth and Fifth Empires. 61

ducees who denied, the doctrine, that the chief captain Lysias was obliged to rescue him, and sent him secretly by night to Cæsarea, where Felix, the Procurator, resided.

At Cæsarea he remained two years (58—60), during which time Porcius Festus succeeded Felix as Procurator. The High Priests and the chief of the Jews desired Festus to put Paul on his trial at Jerusalem, "laying wait on the way to kill him." Paul learning that an attempt would be made on his life claimed the right of a Roman citizen and appealed to Cæsar. Festus had no choice; "thou hast appealed unto Cæsar, unto Cæsar shalt thou go."

After having testified to the Saviour's kingdom in the capital of Greece, he was now to bear similar witness in the capital of the world. In the autumn of A.D. 60 he started for Rome. His journey thither; his shipwreck and consequent detention for three months on the barbarous island of Melita (Malta); his landing and sojourn for seven days·at Puteoli (Pozzuoli); his detention at Rome for two years (61—63); his being permitted, fastened to the arm of a Roman soldier, to reside in his own house, and to preach "the kingdom of God . . . . no man forbidding him;" —these events are narrated in the concluding chapters of the Acts of the Apostles.

In the second year of St. Paul's imprisonment occurred the martyrdom of St. James, Bishop of Jerusalem, surnamed, probably from his stature, the Less, and from his high character both with Jews and Gentiles, the Just. On the death of Festus, Judæa was left for a time without a governor. St. James in his recently written Epistle to "the twelve tribes which are scattered abroad," reproved them with having "condemned and killed the Just." Taking advantage of the anarchy prevailing during the interregnum, the Scribes and Pharisees placing him upon a pinnacle of the Temple, ordered him to address the multitude below concerning "Jesus, the crucified one." "Why do ye ask me about Jesus, the Son of Man?" he asked them. "He sitteth at the right hand of the great Power, and is about to come in the clouds of Heaven." They waited to hear no more; hurling him down headlong, they stoned him, his last words being those of the Saviour, "Father, forgive them, for they know not what they do;" and whilst he was still praying a fuller despatched him with his beam.

In the same year as the martyrdom of St. James occurred that of St. Mark the Evangelist, the founder of the great See of Alexandria. That Mark laboured in Egypt is stated by Epiphanius and St. Jerome, and Eusebius mentions it as an event of which he had heard; "*They say* (φάσιν) [h] that this Mark was the first *that was sent* to Egypt.... and first established Churches in Alexandria," and from the statement of Eusebius [i], that in the eighth year of Nero (i.e. 62) Annianus succeeded him in the parish (i.e. the Diocese) of Alexandria, we may infer that Mark died (and it is believed that he suffered martyrdom) in that year or shortly before.

The mission of St. Mark to Alexandria is generally supposed to have been undertaken not later than A.D. 50, but this does not imply that there were not Christians in that city before his arrival. The Gospel was already known in Africa. Simon, whom "they compelled to bear the cross [k]," was "a man of Cyrene" in Africa. Amongst those who were present in Jerusalem on the great Day of Pentecost were dwellers "in Egypt and the parts of Libya about Cyrene;" and the eunuch of Queen Candace must have passed through Egypt on his return journey to Ethiopia or Abyssinia. Simon Zelotes is supposed to have preached in Egypt and Cyrene, and amongst the Prophets and Teachers at Antioch (Acts xiii 1), was Lucius of Cyrene.

But St. Mark is believed to have been the founder of the See of Alexandria, whence it gloried in the title of the Evangelical See, and the Bishops of that See, of whom

---

[h] H. E , II. 16   [i] Ibid., XXIV.
[k] ἠγγάρευσαν, *pressed into the service*, Matt. xxvii. 32.

The Conflict between the Fourth and Fifth Empires. 63

Annianus was the first[1], as early as the middle of the Third Century was specially designated Popes[m].

We have now traced the foundation of the two first in date of the Patriarchal Sees of Christendom. The foundation of the great Patriarchate of Rome properly belongs to a history of the Latin Church, but as the unhappy contentions between the Eastern and Western Churches mainly turned on the question as to *who* was the founder of the Church of Rome, it cannot be passed over in silence. Its origin is veiled in mystery; that St. Peter was its sole founder is an historical impossibility; the legend, based on a mistake, and supported by a forgery, when once it took root, "filled the land."

After the Council of Jerusalem (A.D. 50), Peter suddenly disappears from the Acts of the Apostles; it may be because he was overshadowed at Jerusalem, as well as amongst the Jewish Christians of the Dispersion, by St. James, Bishop of Jerusalem, and amongst the Greeks by St. Paul, to whom the Apostleship of the Gentiles particularly fell. We know that he was a married man[n], and that he was accompanied in his missionary tours by a Christian sister[o]; whether this was his wife or not we have no means of judging, except that Tertullian in reference to the passage thinks that St. Paul means, not "uxores sed simpliciter mulieres" Tradition tells us of his having a daughter named Petronilla, and St. Clement of Alexandria that he had sons, and some have imagined[p] that the "Marcus, my son," mentioned in the First Epistle of St Peter, may have been his own son.

Peter's missionary work was especially amongst the Jews

---

[1] Eus. H. E., III. 14.

[m] Theodore Balsamon says that, correctly speaking, the Bishops of Rome and Alexandria were Popes, of Antioch, Patriarchs, of Constantinople and Jerusalem, Archbishops.

[n] Some commentators have suggested that I Pet. v. 13, "the co-elect," συνεκλεκτή, in Babylon may have been his wife.

[o] ἀδελφὴν γυναῖκα; I Cor. IX. 5.

[p] See Farrar, Early Days of Christianity, II. 112.

of the Dispersion mentioned in his first Epistle, which it seems reasonable to infer that he wrote from Babylon on the Euphrates, although it is true that in the Revelation (xvii. 5) Rome is figuratively called Babylon; for that he should have spoken of Babylon when he meant Rome is unintelligible.

Lactantius says that Peter first went to Rome in Nero's reign, and Origen that he arrived there shortly before his death. Clement, Bishop of Rome, whilst relating the martyrdom of SS. Peter and Paul, does not specify that it occurred in Rome, nor does any statement leading to the conjecture occur till made A.D. 170 by Dionysius, Bishop of Corinth, and later on at the end of the Second Century by St. Irenæus and Tertullian. As the tradition was all but universal, and as there is no counter tradition, we may perhaps accept Peter's martyrdom in Rome (there is nothing to justify the legend that he was crucified with his head downwards); but it is historically certain that he could not have reached Rome till towards the end of Nero's reign.

The assertion of Eusebius[q] that Peter visited Rome in the reign of Claudius is founded on an error made by Justin Martyr[r]. All authorities agree that Simon Magus, mentioned in the Acts of the Apostles, visited Rome at some time or another; he was certainly there when Peter arrived, which we conclude was A.D. 67, and there is little doubt that he followed Peter thither, as his manner always was, to oppose and attack him. Justin Martyr says that Simon Magus went to Rome in the reign of Claudius, that he was honoured there as a god, and that a statue was erected to him between two bridges over the Tiber bearing the inscription, *Simoni Deo Sancto* (to Simon the holy god). What reason could the Romans possibly have for venerating a Samaritan sorcerer as a god? But Justin was misled by the statue and the inscription. In 1574, in the Pontificate of Gregory XIII., the very statue was dug up in an island of the Tiber, now called *Isola di San Bartolomeo*, with its

[q] H E., II. 2, 13, 14.   [r] Apol., I. 16.

inscription, *Semoni Sanco Deo Fidio Sacrum*, Sancus being a god of the Sabines, by whom he was held to be *deus fidius*, i.e. a god in whom they believed [s].

The year 44 was the year of the martyrdom of St James, the brother of St. John, and Peter also was thrown into prison by King Agrippa. On his release he went, we are told, "into another place" (Acts xii. 17) St. Luke, who had before specified such unimportant places as Lydda and Joppa, would not have dismissed the great capital of the world as "another place." The place referred to was probably Cæsarea, "where he abode." In A.D. 50 Peter was in Jerusalem at the Council. The late Professor Blunt, of Cambridge University, considers that Peter started on his long mission to Asia A.D. 54. In 58 St. Paul wrote his Epistle to the Romans; yet he makes no mention of Peter, not even in the long list of salutations to the Roman Christians, which he certainly would have done if Peter had been their Bishop. In that Epistle he spoke of his desire to "preach the Gospel to you that are in Rome also," in order to "impart some spiritual gift, to the end that ye may be established." But he tells the Romans (Rom. xv 20) that it was his rule not "to build upon another man's foundation," but to preach the Gospel where Christ was not already known. And what spiritual gift could St. Paul impart which St. Peter could not equally have imparted, had he been Bishop of Rome? It seems therefore impossible that Peter could have been in Rome before A.D. 58.

In A.D. 60 Paul was sent a prisoner to Rome, where he remained two years. After he had been a prisoner three days he called the chief of the Jews together (Acts xxviii. 17). They told him they had heard nothing against him, but "we desire to hear of thee what thou thinkest. for as concerning this sect we know that everywhere it is spoken against" Is it possible that if Peter had been Bishop of Rome they would not have obtained from him information

---

[s] A statue of him, found in 1879 on the slopes of the Quirinal, is now to be seen in the Vatican Museum at Rome

about the great Apostle of the Gentiles; that they would not have learnt the accusations that were brought against him; the persecution which he suffered from their own brethren? Paul was released from his imprisonment in A.D. 63, in A.D. 64 Peter wrote his First Epistle from Babylon.

St. Paul was sent for a second time a prisoner to Rome, A.D. 67. It cannot be believed that St. Peter was at Rome at that time, for in his Second Epistle to Timothy, written in that year, Paul says (2 Tim. iv. 16), "At my first trial .... all men forsook me: I pray God it may not be laid to their charge," and (2 Tim. iv. 11) " Only Luke is with me." Would he so have written if Peter had been Bishop of Rome? or if Peter had been in prison at that time at Rome, would not Paul have mentioned it?

There is no reason for supposing that Peter left Babylon immediately after he wrote his epistle, A.D. 64. Even had he done so, weighed down as he was with age, the journey would have occupied a considerable time. He would revisit on his way several Churches which he had planted. We have no reason to suppose that he as yet ever visited Europe. St. Paul in his Epistle to the Corinthians (1 Cor. iii. 6) says, "I have planted, and Apollos watered," but he makes no mention of Peter. At Corinth Peter had many followers, for Paul rebuked the Corinthians (1 Cor. i. 12) for being broken up into several sects, some followers of Paul, some of Apollos, some of Peter. Peter on his way to Rome would naturally wish to preach to his followers in Corinth; so that if Peter went to Rome at all, the journey from Babylon would have taken a considerable time.

We may conclude, therefore, that Peter arrived for the first time at Rome A.D. 67, after St. Paul wrote his Second Epistle to Timothy. On the Day of Pentecost there were at Jerusalem "strangers of Rome." St. Paul in his Epistle to the Romans sends a salutation to his kinsmen Andronicus and Junia, the partners of one of his imprisonments, "who were in Christ before him," and "of note among the Apostles" (Rom. xvi 6). To them and such like Apostolic men a great extension of the faith in Rome was probably due, so that St. Paul could speak of the faith of the Romans as "being spoken of by the whole world." During his first imprisonment at Rome, Paul preached the Kingdom of God with all confidence to all that came to him, no man forbidding him But as yet there was nothing that could be called a Church; no one to ordain Bishops, Priests and Deacons to the ministry. The Apostle of the Jews and the Apostle of the Gentiles were now in Rome together, and the Fathers speak of them as the joint-founders of the Roman Church; and if this was so, it must have been at this time.

The Christian Church had not, before the reign of Nero, been brought into contact with the Fourth Empire Tiberius, so far from consulting the Senate, as he is reported to have done, as to admitting Jesus among the gods, probably never heard of the Christians. Claudius was too much occupied with troubles from the Jews, whom he expelled from Rome, to concern himself with a religion so humble and harmless as Christianity. But his successor was Nero (A.D. 54-68), a monster in human form. Nero, says Eusebius[t], was the first of the Emperors who showed himself an enemy of the divine religion. On July 18, A D. 64, broke out the fire of Rome, which in its course of six days destroyed the greater part of the city. The crime was at once imputed to Nero[u], who to avoid public execration alighted on the Christians, already the subjects of popular hatred, against whom any accusation would be readily accredited. A fearful persecution ensued. Josephus, the Jewish Historian, makes no mention of a persecution of the Jews under Nero, who had his reasons for favouring them Nor was the persecution under Nero so much directed against the Christian Church as against the Christians themselves, "a set of people," says Tacitus, "the Founder of whom was Christ, who were held in abhorrence for their crimes." Still it is reckoned as the

[t] H. E., II 25.   [u] Tacitus, Ann, XV. 39

first and one of the most cruel of the ten persecutions of the Christian Church, and gave the Christians an insight into the terrible conflict which ensued with the Roman Empire. No kind of insult and cruelty was wanting. At the time when SS Peter and Paul reached Rome the persecution was at its height. The legend goes that Peter was induced by the Christians to fly from Rome. St. Ambrose, or a pseudo-Ambrose, relates that just outside the gates he met the Saviour, who to his question, " Lord, Whither goest Thou ? " (*Domine quo vadis ?*), replied, " I go to Rome to be crucified a second time " (*Vado Romam iterum crucifigi*). The place of meeting is represented by the Oratory now standing on the Appian Way. Returning in shame and sorrow to Rome, Peter was imprisoned in the Tullianum, a name in later times changed to Mamertinum, after the God of War, Mars or Mamers

The martyrdom of the two Apostles is said by St. Jerome to have taken place on the same day, which is supposed to have been June 29, A D. 68, the last year of Nero's reign. According to an ancient tradition, Peter, having first witnessed the martyrdom of his wife, was crucified on the precise spot where now stands the obelisk in the centre of the Piazza di San Pietro. St. Paul being a Roman citizen was beheaded, as is supposed on the Ostian way, at a place called Ad Aquas Salvias, on the spot where now stands the Abbadia delle Tre Fontane, so called from the legend that three fountains sprang up on the spot where the martyr's head struck the ground

Mention has now been made of the martyrdom of four of the Apostles, James the brother of St John, James, Bishop of Jerusalem, Peter and Paul. With regard to the other Apostles, with the exception of St. John, next to nothing is known for certain. Omitting what is obviously false, the sum of what general tradition asserts need only be given.

Andrew having preached among the Scythians returned to Jerusalem, and afterwards went to Byzantium, where he is said to have founded the Church and appointed Stachys Bishop, and after other travels suffered crucifixion at Patræ at the hands of the Proconsul of Achaia.

Philip was Bishop of Hierapolis in Phrygia, where he died at an advanced age.

Bartholomew or Nathaniel preached in India, into which country he carried a copy of St Matthew's Gospel, which Pantænus, head of the Catechetical School of Alexandria, when he went on a missionary tour to that country at the end of the second century, found there amongst the Christians. He suffered crucifixion at Albanopolis in Armenia.

Thomas, the Apostle of India, was the founder of the community called the Christians of St. Thomas, and suffered death at the hands of the Brahmins.

Simon Zelotes preached in Egypt and Mauretania, and was martyred in Persia.

Jude, called also Lebbeus and Thaddeus, was sent by St. Thomas to Abgarus, King of Edessa, and suffered martyrdom at Berytus.

Matthew or Levi preached in Parthia and Ethiopia, and died a natural death at Hieria in Palestine.

Matthias, of whom little is known, is supposed to have lived and died in Jerusalem.

St. John, the beloved Apostle, is the only one who is known to have survived the destruction of Jerusalem, thus fulfilling the prediction of our Lord, "If I will that he tarry till I come (i.e. in judgment on Jerusalem), what is that to thee?"

Nothing short of the direct interposition of God in the destruction of Jerusalem, and the impossibility of their carrying out the Mosaic Dispensation, could have convinced the Judaizing Christians of their fallibility, and that, under the New Dispensation, the worship of the Temple and the observances of the Mosaic Law were not necessary requirements. The time had come when the Old Testament was to have its fulfilment, when it was to be shown that the Law of Moses had only a typical meaning, and that the promises related not to the temporal Israel, but to the

Church of Christ   In A.D 70, Jerusalem fell under the arms of Titus, the son of the Roman Emperor Vespasian (69—79). The Christians, mindful of the warnings of their Saviour, and commanded, says Eusebius, by a divine revelation[1], had fled to Pella beyond the Jordan. Josephus, the Jewish Historian, ascribes the cause of the destruction of Jerusalem to the murder of St. James its Bishop. The days had come when the Jews saw the hated Romans "casting a trench about it, compassing it around, and keeping it in on every side." It is not necessary to recount the horrors that filled up the cup of unhappy Israel. Not one element of misery was absent. The city was levelled with the ground, and a plough passed over it in fulfilment of our Lord's prediction that "one stone should not be left upon another." Titus wished to save the Temple, a fire-brand cast into it by a Roman soldier caused a conflagration, and on Aug 10 the Temple was destroyed. The number of those who perished during the whole war, not including those who died of famine and other miseries, was reckoned at 1,337,490, the number of captives at 101,700. Part of the latter were consigned to perpetual imprisonment in the mines, part to fight in the Roman games with wild beasts and gladiators. Well might the Jews exclaim, "Zion is a wilderness and Jerusalem a desolation. Our holy and beautiful House, where our fathers praised Thee, is burnt up with fire, and all our pleasant things are laid waste" (Is. lxiv. 10, 11)

According to Sulpicius Severus, Titus thought to destroy Jerusalem, and with it Christianity, at one blow. After the fall of the City the Christian Church returned from Pella to its ruins, and probably at that time elected Simeon, the brother of James the Less, as their Bishop, and the Gentile Christians were thenceforward delivered from the bondage of the Mosaic Law.

Titus, a man distinguished for his virtues, succeeded his father Vespasian as Emperor, and after a short reign of two years was succeeded by his brother Domitian (81—

---

[1] H. E , III. 5.

96), the rival of Tiberius and Nero in vice and cruelty; and under him the second persecution of the Christians broke out, A.D. 95.

The Jews, notwithstanding the destruction of Jerusalem, continued to look forward to the coming of a temporal Messiah. With the Jews the Christians were confounded, and the suspicions of Domitian, who readily lent his ear to secret informers, were aroused on his hearing of Christians speaking of the Kingdom of Christ. Christianity had found its way into the Emperor's family. Two of his relatives, Flavius Clemens, his cousin, who held the Consulate, A.D. 95, and his wife Drusilla, were accused of Atheism (ἀθεότης), a charge commonly brought against Christians; the former suffered death, the latter was banished. Domitian being informed that there were living in Palestine Christians of the race of David, who were dangerous to his throne, in the hope of preventing the possibility of a rival Kingdom, issued an edict for the extermination of the House of David. Two grandsons of St. Jude, the Lord's brother (or rather cousin), were brought before him They acknowledged their relationship to the Messiah; but when they showed him their hands, hardened by toil and in cultivating their small farm, and convinced him that Christ's Kingdom was not an earthly but a Heavenly one, they were contemptuously dismissed.

To the persecution under Domitian the Church is indebted for the Revelation of St. John the Divine Of the ministerial course of St. John, considering how eminent an Apostle he was, little is known. During the life-time of the Virgin Mary he would, if she resided there, in fulfilment of the Saviour's injunction, have lived in Jerusalem.

Of the Virgin Mary, since just before the Day of Pentecost, no mention is made in the Acts of the Apostles; no mention is made there of her death, although it probably came within the period which it covers; no mention of her is made in the Epistles; and Revelation xii. 1 cannot refer to her She disappears from the Bible; she disappears from early Church history. Whether she died at Jerusalem, where her supposed tomb, close to Gethsemane, is now shown, or whether she accompanied St. John to Ephesus and died and was buried there, we nowhere learn.

Epiphanius says it is not known whether she died or did not die; whether she was buried or was not buried; simply Scripture is silent from the overwhelming weight of the wonder (διὰ τὸ ὑπέρβαλλον τοῦ θαύματος). The sword which "pierced her soul" (Luke ii. 35), is interpreted by the Fathers to apply to the pain of a mother on the Crucifixion of her son The Festival of the Nativity of the Blessed Virgin was introduced into the Greek Church in the VIIth Century, and is commemorated on September 8th; in the Latin Church in the VIIIth Century. Her death is in the Greek Church commemorated on August 11th, simply as "her falling to sleep," (κοίμησις); whilst in the Latin it is commemorated as the Assumption, to signify that her body was taken up into Heaven. The scanty details of her in the Fathers, some of whom go so far as to speak of our Saviour reproving her (Luke ii. 49), and charging her with unbelief (John iv. 2), and the fact that no special cultus was accorded her in the earliest ages of the Church, condemn the medieval error of paying her excessive adoration.

After the Council of Jerusalem we do not again hear of St. John in the Acts of the Apostles. His name occurs only once in the Epistles of St. Paul (Gal ii. 9) as one of the "pillars" of the Church. He is believed to have resided principally at Ephesus, the most important of the Asiatic cities. The next time after the Council that we hear of him is from himself (Rev. i. 9), "I, John, ... was in the Isle that is called Patmos, for the word of God, and for the testimony of Jesus Christ." This was probably in the persecution under Domitian. Tertullian speaks of his having been harmlessly plunged into a cauldron of "boiling oil, and afterwards being banished to an island." The former of these events, which is supposed by Roman Catholics to have occurred at Rome outside the gate leading to Latium, is commemorated in the Western Church on March 6, as the Festival St. John "Ante Portam Latinam" The whole legend may be dismissed as false, and there is no evidence of St. John's ever having been at Rome. Domitian contented himself with banishing him to Patmos, where, being in the Spirit on the Lord's Day (for the Day of our Lord's Resurrection supplemented, although it did not as yet supersede, the Jewish Sabbath), he received the Revelation, which on his return from Patmos after the persecution was ended he committed to writing, and sent to the Angels or Bishops of the seven Churches of Asia.

Domitian was succeeded by Nerva (96-98), an Emperor of humane and just character, and averse to the secret informers who had prejudiced his predecessors against the Christians. He forbade accusations brought by slaves against their masters to be accepted; ordered such informers under Domitian to be put to death, and issued an edict recalling the exiled Christians. After his return, St. John, making Ephesus his centre, travelled through the neighbouring countries, organizing and regulating Churches, probably on the model revealed to him at Patmos. Tertullian states that the Order of Bishops, if traced back, will be found to rest upon St. John, meaning thereby that under him the Episcopate was regulated and fully established in the Church. When too old and infirm to walk, he would be carried into Church, preaching the few words, "Beloved children, love one another;" this he would tell them afterwards was "the commandment of our Lord, and if this is obeyed it is enough." He died at Ephesus in extreme old age, in the last year of the First Century.

There is reason for believing that by the end of the First Century the Gospel had been preached throughout the world. The history of the Church during the Second and Third Centuries is mostly the history of the persecutions which it suffered in its conflict with the Roman Empire.

The blood of martyrs was the seed of the Church (*sanguis martyrum semen Ecclesiæ*). We have hitherto seen monsters of vice, like Nero and Domitian, men who delighted in cruelty for its own sake, persecuting the Christians; we shall now find the worst Emperors often the most humane, and the best Emperors, those who concerned themselves most in the well-being of the State, the bitterest and cruellest foes of the Christians.

A few words must be said in explanation of this otherwise unintelligible state of things. Amongst the Romans religion was closely connected with politics. From the time of Numa the Roman Kings held the title, and frequently performed the offices, of Pontifex Maximus, which Augustus and his successors continued to hold under the Empire. The Laws of the Twelve Tables forbade foreign and unlawful religions (*illicitæ religiones*); and, although it was tolerant of the national religions of the countries which it vanquished, the State kept to itself the right of determining what religions were, and what were not, lawful. But Christianity was not the religion of one nation, but a catholic religion, comprising all nations and languages. Nor was it a tolerant but a proselytising religion; the polytheistic worship of the Romans was incompatible with the worship of the One True God; the Christian religion must be the religion of the whole world, which in the eyes of the Romans was only a mode of expressing the Roman Empire.

Thus Christianity was at once brought into contact with the Empire. Loyalty to the Emperor was part of the Christian creed, but the divinity of the Emperor, whom the Romans enrolled amongst their gods, the Christians could not acknowledge. To them the heathen sacrifices were an abomination; to the Roman merchants and mechanics, the more gods and the more sacrifices there were, the greater the profit, and this profit Christianity threatened to destroy. Thus Christianity was thought not to be compatible with subjection to the Empire; whilst the Christians also loathed the popular spectacles of the arena which were bound up with Paganism. Religious societies (*collegia*, ἑταιρεῖαι) and nocturnal associations were forbidden by the Roman law, and the Christians held their religious meetings by night. For such reasons they were branded as dangerous, as morose, and even enemies of the human race

Under the short reign of Nerva, when persecution was suspended, Christianity rapidly advanced ; but so long as it was a forbidden (*illicita*) religion, there could be no lasting security, and under his successor, Trajan (98-117), it broke out again, and now entered upon a new stage. A statesman like Trajan could little brook a community so thoroughly at variance with the Roman spirit. Pliny, a man of unimpeachable character, the Pro-consul of Pontus and Bithynia, countries in which the Christians were very numerous, finding that they refused to sacrifice to the gods or to take part in the heathen sacrifices, wrote to Trajan for instruction as to how he was to deal with them. With their character he concerned himself but little ; Paganism he regarded as a matter of State, and Christianity as a violation of its laws. He could find no fault in them except that they met before daylight, and sang a hymn alternately to Christ as God, and bound themselves by an oath (*sacramentum*) against sin Trajan in his rescript told Pliny that Christians were not to be sought out, but if they were brought before him and convicted they should be punished ; what the punishment was to be (although probably it was death) he does not state. But in no case should an accusation be received without the signature of the informer ; and any Christian on showing his repentance by sacrificing was to be pardoned.

The martyrdom of St. Clement, Bishop of Rome, must be dismissed as a fiction of the Ninth Century. He is said to have been first banished to the Crimea, and afterwards, by order of Trajan, to have been cast into the sea with an anchor fastened round his neck. The third persecution, that under Trajan, extended as far as Syria and Palestine. In

A D 104, before the correspondence took place between Trajan and Pliny, occurred the martyrdom by crucifixion of St. Simeon, the Bishop of Jerusalem, venerable with one hundred and eleven years of age. No other accusation seems to have been brought against him except one by some Gnostic heretics of being a descendant of the House of David, and, as such, an imaginary aspirant to the throne.

After the publication of Trajan's edict, the most notable martyr of the reign was St. Ignatius (called Theophorus), a disciple of St. John and the successor of Evodius in the See of Antioch. At the time that Trajan was at war with Parthia and was passing through Antioch (A.D. 115), the city was visited by an earthquake, by which the Emperor's life was endangered. The calamity, as such calamities usually were, was attributed to the wrath of the gods for the toleration granted to the Christians, and the cry *Christianos ad leones* was at once raised. Ignatius having voluntarily surrendered himself was brought before the Emperor. It may be that his excessive zeal for martyrdom provoked the Emperor, and he was sentenced to be taken in chains to Rome and thrown to the wild beasts. A morbid desire of martyrdom was condemned by the early Church; "Whoever," says St. Clement of Alexandria, "does not avoid persecution . . . becomes an accomplice with the persecutor, and if he provokes and challenges the wild beasts, he is certainly guilty." Such, however, was not the feeling of St. Ignatius. "I thank Thee, O Lord," he said, when sentence was passed on him, ". . that Thou hast made me to be put in iron bonds, with Thy Apostle Paul."

On his journey towards Rome, several Bishops of the neighbouring Asiatic Churches met him in order to take a solemn farewell, amongst others being Onesimus, now Bishop of Ephesus, undoubtedly the same as the run-away slave mentioned in the Epistle to Philemon. At Smyrna, Ignatius stopped several days with its Bishop, Polycarp, once his fellow-disciple under St. John, and soon to become

The Conflict between the Fourth and Fifth Empires. 77

his brother in martyrdom. From Smyrna and again from Troas he wrote letters, in all seven, to various Churches, in which he lays particular stress on the necessity of the Episcopate. To the Trullians he speaks of the three Orders in the ministry, " without which there is no Church." " Every Bishop," he tells them, " is the Vicar of Christ." The Magnesians he enjoins : " Be subject to your Bishop . . . as Jesus Christ to the Father, according to the Flesh." To the Church of Smyrna, " Without authority of the Bishop it is not lawful to baptize nor to celebrate the Communion;" " Hearken unto your Bishop, that God also may hearken unto you."

The morbid hankering after martyrdom clung to him to the last; and apparently in the fear that they might take some step to avert it, he wrote in his epistle to the Romans; " I fear your love, lest it do me injury.... Ye cannot do me a greater kindness than by suffering me to be sacrificed unto God.... Suffer me to be food for the wild beasts. ... My birthday is at hand. . . Encourage the beasts, that they may become my sepulchre, and may leave nothing of my body."

In his long and tedious journey to Rome, the fatigue of which an old man was ill able to endure, he suffered much cruelty from the soldiers who attended him; he had to fight, he said in his letter to the Romans, "with beasts both by sea and land, by night and day, being bound to ten leopards, that is to a band of soldiers." Arrived at Rome his desire was at once accomplished. It was the last day of the Saturnalia, A.D. 115, being thrown to the lions, he was speedily despatched, nothing but the larger bones remaining.

Trajan was succeeded by Hadrian I. (117—138), who, Tertullian says, was not a persecutor of the Christians. In his reign we have the first of a series of the Apologies published by Christians in the defence of their faith. Dionysius the Areopagite is said to have been the first Bishop of Athens, and to have been succeeded by Publius, who (although the date is uncertain) suffered martyrdom. The first of the Apologies addressed to Hadrian was written by his successor, Quadratus, and another soon afterwards by Aristides, a converted philosopher[y]. These drew forth from the Emperor a rescript which was even more favourable to the Christians than that of Trajan; if Christians acted contrary to the laws, they were to be punished in proportion to the offence; but the greatest care was to be taken (*magnopere curabis*) that calumnious accusations be visited as they deserve.

Favourable as he was to the Christians, Hadrian's reign was terribly calamitous to the unhappy Jews. So recently as A.D. 115, the Jews of Cyrene had broken out into open rebellion. To curb their insurrectionary spirit and to dissipate their hopes of a national restoration, Hadrian inflicted on them the grossest indignities; he refounded Jerusalem under the title of Ælia Capitolina, forbade them to practise the rite of Circumcision, and built a temple to Jupiter on Mount Moriah. A formidable rebellion of the Jews, A.D. 132, under a pretending Messiah, who assumed the name Barcochebas (the Son of a Star, a name meant to signify that he was the Star predicted by Balaam), was the consequence. The Christians now suffered from two opposite causes; one from the Romans through their being confounded with the Jews, the other from the Jews because they refused to "deny Jesus of Nazareth" and to recognize the impostor. After a repetition of the horrors of the first siege, Jerusalem was reduced to a state of ruin; 80,000 persons, beside large numbers who died from hunger and other causes, are said to have perished in the war. The Jews were expelled from Jerusalem; thenceforward no Jew was allowed to enter the City, except on one day in the year, the anniversary of its destruction, and then only by payment of a heavy fine.

[y] A fragment of the Apology of Aristides was found in 1878 in the Armenian Convent in Venice, and in 1889 a complete Syrian translation in the Convent on Mount Sion.

The Conflict between the Fourth and Fifth Empires. 79

The Christian Church now finally emancipated itself from the trammels of the Synagogue. Fifteen Bishops, all of them Jews, had presided over the Church of Jerusalem. Between the death of Simeon and the second destruction of Jerusalem no fewer than thirteen Bishops presided over the See, a fact that seems either to show that the most aged Presbyters were selected, or to point to a severe persecution. The Christians, who had hitherto observed the outward ceremonies of the Law, now felt their deliverance from the bondage, and as a significant result, elected an uncircumcised Gentile, Mark, as Bishop of Jerusalem. Gentile, or only such of the Jewish, Christians as were ready to abandon the Law of Moses were allowed to inhabit Jerusalem. The Judaizing Christians again retired to Pella where they became split up into two sects, Nazarenes and Ebionites. The former name, hitherto the common appellation of Christians, was restricted to a party which accepted the Epistles of St. Paul, and held that the Mosaical Law was not binding on Gentile Christians. The Ebionites, who took their name from a Hebrew word signifying *poor*, were the virulent opponents of the memory of St Paul, and favourers of St. Peter; they regarded Christ as a mere Man, and held that the Law of Moses was binding on Jews and Gentiles alike.

* * * * * * *

The history of the first three centuries of the Christian Church has been so often and so fully written, that we must content ourselves with giving little more than the names of the most famous sufferers in the conflict which continued between the Christian Church and the Roman Empire before the final victory was achieved [1].

The gentle Emperor, Antoninus Pius (138—161), though personally favourable to the Christians, had his hands tied by the tumultuous charges brought against them on account of a prevailing pestilence; to annul the decrees of his

---

[1] The writer has himself given a full account in a work entitled *History of the Church Catholic*.

predecessors at such a time would have been the signal of a revolution; and the martyrdom, in his reign, of Telesphorus, Bishop of Rome (128—139), called forth, A.D. 139, the first Apology of Justin Martyr, a converted Pagan Philosopher. He demonstrated that Christ's Kingdom was not a temporal but a spiritual one; he dwelt on the fulfilment of prophecy in the Person of the Saviour; on the conversion of the Gentiles, and the destruction of Jerusalem, on the innocent lives of the Christians, and their patient endurance under persecution.

The peace of the Church was rudely interrupted in the reign of the successor of Antoninus, the Stoic philosopher Marcus Aurelius (161—180), an Emperor generally distinguished for his wisdom and justice, as well as the simplicity and gentleness of his character; but who was, next to Nero, the worst foe that Christ's Kingdom had as yet encountered. Between Stoicism and Christianity there was no affinity; devoted to his philosophical pursuits, he had little time or opportunity of contrasting the lives of the Christians with those of the heathens; Christianity he despised as obstinacy ($\psi\iota\lambda\dot{\eta}$ $\pi\alpha\rho\acute{\alpha}\tau\alpha\xi\iota\varsigma$), and could not understand the convictions of men who preferred death to idolatry. The numerous calamities which assailed Italy during his reign were all attributed to the anger of the gods which the Christians had provoked. Under Aurelius persecution entered on a new stage; the limited protection which his predecessors had granted was withdrawn; Christians were now to be sought for, and to be subjected to the cruellest tortures in order to induce them to recant.

In the early part of the reign, Justin Martyr published his second Apology. Even if the Emperor ever saw it, which it is doubtful, it was ineffectual in deflecting him from his purpose; Justin was, A.D. 163, beheaded in Rome, and gained the title of Martyr, which has been accorded him from the earliest times to the present day. His martyrdom was followed (perhaps A.D. 166) by that of St. Polycarp, Bishop of Smyrna, the disciple of St. John, and probably the Angel of the Church addressed in the Apocalypse.

A terrible persecution of the Churches of Vienne and Lyons in Gaul, which had shortly before been founded by missionaries from Asia Minor sent by St. Polycarp, took place A.D. 177. Some heathen slaves accused their Christian masters of eating human flesh, like Thyestes, and living in incestuous marriage, like Œdipus; charges which arose from mistaken ideas of the sacrifice of the Christian Eucharist, and of the Agape or Love Feast. The venerable Bishop Pothimus, already broken down in health, and sinking under the weight of ninety-six years, after being unmercifully beaten and stoned by the mob, was thrown, in an almost lifeless state, into prison, where he died in two days. He was succeeded in the See of Lyons by St. Irenæus (177—202), whose name is derived from a Greek word, εἰρήνη, signifying peace.

A memorable event in Polycarp's Episcopate was a conference between him and Anicetus, Bishop of Rome, with regard to the time of keeping Easter The Asiatics following the time of the Jewish Passover, celebrated the Paschal Supper on the fourteenth day of the first Jewish month, Nisan, whence they were called Quarto-Decimans; and three days later, whether the day was Sunday or not, the Lord's Resurrection. The Western Church, on the other hand, always kept their Easter on a Sunday. The two Bishops failed in coming to an agreement, but the conference was carried on in a friendly spirit, Anicetus, in his Church at Rome, requesting Polycarp to celebrate at the Holy Eucharist, at which he himself was present.

The question as to the proper time of keeping Easter was renewed under very different auspices in the Patriarchate of Victor I., Bishop of Rome (190—202). Victor conceived the idea that the Church of Rome had the right of coercing the Eastern Churches, and ordered them, under pain of excommunication, to follow the Western observance, and on their refusal excommunicated them. Irenæus, now Bishop of Lyons, whose own practise was in agreement with that of Rome, acted as mediator, and through him peace was restored, but he recalled to the mind of Victor the different spirit in which the question had been discussed between Anicetus and Polycarp.

Under Victor we find the first beginnings of the claims of the See of Rome, and since the claims of that See so materially affect the history of the Greek Church, it will be as well to inquire whether between the Pontificate of Anicetus and that of Victor anything occurred which gave the handle to Roman claims over the Sees of Eastern Christendom.

There is no necessity for accusing a sister Church of wilful fraud, or of anything beyond a reckless credulity, but about this time the Church of Rome lent a ready ear to one of the most monstrous forgeries on the page of history. An Ebionite, that is to say a heretic of the sect which strove to magnify St. Peter, the Apostle of the Jews, and to discredit St. Paul, the Apostle of the Gentiles, makes St. Clement, Bishop of Rome, address a letter to St. James, Bishop of Jerusalem, saying that Peter, when on the point of death, appointed him as his successor, and forced him into his chair; hence arose the notion of Cathedra Petri, *the chair of Peter*. But Eusebius[a], quoting from St. Irenæus, gives the succession of the earliest Bishops of the Roman See; he says:—" The blessed Apostles having founded and established the Church entrusted the office of the Episcopate to Linus; Anencletus succeeded him, and after him in the third place from the Apostles, Clement received the Episcopate." So that, even had Peter ever been Bishop of Rome, two Bishops intervened between him and Clement, and as the Episcopate of Clement began A.D. 92, it was impossible that Peter, who was martyred A.D. 68, could have ordained him as his successor. This romance gained credence and laid the foundation of the claims of the Popes of Rome, and Tertullian, who wrote about A.D. 200,

[a] H E., V. 6.

at the time that Victor was Bishop, mentions a belief prevalent in Rome that Clement was ordained by Peter to be his successor. But even the romance itself, the object of which was to magnify not the Roman Church but St. Peter, is fatal to the papal pretensions of supremacy, and if one part was deserving of credit, the first paragraph was equally deserving of credit; the letter is addressed, "Clement to James, the lord and *Bishop of Bishops* .... *and of the Churches everywhere.*"

The fifth persecution of the Christians occurred in the reign of Septimius Severus (193—211). Septimius, who was at first favourable to Christianity, whilst passing through Asia and the East came in contact with the Montanists, one of whose crotchets was that the end of the Roman Empire and of the world was at hand. Alarmed at such a prediction, and confusing Montanists with the orthodox Christians, he issued, A.D. 202, an edict forbidding his subjects to embrace either Judaism or Christianity. A terrible persecution of the Christians in Egypt and North Africa ensued. At Alexandria, the most famous of its victims was Leonidas, the father of the famous Origen. Amongst the martyrs, the names of two females of Carthage, a wealthy married lady named Perpetua, only twenty-two years of age, and a married slave, Felicitas, have ever since been household words; the gaoler, we are told, was so struck with the fortitude of these and his other prisoners, that he himself became a convert, and to be a convert under such a circumstance was to be a martyr, for Christianity.

It was probably at the commencement of the persecution that Tertullian (*circa* 160—230) wrote his famous Apology. A native of Carthage and a Pagan by birth, he was converted to Christianity about A.D. 196, and being ordained at Carthage, was for a time its powerful literary defender, but soon afterwards attaching himself to the Montanists, became the bitter opponent of the Church. The Montanists derived their name from their founder Montanus, in the latter half of the Second Century, a native of Phrygia, whence they were called Phrygians and Cataphrygians. Montanus was accused of calling himself the Paraclete or Comforter; and he and his followers, although they received the Old and New Testaments, and were orthodox on the doctrine of the Trinity, gave much trouble to the Church; claiming for themselves a greater sanctity and superior light to that vouchsafed to the Church, and refusing to hold communion with persons who fell into sin after Baptism. It may be remarked that Tertullian, though a native of Carthage, was the first of the Fathers of the Church who wrote in Latin. The persecution smouldered on till the death of Severus, which occurred at York.

The sixth persecution broke out under Maximin the Thracian (235—238). Earthquakes, which destroyed several cities, stimulated the fury of the populace against the Christians; the Emperor lent his ear to accusations brought against them, and thinking thus to destroy the Church, issued an edict against the clergy. The persecution, however, was not violent, and was cut short by his death. Under his successor, Gordian (238—244), the Christians had rest. Gordian being murdered, was succeeded by Philip the Arabian (244—249), who is supposed to have been a Christian, and it is said that when he was passing through Antioch, Babylas the Bishop subjected him to penance, on the ground of the murder of his predecessor, before admitting him to Church privileges.

Philip being killed in a rebellion at Verona, was succeeded by Decius (249—251), under whom the seventh, the most terrible of all, except the tenth persecution, took place. Actuated by hatred of his predecessor he determined to exterminate Christianity; every imaginable kind of torture and cruelty was resorted to, and a universal panic prevailed[b]. The zeal and courage which characterized

---

[b] It was in this persecution that Paul, the first of the Hermits, at the age of twenty-two retired to the desert, where he dwelt for ninety years

the Church in its adversity had deserted it in its late period of comparative rest, and many Christians under torture and threat of the loss of their goods now succumbed. Of these lapsed (*lapsi*) Christians there were three classes, the most criminal being those who offered sacrifice to the heathen gods (*sacrificati*); a scarcely less criminal class was that of those who offered incense (*thurificati*); a third class consisted of those who had purchased certificates of having complied with the Emperor's commands (*libellatici*). In the West, Fabian, Bishop of Rome (236—251), in the East, St. Babylas[c], Bishop of Antioch (237—251), and Alexander, Bishop of Jerusalem, who had already forty years before been a Confessor in the persecution of Severus, were in the list of martyrs. The celebrated Origen, thrown into prison and laden with chains, with an iron collar round his neck, his feet in stocks, and his body daily stretched on the rack, was a Confessor in the persecution.

Origen, born about A.D. 185 of Christian parents at Alexandria, who, as before stated, lost his father in the persecution under Septimius Severus, succeeded, at the age of 18 years, Clemens Alexandrinus in the headship of the famous Catechetical School at Alexandria. In A.D. 228, when on a visit to the Holy Land, whither the fame of his learning had preceded him, he was at the age of 43 ordained Priest by Alexander, Bishop of Jerusalem, and Theoctistus, Bishop of Cæsarea. This infringement on his episcopal rights, and perhaps envy of the increasing fame of Origen, excited the anger of his former friend, Demetrius, Bishop of Alexandria, by whom, after two Alexandrine Synods (A.D. 231—232), he was excommunicated, his Orders being annulled; he was also deposed from the Catechetical School; nor was the sentence removed under Heracleas and Dionysius, the two successors of Demetrius. Finding his position untenable at Alexandria he went to Cæsarea, where for a quarter of a century he delivered lectures on philosophy; one of his pupils being the famous Theodore or Gregory, who was

[c] He is commemorated in the Eastern Church on September 4.

converted by him to Christianity. Gregory became Bishop of Neo-Cæsarea (*circa* 230—270), where, by the miracles which he performed, he gained the name of Thaumaturgus, and continued for Origen so strong an affection that he compared it to that between David and Jonathan.

The object of Origen was the legitimate one of reconciling philosophy, especially that of Plato, with Christianity, and the amount of his literary work was immense. He survived his imprisonment under Decius, but died immediately afterwards from the effects of his cruel treatment. Thus the father was a Martyr, and the son, if not a Martyr, a Confessor. His life-long opposition to heresy; his great work, the Hexapla (so called from the six parallel columns of Hebrew and Greek versions of the Bible under which it was arranged), were enough to gain him esteem, but he was placed under the permanent ban of the Church. Dionysius, a man of almost universal knowledge, whom Eusebius calls "the great Bishop of Alexandria," and St. Athanasius terms "teacher of the Catholic Church," although he always bore him a sincere attachment, did not, as we have seen, remove the sentence of excommunication [d].

About the same time as Origen, lived St. Cyprian, Bishop of Carthage (248—258), the second writer after Tertullian, or, as some think, the greatest, in the Carthaginian Church. In the second year of his Episcopate the Decian persecution broke out, and the cry "Cyprian to the lions" was at once raised. Cyprian, like his great contemporaries, Dionysius of Alexandria and Gregory Thaumaturgus, did not court martyrdom, but pleading a divine command, sought a neighbouring refuge, from which he continued to govern his Diocese, waiting till the tyranny should be overpast. Returning after a year to Carthage he found himself overwhelmed in a sea of troubles.

Soon after his return he convened a Council of Bishops

---

[d] Dionysius was, says Dean Farrar, "one of the most interesting and beautiful characters of ecclesiastical history" "The loss of his writings is," says Dr. Neale, "one of the greatest that has been suffered of ecclesiastical history."

to consider the case of those who had lapsed, in which a moderate course was resolved on; those who had offered sacrifice or incense were to be re-admitted into the Church after penance, whilst the *libellatici*, who were guilty of a lighter offence, were to be received at once. Against this course, Novatus, a Presbyter of Carthage, of evil notoriety, who had before opposed Cyprian, veering round from his former clemency for the lapsed, created a party of rigorists who succeeded in obtaining the consecration of one Fortunatus, a well-known opponent of Cyprian, to the See of Carthage. Novatus having done all the harm in his power in the African Church proceeded to Rome, where two rival Bishops had been elected in succession to the martyred Fabian, Cornelius, by the unanimous voice of the clergy and people, and Novatian, who had been originally a Stoic philosopher, and had received clinical Baptism, and was uncanonically ordained to the Priesthood. Cyprian despatched two Bishops to Rome to enquire into the schism, with the result that Cornelius was recognised by the Carthaginian Church as the rightful Bishop, whilst a Council at Rome excommunicated Novatian and adopted with regard to the lapsed the same course that had been determined on at Carthage. Novatus succeeded in getting Novatian over to his side, and a sect of Novatians arose, holding the same doctrines, but differing from the Catholics in refusing to receive back the lapsed, and those who fell into sin after Baptism. The Novatians held much the same position towards the Church as the Montanists, and after a few years claimed the name of Cathari, or Pure, the Puritans of the Anglican Church. They found a supporter in Fabius (251—252), the successor of St. Babylas in the See of Antioch, but were condemned, A.D. 252, by a Council of Antioch under Demetrius (252—260), the successor of Fabius.

Decius having been slain in battle by the Goths was succeeded by Gallus (251—253), who, following the example of his predecessor, issued an edict ordering the Christians to sacrifice. Gallus being assassinated was succeeded by

Valerian (253—260), who associated with himself his son Gallienus in the government (253—268).

Cornelius and his successor, Lucius I., having suffered martyrdom, the See of Rome was next occupied by Stephen I. (253—257), who allowed himself to be governed by the same arrogance that had marked the conduct of his predecessor, Victor, in the matter of the Asiatic Churches. With regard to the lapsed, Stephen and Cyprian were at one, but on a question which sprung up at this time, Baptism administered by heretics, they were hopelessly at variance. The question has a double importance, both intrinsically, and also as showing the relative position of the Eastern and Western Churches. At Rome Baptism conferred by heretics was held as valid; but in Asia and Africa, on the ground that Baptism could only be conferred by the Church, such Baptism was considered no Baptism at all, and this view was adopted in two Councils held under Cyprian at Carthage, one A.D. 255, the other in the beginning of A.D. 256. Stephen branded and denounced Cyprian as a false prophet, and excommunicated the Asiatic and African Churches. Dionysius, the great Bishop of Alexandria, in a vain attempt to act as mediator, wrote several letters to Stephen, begging him to consider the grave consequences of his conduct. Cyprian wrote, A.D. 256, to Firmilian, Bishop of the Cappadocian Cæsarea, a man eminent as a theologian and a philosopher, on the subject; Firmilian strongly supported the view of Cyprian and the Eastern Church, that heretics ought to be re-baptized.

Whilst the intemperate and arrogant assumption of Stephen must be condemned, on the point of doctrine the Easterns were wrong and Stephen right, as was afterwards determined in the Council of Arles (A.D. 314). To the excommunication of the Roman Bishop the Eastern Church paid no regard, and Firmilian told him that he separated himself from the other Churches (*excidisti te ipsum*), and not those Churches from him; he tells him not to deceive himself, and calls him a schismatic for that he had withdrawn himself from the unity of the Church. It is evident that Firmilian knew of no distinctive dignity between his own See and that of Rome. In the autumn of A.D. 256 was held at Carthage a Council, attended by eighty-seven Bishops from Africa, Numidia, and Mauretania, besides other clergy and a large body of laity, and there Cyprian, with an evident reference to the Bishop of Rome, laid it down as a maxim ; "None of us constitutes himself Bishop of Bishops, nor tyrannically frightens his colleagues into a necessary obedience (*tyrannico terrore ad obsequendi necessitatem, collegas suos adigit*), since every Bishop ... is as incapable of being judged by another as he is of judging another." The Council unanimously affirmed its previous decisions.

Cyprian, whilst supporting the independence of the Episcopate, conceded a precedence of dignity to the See of Rome, on account of the importance of the city (*pro magnitudine suâ debet Carthaginem Roma precedere*); and he speaks of it as the Chair of Peter (*Petri Cathedra*). The precedence of dignity accorded to the See of Rome is that afterwards, and for the same reason, accorded it by the Œcumenical Councils, viz. because it was Old Rome, the seat of Empire. His calling it the Chair of Peter shows that the Clementine fiction had now done its work ; it is evident that, if Peter was never Bishop of Rome, Cyprian had been deceived by what he had heard, and as he was speaking nearly two hundred years after Peter's death he is not an authority on that part of the subject.

Cyprian's own conduct is the best evidence of the independent jurisdiction of the Episcopate, and of the primitive custom of Bishops seeking the counsel and advice of their brother Bishops. Two Spanish Bishops, Basilides and Martiales, were, on their confession of crimes with which they were charged, canonically deposed ; they then went to Rome and consulted Stephen, who took their part. Thereupon a deputation from the Spanish Churches waited upon Cyprian, who saw that the deposition of the Bishops was in accordance with the canons of the Church; and after a Council attended by thirty-seven Numidian Bishops, without consulting Stephen, he wrote, in the name of the Council, to the Spanish Church, to adhere to what it had done, without regard to the opinion of the Bishop of Rome [e].

The Emperor Valerian was at first favourable to the Christians, but in his fifth year the eighth persecution broke out. In A.D. 257, Dionysius, accompanied by Maximus, then a Priest, but afterwards his successor in the See of Alexandria, was brought before the Prefect Æmilian (one of the so-called thirty tyrants who invaded the Imperial power in Egypt), and Dionysius was ordered to recant, and "adore the gods who preserve the Empire." "We reverence and adore," said Dionysius, "one God, the Maker of all things, Who gave the Empire into the hands of Valerian and Gallienus, beloved of God, and to Him we pray continually that their government may remain unshaken;" he was then banished, first to Kephro in the Libyan desert, and afterwards to Coluthion, a city of Maræotis. After the persecution was ended he returned to Alexandria, of which he died Bishop in the beginning of 265.

On August 2, of the first year of the persecution, Stephen, Bishop of Rome, and in 251 Sixtus II., his successor, together with his Archdeacon Laurence, suffered martyrdom. Cyprian was sent into banishment to Curubis, a place about forty miles from Carthage, but on the appointment of a new governour was enabled after a year to return, only to die a Martyr, A.D. 258.

During the Valerian persecution an outbreak of the Sabellian heresy, or the denial of the real distinction of Persons in the Trinity, occurred in Alexandria. The heresy had been taught, A.D. 200, by Praxeas, a native of Asia Minor, and, about A.D. 235, by Noetus, a native of Smyrna, who communicated it to his pupil Sabellius, an Italian. Meeting with much opposition in Rome, Sabellius

[e] Neander I., Bohn's Ed. Burton, Eccl. Hist., p. 549.

went to the East, where he found a readier acceptance of his doctrine, and was ordained a Presbyter at Ptolemais. On account of the prevalence of Sabellianism in Alexandria, the matter was brought before Dionysius at the time he was an exile in Libya. Dionysius condemned the heresy, but, in doing so, laid himself open to what was afterwards known as Arianism, by asserting that the Son was made and produced and therefore was not before he was produced; and his words were reported by the Catholics of Pentapolis to Dionysius (259—269), the successor of Sixtus in the See of Rome. A Council at Rome condemned the extracts submitted to it, and the Bishop of Rome wrote to his namesake of Alexandria for an explanation. That this was no unusual course we have seen in the case of two Spanish Bishops appealing to St. Cyprian ; the Bishop of Alexandria, in a work entitled a *Refutation and Apology,* gave the explanation required, and was pronounced innocent of the charge of Sabellianism. Notwithstanding this acquittal, St. Basil the Great unjustly, and perhaps at second hand, charged him with being the originator of Arianism [f].

About the same time another form of Sabellianism was accredited to Paul, a native of Samosata on the Euphrates, who, about A.D. 261, succeeded to the Bishopric of Antioch, and possesses the unenviable notoriety of being the first Episcopal heresiarch. Paul, a mere ecclesiastical mountebank, and a man of low origin, having obtained the See of Antioch by simony regarded it in the light of a profitable speculation. Through the interest of Zenobia a Jewess, (widow of Odenathus, King of Palmyra), who was for some years virtually Empress of the East, he obtained the lucrative post of Ducenarius, under which title rather than that of Bishop he preferred to be called, affecting all the pomp of a Roman magnate, appearing in public with a large retinue of attendants, whilst he introduced a theatrical affectation into his church. His moral character also was far from blameless.

[f] Farrar's Lives of the Fathers.

These matters caused scandal enough, but they were brought to a head by his heretical teaching on the Incarnation and the Trinity. Zenobia placed herself under Paul for instruction in the principles of Christianity, and the scheme which he presented to her was one which was reconcileable with Judaism. He taught that Christ had no existence before he was born of the Virgin Mary; that there were not Three Persons in the Godhead but literally One God; that the Logos, *Word*, was not a distinct Person; that Jesus is only called God because the Logos descended on Him, without Personal union being inherited; and the Christians in Antioch he forbade to worship the Saviour or to sing hymns in His honour.

Paul was opposed by Dionysius of Alexandria and Dionysius of Rome, and having been condemned in two Councils at Antioch, one A.D. 264 under Firmilian, Bishop of Cæsarea [g], after which he promised amendment; and in a second Council, A D. 269, was, on his relapsing into his heresy, deposed, Domnus being appointed to succeed him in the See of Antioch.

Valerian dying A.D. 260, his son Gallienus, in the interest of peace rather than from any attachment to Christianity, issued an edict for toleration; the persecution came to an end, and till A.D. 274 the Church's peace was uninterrupted. In that year the Emperor Aurelian (270—275) planned what is called the ninth persecution; it was, however, averted through his assassination in the same year at the hand of a pagan officer.

The Church now enjoyed an immunity from persecution till the reign of Diocletian (284—305), under whom the tenth and last, but the severest, of all the persecutions occurred.

[g] This Council rejected the word Homoousion, but in a different sense to that under which it was adopted at the Council of Nice.

CHAPTER II.

The Victory of Christ's Kingdom.

THE Tenth Persecution—Constantine becomes Emperor—Battle of the Milvian Bridge—Constantine's Vision of the Cross—Mode of election of the Alexandrine Bishops—Edict of Milan—The Donatists—Council of Arles—Of Ancyra—Of Neo-Cæsarea—Defeat and Death of Licinius—Constantine sole Emperor—Christianity the Religion of the Roman Empire—Monasticism—The Pillar-Saints

DIOCLETIAN, a man of low birth, elected by the soldiers at Chalcedon after the murder of his predecessor Numerian, commenced, A.D. 284, the reign known in history as the era of Martyrs, and chose Nicomedia in Bithynia as the Imperial residence [a]. In A.D. 286 he took as his colleague Maximian, a man like himself of low birth, to whom he gave the command of the West, whilst he himself kept that of the East. These two reigned as Augusti, and in 293 associated with themselves Constantius Chlorus (χλωρός, *the pale*), who divorced his wife, Helena, and married Maximian's step-daughter, Theodora, and Galerius, who married Diocletian's daughter, Valeria; these two bore the title of Cæsars, the former governing Gaul, Spain, and Britain, the latter reigning in the East.

With Maximian is connected the legend of the Theban Legion. According to the Martyrologies, or, as they are called in the Greek Church, Menologies (μήν, *a month*), the Emperor when about to proceed, A.D. 286, against an insurgent tribe, summoned from the East a Legion under its leader Maurice, entirely composed of Christians, which, from its having been enrolled in the Thebais was known as the Theban Legion. When called upon to sacrifice to the heathen gods, they to a man refused, and after being

[a] The year of his accession formed the basis of Chronology till it was superseded by the Christian Era of Dionysius Exiguus.

twice decimated without effect, were put to a wholesale massacre, the entire Legion to the number of 6,600 dying as Martyrs to the Faith. The scene of the massacre was the present St. Moritz, in the Engadine, which received its name from the leader, St. Maurice, one of the slain. Whatever degree of truth may attach to the legend, Maximian, a man of harsh and savage disposition, was imbued with a bitter hatred of the Christians, whilst his colleague in the West, Constantius, was favourably disposed towards them.

In the interval of rest which followed the last persecution, the influence of the Christian Church had so increased that the heathen regarded it no less with astonishment than alarm. Christ, says Eusebius, was honoured amongst all men, Greeks and barbarians [b]. Christians were appointed to high offices in the State and in the Imperial household; spacious Churches with architectural adornments were built, conspicuous amongst them being the Church of Nicomedia, the city where Diocletian resided; gold and silver vessels were used in the Eucharist; persons of high station allowed not only their servants but their own families to embrace Christianity, and Diocletian's wife, Prisca, and his daughter, Valeria, the wife of Galerius, were favourably disposed towards it, and if not actually Christians, were probably Catechumens. Diocletian himself, not only by his naturally benevolent disposition, but also from political consideration of the large Christian population, was inclined to be tolerant; the victory was almost gained, but one battle more had to be fought, one persecution more to be suffered, by the Christians.

Galerius, a man without education, under the influence of his pagan mother, and his own innate aversion to Christian morality, was a bitter foe to Christianity, and strongly in favour of the old superstition. During a visit to Nicomedia at the end of the year 302, he availed himself of the opportunity for instilling into the mind of Diocletian his

[b] H E., VIII. 1.

The Victory of Christ's Kingdom. 95

own hatred to the Christians. Whilst the Pagan priests were offering sacrifices in the presence of the Emperor, some Christian officers in attendance signed the Cross upon their foreheads; and when on several subsequent occasions they persisted in the practice and refused to obey the Emperor's order to join in the sacrifice, they were deprived of their offices, and several of them, perhaps as insubordinate soldiers, executed.

Galerius seized the occasion to urge the Emperor to more active measures, and Diocletian under his incessant importunities grew irresolute; but, still averse to persecution, he consented to consult the oracle of Apollo at Miletus. The answer being unfavourable to the Christians, February 23, A.D. 303, the Feast of the Roman Terminalia, was chosen as the day for issuing a first edict for persecution, and at break of day the Church of Nicomedia was set fire to and burnt, the books and furniture being seized. On the following day an edict was passed for a general demolition of the Christian churches, and of the Sacred Books, the deprivation of officials, and the enslavement of other Christians. The edict was no sooner posted than it was torn down, the Christian who had the rashness to perform the act paying the penalty by being roasted alive over a slow fire. Twice the Emperor's palace at Nicomedia was in flames, and the guilt imputed by Galerius to the Christians. Diocletian goaded to fury now compelled his wife and daughter to free themselves from suspicion by offering sacrifice. Another edict was issued ordering all the clergy to be imprisoned, and many Christians, amongst them Anthimus, the Bishop of Nicomedia, were put to death.

An order was now sent into the West for the adoption of similar measures as had been adopted in the East, an order which Maximian willingly followed, and in Rome, where he was governor, 60,000 persons were said to have received the crown of martyrdom. A well-founded tradition, the truth of which however St. Augustine denies, asserts that Marcellinus, the Bishop of Rome (296—304), together with three of his Presbyters, who became his successors in the Papacy, Marcellus (304—310), Melchiades (311—314), and the famous Silvester (314—335), delivered up the Sacred Books and offered sacrifice [c]; that Marcellinus afterwards suffered martyrdom is an invention. In Britain Constantius could not entirely disobey the order, and it was in this persecution that St. Alban, the Protomartyr of Britain, is supposed to have suffered martyrdom at Verulamium. But Constantius exercised mercy, and generally only so far complied as to allow the Churches, which could be rebuilt, to be destroyed, but "the true temple of God, the human body, he preserved intact."

In 305, Diocletian and Maximian abdicating the throne, Constantius and Galerius became Augusti. Constantius died at York, A.D. 306, and was succeeded by Constantine, his son by his first wife, Helena, who was according to some the daughter of a British Prince, but more probably a woman of humble birth. In 307 Maximian resumed the purple, and in that year the government of the Roman Empire, after having undergone several changes, was divided between six emperors, Maximian, his son Maxentius, Galerius, his nephew Maximin Daza, Constantine and Licinius. Constantine's first wife, Minervina, by whom he had a son named Crispus, having died, Constantine in 307 married Fausta, the daughter of Maximian, and sister of Maxentius. Constantine was from the first inclined to favour the Christians.

The two following years were the cruellest and the most sanguinary of all the persecutions. In 310 Maximian died, as is supposed by his own hand, at Marseilles. In 311 Galerius, smitten with the same loathsome disease that carried off King Agrippa (Acts xii. 23), brought on by his

---

[c] Eusebius, H. E., VII. 32, only says of Marcellinus, κατείληφεν ὁ διωγμός, "he was overtaken by the persecution." Theodoret speaks of him with praise, ἐν τῷ διωγμῷ διαπρέψαντα But see Wace and Schaff's Eusebius, p. 317, and Smith's Dict. of Christ Biog , III 805.

The Victory of Christ's Kingdom. 97

own excesses, seized with remorse or superstition, issued, in conjunction with Constantine and Licinius, an edict for toleration, with permission to the Christians to rebuild their churches, and in return implored them to pray to their God for his recovery. A few days afterwards he died, and with his death the persecution in Palestine came to an end.

Maxentius, the son of Maximian, defeated by Constantine, on October 28, 312, in the battle of the Milvian Bridge (the present Ponte Molle), about a mile from Rome, was swept away by the waters of the Tiber, and Constantine entered Rome in triumph. He was now sole Emperor of the West, and the persecution in the West was ended. It was two days before the victory that he saw, or supposed he saw, in the Heavens the luminous Cross. The story of the vision his biographer Eusebius asserts was communicated to him by Constantine himself, when the latter was an old man, and consequently after he had had a long time for reflection. The story runs [d], that on his way from Gaul to Rome, Constantine, whose mind was wavering between Christianity and Paganism, aware that his enemy was seeking the aid of magical and supernatural rites, pondered on what god he himself might best rely for protection and assistance. Remembering that the persecuting Emperors had trusted in a multitude of gods, and had all come to an unhappy end, whilst his own father, who honoured the One Supreme God, had found in Him a saviour and protector, he determined to honour the God of the Christians. Whilst engaged in such thoughts and in prayer to God that He would reveal Himself, he saw, shortly after noon, a luminous Cross in the sky bearing the inscription, $\dot{\epsilon}\nu$ $\tau o \acute{u} \tau \wp$ $\nu \acute{\iota} \kappa a$ (in this conquer). The whole army also witnessed the miracle. In the night, the Christ of God appeared to him in a dream, holding before him the same symbol which he had seen in the Heavens, and which He ordered him to use as a safeguard against his enemies. On the following day Constantine ordered the Cross, with the monogram of the

[d] Eus V C, I. 27.

first three letters of the Saviour's name, to be inscribed on the Imperial standard (*Labarum*)[e]. The Labarum, the derivation of which is uncertain says Gibbon[f], was a long pike intersected with a transversal beam; the upper part was in the shape of a cross, with the sacred monogram on the top, so that it was an expression of the figure of the Cross and the initial letters of the name of Christ.

Of all the persecuting Emperors, Maximin Daza, under whose tyranny the provinces of Syria, Asia, and Egypt groaned for six years, was the cruellest. Beyond all the others his character was the most disreputable; and he "stands forth as pre-eminent for brutal licentiousness and ferocious cruelty, 'lust hard by hate[g].'" His mind, says Eusebius, was deranged by drunkenness, he suffered no one to surpass him in debauchery and profligacy, and tutored others, both rulers and subjects, in wickedness[h], and he prided himself that he was the most vigorous enemy of Christianity who had appeared. To the martyrs of Palestine, many of whom suffered under the eyes of Maximin, Eusebius devotes a whole book. In 309, Pamphilus, a Presbyter of Cæsarea, the friend of Eusebius ("a man thrice dear to him"), after two years spent in prison, during which the historian frequently visited him, was, with eleven others, put to death by Firmilian, Prefect of the city[i].

The See of Alexandria had hitherto enjoyed a comparative immunity from persecution; nothing seems more clearly to show this than the fact that, whilst at the commencement of the tenth persecution twenty-nine Bishops had presided over the See of Rome, there had only been seventeen in Alexandria[j]. In the persecution which now

---

[e] This representation on Constantine's Labarum, Eusebius asserts that he himself had seen. Julian the Apostate removed the Labarum and substituted a heathen symbol.   [f] III. 258
[g] Dict of Christ. Biog, III. 872.   [h] Eus H E, VIII. 14
[i] Eusebius, Martyrs of Palestine, Chap II   After the execution of Pamphilus, Eusebius styled him Eusebius Pamphili.
[j] Neale's Alexandria, I 90

The Victory of Christ's Kingdom. 99

assailed Alexandria, apostasy, which was so prevalent during the Decian persecution, was almost unheard of; the martyrs in the Thebais alone were reckoned at 144,000; of one Confessor, the Bishop Paphnutius, we shall have occasion to speak in the next chapter.

In A.D. 300, Peter I. succeeded Theonas in the See of Alexandria. Some difficulty exists as to the mode of election of the Bishops of the Alexandrine See. St. Jerome says;—" At Alexandria, from Mark the Evangelist down to the Bishops Heraclas and Dionysius (i.e. to A.D. 249), it was the custom of the Presbyters to choose out of their own body one whom they placed in a higher dignity of Bishop." Eutychius, Patriarch (933—940), and the Historian, of the Alexandrine Church, tells us that this system prevailed till the time of Alexander, who was Bishop of Alexandria at the Council of Nice. We will dwell further on this subject when we come in the next chapter to the Episcopate of Alexander; but here (*valeat quantum*), in fairness to those who hold Presbyterian views, it must be mentioned that Peter is said by Severus, an Arabic Historian, to have been constituted Bishop by the imposition of the hands of the clergy and laity.

In A.D. 311, the aged hermit Antony left his cell to comfort the suffering Christians of Alexandria, and exhort them to steadfastness in the faith. In that same year Peter, "one of the most excellent teachers of Christ's religion," Eusebius calls him, "was advanced to the crown of martyrdom [k]."

We need not dwell on the persecution within the See of Antioch, as it is only a repetition of the same horrors, during which the names of many illustrious martyrs are recorded. One name, however, must be mentioned, that of St. Lucian, a Priest of Antioch and editor of the Septuagint, who was one of the founders of the famous Antiochene school of divines. At one time he was accused of heresy, but afterwards moderated his views, and lived

[k] St. Peter is commemorated in the Greek Church on November 24

to die a Martyr for the faith; after being for a long time starved, he was tempted with meat offered to idols, and eventually put to death in his prison at Nicomedia.

The end of the persecutions was now at hand. The superstitious tyrant would at one time vow to Jupiter that, if he were successful in battle, he would blot out the Christian name from off the earth; at another pray to the God of the Christians for victory On May 1, A.D 313, Licinius, who had shortly before married Constantine's half-sister Constantia, routed him in the battle of Hadrianople. In that year Constantine and Licinius issued the famous edict of Milan for a universal toleration (*et Christianis et omnibus*). Maximin, who ascribed his defeat to his Pagan gods, now turned against the Priests and soothsayers who had urged him on, and issued a decree for a toleration of Christians and restitution of their property, but shortly afterwards, in a fit of despair which he endeavoured to drown by intoxication, he ended his life by poison at Tarsus in Cilicia; the long agony of death wringing from him a piteous appeal to the Saviour.

About the same time that the Edict of Milan was issued, Constantius wrote two Letters to Anulinus, Proconsul, conferring special privileges in "the Catholic Churches" of Africa, over which Cæcilian, Bishop of Carthage, presided; having suffered more than other Churches in the late persecution, they were considered to be in greater need of assistance[1].

There were now two Emperors left, Constantine, who governed in the West, and Licinius in the East. Diocletian survived to learn of the toleration granted at Milan to the Christians, but he had lived to excite the suspicion and enmity of the two Emperors, and died, according to one account of poison, in the same year. His wife Prisca, and his daughter Valeria, the widow of Galerius, survived him. After the death of Galerius they had taken refuge under the roof of Maximin, but on the refusal of Valeria

[1] Eus H E, X 15.

The Victory of Christ's Kingdom

to listen to his lustful desires, they were driven into exile, and their goods confiscated. After the death of Maximin they were for a time sheltered in the Court of Licinius, whose wife, Constantia, was a Christian. At the commencement of the persecution they had been, at the least, favourers of Christianity, which it is probable they now, under the influence of Constantia, embraced. Licinius, though he had given a half-hearted support to Constantine, in issuing edicts of toleration, still hated Christianity, opposed the Christians in his dominions, and destroyed their Churches It may be that on the ground of their Christianity, the wife and daughter of Diocletian incurred his enmity. At any rate, they had grounds for dreading his cruelty; through fear of him they escaped from his palace, and wandered about in disguise from place to place, outcasts on the face of the earth, in a state of abject poverty, till at last being discovered at Thessalonica, they were executed, and their bodies cast into the sea. Such was the terrible fatality that attended the end of the last of the ten persecutions.

The province of Africa had by the death of Maxentius fallen to Constantine. There was nothing that Constantine more desired than peace, but peace he did not find in the Church of Africa. At Carthage continued divisions had arisen out of a disputed election which ensued in 311, on the death of its Bishop, Mensurius. Mensurius had given offence to many Christians by resorting, during the persecution under Maxentius, when required to give up the Holy Scriptures, to the subterfuge of hiding them, and passing off heretical books in their stead. And he gave still greater offence by opposing, as he felt bound in duty, the morbid desire of martyrdom, even amongst people who led licentious lives, which was then in vogue, and the mistaken reverence in which they were held as Confessors or Martyrs. On his death, Cæcilian, who had been his Archdeacon and supported and consequently shared his unpopularity, was elected as his successor, and consecrated by Felix, Bishop of Aptunga, a See of which, further than that it was in Africa, the situation is uncertain. Felix was accused of being a Traditor, i.e. one who during the persecution had delivered up the Scriptures. The Bishops of Numidia, who were under the jurisdiction of Carthage, urged on by one Donatus, Bishop of Casa Nigra, further complained that the election had taken place in their absence, and that, instead of being consecrated by Felix, Cæcilian ought to have been consecrated by Secundus, Bishop of Tigisis, Primate of Numidia. They, in consequence, in a Synod at Carthage, excommunicated Cæcilian and appointed Majorinus in his place, thus causing a schism in the Church of Africa. The Donatists, to anticipate the name which they derived from another Donatus, were also exasperated by the Letters, above referred to, of Constantine to the Proconsul Anulinus, confining his benefactions to the Catholics of Africa under Cæcilian. The matter being referred by the Donatists to Constantine, was decided by him in favour of Cæcilian, and Felix was acquitted of the charge brought against him; whilst throughout Christendom, except by the Donatists in Africa, Cæcilian was regarded as the canonical Bishop.

The Donatists laid themselves open to the charge of being the first Christians who called in the civil arm to decide an ecclesiastical cause. Having so done, they next asked Constantine to order it to be tried by the Bishops of Gaul, who, their country not having suffered in the late persecutions, might be expected to be impartial judges. Constantine in compliance with their request wrote to Melchiades, Bishop of Rome, and Marcus (who this latter person was is only a matter of conjecture), professing his own reverence for the legitimate ($\dot{\epsilon}\nu\theta\dot{\epsilon}\sigma\mu\omega$) Catholic Church, and bidding him summon a Council of enquiry at Rome, at which he had commanded Retecius, Bishop of Autun, Maternus of Cologne, and Marinus of Arles, to be present, and before which Cæcilian and ten of his accusing Bishops were to appear. The Council, consisting of the three Bishops summoned by Constantine, and fifteen from Italy, met under the Presi-

The Victory of Christ's Kingdom.

dency of the Bishop of the See in the Lateran Palace, the residence of the Empress Fausta. Cæcilian was, on October 2, A.D. 313, again acquitted, his Ordination by Felix declared to be valid, and Donatus condemned. The case of Felix was not entertained by the Council, but was afterwards tried by the Proconsul, who found the evidence brought against him a malicious scandal.

The Donatists, still dissatisfied, appealed against the decision of Rome to the Emperor, and asked for a Council of all the Western Bishops. Constantine then arranged for a Council to be held at Arles in Gaul. The sentence of the Council of Rome having been impugned on the ground that "those who expressed their opinions and decisions were few, and their judgment hasty [m]," Constantine in a letter to Chrestus, Bishop of Syracuse, assigns this as a reason for summoning a larger Council. The Council of Arles accordingly met on Aug. 1, 314 [n], under the nominal presidency of Marinus, the Bishop of the See, Constantine having entrusted the general guidance to Chrestus; Silvester, now Bishop of Rome, was represented by four Prelates [o].

St. Augustine says that the Council of Arles consisted of about two hundred Bishops and was "a plenary Council of the whole Church." But no Bishop (if we except Cæcilian) of the Eastern Church was present, nor were the Eastern Bishops even invited; indeed the Donatist Schism was ignored in the East. It cannot, therefore, be termed an Œcumenical Council, nor would it be mentioned here except for the reason that, not confining itself to the Donatist Schism, it included matters affecting the whole Church, such as the Paschal controversy, and its canons, twenty-two in number, concerned the Eastern as well as the Western Church.

A few of these canons must be mentioned;—Canon I.

---

[m] This seems to show that no superior importance at that time attached to the See of Rome.

[n] At this Council three British Bishops were present.

[o] Eus. H. E., X. 5

enacted that Easter should be celebrated everywhere on the same day, and that the Roman computation should be followed. VI. that those who had been received into the Church in sickness (*in infirmitate conversi*) should afterwards receive imposition of hands. VIII. against the Donatists, who re-baptized their converts, that converts from heresy who had been baptized in the name of the Trinity should not be re-baptized but receive imposition of hands. X. forbade a second marriage even to a man whose wife had been convicted of adultery. XIII., concerning Traditors, was directed against the Donatists. XV. prohibited Deacons from celebrating the Holy Eucharist. XX. enacted that no Bishop should be consecrated by fewer than three Bishops.

By the Council of Arles, Cæcilian was again acquitted. Majorinus dying A.D. 315, was succeeded by Donatus, who was called, in distinction to the Bishop of Casa Nigra, the Great Donatus. The Donatists still continuing to give trouble, Constantine granted them and Cæcilian a conference, first at Rome in 315, and then in 316 at Milan, and Cæcilian was again acquitted. But they were no better satisfied than before, denounced the Catholic Church, calling themselves the only true and the whole Church, and all other Christians schismatics, and continued, notwithstanding the Council of Arles, to re-baptize converts, and wrote to the Emperor that they would have nothing to do with his "fool of a Bishop." Constantine at first thought of punishing them with death, but eventually contented himself with depriving them of their Churches and banishing them. But the heresy continued; Donatists, if they gained possession of the Churches of the Catholics, purified them as unconsecrated and contaminated places; burnt the Altars, cast the Eucharist to the dogs, and even dug up the graves, ejecting the bodies of the dead. Donatus became the rallying personage of all discontented people, civil and ecclesiastical. But his followers soon broke up into several parties. One fanatical sect, the Circumcellions (so called from their going round the cells or cottages of the poor), begged, and if they could not succeed, under pretence of religion, stole what they wanted. They laid claim to inspiration ; but they were in reality nothing but common highway robbers, destroying harvests, laying violent hands on whoever they met, burning Churches and maltreating the Catholic clergy. Death they courted, consoling themselves that thereby they would win honour and be accounted martyrs. They found an opponent in the great St. Augustine of Hippo, in whose Diocese they had their own Bishop and were more numerous than the Catholics ; and it was not before the Seventh Century that the last sparks of the schism were stamped out in the universal ruin, under the Saracens, of the Church of Northern Africa.

About the same time as the Council of Arles two Councils were held in the East (perhaps A.D. 315), those of Ancyra, the Metropolis of Galatia, and of Neo-Cæsarea in Cappadocia. Vitalis, Bishop of Antioch, accompanied by eighteen Bishops, was present at both the Councils, the object of which was the same, viz. to regulate the penances of those who had lapsed during the late persecution, and to restore discipline to the long afflicted Church of Antioch. Of the 25 Canons of Ancyra, the first nine and the twelfth dealt with the former subject. Canon X. forbade Deacons to marry, unless at their Ordination they had expressed their intention to do so, XIII prohibited Chorepiscopi (or rural Bishops) to ordain without permission of the Bishop of the Diocese ; by XIX. Deacons who broke their promise of celibacy were to be treated as digamists ; by XX. those guilty of adultery were to be subjected to a penance of seven years, before being admitted the full rights of the Church.

The Council of Neo-Cæsarea was also attended by about eighteen Bishops, mostly the same that had attended at Ancyra. Of the 15 Canons, I. forbade Priests to marry ; II. decreed excommunication against any woman who marries two brothers, VIII. forbade a layman whose wife had been guilty of adultery to marry; XI. prescribed thirty years as the earliest age for Ordination to the Priesthood; XII. enacted that one who has been baptized in illness (ἐὰν νοσῶν τὶς φωτισθῇ) should not be ordained a Priest; XIII. forbade Country Priests to consecrate or celebrate the Eucharist in the presence of the Bishop or Priests of the city.

Constantine had now become Emperor of the West and of Africa; but one more enemy had to be overcome before the victory of Christianity was complete, and the Pagans made a last stand under Licinius. Before the battle of Hadrianople, in which he defeated Maximin, Licinius had put his army under the protection of the God of the Christians; it was scarcely possible but that he should feel some gratitude to God for the victory, and under such a transient feeling he immediately afterwards issued the edict of Milan But he was never in his heart anything but a Pagan, and soon the feeling passed away. He forbade the Bishops to hold Councils, interfered with their services, destroyed the Churches, and it was said that he was on the very point of issuing an edict for a general persecution of the Christians. But this was not to be; the battle that ensued between him and Constantine was really a religious one between Christianity and Paganism, he told his soldiers, "the present occasion shall prove which is mistaken in his judgment, and shall decide between our gods and those whom our adversaries propose to honour [p];" Constantine before the battle appealed to the God of the Christians.

On July 3, 323, Constantine defeated him in a second battle at Hadrianople, and pursued him to Byzantium, and on September 10 gained over him another and more decisive victory at Chrysopolis. Licinius was taken prisoner, but at the entreaty of Constantia, his life was spared, and he was allowed to live at Thessalonica. His restless spirit led him on to further agitation and intrigue, for which

[p] Eus. V. C., II. 5

The Victory of Christ's Kingdom.

in the next year he paid the penalty of death. Thus the victory of Christ's Kingdom over the Roman Empire was complete; after this, says Eusebius [q], "those who had so long been divided by false deities acknowledged with unfeigned sincerity the God of Constantine, and openly professed their belief in Him as the only true God." From A.D. 324—337 Constantine was sole Emperor. The edicts issued by Licinius against the Christians were repealed; and a proclamation followed by many similar acts issued in their favour. Paganism was not extinguished, but thenceforward Christianity was the religion of the Roman Empire.

The mention made of St. Antony in connexion with the late persecution at Alexandria, brings into prominence the subject of Monasticism, which took its rise in the East, and which has been an integral part of Greek Christianity, from its rise to the present day. In its earliest form, that of Asceticism (ἄσκησις, *the discipline of athletes*), which existed from the earliest time, monasticism did not necessitate retirement from the world. The next form was that of the monk (μόναχος, *living alone*), strictly so called, hermit (ἐρημίτης, *dweller in a desert*), or anchoret (ἀναχωρητής, *retirer from the world*), which had its rise in Paul, a native of the Thebaid, in the time of the persecution of Decius. The next transition was one to less solitary dwellings, or Λαῦραι (λαῦρα, *alley*), corresponding with the Latin Claustra, and the English Cloisters, a system founded by the famous St. Antony, which developed into the Cænobitic life (κοινὸς βίος), under his pupil Pachomius. Antony and Pachomius were both, like Paul, natives of the Thebaid. Pachomius associated a number of monks in one building (μάνδρα, *a fold*) with an Abbot (ἄββας), or Archimandrite, at its head.

The regulations which Antony made for his monks were introduced into Palestine and Syria by Hilarion, who had been sent by his pagan parents to Alexandria for education, where he was converted to Christianity, and lived for some time in St. Antony's monastery in the Thebaid. This rule

[q] V. C., II. 18.

of St. Antony formed the basis of the system which St. Basil the Great adopted, and which became, and has ever since remained, the pattern of all subsequent monasteries of the Eastern Church.

When, imitating the example of the rich young man in the Gospel, who was told by Christ to sell all that he had and give to the poor, Antony commenced his ascetic life near his native village, Coma, we are told by his biographer, who is supposed to be St. Athanasius, that he placed his sister in a house of virgins ($\pi\alpha\rho\theta\epsilon\nu\hat{\omega}\nu\alpha$); this is the first allusion to a Nunnery ($\nu o\nu\iota s$), an Egyptian word, signifying Nun[r].

So rapid was the advance of monasticism, that Antony's first disciple, Pachomius, found himself the superior of ten thousand monks; in the district of Nitria alone there were no fewer than fifty monasteries; and when St. Athanasius visited the desert, three thousand monks passed in his presence. By degrees the land first in the East and then in the West, into which Monasticism was introduced by St. Athanasius, was covered with monasteries.

The ideal of monasticism was the perfecting of the spiritual life; many thought and many were deceived in thinking that in the deserts they would be free from temptation, and there can be no doubt that many people embraced the monastic life from holy motives. But in time not religion, but idleness, or the desire to escape the duties and dangers of the military life, or the burden of taxes and imposts, attracted men to the monasteries, and so depopulated the lands, that the civil government was compelled to interfere, and to place a restriction on their numbers. Notwithstanding their degeneracy, the most distinguished Bishops, e.g. the great St. Basil, felt it their duty to take the monasteries under their special care and supervision, and under such direction they became beneficial as places of refuge for the oppressed and persecuted, and benevolent institutions for the sick and poor.

[r] Bingham's Antiquities, Bk. VII. Ch. IV.

The Victory of Christ's Kingdom. 109

From the first Greek monasticism was of a contemplative and less practical character than in the West, and little distinguished in literature and missions. A monk, said St. Antony, could no more live out of his cell than a fish out of water; when a traveller demanded of a Greek monk how he spent his time and where his books were, the latter pointed to, "pour toute reponse, la terre et les cieux," and St. Antony himself made a similar remark to a pagan philosopher, "My book, O philosopher, is Nature."

With the Acæmetæ (*sleepless*), a class of monks in the monastery of Studium, near Constantinople, so called from their keeping watch night and day, we shall meet in the course of our narrative; but we must not omit mention of the Stylites (στυλίται), or Pillar-monks, a name derived from their practice of living on a pillar. Most famous of the number was the Syrian Anchorite, St. Simeon, who for more than thirty years, from A.D. 423, lived with a weighty chain round his body, at a place about forty miles from Antioch, on the summit of a pillar, a yard in diameter, and raised sixty feet from the ground. There to the people who flocked to him from all quarters he gave counsel and preached repentance; Bishops and Emperors, and the King of Persia, sought his advice, and consulted him as an oracle; and to his memory, soon after his death, a magnificent Church was erected, built round an hypæthral court, in the centre of which stood the world-famed pillar.

Two other famous Stylites alone are known; St. Daniel, who lived on a pillar four miles from Constantinople for forty years, and died, A.D. 494, at the age of eighty, and a younger Simeon, who died at Antioch A.D. 596.

It is probable that, previously to the general relaxation of discipline which followed the Saracenic invasions, the Eastern monasteries never fell into so deep a degradation as the monasteries of the West, which by the evasion of their Rule were constantly necessitating reform and the creation of new Orders. The same conservative spirit which has always characterized the Greek Church, the same veneration for antiquity, tended to preserve a fraternity amongst the monks of the East, and to retain the ancient unity of the Order of St. Basil, which has subsisted ever since his time with its original simplicity.

CHAPTER III.

The First Œcumenical Council.

THE Antiochene School—Arius—Mode of Election to the Alexandrine Episcopate—The heresy of Arius—Constantine summons the First Œcumenical Council of Nice—The Homoousion adopted as its watchword—The Nicene Creed—The Meletian Schism—Time for observing Easter arranged—The celibacy of the clergy condemned—Τὰ ἀρχαῖα ἔθη κρατείτω—Prayers to be offered in Church by people standing—St. Athanasius elected Bishop of Alexandria—Some account of him—Constantine leaves Rome for ever— St Helena's Pilgrimage to Jerusalem—Foundation of the Basilica of the Holy Sepulchre and other Churches in Palestine laid—Discovery of the Holy Cross—Constantine builds several Churches in Rome—Dedication of Constantinople—Transference of the capital thither—It was the foundation of the Papal power—Disadvantageous to the Bishops of Constantinople —Difficulties with which the Eastern Church had to contend.

UNDER Constantine, Christianity had gained the victory over the Roman Empire; but was Constantine himself yet at heart a Christian? From the first he had been averse to persecution; he inherited his father's favour towards the Christians, and he had learnt to despise the religion of Greeks and Romans whom he had so often conquered. Since the vision of the Cross, which he thoroughly believed to have been miraculously revealed to him, he professed his belief in the God of the Christians. But even amongst the Pagans a kind of mysterious dread, a mistrust in their own gods, had begun to prevail, and preceded the final victory of Christianity. Licinius, before engaging in his last battle, counselled his soldiers not to attack the Labarum, not even to let their eyes rest incautiously on it [a]. Constantine, before the battle, prayed with a Cross erected in his tent, and after the victory assumed an attitude more distinctly favourable to the Christians. The victory he ascribed to the One God, and after it commended the religion of the Christians [b], recalled the exiles, restored the property

[a] Eus. V. C., II 16.   [b] Ibid., II. 19.

taken from the Church, commended the observance of Sunday [e], built Churches, and adorned them with Crosses of precious stones. Still he hesitated to take the irretrievable step of becoming the first Christian Emperor by accepting Baptism.

Henceforward the history of Christianity and of the Roman Empire ran in the same channel; the long death-struggle had ended; and the Christian Church entered on a new phase of existence. A series of religious controversies ensued, the first of which was on the subject of the Incarnation At the very time when a community of faith and worship was most required for cementing the foundation of the Church, a controversy arose as to the relation in the Godhead of the Son to the Father. In the earliest times the Eternity of the Logos, as declared in the Gospel and Epistles of St. John, had been firmly established in the Church. But in time false doctrine, especially in the East, had been taught, although not in so dogmatic or positive a manner as to call forth any public formula of the Church. In Antioch the teaching of Paul of Samosata had left its mark, and a famous school was formed which, whilst it produced such distinguished divines as Lucian, a native of Samosata, St. Chrysostom and Theodoret, produced also Diodorus and Theodore of Mopsuestia, as well as the chief leaders in the Trinitarian controversy. Lucian afterwards moderated his opinions and died a Martyr for the faith, but his rationalizing views had their influence on the school of Antioch.

The author of the great Trinitarian controversy was Arius (256—336), a native of Libya, who had been educated in the school of Antioch under Lucian. Arius is described as a man of imposing appearance and unblemished character; "a subtle-witted and marvellous fine-spoken man," Hooker calls him. He had been an adherent of the schism of Meletius, Bishop of Licopolis, who (A.D. 306) was deposed by Peter, Bishop of Alexandria, in his recon-

[e] Under the heathen name, however, *Dies Solis*.

The First Œcumenical Council. 113

ciliation to the Church he was ordained Deacon by Peter, but on his return to the Meletian schism, Peter excommunicated him, and so badly did he think of him that, though Arius prevailed on some Presbyters of Alexandria to intercede for him, Peter shortly before his death anathematized him. On the martyrdom of Peter, Achillas succeeded him in the See of Alexandria, and by him Arius was re-admitted to communion, ordained Priest, and, A.D. 313, appointed to the most important charge in Alexandria, that of Baucalis, in which he attained considerable popularity After the short Episcopate of Achillas two candidates presented themselves for the vacant See, Alexander and Arius, the latter of whom was disappointed in being passed over in favour of Alexander (313—326).

We have before[d] alluded to the early mode of election to the Alexandrine Episcopate as related by the historian Eutychius. This, the same author continues, was changed by Alexander; "he ordained that upon the vacancy of the See the Bishop should meet to consecrate the successor, and that the power of election should be in their hands without confining themselves to the twelve Presbyters." Those who ground on this a precedent for a Presbyterian form of Church government fortify their case by an incident which occurred the year before the Council of Nice. Colluthus, a Priest, had taken upon himself to confer holy Orders, one so ordained being Ischyras In a Council at Alexandria, A.D. 324, by which both the Meletian schism and Arius were condemned, it was decided that Episcopal Ordination was necessary; whereupon Colluthus submitted to the Church, and Ischyras was, on the ground that Colluthus was not a Bishop, pronounced a layman.

Friendly relations between Arius and his Bishop seem to have been maintained until A.D 319 In that year Alexander issued an address to his clergy on the mystery of the Trinity, insisting especially on the Unity, in which Arius professed to detect Sabellianism and a confusion of Persons. In

[d] See p 99

Chapter III.

attacking Alexander he denied the eternity and uncreatedness of the Son; he contended that as He was begotten by the Father, there must have been a time before He was begotten, and that He was not from all eternity (ἦν ὅτε οὐκ ἦν); that He was consequently created like all creatures out of a substance which had no previous existence (ἐξ οὐκ ὄντων ἔχει τὴν ὑπόστασιν) His opinions spread rapidly in Egypt, where many Bishops adopted them Alexander called upon Arius to retract his statements, and as he refused to do so, convened, A.D. 321, a Synod at Alexandria, which was attended by nearly 100 Egyptian and African Bishops, and in which the teaching of Arius was condemned, and he with two Bishops, Secundus and Theonas, who supported him, were anathematized Amongst other Bishops, Arius had on his side the influential Eusebius, his fellow-pupil in the school at Antioch, who, having been first Bishop of Berytus, was translated to the See of Nicomedia, a See of great importance, not only as the capital of Bithynia, but also as the See of the Imperial residence.

Driven away from Alexandria, Arius went first to Palestine, whence he wrote to Eusebius of Nicomedia, setting forth the persecution he had suffered from the Bishops (whose doctrine he misrepresented), and his expulsion from Alexandria. Whilst in Palestine he made a favourable impression on Eusebius, Bishop of Cæsarea, the Church historian. He then went to Nicomedia, where he wrote the *Thalia*, a work which contained Arianism in its most developed form, speaking of the Son not only as not equal to, but not of the same essence with, the Father. In 323, availing himself of the confusion which existed in consequence of the war between Constantine and Licinius, he returned to Alexandria, where he was condemned in the Synod of 324.

Constantine, when Emperor of the West, had to contend with the Donatist schism, but in the Eastern Church, of which the See of Alexandria was the most important, he had hoped that he should find peace; "Disunion in the Church," he said

The First Œcumenical Council. 115

to the Fathers assembled at Nice, "I consider a more grievous evil than any kind of war." On his arrival at Nicomedia, after the defeat of Licinius, he had to contend with a more serious and wide-spreading schism than that of the Donatists, and encountered a far greater difficulty in the subtleties of Eastern theology.

He wrote, through Hosius, Bishop of Corduba, who had been a confessor under Maximian, a letter to Alexander and Arius, in which he showed, as might have been expected in one whose life had been spent in the West, and whose mind was trained in war, a complete ignorance of the character and importance of the subject in dispute. Arius by denying the Eternity had denied the Divinity of the Saviour, thus destroying the very essence of Christianity. Yet Constantine wrote of it as a trivial matter which Arius had better not have given trouble about, and Alexander ought to have taken no notice of; and he gave advice such as an Emperor might well give, and which came within his province, to forgive one another. Arius answered in a tone of remonstrance which irritated the Emperor into retorting with a letter of coarse invective, he sneered at his dismal and emaciated figure, and called him "a shop of iniquity," and ordered him peremptorily to recognize the Son as of one Essence with the Father [e].

Constantine in his desire for union in the Church would persecute all kinds of sectaries, prohibit their assemblies, and confiscate their revenues. He was acting more strictly within his rights when he determined to call an Œcumenical Council, i.e. a Council of the universal Church, the only kind of Council to which the whole Church would defer, to decide the matter. There had before been what we should call Diocesan and Provincial Synods, but these would only have a limited authority. The creed of the Church had existed since the time of the Apostles, but in the days of the persecutions it was impossible that a Council of the whole Church could assemble, or such fixed rules

[e] Bright's History of the Church, p. 20.

of doctrine and discipline be laid down as would receive the sanction of the collective Church. Nor could any one but the Emperor convene an Œcumenical Council, for there was no one recognized Bishop of the universal Church who could exercise such a power. The statement made in the Sixth Œcumenical Council, three hundred and fifty-five years afterwards, when, in consequence of the heresies in the East, the Pope of Rome had gained a pre-eminence which he had not before, that Constantine and Silvester, Bishop of Rome, together assembled (συνέλεγον) the Council of Nice, can have no weight whatever against the authority of Constantine's biographer, Eusebius, who was himself present at the Council; Eusebius expressly states that Constantine invited "the Bishops of every country to proceed to Nicæa."

Nice was selected as a central place, and also as being in the neighbourhood of the Emperor's Palace at Nicomedia. The Council, attended by 318 Bishops (whence it is called the Council of the 318 Bishops), met on June 19, 325 Thither came Syrians and Cilicians, men of Phœnicia and Palestine, of Libya and Egypt; Pontus and Asia, Phrygia and Pamphylia sent their best. Others came from Thrace and Macedonia, from Achaia and Epirus, and the regions beyond[f]. The Council was almost wholly composed of Eastern Bishops. Alexander of Alexandria, and with him his Deacon, Athanasius, Eustathius of Antioch, Macarius of Jerusalem, were present; two Roman Priests, Victor and Vincent, represented Silvester, Bishop of Rome, whom his great age would prevent from attending. The two Eusebii, Paphnutius, Bishop of the Upper Thebais, who had suffered banishment and mutilation during the Diocletian persecution, John, Bishop of Persia, Theophilus, "Bishop of the Goths," and Acesius, a Novatian Bishop, were amongst those present. Theognis, Bishop of Nice, attended, as also the two Bishops, Secundus and Theonas, who had been excommunicated with Arius at the Council of Alexandria.

[f] Socr., V. 22.

The First Œcumenical Council.

One other Bishop may be mentioned, not from any important part which he took in its deliberations (his name does not appear amongst the signatories), but as the Patron Saint in the present day of the Ionian Islands, St. Spiridion, Bishop of a See in Cyprus [g].

The Presidency of the Council would in ordinary circumstances belong to the Bishop of Alexandria, but, as chief accuser, he would be incapacitated, the next in rank was Eustathius of Antioch, and the Presidency of the sessions was probably shared by him and Hosius. Constantine, magnificently attired, attended, but, Eusebius tells us, declined to take his seat on the golden throne until invited to do so by the assembled Bishops. He delivered a Latin speech, which the interpreters translated into Greek, the language of the great majority, and himself took part in the debates.

Arius being called upon for his defence declared that the Son was a created Being, that at one time He did not exist, and was capable of sinning. The Eusebians, as the party of Eusebius of Nicomedia were afterwards termed, defended Arius; on the other side Athanasius took the prominent part, exciting the admiration of all, but at the same time the jealousy of many. Henceforward he was the recognized champion of the Orthodox party, thus provoking the implacable enmity of the Eusebians, which pursued him to the end of his life.

The Homoousion (*of one essence*) was adopted as the watchword of orthodoxy. Constantine himself, probably at the suggestion of Hosius, insisted on it. In vain Eusebius of Nicomedia opposed it. Eusebius of Cæsarea presented a Creed, which, though it used the words " begotten before all creation, having been begotten of God the Father before all the ages; by Whom all things are made," yet

---

[g] Dean Stanley mentions that his body was, on the capture of the city the Turks, transferred from Constantinople, where it was buried, to Corfu, where it is annually carried round the island in procession.

because it omitted the words ἀληθινόν and ὁμοούσιον, was rejected.

Hosius then, commissioned by the Council, drew up the Creed which has ever since been universally known as the Nicene, on the formula of the Creed of Eusebius, but with the addition of the word ὁμοούσιος :—

"We believe in One God (πιστεύομεν εἰς ἕνα Θεόν) the Father Almighty, Maker of all things, both visible and invisible. And in one Lord, Jesus Christ, the Son of God. Begotten of the Father, that is, of the Substance of the Father (ἐκ τῆς οὐσίας τοῦ Πατρός). God of God Light of Light. Very God of Very God. Begotten, not made. Of one Substance (ὁμοούσιος) with the Father. By Whom all things were made, that are in Heaven and earth. Who for us men and our salvation came down, and was Incarnate, and was made Man. He suffered and rose again the third day, and ascended into Heaven. And He shall come again to judge the quick and the dead.

"And in the Holy Ghost."

The Council added the following declaration :—

"And as to those who affirm that there was a time when the Son of God was not (ὅτι ἦν ὅτε οὐκ ἦν) ; and that before He was begotten He was not (πρὶν γεννηθῆναι οὐκ ἦν) ; and that He was made out of nothing (ἐξ οὐκ ὄντων γεννηθῆναι) , or that He is of a different Substance or Essence (ἐξ ἑτέρας ὑποστάσεως ἢ οὐσίας φάσκοντας εἶναι) ; or that He is created, or subject to change or alteration (ἢ κτιστὸν, ἢ τρεπτὸν, ἢ ἀλλοίωτον) ; they are anathematized by the Holy Catholic Church."

Seventeen Arian Bishops, as also Eusebius of Cæsarea, at first refused to sign the formula. Eusebius soon gave way and subscribed. Eusebius of Nicomedia and Theognis of Nice signed the Creed, but not the condemnatory clauses. Ultimately the number of non-subscribers dwindled down to two, Secundus and Theonas, who stood firm to their convictions. Constantine was now a zealot for orthodoxy, which he tried to enforce by penal laws against the Arians.

Secundus and Theonas, together with Arius and two of his friends, Euzoius and Pistus, the former of whom was afterwards intruded by the Arians into the See of Antioch, the latter into that of Alexandria, were banished to Illyria. Arius' books were ordered to be burnt The sentence of banishment was afterwards pronounced against Eusebius of Nicomedia and Theognis, the former of whom, by his opposition to his plans for peace, had offended Constantine.

Another matter brought before the Council was the Meletian Schism [h]. Meletius himself was dealt gently with. He was admitted to communion and allowed to be styled a Bishop, but deprived of the power of Ordaining; those who had received their Orders from him were subjected to a second Ordination, and to hold afterwards a secondary rank amongst the Clergy. By such clemency the Council hoped to gain the Meletians, but so far from this being the case, they entered into a union with Arians which was long unfortunate to the Church, and especially to Athanasius, nor do they disappear from history till the end of the Fifth Century.

The diversity between the Asiatic and the Western Churches, as to the observance of Easter, with regard to which Polycarp, Bishop of Smyrna, and Anicetus, Bishop of Rome, had failed to come to an agreement, and Victor, Bishop of Rome, had issued the sentence against the Eastern Church, which brought on him the remonstrance of St. Irenæus, continued till the time of Constantine. The different times of its observance, some Churches continuing the fast of Lent whilst others were celebrating their festivities, must have offended the scrupulous uniformity of the Emperor in only a less degree than doctrinal differences. The conservative spirit of the Easterns would incline them to adhere to the custom which had prevailed in the earliest times. But its observance on the same day on which it was kept by the descendants of the murderers of the Saviour now induced

[h] Not to be confounded with the Meletian Schism which agitated the Church of Antioch half a century later.

them to join the practice of the Western Church. The Synod of Arles being a Western Synod had little weight with the Eastern Church, and so failed to establish one uniform practice throughout Christendom. But the Council of Nice was composed almost entirely of Eastern Bishops, and the decree as to the future observance of Easter was determined " by common consent," and, with a few isolated exceptions, at once adopted. The Council decided that Easter should be kept on the next Sunday after the full moon following March 21st, and the Bishops of Alexandria (that See enjoying the highest reputation in the branch of astronomical science) were deputed to ascertain the exact day in each year for its celebration, and to communicate it, through the Bishops of Rome, to the Western Church.

With the Novatians Constantine appears to have had greater sympathy than with the other sectaries, and had invited their Bishop, Acesius, to the Council. The Emperor asked him afterwards whether he was satisfied with its decrees. Acesius answered in the affirmative, for they were conformable to Apostolical authority, though he could not admit the right of the clergy to grant Absolution to those who fell into post-baptismal sin. "Then," said Constantine, "you had better take a ladder and climb up to Heaven by yourself[1]."

Since at the time of the Nicene Council no controversy with regard to the Holy Ghost had been brought into prominence, the Creed ended with the clause, " And the Holy Ghost."

Twenty Canons were enacted, the most important of which were,—III., which forbade the clergy having in their houses a συνείσακτος (*subintroducta*, meaning an *introduced woman*), with the exception of a mother, sister, aunt, or such relative as was free from suspicion. An attempt was made to introduce, what Socrates, the ecclesiastical historian, calls " a new law " (νόμος νεαρός) of clerical celibacy, into the Church. But a proposal that the married clergy should be

[1] Socr., I. 10.

compelled to put away their wives was met with a burst of indignation from the aged confessor Paphnutius, himself educated in a monastery and unmarried. He insisted on the Gospel precept that "marriage is honourable unto all," and on the old tradition of the Church (τὴν Ἐκκλησίας παράδοσιν); that it was sufficient that a man should be precluded from marrying after, but that he should not separate from a wife to whom he was already married before, his Ordination, and his voice decided the matter. This rule was confirmed at the Council of Gangra in Paphlagonia about A.D. 340; "If any man make a distinction (διακρίνοιτο παρά) between a married and unmarried Presbyter let him be anathema." The custom as approved by the Nicene Fathers has always been observed in the Greek Church, but in the Roman Church clerical celibacy is compulsory.

Canon V. allowed an appeal to provincial Synods, for which purpose two such synods were to be held every year, one before Lent, the other about Autumn. Canon VI., probably passed against the Meletians who had invaded the rights of the Bishop of Alexandria, decreed that ancient customs in Egypt, Libya and Pentapolis should be observed (τὰ ἀρχαῖα ἔθη κρατείτω), that over them, "as was customary with the Bishop in the City Rome," the Bishop of Alexandria should hold jurisdiction. In like manner Antioch and all other Provinces (ἐπαρχίαι) should preserve their rights (πρεσβεῖα) [k]. It is evident that the Nicene Fathers recognized no special preeminence in the See of Rome, had they done so, they would certainly have mentioned it, they put "the Bishop in the City Rome" on the same level as the other primatial Sees.

Canon VII., perhaps at the instance of its Bishop Macarius, gave a special privilege (τὴν ἀκολουθίαν τῆς τιμῆς, i.e. probably after the three great Sees) to the See of Ælia

---

[k] These Provinces were probably Ephesus and Cæsarea, which latter comprised Jerusalem, to which a higher dignity appertained, second only to the three great Sees, Rome, Alexandria, and Antioch.

(the name given by Hadrian to the new colony founded on the ruins of Jerusalem), "saving the dignity (ἀξιώματος) belonging to the Metropolis," i.e. Cæsarea. The saving clause was probably inserted at the instance of Eusebius, Bishop of Cæsarea. It is worthy of remark that, notwithstanding this clause, Macarius signs in the fourth place, immediately after the two papal Legates, Hosius signing first. It is also deserving of notice that though he is commemorated in the Western Church on March 10th, no notice is taken of him in the Greek Menæa.

Canon VIII. treated the Novatians, or as they were called καθαρούς (puritans), with the same forbearance as it had shewn to the Meletians, and decided that if they would adhere to the decrees of the Catholic Church and communicate with those who contracted a second marriage (διγάμοις), and with such as had lapsed during persecution, they should be allowed to hold their Orders, but with an inferior status to the Catholic clergy.

Canons XV. and XVI. forbade the translation of Bishops, Priests and Deacons; a canon which circumstances rendered it impossible to carry out, and which was frequently violated.

Canon XIX. ordered the Paulianists, as the followers of Paul of Samosata were called, to be re-baptized, and their clergy to be re-ordained.

Canon XX. enacted that, in order that there might be uniformity in every Parish, prayers should be offered in Churches by the people *standing*, a rule which has always been observed in the Greek Church.

A fable was afterwards invented and found favour in the Western Church, that, on the receipt of the Nicene Canons, Pope Silvester convened a Council of 277 Bishops at Rome, in which the Canons were sanctioned and enforced by the Pope's authority.

The most conspicuous figure in the Church during the Fourth Century was the great Athanasius, whose life is little short of a history of Christianity during his time.

The First Œcumenical Council. 123

On the death of Alexander, which occurred shortly after the Council of Nice, Athanasius was, in accordance with his dying request, elected by the suffrages of the whole people as his successor in the See of Alexandria (326—373). He reluctantly accepted, and even tried to avoid, the election by flight[1].

Born at Alexandria about A.D. 296, his youth saved him from the persecution under Maximin. An interesting story is told by Rufinus, Socrates, and Sozomen, how that Alexander the Bishop once saw from his window a group of children playing on the sea-shore a game of religious ceremonies, and imitating the Sacrament of Baptism. Athanasius performed the part of the boy-bishop, dipping the others in the sea, the ceremony being accompanied with the usual questions and responses. Alexander sent for them, and whilst he determined that the Baptism so conferred was valid, himself completed the ceremony with the Sacrament of Unction with Chrism, whilst he was so struck with the knowledge and seriousness of Athanasius that he took him into his service. Under his careful eye the education of Athanasius was conducted, till in time he became the Archdeacon, or head-Deacon of the Bishop, in which capacity we have seen him attending the Council of Nice.

He is described as being of diminutive stature [m], almost angelic countenance, hook-nosed, with auburn hair, and a slight stoop. That he was the greatest theologian of the day is acknowledged not only in the East but the West also. "The Great" was the title which the next generation conferred on him. He has been considered the Father of theology, and, says Dean Stanley, was the Father of orthodoxy; his life to his death was, he says, a witness to, and a struggle for, the Homoousion.

It speaks wonders for him that he was a man who kindled

---

[1] Dean Stanley, Eastern Church, p 267, relates how to the present day his successors in the See are brought to Cairo loaded with chains, and strictly guarded so as to provide against escape

[m] The Emperor Julian sneered at him as ἀνθρωπίσκος (*manikin*)

the enthusiasm of Gibbon. In order to appreciate what he was and what he did, we must understand the evil against which he had to fight, and how thoroughly Arianism, during his whole life-time, permeated the Court, the Church, the legislature, even the Church Councils. Soon after the Council of Nice, the vacillating Constantine went over to the side of the Arians, and at one time Athanasius was almost the only Churchman of eminence who stood out firmly and openly against them. Hooker well sums up his position, "the heart of Constantine stolen from him; Constantius using every means to torment him which malice and his sovereign power could invent, no rest under Julian; as little under Valens; crimes of which he was innocent laid to his charge, his accusers and judges being the same persons; Bishops and Prelates feeling it unsafe to befriend him and falling away from him; his life was a long tragedy.... During the space of 46 years from the time of his Consecration.... till the last hour of his life in this world, they (the Arians) never suffered him to enjoy the comfort of a peaceable day[n]." The history of the Church in his time is concentrated in the apothegm, "Athanasius contra mundum."

In the year following the Council of Nice, Constantine, after his long sojourn in the East, went to Rome; there he stopped only a short time, but it was a turning-point in the history of the world. In the East, if his character had not been softened by its influence, he had been brought into close contact with Christianity and had taken Hosius (ὅσιος, *holy*) as his guide. At Rome he found Paganism, which in the East had been got under control, triumphant, and he viewed with disgust the pagan superstitions prevalent in the leading families; the people resented his preference for Oriental manners and customs and for the religion which they had in vain tried to stamp out; and he soon left it, never to return. The concluding years of his life have left an indelible stain on Constantine's name. In A.D. 326, for

---

[n] Hooker, V. 42.

reasons, it was supposed, of political and domestic jealousy, he ordered the execution of his son, Crispus, a youth of brilliant promise and heir to his throne. In the same year, the young Cæsar Licinius, son of his sister Constantia, shared the same fate Some attribute the fate of Crispus to the false accusations of his step-mother Fausta, who desired the succession to the throne for her own sons. However this may be, Fausta herself soon fell a victim to his suspicious jealousy, and was found strangled in her bath.

Zosimus, a heathen historian who probably flourished in the middle of the Fifth Century, would convey the idea that Constantine was at this time a Pagan. He relates that after the murder of Crispus Constantine resorted for comfort and absolution to the pagan Priests, who told him that for such sins as he had committed there was no expiation He thereupon betook himself to a Spaniard (probably Hosius, Bishop of Corduba), through whom he was induced to embrace Christianity. That he did resort to Hosius is probable ; Eusebius tells us[o] that Constantine converted his mother, Helena, to Christianity ; we may therefore, perhaps, conclude that, although he deferred his Baptism from religious scruples and perhaps political motives, he continued to profess Christianity ever since the Vision of the Cross

Now that there was a Christian Emperor, the recovery of the Holy Sepulchre at Jerusalem, which Eusebius says was a divine impulse and long contemplated by the Emperor, was possible, and to that the mind of Constantine and his pious mother, Helena, at once turned. Macarius, Bishop of Jerusalem, had, as we have seen, been present at the Council of Nice, and in the year after the Council, Helena started on her pilgrimage to the Holy Land. Constantine wrote to Macarius enjoining him to provide her with money at the public cost for the erection of a magnificent Basilica, the Church of the Holy Sepulchre, he also purposed to build other churches in Palestine, one at Bethlehem to com-

[o] V. C., III. 57.

memorate the Nativity, another on the Mount of Olives, the Ascension, and a third at Mamre, where the Saviour and two Angels appeared to Abraham. Pilgrimages to the Holy Places were coming in vogue, and were often thought necessary as an atonement for some great crime No doubt the journey was an act of piety on her part, and perhaps a vicarious expiation for the crimes of her son; but one object was to expedite the works which Constantine had undertaken

Though nearly eighty years of age, Eusebius says she entered upon her purpose "with youthful alacrity." Arrived at her destination, she was directed, we are told, by the local tradition to the site of our Lord's Burial. Everything, no doubt, had been done by the heathen to desecrate and obliterate it. Hadrian had built a Temple over it; the heathens had heaped up rubbish around it. But instead of obliterating it, the means which they adopted would only serve to draw attention to it. "The Church had never," says Mr. Williams [p], "been absent from Jerusalem for more than a few years, probably not more than two, and would any Christian who had once known the place Golgotha fail to identify it, however accident or design might have altered its character?" The first thing that Christian pilgrims would ask would be to be directed to the Sepulchre of their Lord. There could have been no doubt, no mere local *tradition*, as to the site, and Helena could have had no difficulty in discovering it.

She immediately ordered the stones and rubbish which concealed it to be cleared away, the Temple which had been built on it to be demolished; and the Holy Sepulchre was brought to light. Near the Sepulchre the three Crosses were found lying, the true Cross being distinguished, according to SS. Chrysostom and Ambrose, by its inscription, according to later authorities by the operation of a miracle. The Sepulchre Helena caused to be separated from the cave in which it was built, and enclosed in a Chapel. Part,

[p] Holy City, II 70

The First Œcumenical Council. 127

together with two nails, of the Cross she sent to Constantine, one of which he placed in his crown, the other he used for his horse's bit.

As early as the Fifth Century the discovery of the Cross by Helena was credited in the Church. But the Pilgrim who went, A.D 333, a few years therefore after the supposed event, from Bordeaux to Jerusalem, in the description which he gives of the Scriptural places of the latter city, neither mentions Helena, nor the discovery of the Cross ; and Eusebius, writing only a few years later, whilst he speaks of the visit of Helena, is equally silent as to the discovery. From the pontificate of St. Gregory the Great, the Invention of the Cross has been commemorated in the Western Church on May 3 , but in the Eastern Church the Festival of the Σταυροφανεία (appearance of the Cross), on September 14, commemorates not the discovery by Helena, but its recovery from Chosroes, King of Persia, by the Emperor Heraclius. The date and place of Helena's death are uncertain. It is generally supposed that she died about A.D. 328. Between the time that she started on her pilgrimage and the time of her death, Constantine had left Rome. Eusebius says that she died in the presence of the Emperor, but he does not say where (probably it was in the palace at Nicomedia) ; and that her body was carried with great pomp to the Imperial city, which would be Constantinople, the foundations of which had been lately laid ; and that she was buried in a royal tomb[q], that is, in the Church of the Holy Apostles which Constantine built.

Shortly before this, and probably in expiation of his crimes, Constantine provided for the building of several churches in Rome ; one on the site now occupied by St. Peter's, two others in memory of SS. Laurence and Agnes, the former Archdeacon of Rome, who perished in the Valerian persecution, the latter a martyr under Diocletian. To Constantine also, probably at this time, the foundation of the

---

[q] Eus. V C., III 47

Lateran Basilica where the Palace of Fausta stood is ascribed.

In 327, Constantine's half-sister, Constantia, widow of the Emperor Licinius, died at Nicomedia. There she had been brought by Eusebius, Bishop of the See, under Arian influence, with what disastrous results to the religion of the impulsive Emperor will be seen in the next Chapter.

On May 11, 330, took place the Dedication of New Rome, or Constantinople. Constantine, though he still held the title of Pontifex Maximus, determined to found a new Capital which should be from its foundation Christian; and having first turned his thoughts to Sardica, Thessalonica, and Troy, he eventually settled on the ruined city of Byzantium. He did not destroy the pagan monuments which he found existing there, but he forbade any new ones to be erected; he became there the same prodigal builder of churches as he had been before in Palestine and Rome; the chief was the one dedicated to the Wisdom of God, which afterwards received the name of St Sophia; another was the Church of the Holy Apostles; and Metrophanes was consecrated its first Bishop by Eustathius, Patriarch of Antioch The transference of the capital of the Roman Empire to Constantinople was one of the most important events in the history of the world. Its geographical and political importance is unhappily familiar to all in the present day, and its political founded its ecclesiastical importance; it was so with Old Rome, it was the same with New Rome.

So long as the Old Rome was the metropolis of the Empire, an honorary precedence of a vague and undefined nature had attached to the Roman Bishop, and that he never lost. In addition to Rome being the capital of the Empire, many circumstances favoured the Roman Church and increased its importance; its foundation not by one but by two, and those the two greatest, Apostles; the number of its martyrs; the high character of its Bishops; the purity of its faith Bishops of neighbouring Churches, before the faith was clearly defined at Nice, naturally consulted the Bishop of the Imperial city on matters in which they differed amongst themselves. Nor was this deference entirely confined to the West. The Church historian, Socrates, himself a Greek, speaks of a similar reverential feeling existing in the Eastern Church[r]: Μὴ δεῖν παρὰ τὴν γνώμην τοῦ Ἐπισκόπου Ῥώμης τὰς Ἐκκλησίας κανονίζειν. The fact that the Bishops of Rome afterwards put forth extravagant claims, on the fictitious supposition that St. Peter had been its Bishop and delegated to them his authority, does not derogate from the historical fact that in the earliest times an honorary precedence was accorded, both in the East and West, to their predecessors.

Through the transference of the Imperial throne to the East, New Rome in one sense gained whilst Old Rome lost. It was the metropolis of the whole Empire whilst it was united, and remained the metropolis of the East after it was divided; the Empire of the East still continued to be styled the Roman Empire, and the Eastern Emperors claimed to be the legitimate successors of the first Roman Emperor, Augustus.

But in the long run old Rome was the gainer. The removal of the seat of Empire to Constantinople, if it did not consummate, laid the seeds of the separation between East and West. It was, says Dean Stanley, the foundation of the Papal power. East and West became ranged under two spiritual and rival Heads. Old Rome, when it ceased to be the metropolis of the Empire, aimed at being the metropolis of the whole Church, and towards the attainment of that end, for which it was never over scrupulous as to the means, it had everything in its favour[s]. In the first place it possessed, what the See of Constantinople lacked, an Apostolical foundation, of which it promptly availed itself. It was also the only Patriarchate in the West, whereas

---

[r] Eccl. Hist., II. 8.

[s] It is difficult to explain away the Forged Clementines, the Forged Donation of Constantine, and the Forged Decretals.

in the East there were two other Patriarchates, those of Alexandria and Antioch, both of which were inclined to resent the pre-eminence allowed by the Œcumenical Councils to the Patriarch of Constantinople.

The residence of the Emperors at Constantinople and the remoteness of Old Rome from the new seat of government, were advantages which immensely told in favour of the latter. The position which Constantine claimed, viz. to be Head of the Church in external matters, had some appearance of reason[t]; but he went beyond this, and whereas his predecessors had persecuted it, he was the first Emperor who interfered in the guidance of the Church, not only in merely external matters, but also in its internal government. Following his example, his successors claimed and exercised the temporal Headship of the Church, and in that capacity the Emperors convened all the great Œcumenical Councils.

The temporal Headship exercised by the Emperors told differently in the East and in the West. The history of the Eastern Empire is, says Professor Freeman[u], largely a history of ecclesiastical disputes; yet we never find there the same kind of disputes between Church and State, between the ecclesiastical and temporal powers, which make up so great a part of Western history. The reason is obvious. In the East the Emperors were close at hand, and if only the Patriarch, in the conscientious discharge of his duties, opposed the arbitrary will or any unrighteous act of the Emperor, he was subject to deposition and banishment.

But it would be erroneous to suppose that the Emperors limited the exercise of their temporal Headship to the Eastern Church. To some extent the dependence of the Church on the temporal Ruler must have been still more galling in the West than it was in the East. After the fall of the Western Empire, the Emperors, who resided at Constantinople, theoretically governed the West through the

---

[t] Ὑμεῖς μὲν (the Bishops) τῶν εἴσω τῆς Ἐκκλησίας, ἐγὼ δὲ τῶν ἐκτὸς ὑπὸ Θεοῦ καθιστάμενος ἐπίσκοπος ἂν εἴην. Eus., IV. 24.

[u] General Sketch, p. 116.

Kings of Italy, who were practically independent of them, and, though Arians in religion, claimed authority in the confirmation, and even in the election, of the Popes of Rome[x]. And after the Western Empire was restored by Charlemagne, the example set by the Eastern Emperors was continued under the Holy Roman Empire, the German Emperors, more than once called in by the people of Rome to reform the Papacy, themselves deposed and appointed the Popes, and, it must be allowed, much better Popes, at their own will. But even then the continued absence of the Emperors from Rome fought for the Popes, the circumstances of the times enabled the latter in their conflict with the Emperors to exercise the fearful engine of excommunication, by which the consciences of the people were worked upon to believe that they must either be traitors to their sovereigns, or that by disobeying Rome be cut off from all hope not only in this world but also in the next. It was by such means that the Popes gained the victory over the Emperors.

Other circumstances, to which we need not allude at present, occurred, owing to which the Western Patriarchate went on and on, whilst the Eastern, though saved from the abyss of degradation which overwhelmed the Papacy, went back and back. It is necessary to take into consideration the difficulties with which the Patriarchs of Constantinople had to contend. The Eastern Church is often accused of subservience to the Emperors. The accusation is true, and from it the Western Church was free. But the different circumstances between East and West, to which the aggrandisement of the one Patriarchate and the decadence of the other is attributable, must be taken into account.

[x] Thus a disputed election to the Papacy was settled by the Arian King Theodoric, A.D. 498, in favour of Pope Simplicius, and, A.D 526, Theodoric himself appointed Pope Felix IV.

CHAPTER IV.

The Struggle for the Homoousion.

CONSTANTINE goes over to the Arians—The struggle for the Homoousion commences—Eusebius of Nicomedia—Eustathian Schism in Church of Antioch —Persecution of Athanasius commences—Council of Tyre—Eusebius of Cæsarea—Marcellus of Ancyra—Council at Constantinople—Athanasius banished to Tréves—Death of Constantine—Fiction of the Baptism and Donation of Constantine—Constantine's three sons—Recall of Athanasius —Julius, Bishop of Rome—The Dedication Council—Athanasius deposed, and goes to Rome—Council at Rome—Councils of Sardica and Philippopolis—Apiarius and the African Bishops—Councils of Laodicea and Gangra—Athanasius restored—Battle of Mursa—Athanasius banished— Homoiousians, Homoians, Anomœans—Lapse of Hosius of Corduba and Liberius of Rome—Councils of Rimini and Seleucia—Macedonius matures his heresy as to the Holy Ghost—Julian the Apostate—Athanasius recalled —Attempt to rebuild Jerusalem—Athanasius banished—Death of Julian and recall of Athanasius—Valentinian and Valens Emperors—Athanasius banished—But soon recalled—His death—The Three Cappadocians— "Rule" of St. Basil—Victory of the Homoousion

THE Council of Nice had given its Creed to the Church, Constantine himself approving and even suggesting the Homoousion. The Bishops had scarcely returned to their Sees than he went over to the side of the Arians, recalled, A.D. 330, without any stipulation being required that they would obey the voice of the Church, Arius and his allies, and ordered Athanasius, on pain of deposition, to admit Arius to communion.

There is no reason for believing that at any time of his life Constantine's religious convictions disposed him to embrace orthodoxy. He had favoured Christianity because it was congenial to his reason. He wanted peace and uniformity, so he supported the Orthodox against the Donatists, as he again supported them at Nice. He let himself be guided for some time by the orthodox Hosius, and considered the Council of Nice the bulwark of the Christian faith, yet immediately afterwards he gave himself over to the influence of Eusebius, the Arian Bishop of

Nicomedia. His rude intellect could never really grasp the points at issue between the Orthodox and the Arians; whether the Son was of the same essence (ὁμοούσιος) or only of like essence (ὁμοιούσιος) with the Father was to him one and the same thing. But it was the very question which he had summoned the Council of Nice to decide; and having called that Council, and himself having approved the ὁμοούσιον, he should have abided by the decision of the universal Church, or have summoned another Œcumenical Council. At any rate he should not have listened to what he himself knew to be absurd and false accusations, nor have allowed Orthodox Bishops to be deposed and exiled, simply because he imagined them, instead of their false accusers, to be the disturbers of the peace. The result was that instead of making peace he added to the divisions of the Church, and the Council of Nice, so far from ending, was only the commencement of a contest which lasted more than half a century, during which Arians and Semi-Arians applied themselves to the rejection of the word ὁμοούσιον. And now the Arians under the leadership of Eusebius of Nicomedia, and in a lesser degree of his namesake of Cæsarea, had the Emperor and the Court as their allies.

The first object of their attack was Eustathius, Bishop of Antioch, who as the defender of the Nicene Faith takes rank second only to Athanasius. Eustathius had been Bishop of Berrhœa, from which See he was translated to Antioch about A.D. 324. He was a man of holy life and great learning, who had taken a prominent, perhaps the most prominent, part amongst the Bishops at the Council of Nice, and afterwards had exerted his authority in counteracting heresy. The Arians, about the beginning of 331, accused him of Sabellianism (a common charge of the Arians against Athanasius and the Orthodox party), and in order that they might have more weapons in case one failed, they fabricated against him an accusation of immorality. Eustathius was summoned before their self-constituted tribunal at Antioch, condemned and sentenced to banishment into Illyria, the

Emperor ratifying the sentence; and he died in banishment about A.D. 337. A lamentable schism in the Church of Antioch, which lasted nearly a hundred years, and which was not completely healed till the episcopate of Alexander (413—420), was the result. Arian Bishops were appointed to the See, and the schism was rendered doubly disastrous by schism amongst the Orthodox Christians themselves.

The Arians availed themselves of the deposition of Eustathius to ordain Eudoxius, whom Eustathius had rejected on the ground of the unsoundness of his doctrine, and appointed him to the Bishopric of Germanicia.

Their vengeance, however, was especially directed against Athanasius, whom they assailed with a series of charges of a personal character, which it cannot be supposed that they believed, but under which they veiled their theological hatred. One only need be mentioned, as a specimen of the rest. They accused him of having cut off the hand of a Meletian Bishop, named Arsenius, and having used it for magical incantations. Constantine thought it so serious that he summoned, in 334, a Council to Cæsarea to enquire into the charge Athanasius feeling that no justice would be meted out to him in a city where the Bishop was one of his principal accusers, refused to attend, and wrote to the Emperor that an investigation had been made which disproved the story about Arsenius. The Emperor recognizing the deceit practised upon him stopped the investigation.

The Arians being thus outwitted, next bethought themselves that something might be done against Athanasius, through means of a Council. The thirtieth anniversary of Constantine's reign was approaching, on which the Basilica of the Holy Sepulchre which the Emperor had built at Jerusalem was to be consecrated. They represented to Constantine how noble a thing it would be if that event could be inaugurated by the cessation of ecclesiastical disputes. Constantine fell into the trap thus laid for him, the healing of the troubles in the Church, even after he had joined the Arians, was a thing he had still at heart; he arranged that the Bishops should meet together at Tyre, and after the desired reconciliation had been effected, proceed to Jerusalem.

He consequently summoned a Council to Tyre (A.D. 335), under Flaccillus, or Placillus, Bishop of Antioch, and notwithstanding the deceit practised by the Meletians was known to him, he compelled Athanasius, who was still reluctant to entrust his cause to the Eusebians, to attend. Athanasius went to the Council, which, besides his own Bishops, was attended by sixty Bishops, mostly his enemies. The Meletians were his accusers, the Eusebians his judges, and his enemy, Eusebius of Cæsarea, took a prominent part. The Count Dionysius, who was appointed by the Emperor to represent him at the Council, was influenced by the Eusebians.

An aged Egyptian Bishop, named Potamon, who had suffered mutilation in the Diocletian persecution, tauntingly asked Eusebius; "Were we not in prison together, Eusebius, in the time of persecution? How came you to escape without betrayal of the Lord's cause, when I was thus maimed in upholding it? and how come you to sit as judge of the innocent Athanasius?"

Several new charges were now brought against Athanasius, and whilst his slanderers were listened to, his own Bishops were refused a hearing. The story of the murdered Arsenius was revived, and the hand was produced in a wooden box. The Meletians had persuaded their murdered man to go into hiding in a monastery of the Thebaid, and when that place was found to be too public, they next sent him to a private house in Tyre. There being discovered, he denied his identity, until confronted by Paul, the Bishop of Tyre, who had known him of old and now convicted him of the fraud. The man whom the Eusebians had thought in safe concealment was introduced before the Council muffled in a cloak from head to foot. Athanasius, who had hitherto sat silent under the clamour and objurgations of the opposite faction, asked them, "Is this the Arsenius whom I murdered?" First he drew out one hand and then another, and then, with pointed irony and humour which was a well-known trait of his character, he added, "No need to ask for a third hand, for two hands, and two only, has the Creator of all things bestowed."

We have given the story at length (as it has been handed down), for it may give some insight into the character of Constantine, who notwithstanding such absurd and notorious calumnies could still lend his ear to Arian calumnies, and send the confessor of the Orthodox faith into banishment. Other charges brought against him, such as one of immorality with a consecrated virgin, need not be entered into; they were one and all unfounded impostures.

Incredible as it may appear, the Arians still persisted in accusing him of magic arts. Two Arian Bishops, who had in their early years been degraded from the Priesthood, Valens, Bishop of Mursa, and Ursacius of Syngidon, now appear on the scene at Tyre with fresh accusations against him, and such was the feeling against Athanasius, that the civil authorities were called upon to rescue him, and by them he was conveyed by night on board a ship to Constantinople. The Council of Tyre pronounced against him a sentence of excommunication, the ex-murdered Arsenius signing the decree of condemnation.

In consequence of the tumultuous proceedings at Tyre, Athanasius now determined to bring his cause before the Emperor himself at Constantinople. Meeting Constantine, who was riding on horseback and tried to avoid the man whom he considered the disturber of the peace of Egypt, Athanasius demanded that either a lawful Council should be summoned, or the opportunity afforded him of meeting his accusers face to face in the presence of the Emperor. The demand was one which Constantine could not refuse. The Bishops had gone from Tyre to Jerusalem to attend the consecration of the new Church. He accordingly wrote to them complaining of the riotous proceedings at Tyre, and ordering them to appear on their return from Jerusalem

The Struggle for the Homoousion

to justify their proceedings at Constantinople. During the short time which they spent in Jerusalem the Arians had occupied themselves in attacking Marcellus of Ancyra, an Orthodox Bishop who had been one of their opponents at Nice, and had since defended Athanasius. Further proceedings, however, against him were stopped through Constantine's peremptory order for them to proceed to Constantinople.

Maximus, who had recently succeeded Macarius, was at that time Bishop of Jerusalem. He had been an Othodox Bishop, a Confessor in the Diocletian persecution, and attended the Council of Nice. But even then his brother Confessor, Paphnutius, had discovered in him a vacillating spirit, and now the Arians had during their stay in the Holy City succeeded in bringing him over to their party.

Most of the Bishops alarmed at the summons, and the apparent change in the mind of the Emperor, instead of obeying it, fled in terror to their Dioceses. Only six, but amongst them Athanasius' greatest enemies, Eusebius, Theognis, Ursacius, and Valens, obeyed. They now brought a charge of a different nature against him, and accused him of forbidding the exportation of corn from Alexandria, which was the principal granary of the East, to Constantinople. The accusation was as groundless as the rest, but such as they were well aware was well suited to influence the Emperor's mind. "How could I, a private person, do such a thing?" Athanasius asked. But the Emperor was entirely in the power of Eusebius of Nicomedia; at any rate he thought it desirable, as a means of bringing peace to the Church, to get rid of Athanasius, he affected to believe the charge, and Athanasius was banished in February, 336, to Tréves. At the same time the Emperor rejected the petition of Eusebius, that another Bishop should be appointed to the See of Alexandria. At Tréves he was received with marks of great honor and reverence by the Bishop Maximin (afterwards canonized), and there he made the acquaintance, which was afterwards of much value to him, of Constantine, the Emperor's eldest son, an orthodox Prince who was at the time resident in the Palace.

At Constantinople the Arians renewed the charges which they had brought at Jerusalem against Marcellus, adding another, with perhaps some truth, of his holding the views of Paul of Samosata, and he was sentenced to deposition from his Bishopric. Marcellus then repaired to Rome, where he was received into communion by Pope Julius.

Arius had not ventured till the condemnation of Athanasius to return to Alexandria. He now, however, thought it a favourable opportunity to do so, but the Alexandrians, faithful to their Bishop, refused to admit him to communion. Constantine knowing that Alexandria was too remote, and its people too staunch to Athanasius for him to use compulsion, summoned Arius to Constantinople, and ordered its aged Bishop, Alexander (317—336), to admit him to communion. The Eusebians threatened him with deposition and exile if he refused to do so. He could not, he told the Emperor, receive the Heresiarch. On the evening of the day before he intended to offer himself, or early on the Sunday morning, Arius died, his death being accelerated by excitement.

In the same year (336), Alexander, the Bishop of Constantinople, at the age of nearly a hundred years, and in the following year the Emperor, died. To the end, although entreated by the aged hermit, St. Antony, whom he held in high respect, Constantine persisted in refusing to recall Athanasius; Athanasius was, he wrote to him, a quarrelsome man, a promoter of dissension, and it was impossible that so many excellent Bishops could be wrong in their judgment respecting him. Constantine had persisted to the last in deferring his Baptism. There are few characters in ecclesiastical history which present such flagrant contradictions as that of Constantine the Great. Abjuring Paganism yet continuing to hold the title of Pontifex Maximus; professing to be a Christian and inscribing the sacred monogram on his banner, yet rejecting the initiatory rite of Christianity, which both Orthodox and Arians accepted, sanctioning the decrees of the Council of Nice, yet immediately afterwards persecuting the Homoousians, he in his self-confidence made shipwreck of his faith till he was brought face to face with death Being seized with illness and feeling that his end was near, he became a Catechumen, and soon afterwards sent for Eusebius, the Arian Bishop of Nicomedia, and from him received the Sacrament, he had he said delayed it in the hope that it might be conferred in the waters of Jordan. On Whit Sunday of the same year, wearing to the end the white robes of his Baptism, he died

We cannot omit a story which sprang up about the end of the Fifth Century, as it materially conduced to the aggrandisement of the Roman over the Eastern Patriarchate. The story runs that Constantine had received Baptism at an earlier time in his life from Silvester, Bishop of Rome, and on that fictitious event was grounded the further fiction of the Donation of Constantine. Of Silvester little is known, and of that little, it may we think be said with certainty, every item is a fiction.

The See of Rome in his Pontificate was, as always, held in high reverence. Silvester was Bishop of Rome at the time of the Council of Arles, but Constantine took no notice of him, and committed the arrangements of the Council to the Bishop of Syracuse. His Episcopate extended over the Council of Nice, which old age, if no other reason, would have prevented his attending. But we hear nothing of him in connexion with that Council, Hosius, Bishop of Corduba in Spain, was at that time Constantine's chief confidant among the Bishops, and perhaps presided, but whoever presided, it was in his own name and not in that of the Bishop of Rome.

It may be hoped that the accusation brought against him of having, when still a Presbyter, in company with his three predecessors in the Papacy, offered incense to the Pagan deities, may be as unfounded as are the other statements with regard to him. It is with the strangest of all, his alleged Baptism of Constantine, and the famous Donation, that we are concerned. Eusebius, Constantine's biographer, tells us that the Emperor, when he was "convinced that his life was drawing to a close," received Baptism at Nicomedia. The Roman story as to his Baptism by Silvester states:— Silvester, in order to escape the persecution under which the Christians were suffering, had fled to Soracte. Constantine being at that time afflicted with leprosy was advised by the soothsayers to seek a cure by bathing in a tub filled with the blood of a child. Moved by the cries of the child and the tears of the mother, he abandoned the idea, and in a vision by night of SS. Peter and Paul he was directed to recall Silvester, by whom he was cured of his leprosy and baptized. The Emperor, in gratitude, not only destroyed several heathen Temples and built Christian Churches, but conferred on the Papacy the temporal dominion of the City of Rome and of all the provinces of Italy and the Western Empire, together with the Lateran palace. As a residence for himself, Constantine founded Constantinople, considering it unfit (*justum non est*) that the place where "the Head of Christ's Church was settled by its Heavenly Ruler (*ubi religionis Caput ab Imperatore cœlesti constitum est*) should be subject to an earthly Head."

The "Donation of Constantine" was long accredited, and was the foundation of Rome's claim to temporal power. It was incorporated in the Forged Decretals, known as the Pseudo-Isidore, in the middle of the Ninth Century, which were long accepted as genuine and acted on by the Popes; their spuriousness was only fully exposed in the revival of learning in the Fifteenth Century, and then, but not till then, the Roman Church itself discarded them.

On the death of Alexander, Bishop of Constantinople, a conflict occurred between the orthodox party and the Arians on the election of his successor. Two candidates were brought forward, Paul, who had been secretary to the late

The Struggle for the Homoousion. 141

Bishop, and Macedonius, soon to become of heretical notoriety as the Head of the Pneumatomachi. Paul was elected, but his election was the cause of much trouble to the See of Constantinople. The Bishops of Constantinople were consecrated by the Metropolitan of Heraclea, whom it was an obvious advantage for the Arians to gain over to their party. They now, under the influence of Eusebius of Nicomedia, complained that he had not been so consecrated: Paul was consequently deposed by a Synod of Arian Bishops, and banished.

Constantine the Great divided his dominions between his three sons, Constantine II., the eldest, having Great Britain, Spain and Gaul, with a certain precedence over his two brothers, and Constantinople the capital; Constantius, the second, Asia, Syria and Egypt, whilst Italy and Africa fell to the youngest, Constans. Constantine II. was a pious and orthodox Prince, and, as was also Constans, a favourer of Athanasius; whilst Constantius, who was first Emperor of the East but afterwards became sole Emperor, was a persecuting Arian, and from first to last the bitter enemy of the Homoousians.

Constantine II. carrying out, as he said, his father's intention, immediately sent back Athanasius from Tréves to Alexandria, where he, after two and a half years' exile, arrived in November, A.D. 338, and was triumphantly received by the people. Paul also was enabled to return to Constantinople. An orthodox Bishop was however distasteful to Constantius, and Paul was, in A.D. 339, deposed by an Arian Council, and Eusebius translated from Nicomedia to the See of Constantinople.

Eusebius the historian, dying A.D. 340, was suceeeded in the See of Cæsarea by Acacius, an Arian, known from a personal deformity as the one-eyed ($\mu o\nu \acute{o}\phi \theta a\lambda \mu o\varsigma$), of whose relations with St. Cyril of Jerusalem more will be said further on.

In 340, Constantine II. was, unhappily for the Church, slain in battle with his brother Constans.

Eusebius only survived his translation to Constantinople a short time, and on his death in 341 Acacius became the Head of the Arian party Paul was now again restored to the See of Constantinople, but Macedonius, being again brought forward by the Arians, was consecrated by the Metropolitan of Heraclea

The Arians were not inclined to leave Athanasius or Paul in peace But now both they and Athanasius consulted Julius, the Bishop of Rome (337—352), who proposed that the two parties should attend a Council at some place in the West to be selected by Athanasius. The Eusebians, however, as the majority of the Arian party were called, unwilling to attend a Western Council, availed themselves of the opportunity offered by the dedication of the Church at Antioch, called the Golden Church, commenced ten years previously by Constantine the Great, to hold a Council in that city. The Council known as the Council in Encæniis, or the Dedication Council, and attended by ninety-seven Bishops, of whom thirty-six were Arians, was held in the early part of 341 under Flaccillus, a Eusebian, Bishop of Antioch, Constantius himself being present.

Four Creeds, the second of which became known as the Dedication Creed, and twenty-four canons, all of a vaguely orthodox character, by way of persuading the Western Church of its orthodoxy, were drawn up; the more objectionable tenets of the Arians were avoided; the Son of God was pronounced to have been begotten before the Creation of the world, but the word Homoousion was studiously avoided. The Canons were of importance as having been adopted by, and therefore having the authority of, the Eastern and Western Church. Of these the principal ones may be here mentioned ;—Canon I. renewed the decree of the Council of Nice with regard to Easter, III., in agreement with Canons XV. and XVI. of Nice, related to Priests migrating from one Diocese to another; V. condemned schism and forbade Priests and Deacons setting up an Altar against their own Diocesan; VII. and VIII.

The Struggle for the Homoousion.

ordered commendatory Letters (κανονικαὶ ἐπιστόλαι) to be adduced by strangers from another Diocese with a view to their admission to communion; IX. shows the antiquity of the Apostolical Canons; X. forbade Chorepiscopi to ordain without leave of the Bishop of the See to which they were subject; XI., XII., XIV, XV, XX. (evidently directed by the Arians against Athanasius) forbade appeals to the Emperor against the judgment of Synods[a]; XXI. forbade the translation of Bishops; XXII. forbade a Bishop, even at the point of death, from electing his successor.

It has been surmised that after these orthodox Canons were passed, most of the Catholic Bishops returned to their Dioceses, and that the Arians remaining took advantage of their majority to turn the Canons against Athanasius Certain it is that the Council took high ground against him, and insisted that, though his return had been sanctioned by the Emperor, Constantine II., yet, that having been deposed by a Synod he could only be re-instated by the same authority. It confirmed the sentence of the Council of Tyre, and by means of the Canons of the Dedication Council, Constantius was brought to sanction his deposition. One Pistus, an excommunicated Arian, was appointed, and when he, on account of his notorious incompetence, was set aside, Gregory of Cappadocia was intruded into the See of Alexandria Athanasius then went to Rome. Troubles also occurred in Constantinople, and Paul was again ejected. To this unjust treatment of their Bishop the people of Constantinople would not however submit; riots between the adherents of Paul and Macedonius, and civil war, followed, which the Imperial forces were sent to quell; much bloodshed ensued, Hermogenes the General being killed and torn in pieces by the population. Paul driven out from Constantinople went to Rome, where Athanasius and Marcellus of Ancyra had arrived.

[a] These canons, passed in the presence of the Emperor by a Council in which the Arians were in a minority, show the influence which they had gained over him.

The three exiled Bishops took counsel with Pope Julius, who in December, 341, held in Rome the Council which he had before proposed to the Eusebians, and sent two Priests to invite their attendance. The Council was attended by more than fifty Bishops, but the Eusebians did not present themselves, the result was that Athanasius and Paul were acquitted, and Marcellus, who had been deprived at the Arian Council of Constantinople, was declared orthodox. The Pope sent by two Priests a letter of strong rebuke to the Eusebians, and another letter to the Emperor Constans. In January, 342, the two Priests were sent back from the East with a defiant reply to the Pope's attempt at mediation.

It was now evident that a General Council of East and West was the only remedy for the distracted state of the Eastern Church; and Constans prevailed with Constantius that such a Council should be convened to Sardica (the modern Sophia), in Bulgaria, as a place conveniently situated on the confines of both Empires. The Council of Sardica, convened by the Emperors Constantius and Constans, met about the end of 343, Julius, the Pope of Rome, being represented by two legates [b]. The Eusebian Bishops who were in a minority, as soon as they arrived at Sardica, knowing that Athanasius and Marcellus had been acquitted in the Council of Rome, and fearing that they might be acquitted now, refused to attend the Council, unless they and their other opponents were excluded from it. They were told that it was a General Council, and that a full hearing would be accorded to both parties. The Eusebians, however, still continuing their objection, two contemporaneous assemblies were held, one the Council of Sardica, consisting of Western Bishops, with Athanasius and a few Orthodox Bishops from the East, under the Presidency of Hosius, Bishop of Corduba; the other a "Conciliabulum" of Eastern, with a few Western, Bishops,

[b] The date given is that adopted by Hefele, whom the writer has generally followed when treating of the Councils.

under Stephen, Bishop of Antioch, at Philippopolis, within the Eastern part of the Empire The Sardican Council acquitted Athanasius and Marcellus, and their brethren (among whom doubtless Paul was included), and excommunicated Stephen the Bishop of Antioch, Theodore of Heraclea, Acacius of Cæsarea, Ursacius and Valens, and other leaders of the Eusebian party. The Bishops at Philippopolis in their turn excommunicated Julius, Hosius, Athanasius, Paul, and their adherents, and they drew up a Creed of a more Arian character than the Dedication Creed Thus there was an open schism between the Eusebians and the Western Church.

The Council of Sardica drew up twenty-one Canons. In consequence of the secession of the Eastern Bishops, it was only a Western Council, and its Canons, although adopted in the Trullan Council, were never received into the code of the universal Church They are, however, of importance, since they gave rise to Rome's appellate jurisdiction. The provision with regard to the See of Rome is contained in the third and two following Canons. They allowed a Bishop, deposed by his provincial Synod, to demand a new trial and to appeal for that purpose to the Bishop of Rome (Can. IV., V.); in which case his comprovincial judges should also write to the Roman Bishop (Can. III), who, if he thought it reasonable, might send the case to the Bishops of the next adjacent Province, and, at the appellant's special request, might depute one or more Presbyters *de latere suo* to act with them as holding his authority. The words of Hosius, who proposed the Canons, were ;—" If it is your pleasure (*si placet*) let us honour the memory of the Apostle Peter." The reasonableness of the Canons at that particular time is evident. Julius had given an asylum to Athanasius and Paul when they were persecuted by the Arians, and had extended to them justice, which it was impossible for orthodox Prelates to find in the East. The kindly reception of the great Athanasius by Julius had reflected a glory upon the See of Rome. Canons IV. and V. are supposed to have been personal to Julius. In consequence of the absence of the Eastern Bishops the character of the Council of Sardica, which was originally intended to be a General Council, was completely altered; and, although the Roman Church tacked the Sardican Canons on as an appendix to the Nicene Canons, it could not possibly bind the Eastern Church.

Zosimus, Bishop of Rome (417—418), the first Bishop of that See who claimed to "inherit a divine authority equal to that of St. Peter [c]," quoted them as Nicene Canons; and the example once set was followed by his successors, Boniface I. (418—422), Cœlestine I. (422—432), Leo I. (440—461), who in like manner appealed to them as Nicene Canons.

The Pontificate of Zosimus, though short, was of much importance, and we shall have to refer to it again further on; but the celebrated case of Apiarius affords evidence of the relations at that time existing between the Roman and African Sees. Apiarius, an African Priest, who had been deposed and excommunicated by his own Bishop for gross offences, enlisted the sympathy of Zosimus, who ordered him to be reinstated; the order was not obeyed by the Bishop, whilst the African Church resented the Pope's interference. To a Council which was held at Carthage, Zosimus sent a Bishop and two Priests with a Commonitorium which claimed jurisdiction for the Pope on the ground of the Nicene Canons. The African Bishops, knowing nothing about Sardican Canons, were willing to abide by anything that was Nicene, but on their referring to the Patriarchs of Constantinople, Alexandria, and Antioch for a copy of the Nicene Canon, they found the Canon adduced by Zosimus "conspicuous by its absence [d]."

Still the Sardican Canons laid the foundation of Rome's appellate jurisdiction; Romanists grounded on it the right of the Pope to receive appeals from the whole Church; and thus jealousy between the Eastern and Western Churches was engendered.

The Council of Sardica acquitted Marcellus and restored

[c] Mansi, IV 366   [d] Bright's Roman See in the Early Church, p. 139.

him to his See, but, though he lived on till A.D. 374, he never appears to have been reinstated. The accounts given of this Prelate are so confused that it is impossible to form a real estimate of his character and teaching. He is accused by the historian Eusebius of holding the doctrines of Paul of Samosata and Sabellianism Orthodox Bishops also were subjected by the Arians to the same accusations. He certainly professed orthodoxy at the Council of Nice, and afterwards boasted of the friendship of both Julius and Athanasius. There is reason for believing that he imposed on both. At any rate he outlived his character for orthodoxy and became, rightly or wrongly, an object of suspicion to all parties, Orthodox and Eusebian, alike.

Two Eastern Councils, those of Laodicea in Phrygia, the Church addressed by St. John in the Apocalypse, and of Gangra in Paphlagonia, were held about the same time as the Council of Sardica. The former Council consisted of thirty-two Bishops, and passed fifty-nine Canons. Canon VIII. enacted that the Phrygians (i.e. the Montanists) must be re-baptized; XLIX. that "Bread ought not to be consecrated during Lent, save on the Sabbath-day and the Lord's Day," in other words, on ordinary days in Lent, the *Missa Præsanctificatorum*, as observed in the Greek Church, was to be used. Canon LIX. prescribed the Books of the Old and New Testaments which were to be read in Church, the Revelation being omitted from the Catalogue. It must be borne in mind that the Council was held at Laodicea, the Church of which was strongly reprobated by St. John; thou "knowest not that thou art wretched, and miserable, and poor, and blind, and naked." This will account for its omission. At what time the Apocalypse was inserted in the Bible cannot be determined, but it certainly was so before the last of the Œcumenical Councils was dissolved.

The Council of Gangra, attended by fifteen Bishops, passed twenty canons, of which the most important was Canon IV., which was to the same effect as the previous

decree of Nice and sanctioned the marriage of the clergy;—
"If any one maintains that when a married Priest performs
the Liturgy, no one should take part in the Service, let
him be excommunicated."

The Sardican Council stimulated the advisers of Constantius to further measures against Athanasius, and an
order was sent to the magistrates of Alexandria to put him
to death if he should attempt to re-enter the City. In 349,
Gregory, the intruded Bishop of Alexandria, died, or,
as some say, was murdered. Constans then wrote to Constantius threatening that he would himself, if necessary, by
a fleet and army restore Athanasius and Paul to their Sees.
The threat had the desired effect. Still Athanasius would
not, till he had been thrice invited by him to return, trust
the word of Constantius. On his homeward journey he
visited Constans at Milan and Julius at Rome. From the
latter he received letters to the Church of Alexandria congratulating it on the return of its Bishop, and expressing
his own happiness in having made such a friend. At
Antioch he was favourably received by Constantius, who
promised that the past should be banished from his mind,
and that never again would he credit accusations against
him. Passing through Palestine he was welcomed by Maximus, Bishop of Jerusalem, and the other Bishops, Acacius
of Cæsarea being the almost sole exception, and at a Council
at Jerusalem he was commended to the love and duty of
the people of Alexandria. Athanasius again entered Alexandria in triumph. St. Gregory Nazianzen describes his
return and compares it to the triumphal entry of the Saviour
into Jerusalem. He likens it to the flow of the Nile at the
height of its flood. The population of the city streamed
forth in a preconcerted arrangement to meet him; men in
one company, divided according to their trades and occupations, the women in another, the children forming a third
body by themselves. Branches of trees waved overhead;
the richest carpets were strewed under his feet; thousands
of hands were clapped with an unbroken shout of joy; at

night the city was a blaze of illuminations; public or private entertainments were given in every house; the poor and hungry were fed; men, women, and even children, determined to devote themselves to the monastic life, and long afterwards the reception given to Athanasius was a byword throughout the Patriarchate of Alexandria.

Paul also returned to Constantinople. Five Arian Bishops in succession had presided over the See of Antioch. Stephen, the last of the Arians, was deposed A.D. 348, and Leontius (348—357) appointed by Constantius in his place. There still continued two parties, one the Eustathians, the other the sympathisers with the Arians. Leontius tried to take a *via media*, and neither party could make more out of his religion than that in the Doxology the only words which he recited audibly were "unto ages of ages. Amen;" Athanasius when at Antioch communicated with the Eustathian party. The worst that could be said against Leontius was that if he was not strictly Arian, neither was he strictly orthodox.

The victory of the Homoousion seemed now to have been gained, and the Arians regarded their cause as lost. The two Bishops, Valens and Ursacius, who had been the most violent opponents of Athanasius, went, under fear of deposition, to Rome, where they confessed that their accusations against him were false, anathematized Arianism, and requested Julius and the clergy to admit them to communion.

But the hopes of the Homoousians were soon dashed to the ground. On Feb. 15, 350, the Emperor Constans was killed in an insurrection under one of his generals, Magnentius, who then assumed the government of the Western Empire. In that year also Paul was finally expelled from Constantinople, and sent, loaded with chains, to Cucusus where it was supposed he was strangled. On the deposition of Paul, Macedonius was appointed to the See.

In the same year (350) Maximus, the weak and vacillating Bishop of Jerusalem, died. After he had been gained over by the Arians he returned to orthodoxy, but knowing too well the danger of trusting his own will, he declined to attend the Dedication Council. By such means he managed to preserve his orthodoxy to the end, and on his death was succeeded in the See of Jerusalem by St. Cyril (350—386), who was consecrated by Acacius of Cæsarea.

No sooner was Constans dead, than Valens and Ursacius saw that the tide had turned, and again went over to the Eusebians.

In 351 Magnentius suffered a defeat at Mursa under the avenging hand of Constantius. Constantius attributed his victory to the prayers of Valens, the Bishop of Mursa, who thus regained his confidence, which he determined to turn against Athanasius. In 353 Magnentius died by his own hand; thus Constantius became undisputed Emperor, and the whole Roman Empire was subjected to the rule of an Arian. Constantius was also now much under the influence of his Arian wife, Eusebia, whom he had lately married.

Two Councils were held under Eusebian influence in the West, one, A.D 353, at Arles, where Saluminus the Bishop was a Eusebian; the other at Milan, in 355, under its orthodox Bishop, Dionysius. In vain in the latter Council the Bishops insisted that Athanasius ought not to be condemned unheard, they were opposed by Valens and Ursacius and intimidated by the Emperor; "What I will," he declared, "let that be regarded as a Canon of the Church;" thus they were intimidated into submission, and the sentence for his condemnation was signed or confirmed by nearly all the Bishops both of the East and West. Now it was truly *Athanasius contra mundum.* Those who refused to subscribe the Councils of Arles and Milan were deposed. Liberius of Rome, Hosius, Hilary of Poitiers, Eusebius of Vercelli, Lucifer of Cagliari and Dionysius of Milan were amongst these deposed Bishops, their Sees being conferred upon Arians. Liberius, Bishop of Rome, was banished to Berrhœa, and Hosius to Sirmium.

It is needless to wade through the various plans and

intrigues by which Constantius was led to forget all his promises, and to enter on so severe a persecution against Athanasius that it was compared to those under Nero and Domitian. On February 9, A.D. 356, whilst Athanasius and his clergy were employed in their midnight service in the Church of St. Theonas, the Emperor's officers, conducted by the Eusebians, surrounded the Church with 500 soldiers, thus making escape almost impossible. The presence of mind for which he was distinguished did not for a moment desert the Bishop. Seated on his throne behind the Altar, and having ordered the 136th Psalm to be repeated, of which each verse concludes with the words, " For his mercy endureth for ever," he calmly awaited what appeared to be certain death In the tumult and darkness that pervaded the Church, and perhaps owing to the smallness of his person, he was enabled at length to pass unobserved through the crowd; as it was, he was carried out in a swoon. Whither he went no one knew, but from that night he disappeared from Alexandria, and for six years (356—362) lived in unsuspected concealment somewhere in the deserts of Egypt. In vain Constantius sought him out in all parts of the Empire, offering rewards for his apprehension and threatening any who sheltered him. George of Cappadocia, an illiterate man, a stranger alike to humanity and morality, was intruded into his See, in which he showed himself the scourge of Christianity, and became an object of detestation not only to the Orthodox and the Eusebians, but also to the Pagans.

Thinking that Athanasius had taken refuge in Abyssinia, Constantius wrote to the Princes of that country not to give him an asylum; at the same time he requested them to send their Bishop Frumentius, who had lately converted the country, and whom Athanasius himself had consecrated, to receive instruction in the faith from the Arian Bishop of Alexandria. For those six years, except that he employed much of his time in literary work, little is known of Athanasius.

It seemed now that the victory of Arianism was in its turn complete; the Nicene Creed was almost entirely suppressed, and the ranks of the Eusebians were increased by many orthodox Bishops who were persuaded into the belief that the Homoousion sheltered many who held Sabellianism But just when Arianism seemed to be everywhere triumphant, it became broken up into several conflicting sects. There were the advanced Arians, the followers of the doctrine as it had been held by Eusebius of Constantinople, the root and branch opponents to the Homoousion; there were the Semi-Arians or moderate party, followers of Eusebius the Historian, who were called Homoiousians. And now another party owed its origin to Acacius of Cæsarea. In 357, Valens and Ursacius prevailed with Constantius to summon the Arian Council, the Second of Sirmium. In that Council the term οὐσία was laid aside as unscriptural; both the Homoousion and the Homoiousion were rejected, and a formula was agreed to that the Son was *like* the Father; whence the new party were called Homoians. It is to this formula that St. Hilary of Poitiers, the Athanasius of the West as he has been called, refers when he speaks of "the blasphemous faith of Sirmium[e]." But now the saddest blow of all befell the orthodox cause; after two years of exile the aged Hosius, after suffering various acts of cruelty, and Liberius, Bishop of Rome, gave way, abandoned the Nicene faith, and subscribed the Arian Creed of Sirmium; they were thereupon permitted to return to their Sees. Whether the Creed signed by Liberius was that denounced by St. Hilary has been questioned; there is no doubt, however, that it was an Arian formula, or Hilary would not have spoken of him in such uncompromising language:—"Anathema I say to thee, Liberius, with the Arians; again and a third time I say anathema, prevaricator Liberius." Both Bishops afterwards returned to orthodoxy.

---

[e] A previous Council in 351 had been held at Sirmium, the Creed of which Hilary pronounced to be orthodox

The Struggle for the Homoousion. 153

Another party only carried the Arian doctrine to its logical conclusion in teaching that the Son was unlike the Father, whence they were called Anomœans (*unlike*) Finding that no others were prepared to go to this extreme length with them, they separated themselves, and created a schism which wrecked the cause of the Arians. The first Head of this party was Ætius, a native of Cappadocia, an ignorant charlatan of low origin. Ætius "was," Gibbon says of him, "successively a slave, or at least a husbandman, a travelling tinker, a goldsmith, a physician, a schoolmaster, a theologian, and at last the apostle of a new Church, which was propagated by his pupil Eunomius." He managed to obtain Orders, *circ.* 350, from Leontius, Bishop of Antioch, whose pupil he had been, and served as Deacon under George of Cappadocia; but being unwilling to be consecrated by Arian Bishops, he refused a Bishopric.

His pupil Eunomius, after whom the Anomœans were also called Eunomians, had the credit of being a man of unblemished character, and of a sturdy honesty which disdained everything like dissimulation. He carried out his views, however, to such an extreme, that Homoousians and Homoiousians alike were horrified with the blasphemies of the $\dot{a}\nu o\mu o\hat{\iota}o\nu$. The Emperor also was opposed to the party, although Eudoxius, who had, A D 357, succeeded Leontius as Bishop of Antioch, managed to obtain for Eunomius the See of Cyzicus.

With the view of restoring peace amongst the discordant Arians, Constantius, himself a Semi-Arian, determined to call a General Council to Nicomedia. That city was, however, A.D. 358, destroyed by an earthquake; the Anomœans, then, fearing that in a General Council Homoousians and Arians might prove too strong a combination against them, prevailed on the Emperor, through Acacius of Cæsarea, to split the Council into two parts, to convene the Western Bishops to Ariminum or Rimini on the shores of the Hadriatic, and the Easterns to Seleucia in Isauria.

Chapter IV.

The Seleucian Council, composed of one hundred and sixty Bishops, the large majority of whom were Semi-Arians, some Arians, some Anomœans, and a few Catholics from Egypt, met on September 27, A.D. 359, under Acacius. At Seleucia, says Dean Milman, "the Arians, Semi-Arians, and Anomœans hurled mutual anathemas at each other." Acacius brought forward a formula which had been drawn up in a Third Council of Sirmium, called the *Dated Creed*, which rejected the words Homoousion and Homoiousion alike. This Creed the Semi-Arians rejected, and Acacius was deposed. Ultimately the *Dedication Creed* was adopted, and in a few days, after several acrimonious debates, the Council separated without arriving at any practical conclusion. At the Council, Macedonius, Bishop of Constantinople, and Eudoxius of Antioch were present, the latter of whom was deposed by the less heretical party. The majority signed the Dedication Creed.

Meanwhile, the Council of Rimini had met in May of the same year, and was attended by more than 400 Bishops from Africa, Italy, Spain, Gaul, Britain, and Illyricum, about eighty being adherents of the Arian party. Valens presented to the Council the Third Creed of Sirmium, and called upon the Bishops in the name of the Emperor to accept it. In vain the majority pleaded that they were content with the Nicene Creed; after having sat six months they wrote to Constantius asking that, inasmuch as they were worn out with age and poverty, they might be allowed to return to their own Dioceses. But the Prefect of the City had received orders from the Emperor that the Council should not be dissolved before it had arrived at a unanimous decision. The Emperor now insisted on the exclusion of the word οὐσία and the ὁμοούσιον. The Homoousians dreading detention at Rimini during the winter months; cajoled and out-manœuvred by Valens and Ursacius, who assured them that the difference was a mere question of words, surrendered the οὐσία and the ὁμοούσιον and set their names to an uncatholic formula.

The Struggle for the Homoousion. 155

Amongst those who subscribed the Creed of Rimini must be mentioned Dianius, Bishop of the Cappadocian Cæsarea, a man venerated for his saintly character, by whom St. Basil the Great was baptized ; to Basil, Dianius shortly before his death in 362, after he had held the See of Cæsarea for twenty years, bitterly lamented his fall, and declared that he had acted in the simplicity of his heart, and had never intended to impugn the Nicene Faith. Another was Gregory, who held the See of Nazianzus for forty-four years, and had the honour of being the Father of St. Gregory Nazianzen , before and again after his fall he was regarded as a pillar of orthodoxy, and was one of the consecrators of St. Basil to the Episcopate.

From Seleucia Acacius fled to Constantinople, where he succeeded in gaining the ear of the Emperor, with a view to which he made a scape-goat of Ætius, who was deposed from the Diaconate and sentenced by the Emperor to banishment. A fresh Council wholly under the influence of Acacius was held in 360 at Constantinople, in which the Homœan Creed was adopted. " We do not despise," it said, " the formula of the Antiochene Synod in Encæniis ; but inasmuch as the words ὁμοούσιος and ὁμοιούσιος have occasioned confusion, and some have recently set up the ἀνόμοιος, we reject ὁμοούσιος and ὁμοιούσιος as unscriptural, and anathematize the ἀνόμοιος ; and acknowledge the Son to be similar to the Father, agreeably to the words of the Apostle, who calls Him the Image of the Invisible God . . . . Whoever declares anything else outside this faith has no part in the Catholic Church."

Eudoxius, after his deposition at Seleucia, also took refuge at Constantinople, where he circumvented the deposition of Macedonius, and, by the help of Acacius, his own appointment to the See of Constantinople The irregularities of Macedonius, accompanied with violence and cruelty, had so excited universal detestation, that the Emperor was glad to get rid of him. It was after his deposition, and apparently to console his solitude, that Macedonius matured the heresy with which his name is associated. Eudoxius was now Patriarch of Constantinople, and he has descended to posterity with the character of "the worst of all the Arians." Well might St. Jerome exclaim that "the whole world groaned in amazement at finding itself Arian." The only gleam of light was a disposition on the more moderate part of the Arians, who were horrified with the impiety and blasphemy of the Anomœans and the Homœans, to renounce Arianism and accept the Homoousion of the Nicene Creed

Meletius, Bishop of Berrhœa, was appointed to succeed Eudoxius in the See of Antioch. Both parties in Antioch, the Eustathians and the Eudoxians, regarded him as their adherent, and both recommended him to the Emperor. But on his proclaiming himself the holder of the Homoousion, the Eudoxians accused him of Sabellianism to Constantius, and he was deprived and banished, his See being conferred on Euzoius, the former friend of Arius. Never before nor since was the Church so near a general apostasy, when in the same year (361) Constantius died, having like his father postponed his Baptism to the last, when he received it from the Arian Euzoius. He was succeeded in the Empire by his cousin Julian (361—363), thirty years of age, commonly known as the Apostate.

The new Emperor was the younger son of the half-brother of Constantine the Great, and was, with his elder brother Gallus, the sole survivor of a massacre of the male branches of the family of Constantine, made, it was supposed, at the instigation of Constantius. In 354 Gallus was executed, and Julian, who had in 351 been created Cæsar, was thus left heir to the Imperial throne; having become an object of suspicion to Constantius he was for a time imprisoned, but after his release married the Emperor's sister, Helena.

His early education had been conducted under Eusebius the Arian Bishop of Nicomedia. Julian became by Baptism outwardly, but by no means willingly, a Christian; he must also have acquired some knowledge of the Bible, for he was ordained a Reader in the Church of Nicomedia. Having before him the example of Constantius, the murderer of his relatives, the oppressor of his youth ; having witnessed the persecuting spirit of the Arians, and the constant change in their Creeds, which elicited from the Pagans the remark that the Christians had yet to learn in what their faith consisted ; Christianity, into which he had been forced against his will, had few attractions for him ; and although during a short residence in the schools of Athens, he made the acquaintance and even friendship of such men as SS. Basil the Great and Gregory Nazianzen, it was too late to eradicate his dislike But it seems unreasonable that the title of Apostate should for ever attach to him ; it is true that for a time he dissembled his views, but when he was free to act for himself, he did what others do, and what, if Christianity and Paganism were reversed, he would be praised for doing, and adopted the religion which he had always regarded as the right one.

In everything else than what concerned Christianity he was one of the best of the Roman Emperors. His manner of living was of the simplest, even of a severe, character ; he took Alexander the Great as his model in war, and the philosopher, Marcus Aurelius, as his model Emperor. The pagan religion flattered his intellect ; the Christians he called "atheists" and "Galilæans," and could not understand how people could abandon the religion of philosophers to follow that of a few poor ignorant fishermen ; and he aimed at restoring Paganism as the religion of the Roman Empire. His first act was the recall from exile of the Christian Bishops and the restoration of their property ; this was not done as an act of justice but out of contempt for Christianity ; experience had taught him that their quarrels would be thus increased and would favour the restoration of Paganism.

Under the general amnesty Athanasius returned to Alexandria, where the pagan population, more incensed even than the Christians, Orthodox or Arians, against the cruelties and impiety of the usurper, had lately murdered George of Cappadocia. Julian advocated toleration of all sects which were opposed to Christianity. This toleration was in particular applied to the Jews, because they rejected Christ as the Saviour of the world; and although he had little sympathy with a people who were the worshippers of One God, yet he approved of their sacrifices; Christ he imagined that he might enlist as an inferior deity. Naturally of a gentle and amiable disposition he was averse to cruelty and persecution; history taught him that the Christians were ready to die for their faith, and that the blood of the Martyrs had conduced to the spread of the Christian Faith. The old Paganism he felt to be effete, so he determined to reform it on the principles of Neo-Platonism, which he himself held, and of Christianity.

At the same time he determined by every means in his power short of bloodshed to abolish Christianity. He wrote against it; the Christian Monogram was expunged from the Labarum; Christians were prohibited from holding military or civil offices, and from following the medical and legal professions. Thinking to force them into the pagan schools, he forbade Greek and Roman literature to be taught in the Christian schools, for why, he asked, should they teach the authors whose very gods they denied?

One thing which he had at heart was the falsifying our Lord's prediction as to the everlasting destruction of Jerusalem; the reversal of the prophecy would, he thought, inflict a fatal blow on Christianity. So he gave the Jews permission to rebuild the Temple. But so direct a violation of God's decree was providentially and signally defeated. An earthquake, a whirlwind, and a fiery eruption scattered the new foundations of the Temple. The pagan Philosopher, Ammonius, describes what happened,—"fearful balls of fire breaking out near the foundations, with reiterated assaults, and several times burning the workmen, rendered the place inaccessible; and by frequent repulses under the determined fury of the elements (*elemento repellente*) the undertaking had to be abandoned"

The Alexandrine Church was dismayed by the acccession of Julian Athanasius, alone untroubled, at once set himself to the task of restoring peace which had been so long disturbed in the city, and to reconciling the discordant factions. Theodoret relates how that the pagan Priests represented to Julian that if he was allowed to remain in the city, not one worshipper of their gods would be left. Julian accordingly issued an edict that he had never intended that Athanasius should resume his Episcopal office; he denounced him as a foe to the gods, who had dared to baptize Greek ladies; and in 362 he again sent him into exile. Athanasius assured the weeping crowds that gathered around him that it was only "a little cloud which would soon pass." Scarcely had he embarked on board the vessel which took him from Alexandria than Julian sent messengers to intercept him. They saw a boat descending the Nile; "Where is Athanasius?" they asked. "Not far off," was the reply. It was the boat which conveyed him, and the voice was perhaps his own. Taking advantage of a bend in the stream he was enabled to evade his pursuers and unexpectedly returned to Alexandria; whence after a short time he withdrew to the Thebaid to find an asylum among his old friends the monks.

The little cloud, as he foretold, soon passed away. In March, 363, Julian started on an expedition against the Persians, the same enemy of the Empire by whom Valerian had been slain. He wrote to his former friend, Basil, demanding a thousand pounds in gold towards the expenses of the war, with a threat of razing Cæsarea to the ground in case of refusal. Basil reminded him of the time when he, who was now exalted by demons against the Church, used to study with him the Bible, and reprimanded him for his folly in demanding so large a sum from one who had not enough to buy a meal. Basil was saved from further danger by the death of Julian on June 26, 363.

Julian, after a short reign of little more than eighteen months, died of wounds received in the battle with Persia, with a bitter reproach, it is said, to the pagan gods for their desertion; and with the last words on his lips, "Thou hast conquered, O Galilean." The army immediately elected as his successor, Jovian (363—364), a Christian and favourer of the Homoousion, and thus the first pronounced orthodox Emperor. He had already proved his faith under Julian. When Julian ordered his Christian officers either to renounce their faith or abandon his service, Jovian, who held an important rank in the army, offered to give up his sword; but Julian gave way, he could not afford to part with so good an officer, whose example he knew many others would follow

Jovian immediately on becoming Emperor adopted the Labarum as his standard, and induced the soldiers, many of whom had under compulsion professed Paganism, to return to the Church, whilst allowing toleration to the Pagans, he repealed the acts of Julian and restored to the Christian Church its property and immunities He wrote to Athanasius re-instating him in his See, requesting him to return, and asking his prayers. Athanasius had already arrived in Alexandria before he received the letter. At the request of the Emperor that he would draw up a statement of the orthodox doctrines, he immediately summoned a Council at Alexandria, and wrote in its name a Synodal letter to Jovian, commending to him the Nicene faith, to which he appended the orthodox doctrine with respect to the Holy Ghost. All seemed now to point to orthodoxy and the peace of the Church. Within a week after the return of Athanasius, Jovian, after a short reign of eight months, on his road through Asia Minor to Constantinople was found dead in his bed; St Chrysostom says he was poisoned, others that he was suffocated through a charcoal fire in his apartment. He was succeeded by Valentinian (364—375), a Catholic.

In the reign of Julian, Valentinian had shown a marked abhorrence of Paganism. When Julian was entering a pagan Temple, a Priest of Jupiter stood at the door sprinkling the lustral water, some of which fell on Valentinian, who, considering himself defiled, ventured to strike the Priest, and was in consequence banished. Valentinian's reign was marked by a tolerant spirit towards both Arians and heathens ; but we now find that heathenism discountenanced in the towns took refuge in the villages (*pagi*), where their meetings would be less noticed ; its votaries hence acquired the name (which for convenience' sake we have anticipated) of Pagans (*villagers*). The Emperor does not, however, seem to have been equally tolerant in his own family. His wife, Justina, whom he took to himself after having repudiated his first wife, Severa, the mother of the future Emperor, Gratian, he compelled to accept the Nicene Faith. By her he became the father of Valentinian II, and of a daughter named Galla, afterwards the wife of the great Emperor, Theodosius I. As the result of this compulsory act, Justina after his death became the violent opponent of the Catholics, and supporter of the Arians.

Soon after his accession he gave the command of the East to his brother Valens (364—378), who was at first orthodox, but, A.D. 368, received Baptism from Eudoxius, the Arian Bishop of Constantinople, and became the violent persecutor of the Homoousians. He issued an edict for the banishment of all the Bishops who had been reinstated under Julian, an edict under which Athanasius was included. On the death of Eudoxius, A.D. 370, the Catholics, during the absence of Valens from the city, elected an orthodox successor, Evagrius. But no sooner was the news of his election conveyed to Valens than he ordered troops from Nicomedia to Constantinople ; Evagrius and his consecrator (whoever he might have been) were expelled and banished to Thrace; and Demophilus, Bishop of Berrhœa, who had induced Liberius, Pope of Rome, to join the Arians, was elected Patriarch in his place, and consecrated by Theodore, Metropolitan of Heraclea.

A violent persecution of the Orthodox soon commenced. It is recorded that, A.D. 370, fourscore orthodox Bishops, having, in consequence of their presenting a petition to Valens at Nicomedia, imploring him to adopt a more lenient course, been put on board ship to be conveyed across the Black Sea into banishment to Thrace, were to a man burnt to death, whilst all the sailors abandoned the ship and made good their escape.

The edict for his expulsion reaching Alexandria, Athanasius again left the city, and for four months concealed himself in the country, according to one account in his father's tomb[f]. This was his last banishment. Valens, apprehensive of an insurrection, sanctioned his return, after which he was allowed to pass the remainder of his life amongst his own people, dying on May 2, 373, at the age of seventy-six, after an episcopate of forty-six years.

The mantle of Athanasius fell on "the three Cappadocians:" Basil the Great, his brother, Gregory of Nyssa, and Gregory Nazianzen. The parents of the first two were Christians, and gave three Bishops to the Church, Basil, Bishop of Cæsarea in Cappadocia, Gregory, Bishop of Nyssa, and Peter, Bishop of Sebaste; whilst their daughter, Macrina, the eldest of their children, is reckoned amongst the Saints of the Greek Church. St. Basil together with St. Gregory Nazianzen had been, as before stated, fellow-pupils with Julian the Emperor in the schools of Athens. Leaving Athens, after a stay there of about five years, in A.D. 357, when he was eighteen years of age, and having about that time received Baptism, Basil visited the most celebrated monasteries in Palestine and Egypt with a view of learning the mode of life in these communities, and embraced the life of a monk at Pontus, where he induced Gregory Nazianzen to join him. Finding the life of an anchorite too selfish and individual, and conflicting with his idea of Christian love, he adopted the cœnobitic system, and together with Gregory drew up the "Rule" which has ever since been that followed in the Orthodox Greek Church. What his idea of the monastic life was we gather from

[f] Soc. Hist., IV. 13.

one of his Homilies:—" To live in monasteries and deserts ; to eat only once in the day ; to refrain altogether even from bread and water in fasting ; to wear sackcloth, and the like, is the tradition of holy men derived from God ; but those who do these things ought first to keep the Lord's commandments, humility and temperance, forgetfulness of injuries and indifference to worldly things ; those of faith and patience and charity unfeigned, without which it is impossible to please God."

In 359 he was called from his monastic life to other duties; but, finding that Dianius, the Bishop of Cæsarea, had signed the Arian formula at Rimini, and being unable to hold communion with him, instead of returning to his native place (Cæsarea), he went to live with his friend Gregory at Nazianzus. In 362 he was summoned to Cæsarea at the dying request of Dianius, who died in his arms, protesting his innocence of any intentional desertion of the Nicene Faith.

On the death of Dianius, dissensions arose amongst the clergy as to his successor, till at length the people of Cæsarea insisted on the election of Eusebius, as yet an unbaptized layman of high position and character; the Bishops of the Province, under military compulsion, were forced to perform first the Baptism and then the Consecration of the Bishop ; and were afterwards dissuaded by the father of Gregory Nazianzen from their intention of annulling the Consecration. On the death of Eusebius in 370, Basil was elected as his successor, one of his consecrators being the aged father of Gregory Nazianzen ; and his election was greeted with joy by the people, and the congratulations of Athanasius. As Bishop of Cæsarea, Basil was Metropolitan of Cappadocia, and in the latter capacity he, A.D. 372, appointed to the See of Nyssa his brother Gregory, who was one of the greatest Fathers of the Church, and if in the practical importance of his life he was inferior to them, was in ability and theological attainments at least the equal of Basil and Gregory Nazianzen.

Gregory Nazianzen, a man prominent amongst his contemporaries in every branch of learning, was born, probably a few years before Basil, at Arianza, a village near Nazianzus, from which latter place, over which his father presided for forty-five years, he received the title by which he is familiarly known. He was the life-long friend of St. Basil, although the friendship was for a short time intermitted by an arbitary act on the part of the latter. Basil had, as a safeguard against the Arians, erected several new Sees, amongst them one at Sasima, a little dirty and unhealthy town, without any marks of civilization, and for which a man of Gregory's intellectual and sensitive mind was wholly unsuited. This See he in 372 forced upon Gregory, who reluctantly, at the request of his father, accepted it.

Valens had lately divided Cappadocia into two provinces. Anthimus, Bishop of Tyana, a town about thirty miles from Sasima, thereupon claimed Metropolitan rights over one province; an open rupture between Basil and Anthimus was the consequence, and Gregory, a man of peace, felt that Anthimus would be a disagreeable and even dangerous neighbour. Though he had accepted the Bishopric, on learning that Anthimus was prepared to oppose his entrance by force of arms, he resigned it and assisted his father at Nazianzus till the death of the latter, A.D. 374; after which he continued to reside at Nazianzus. There we will for a time leave him.

In 371, the year after Basil's appointment to the See of Cæsarea, he, who next to Athanasius was the chief champion of Orthodoxy in the East, was brought into contact with Valens. Valens, hitherto everywhere successful in his campaign against the Orthodox, determined to reduce Cæsarea to submission, and sent Modestus, the Prefect of Cappadocia, to Basil, offering him the alternative of Arianism, or deposition, together with confiscation of his property, torture, banishment and death. As to loss of property, Basil told him, he had only a ragged cloak and a few books; as to banishment, wherever God is, there was the Christian's home; as to torture and death, his body was so frail that the first stroke would kill him, and death would be a kindness, for it would bring him nearer to God. The Emperor was so struck with the pious firmness of the Bishop that he forbade any to harm him, and contented himself with requiring that he should receive the Arians to communion. On Basil's refusal, the Emperor attended the service on the Feast of the Epiphany, A.D. 372, in the Cathedral of Cæsarea; Basil himself celebrated; the imposing grandeur of the service visibly affected his impressionable mind; but the Arians were at hand to counsel him, and Valens was induced to order his banishment.

On the night that Basil was about to leave the city, the Emperor's only son was seized with an alarming illness, and the Arian Empress, seeing in it the hand of God, sent for Basil to pray over him. He consented on the condition that if the child recovered it should receive Catholic Baptism; the child recovered, but the promise was broken, and on the same day that it received Arian Baptism the malady returned and the child died. The Arians still schemed for Basil's banishment, but the Emperor was recalled from Cæsarea before the decree was signed, and Basil was thenceforward left untroubled.

Peter, agreeably to the wish of Athanasius, was elected to succeed him in the See of Alexandria; but soon, after fearful scenes of blasphemous orgies in the Church of St. Theonas, he was, at the instigation of the Arians, driven away by the pagan Prefect. Lucius, who had been ordained by George of Cappadocia, was then conducted to Alexandria by Euzoius, the Arian Bishop of Antioch, and by order of Valens installed in the See, the Pagans welcoming the election as of one who did not worship the Son of God, but their own god Serapis. Peter then made his way to Rome, where he was welcomed by Pope Damasus (366—384). The Emperor Valentinian died in 375, and in 378 Valens was killed in the battle of Hadrianople, in which his troops suffered a disastrous defeat from the Goths. Before he started on his campaign he had put an end to the persecution. With the death of Valens the Arian supremacy came to an end; Arianism, although not extirpated from the Roman Empire, was thenceforward relegated to the Goths and other barbarous nations, and the victory of the Homoousion was complete.

CHAPTER V.

The Second Œcumenical Council.

GRATIAN Emperor—Theodosius the Great, Emperor—Intolerance of Gratian and Theodosius—Gregory Nazianzen, Bishop of Constantinople—Theodosius summons the Second Œcumenical Council—Creed of Constantinople—Precedence over Alexandria and Antioch given to Constantinople—Theophilus of Alexandria—Destruction of the Serapeum—The effect of intolerance on the Church—Division of the Empire into East and West—John Chrysostom, Patriarch of Constantinople—Corrupt state of the Church—Origenist Controversy—The Tall brothers—Synod of the Oak—Eudoxia—Chrysostom banished—His sufferings and death—End of the Eustathian schism at Antioch—St. Jerome at Bethlehem—The Vulgate—Conversion of Augustine—His *De Civitate Dei*—Pelagianism.

ON the death of Valentinian, his son Gratian, who had been for eight years associated with him in the government, became sole Emperor in the West, and after the death of Valens, he, being then eighteen years of age, made his half-brother Valentinian II. co-Emperor in the government of the East. The insecure state of the Empire from the Goths who had lately defeated and killed Valens in the battle of Hadrianople induced him, in January, 379, to confer the Empire of the East upon Theodosius, a Spaniard by birth, a man about thirteen years older than himself, who was afterwards styled the Great.

Gratian was a Catholic much under the influence and guidance of Ambrose, Bishop of Milan. In 377 he ordered the Churches taken by the Donatists to be restored to the Catholics, but he granted a general toleration of religion for all, with the exception of Manichæans, Photinians [a], and Eunomians. Lucius was expelled and Peter returned to Alexandria, and Meletius was restored to Antioch, where the Arian Bishop Euzoius had died in the previous year. Gratian's step-mother Justina took the opportunity of shak-

---

[a] Followers of Photinus of Sirmium, a disciple of Marcellus, condemned in a Western Council (Milan), A.D 347.

ing off the trammels imposed upon her by her late husband, and did her best to promote the cause of Arianism. Theodosius, when elected Emperor, was, though a Catholic, only a Catechumen, but in the first year of his reign (379—395) he received Baptism from Ascholius, the orthodox Bishop of Thessalonica. So that now the whole Roman Empire, both East and West, was governed by orthodox Emperors.

Whilst the Eastern Empire had been troubled by Arianism, Paganism was extensively prevalent in the West. The principle of toleration had been the ruling maxim of the Roman government, the Emperors who persecuted the Christians having acted on political rather than on religious grounds; but from this principle both Gratian and Theodosius departed, and the fall of Paganism forms a less noble chapter in the history of the Christian Church than its triumph over Arianism.

On January 1, 379, Basil of Cæsarea terminated his troubled life. He had been during his episcopacy the victim of misrepresentation even from the Orthodox. He was accused at times of being a Sabellian, an Arian, a Macedonian, the last two accusations being grounded on a form of Doxology which he had used; "Glory be to the Father, through the Son, in the Holy Spirit." He lived just long enough to witness the triumph of orthodoxy, to which he had devoted his life, and died worn out with trouble before he had ended his fiftieth year. His brother, Gregory of Nyssa, who had been in 376 deposed by an Arian Synod, an Arian being appointed in his place, was now restored by Gratian.

In the summer of the year in which Basil died, Gregory Nazianzen accepted an invitation, backed by several Bishops, from the small remnant of orthodox Christians, to go to Constantinople. Constantinople had long been the hot-bed of heresy, the See for forty years having been presided over by Arian Bishops. Gregory began his mission services in a room of a private house; the room soon grew into a chapel, the chapel into a spacious Church, to which the name of Anastasia (*resurrection*, to signify the resurrection of the Nicene Faith) was given. Here he gained his title of the *Theologian*, and people of all classes, many Arians included, thronged to hear him. The greater part, however, mocked, jeered at his poverty, the meanness of his dress, the rusticity of his manners. A violent opposition headed by Lucius, who since his expulsion from Alexandria had resided at Constantinople, was raised against him; riots ensued in which his life was endangered; the doors of the Anastasia were broken down, and great damage and even bloodshed ensued.

In February, 380, Theodosius, immediately after his baptism, issued to the people of Constantinople from Thessalonica, where he had taken up his residence, his first edict concerning religion, ordering that the religion as held by those saintly Prelates, Damasus of Rome and Peter of Alexandria, should be the standard of orthodoxy. Peter had shortly before this died, but of this the Emperor had evidently not heard. Those only who held the co-equal majesty of the Three Persons in the Trinity were to be accounted Catholics, to them the Christian Churches were to be restored, and all other persons were to be accounted heretics, liable to punishment.

Towards the end of the year he made his first entrance into Constantinople, where he determined to enforce religious unity on the basis of the Nicene Faith. He offered to confirm the Patriarch Demophilus in the See on condition of his subscribing the Nicene Creed, and on his refusal he was deposed, and together with Lucius was forced to leave Constantinople, and Gregory Nazianzen was appointed in his place.

There had lately been living in Constantinople a disreputable fellow, a Cynic philosopher, named Maximus, a native of Alexandria, who represented himself as having been a Confessor for the Nicene faith and an opponent of heretics. He lived there the life of an ascetic, and at first imposed upon Gregory, as he had before on Peter of Alexandria, and managed to get himself uncanonically consecrated a Bishop by some Egyptian Bishops commissioned by Peter. This impostor having been driven out by the people of Constantinople, applied first to Theodosius at Thessalonica and afterwards to Peter at Alexandria, but, Peter having in the meantime discovered his real character, received a cold reception from both, and was expelled from Egypt by the civil magistrate. No sooner was Gregory installed in the See of Constantinople than Maximus showed himself his bitter enemy, and took every means in his power to get him deposed and himself appointed in his place. Peter of Alexandria was, in February, 380, succeeded by his brother Timothy. A struggle for pre-eminence between the Sees of Constantinople and Alexandria was even then apparent, and Maximus taking advantage of this, succeeded in gaining over Timothy, as he had before his brother Peter, and persuading him that the translation of Gregory was uncanonical, and in getting himself elected to the Patriarchal throne [b].

Gregory was Patriarch of Constantinople for barely seven months. In order to secure the triumph of the Nicene faith and to end the troubles of the Church, Theodosius determined to convene the Second Œcumenical Council, the First of Constantinople. Macedonius had during his exile brought into prominence the heresy that took his name, which taught that the Holy Ghost is not Very God, but a creature and minister of God; a heresy which had been held, but not brought into such prominence by the Arians, as to require notice at the Council of Nice. Athanasius when in exile in the desert had heard of and reprobated the heresy.

The Council met on May 2, A.D. 381. It was attended by one hundred and fifty Bishops (whence it was called the Council of the One Hundred and Fifty Fathers), from

---

[b] This seems the only way of reconciling the dates: Peter might have appointed Maximus a Bishop, but Gregory was not appointed to the See of Constantinople till after the death of Peter.

The Second Œcumenical Council. 171

all parts of the East, except Egypt, the most famous Bishops being Meletius of Antioch, Gregory Nazianzen, Timothy of Alexandria, Cyril of Jerusalem, Gregory of Nyssa, and his brother Peter of Sebaste. Thirty-six Macedonian Bishops were likewise invited by the Emperor to attend, but, refusing to be reconciled to the Church, soon left the Council. The first President was Meletius, and Gregory was confirmed in the See of Constantinople. Soon afterwards Meletius died, and Gregory unwillingly accepted the presidential seat. The post was distasteful to him, and he was personally unfitted to cope with the scenes of faction and disorder which he describes as having pervaded its deliberations. A difficulty at once arose.

Meletius, soon after he had been translated to the See of Antioch was, as we have already seen, driven out by the Arians; he was banished, in all, three times. But he had other opponents binding the Arians in the Orthodox followers of the former much-beloved Bishop, Eustathius, who under Paulinus, a Priest of Antioch, objected to him on the ground that he had been consecrated by Arians. Just when a concordat was on the point of being arranged in a Council of Alexandria in 362, the hot-headed Priest, Lucifer of Cagliari, returning from his exile in the Thebaid, in his intemperate zeal for orthodoxy, consecrated Paulinus Bishop. The schism thus caused extended to the whole Church, Egypt as well as the Western Church siding with Paulinus, whilst the Eastern Church generally took the side of Meletius. At Antioch, however, the schism was accommodated by an understanding that on the death of either, the survivor should be recognized as Bishop.

Gregory now thought that the death of Meletius might be the means of healing the long-existing schism, and that Paulinus should be recognized by both parties as his successor. It had been well for Antioch if Gregory's plan had been adopted. But the Asiatic Bishops, thinking that this would be a triumph to the West, and to Pope Damasus who had been the advocate of Paulinus, set aside the agreement and consecrated Flavian, an orthodox and highly-esteemed Priest of Antioch, to the See, thus continuing the schism, for, popular as Flavian was, many of the people of Antioch, together with the West, still continued their adherence to Paulinus.

Timothy, Patriarch of Alexandria, together with the Egyptian Bishops, now arrived at the Council. They expressed their displeasure at proceedings having been commenced without them, and at the deposition of Maximus, and objected to the translation of Gregory as being opposed to the Canon of Nice. The Asiatics were equally displeased with Gregory's opposition in the matter of the election of Flavian.

Gregory had reluctantly accepted the See of Constantinople, and had only done so in the hope of being able to reconcile the Eastern and Western Bishops. In this he had signally failed, and he now asked to be delivered from the Presidency of the Council and for leave to resign the See. His resignation was unwillingly accepted by Theodosius, but not so unwillingly by the Bishops; he then returned to Nazianzus, visiting on the way Cæsarea, where he pronounced the funeral oration at the grave of St. Basil, thus showing that between the two no permanent ill-will had been engendered.

Maximus was not reinstated, but, as successor to Gregory, Nectarius, an unbaptized layman, a man of noble family, venerable appearance and gentle and winning manners which recommended him to the Emperor, was appointed to the Patriarchate. A native of Tarsus he was a man thoroughly ignorant of theology, and fond of luxurious living, in fact nothing more than a highly respectable old gentleman; he was baptized and consecrated Patriarch of Constantinople, and presided over the See, A.D. 381—397.

The Council amplified the Nicene Creed, adding particularly the clauses respecting the Holy Ghost against the Macedonians or Pneumatomachi, who had left the Council before the Creed was drawn up and rejected it afterwards;

so that the Creed which is usually called the Nicene Creed, and was so read at the General Council of Ephesus, might with greater strictness be called the Creed of Constantinople. The Constantinopolitan Creed ran thus (as the English rendering is familiar to all, we give it in its original language) :—

Πιστεύομεν εἰς ἕνα Θεὸν Πατέρα παντοκράτορα, ποιητὴν οὐρανοῦ καὶ γῆς, ὁρατῶν τε πάντων καὶ ἀοράτων· Καὶ εἰς ἕνα Κύριον, Ἰησοῦν Χριστὸν, τὸν υἱὸν τοῦ Θεοῦ τὸν μονογενῆ, τὸν ἐκ τοῦ Πατρὸς γεννηθέντα πρὸ πάντων τῶν αἰώνων, Φῶς ἐκ Φωτός, Θεὸν ἀληθινὸν ἐκ Θεοῦ ἀληθινοῦ, γεννηθέντα οὐ ποιηθέντα, ὁμοούσιον τῷ Πατρί· δι' οὗ τὰ πάντα ἐγένετο· Τὸν δι' ἡμᾶς τοὺς ἀνθρώπους καὶ διὰ τὴν ἡμετέραν σωτηρίαν κατελθόντα ἐκ τῶν οὐρανῶν, καὶ σαρκωθέντα ἐκ Πνεύματος ἁγίου καὶ Μαρίας τῆς Παρθένου, καὶ ἐνανθρωπήσαντα· Σταυρωθέντα τε ὑπὲρ ἡμῶν ἐπὶ Ποντίου Πιλάτου, καὶ παθόντα, καὶ ταφέντα· Καὶ ἀναστάντα τῇ τρίτῃ ἡμέρᾳ, κατὰ τὰς γραφάς· Καὶ ἀνελθόντα εἰς τοὺς οὐρανοὺς καὶ καθεζόμενον ἐκ δεξιῶν τοῦ Πατρὸς, Καὶ πάλιν ἐρχόμενον μετὰ δόξης κρῖναι ζῶντας καὶ νεκρούς· οὗ τῆς βασιλείας οὐκ ἔσται τέλος·

Καὶ εἰς τὸ Πνεῦμα τὸ Ἅγιον, τὸ Κύριον, καὶ τὸ ζωοποιὸν, τὸ ἐκ τοῦ Πατρὸς ἐκπορευόμενον [c], τὸ σὺν Πατρὶ καὶ Υἱῷ συμπροσκυνούμενον καὶ συνδοξαζόμενον, τὸ λαλῆσαν διὰ τῶν προφητῶν· Εἰς μίαν ἁγίαν [d] καθολικὴν καὶ ἀποστολικὴν Ἐκκλησίαν· Ὁμολογοῦμεν ἓν βάπτισμα εἰς ἄφεσιν ἁμαρτιῶν· Προσδοκῶμεν ἀνάστασιν νεκρῶν, Καὶ ζωὴν τοῦ μέλλοντος αἰῶνος. ἀμήν.

The new clauses added to the Nicene Creed were ; "Before all worlds ;" "From Heaven ;" "By the Holy Ghost of the Virgin Mary ;" "Was crucified also for us under Pontius Pilate ; and was buried ;" "Sitteth on the right hand of the Father ;" "Whose Kingdom shall have no end,"

[c] Bishop Wordsworth (Church Hist., II.) draws the distinction between the Greek ἐκπόρευσις and the Latin *processio*, and shows how in the restricted sense of the former word the Holy Ghost only proceeds from the Father, in the wider sense attached to the latter, He may be said also to proceed from the Son.

[d] The word ἁγιάν, *holy*, is omitted in one version of the Creed.

and all the clauses following the words, "And in the Holy Ghost[e].

The drawing up of the expanded Creed is generally attributed (although there is much doubt on the subject) to St. Gregory of Nyssa, to whom was given by the Seventh Œcumenical Council the title of "Father of Fathers."

Besides the enlargement of the Nicene Creed, the Council drew up Canons, which some suppose to have been seven in number, but of which the last three are generally attributed to a later date. The First Canon confirmed the Nicene Creed and anathematized the heresies of the Eunomians, the Eudoxians, the Semi-Arians or Pneumatomachi, the Sabellians, the holders of the doctrines of Marcellus of Ancyra, and of his pupil Photinus, Bishop of Sirmium, and Apollinarius. Apollinarius, Bishop of Laodicea, whilst he held the true Divinity of Christ, denied the completeness of the Human Nature, teaching that Christ had a human Body without a reasonable Soul ($\sigma\hat{\omega}\mu\alpha$ with $\psi\upsilon\chi\grave{\eta}$ $\check{\alpha}\lambda o\gamma o s$), the latter being supplied by the Divine Logos. As Arius had assailed the Divinity, so Apollinarius assailed the Humanity of Christ; the Council of Nice established the perfect Divinity, the Council of Constantinople the perfect Humanity. Notwithstanding this condemnation by the Council Apollinarius continued to hold his Bishopric till his death, about A D. 390; he was the originator of the first of the Christological controversies which had their termination in the Monophysite, and in that which necessarily resulted from the latter, the Monothelite heresy. The Canon identifies the Pneumatomachi, or followers of Macedonius, with the Semi-Arians, from which party they sprang and whose doctrine with regard to the Saviour they extended to the Holy Ghost.

Canon II. enacted that Bishops of one Diocese may not intrude into the Diocese of another, and the ecclesiastical were arranged on a general conformity with the civil Dioceses. It has been thought probable that the second

---

[e] The Procession of the Holy Ghost from the Son (*Filioque*, and the Son) was not inserted in the Creed till the Council of Toledo in Spain, A.D. 589.

The Second Œcumenical Council. 175

Canon was occasioned by the recent action of the Patriarch of Alexandria appointing Maximus the Cynic to the See of Constantinople. The Council, whilst confirming the See of Alexandria and Antioch in their just rights, forbade their interference with Sees outside their proper jurisdiction. It enacted that the Bishop of Alexandria "should govern the affairs of Egypt only, and the Eastern Bishops shall have charge of the East only, whilst the rights (τὰ πρεσβεῖα) of the Church of Antioch should be preserved agreeably to the Canons of Nice;" at the same time the Bishops of the diocese of Asia (Ephesus) should only have jurisdiction over Asia, those of the diocese of Pontus (Cæsarea) over Pontus, those of the diocese of Thrace (Heraclea) over Thrace.

Hitherto the Bishops of Constantinople had been under the Metropolitan of Heraclea, and held a lower position than those of Alexandria and Antioch. By the second Canon it had been enacted that the Bishop of Alexandria should govern the affairs of Egypt only. The third Canon went further and enacted that "the Bishop of Constantinople shall hold the first rank after the Bishop of Rome (τὰ πρεσβεῖα τῆς τιμῆς μετὰ τὸν τῆς Ῥώμης ἐπίσκοπον) because it is the New Rome." Since the Council of Nice, when the three principal Sees were those of Rome, Alexandria and Antioch, Constantine had founded the Imperial city of Constantinople and conferred on it the same rank and privileges as before belonged to the old Imperial city Rome. An honorary precedence attached to the See of Rome when it was the capital of the Empire. The Canon recognized such a precedence, but enacted that an honorary precedence should also be accorded to New Rome on the same ground as that on which it had been granted to Old Rome, viz because it was the Imperial City, or New Rome [f].

A law passed as late as A.D. 445 in the reign of Valentinian III. shows that it was a matter of civil arrangement, "We ordain by a perpetual sanction .... that the privileges which our fore-fathers have granted to the See of Rome be preserved inviolate."

Socrates speaks of the Patriarchal dignity being established by the Council; we shall therefore henceforward speak of the Bishops of Constantinople, Alexandria and Antioch under the titles of Patriarchs, and of the Bishops of Rome under the title which they prefer, that of Pope.

Œcumenical, in the sense of being representative of the whole Church, the First Council of Constantinople was not, for it was wholly comprised of Eastern Bishops. But the test of an Œcumenical Council is not the number of Bishops who attend it, nor the countries represented in it, but its acceptance by the Catholic Church at large and its confirmation by subsequent Councils. A second Council held in Constantinople in the following year sent the Canons to the Latins, and expressly called the Council of 381 Œcumenical. The Creed of Constantinople was readily received in the West as well as in the East, but not so the Canons: Both Rome and Alexandria were opposed to the precedence given to Constantinople. To the third General Council, that of Ephesus, the Pope sent two legates to uphold the dignity of Rome and to support the See of Alexandria; this accounts for the silence at Ephesus of the second Œcumenical Council [g]. Popes Leo the Great and Gregory the Great, although the latter allowed that the Council was Œcumenical and spoke of four Œcumenical Councils, refused to receive the objectionable Canon, the former asserting that it had never been sent to Rome; whilst he contended that it was the Apostolic origin of a Church, not its civil rank, which gave it the pre-eminence.

But all cavilling is superseded by the fact that its œcumenical character was recognized by the Fourth Œcumenical Council, that of Chalcedon, in which the Creed of Constantinople was twice repeated and received into its acts. Succeeding Popes of Rome, after the Council of Chalcedon, did their best to ignore the First Council of Constantinople,

---

[g] The Latrocinium, or Robber Council, speaks of the Council of Ephesus as the Second Council, ἡ δευτέρα Σύνοδος.

The Second Œcumenical Council. 177

and spoke of three Councils, those of Nice, Ephesus and Chalcedon. But after the conquest of Constantinople, A.D. 1204, by the Latins, when a *Latin Patriarchate under the Pope* was established there, Pope Innocent III. acknowledged the Patriarchal rank of Constantinople, which was confirmed by the Fourth Lateran Council, A.D. 1215.

After the abdication of Gregory, Timothy, Bishop of Alexandria, probably became President of the Council till Nectarius was appointed Bishop, when he assumed the Presidency; Timothy was evidently outvoted in the passing of the Canon, and his sympathy as Bishop of Alexandria naturally went with Rome in opposition to it. Alexandria and Antioch descended a scale, and had to give place to a See which had hitherto been, as before stated, a subordinate See under the Metropolitan of Heraclea. A feeling of jealousy at the priority given to Constantinople over his own See and disgust with the conduct of the Eastern Bishops who voted for the Canon, so influenced Timothy that he took his departure for Alexandria and refused again to return to Constantinople.

The Fourth Canon related to Maximus the Cynic. It decreed that he "never became a Bishop and is not one now," and therefore all the Orders conferred by him were invalid.

St. Cyril, who had succeeded Maximus in the See of Jerusalem, took a prominent part in the Council. He had at one time been accused of Semi-Arianism, but was sent into banishment by Valens for his orthodoxy; at the Council he gave his full assent to the Nicene faith, and the catechetical lectures which he delivered when a Presbyter at Jerusalem, though the Homoousion does not occur in them, show that he was sound in the faith before he was consecrated a Bishop. He and Acacius, Bishop of Cæsarea, his Metropolitan[h], had been engaged in a long controversy

[h] It must be borne in mind that there were three Cæsareas; (1) in Palestine, to which See the Bishop of Jerusalem was subject; (2) in Cappadocia, of which Basil the Great had been the Bishop; (3) Neo-Cæsarea in Pontus.

as to the precedence of their Sees, Cyril basing his claim on the Apostolical foundation of his See; twice Acacius gained the victory, which was followed in each case by Cyril's deposition. On the accession of Julian he, together with the exiled Bishops, returned, to be banished a third time under Valens; but the contest continued till the death of Acacius, A D. 366, when Cyril claimed the right of appointing to the See of Cæsarea, and appointed his own nephew. But we do not find the subject brought into prominence at the Council of Constantinople.

In July, 381, Theodosius issued an edict prohibiting all assemblies of Arians, Photinians, and Eunomians, and ordering all their Churches to be given up to the Orthodox Church; and a few weeks later two more edicts prohibiting them from building Churches in place of those which they had surrendered. In March, 382, he issued an edict against the Manichæans. Gratian, from the beginning of his reign, had showed his strong aversion to Paganism, and was the first Emperor to refuse for himself the title of Pontifex Maximus. In 382 he issued an edict for the destruction of the Temple of Victory at Rome, which was soon followed by another for the confiscation of its revenues and of the property of the Vestal Virgins.

In 382 Theodosius summoned a second Council to Constantinople. St. Gregory Nazianzen, on his return to Nazianzus from Constantinople, finding the Church much troubled by Apollinarians, felt it his duty to undertake the duties of the vacant Bishopric till such time as a Bishop should be appointed. The Emperor invited him to attend the Council, but Gregory objected on the ground that Councils only aggravated the evils they were intended to remedy. In vain he wrote to his Metropolitan, Theodore, Bishop of Tyana, like himself a native of Arianza, imploring him to appoint a Bishop who might stem the tide of heresy; and when at length he succeeded in his object, he retired to Arianzus, where he spent the remainder of his life, dying A.D. 389.

The Second Œcumenical Council. 179

The Council of 382, composed of the same Bishops who had attended the previous Council at Constantinople, addressed a letter, signifying its adherence to the Nicene Faith, to a Council that was then sitting under Damasus at Rome, and drew up two Canons, " which," says Hefele, " have been erroneously adopted as the vth and vith Canons of the Second General Council [1]." In a third Synod at Constantinople, A D. 383, the Arians under Demophilus, the deposed Bishop of Constantinople, and the Anomœans under Eunomius, were called upon by the Emperor to present their Creeds, the latter of which asserted that the Holy Ghost, though higher than other creatures, was still created, and therefore subject in all things to the Son. This so horrified the other Arians that many abjured Arianism altogether and joined the Orthodox Church; and Theodosius, in a decree of July 25, A.D. 383, forbade all sectaries, except Novatians, who accepted the Homoousion and differed from the Church rather in discipline than in doctrine, to hold their services or disseminate their doctrines under threat of severe punishment. In that year Gratian also issued an edict against apostates from Christianity, and converts to Paganism, Judaism, or Manichæism.

In the same year occurred the rising in Britain under Maximus; Gratian, being defeated in a battle between the Imperial and insurrectionary armies near Paris, fled to Lyons, where he was assassinated by his own troops; and Maximus assumed the sovereignty of Britain, Gaul, and Spain.

Timothy, Patriarch of Alexandria, died A.D. 385. Under his two successors, Theophilus (385—412), who had been secretary to St. Athanasius, and his nephew Cyril (412—444), the See of Alexandria reached its highest eminence; " the power of its Prelates was in some respects greater than that of the Bishops of Rome over its own Prelates [k]."

In 386, Theodosius issued an edict for the proper observance of the Lord's Day. Maximus having in 387 invaded

[1] Hefele, II. 381. [k] Neale's Alexandria, I. 210.

Italy, Justina, with her young son Valentinian and her daughter Galla, sought the protection of Theodosius at Thessalonica. In the following year, Theodosius having just before issued an edict against the Apollinarians, defeated Maximus in battle, driving him to Aquileia, where he was murdered by his own soldiers. In August of the same year the Empress Justina, the strenuous supporter of the Arians, died, and the young Emperor Valentinian was now left wholly under the control of St. Ambrose. We may also mention another important event which took place in that year, the Baptism of the great Father of the Church, St. Augustine, which was administered at Milan by Ambrose.

In 388 also died Paulinus of Antioch, having uncanonically consecrated in his sick chamber Evagrius as his successor, thus continuing the schism in the Antiochene Church; but on the death of the latter, Flavian remained sole Bishop till his death, A.D. 404.

Only three quarters of a century had elapsed since the last of the persecutions ended, when an event occurred which showed the great advance which Christianity had made, and the moral control which the Church exercised. In A.D. 390, an indiscriminate massacre at Thessalonica, in which more than seven thousand persons were killed, had occurred by order of Theodosius. Ambrose, when he heard of the event, filled with sorrow, wrote a letter to the Emperor urging him to repentance, without which he could not admit him to Communion. From Thessalonica the Emperor, overwhelmed with the reproaches of his conscience, went to Milan, and was about, as usual, to enter the Cathedral, when Ambrose stopped him, as one defiled with innocent blood. The Emperor signified his repentance, and pleaded in his defence the sin of David; "You have imitated," said Ambrose, "David in his sin, imitate him also in his repentance." The great Emperor was sentenced to undergo the penance of the Church, from the rites of which he was for eight months excluded. When Christmas came, and he again attempted to enter the Cathedral, Ambrose, still inflexible, barred the way; if he would enter the Church, it must be over his body. The Emperor accepted the terms which Ambrose imposed. Stripped of his Imperial robes, and assuming the dress of a penitent, he publicly did penance in the cathedral at Milan; and not even then was his absolution granted, nor till he promised to issue an edict, that no criminal should thenceforward be put to death till an interval of thirty days had elapsed between the sentence and its performance.

In A.D. 389 took place an indiscriminate destruction of the pagan Temples in Egypt. Already by a law of A.D. 385, Theodosius had, under penalty of death, prohibited pagan sacrifices and divinations, and entrusted Cynegius, Prefect of the East, with the duty of carrying out the decree. A rage for the destruction of the pagan Temples seized upon the monks of Syria, but the inhabitants of Arabia, Palestine, and Phœnicia offered a sturdy resistance; Marcelius, Bishop of Apamea ("a man of Apostolic zeal and fervour" Theodoret calls him), at the head of a body of soldiers and gladiators, was about to demolish a stately Temple, but paid the penalty of his rashness by being burnt alive by the indignant populace [1].

In 390 the Emperor found a ready accomplice in Theophilus, the headstrong, and, there is much reason for believing, the profligate, Patriarch of Alexandria. In that year Theodosius ordered the demolition of the Serapeum, the magnificent Temple founded by the first Ptolemy, at Alexandria. On the goodwill of the pagan god Serapis, the rise and fall of the Nile, on which depended the very existence of Egypt, was thought to hang, and the belief prevailed that if the sacred shrine of their god was violated, Heaven and earth would be involved in a common ruin.

The conversion by Theophilus of a Temple of Bacchus into a Christian Church had excited the alarm of the people of Alexandria, and led to an insurrection under the Pagan philosopher, Olympias, who exhorted them to die in defence

[1] Socr., VII. 15; Theod., V. 21.

of their altars. At first the Pagans were successful, and in their short hour of victory perpetrated inhuman cruelties on the Christians. But a truce was agreed upon by the two parties, until instructions from the Emperor as to the fate of the Serapeum should arrive. To the dismay of the Pagans, and the exaltation of the Christians, the Imperial decree went forth for the destruction of every pagan Temple in Alexandria. Theophilus at once applied himself to the demolition of the Serapeum, which involved that of the god Serapis. Even Christians shared the superstition which had so long attached to the tutelary god of Alexandria, and were filled with doubt and dismay while the work of destruction was being carried on; but the Serapeum fell; and their fear gave place to ridicule, when a swarm of rats and mice from the severed head of the idol convinced even the Pagans of, at least, the impotence of their worship.

The work of destruction still went on; the pagan Temples throughout Egypt were deserted or destroyed, or sometimes, a Cross being affixed to the summit, were converted into Christian Churches. A still more rigorous edict in the same year forbade alike magistrates and private citizens, whatever their rank or condition, throughout the Empire, to worship any inanimate idol by the sacrifice of an innocent victim, condemning the practice as a crime of High Treason punishable with death. Many Pagans, far from exhibiting the fortitude of the Christians in their persecutions, instead of maintaining to death that obedience to their gods was superior to that due to the Emperor, having for a time tried to elude the laws and disguise their religious meetings under the character of social gatherings, were ultimately led, from fear rather than conviction, to embrace the Gospel; and thus the Christian Churches became filled with multitudes of lukewarm and hypocritical proselytes.

On May 15, A.D. 392, the young Emperor Valentinian II., who from a mistaken idea too prevalent at the time, had deferred, till it was too late, his Baptism, was at the age of nineteen assassinated at Vienne in Gaul. His desire had been to be baptized by Ambrose, and he had even sent for him to come to Gaul for the purpose. His body was conveyed to Milan to be buried by the side of his brother, and Ambrose himself, overwhelmed with grief, in a sermon which he preached in the Cathedral, commemorated his virtues and misfortunes, and comforted his sisters with the assurance that a sincere desire for Baptism, if accidentally frustrated, ensured its benefits, his case being like that of the Martyrs who "were baptized in their own blood [m]."

A puppet Emperor, the rhetorician Eugenius, was set up as Valentinian's successor, but in September, 394, he was defeated and slain in battle by Theodosius, and with his death disappeared the last vestiges of open Paganism to which, even if he outwardly professed Christianity, he was secretly attached.

In January, A.D. 395, the Emperor Theodosius at *the age of fifty* died in the arms of St. Ambrose at Milan, the only Emperor, except Constantine, since the commencement of the century who had died a peaceful death in his bed. Among the benefactors of the Church, says Gibbon, the fame of Constantine was rivalled by the glory of Theodosius. "If Constantine erected the standard of the Cross, Theodosius subdued the Arian heresy and abolished Paganism." The heathen Emperors, he continues, had persecuted the Christians because they thought them a dark and dangerous faction to the civil power. But, he says too truly [n], "the same excuses of fear and ignorance cannot be applied to the Christian Emperors, who violated the principles of humanity and the Gospel." "Religio cogi non potest" is a maxim useful at all times, and the religion of Christ needs no such support; "non tali auxilio nec defensoribus istis." Even the pagan Sophist, Libanius, whom Theodosius himself, at the very time when he was

---

[m] St. Gregory of Nyssa wrote a treatise "Against those who defer Baptism."
[n] Vol. V. 118.

persecuting the Pagans, distinguished with his friendship and on whom he conferred special marks of honour, appealed to the consciences of Christians that religion ought to be grounded on conviction, not compulsion. And the Church paid the penalty. There were already too many professing Christians whose evil lives were in marked contrast with the lives of the Pagans. St. Chrysostom, when in the early years of his life he was the great preacher at Antioch, complained that the lives led by Christians in that place were in strong contrast with the early days of Christianity, and the lives of the early Christians; he told them that their loose living was the great obstacle to his work amongst the Pagans, and that he even feared that Paganism might reconquer the Church. This was the strong argument which Libanius used against him at Antioch, when Chrysostom tried to impress on him the truths of Christianity.

Although under Theodosius the outward observance of Paganism was forbidden and the laws rigidly executed, the profession of Christianity was not enforced, nor required as the necessary condition for holding civil or military offices; ability in Pagans was still recognized, and they continued to retain important posts even in the Palace. Paganism was not abolished by Theodosius, it was driven into the background. But when once the exercise of its public worship was prohibited, and the laws rigidly enforced against its ceremonial, Paganism received its death-blow, and its disappearance was only a question of time.

Gratian, though twice married, left no children, and by the death of Theodosius, the Empire became divided between his two imbecile sons, Arcadius, a youth, eighteen years of age, who ruled over the East (395—408), and Honorius, a boy of eleven, who ruled over the West (395—423). The division of the Empire at the very time when a community of feeling was most required against the coming inroads of the Barbarians, was most disastrous; what were really two separate nations came into existence, thoroughly out of sympathy with each other, so that their enemies were enabled to attack them in detail. The division in the Roman Empire materially affected the history of the still undivided Christendom.

The tutor of the two Princes had been the holy Arsenius, a man of noble family (still commemorated in the Greek Church as Arsenius *the Great Father*), who, A.D. 394, in obedience to a heavenly call gave up his charge and renounced the world, to lead a hermit life, with even greater than the usual austerities, in the Scetic desert. Theodosius then confided them to the care of St. Ambrose (who followed him to the grave two years afterwards), leaving them with the dying charge to remember that true religion was the safeguard of the Empire. In the matter of religion they were at least orthodox, but they followed their father's example, even with greater serenity, in extirpating whatever of Paganism survived. All remaining images of pagan worship were ordered to be destroyed, all pagan Festivals abolished; the Bishops being entrusted with the duty of seeing that the edict was carried out, whilst the civil magistrates were to assist the Bishops in the task.

In 398, three years after the death of Theodosius, Chrysostom succeeded the popular, because easy-going and luxurious, Nectarius in the Patriarchate of Constantinople.

John, surnamed, on account of his eloquence, Chrysostom, the golden-mouthed ($\chi\rho\acute{v}\sigma os$, $\sigma\tau\acute{o}\mu a$), was born at Antioch about A.D. 347, of good birth both on the side of his father and mother, and having studied rhetoric under the famous pagan Sophist Libanius, and at first practised as an advocate, he was, in A.D. 370, baptized by Meletius, Bishop of Antioch, and by him ordained a Reader. After the death of his mother, the pious Anthusa, with whom he had resided at Antioch, practising even there the most rigid asceticism, he carried out the intention, which he had had long at heart, of being a monk, and together with two of his fellow-pupils in the school of Libanius, one of whom was the famous Theodore of Mopsuestia, retired to a neighbouring monastery, presided over by Diodorus, who, about A.D. 379, became Bishop of Tarsus. Worn out by the severe discipline which he exercised, he returned to Antioch, and was, A D. 381, ordained Deacon by Meletius, and five years afterwards Priest by Flavian, by the latter of whom he was appointed preacher in the principal Church at Antioch, living in the same street, as he was wont to relate, in which SS. Paul and Barnabas resided, when they first preached to the Gentiles. Here amidst a dissolute population of 100,000 souls he preached and laboured for twelve years, abolishing abuses, and entirely changing the moral aspect of the city, so that the fame of the great preacher spread throughout the whole Roman Empire.

On the death of Nectarius he was inveigled by the eunuch Eutropius, the chamberlain and chief adviser of Arcadius, to Constantinople. Eutropius had on a visit to Antioch been attracted by his eloquence; but feeling that Chrysostom would decline the Episcopate, and that the people would oppose his removal, he had recourse to a stratagem, and no sooner had Chrysostom arrived at Constantinople, a city 800 miles distant from Antioch, than he was told for the first time that he had been elected to the vacant Patriarchate. In vain he remonstrated, pleading his unfitness and unworthiness; he was told that the Emperor's wishes must be obeyed; "Would God that it might be otherwise, but God's will be done," he exclaimed; and he was forced to accept the Patriarchate.

Theophilus, the worthless Patriarch of Alexandria, had a candidate of his own, an obscure Egyptian Priest, named Isidore, whom he wished to be elected, thinking to use him as his tool in advancing his own Patriarchate over that of Constantinople. For this reason, as also because he saw in Chrysostom one who would make a more earnest Patriarch than suited his views, he not only instigated the Provincial Bishops against him, but refused to perform his Consecration. But on Eutropius, who had his life in his hands, threatening to expose his many misdemeanours, Theophilus reluctantly assented, and Chrysostom was consecrated Patriarch of Constantinople on Feb. 26th, 398.

In order that we may understand the persecutions which this great Patriarch had to undergo, we must bear in mind the state of the Church in his time. It had triumphed over the so-called ten persecutions, over Arianism, and, by state-aid, over Paganism, but it had not advanced in godliness since the earliest days of Christianity. Pliny had written to the Emperor Trajan, that in his time Christianity had so prospered even in Bithynia as to empty the Temples of the Pagan gods. The age of the persecutions followed; the Church prospered in adversity and triumphed. But the smiles of the Emperors were more fatal to it than the sword of the executioner. Outwardly, it had spacious Churches and grand services; but even religious Pagans complained that it had degenerated from its ideal, and was more material and corrupt than their own Neo-Platonism; that it had lost the virtues and assimilated the acknowledged vices of the heathen

We have seen the state of things which existed at Antioch; it was still worse in Constantinople. The same was the case throughout Thrace and Asia Minor. The See of Alexandria was occupied by a Patriarch who was notorious for his vices. St. Gregory of Nyssa complained of the scenes of debauchery which attended the pilgrimages to Jerusalem, and that the Holy City was defiled with violence and debauchery. Equally did corruption prevail in Ephesus, a See second only to the great Patriarchates. Antoninus, the Metropolitan of Ephesus, was accused by a brother Bishop, Eusebius of Lydia, of simony and other enormous crimes, and St. Chrysostom was himself called upon to investigate the charges. Eusebius professed to be moved by conscientious motives and a righteous horror of the crimes which he revealed; he proved to be a pious hypocrite, as wicked himself as the man he accused, and was sentenced to excommunication. The charges against

Antoninus were gone into; six Bishops at first denied, but afterwards confessed their guilt of having purchased from him their Bishoprics, and were sentenced to deprivation of their Sees, the heirs of the now deceased Antoninus being required to refund the proceeds of the simony.

The same state of things meets us as we proceed Westwards, to Milan and to Rome, the last of which cities St. Jerome left an account of its corruption, denouncing it as Babylon, and shaking off the very dust from his feet.

We need, therefore, wonder little at the opposition which Chrysostom met with at Constantinople, especially from a Patriarch like Theophilus. Under the lax rule of Nectarius, the clergy of Constantinople had become thoroughly worldly-minded and dissolute, and were accused of various different crimes, not excluding murder, adultery, and entertaining " spiritual sisters" ($\sigma\upsilon\nu\epsilon\iota\sigma\alpha\kappa\tau\omicron\iota$), the last practice being that condemned by the third Canon of the Council of Nice. Many of them had also intrigued and bribed for the Patriarchate which Chysostom so reluctantly accepted.

The weak and indolent Emperor of the East was naturally inclined to admire the holiness of Chrysostom's character, but he was at the same time wholly under the influence of his wife, Eudoxia. The Empress imagined herself to be religious because she was liberal in almsgiving, and in building Churches, attended the Church services, reverenced the relics of Martyrs, and patronized the clergy, so long as they let her have her own way. But she was superstitious, thoroughly worldly-minded, avaricious, absorbed in luxuries and pleasures, and those of a not very innocent character. She at first welcomed Chrysostom, and assured him of her favour, but soon turned against him.

These were some of the evils with which Chrysostom had to contend, and the corrupt clergy of the Patriarchate found a leader in one worse than themselves, Theophilus of Alexandria.

Amongst the better classes of Constantinople Chrysostom soon acquired even a stronger influence than he had done at Antioch. But a Patriarch who was in earnest and resolved to effect a reformation, was at such a time little likely to suit the careless and pleasure-loving portion of the community. For such a task as his, discretion was necessary; but here was Chrysostom's weak point. A hot and impulsive temper, want of tact, and sometimes error of judgment, added to the list of enemies those who might have been his friends. The neighbouring Bishops and clergy when they visited Constantinople professed a grievance that the Patriarch was not given to hospitality, as St. Paul says a Bishop ought to be. To him princely grandeur and magnificent revenues had no attraction. He eschewed sumptuous banquets and the luxurious living of his predecessor, preferring a quiet life and the frugal meal in his solitary chamber. We must hear his own idea of hospitality;—"He is given to hospitality," he says in one of his sermons, "who makes himself a partaker in all that he has with the poor." In his condemnation of sin he determined that the trumpet should give no uncertain sound, and of vicious pleasures he was the uncompromising enemy; yet even his compassion for the returning penitent, and the gentleness with which he spoke of heretics, excited the ire of the ill-disposed, but rigidly orthodox, Bishops.

Theophilus prided himself on his orthodoxy. A sharp controversy was going on as to the writings of Origen, probably the most learned theologian in the early Church; his father had died a Martyr, whilst he himself had been a Confessor for the faith, and he deserved better treatment from the Church than fell to his lot. Some people thought (not apparently without reason) that his writings had been, after his death, garbled and interpolated by heretics; at any rate the speculative character of his theology required a more thorough and impartial handling than it met with, whilst any serious unorthodoxy is negatived by the fact that St. Athanasius greatly admired his works; and if Arians appealed to them in support of their opinions, so also did the orthodox party in support of theirs.

John, the successor of Cyril in the Bishopric of Jerusalem, and who held that See for 30 years (386—417), was a favourer of Origenism, as was also Rufinus the historian, who from 371—397 resided in Palestine, but it was opposed in his latter years by St. Jerome, who from 386 had taken up his permanent abode in his cell at Bethlehem, and even more vehemently by Epiphanius, Bishop of Salamis, in the island of Cyprus (376—403), who thought he detected in Origen the taint of Arianism.

Rufinus and Jerome, the latter of whom had been at first amongst Origen's most ardent admirers, were once intimate friends, but the same cause which had cemented their friendship, viz. their admiration of Origen, now rendered them bitter opponents. Epiphanius, a man of saintly character, but narrow views, the friend of Jerome, went in 394 to Palestine, where he was kindly received by John, the Bishop of Jerusalem, for which he made a bad return on the ground of his attachment to Origen, opposing him by every means in his power and stirring up his own people against him; and proceeded so far that a Bishop of less gentle disposition than John would have excommunicated him. By Epiphanius, Jerome was induced to take part against his own Bishop, and became the violent opponent, as he had before been admirer, of Origen.

Theophilus of Alexandria at that time sided with the Origenists and stigmatised Epiphanius as a heretic. A violent controversy ensued between Jerome and Rufinus; Siricius, the Pope of Rome, took the side of the latter; but Anastasius I., his successor, although he afterwards confessed that till then he "did not know who Origen was or what language he had used[o]," sided against him, and summoned him to Rome (a summons which, needless to say, Rufinus did not obey), to defend his opinions.

Meanwhile Theophilus changed round, and in a Synod at Alexandria condemned Origenism. In the Monastery of Nitria, which was in his diocese and the stronghold of

[o] Bright, p. 236.

Origenism, were four Monks known as the *Tall Brothers*. Being, in consequence of their opinions, expelled by Theophilus, they fled to Palestine, hoping to find protection under John of Jerusalem; thither, however, the wrath of Theophilus pursued them, and John was afraid to give them anything further than sympathy. They then went to Constantinople, and threw themselves on the clemency of Chrysostom.

Chrysostom, as might be expected from one of his generous disposition, sympathised with, boarded and lodged them, and gave them the Church of the Anastasia for their services; but, as the Monks of Nitria were under the jurisdiction of the Patriarch of Alexandria, he refrained from giving any cause for a breach, and refused to admit them to communion. He however intervened on their behalf with Theophilus, who resented this charitable act as one of uncanonical interference.

The Tall Brothers then represented their case to the Emperor Arcadius, who ordered Theophilus to appear in his defence at Constantinople. This was a rash proceeding on the part of the Emperor, for Theophilus was almost equal in power to Arcadius himself, and the Patriarchs of Alexandria had attained such a height of power, not only in ecclesiastical but civil matters, as to be almost sovereign Princes[p]; the whole Egyptian nation regarded the Patriarch as a King, and cared little for the distant Emperor[q].

Theophilus delayed as long as possible, but eventually, attended by his nephew Cyril, and a splendid retinue of Egyptian and Abyssinian Bishops, with all the pomp of a monarch, made his appearance in June, 403, but he refused to hold any intercourse with Chrysostom. Meanwhile, the reforms of Chrysostom had raised up many enemies against him in Constantinople, chief amongst them being the Empress Eudoxia. The wily Patriarch of Alexandria now saw and seized the opportunity of increasing the prestige

---

[p] Neale's Eastern Church, I. 112.
[q] Butcher's Story of the Church in Egypt, I. 232.

of his own Patriarchate by deposing Chrysostom and thus lowering that of Constantinople. He assumed a jurisdiction in the Patriarchate of Alexandria over the Patriarchate of Constantinople. Instead of appearing as defendant at his own trial, yet fearing to hold a Council of his own in Constantinople, where he knew that Chrysostom's friends would be too powerful for him, he passed over to Chalcedon, where the Bishop Cyrinus, an Egyptian, and his own cousin, was the violent enemy of Chrysostom. There he summoned, in July, 403, the Council of the Oak, which was attended by 36 Bishops, almost entirely Egyptians, and therefore his own suffragans, and presided over by the Bishop of Heraclea, the Bishops of which See were never favourable to the Patriarchs of Constantinople, whose Metropolitans they had once been, but whose suffragans they now were.

Chrysostom, though four times summoned, refused to attend a Council which had no right to judge him, and of which the principal members were his avowed enemies. He sat quietly at home with forty Bishops of his own, who in vain sent a deputation to remonstrate with Theophilus. A number of frivolous, and mostly false, accusations were brought against Chrysostom, one a charge of high treason in reviling the Empress Eudoxia. He was condemned as contumacious and sentenced to deposition, and a request made to Arcadius that he should be banished. The weak Emperor, who was wholly under the control of his wife, consented, and Chrysostom was sentenced to banishment for life.

Scarcely had he crossed the Bosphorus, when Constantinople was convulsed by an earthquake, and the alarmed Empress regarding it as a divine judgment on her injustice prevailed on Arcadius to recall him. So strong was the feeling of the populace in favour of Chrysostom, that Theophilus in fear of his life fled away at midnight to Alexandria, from which safe distance he continued to direct the plots of the enemies of Chrysostom. A synod of sixty

The Second Œcumenical Council.   193

Bishops at Constantinople, annulling the proceedings of the Council of the Oak, decreed that Chrysostom was the lawful Patriarch of Constantinople, and he consequently resumed his office.

The Empress, who could neither forget nor forgive, availed herself, in her enmity against Chrysostom, of an incident which, accompanied with heathenish and boisterous dancing interrupting the Church-services, occurred in September, 403, at the dedication of a silver statue to herself in front of the Cathedral of St. Sophia. Chrysostom, who was righteously indignant, was represented to her as having used in his sermon the unguarded words, " Again Herodias rages ($\mu\alpha\acute{\iota}\nu\epsilon\tau\alpha\iota$), again Herodias dances, and demands the head of John on a charger." Theophilus, little caring that the Canon of a Council of doubtful orthodoxy had been used against his own great predecessor, St. Athanasius, sent three Bishops to Constantinople with a copy of the Canon of the Dedication Synod at Antioch, which ordered the deprivation of any Bishop who having been deprived by a Synod appealed to the secular power. A fresh Synod, composed of Bishops hostile to Chrysostom, was held at the end of the same year at Constantinople ; it was nothing to them that a larger Synod than that of the Oak had restored him ; the Canon of Antioch was put in force ; Arsacius, an old man, eighty years of age, brother of Nectarius, who had been one of his principal accusers at the Oak, was intruded into the Patriarchate , and Arcadius, in June, 404, signed an edict for the banishment of Chrysostom. The hatred of Eudoxia only ended with her death in October of the same year. In November a law was passed enforcing Communion with Arsacius, Porphyry, the profligate Patriarch of Antioch, and Theophilus of Alexandria.

The place appointed for his exile was Cucusus in Armenia, where Paul, his saintly predecessor, had been strangled in banishment little more than fifty years before. His banishment was somewhat mitigated by Adelphius, the excellent Bishop of Cucusus, who offered to resign to him his See, and by the kindness of the neighbouring Bishops, whilst Dioscorus, a man of rank, gave him his own house, fitting it up for his requirements. His wants were ministered to by a Deaconess of great holiness, Sabiniana, his father's sister. Innocent I., the Pope of Rome, wrote to him; Honorius, Emperor of the West, interceded with his brother Arcadius; and his name and innocence were revered throughout Christendom. Cucusus was a miserable little place, in which he suffered much from intense heat in summer and cold in winter. His life was constantly in danger from Isaurian freebooters, who made frequent inroads into the neighbourhood. But in his exile Chrysostom was able to exercise even a more powerful influence than he had done from his own diocese, his advice being sought from all countries. His friends from Constantinople sent him large sums of money, by which he was able to set on foot missions to the Pagans of Phœnicia, to the Goths, and to the Persians. In the winter of A D. 405, danger from the Isaurians forced him to seek refuge in the Castle of Arabissus, about 60 miles distant; there he suffered from the inclemency of the climate even worse tortures than at Cucusus, so that he gladly welcomed the possibility of returning to the latter place in the spring of 406.

In that year Atticus (406 –426) succeeded Arsacius in the Patriarchate of Constantinople. He had been one of Chrysostom's accusers at the Oak, and was still his bitter opponent. Jealous of the influence which he exercised from Cucusus, Chrysostom's enemies now determined on his death, which they had in vain hoped that the rigour of the climate would have effected. Flavian, Patriarch of Antioch, having died A D. 404, was succeeded by Porphyry (404—413), a man of disreputable character. He wrote to Atticus a letter of complaint, that Chrysostom was directing missions to Persia and Phœnicia, that he was uniting the sympathies of the Pope of Rome and the Western Bishops against the Eastern

The Second Œcumenical Council. 195

Patriarchs, and that Arcadius must be prevailed on to banish him to some more distant place; adding that if on the way he fell into the hands of the Huns or the Isaurians, so much the better. Atticus succeeded in persuading the Emperor that Chrysostom was fomenting a conspiracy of the Western against the Eastern Church. Arcadius, who, though no longer under the influence of Eudoxia, was always ready to lend his ear to the last speaker, now yielded to the episcopal maligners, who, as a salve to his conscience, assured him that the guilt would be on them and not on the Emperor's head. Thus he was prevailed upon to accede to the murderous project, and ordered his removal to Pityus, on the shores of the Euxine sea, the most bleak and inhospitable clime in the whole Empire; and Chrysostom was committed to two brutal guards who were charged to hurry him on without regard to his health or strength. Forced along for three months, more dead than alive, through the scorching heat and drenching rains of summer; all places where he might find ordinary comfort avoided, and the most squalid villages selected as halting-places, he reached Comana in Pontus. There it was evident that his strength was gone and his end near; still without halting they dragged him six miles further, resting the night in the Church of St. Basiliscus, a former Bishop of Comana, who had died a Martyr in the Diocletian persecution. In the morning (September 14, 407), he in vain asked for a little longer rest, and again was hurried off. They had not proceeded far when seeing evident signs that he was dying, the guards retraced their steps to the Church. There, being carried to the Altar, and having received the Sacrament of the Eucharist, Chrysostom, with the Doxology on his lips, calmly expired, and there by the side of the Martyr Bishop he was buried.

The Emperor Arcadius died A.D. 408. Theophilus was found dead in his bed on Oct. 15, 412. Under Porphyry, with whom the respectable people of Antioch refused to communicate, the Eustathian schism continued. Porphyry was succeeded by Alexander (413—420), in whose Patriarchate the schism, having lasted more than eighty years, came to an end. He is described as a man of holy and ascetic life; he replaced the name of St. Chrysostom on the Diptychs of the Church at Antioch, and personally visited Constantinople, where he used his influence to obtain from the Patriarch Atticus the same act of justice which was tardily extorted by the threats of the people.

The fate of Chrysostom, says Dean Farrar, produced age-long consequences both over the Eastern and Western Empires. Thenceforth the Patriarchate of Constantinople produced no mighty Church-leader to confront the banded unions of civil tyranny; in the long lapse of the ages not one great Saint or orator, like Chrysostom, swayed the diminished power of the Church of the Great Eastern Metropolis. Whilst it weakened the Eastern, it strengthened the Western Church. The dwindling power of the Western Empire till Romulus Augustulus increased the ever-deepening influence of the Popes; the distracted age looked for guidance, and could find it only in the chief Bishop of the West.

St. Chrysostom was the last of the Four great Fathers of the Greek Church, the others being SS. Athanasius, Basil the Great, and Gregory Nazianzen. The Four Latin Fathers are SS. Ambrose, Jerome, Augustine of Hippo, and Gregory the Great, but in two of them SS. Jerome and Augustine, the Greek Church must claim a share.

Of the former, whom Erasmus styled the chief of the Latin Fathers, although all his works were written in Latin, the real names Eusebius Hieronymus are Greek. Born about A.D. 346, of Catholic parents, at Stridon, near Aquileia, he was sent early in life to complete his education in Rome, where he acquired the knowledge requisite for his subsequent translation of the Scriptures, and where he was baptized by Pope Liberius. Between A.D. 374—378 he lived a monastic life in the desert of Chalcis; during which he studied Hebrew from a converted Jew, a task of the greatest consequence to the Church, as it enabled him to read the Old Testament in the original language. He was ordained

Priest about A.D. 379, by Paulinus at Antioch. Thence he went to Constantinople, where he was much impressed with the sermons which Gregory Nazianzen was at the time preaching in the Church of the Anastasia. One of the most eventful periods of his life was a visit to Rome between 382 — 385, where he became secretary to Pope Damasus, a man of considerable learning, by whose advice he set about his translation of the Bible. In Rome, his learning and eloquence and the austerity of his life at first gained him universal popularity, and at one time he was regarded as a probable successor to the Papacy. Like St. Chrysostom at Constantinople, he was intolerant of the vice and imposture which he found existing alike amongst Priests and people. But he was not a man of Chrysostom's saintly charity; and, moreover, in trying to effect a reformation, he adopted the very course which common sense would have condemned; and in one way or another contrived to offend all classes of society, the religious no less than the irreligious. Ever since St. Athanasius' visit, A.D. 340, in company of two monks, to Rome, a permanent impression favourable to the monastic life had existed in the city, and many, especially Roman matrons, regarded it as the ideal of the Christian life. This feeling Jerome encouraged, and, as their spiritual adviser, induced several ladies of high position to become the brides of Christ, to adopt celibacy, and a life of the strictest asceticism.

Amongst his followers were Paula, a widow belonging to one of the noble families in Rome, and her two daughters, Blesilla and Julia Eustochia. Blesilla dying in consequence, as was supposed, of her severe fastings, increased the feeling against Jerome. On the death, in 384, of his patron, Damasus, and the accession of Siricius (384—398), who was by no means well affected towards him, his position in Rome became no longer tenable; and smarting under the treatment he received, with a curse on his lips for its Babylonish wickedness, he left the city accompanied by his younger brother, Paulinian, and was soon afterwards joined at Antioch by Paula and Eustochia. In 386 he settled down in his cell at Bethlehem, where by the sale of his patrimony he was enabled to build a monastery, over which he himself presided till his death, A.D. 420, a period of thirty-four years. There he completed his great work, which he had commenced at Rome at the instigation of Damasus, the Vulgate or Latin Version of the Bible.

Aurelius Augustine (354—430), who is generally considered the greatest of the Latin Fathers, was born at Tagaste in Numidia. His father, Patricius, a heathen and a man of indifferent character, was won over to Christianity by his pious wife Monica. St. Augustine is known to have had a brother named Navigius and a sister whose name is not known, but who became Abbess of a community of Nuns. In his "Confessions," written in his forty-sixth year, he has given the history of his own life.

When he was seventeen years of age his father died, and his mother Monica being left in straightened circumstances, a rich neighbour took upon herself the expenses of his education. He was sent to the famous school in the dissolute city of Carthage, where he fell into bad company and vicious habits, and had a natural son named Adeodatus, who grew up to be a youth of great promise. At twenty years of age he imbibed the Manichæan heresy, which at that time had many adherents in Africa. Having followed this form of worship for about ten years, and failing to find in it the truth which he sought, he adopted Neo-Platonism, which, as it embodied many doctrines of the Bible, brought back to his mind the reminiscences of his mother's instructions, and led him to a closer study of the Holy Scriptures. In A.D. 383 he left Africa and went to Rome, where he opened a school, but not meeting with success he went to Milan, where, in 385, he was joined by Monica Here, he says, he was led by God to the great Bishop Ambrose. First he went to hear him from curiosity, but Ambrose was always accessible to him, and received him, as he says, "like a true father;" and he became a

Catechumen, reading carefully St. Paul's Epistles. His eyes fell on the words, " Let us walk honestly as in the day ; not in rioting and drunkenness, not in chambering and wantonness, not in strife and envying, but put ye on the Lord Jesus Christ, and make not provision for the flesh, to fulfil the lusts thereof." There he read the history and saw the vileness of his own life, and on the following Easter, April 25, A.D. 387, when he was thirty-three years of age, he together with his son Adeodatus, then fifteen years of age, and his friend Alypius, was baptized by Ambrose. This joyful news, as a return for her life of prayer, greeted Monica soon after her arrival at Milan.

A year after his Baptism he determined to return to Africa, but had only arrived at Ostia when Monica died. From Ostia he went to Rome, where he stayed about a year, and then left for Carthage, arriving there about September A.D. 388. At his native Tagaste he devoted three years to prayer and study, and there his son Adeodatus died. Avoiding, as he thought, all places where there was fear of his being seized by force and Consecrated a Bishop, he, at the request of a friend who wished to receive from him instruction, went to Hippo, of which Valerius was Bishop. There he was ordained to the Priesthood, and notwithstanding his objections was in 395 Consecrated by Valerius as his Coadjutor Bishop. In the next year Valerius died and Augustine succeeded him in the See of Hippo. At Hippo Augustine founded a monastery, in which he himself resided as a monk, and also a nunnery; and in that humble and obscure See, this great Bishop of the African Church spent the remaining thirty-four years of his life, writing numerous works and upholding the doctrine of the Church against heretics.

Not the least famous of his works is his "De Civitate Dei," which occupied him for thirteen years (413—426), and which was called forth by the reproach of the heathens that the victories of their enemies over the Roman Empire were due to its advocacy of Christianity and its renunciation of the Pagan gods. Rome had already fallen under Alaric, and it was felt that still worse things were in store for it. He contrasts the destiny of the world with that of the Church. He shows how the misfortunes of the Empire were due, not to its advocacy of Christianity, but to the vices and corruptions of Paganism, and to the luxury and effeminacy of the people; how the earthly city with its false gods and sacrifices had passed away, whilst the City of God grew more glorious and the Church of Christ is eternal and immutable.

He lived to see Hippo surrounded by the armies of the Vandal Genseric, but, "felix opportunitate mortis," he was saved from witnessing the crowning disaster which befell, A D. 430, his beloved Hippo. He was the last Bishop of the See. His valuable library, which was his only earthly possession and the only thing which escaped the conflagration of the siege, he left to the Church. In learning he was unacquainted with the original language of the Old and only moderately versed in that of the New Testament; in depth of thought, in eloquence, and administrative power, he had superiors in the Four Fathers of the East and in St. Jerome in the West; but in the combination of these qualities he had no superior, if indeed an equal. His Western characteristics caused him to be less understood and less appreciated in the East than in the West; but no other Father since the Apostles has equally influenced the succeeding generations of the Church at large.

Between 400—411 St. Augustine was engaged in controversy with the Donatists, but a far more important one with Pelagianism engaged him to the end of his life. Pelagianism, or the denial of original sin, is the heresy condemned in the IXth Article of our Church. The heresy which convulsed the West exercised comparatively little influence on the Eastern Church. The controversies of the East were generally with regard to subtle matters of theological speculation, such as the relations of the Persons in the Trinity, the Incarnation, the union of the Divine and

Human Natures in our Lord; whereas those of the West were of a more practical nature, such as original sin, Predestination, and free-will in man.

Yet the Pelagian heresy is generally supposed to have had its origin in the East, and its author to have been Rufinus, who was called the Syrian to distinguish him from his contemporary namesake of Aquileia. Rufinus, a friend of St. Jerome, and one of his community at Bethlehem, was sent by him, A D. 390, on a mission to Rome, where he broached the doctrine that Adam's fall had no influence on his descendants, and that man is now born, just as Adam was, without sin.

At the commencement of the Fifth Century a Welsh monk named Morgan, a name which was Grecized into Pelagius (πέλαγος, *sea*), went to reside at Rome, where he is supposed to have been inoculated with the doctrines of Rufinus. That he was a Briton seems evident, for Prosper stigmatizes him as the "snake of Britain" (*coluber Britannicus*), and Jerome as the "dog of Albion." At Rome he became acquainted with Celestius, who is supposed to have been a Scot, which at that time meant a native of Ireland, and to have imbued him with his doctrines.

Pelagius, who had not fallen so deeply as Augustine into actual sin, instead of ascribing it to the Grace of God, and recognizing that freedom from evil and the power of doing anything that is good is the gift of the Holy Ghost, ascribed it to the power inherent in human nature and to man's free-will. When residing in Rome he witnessed the same sins prevailing which drove St. Jerome from it, and he heard people excusing themselves on the ground of the weakness and corruption of their nature. In condemning this error he fell into the opposite extreme of asserting that man's nature is not corrupt, that it is not worse for, nor influenced by, the fall of our first parents, that man can by his own natural strength avoid sin and do works pleasing and acceptable to God. Augustine having himself gone through the fiery trial and yielded to temptation, felt and taught against the Pelagians the need of God's Grace to enable men to will and to do anything that is good. The doctrine of Pelagius was condemned by the African Church in Synods at Carthage, A D 412 and 416, and by another in the latter year at Milevum in Numidia. It would appear that the Eastern Bishops generally did not trouble themselves much about the matter, and they seem to have recognized the co-operation of Grace and Free-will, without determining their limits. They held less rigid views than the Bishops of Africa as to the efficacy of the human will, and were opposed to the extreme doctrine of St. Augustine. John of Jerusalem, in a Synod held in that city in June, 415, declined to accept the decision of the African Bishops, and if he did not actually acquit Pelagius and Celestius, was so far in their favour as to draw upon himself a remonstrance from Augustine for his toleration of heresy; and again in a Synod at Diospolis in Palestine, at the end of the same year, under Eulogius, Metropolitan of Cæsarea, Pelagius was acquitted.

John of Jerusalem died at the end of A D. 416, and was succeeded by Praylius (416—420), who addressed a letter to Innocent I., Pope of Rome, expressing his belief in the orthodoxy of Pelagius. But a work written by Pelagius being forwarded to Innocent, he pronounced it blasphemous, and excommunicated its author and his friend Celestius; and this it was which drew from St. Augustine the famous apothegm, "Roma locuta, causa finita." Innocent died shortly afterwards, and was succeeded by Zosimus. Meanwhile Celestius, having been expelled from Africa, went to Ephesus, whence, having received Priest's Orders, he repaired to Constantinople. Expelled thence for propagating his opinions by the Patriarch Atticus, he went to Rome and laid his version of the case before Zosimus, who had before him the conflicting judgments of the African and the Eastern Bishops. A modern Pope would have decided that the judgment of his predecessors was infallible and immutable. The mind of Zosimus seems to have been little fitted to decide such minute points of theology ; but instead of considering himself bound by the judgment of Innocent, he reheard the case, and gave an exactly opposite judgment, took the side of the Council of Diospolis, acquitted Pelagius, and pronounced him to be Catholic, and wrote to the African Bishops upbraiding them for their condemnation of his doctrine.

Through the influence of Augustine, a man of greater ability and greater spiritual influence than the Pope, the Emperor Honorius in the West, and Theodosius, who had succeeded Arcadius in the East, in order to bring to an end a controversy which convulsed the Western Church, issued an edict, notwithstanding the decision of Zosimus, banishing Pelagius and Celestius from Rome. Under such opposition Zosimus investigated the matter anew, withdrew from them his support, censured their opinions as opposed to the Catholic faith, confirmed the decisions of the African Bishops, and compelled the Italian Bishops to obey his latest decision.

CHAPTER VI.

The Third and Fourth Œcumenical Councils.

NESTORIUS, Patriarch of Constantinople—Theodore of Mopsuestia—Nestorius opposes the word Theotokos - Cyril, Patriarch of Alexandria—Murder of Hypatia—The Emperor, Theodosius II., summons the Third Œcumenical Council to Ephesus—Council deposes Nestorius—Conciliabulum of Ephesus—Theodoret, Bishop of Cyrus—Brutal treatment and death of Nestorius—Dioscorus, Patriarch of Alexandria—Eutyches—The Latrocinium—The "Tome" of Pope Leo—Dioscorus excommunicates Pope Leo—Marcian summons the Œcumenical Council of Chalcedon—Dioscorus deposed—The See of Jerusalem raised to a Patriarchate—Precedence given to See of Constantinople— Ulfilas, the Apostle of the Goths—Anger of Leo with the Canons of Chalcedon—Rise of the Monophysites—Zeno's Henoticon—Great Confusion in the Eastern Church.

AT the time at which we have now arrived, Cyril had succeeded his uncle Theophilus in the See of Alexandria (412—444); Theodotus was Patriarch of Antioch (420—429), to be succeeded by John (429—448); and Juvenal, Bishop of Jerusalem (420—458). On the death of Atticus, the Patriarch of Constantinople, one party favoured the election of Proclus, a disciple of St. Chrysostom, who was, however, passed over in favour of Sisinnius (February, 426—December, 427), as he was again passed over, when, on the death of Sisinnius, Nestorius was on April 10, A.D. 428, consecrated Patriarch (428—431).

The See of Antioch had been more troubled with heresy and discord than any of the great Sees. It was the first whose Bishop, Paul of Samosata, fell into heresy and was deposed. Then followed the eighty years' schism. And now from Antioch proceeded the Patriarch of Constantinople, whose heresy, or perhaps the heresy imputed to him, caused a schism in the Greek Church which has never been healed.

Diodorus, afterwards (379—394) Bishop of Tarsus, the head of the famous school of Antioch, had once been the intimate friend of SS. Basil and Chrysostom, and the defender of orthodoxy against the Arians; but, in his fear of Apollinarianism, he fell into the heresy which afterwards bore the name of Nestorius, and he has been considered the father not only of Nestorianism, but also of Rationalism. His views were further developed by Theodore, a native of Antioch, who afterwards (392—428) became Bishop of Mopsuestia, and who had been one of his pupils in the school of Antioch. Nestorius had been a pupil of Theodore of Mopsuestia, who lived just long enough to receive a visit from him on his way from Antioch to Constantinople.

Nestorius, once a monk in the neighbourhood, afterwards a Priest at Antioch, was a man of exemplary and ascetic life; he was also a man of some learning; and gained a name at Antioch for his preaching, in connexion with which he was accused of great vanity and love of applause. Such was his fame, that the people of Constantinople expected to find in their new Patriarch a second Chrysostom. He was also a firm opponent of heretics. "Give me," he said to the Emperor, "the Earth cleansed from heretics, and I will in return give you Heaven." The Pelagians alone amongst heretics found favour with him; but although he agreed with them as to the sufficiency of man's Will, and received Celestius and other leaders of the sect, and even interceded for them at Rome, yet he disagreed with their view on original sin.

On his arrival at Constantinople he immediately showed himself a zealous and somewhat intemperate opponent of heretics. But from Antioch he had brought with him a Priest of the name of Anastasius, a follower of the teaching of Theodore of Mopsuestia. On Nov. 22, A.D. 428, Anastasius in the presence of Nestorius preached a sermon in which he denied that the Virgin Mary was Θεοτόκος (the *Mother of God*), and the people appealed to the Patriarch to discountenance such teaching. Nestorius himself disliked the word Θεοτόκος, not only because under it Arians and Apollinarians sheltered themselves, but it seemed to him to imply that the Godhead of Christ had its commencement through the Virgin Mary.

In a sermon on the following Christmas-day, and in two subsequent sermons in the following January, Nestorius insisted that Mary was not the Mother of God. He did not deny that she was the Mother of Christ; he spoke of the two Natures as a connexion (συνάφεια) or indwelling (ἐνοίκησις), but denied that there was a communication of attributes (κοινωνία ἰδιωμάτων), or a supernatural union of the two Natures. The doctrine was a denial of the personal union between "God the Word" and the Son of Mary, and seemed to imply that there were in the Saviour Two Persons.

Eusebius, at the time a layman and advocate at Constantinople, who afterwards became Bishop of Dorylæum, took the lead as accuser of Nestorius, whom he charged with holding the same views as Paul of Samosata, both of them denying that the Son of Mary was the Eternal Logos. As his great predecessor, St. Athanasius, had been the champion of the Homoousios, so the champion of the Theotokos was Cyril, Patriarch of Alexandria; a man, who, however great as a theologian, was of as an irascible temper as his uncle, not sorry of an opportunity for crushing his rival Bishop; and he now entered the lists against Nestorius.

The character of Cyril has not been handed down in altogether favourable colours; but as the champion of the Theotokos he did a work corresponding in importance with that done by St. Athanasius But for him, says Bishop Wordsworth [a], "it is probable that Jerome's words . . . . might have been applicable to an equally deadly heresy; the world would have been astounded and wondered to find itself Nestorian."

After a contested election with the Archdeacon Peter, Cyril entered on his episcopal duties under unfavourable auguries. Like Nestorius he began with persecution; he refused to put the name of St. Chrysostom, who had been persecuted by his uncle, on the diptychs; "He would as soon," he is reported as having said, "put the name of Judas on the roles as that of Chrysostom." He closed the

---

[a] Church Hist, IV. 229.

The Third and Fourth Œcumenical Councils.   207

Churches of the Novatians and confiscated their property; and in 415 he seized on the Synagogues of the Jews and expelled them from Alexandria.

This last act of Cyril brought him into contact with the Prefect Orestes, who appealed against it to the Emperor; nor did Cyril, with the exception of the monks, meet with the support of the people, and when, in consequence, he sought a reconciliation with Orestes, he suffered a rebuff The cruel murder of Hypatia brought obloquy upon him. She, the pagan daughter of a learned mathematician, Theon, by her beauty, modesty, and learning was universally respected. She delivered lectures in philosophy, and it was thought that Cyril was jealous because more people went to hear her lectures than his sermons. But she was a friend of Orestes. A band of furious zealots, swelled by the Parabolani [b], and headed by a Reader named Peter, attacked her, as she was returning from one of her lectures, in the streets of Alexandria, dragged her from her carriage and literally tore her to pieces. The deed was imputed to the followers of Cyril, and has left a stain on his memory.

In 430, Cyril, in a Council at Alexandria, hurled twelve Anathemas against Nestorius. To the supporters of the latter these savoured of Apollinarianism, and on that account offended both John, who had succeeded Theodotus in the Patriarchate of Antioch, and Theodoret, Bishop of Cyrus, the latter probably, since St. Augustine, the leading theologian of the Church. Each party tried to enlist Celestine, Pope of Rome, on its side, for so great was the jealousy and rivalry of the Sees of Constantinople to Alexandria, that each was desirous, almost at any sacrifice of independence, to have the Western Bishop as its adherent The Pope, who was no theologian, sided with Cyril, and in a Council at Rome in August, 430, threatened Nestorious with excommunication, unless within ten days

[b] A guild employed in attending the sick and burying the dead, but who often abused privileges conferred on them by taking part in popular riots.

after he received the notice he recanted his error. He also wrote to John of Antioch and Juvenal of Jerusalem announcing his intention. The Syrian Bishops, with John of Antioch at their head, sided with Nestorius, although John advised him to withdraw his statement with regard to the Theotokos. Egypt was foremost in the cause against Nestorius and in favour of its own Bishop. Nestorius, so far from humbling himself before the Pope, set both his monition and Cyril's anathemas at defiance.

Both the adherents of Nestorius and those of Cyril now demanded an Œcumenical Council. The Emperor Arcadius had been succeeded by his son, Theodosius II. (408—450), or, as he is sometimes called, Theodosius the Younger, a boy eight years of age at his succession, who grew up a pious but feeble Emperor, and during his long reign was little more than nominal Head of the Eastern Empire, entirely under the guidance of his pious and able sister Pulcheria. The Emperor Honorius, having died A.D. 423, was succeeded by Valentinian III. (425—455), a boy six years of age, the last and worst of the family of the great Theodosius, under the guardianship of his mother Galla Placidia. Thus two women virtually ruled the Roman Empire, Pulcheria in the East, and Placidia in the West.

The Emperor, Theodosius II., who was at first under the influence of Nestorius, was prejudiced by him against Cyril; and being unwilling to allow the Pope's interference with his own Bishop, he, in his own name and that of Valentinian II., issued on November 19, 430, a summons for a Council to meet at Ephesus at Whitsuntide in the following year, with the view of remedying the troubles and disorder of the Church. At the same time Theodosius wrote to Cyril blaming him as the real cause of trouble, and also for having addressed two separate letters to his wife Eudocia and his sister Pulcheria, as if there had been dissensions at the Court. He also wrote to the great Augustine of Hippo inviting him to attend the Council, but before the letter reached its destination Augustine was dead.

The winter passed in mutual recriminations between the two rival Bishops; Nestorius complained of the dealings of Alexandria with Antioch and Constantinople; how that "by it Flavian and Nectarius suffered, and Meletius, now reckoned amongst the Saints; how by it John Chrysostom, whose holiness they had been obliged to acknowledge, had suffered;" and he issued twelve anathemas as a reply to those of Cyril.

Both Nestorius and Cyril set out for Ephesus, the former accompanied by ten of his Bishops and Count Candidian, the commissioner of both the Emperors; and in the first week of June Cyril arrived to find Nestorius already there. Juvenal of Jerusalem arrived about a week afterwards. John of Antioch and the Syrian Bishops being detained, John wrote to Cyril excusing the delay on the ground of exceptional circumstances, but saying that they might be expected in five or six days. Theodoret, Bishop of Cyrus, had also arrived, and he, always the counsellor of peace, advocated delay. Cyril well knew that John was opposed to his Anathemas, and that the Syrian Bishops were in favour of Nestorius. Cyril, who had a devoted adherent in Memnon, Bishop of Ephesus, notwithstanding the announcement of John, determined not to wait.

The Third Œcumenical Council, that of Ephesus, was opened on June 22, 431, about one hundred and fifty-eight Bishops being present: Cyril presided[e]; Juvenal occupied the next place of honour, and next to him Memnon. In vain Nestorius, in vain Candidian protested against the unseemly haste. Nestorius, though thrice summoned, refused to attend until all the Bishops should arrive; Candidian surrounded the house of Nestorius with soldiers to prevent the entrance of the deputations which were sent to summon him. After sermons and other writings of Nestorius had been read, a unanimous cry arose in the

[e] For the statement that he presided as plenipotentiary of the Pope there is not the shadow of foundation.

Council;—"We all anathematize the impious (ἀσεβῆ) Nestorius, and every one who will not anathematize him;" and the sentence, which was subscribed by Cyril, Juvenal, and the Bishops present, others afterwards giving their adhesion, was pronounced against him; that since he had refused to obey the citation, and was convicted of impious doctrines, the Council was compelled by the Canons, in accordance with a letter of their most holy Father and colleague (συλλείτουργον) Celestine, Bishop of the Roman Church, to pronounce with many tears (δακρύσαντες πολλάκις) the sorrowful sentence, that our Lord Jesus Christ Whom he had blasphemed, declares by this holy Council that he is deposed from the Episcopal dignity, and from all Priestly communion. Candidian caused the placards which announced the sentence to be torn down, but the Council sent the Acts to Theodosius.

John of Antioch, with about fifteen Bishops, arriving on June 26 or 27, learnt with indignation of the hasty proceedings of the Council. He immediately, "whilst the dust of the journey was still on his robes," held at his residence a Conciliabulum, attended by forty-three Bishops, which he declared to be the Council of Ephesus, assembled by the Grace of God and command of the pious Emperors, by which Cyril and Memnon were deposed and excommunicated, Theodoret, who was present, subscribing the sentence. It excommunicated all those who had given their assent to the Council of Ephesus, until such time as they should repent; accepted anew the Nicene Creed, and anathematized the propositions of Cyril. It however made no mention of Nestorius, nor sanctioned his doctrine. The real Council, in another Session, excommunicated John and his adherents.

It is unnecessary to follow on the protracted and unseemly wrangle between the Sees of Alexandria and Antioch. Both represented their side of the matter to Theodosius, each attacked the other with unmeasured reproaches. The perplexed Emperor sent Count John as his commissioner to Ephesus, who arrived late in July, with the result that Nestorius, Cyril, and Memnon were all placed under arrest

Nestorius, who had hitherto relied on the Emperor, now found the danger of putting his trust in Princes. Cyril understood better than Nestorius the feeble-minded Theodosius, and cared nothing for an Emperor, except so far as he could bend him to his purpose. For this he left no stone unturned, and enlisted on his side the monks of Constantinople. The Archimandrite, Dalmatius, who had not left his cell for forty-eight years, now at Cyril's bidding, at the head of the monks and Archimandrites (one of whom was the afterwards famous Eutyches) of the neighbouring monasteries, gained an audience of the Emperor and terrified him into submission. Cyril, to the great impoverishment of the Church of Alexandria, lavished bribes on all sides to gain the Princess Pulcheria over to his side. This does not redound to her credit, but it must be attributed to the custom of the times. The Emperor veered round to the side of Cyril; ratified the Synodical deposition of Nestorius, and consented to the appointment as his successor of Maximian, 431—434, a man of pious and peaceful character, long resident as an orthodox Priest at Constantinople, who had already been consecrated by Cyril. Cyril returned to Alexandria, and Memnon was reinstated in the See of Ephesus.

In the Eighth and last Session, on August 31, of the Council of Ephesus, an important Canon affecting the Cypriot Church was decreed. Canon IV. of the Council of Nice had enacted that Bishops should be Consecrated by all the Bishops of the Province. The Cypriots now, by Rheginus, Bishop of Constantia, contended that from Apostolic times their Bishops had been Consecrated by the Bishop of the Province, and not by the Bishop of Antioch. The Council thereupon determined that "the Churches of Cyprus should be confirmed in their independence and in their right to elect and Consecrate their own Bishops."

It must, however, be borne in mind that John of Antioch did not take part in the Council.

The Emperor Theodosius now took counsel with Maximian and other Bishops and clergy of Constantinople "in a kind of Synod[d]," in the hope of effecting peace in the Church. By their advice an Imperial letter was addressed to John of Antioch, exhorting him to subscribe to the deposition of Nestorius and to condemn his doctrine. Another letter was sent to the famous Pillar-Saint, St. Simeon Stylites, seeking his co-operation. Theodosius recommended that Cyril should confine his anathemas to those who held false doctrine on the Sonship, and not extend them to the teaching of Nestorius, which the Antiochenes held to be correct. Cyril was thereby induced to make such explanations as satisfied both Theodoret and John of Antioch. John sent Paul, Bishop of Emesa, one of the Bishops who had joined in the deposition of Cyril and Memnon, with a conciliatory letter to Cyril which, while it expressed regret for his Twelve Anathemas, contained a Creed which Theodoret had drawn up, and which Cyril approved as orthodox. Still Cyril stood firm; nothing short of the consent of John to the deposition of Nestorius and the condemnation of his doctrine would satisfy him. In the end John gave way, and early in 433 abandoned Nestorius and Nestorianism. He wrote to the Emperor Theodosius and to Cyril that "he had determined to agree to the judgment pronounced against Nestorius, to recognize him as deposed, and to anathematize his infamous teaching;" and he allowed the Consecration of Maximian. He also wrote to the two Emperors, advocating the restoration of the deposed Bishops, not, however, including Nestorius.

Nestorius, deserted by all his friends, even Theodoret, though he persisted in refusing to anathematize him, condemning him as the cause of all the trouble, was permitted by the Emperor to retire to his former monastery near Antioch, where "he was loaded with presents and treated

[d] Hefele's Councils.

The Third and Fourth Œcumenical Councils. 213

with the highest respect [e]." But his residence in the neighbourhood of Antioch was a standing reproach to John, and at the request of the latter, Nestorius, after the space of four years, was banished to the Oasis of Libya (the Botany Bay of the time for the worst criminals), where he suffered much from marauders; and after being dragged about from place to place, and suffering from Catholics cruelties equal to those inflicted on St. Chrysostom, died from the effects of his ill-treatment about A.D. 439.

Theodoret consented to a reconciliation on the understanding that he would not anathematize Nestorius, but only the doctrine imputed to him. He did not at that time believe that Nestorius held the doctrine with which he was charged; he would rather he said have both his hands cut off than condemn the doctrine of Nestorius. It was not till ten years afterwards, at the Council of Chalcedon, that he assented to his condemnation.

Peace was now to outward appearance restored between the Eastern Bishops; but the last act of John was the first act in a long drama, and laid the foundation of a deplorable schism in the Eastern Church which has never since been healed [f].

Maximian dying A.D. 434, was succeeded by St. Proclus (434—447), titular Bishop of Cyzicus, who was at the time officiating as Priest in St. Sophia's. He had been the secretary of St. Chrysostom, and by his request Chrysostom's body was, on January 27, A.D. 438, translated with great pomp from Comana to Constantinople, and deposited near the Altar in the Church of the Holy Apostles, the place of sepulture of the Emperors and of the Bishops of Constantinople; the Emperor and Pulcheria assisting at the ceremony, and asking the pardon of Heaven for the grievous wrong inflicted by their parents on the sainted Bishop. St. Proclus died in October, 447, and was succeeded by Flavian. John of Antioch dying A.D. 441, was succeeded by his nephew Domnus (441—449); on the

[e] Evag. Schol. [f] See Chapter on the Separatist Churches.

death of Cyril in June, 444, his Archdeacon, Dioscorus, succeeded him at Alexandria, a violent and notoriously immoral man, who gained the See by the unscrupulous bribery of the eunuch of the weak Theodosius, and who brought with him the faults without the theological learning of St. Cyril. Juvenal was still Bishop of Jerusalem.

The reconciliation of John and Theodoret brought about to a certain extent a reconciliation between the latter and Cyril. But between the violence of Cyril and the amiable character of Theodoret there was little in common; another quarrel between them as to the works of Theodore of Mopsuestia ensued, Cyril attacking and Theodoret defending them, which was only ended by the death of Cyril.

Dioscorus having gained the ear of the Emperor at once set himself to ruining Theodoret. The heresy of Eutyches, whom Dioscorus favoured, was now coming into prominence. Theodoret was one of the first to expose the heresy, and on this and other grounds Dioscorus was his enemy. By accusing Theodoret of being a restless and turbulent man, the abettor of Nestorius, he obtained an Imperial edict that Theodoret should confine himself to his diocese, and even publicly anathematized him in Church. In order to crush both him and Flavian, Dioscorus prevailed on the Emperor to summon the Robber-Synod of Ephesus (A.D. 449), which Theodoret was forbidden by a second edict of the Emperor to attend.

The heresy of the Two Natures of our Lord had found no more strenuous opponent than in the aged Eutyches, who had been for seventy years the inmate of a monastery, and was at the time the Archimandrite of one near Constantinople. But in avoiding the heresy of the Two Natures he ran into the opposite extreme of attributing only one Nature to Christ. A charge was brought against him before Flavian by Eusebius, now Bishop of Dorylæum in Phrygia, who twenty years before had been the accuser of Nestorius. In vain the gentle and peace-loving Flavian recommended a private arrangement between the two who, as the opponents of Nestorius, had before been friends. Eusebius persisting in demanding an enquiry, a Council was appointed to be held in A.D. 448, at Constantinople, before which Eutyches was summoned to appear. In vain the aged Archimandrite thrice excused himself on the ground of his infirmities, and not before Flavian threatened him with deprivation as a Priest did he consent to appear. Being interrogated by the Imperial commissioners, Eutyches stated his belief that our Lord "before the union of the Godhead and Manhood had Two Natures, but after the Union only One;" he was then condemned to excommunication and deprivation. The monks rallied round their Archimandrite, who also gained the patronage, whilst Flavian fell under the disfavour, of the Court.

Celestine was succeeded at Rome by Sixtus III. (432—440), and he by Leo I. (440—461), to whom Eutyches and, as it would appear, Flavian also wrote. Leo in his answer complained that Flavian had acted without consulting him, and requested to know why Eutyches had been so hastily punished; but, on receiving a second letter from Flavian, he sided with him and expressed his sympathy. At the request of Dioscorus and Eutyches the Emperor summoned the Council which gained the name of Latrocinium or Robber-Council (σύνοδος ληστρική) to meet at Ephesus.

The Council accordingly met at the beginning of August, 449, in St. Mary's Church at Ephesus (the same Church in which the great Council had sat), but not under the presidency of Domnus, Bishop of Antioch, who was deprived of his right by an Imperial rescript, but under Dioscorus, the hereditary enemy of the Bishop of Constantinople, and himself a holder of the views of Eutyches. The next seat of honour was accorded to Julius, Bishop of Puteoli, who, with a Deacon named Hilary (destined to become the successor of Leo in the Papacy), represented the Pope of Rome; the usual order was reversed, Juvenal of Jerusalem occupying the third, Domnus the fourth, whilst the fifth place was accorded to Flavian.

The papal legates brought with them to Flavian the famous *Tome* of Pope Leo, which clearly set forth the orthodox doctrine of the One Person of God and Man; the inferiority of the Son as touching His Manhood, His equality with the Father as touching the Godhead.

Theodosius, who as we have seen was prejudiced in favour of the teaching of Eutyches, had allowed Barsumas, a furious Monophysite monk, as representative of the malcontent monastic body, to be summoned, who brought with him a turbulent band of one thousand monks to coerce the Synod to vote according to their wishes. The Council packed with gross unfairness by Dioscorus, who showed himself from first to last a thorough partizan, was marked from the commencement with violence; Dioscorus encouraged the ring-leaders, and so turbulent a scene was presented that the Imperial soldiers were called in to preserve order. When the Pope's Letter or Tome was handed in by Hilary, Dioscorus refused to allow it to be read; and when Flavian suggested that Eusebius the accuser of Eutyches should be called, his reasonable proposal was negatived. The weak Domnus of Antioch, who had been one of the first to impeach Eutyches in a synodal letter to Theodosius, now expressed his regret for having condemned him. The end was that Eutyches was acquitted, his doctrine pronounced orthodox, and the sentence against him annulled, Juvenal of Jerusalem assenting to the judgment. The Council also attacked Theodoret, in his absence, as the enemy of the Council of Ephesus and of the writings of the blessed Cyril. Dioscorus led the attack against him, as an impious wretch whose impiety was of long standing; who by his false teaching had led astray innumerable saints. The Synod sentenced him to be deprived not only of the Priesthood but of lay communion, as one unfit for people to associate with; and the sentence was approved by Domnus, whose own deposition and banishment was to follow the next day.

The question was brought forward whether Flavian and

Eusebius ought not to suffer the punishment to which Eutyches had been condemned. Several Bishops, and amongst them Thalassius of Cæsarea, though he held the doctrine of Eutyches [g], declared that whosoever went beyond the Nicene Creed was not orthodox. Dioscorus, in proposing the Nicene Creed as a test, had evidently aimed at Flavian, who in the late Synod of Constantinople had used the expression "Two Natures." "It follows," he said, "that Flavian of Constantinople and Eusebius of Dorylæum must be deposed from their ecclesiastical dignity; I pronounce, therefore, their deposition." Juvenal and Domnus signed the sentence. In vain Flavian protested, as did also the papal legates, against the action of Dioscorus. Dioscorus accused those who opposed him with exciting to sedition, called in the soldiers, and demanded that the Bishops should sign the deposition. The Bishops, many of whom had during the tumult tried to conceal themselves in obscure parts of the Church, were dragged forth, and eventually one hundred and thirty-five, forced by the threats of Dioscorus and the blows of the soldiers, signed the sentence. Flavian, brutally kicked and beaten by the agents of Dioscorus and Barsumas, and, it was said, by Dioscorus himself, was sentenced to banishment to Epipas, a village of Lydia, and thrown into prison, only surviving his cruel treatment three days. Eusebius managed to effect his escape to Rome. Dioscorus next turned against those who, though they had supported him at the Latrocinium, had previously opposed him; and Domnus was deposed and eventually retired to a monastery. As a just judgment on their conduct in the Council the names of Juvenal and Dioscorus were erased from the diptychs of the Orthodox Church.

Julius, the Papal Legate, who took a less conspicuous part in the Council than Hilary, although he opposed the deposition of Flavian, was left in peace and safety. Hilary, who met the decisions of the Council with unflinching

[g] He, however, on his retraction of the doctrine was acquitted at the Council of Chalcedon.

opposition, threatened by Dioscorus, and finding his longer stay at Ephesus unsafe, got off the best way he could, and fled by a clandestine and circuitous route (*per incognita et invia loca*) to Rome.

Anatolius, through the influence with the Emperor of Dioscorus, whose agent he had been at the Latrocinium, succeeded Flavian as Patriarch of Constantinople (449—458). Maximus chosen by Dioscorus, and appointed by Theodosius uncanonically without the clergy and people being consulted, to succeed Domnus, was consecrated Patriarch of Antioch (449—455) by Anatolius; he however proved himself to be an orthodox Bishop. The Emperor Theodosius, notwithstanding the protests of Pope Leo, confirmed the Latrocinium, and Dioscorus, now master of the whole Eastern Church, pronounced a sentence of excommunication against Leo. But it was impossible that the scandal and confusion caused by the Latrocinium could long be acquiesced in. Leo wrote to Theodosius in October, 449, stating that Flavian had appealed to Rome (to what other See could he appeal, persecuted as he was in the East?), and that in agreement with the Nicene Canons a General Council should be held in Italy. As we have already seen in the case of Zosimus, it was a favourite plan of the Bishops of Rome to confound the Canons of the comparatively unimportant Council of Sardica with those of the great Council of Nice. The Western Emperor, Valentinian, supported Leo, who also enlisted the sympathy of the orthodox Pulcheria on his side. But Theodosius remained inflexible and adhered to the Latrocinium, and to the belief that Flavian had been justly deposed.

The cause of Dioscorus was, however, wrecked through the death on July 19, 450, by a fall from his horse, of Theodosius. Pulcheria, who since she was sixteen years of age had reigned with him as co-regent with the title of Augusta, succeeded to the Empire. She with her two sisters had dedicated themselves to a life of virginity. But as a woman had never before been sole ruler of the

The Third and Fourth Œcumenical Councils. 219

Roman Empire, feeling that a prejudice would attach to her sex, she now took as her nominal husband Marcian, a Thracian of humble birth, a man much esteemed for his piety, who from being a common soldier had risen to be one of the most distinguished Generals and Statesmen of the time. Marcian was crowned Emperor on August 24, 450, and proved one of the most virtuous Princes that ever ruled over the Roman Empire (450—457).

Marcian and Pulcheria were both orthodox and opposed to Eutyches; the influence of Dioscorus was at an end; the Bishops and orthodox Confessors of the faith who had been banished after the Latrocinium, and amongst them Theodoret, were at once recalled; whilst many of the Bishops who had, under fear, subscribed the decrees of the Latrocinium signified their repentance.

The difficulties in the way of holding an Œcumenical Council being removed, Marcian acceded to the request which the Pope had made to Theodosius, that a Council should assemble; but not, as Leo desired, in Italy. But now that orthodoxy was re-established, the desire for a General Council had abated, the Catholics, and amongst them Pope Leo, feared lest a Council, in condemning Eutychianism, might favour Nestorianism.

The Emperor, however, thought differently to the Pope, and in obedience to his summons, the Bishops met at Nice, on September 1, 451. But as he was occupied with the invasion of Illyria by the Huns and other important affairs of State, he wrote to them requesting that they would transfer the Synod to Chalcedon, "because it was so near the capital that he could attend in person both to his affairs in Constantinople and to those of the Council." The Fourth General Council, at which as many as six hundred and fifty Bishops at different times attended, held its first meeting on October 8, A.D 451, at Chalcedon, in the Church of St. Euphemia the Martyr. The Emperor, having opposed the Pope's wish, first to have the Council in Italy, and then to have any Council at all, would feel inclined to make some amends to one who had assumed so firm and consistent an attitude with regard to the Latrocinium. This may account for the fact that the Roman legates presided, and for the first time, in an Œcumenical Council. Though addressing a meeting composed almost entirely of Eastern Bishops, they spoke in the Latin language, their speeches having to be translated into Greek. Anatolius, Patriarch of Constantinople, held the next place of dignity to the legates; then Maximus of Antioch, then Dioscorus, who, however, on the protest of one of the legates against his being a judge whilst he himself was to be judged, was obliged to sit aside; and last, but not till after the Fourth Session, the time-serving Juvenal, who finding that his name had been erased from the diptychs, and himself regarded with general indignation, had completely veered round to orthodoxy. So strong had been the feeling against him that he was not at first included in the general amnesty.

There were in all sixteen Sessions, the first of which was marked by riots as disgraceful as the Latrocinium. The introduction of Theodoret, whom the magistrates ordered to appear, created a fearful storm. No sooner had he entered than the Egyptians and the party of Dioscorus shouted that the teacher of Nestorianism should be turned out; the Eastern Bishops declared that they had been beaten and forced to sign the Latrocinium, and shouted "Turn out the enemies of Flavian and of the faith;" next the cry was turned against Dioscorus, "out with the murderer of Flavian .... that Pharaoh, the homicide Dioscorus." The storm was only abated through the interference of the magistrates, who begged them to remember that they were Bishops. In the Second Session, October 10, first the Nicene and immediately afterwards the Constantinopolitan form of the Creed was read, both forms being received with shouts of adhesion. In the Third, on October 13, Dioscorus was charged with his conduct at the previous Council as well as of moral offences, with refusing to allow

The Third and Fourth Œcumenical Councils. 221

the Pope's Letter to be read and with excommunicating him, and the Papal Legates gave the sentence that "the most holy Archbishop of Rome, Leo, through us and this Council" deprived him of his episcopal and all sacerdotal ministry.

In the Fourth Session, commencing Oct. 17, the Tome of Leo was accepted as being in agreement with the Creeds of Nice and Constantinople. Five Bishops who had been deposed for the part they had taken in the Latrocinium, and amongst them Juvenal, were restored.

In the Fifth Session, Oct. 22, the Synodical Letter of Cyril to Nestorius and the Eastern Bishops, and the Tome of Leo, were accepted as a Rule of Faith against the evil teaching of Eutyches. The Council confirmed the Faith of the Councils of Nice and Constantinople. It then condemned several heresies and declared ;—"We with one consent (συμφώνως), teach men to confess One and the same Son, the Lord Jesus Christ, perfect in Godhead, perfect in Manhood, truly God and truly Man, of a reasonable soul and body (ἐκ ψυχῆς λογικῆς καὶ σώματος) ; co-essential with the Father as touching the Godhead, and co-essential with us as touching the Manhood, in all things like unto us, sin only excepted (χωρὶς ἁμαρτίας) ; Begotten of the Father before all ages, as touching the Godhead, and in these latter days for us and our salvation Born of Mary, the Virgin Mother of God, as touching the Manhood, One and the same Christ, Son, Lord, Only-begotten, to be recognized in Two Natures, without confusion (ἀσυγχύτως), without change (ἀτρέπτως), without division (ἀδιαιρέτως), without separation (ἀχωρίστως), the distinction of Natures being in no wise removed by the union, but rather the property of each Nature being preserved, and continuing in One Person and hypostasis ; not parted and divided into two Persons, but one and the same Son, Only-begotten, God the Word, the Lord Jesus Christ, even as we have been taught from the beginning by the Prophets and the Lord Jesus Christ Himself, and the Fathers have delivered to us."

At the Sixth Session, October 25, Marcian and Pulcheria were present, the former delivering a speech in Latin, which was translated by an interpreter into Greek.

By the Seventh Canon of Nice an honorary precedence had been accorded to Jerusalem, "Saving the rights of the Metropolitan," i.e of Cæsarea. We find accordingly, Acacius, Bishop of Cæsarea, under that Canon, deposing St. Cyril, Bishop of Jerusalem. The chief object of Juvenal, during his long but not very creditable Episcopate, was to raise his See from the secondary rank, accorded it at Nice, into a Patriarchate. In the Seventh Session, October 25, of Chalcedon, the See of Jerusalem was, at the claim of Juvenal, raised into a Patriarchal See, with jurisdiction over the three Provinces of Palestine, which had before been subject to the Patriarch of Antioch, whilst Antioch was to have jurisdiction over Phœnicia and Arabia. At the Latrocinium Juvenal had subscribed before Domnus of Antioch. Elated probably by this success, he now put forth an arrogant claim for precedency over the Patriarch of Antioch, which was opposed by Maximus, Patriarch of that See, and rejected.

In the Eighth Session, October 26, the cause of Theodoret was brought forward, and he was, as the condition of his being admitted to communion, required to anathematize Nestorius. Menaced and wearied out, he gave way, and with some demur said; "Anathema to Nestorius and to every one who refuses to call the Holy Virgin Theotokos, or who divides the Only-begotten Son into two. I have subscribed the definition of faith, and the Letter of the most Holy Archbishop Leo; and this is my mind."

In the Ninth and Tenth Sessions, Oct. 27, Ibas, Bishop of Edessa, of whom we shall hear more further on, who had been condemned at the Latrocinium, was, on his subscribing the Letter of Leo, and adding an anathema of Nestorius, pronounced to be orthodox.

In the Fifteenth Session, Oct. 31, at which the Papal legates were absent, thirty Canons were passed, of which

The Third and Fourth Œcumenical Councils. 223

the Ninth and the Twenty-eighth are of special importance.

Canon IX. forbade a clergyman to apply to the secular Courts, and enacted, that if he had a controversy with another, he should apply to his own Bishop, or if he had a complaint against his own or another Bishop, to the Metropolitan, or if the Bishop or clergyman had cause against a Metropolitan he should apply to the Exarch of the Diocese (διοίκησις, a group of Provinces), or to the throne of Constantinople.

Canon XXVIII., after reciting and confirming the Third Canon of Constantinople, enacted, "We following in all respects the decrees of the Holy Fathers, and recognizing the Canon of the 150 Bishops most beloved of God (i.e. of the Council of Constantinople) decree, and vote the same as they did concerning the privileges (τὰ πρεσβεῖα) of the most holy Church of Constantinople, which is New Rome. For the Fathers have with good reason granted its privileges to the throne of Old Rome, on account of its being the Imperial city, and the 150 Fathers, most beloved of God, acting under the same consideration, have given the same privileges to the most holy throne of New Rome, rightly judging that the city which is the seat of Empire, and is equal to the Imperial Rome in other privileges, should be also honoured as she is, in ecclesiastical affairs, as being the second and next after her."

This Canon was objected to by the Papal legates, who in the Sixteenth Session, November 1, remonstrated against it. But when one of the legates asserted that the Bishops had been forced to sign, he was met with an indignant denial; and Ætius, Archdeacon of Constantinople, said that the Canon had been regularly brought forward and enacted, and had been subscribed by one hundred and ninety-two Bishops.

At the Council of Chalcedon both forms of the Creed, the Nicene and the Constantinopolitan, were recited, and in the Fourth Session the Council declared that the Creed taught what was perfect (τὸ τέλειον) concerning the Father, Son, and Holy Ghost. It also decreed that "it was not lawful for any one to propose, compile, hold, or teach any other faith, under pain of being deposed, if they were amongst the clergy, of being anathematized, if amongst the laity." The decree was recited, word for word, and re-affirmed with equal solemnity in the Fifth and Sixth Œcumenical Councils; not a word was to be added to, or taken from, the Creed. Most explicit on this head was the oath taken by the Popes themselves. They swore at their election to preserve unmutilated the decrees of the First Six Œcumenical Councils, with an imprecation on themselves, if they were unfaithful to their oath; *Si præter hæc aliquid agere presumpsero, vel ut præsumatur permisero, erit mihi Deus in illâ terribili die judicii depropitius.* We look in vain for any General Council, we look in vain for any Papal Encyclical, authorizing the insertion, yet we find for the first time an alteration made in the Pontifical oath of the Eleventh Century, and all the Churches of the West, with that of Rome at the head, using the Creed with the Filioque Clause appended to it [h].

The Pontificate of Leo I. marks an era in the Papacy, and in its connexion with the Eastern Church. When he became Pope, Alexandria was, under St. Cyril, probably reputed the highest of all the five Patriarchal Sees. Leo was the most able Bishop that had as yet presided over the See of Rome, and was the foremost man, not only in the Church, but also in society. Under him the tide turned, and whilst the Eastern Patriarchs were engaged in an internecine struggle, Leo was laying the foundation of the pre-eminence of the Roman See, which it has never since lost.

If the Roman Emperors had, the Roman Empire had not, either in the East or in the West, become Christian; it needed new blood to regenerate it, and in the Western part of the Empire the new blood was now at hand. The

[h] Ffoulkes, The Church's Creed or the Crown's Creed?

great tide of German nations, one tribe pushing on another, was sweeping over Europe, to settle and make nations in the West, whilst the Germans could never effect a permanent settlement in the East. Barbarians as they were, they had in them the seeds of the civilization which the Roman Empire wanted, and they brought with them the material which was most needed for building up the future Christendom.

Most of them were already Christians, although in the imperfecting form of Arianism. Theophilus, a Gothic Bishop, was present at the great Council of Nice. His successor, in A.D. 348, Ulfilas, translated the Scriptures into the Gothic language, suppressing the Books of Samuel and Kings for fear of irritating the fierce and sanguinary spirit of the Barbarians[1]. The *Apostle of the Goths*, as he was styled, exercised over them an unbounded influence, and through him the whole nation, both Goths and Visigoths, embraced Christianity in the Arian form. From them, Arianism spread through the other tribes of Germany and became the Creed of the nations which conquered the Roman Empire. They subverted the Western Empire, but embraced the Catholic religion of the Romans; they gave new life to and regenerated the West, but some great Providence (as Professor Kingsley says in his *Hypatia*) prevented all their attempts to do the same for the East; and under the army of Belisarius disappeared the last chance of their restoring the East, as they had the West, to life.

The personal character and unflinching orthodoxy of Leo marked him out as the very man whom the circumstances of the Empire needed, and he paved the way for the future grandeur of the Roman and the decadence of the Eastern Church. When the Western Empire was tottering to its fall, and Attila, fulfilling his destiny as the *scourge of God*, was marching on Rome, and encamped on the shores of Lake Benacus; when the cowardly Emperor Valentinian sent an embassy to deprecate his wrath, the

[1] Gibbon, VI. 269.

Pope, risking his life for the safety of his country, entered the Barbarian's tent, and through his venerable and majestic appearance and commanding eloquence, succeeded in obtaining peace for the Empire. When, again, Genseric was completing the work which Attila had left unfinished, the good services of Leo were again requisitioned, and if he did not meet with the same success, nor was able to avert the sacking of Rome, he was at least able somewhat to mitigate its horrors.

Whilst the Eastern Patriarchs were quarrelling amongst themselves, and the Greek Church was agitated with subtle distinctions as to the Homoousion or Homoiousion, the One or Two Natures in our Saviour, the Western Church, if slightly ruffled by the Donatists and Pelagians, had been enjoying peace and rest, and under Leo it was the rallying-point of Orthodoxy, as the See of Carthage had been under St. Cyprian. The Bishops of Constantinople and Alexandria, mutually jealous of each other, sought the alliance of the Western Patriarch, who, apprehensive of the rival See of Constantinople, threw his ægis over the latter. The Clementine fiction that St. Peter had been Bishop of Rome now became magnified into the claim of the Popes that St. Peter was the *Rock* on which Christ built His Church. St. Augustine, the greatest of the Latin Fathers, who had not been dead twenty years when Leo I. entered on his Pontificate, shows that that was not the belief of the Church, for he expressly states that that Rock was Christ Himself[k].

When the Canon of Chalcedon was reported to Leo, he wrote angry letters to Marcian, Pulcheria, and the Patriarch Anatolius, the last of whom he accused of having influenced the Council. The Patriarchs of Alexandria and Antioch had subscribed the Canon, but the Pope of Rome rejected it on the ground that it was an usurpation of the rights of other Bishops, especially of the two Patriarchs, who, he said, possessed the precedence next to Rome;

---

[k] " Super hanc Petram quam confessus es . . . . ædificabo Ecclesiam meam ;
i e *Me Ipsum* . . . . *Petrus ædificatur super Petram, non Petra super Petrum.*"

and he rested his case on a Canon of Nice which, there is reason for believing, except in a Roman Version, had no existence. Anatolius adhered to the Canon because it was "decreed by the whole Synod." And Anatolius had the better of the argument, for both Greek and Latin Churches profess that the Œcumenical Councils sat under the guidance of the Holy Spirit, so that if one part of the Canons is accepted on that ground, the whole must be accepted also. Leo signified to the Emperor his consent to the doctrinal decrees and the condemnation of heretics, but persisted to the end in refusing the twenty-eighth Canon. It, however, remained in force, and his great successor, Gregory I., acknowledged the Four Œcumenical Councils, and said that they are to be received with the reverence paid to the Four Gospels.

The Canon, however, increased the jealousies between the Sees of Rome and Constantinople, and was the principal cause which led to the schism of the Eastern and Western Churches. Notwithstanding the new life infused into the Western, new life was not infused into the Eastern part of the Empire; under the union between Church and State, the Eastern Church suffered more from the Emperors than the remote Western Church, and whilst the latter was able to develope its resources, the downward career of Eastern Christianity went on increasing till it was overwhelmed by its Mahometan invaders. The Council of Chalcedon defined clearly the doctrine of the Catholic Church when it anathematized those who held that there were in our Lord Two Natures before the union and only One after it, but so far from giving peace to the Church, it intensified theological difficulties. In avoiding Eutychianism, it seemed to some to fall into Nestorianism, and to condemn their great champion, St. Cyril. Such was the case amongst the Copts, who formed the majority of the Christians in Egypt, and out of it grew the great Eutychian or Monophysite controversy.

The population of Egypt was made up of two distinct

races, the native Egyptian and the Greek residents; the latter accepted the decrees of the Council of Chalcedon; the former made the Council a national question, threw off their adherence, which had never been more than a merely nominal one, to the Patriarch of Constantinople, rejected the Orthodox Church as a State-made Church, and stigmatized its adherents as Melchites or Imperialists.

The deposition of Dioscorus was confirmed by the Emperor, and he was banished to Gangra in Paphlagonia, where he died A.D. 454. St. Proterius, Arch-Priest of Alexandria, who had been deputed by Dioscorus himself to take charge of the Church during his absence, was elected by Imperial mandate to succeed him. When news of the deposition of their Bishop reached Egypt, the indignation of the native population knew no bounds; with one consent they refused to acknowledge the decision of the Council, or, if their Bishop was excommunicated, they would be excommunicated too; so long as he lived they would acknowledge no other Bishop. Proterius was from the first regarded as the Emperor's Bishop; he had removed the name of Dioscorus from the Diptychs, and inserted the Council of Chalcedon; he was a heretic who had intruded himself into the fold when it was bereft of its shepherd. When Dioscorus died, though still refusing to acknowledge Proterius, they at first refrained from electing their own Bishop. But, A.D. 457, four years after his virgin-wife Pulcheria, who was canonized by the Church, the Emperor Marcian died. The Patrician Aspar might, if he would have subscribed the Nicene faith, have placed the diadem on his own head; as he was unwilling to do so, Leo I. (457—474) was by his recommendation elected, and received the Imperial Crown from the hands of the Patriarch (Anatolius). To Leo the title of Great was conferred by the Greeks, but rather in reference to his orthodoxy and his opposition to Nestorianism and Eutychianism, than for any other cause.

When the news of the death of Marcian reached Egypt, the hopes of the Monophysites were raised, and the malcontent party now elected Timothy, a Priest of Alexandria, whom Proterius had excommunicated and banished ; a man to whom the nickname of Ælurus (*the Cat*) was applied, on account, it has been supposed, of his creeping by night into the cells of the monks to induce them to elect him as their Bishop ; assuring them that he was an Angel sent by God to deliver them from Proterius. An outbreak occurred in which Proterius, who took refuge in his Baptistery (thinking that the sacredness of the place and the day, for it was Good Friday, would protect him), was murdered ; Timothy was intruded into the See, and publicly renounced the communion of the Egyptian Chuich with Rome, Constantinople, and Antioch.

Equally unacceptable were the decrees of Chalcedon to the Archimandrites and monks of Palestine, and Juvenal had, in 452, to give place to a monk of disreputable character named Theodosius, and was forced to fly to Constantinople[1]. Theodosius was a native of Alexandria, and probably one of the gang of turbulent monks whom Barsumas had taken with him to the Latrocinium, and he afterwards attended the Council of Chalcedon. Hurrying away from Chalcedon to Jerusalem he persuaded the monks that the Council had betrayed the true faith, and favoured Nestorianism. In vain he attempted to gain to his side St. Euthymius, the famous anchorite of Palestine, but he found a patroness in the widow of the Emperor Theodosius II., Eudocia, who was living in Jerusalem in exile, and for a time held the Eutychian heresy. For twenty months he managed to hold the See ; but on Eudocia being induced by Euthymius to join the orthodox party, her example was followed by a large number of the monks. Juvenal was then, in 453, enabled to recover his own ; Theodosius seeking refuge amongst the monks of Syria. But no one, Orthodox or Monophysite, could place confidence in the time-serving Juvenal, and a cloud hung over him to his

[1] Theodosius "had been expelled a monastery and publicly whipped at Alexandria for sedition." Evag. Schol.

death, A.D. 458, when he was succeeded by Anastasius (458—478). The schism continued under Gerontius, who gave great trouble by his factious endeavours to uproot the Council of Chalcedon, but was at length healed under Martyrius, the successor of Anastasius in the Patriarchate of Jerusalem.

In the same year as Juvenal, died Anatolius, Patriarch of Constantinople. He had once been, as we have seen, a favourer of Dioscorus, but after his consecration he publicly condemned both Nestorius and Eutyches, and in the difficult circumstances of the times he seems, especially at Chalcedon, to have been a wise and prudent Bishop. He is the first of the Greek hymn-writers of whom we have any record, and is the author of the three beautiful hymns in Hymns Ancient and Modern; the well-known Evening hymn, "The Day is past and over;" and the hymns beginning, "Fierce raged the tempest o'er the deep;" "The Son of God goes forth to war;" the first two translated by Dr. Neale, the last by Bishop Heber. Of his Evening hymn, Dr. Neale says, "it is to the scattered hamlets of Chios and Mitylene what Bishop Ken's Evening hymn is to the villages of our own land, and its melody singularly plaintive and soothing."

The Monophysites having overwhelmed the Bishoprics of Alexandria and Jerusalem, soon got possession of that of Antioch. Maximus, dying A.D. 455, was succeeded by Basil (456—459), and he by Acacius (459—461), after whom followed Martyrius (461—471). Peter, a monk of Constantinople, surnamed, from the trade which he had sometime followed, the Fuller (ὁ γναφεύς), gained the ear of Zeno, the son-in-law of the Emperor Leo, with whom he proceeded to Antioch, and there formed so strong a faction against Martyrius, that the latter, who was accused of being a Nestorian, as those who, not Monophysites, commonly were, abdicated the See, and sought an asylum with Gennadius (458—471), who had succeeded Anatolius as Patriarch of Constantinople.

The Third and Fourth Œcumenical Councils. 231

Peter, in order to establish his own Monophysite views against the Council of Chalcedon, introduced into the hymn called by the Greeks Trisagion, the words, "Who was crucified for us [m]" (ὁ σταυρωθεὶς δι' ἡμας), meaning thereby to imply that Jesus suffered, as God, on the Cross; hence his followers were called by the Greeks, Theopaschites [n]. The Orthodox Emperor was, however, indignant at this uncanonical usurpation, and after a Synod held at Antioch, sentenced Peter to banishment in the Oasis, and Julian (471—476) was appointed by the orthodox party in his place. Peter, however, contrived to escape to Constantinople, where he lay hid in the monastery of the Acœmetæ. The reign of Leo was one of comparative peace, and Eutychianism yielded to the orthodoxy of the Emperor. Unwilling to call together another General Council, he consulted the Bishops and orthodox clergy, amongst others the Pillar-Saint Simeon Stylites, concerning the troublous state of the Church of Alexandria; and by their advice he sent orders, A.D. 460, to the military commander at Alexandria, to expel Timothy Ælurus, and also to summon a Council for the election of an orthodox successor. Timothy then professed himself ready to accept the decrees of Chalcedon, but the Emperor refused to accept his submission and banished him to the Chersonese.

Another Timothy, called Salophaciolus (*wearer of the white cap*), an Orthodox Churchman, was, on account of the gentleness, which he carried to a fault (replacing the name of Dioscorus on the Diptychs), as well as the purity, of his character, appointed in his place. For sixteen years he so successfully presided over the See as to gain him the affection even of the Monophysites, who were wont to

---

[m] The hymn, says Bingham, B. xiv. ch. ii., though really much older, was in the Orthodox form ascribed to Proclus, Patriarch of Constantinople.

[n] This addition the heretic Severus, whom the Emperor Anastasius I. intruded into the See of Antioch, continued to use, and all the separatist communions of the East, except the Nestorians, who separated before the addition was made, persist in retaining it to the present day.

say, "though we do not communicate with thee, yet we love thee."

In 471, Gennadius, Bishop of Constantinople, died, and was succeeded by Acacius (471—489), and he, after the short interval of Favritta, by Euphemius (489—496), an uncompromising supporter of orthodoxy.

In 474 the Emperor Leo died. By an edict issued in his reign, the title of "Mother of all the Churches and of the Orthodox Religion" was conferred on the Patriarchate of Constantinople. Leo was succeeded by his grandson, Leo II., the son of Zeno by his daughter Ariadne, and on the death of the boy-emperor in the same year, Zeno himself, an Isaurian by birth, who was unpopular amongst the Greeks, for a double reason, that they regarded him as heterodox and a barbarian, became Emperor (474—476; and again 477—491).

The treatment of the Eastern Church at this period by the Emperors has its counterpart (if we may be pardoned the homely comparison), in what children call the game of see-saw; the Emperors favoured now orthodoxy, now Monophysitism, to suit their political interests. The Patriarchate of Constantinople under Acacius was taken up with these controversies, and ended in a thirty-five years' schism between the Eastern and Western Churches.

The Emperor Zeno ($αὐτοκράτωρ\ Καῖσαρ\ Ζήνων$, as he styled himself) was a contemptible ruler whom no one could trust, at heart a Monophysite, he was always wavering between Orthodox and Monophysite views, and at first found it to his interest to favour the former. In 476 he was driven out by Basiliscus, the brother of the widowed Empress Verona; Basiliscus, being desirous of obtaining the aid of the Monophysites, issued in condemnation of the Council of Chalcedon and the Tome of Pope Leo, an Encyclical Letter, which he called upon all the Bishops to subscribe under pain of deposition. This letter was subscribed by Peter Fuller, Anastasius, Bishop of Jerusalem, and Timothy Ælurus, Acacius of Constantinople refusing to sign. Timothy

The Third and Fourth Œcumenical Councils. 233

was thereupon reinstated in the Bishopric of Alexandria, and the gentle Salophaciolus withdrew into the monastery of Canopus, in a suburb of Alexandria. Julian was deposed and Peter Fuller restored to Antioch.

In 477, the Patriarch Acacius effected a rising against Basiliscus, by which Zeno was restored; Peter Fuller was deposed by an Antiochene Synod; and Timothy Ælurus dying in that year, the Monophysites elected as his successor his Archdeacon, Peter Mongus (*stammerer*). The orthodox party, however, were now in the ascendant, and Salophaciolus was restored, and through his wise moderation the Church of Alexandria enjoyed peace till his death, A D. 482.

John Thalaia, who had been recommended to Zeno by Salophaciolus, was elected by the orthodox party as his successor. Simplicius (468—483) was now Bishop of Rome. Thalaia sent the usual Encyclical Letter announcing his election to the Patriarchs, and amongst them to Simplicius; but the Patriarch Acacius was offended that the announcement (owing to neglect on the part of Thalaia's messenger) had not also been made to him. Thalaia seems also to have promised Zeno that he would never accept the See of Alexandria. Acacius now took the side of the Monophysites against Thalaia, and persuaded the Emperor, who considered Thalaia a perjurer and was exasperated by the preference apparently shown to the Pope of Rome over the Patriarch of Constantinople, to request Simplicius to condemn him as unworthy of the Episcopate. At the same time he suggested to Simplicius the appointment of Peter Mongus as the means of restoring peace to the Church. Simplicius replied that he would suspend his judgment till the charges brought against Thalaia were investigated, but that he could not possibly recognize a heretic like Peter as Patriarch. Zeno then sent orders to Alexandria that Thalaia should be expelled and Peter appointed. Thalaia went to Rome, where he enlisted the sympathy of Simplicius, but eventually finding his chance of the Patriarchate hopeless, accepted the Bishopric of Nola in Campania.

"With Thalaia," says Dr. Neale[o], "the Catholic succession of Alexandrian Bishops ceased for nearly sixty years."

In 482 Zeno, by the advice, and probably in the very words, of Acacius, issued his celebrated Henoticon, or *Instrument of Union*, addressed to the Bishops and clergy, and to the monks and laity throughout Alexandria, Egypt, Libya and Pentapolis. It pronounced an anathema on both Nestorius and Eutyches; and approved the faith as laid down in the Councils of Nice, Constantinople and Ephesus, without recognizing the Council of Chalcedon. It declared Mary to be the Mother of God, and Jesus Christ to be ὁμοούσιος with the Father as touching the Godhead, ὁμοούσιος with us as touching the Manhood; and anathematized all those by whom the Natures "are divided, confused, or reduced to a phantom;" and censured all other doctrines, if any such have been taught "either at Chalcedon or any other Council whatever" (ἢ ἐν Χαλκηδόνι ἢ ἐν οἵᾳ δήποτε συνόδῳ).

Peter Mongus by subscribing the Henoticon commended himself to Zeno, by whom his election to the Patriarchate of Alexandria was, through the influence of Acacius, confirmed. Peter Fuller also on signing the Henoticon was reinstated in the Patriarchate of Antioch, where he renewed his violence against the orthodox party, banishing the Bishops who refused the Henoticon.

It could not be expected that such a compromise as the Henoticon would satisfy every, or indeed any, party. It was, however, accepted by the Patriarchs of Constantinople, Alexandria and Antioch, and found many adherents in the Churches of the East. The orthodox party resented the Emperor's taking upon himself to dictate to them on spiritual matters, as well as the ambiguous language of the Henoticon with respect to the Council of Chalcedon, whilst they suspected Acacius of a leaning towards Monophysitism. It was, however, generally acquiesced in as a reasonable toleration.

[o] Alexandria, II. 21.

The Third and Fourth Œcumenical Councils. 235

Peter Mongus, now Patriarch of Alexandria, anathematized the Council of Chalcedon and the Tome of Leo, and deprived and banished some Egyptian Bishops who adhered to the Chalcedonian Faith. But the extreme Eutychians were disgusted with the double dealing of their unprincipled and time-serving Patriarch, who, though he anathematized the Council of Chalcedon and the Tome of Leo, accepted the Henoticon; so they disowned him, omitted his name from their Diptychs, and became henceforward known as Acephali, or those who own no Head or Bishop.

The Henoticon was never accepted in Rome, which was now practically independent of the Eastern Empire. Simplicius addressed a letter to Acacius signifying disapproval of his conduct on the ground of his communicating with Mongus in respect of the latter being a Eutychian. Acacius replied that he was not only Patriarch of Alexandria, but an orthodox Bishop. Shortly afterwards Simplicius died and was succeeded by Felix III. (483—492), who at once rejected the Henoticon, and anathematized all the Bishops who had subscribed it. We now witness the deep degradation to which the dissensions of the Patriarchs had brought the Eastern Church. Felix took the unprecedented step of summoning the Patriarch of Constantinople to Rome, and, on his not obeying the summons, issued, in July, 484, a sentence of excommunication against him. The sentence was communicated to Acacius by the Acæmetæ, the society of monks which derived their name from their keeping up night and day an uninterrupted series of services.

Acacius was sentenced by the Roman Prelate to deprivation of his Episcopal and Priestly Orders, and separation from the Communion of the faithful. Felix also wrote to Zeno to separate himself, under pain of excommunication, from Mongus. The sentence had little effect on the Patriarch, who did not acknowledge any superiority in the See of Rome, and took no notice of it, except to retaliate by issuing, Aug. 1, 484, a counter-sentence of excommunication against Felix. Thus by the Henoticon was caused a schism between the two Patriarchates which lasted thirty-five years.

In A.D. 476, the succession of the Western Emperors had come to an end. It could not be expected that the Romans, with the experience of such a succession of Popes as Leo the Great, Hilary, and Simplicius, would tolerate for ever the humiliation to which their Emperors had brought them. The last act in the long reign of the despicable Valentinian III. was the murder of Ætius, the greatest General of the time. The debauched Emperor had treacherously outraged the chaste and unsuspecting wife of a Roman Senator, named Maximus, by whose adherents he was, in revenge, murdered, Maximus being elected to succeed him. The murder of Ætius was followed by the sacking of Rome by the Vandals. Maximus only reigned three months, but long enough to force the unwilling Eudoxia, the widow of the Emperor whom he had murdered, to become his wife; Eudoxia in revenge called in the Vandals from Africa, on whose approach Maximus was murdered by his own soldiers. Between A D. 455—475, no fewer than nine Emperors ruled over the West, and, A.D. 476, Romulus Augustus, derisively nick-named Augustulus, yielded to Odoacer, King of the Heruli, and signified his resignation to the Senate. The Roman Senate voted that one Emperor was sufficient, and wrote to Zeno that he should rule over the whole Empire with the seat of government at Constantinople. Under Leo the Great, the Papacy had become the rallying-point of orthodoxy to East and West, and such it continued to be under Simplicius. Is it to be wondered that, with such a contrast before them of their temporal and spiritual rulers, the Romans preferred to be governed, spiritually as well as temporally, by their Popes? They could not have been enamoured of such Emperors in the East as the heretical Basiliscus and Zeno; and the application of the Roman Senate to the latter must have been prompted by the desire and expectation of their being some day able to shelve the Empire altogether.

An Emperor resident at Constantinople would interfere, they imagined, but little in affairs at Rome. The abeyance of the Western Empire immensely conduced to the prestige of the Papacy, and the Popes became practically the rulers of Rome. But the Romans were disappointed in their expectation; and they were now to be subjected to an Arian King instead of an Emperor who would, at least, have been orthodox. Odoacer did not assume the title of Emperor, but ruled over Italy with the title of King, having his residence at Ravenna, and when he was, A.D. 493, murdered, the Kingdom of Italy was transferred to the Ostrogoths in the person of Theodoric the Great (493—526). Theodoric was also an Arian, but whilst he allowed the Catholics the free exercise of their religion, he claimed, as Constantine and his successors had, to be supreme over the Church, and to confirm the election of, and even himself to appoint and depose, the Pope.

Zeno having, in 489, destroyed the famous school of Edessa, the stronghold of Nestorianism in the Empire, died A.D. 491, and was succeeded by Anastasius I. (491—518). Zeno's plan of governing the Church by an Imperial concordat had proved a signal failure, and at the time of his death it appeared as if the whole Eastern Church would be swallowed up in the gulf of Monophysitism. The Emperor Anastasius, who owed his succession to his marriage with Zeno's widow, Ariadne, is described as a man of profound piety; he was, however, a Monophysite of the extreme sect of the Acephali; and but for his heretical opinions would have been regarded as a model Emperor. He desired a comprehension in the Orthodox Church of all sects of religion, his watchword being the Henoticon to which he endeavoured to bind all the Bishops; but being a Monophysite he was looked upon with suspicion by the Orthodox.

The schism between the Church of Constantinople and the Western Church continued; but it may elucidate matters, if, before proceeding further, we take stock of the occupants of the principal Sees at this time. Acacius, Patriarch of Constantinople, died A.D. 489; and the Popes of Rome, no longer able to contend with the living, kept up the controversy against the dead, Patriarch. Acacius was succeeded by Favritta, who in his Synodal Letter to Peter Mongus, sought communion with him, whilst in his Synodal Letter to the Pope he sought reconciliation with Rome, but without undertaking to erase the names of Acacius and Peter Mongus from the Diptychs. His Pontificate, however, was, after a few months, before the Pope's reply reached Constantinople, cut short by his death, and he was succeeded by Euphemius (489—deposed 496, died 515). Peter Fuller, Patriarch of Antioch, dying A.D. 488, was succeeded by Palladius (488—498), a Monophysite. On the death of Peter Mongus, A.D. 490, the Patriarchate of Alexandria devolved on Athanasius (490—497), also a Monophysite. Sallustius was, in succession to Martyrius, Patriarch of Jerusalem (486—494); he was the friend and patron of St. Sabas, the Founder of the Lavra which bears his name, and was probably inclined to orthodoxy, although he, as is supposed in the cause of peace, accepted the Henoticon, and communicated with Athanasius the Monophysite Patriarch of Alexandria. Peter Mongus' answer to Favritta's Letter, arriving after the death of the latter, fell into the hands of his successor Euphemius, who, as it anathematized the Council of Chalcedon, renounced communion with him. Euphemius sent the usual Synodal Letter announcing his election to Pope Felix, who refused to acknowledge him as Patriarch, unless he removed from the Diptychs the names of his two predecessors, Acacius and Favritta. Pope Felix died in February, A.D. 492, and was succeeded by Gelasius I. (492—496), who put forward the highest pretensions for the Roman See, nor did he write, as was usual, to the Patriarch of Constantinople announcing his succession. Notwithstanding this, Euphemius twice again wrote to him, expressing a desire for the reconciliation of the Churches, but stating that the people of Constantinople would never allow the name of Acacius to be removed from the Diptychs, for that he had only communicated with Peter Mongus, after that the latter had publicly renounced his heresy. Gelasius in his reply refused all terms except unconditional surrender to the See of Rome; he spoke of the custom of the Roman Prelates announcing their election to *inferior* Bishops as a condescension. The Pope's sneer at the Patriarchate of Constantinople was of course no proof nor argument, but only showed that the Patriarch of Constantinople was the superior of the Pope of Rome in manners. Gelasius also made one of those slips which were now becoming so common with the Popes; he based his pretensions on the Canons of the Church, meaning thereby the Canons of Nice, whereas there was only one, the doubtful one of the inferior Council of Sardica, which could possibly be construed into giving supreme jurisdiction to Rome. He demanded the erasure of Acacius' name from the Diptychs; the end was that Gelasius' own name was erased from the Diptychs of the Eastern Churches, and any further result was frustrated by the death of the Pope.

Euphemius soon put himself in opposition to the Emperor Anastasius, whom he accused of being a heretic, and, notwithstanding the entreaties of the Empress Ariadne, refused to crown him until he had bound him by a solemn promise to respect the Council of Chalcedon, and to uphold the Catholic faith.

The Patriarch still continued to thwart the Emperor; it may also well be doubted whether Euphemius was the wisest of counsellors. The Emperor, who chafed under the severe restriction imposed upon him at his coronation, only awaited an opportunity for deposing him. The opportunity presented itself through an act of imprudence on the part of Euphemius, in a secular matter, which determined the Emperor to get rid of him; he brought it before a Synod in 496, at Constantinople, with the result that the obsequious Bishops excommunicated and deposed the Patriarch.

Macedonius, his successor, was, like Euphemius, a Catholic, and on that account little more acceptable to the Emperor; but he was the nephew of a former Patriarch, Gennadius (458—471), and Anastasius knew that his election, which was also favoured by the Empress, would for that reason be popular. In vain the Emperor tried to persuade him to condemn the Council of Chalcedon and to release him from his promise to Euphemius; and even went so far as to induce the Eutychian monks and disaffected clergy of the city to outrage and insult him. But the people of Constantinople were well affected both to the Council and to their Patriarch; riots, in which the statues of the Emperor were destroyed and his life was imperilled, ensued; for three days he lay concealed in a suburb, and then implored the aid of the Patriarch, who openly charged him with being the cause of the calamities which beset the Church.

But the conflict between an Emperor and a Patriarch was an unequal one. The Emperor was urged on by Severus, one of the Acephali, and Julian, Bishop of Halicarnassus, the principal leaders of the Monophysite party; false accusations of immorality and Nestorianism were trumped up against the Patriarch, and he, A.D. 511, was, like his predecessor, deposed and banished to Gangra, where he died shortly afterwards. The day after his deposition Timothy (511—517), a man of bad character, and, as far as he had any convictions at all, a Monophysite, was appointed to succeed him. Timothy subscribed the Henoticon, and anathematized the Council of Chalcedon, and, in concert with the Emperor, he, in 512, caused the words "Who was crucified for us" to be added to the Trisagion in the Churches of Constantinople.

Thus the Patriarchate of Constantinople was now in the hands of a Monophysite. Alexandria was the hot-bed of Monophysitism; the successors of Athanasius II. were Monophysites; John I. (497—507), and John II. (507—517), Dioscorus II. (517 — 520), Timothy III. (520 — 537). Flavian II., who succeeded Palladius in the Patriarchate of Antioch, was in 512 deposed by Anastasius, and Severus

(512—519), the leader of the Acephali, the extreme section of the Monophysites, appointed The orthodoxy of Sallustius, Patriarch of Jerusalem, was at least doubtful.

The injustice of Anastasius to the orthodox excited the indignation of Vitalian, the Arian General of Theodoret, the King of Italy. At the head of an army of Huns and Bulgarians he appeared before the walls of Constantinople, and the Emperor shortly before his death was forced to sign a treaty guaranteeing justice to the Orthodox Church.

CHAPTER VII.

The Separatist Churches of the East.

RESULT of the Councils of Ephesus and Chalcedon—Question as to how far the Separatist Churches are heretical—And if they are schismatical—The Nestorians or Eastern Syrians—The School of Edessa—Ibas—The School of Nisibis—Synod of Seleucia—Ghengis Khan—Timour—The Uniat Chaldæans—The Nziri—The Mattran—The persecution of the Eastern Syrians by the Turks and Kurds—Archbishop Benson's Mission to them—Christians of St Thomas—Alexis di Menexes—They embrace Jacobitism—The Jacobites—Jacob Baradai—Their Maphrian—Abelpharagius—The Copts—Continued persecution suffered by them—Occupation of Egypt by the French—Christian Churches at Khartoum—Christianity eradicated in Nubia—Failure of Protestant Missions amongst the Copts—A reforming Coptic party—The English occupation of Egypt—The Abyssinians—Foundation of their Church—Prester John—The Portuguese and Jesuits in Abyssinia—Their Abuna—The Judaisers of Christendom—The Armenians—Gregory the Illuminator—Encyclical of Pope Leo XIII—St Mesiob—The absence of their Catholicos from Council of Chalcedon—Synod of Tovin—The Council of Florence—Etchmiadzen part of Russian Empire—Armenian Uniats—The Maronites—St Maro—Become Uniats—The Maronites and the Druses.

THE schisms which resulted from the Councils of Ephesus and Chalcedon arose as much, if not more, out of national rather than ecclesiastical differences, national antipathy seized the opportunity afforded by theological controversy to revolt at the same time from the Orthodox Church and from the Roman Empire. Alexandria and Antioch, next to Rome the two greatest cities in the world, were Greek colonies planted in a soil which was never thoroughly Hellenized; Egypt and Syria, even when governed by Macedonians, who were practically Greek Kings, never willingly acquiesced in what they considered an alien yoke; nor, says Professor Freeman, were their intellectual and theological natures ever subdued by their political conquerors. The schism in the Greek Church was not merely a revolt of Churches from orthodoxy, but of whole nations from the Roman Empire.

As the result of the Council of Ephesus, Nestorianism became the religion of Syria; after Chalcedon, Eutychianism became the religion both of Syria and Egypt. It is

The Separatist Churches of the East. 243

doubtful to what extent some of these Churches were, if at all, heretical, and there seems no reason why in the present day they should not be brought to coalesce with the Orthodox Church. It is possible to resent the condemnation of individuals, even to reject the watchwords adopted by Councils, and to be led thereby into extravagant modes of thought and incautious expressions, without sympathizing with the condemned doctrines. This is not improbably the case with the so-called Nestorians and the Armenians. The Nestorians probably err rather in language than in doctrine, which latter does not seem to be inconsistent with the decrees of Ephesus. The Armenians separated, as we shall see presently, from the Orthodox Church through a misunderstanding, and probably were not at first, as they are not in the present day, heretical at all. Many of us read translations of books and Liturgies without thinking that the original language may be capable of a different construction, and judgment is often warped by an imperfect, a one-sided, and perhaps hostile, version.

To the Œcumenical Councils of the Church we are indebted for the right doctrine of the Incarnation; but their anathemas and excommunications detract much from their usefulness, and the schisms which were the consequence have left a permanent heritage of woe to the Eastern Church.

Such considerations may not be without use in attempts at reunion, and bringing the, at present, schismatical (inasmuch as they do not own allegiance to the Orthodox Patriarch) communions, back to the Orthodox Church. Protestant Missions have failed through taking it for granted that they are heretical, or, if not heretical, differing from themselves, and in trying to proselytize them to their own views. On national rather than on religious grounds a deep-rooted aversion to proselytism exists in the East; a convert is regarded with feelings of contempt as unpatriotic, and to such a height is this feeling carried that it is said to extend to the qualification of Protestant Princesses by the change of their religion. The members of the various

Christian communities discarding religious differences generally live together in perfect amity and agree to differ; and if, in their dealings with each other, their differences are sometimes emphasized, as is the case with regard to the Holy Sepulchre at Jerusalem, it is on national rather than religious grounds. If the desirable object of bringing them back to the Orthodox Church is ever to be achieved, we must put ourselves in their position, above all examine their writings, and try whether a favourable construction may not be put upon them, whether they may not have used expressions in one sense which we have construed in another. It is possible to condemn the schism and yet acquit them of heresy. Some people hold that, being national Churches, they are not even schismatical; "They can hardly," says Dr. Neale, "be called schismatical, because they have constantly maintained their succession, and for many years they had no branch of the Church co-existent with them in their own territories." But their divisions and unseemly strifes are not only a great stumbling-block in the way of the re-union of Christendom, but they excite the contempt of the Turk. No religion is broken up into more sects than the Mahometan; but to the Mahometans the violence and sanguinary conflicts which have taken place (we hope we may speak in the past tense) at the Holy Sepulchre seem a proof against the truth of Christianity.

Some account of the separatist Churches may not be out of place in a narrative of the Orthodox Church, which the separation has so materially affected. They consist principally of two classes, Dyophysites and Monophysites; the former being those who separated after the Council of Ephesus, as the Nestorians; the latter, the Jacobites, Copts, Abyssinians, and Armenians, after the Council of Chalcedon. There is also one remnant of the Monothelite controversy to which we shall come in the next Chapter, the Maronites, who are now members of the Roman Catholic Church. To each we will devote such short space as we have at our disposal.

The Separatist Churches of the East. 245

1. *The Nestorians.* But a difficulty meets us on the threshold, as to their proper appellation. They themselves, claiming that their faith is derived from the very earliest times, abjure the name and refuse to acknowledge Nestorius as their founder. The name is a nick-name given them by outsiders, and is scarcely ever used except by those under European influence [a]. Sometimes they are called Assyrians, but neither does this name adequately describe them, for Assyria is only one province of their Church of Seleucia—Ctesiphon; it is never applied to them in the East, and has only recently been given to them in England as an approach to the name of Syrians [b]. They are sometimes, but incorrectly, called Chaldæans, for that title, which was originally given to astrologers, is now confined to the Roman Uniats at Mosul [c]. Their national name and that by which they call themselves is Syrians, for they consider themselves to be of the same nation as the Syrians of Western Asia and Mesopotamia; and convenience requires that they should be called Eastern Syrians to distinguish them from the Jacobites or Western Syrians.

The Eastern Syrians (to call them by that name) trace their origin to St. Thaddæus, one of the seventy (St. Luke x. 1—20), sent to their sacred city, Edessa, and their king Abgarus, by St. Thomas the Apostle [d]; and to St. Mari, a disciple of Thaddæus. The way for the missionaries is said to have been prepared by the three Magi, who, it is reasonable to suppose, would on their return home have spread in the country the Good News of the Saviour to Whom they had done homage. St. Mari (or Mar Mari, as he is called by the Syrians) established, and according to tradition was the first Bishop of, the See of Ctesiphon, the then capital of Persia, which in subsequent times became the Metropolis of the Church of the Eastern Syrians.

---

[a] Maclean, Some Account of the Eastern Syrians. [b] Report of the Archbishop of Canterbury's Mission, 1896. [c] Badger's Nestorians and their Ritual.
[d] The correspondence between our Saviour and Abgarus must be dismissed as fictitious.

Their Primate was in early times subject to the Bishop of Antioch, by whom he was invested in his office; the title he bore was Catholicos, and the rank which he took in the Church was next after the Bishops of Alexandria and Antioch. The difficulty of reaching Antioch gradually led to his practical independence, which was doubtless favourably regarded by the Persian government. This continued till A D. 431, and the condemnation of Nestorius by the Council of Ephesus.

The famous school of Edessa was the great stronghold of the Eastern Syrians. Rabulas, the Bishop of the See (412—435), who had formerly been a pupil and admirer of Theodore of Mopsuestia, and supported John of Antioch at Ephesus, turned against his former friends, openly anathematized Theodore, and caused his writings to be destroyed. He became a staunch supporter of orthodoxy and expelled the teachers from the school of Edessa. Ibas, who had also been a pupil of Theodore of Mopsuestia, and was one of the expelled teachers, succeeded Rabulas as Bishop of Edessa (435—457); he gave a strong impulse to the Nestorian movement, and the school of Edessa again rose to high importance. Barsumas, another of the expelled teachers, became Bishop of Nisibis and Metropolitan (435—489), and he and Ibas were the zealous upholders and propagators of the teaching of Nestorius.

Notwithstanding that Ibas had the support of the great majority in Edessa, there was an influential party in favour of the anti-Nestorian views of his predecessor; they were also strongly opposed to Ibas on account of his famous letter to Maris, Bishop of Hardaseir in Persia, written A.D. 433, and they obtained from the Emperor Theodosius an order for his deposition. Ibas is said to have been committed from time to time to no fewer than twenty different prisons. At length he was summoned before the Latrocinium; but being at the time in prison at Antioch, and therefore unable to attend, he was condemned unheard, sentenced to deposition from the Episcopate and the Priesthood, and even forbidden lay Communion After the death of Theodosius he was restored to his See and died, A.D. 457.

After Nestorius was condemned by the Council of Ephesus, the Eastern Syrians continued to adhere to the fallen Patriarch. His followers being persecuted in the Roman Empire sought refuge in Persia where the way had been prepared for them through the letter of Ibas to the Bishop of Hardaseir. Persia threw its ægis over the Nestorians; their separation from the Orthodox Church was cordially welcomed as conducive to the weakening of the Roman Empire; and they received in the country, especially at Nisibis[e], shelter and encouragement. Barsumas, the Bishop, persuaded their Catholicos to separate himself from the Orthodox Church, and soon afterwards he and his community abjured the jurisdiction of the Orthodox Patriarch of Antioch.

During the fifty-four years that he presided over the See of Nisibis, Barsumas gained a strong influence over the King of Persia. By persuading him that the Nestorians were the real friends of Persia, he induced him to expel the Orthodox Christians from his dominions, to put the Nestorians in possession of their Churches, and to give to the Catholicos, who about this time assumed the title of Patriarch, Seleucia for his See. To Barsumas, the establishment of Nestorianism in Persia is specially attributable. When the Emperor Zeno suppressed the school of Edessa, which up to that time had been the chief nursery of the doctrine of Theodore of Mopsuestia, Barsumas founded the famous theological school of Nisibis, over which he set Narses, who presided with great ability and success for fifty years The Nestorians afford an almost solitary exception to the inactivity of the Eastern Church in the work of missions, and it was from the school of Nisibis that the missionaries proceeded who in this and the following centuries disseminated Nestorian Christianity in Egypt, Syria, Arabia, India, Tartary, and even China.

[e] For a similar reason the Jacobites were afterwards welcomed in Persia.

Barsumas died, A.D. 489. Still the Church of the Eastern Syrians, being recruited from time to time by persecuted refugees from the Roman Empire, continued, notwithstanding the opposition of the Magi, to enjoy the protection of the King of Persia. In addition to the school of Nisibis, a flourishing school was established in Seleucia, and other schools in various places; till at a Synod of Seleucia, A.D. 499, under the Patriarch Babuæus, the whole Church of Persia finally broke away from the Orthodox Church.

Dropping the more humble title of Patriarch of Seleucia, the Patriarchs assumed the title of Patriarch of Babylon. In the Ninth Century the Eastern Syrians and Jacobites outnumbered all the Greek and Roman Churches together, the former being by far the larger number of the two[f]. In that century they removed their primatical See to Bagdad, the seat of the Caliphs, a town near the ruins of the ancient Nineveh. Their missionary zeal remained unabated till the Thirteenth Century, at the commencement of which the Church of the Eastern Christians reached its culminating point. The Patriarch had at that time under him twenty-four Metropolitans, and "it may be doubted," says Dr. Neale[g], "whether Innocent III. possessed more spiritual power than the Patriarch in the City of the Caliphs."

It appeared at that time that their Church would supersede the Orthodox Greek Church; but from that time it rapidly fell. With the overthrow of the Caliphate by Ghengis Khan their prosperity came to an end. In vain they attempted missionary enterprises amongst the Moguls. Timour (1369—1405), "the scourge of Asia," almost annihilated them, their Churches were destroyed; one by one their branches were exterminated; numberless martyrs laid down their lives for their faith; and the survivors were driven into the inaccessible mountains of Kurdistan, where in the village of Kochanes their Patriarch took up his humble residence.

Pope Innocent IV., A.D. 1246, and Pope Nicholas IV.

---

[f] Neale's Holy Eastern Church, I 144   [g] Ibid

in 1278, tried in vain to draw the remnant over to Romanism. But, A.D. 1552, owing to a disputed election of a Patriarch, they became broken up into two bodies. The smaller body living in the plain of Mosul and the neighbouring hills, consisting of about one-third of the whole, followed the anti-Patriarch, who was consecrated by Pope Julius III., and after many fluctuations they put themselves, A.D. 1778, under the See of Rome. Thus arose the sect known as "the Uniat Chaldæans," whose Patriarch, Mar Elia, styling himself Patriarch of Babylon, has his residence at Mosul, with a population of two thousand seven hundred and forty-three families The larger body of the Church of the Eastern Syrians were the people of the mountains of Kurdistan, and the plains of Azer-baijan, bordering the sea of Urmi. In the present day the Patriarchate contains eleven thousand three hundred and seventy-eight families [h], who living on the Turco-Persian frontiers are politically the subjects of Turkey and Persia They form, as is the case with the other separatist Churches, at once a nation and a Church, under the rule of Mar Shimun (*my Lord Simon*), styled " Catholicos or Patriarch of the East," who, living at Kochanes in Turkey, or as the Patriarch prefers it to be called, " On the banks of Pison, the river of Eden [i]," exercises temporal as well as spiritual authority, which is recognized by the Sultan The office is hereditary, which, even if under existing circumstances it may be necessary, is liable to abuse, the choice being limited, and the post often held by an unworthy occupant. The Eastern Syrians recognize five Patriarchs, of whom their own Patriarch is one ; but to the Patriarch of Jerusalem they assign only a peculiar dignity.

The males in the succession to the Patriarchate are called Nziri or Nazarites, and are forbidden to eat meat or to marry ; nor are their mothers allowed to eat meat during their pregnancy. After the election of the Patriarch these restrictions are removed from them ; but in either case they

---

[h] Stubbs Mosheim.   [i] Athelstan Riley, The Assyrian Church

are debarred from becoming Bishops, since the same restrictions are placed on the Episcopate.

The second in rank is the Mattran, who is the only Metropolitan, and whose Diocese is also within the dominions of the Sultan. His dynastic title is Mar Khnanishu, and by him the Patriarch is Consecrated, and sometimes (but this is generally done by the Patriarch himself) the Bishops also, who are ten in number, three in Persia, and seven in Turkey, some of them with only nominal Dioceses.

Crushed under the iron rule of the Mahometans, and exposed to the pitiless hostility of the Kurdish chiefs, those of the plains exist, rather than live, under the most miserable conditions. The dwellers in the mountains, secure from molestation in the deep and narrow valleys that divide the ranges of Kurdistan, maintain under the rule of their hereditary Maleks or Chiefs, a kind of semi-independence, although at the cost of absolute isolation from the world and from all civilizing influence. In an evil hour, in 1834, the Americans sent a mission amongst them. The want of judgment of the missionaries explains, but it does not excuse, what follows. The suspicion of the Turks and Kurds, fomented by Jewish intrigues, was aroused, and a war of extermination which filled Europe with horror was waged against the mountain-Nestorians, and in 1843 ten thousand, and again in 1845 five thousand of them, were massacred. Those earnest remonstrances with which we are so familiar of late years were made to the Turkish government, with the result that Bedr Khan Beg was exiled to Crete!

In the former year the Eastern Syrians opened, in a letter addressed to Archbishop Howley, their first communication with the Church of England, in consequence of which Dr. Badger[J] was sent out at the expense of the S.P.G. and S.P.C.K.; but owing to the Kurdish insurrection under Bedr Khan Beg the mission was cut short; the Patriarch, Mar Shimun, found for a time a refuge under Dr. Badger's roof at Mosul, but the latter was obliged to return to England.

[J] Author of The Nestorians and their Ritual.

The Separatist Churches of the East 251

Wild and savage as their condition is, the Eastern Syrians, in spite of their barbarism and ignorance, have a devoted attachment to the Scriptures; they cling tenaciously to their ancient ecclesiastical rites and Liturgies, and are most anxious to learn and have schools established amongst them [k]. In other respects (if we omit that they are brave and warlike) their character is not painted in favourable colours. There exist among them two faults, common to almost all Christians living under Mahometan rule, a want of truthfulness and trustworthiness. And yet, says Dean Maclean [l], they have many virtues combined with many glaring defects Amongst those of the Persian plains may be remarked an intense love of money, associated with an unstinted hospitality; amongst the mountaineers of Kurdistan, an incorrigible proneness to quarrel accompanied with the most affectionate warmheartedness. They are incorrigible beggars, "to proceed on a begging tour to England and America is the height of their ambition [m];" they come to England to plead for their oppressed Communion, but many of them when they return home are known to live in greater comfort and wealth than when they left it.

We have dwelt with the Eastern Syrians, or, as they are commonly known, Nestorians, at greater length than our space can well afford on account of the mission started amongst them in 1884 by the late Archbishop Benson, "the little band, which, through constant and ruthless persecution from without and ignorance from within, had so gallantly proved their independence through the ages, but could no longer stand alone [n]. Amongst the clergy who have taken part in the mission have been representatives of the English, Scottish, and American Churches [o], and its object—to strengthen an ancient Church—was

---

[k] "The Assyrian Church." Eastern Syrian Churches. the Assyrian Christians.
[l] Some Account of the Customs of the
[m] Athelstan Riley's Narrative of a Visit to
[n] Report of the Archbishop's Mission, 1896
[o] Leaflet published by the Assyrian Mission, 1896

explained in a Letter from the Archbishop to the Patriarch;—" Not to bring the Christians to the Communion of the Church of England, and not to change any doctrines or customs, except such as are contrary to that faith which the Holy Spirit, speaking through the Œcumenical Councils of the undivided Church, has taught as necessary to be believed by all Christians."

* * * * * * *

A few words must be said about the Christians of St. Thomas. One of the chief missions of the Eastern Syrians was to the coast of Malabar. Uniform tradition makes the Church in India to have been founded by the Apostle St. Thomas. It relates how that, having preached the Gospel in China, he, for a second time, returned to the coast of Coromandel; that the chiefs were well affected to his preaching, and that he baptized the King of the country; but that the many conversions made by him to the Christian faith so enraged the Brahmins, that he suffered martyrdom at their hands at Meliapore near Madras. The scene of his martyrdom is still called the "Mount of St. Thomas," and his remains were believed to have been translated from Meliapore to Edessa. St Bartholomew is also said to have preached in India. St. Jerome relates that about A.D. 188, the Indians sent a deputation to Alexandria for some person to instruct them, and that, in consequence, Pantænus, head of the famous Catechetical school in the city, was sent out, and that he found on his arrival a copy of St. Matthew's Gospel which had been left in the country by St. Bartholomew. It is certain that for many centuries there continued there a flourishing Church, at the great Council of Nice the Canons were subscribed by a Bishop styling himself Bishop of Persia and the Great India, and in process of time the Church, which meanwhile suffered much persecution, came to be recognized as the Church of Malabar.

In the Sixth Century Nestorian missionaries won over the Church of Malabar, or the Christians of St. Thomas, as they were called, to their faith. This was confirmed (although at what date is uncertain) by a rich merchant, holding the Nestorian doctrine, from Syria, named Mar Thomas, who by his riches and virtues gained a strong influence over the Church of Malabar, and persuaded them to accept a Bishop from the Catholicos of the East [p] "One colony alone," says Dean Stanley, "of this ancient dominion (the Nestorians) remains; the Christians of St. Thomas, as they are called, are still clustered round the tomb of St. Thomas, or the Nestorian merchant, who restored, if he did not found, the settlement." The Anglo-Saxon Chronicle relates that King Alfred, at the end of the Ninth Century, sent from England missionaries to those Christians, and that they returned home bringing from them many valuable presents.

In the early years of the Tenth Century the Christians of St. Thomas enlisted the favour and protection of the infidel Kings of Malabar, who, witnessing the respect which was paid to them by their Christian subjects, vied with each other in conferring benefits upon them, and allowed them to build Churches and to propagate their faith in their dominions. So powerful did they become that they were able to throw off the pagan government and elect kings of their own, who assumed the title of Kings of the Christians of St. Thomas. After several generations, the kingdom, through failure of issue to the Christian king, came to an end, and devolved upon the pagan King of Diamper, whom he had adopted as his heir; and afterwards on the King of Cochin.

Under that dynasty the Christians of St. Thomas were living when, A.D. 1503, the Portuguese arrived on the coast of Malabar under Vasco di Gama, to whom they were able to show the sceptre which once belonged to their Christian Kings.

We must pass over the persecutions which they suffered under the Portuguese, who exercised over them an intolerant bigotry with the view of bringing them into subjection to the Pope of Rome. Ninety years of strife between the

[p] But see Neale's Holy Eastern Church, I. 145.

Latins and the Christians of St. Thomas had won over no
appreciable number to the Roman Church, when, A.D. 1594,
the Augustinian, Alexis di Menexes (that "man of iron"),
consecrated Archbishop of Goa, appeared amongst them,
with the result that their Metropolitan Mar Joseph was sent
a prisoner to Rome, and they were forced into the obedience
of the Pope. In vain the Christians of St. Thomas pleaded
that they had never heard of a Pope of Rome, and that they
themselves came from the place where the disciples of Christ
were first called Christians. What conviction failed to do,
that the Inquisition effected. In five years Menexes succeeded in convening the famous Synod of Diamper, in which
the independence of the Indian Church was trampled out
under the heel of the Vatican. By a decree of the Synod
all the Syrian MSS. were destroyed, and their Liturgy and
Service Books altered so as to assimilate them to the Roman
worship. But by the abolition of the ancient Eastern rites
and the enforcement of Latin peculiarities, the people were
rendered so hostile to the Church of Rome that, after the
successes of the Dutch in the middle of the Seventeenth
Century, half of the native Christians threw off the Roman
allegiance, and, being unable to procure a Bishop from
Babylon, they in 1665 passed from Nestorianism into
Jacobitism, procuring Prelates from Alexandria and sometimes from Diarbekr[q]. The decline of the Dutch and the
rise of the British power in Hindoostan did not much affect
them. "The trading companies of Holland and England,"
says Gibbon, "are the friends of toleration, but if oppression be
less mortifying than contempt, the Christians of St. Thomas
have reason to complain of the cold and silent indifference
of their brethren in Europe."

Jacobite the Christians of St. Thomas still remain. They
occupy the narrow strip of land extending about two
hundred miles on the South West Coast of India, known
as Malabar, and number about 250,000 souls, of which about
a third part were Uniats, which means that they acknow-

[q] Neale, I. 151

ledged the supremacy of the Pope, whilst they held their services in the Syro-Chaldaic language, and to all outward appearance were perfectly distinct from Romanists. But in 1862 the Church of Travancore, the country in the South of Malabar, obtained a Bishop from Mesopotamia, and to him about 81,000 Uniats gave their adherence[r].

* * * * * * *

2. *The Jacobites.* Jacobite is the common name under which Monophysites in general are included, but it belongs in particular to the Monophysites of Syria and Armenia. Soon after the Council of Chalcedon, the Monophysites became split up into two sects. Eutyches, who had ranged himself on the side of Cyril of Alexandria, was supported by Cyril's successor, Dioscorus. But whereas Eutyches maintained the union of the two Natures in Christ to be so intimate that they became One Nature, and that, the Divine Nature being the superior, the Human was swallowed up in it; Dioscorus so far modified the doctrine as to declare that the Two Natures were so blended that there was one humano-divine Nature. The latter became the faith of Egypt, the former of Armenia, and the Armenian Church symbolized the doctrine by forbidding the then universal practice of mixing water with wine in the Chalice of the Eucharist[s]. Syria, abandoning Nestorianism, fluctuated between the two, but eventually, under the influence of Severus, the Monothelite Patriarch of Antioch (512—519), was drawn into the Monophytism of Dioscorus. When, owing to its persecution by the Roman Empire, the very existence of the Monophysite communion in Syria seemed on the point of extinction, there arrived amongst them a monk named Jacob Baradai (*the man of rags*), so called because he went about dressed as a beggar. He had been a zealous disciple of Severus, and having, A.D. 541, received Consecration as Bishop of Edessa from some Monophysite Bishops, assumed the leadership of the previously acephalous party in Syria, ordaining Bishops and clergy (it is said to

[r] Colonial Church Chronicle 1862.   [s] Neale's Alexandria, II 8

the fabulous number of 80,000); and he probably composed the Liturgy in which he himself is commemorated.

From Jacob Baradai the Monophysites derived their name of Jacobites. The Jacobites of Syria condemned both the Eastern and Western Churches as heretical, but though holding the principal error of Eutyches they always refused to be called his followers or to bear his name. They claim to be, next to that of Jerusalem, the oldest Church in Christendom; that in Antioch the believers were first called Christians; that of the See St Peter, from whom they trace their succession, was the first Bishop; and that to the See of Antioch the distinctive title of Patriarch first belonged. These prerogatives of the ancient See of Antioch the Jacobites still claim for themselves. Jacob Baradai at his death, after an Episcopate of thirty-seven years, in A.D. 578, left a flourishing community, which usurped and still continues to hold the title of Patriarch of Antioch, its Patriarchs invariably holding, after St. Ignatius the martyred Patriarch of that See, the name of Ignatius.

Since a defection, in 1646, from the Jacobite Patriarch, the Roman Church has continued a succession of Prelates styling themselves Patriarchs of Aleppo.

The Jacobites under the Patriarch of Antioch, whose usual residence is at Diarbekr, the former Amida, but who sometimes resides in the Monastery of St. Ananias near Mardin, are mostly to be found in the extreme North of Syria, but they have a monastery and about fifteen families at Jerusalem. Their Metropolitan or Maphrian (*fruit-bearer*[t]), having with him three Presbyters, an Archdeacon, and a number of Deacons, lives in the present day in the House of St. John Mark on Mount Zion[u]. In the five annual Lents which they observe, both the clergy and laity abstain, not only from flesh and eggs, but even from the taste of wine, oil and fish.

The Syrian Jacobites have from time to time produced

---

[t] Kurtz, Church Hist., I. 339.
[u] Report of the Eastern Church Association, 1894

many distinguished scholars, the last of whom was Gregory Abelpharagius, "poet, physician, historian, philosopher, and divine." The son of a Jewish physician who was converted to Monophysitism, he was first Bishop of Guba and afterwards Maphrian. His noble and benevolent disposition added to his extraordinary learning made him universally beloved not only by Christians of all denominations, but also by Mahometans and Jews, and at his death, which occurred A D. 1286, his funeral was attended by his rival the Nestorian Patriarch with a train of Greeks and Armenians, "who forgot their disputes and mingled their tears over the grave of an enemy [x]."

* * * * * * *

3. The Copts constitute by far the greater part of the population of Egypt. They probably derive their name from Coptos (the modern Kepht), once an important town in Upper Egypt, described by Pliny as the emporium of goods imported down the Nile from India to Alexandria. The opposition of the Monophysites in Egypt to the Council of Chalcedon and its condemnation of their Patriarch, Dioscorus, was increased by injury and injustice inflicted on them by the Greek Emperors No office of honour or emolument was allowed to be conferred on them ; trade and merchandise and servile duties, such as tilling the ground and plying the loom, were alone their lot in life. Socially, politically, and ecclesiastically opposed to the Greek Empire, they were led to hate and abjure everything that was Greek "Every Melchite or Imperialist was, in the eyes of the Copts, a stranger, every Jacobite a citizen ; the alliance of marriage, offices of humanity towards the Greeks, were condemned as deadly sins ; the nation renounced all allegiance with the Emperor, and his orders, at a distance from Alexandria, were obeyed only under the pressure of military force [y]."

Since A.D. 536 they have persisted in choosing a Patriarch of their own, who, residing at Cairo, accounts himself

[x] Gibbon, VIII. 353.   [y] Ibid., 365.

the true successor of St. Mark. Nationally descendants of the ancient Egyptians, and speaking the very language, although in a debased form, which Moses spoke in the court of Pharaoh, they discarded the Greek language in their services; although the Coptic idiom of their officebooks is understood not at all by the common people, and little by the clergy, and is generally supplemented with an Arabic translation in the margin.

We shall see in a future chapter how their hatred to the Greeks led them to afford material assistance to the Saracens in their invasion of Egypt. But the Copts made a miserable bargain; if the Greeks chastised them with rods, the Mahometans chastised them with scorpions. Between them and the Greeks there had been, even if in a different form, an affinity of Christianity; between them and their new masters, who treated their religion with scorn and insult, there was nothing but antipathy. They had, it is true, the advantage of being exonerated from military conscription, but for this they were indebted to the contempt of the Moslems, who did not consider Christians worthy of falling in the Prophet's cause.

We will select a few out of the terrible calamities inflicted on them by the Mahometans[1]. In the Patriarchate of Isaac the Just (686—688), Abdul-Aziz commanded all the Crosses throughout Egypt to be destroyed, and blasphemous inscriptions, proclaiming Mahomet as the Apostle of God, to be attached to the entrances of their Churches. This Dr. Neale calls the first persecution[a]. Under Asabah, the son of Abdul-Aziz, when Alexander was Patriarch, another terrible persecution broke out, in which a large number not only of the laity but of the clergy also abjured Christianity, and went over to the Mahometans. In A D. 710, the orthodox Patriarchate of Alexandria was, after a lapse of ninety-seven years, restored in the person of Cosmas I. Cosmas had been a needle-maker by

---

[1] For a fuller account see Renaudot's *Historia Patriarcharum Alexandrianorum*.
[a] Neale's Alexandria, II. 82.

trade, and was an uneducated man who could neither read nor write, still he was not unequal to the management of the Alexandrine Church. He sought out the Caliph at Damascus and proved to him that he was the rightful successor of St. Cyril, and that his predecessors in the Caliphate had been deceived by the Copts; the Orthodox Church was consequently re-established in its rights, and a vacancy of some years in the Coptic Patriarchate enabled Cosmas to consolidate the orthodox party. In 743 a Coptic Patriarch in the person of Chail I. was again elected. Under Hafiz, the Mahometan governor (*circ.* 742—766), at the time of the political convulsions occasioned by the conflicting dynasties of the Ommiads and Abbassides, Orthodox and Copts alike suffered. Hafiz ordered all Christians throughout Egypt to repeat Mahometan prayers, and by exempting from tribute those who did so, caused many to apostatize; many Coptic Bishops being driven out from their Sees were forced to take refuge in the monasteries; many, together with the Coptic Patriarch, Minas I., the successor of Chail, were compelled to labour for a whole year in the dockyard of Alexandria. In 881, under the Caliph Ahmed, a terrible persecution, from which the Orthodox Church was free, was suffered by the Copts. Chenouda I. (859—881) was at the time their Patriarch. The Caliph required money for a Syrian expedition, for which the tribute hitherto imposed on the Copts was tripled; the Patriarch was falsely accused by a Deacon and a monk, to both of whom he had refused Ordination, of concealing vast sums of money; the Patriarchal chests were ransacked, but nothing but MSS., of which he was a great collector, and vestments were found; all the Churches in Cairo except one were ordered to be closed; the Patriarch imprisoned, and afterwards driven out, was forced to wander about in the deserts, exposed to the greatest hardships. Many again apostatized from the faith.

Nor under the Fatimites did they fare better. Under Hakem, the third of the dynasty, occurred what Dr. Neale calls the tenth persecution, in which the Orthodox as well as the Coptic Church suffered the direst calamities which it had ever experienced since the Saracenic invasions. The Patriarch Zacharias (1005—1032), loaded with chains, was cast into prison, from which he was released only to be exposed to lions which, it was said, refrained from hurting him. Christian Churches were pulled down, the monasteries plundered by soldiers, their endowments confiscated, and Mosques built on their sites. The Copts under successive Fatimite Caliphs were visited with the most severe oppression, which became, if possible, still worse under the Mamelukes. The Coptic Church was in a state of utter stagnation; the Copts, completely driven away from the cities, maintained in their villages a miserable existence.

The whole history of the Coptic Church from their first to their last chapter has been one of misfortune and misery. The occupation of Egypt by the French (July, 1798—September, 1801) was to the Copts a period of trouble and disaster. The French found the necessity of employing the Christian natives for offices of trust; the footing of equality in which they were thus placed drew on them the animosity of the Turks, and at the very commencement of the occupation a proposal made in the Divan for a general massacre at Cairo was, by only a narrow majority, overruled. Their Churches, convents and private dwellings were searched by the Turks for arms; "In a word," says the Moslem historian, Gabbarti, "Egypt became for the moment the theatre of robberies, assassinations and murders." Nor did they fare better from the French. In the struggle for the possession of Cairo, and the revolts which broke out against the French, they were always the first to suffer; and "by the end of the time their quarter was plundered and ruined beyond repair, so that those who survived were compelled to build a fresh one, and a Cathedral, after the French were gone [b]." Why the English after they had driven the French out of Egypt left the Christians to the mercy of

---

[b] Bullock's Story of the Church of Egypt, II. 356.

the Turks, must have surpassed the comprehension of Christendom; but no sooner had the English left the country than a violent insurrection occurred; a second insurrection two years afterwards (May, 1805) made way for Mahomet Ali.

With the accession of Mahomet to power began a new era for the Copts [c]. He found the Copts more intelligent, better men of business, and more trustworthy (the last not a quality in which they are generally supposed to excel), than the Mahometans. But at the same time he invariably chose (if possible) Armenians, Roman Catholics, or other European Christians, anticipating danger if he allowed the Copts of the national Church to gain a preponderating influence in the country [d].

Owing to the persecutions which they have suffered, the number of the Copts has dwindled down from two millions to about 200,000 souls, of whom a large part are in Cairo, but a still larger number in Upper Egypt. They have twelve Bishops, eight in Upper and four in Lower Egypt, and two Metropolitans, those of Alexandria and Minufiyah, who, however, have little power under the present despotic Patriarch [e]. There is also a Coptic Patriarch in Jerusalem, where they have been able to establish themselves in a large monastery near the Holy Sepulchre [f]. There were once Coptic Christians in the Soudan, and when General Gordon, in 1885, arrived at Khartoum, he found a Coptic Bishop still surviving with seven Churches and a Convent of nuns [g].

Their Bishops, like those of the Orthodox Church, are selected from the monasteries. We hope we are speaking in the past tense, and that some improvement is being now effected. But the lower Coptic clergy are described as ignorant, ordained without an Ecclesiastical training (this defect at least has been somewhat remedied), who consequently take but little interest in their work; they are miser-

---

[c] Article in Contemporary Review, May, 1897, by a Coptic layman.
[d] Bullock, II 366   [e] Report of the Eastern Church Association, 1894
[f] Williams' Holy City, 565.   [g] Bullock, II. 368, *note*.

ably poor, their stipend, often not more than £12 a year, having to be eked out by begging; whilst their character, especially with regard to intemperance, stands very low. Their tedious services, performed in their mud-built and often filthy edifices, said in Coptic, but sometimes afterwards in the colloquial Arabic of the country, occupy some four hours. But their lections are always in Arabic, and sermons are more in vogue amongst them than is generally the case in the East; every Sunday there is either a sermon or a homily read from the Book of Homilies, generally of St. Chrysostom [h].

In Nubia, the intervening country between Egypt and Abyssinia, there were once many Churches, but owing to Mussulman persecution and temptations held out to apostatize from the faith, Christianity has entirely disappeared. "Nubia was once a Christian land . . . . now there is not a Christian to be found in the whole land. . . . A traveller not three centuries ago records that he found congregations mourning for lack of Priests. There was then a people, but no Priests; now there are neither a Christian people nor Priests; the only traces left of either are the ruined Churches of God [i]"

The Copts of Egypt, says the author of The Crescent and the Cross, "are considered deceitful, sensual, and avaricious." Notwithstanding this, they are, says Dean Stanley, "even in their degraded condition the most civilized of the native Egyptians." They are industrious and skilled in several trades, and however doubtful their character may be, being intellectually superior to the other inhabitants of Egypt, are extensively employed in matters of trust, and being able to read and write well fill the revenue departments in the Pasha's Offices. But here again they trouble themselves little about honesty, or in resisting the temptations which beset them, and their craft and duplicity are notorious;

[h] Report of the Eastern Church Association, 1894.
[i] Colonial Church Gazette, July, 1849.

whilst, at any rate before the English occupation, they were ready to abet the civil authorities in fleecing the Fellahs.

It must be placed to their credit that, though there are many defections to Islam, the Coptic Christians have, as a body, in the face of persecutions and inducements held out by the Mahometans, remained steadfast to their creed, and in consequence of our occupation of Egypt the Coptic Church has strong claims upon our sympathy. The Copts, it is true, are not fond of, nor well disposed to, the English administration, but the claims which the Coptic Church is now making for our assistance are so many calls which ought not to be neglected. The Roman Catholics in the Eighteenth Century organized a Uniat-Coptic Church, which is said to number 10,000 adherents, with a well-trained clergy under the Jesuits, and a seminary for the Copts at Cairo[1]. But it must be borne in mind that there is still an Orthodox Church, and the true successors of SS. Athanasius and Cyril, and a better way is, instead of proselytizing and weakening the Orthodox Greek Church through withdrawing its members, to strengthen the Church by bringing the Copts back to the allegiance of the Orthodox Patriarch. Whatever they may once have been, the Copts are not now Monophysite. Their return to the confession of Orthodoxy cannot be effected by the Roman Church, for all Easterns have before them the experience of the Uniats, and the Copts know that its object is to bring them under the supremacy of the Pope Protestant missions cannot effect the object, because they try to proselytize to their own views, and Proselytism no Eastern communions will tolerate. The field is open to, and now that we have undertaken the government of Egypt is the duty of, the Anglican Church, and it ought not to be one of insurmountable difficulty. There is a hopeful feature in the growth of a young reforming party amongst the Copts, demanding a greater efficiency in their schools, better education and a more adequate stipend for their clergy,

[1] Contemporary Review, May, 1897

and to this feeling it is due that a Theological seminary was founded in 1893 [k].

A new era, as said above, dawned on Egypt at the accession of Mahomet Ali; his reign and those of his successors have been at least an improvement on former times; religious persecution has since the early years of the present century considerably abated; and Christians, finding favour at Court, began to breathe more fully and to gain strength day by day. After the death, in 1809, of the Coptic Patriarch Mark, the Patriarchal throne was occupied for nearly half the century (1809—1854) by Amba Butros VII. In 1830, a mission under Mr. Lieder was sent out to Egypt by the Church Missionary Society; at that time the four Gospels had been translated into Arabic and Coptic by the Bible Society, and Mr Lieder established friendly relations with the Patriarch and the Copts, and a training school for candidates for Holy Orders was, with the approval of the former, opened. But it appears that the missionaries tried to proselytize the pupils to their own views; the Patriarch then himself sided against them; the Bishops suspected the orthodoxy of the candidates submitted to them, and not one of its pupils was ordained; and in 1848 the school was closed and the mission abandoned.

On the death of Amba Butros in 1854, Cyril X, the former head of the famous monastery of St. Antony, whose reforming tendencies were already known, was called by popular acclamation to the Patriarchal throne. When the Coptic Bishops, who were strongly opposed to reform, were assembled in the Cathedral of Cairo and on the point of secretly consecrating an obscure monk as Patriarch, the people rose in insurrection, and, accompanied by a body of armed Abyssinians, broke into the Cathedral and stopped the election. The Bishops fled away in terror; ultimately a compromise was arranged which left Cyril in possession of the Patriarchate (1854—1861).

[k] The Coptic Era, it may be mentioned, dates from the Era of the Martyrs, so that the present year is with them 1614.

The Separatist Churches of the East. 265

The work abandoned by the C.M.S. was in the year after Cyril's election resumed by the United Presbyterian mission from America, which has been at work ever since, and has been instrumental in widely diffusing the Scriptures, opening schools and establishing prayer and Bible meetings. Its object was, not that of benefitting the Coptic Church, but of converting Mahometans; and by resorting to, what is certain to be fatal in Eastern missions, proselytizing, it gained the ill-will of the clergy. Still the Patriarch's heart was bent on reform; he founded the first school for boys and girls, that which still exists at Cairo, numbering twelve hundred boys and three hundred girls; he entirely rebuilt the Cathedral, destroying, in the presence of an immense crowd of Copts, the existing Icons, whilst he allowed no new Icons to be set up in it. He had also much at heart the re-union of the Coptic with the Orthodox Church. But Cyril's proceedings drew on him the suspicion of the Moslem authorities, and so oppressive was the government of Said Pasha, that he applied to the English government for protection. Sabbatier, the French Consul-General, offered to use his influence, on condition of Cyril's issuing an order for the admission of the Jesuits into Abyssinia, the Patriarch understood what that meant, and refused to purchase protection for the Copts at such a price. Now that application had been made to the English, pressure was brought to bear on Said by some influential Egyptians; but the affair was not forgotten against the Patriarch; and for this and other attempts to improve the Coptic Church he was poisoned by order of the government, and hundreds of Copts were subsequently dismissed from the offices which they held [1].

Thus his pontificate was cut short before he could complete the reforms which he meditated; yet Cyril inaugurated the movement which has been going on ever since. The Copts "of to-day pay no more attention to the pictures on the walls of their houses than we do to the pictures

---

[1] Bullock, II 381, and *note*.

in our stained-glass windows, whilst devotional pictures are rarer in the Coptic houses than in our own [m]."

Demetrius II. (1861—1873), an unlearned, but who was said to have been a good and just, man, the next Patriarch, was unequal to the task of carrying out the reforms begun by Cyril; in the year of his accession, Miss Whateley's schools were started, but they were intended for the Moslems and had little to do with the Copts.

Cyril XI., the present Patriarch, was consecrated in 1875. During the interregnum, two Councils, one lay, for civil, the other clerical, for ecclesiastical matters, were, with the sanction of Mark, Metropolitan of Alexandria, appointed for every Diocese, and were to be under the Presidency of the Patriarch; they also received the sanction of the Khedive. The new Patriarch at first worked harmoniously with the Councils; a Theological College was founded at Cairo, and placed under the charge of the Dean of the Cathedral, and the most intelligent monks from the monasteries were appointed as teachers. But it was represented to the Patriarch that he, as Vicar of Christ, should alone govern as the Spirit moved him; he soon got impatient of control, and abolished the College. The members of Council finding their advice unheeded, refused to attend the meetings, and a struggle between reformers and anti-reformers, which has lasted ever since, commenced. In 1883, the people clamouring for the re-appointment of Councillors, the Patriarch was intimidated into acquiescence, and an election of committees took place, but owing to his secret opposition, everything remained a dead letter.

In 1890, the El Tewfik Society[n] to ameliorate the condition of the Church was founded, nearly every intelligent Copt being enrolled on its list of members. The Patriarch thwarted it, represented it to the government as revo-

---

[m] Bullock, II. 381, 399.

[n] It did not derive its name from the Khedive, but from an Arabic word corresponding with "Pioneer."

lutionary, to the people as atheistic, and to the leaders of the Mahometan party as a device of the English preparatory to the annexation of the country. Nevertheless, the Society advanced. Cyril started a rival Society, which accused the Tewfikists of heresy and schism, and applied to Tewfik, the late Khedive, to forbid the Councils. After hearing both sides, the Khedive advised the Patriarch to accede to the just demands of the people, and after the death of the former, which occurred soon afterwards, the present Khedive, Abbas II., gave orders for its reconstruction.

We need not carry on the disputes between the Patriarch and the Councils, the banishment of the former, and his restoration under a reactionary government. Cyril, after his restoration, at first showed a more conciliatory spirit, and the Theological school was reopened, but under masters so unfitted for their work that the pupils complained that they were taught everything except theology°; and the most sanguine of the reforming party, thwarted by the Patriarch, have abandoned all hope of reforming during the life-time of Cyril.

In 1882, the English entered on the control of Egypt. Soon afterwards the "Association for the Furtherance of Christianity in Egypt" was started for the purpose of assisting the Coptic Church in the attainment of a higher spiritual life, especially for a better system of education, for those designed for Holy Orders. In June, 1883, the late Archbishop of Canterbury soon after his appointment accepted the Presidency. The object of the Association is not to proselytize or to draw them away from their Church, but to improve the spiritual condition of the Copts. In 1891 the Coptic school in Cairo requested the Association to send them out a teacher for the Iktissad school in that city, and accordingly Mr. Oswald S. Norman was sent in the hope that he would give such religious training as

° Article of the Coptic layman before referred

would bring the Copts back to the primitive standard of their Church in faith and practice.

* * * * * * *

4. The Abyssinians maintain that their country is the same as Sheba; that the Queen of Sheba was, on her visit to Solomon, converted to Judaism, and became by him the mother of Menelek, from whom they claim descent. From Judaism they say they were converted to Christianity by the eunuch of Queen Candace, who after his conversion by Philip became the Apostle of Christianity to Ethiopia. To their conversion from Judaism to Christianity is attributable the strange medley of Christianity and Judaism in the doctrines and ritual of the Abyssinian Church.

We stand on surer ground when we attribute the foundation of the Abyssinian Church to two cousins, Frumentius and Adæsius, early in the Fourth Century, who are designated the Apostles of Ethiopia. They were the remnant of a crew which went, under their uncle Meropius of Tyre, about A.D. 316, on a voyage of discovery to the South of Egypt; the ship being wrecked off the coast of Abyssinia, the whole crew, except the two cousins, were murdered by the barbarous inhabitants of the country. Their talents recommended them to the favour of the King, who appointed them tutors to his son Aizanes, and Aizanes, after being instructed in the faith, was baptized by Frumentius. Frumentius was afterwards consecrated by the great St. Athanasius as Bishop of Abyssinia, and by his means many Churches were built, and the Church was rapidly extended throughout Abyssinia and Africa.

It must be remembered how that the Emperor Constantius, supposing that Athanasius in one of his banishments had taken refuge in Abyssinia, wrote to the two Princes, Aizanes and Saizanes, who bore joint government over the country, to deliver him up, at the same time requesting that they would send Frumentius to Alexandria to receive instruction in the faith from the intruded Bishop Gregory of Cappadocia. Frumentius did not avail himself of the request, but thenceforward an intercourse was kept up between Abyssinia and Egypt, and when the Copts broke off Communion with the Orthodox Church, Abyssinia sided with them, and refused to accept the decrees of Chalcedon, and its See has ever since received from Alexandria its Abuna (*father*).

Who the famous Prester John (supposed to have lived about A D. 1200) was, and what Prester means, has always been, and must still remain, a matter of doubt. "The fame of Prester or Presbyter John," says Gibbon [p], "has long amused the credulity of Europe." The general opinion is that he was a mighty king of Ethiopia, and the explanation given by Renaudot is the simplest and perhaps as likely as any other to be right ; viz. that the Kings of Ethiopia were ex-officio Priests or Presbyters ; that John was both King and Presbyter, and that the word Prester or Presbyter is to be taken in its ordinary sense.

From Frumentius to Simeon, A D. 1613, the Abyssinians reckon ninety Abunas, and it is remarkable that during all that time, although only separated by a narrow sea from the gate of Mecca, they withstood the encroachments of the Mahometans. To the Orthodox Greek Church they bear no good will, but are sincerely attached to the faith of their country, in defence of which both rulers and people have stood together, and this attachment has been attributed to their having originally received their faith not by force but from conviction.

In the early years of the Seventeenth Century, the Portuguese, having commercial relations with the country, appeared amongst them, and soon afterwards the Jesuits, conveyed in Portuguese ships, followed. By them the reigning monarch, Sequed, together with several of the courtiers and provincial governours, were induced to abjure Monophysitism and accept the supremacy of Pope Gregory XV. The Abuna, clergy, and monks, stood firm to their faith, and the persecution and cruelty practised by the Jesuits on the believers of the old faith caused a rebellion among

[p] VIII 344.

the people. The King was forced to abdicate in favour of his son Basilides, who returned to the religion of his fathers; and the Jesuits, together with their allies the Portuguese, were driven from the country and forbidden under pain of death to return. Thus ended the short-lived power of the Jesuits in Abyssinia; thenceforward they abstained from proselytizing either the Abyssinians or the Copts, and Monophysitism remains to the present day the religion of the country.

Next in rank to the Abuna is the Kumos, a kind of Archdeacon, an intermediate between a Bishop and a Priest, and since in Abyssinia there are no Bishops, he has no superior except the Abuna. All orders of the ministry, except the monks, of whom there are two principal classes, those of Debra-Libanos and Abba-Eustateos (*St. Eustathius*), are allowed to marry.

The Abyssinians have not the power of electing their Abuna, who, by a special canon, is prohibited from being an Abyssinian, and is chosen and consecrated by the Coptic Patriarch of Alexandria. Nor has the Abuna, although he bears the rank of Patriarch or Catholicos, the power of ordaining Metropolitans or Bishops. Being a foreigner, and living at Axum, he is generally ignorant of the language ordinarily spoken as well as of that in which the Church services are conducted. The language of the Court is the dialect of Amhara, the province in which the Royal Family as well as the nobility usually reside; the public records are written in that of Tigré, whilst the ecclesiastical language is Ethiopic, which has an affinity to Hebrew and Arabic.

The Abyssinian Church presents the spectacle of the benign influence of the Gospel struggling with the cruel surroundings of a savage life; it combines a strange mixture, which has taken deep root in the hearts of the people, of devotion, superstition, and barbarism, combined with Christianity. The utmost extreme of ceremony, with an almost complete abandonment of Christianity, is to be found amongst them. The Emperor and nation are proud of their connection with the land of Judah and make their profession of faith; "This is my faith and the faith of my fathers, Kings of Israel." This accounts for the Jewish or old Egyptian ritual which is still preserved in their Church. "They are," says Dean Stanley, "the only true Sabbatarians of Christendom, observing the Jewish Sabbath as well as the Christian Sunday." He might have added that they are the chief Judaisers of Christendom. They believe that they possess the Ark of the Covenant, and by them the Jewish rite of Circumcision is practised. The flesh of animals which do not chew the cud and have not cloven feet is forbidden. Dancing, as was the case amongst the Jews, forms part of their ritual. Still such Christianity as Abyssinia presents has rendered their country superior to all other countries of Africa; a proof, says Schaff, that even a barbaric Christianity is better than none at all.

* * * * * * *

5. *The Armenians* The Gospel is supposed by some to have been introduced into Armenia by St. Bartholomew; but the Armenians themselves ascribe the foundation of their Church to a mission under St. Thaddæus. Although traces of Christian worship, as early as the time of Tertullian, exist, the real founder of the Armenian Church was St. Gregory the Illuminator ($\phi\omega\tau\iota\sigma\tau\eta\varsigma$), the Apostle, as he is called, of Armenia, in the first years of the Fourth Century. The Emperor Diocletian, to whom the tenth persecution is ascribed, had helped Tiridates III. in obtaining the Kingdom of Armenia, and from him the King imbibed his hatred to Christianity and his persecuting zeal. Gregory, who was the son of a Parthian Prince and a relative of the King, refusing to join in the Pagan worship, was thrown into a mud-pit, the mode of punishment of common malefactors, where for fourteen years he was supported by a Christian woman named Anna. Armenia and the King suffering by the visitation of a plague, Gregory was summoned from his pit, with the result that both the

King and people were restored to health. Gregory having been created Bishop of Armenia, settled his See in his native village, to which he gave the name of Etchmiadzen (the *Descent of the Holy One*), so named from a vision of the Saviour which appeared to him in the Heavens; and A.D. 302, King Tiridates and the people received Baptism in the waters of the Euphrates. This event occurred before the conversion of Constantine the Great; Armenia, therefore, is entitled to the credit of affording the first instance of the conversion of a whole Kingdom to Christianity.

The present Pope of Rome, Leo XIII., in an Encyclical of 1888, desiring "to show" from numerous historical evidences " that the Armenian Church owes its conversion to Rome," uses this remarkable language;—" St. Gregory the Illuminator, the Apostle of Armenia, went to Rome to give an account of his faith, and to present tokens of his obedience to the supreme Pontiff, Silvester." But Silvester did not become Pope till A D. 314; this fiction about St. Gregory having gone to Rome is not older than the Seventeenth Century, but, by a forgery, which Roman Catholics themselves allow, was foisted into a manuscript of the Fourth Century.

The Armenian Church, having been established by St. Gregory, rapidly became so flourishing as successively to resist an attack made upon it, A D. 312, in order to force it back into Paganism, by the Emperor Maximin. In 332, Gregory, who had in the previous year resigned his See to live a hermit life in the desert, died; after him, first his son, and then his grandsons, who, together with him are commemorated as Saints in the Armenian Church, occupied for several generations the Episcopal throne of Armenia, with the title of Catholicos. The last Catholicos of the family was St. Isaac (390—441), who, in conjunction with St. Mesrob, invented for his people a national alphabet and translated the Bible into their new language. On his death, at the age of one hundred and ten years, Mesrob succeeded him as Bishop, but within six months followed him to the grave. The next Catholicos was Joseph (perhaps 441—452). About that time the Persian dynasty of the Arsacidæ made way for the Sassanidæ, who endeavoured to eradicate Christianity, and to bring Armenia back to the doctrine of Zoroaster; and in the fearful persecution of Christianity which followed, the Episcopal See was removed from Etchmiadzen to Tovin. The persecution had a further unfortunate consequence, for in the midst of these troubles the Council of Chalcedon sat (A.D. 451), at which the Armenian Church was prevented from being represented.

To the absence of their Catholicos from the Council, to their ignorance of the Greek language, in which its decrees were written, and to the paucity of their own language, which had only one word to express both Nature and Person, may be attributed the opposition of the Armenians to the Council of Chalcedon, and their separation from the Orthodox Greek Church. In 491 the Armenian Church in full Synod at Vagarshiabad condemned the decrees of the Council, and, A D. 535, under their Patriarch Nierses, separated from the Orthodox Church; and the condemnation was repeated in a Synod held, A.D. 596, at Tovin. But the difference between the Armenian and the Orthodox Church consists rather in the mode of expression than in any point of faith. From the Monophysites they differ in several points both of faith and discipline, and hold no communion with the Jacobites; nor does the Orthodox Church consider them Monophysites. From the Orthodox Church they differ only in that they do not mix water with wine and use unleavened bread in the Eucharist. Thus they hold the central position between the Separatists and the Orthodox Greek Church; there seems to be no hindrance to their return, which would pave the way for the return of the other Separatist Communions to the Orthodox Church.

On the fall of the dynasty of the Sassanidæ, A.D. 651, Armenia was freed from Persian rule only to fall under that of the Caliphs. From the earliest to the present time says

Gibbon [q], Armenia has been the theatre of perpetual war. Yet while suffering severe persecution they have always maintained their Christian profession, and have preferred Martyrdom to embracing the faith of Mahomet. In 1367, the country was overrun by the Mamelukes, from whom they again suffered severe persecution. In its persecutions under the Mahometans Armenia from time to time sought Western help, and the Popes seized the opportunity for extending their supremacy over the Armenian Church; but if it truckled to Rome, even if some Armenian Patriarchs recognized the supremacy of Rome, it was, as was the case with the Greek Emperors, from political motives and proceeded from Court influence, and the mass of the people adhered to their own Church. But after the Council of Florence a not inconsiderable number were led to acknowledge the supremacy of the Pope, and are known as Uniat-Armenians, holding their own Liturgy and Ritual.

A schism effected by the Jesuits was a cause of great weakness to the Armenian Church, but through the intervention of Peter the Great it found protection under Russia, and from that time its condition ameliorated. Further protection was afforded by Catherine II. to the Catholicos Simeon, A.D. 1766; by the treaty of 1828, Etchmiadzen became part of the Russian Empire, and by a Ukase of 1836 the Armenian Church was recognized by the Russian Government.

Still the Roman Church has continued to harass the Armenian Christians, nor has it, in its endeavour to draw them over to Roman doctrine, even left the Uniats in peace. When, in 1867, Pope Pius IX. issued his Bull *Reversurus*, claiming the right of nominating the Patriarchs of the Uniat Churches of the East, a schism of the Uniats was the result; part remaining under the Patriarch Hassoum, whom they had elected in the previous year; the majority, headed by the Mechitarists of Venice, resisting and electing a Patriarch, named Kumelian, for themselves. Kumelian, sorely

[q] VIII. 359.

persecuted on every side, abandoned in 1879 his position, and made his submission to Rome, and in the following year Hassoum was created a Cardinal.

Under the present Pope an Armenian seminary has been established in Rome for the training of Armenians for Holy Orders, with the view to their returning to Armenia to convert their country to the Roman faith; for a similar purpose, with regard to England, the famous College of Douay was founded in the reign of Queen Elizabeth[r]. The recent Encyclical of the Pope only intensified the animosity which Greek Christians in general have always felt for the Roman Church, and the Counter Encyclical of the Patriarch of Constantinople, Anthimus, issued in August, 1896, exposing the intrigues of Rome and maintaining that the Eastern Church has retained a more Apostolical faith, has exposed the weakness of the Roman cause in Armenia.

The Armenian Church is governed by three Patriarchs, the chief of whom resides in the monastery of Etchmiadzen, now in Russian territory, at the foot of Mount Ararat, whose Diocese comprises the Greater Armenia with forty-two Archbishops under his jurisdiction. The second, with twelve Archbishops under him, resides at Cis, with Churches owning his jurisdiction in Cappadocia, Cilicia, Cyprus, and Syria. A third, and last in rank, with eight or nine Bishops under him, resides at Aghtamar, but is regarded by the Armenians generally with suspicion as an enemy of their Church. There are also titular Patriarchs in Constantinople and Jerusalem, and also a Patriarch in Poland, who presides over the Armenians in those quarters; but they all perform their duties subject to the Patriarch at Etchmiadzen. The Uniat-Armenians resident in Poland are under a Bishop who resides at Lemberg.

In wealth and intelligence, Armenia in the present day

---

[r] Part of the oath taken by the Seminarists of Douay was;—"I swear in the presence of Almighty God . . . in due time to receive Holy Orders, and to return to England to convert the souls of my countrymen and kindred."

constitutes, next to Russia, the most important, and, till yesterday, the most prosperous and progressive community in the East Armenia, says Dr. Neale, has always been distinguished for the interest its Church has taken in education; money is regarded by its rich merchants as a gift entrusted to them by God, and Christian benevolence as a matter of principle forms part of the religion of the people. Dr. Buchanan, in his "Christian Researches in Asia," written in 1809, says, Armenians "are to be found in every principal city of Asia; they are the general merchants of the East, and are in a state of constant motion from Canton to Constantinople Their general character is that of a wealthy, industrious, enterprising people. They are settled in all the principal places of India, where they arrived many centuries before the English. Wherever they colonize they build Churches, and observe the solemnities of the Christian religion in a decorous manner. Their ecclesiastical establishment in Hindoostan is more respectable than that of the English. They have preserved the Bible in its purity, and their doctrines are, as far as the author knows, those of the Bible [t]."

The late Armenian massacres are fresh in the memory of all, and need no description or comment here.

* * * * * * *

6. The Maronites, the sole remnant of the Monothelitic heresy (which will be dealt with in the following chapter), derive their name from a monastery, near Mount Lebanon, founded by St. Maro, a contemporary of St Chrysostom. They are said to have elected, about A.D. 700, as their first Patriarch, a man also named John Maro, whom they managed to get Consecrated by some Bishops of the party of Macarius, the Monothelite Patriarch of Antioch, who was deposed by the Sixth Œcumenical Council; Maro won over the monks of the monastery of Mount Lebanon, and the

---

[t] "The dead hand of their first Patriarch is said to be used at the Consecration of their Bishops"—Archdeacon Sinclair's Charge, 1898.

The Separatist Churches of the East. 277

neighbouring people, and assumed the title, which his successors have continued to bear, of Patriarch of Antioch.

When the decrees of the Council of Chalcedon were enforced at the edge of the sword, they took refuge on Mount Lebanon, and there founded a separate community. The Maronites constitute a nation rather than a religion, forming nearly the whole population of Mount Lebanon. In 1182, during the Crusades, they renounced the Monothelite heresy, and the whole nation or Church was brought, through Aymeric, the Latin Patriarch of Antioch, to acknowledge the Supremacy of the Pope, and to embrace the Roman Catholic Church, of which, although they still continue to retain their own peculiar observances, the Syrian Missal and the marriage of their Priests, and enjoy independence in the election of their Patriarch by their own Bishops, they may be considered the most ultramontane section. At the present day they number about 200,000 adherents. Besides their Patriarch, who resides in the convent of Kennobin (*Cœnobium*) on Mount Lebanon, and takes at his Consecration the name of Peter, as his rival of the Jacobite Church, who also bears the title of Patriarch of Antioch, takes that of Ignatius. They have eight Bishops with Sees at Aleppo, Tripoli, Byblus, Heliopolis, Damascus, Beyrout, Cyprus (in which island they have many adherents), Tyre and Sidon.

The Orthodox Greek Church also has at the present day a Church on the Lebanon, although greatly outnumbered by the Maronites. This Church is of course in communion with the Russian Church, which is greatly interesting itself in it, and in the present year (1898) the Greek Priest was able to show to the Bishop of Salisbury a fine set of robes lately sent him from Russia [u].

An interesting account of the Maronites is contained in Pinkerton's travels, published in 1811 [x]. Mount Lebanon, he says, is wholly inhabited by Christians, who do not suffer the Mahometans to settle in it, "nor even the Pashas them-

[u] Salisbury Diocesan Gazette.   [x] Vol. X., p 479.

selves to come up to the hills" It is a place of refuge for Christians from the tyranny of Turkish governors, and " especially for those unhappy wretches, who having denied the faith repent of it and become Christians again." Every village has a well-built Church, and there are almost as many monasteries as villages, the monks belonging to the rule of St. Antony; in their villages and all the Churches there is "a bell, which is an extraordinary thing in those parts." They have also several nunneries, but as the nuns do not take vows, they are only in a state of probation, and but few young women live in them, so that they are generally used as hospitals for old and decrepit women.

"The Maronites," says Dean Stanley, "have lately acquired a more tragical claim to our interest through the atrocities perpetrated in their villages by their ancient hereditary enemies, the Druses, provoked it may be, but certainly not excused, by Maronite aggression and Latin intrigues." This was in 1845. At the hands of the Druses their blood was poured out like water; their Churches and monasteries were sacked and burnt, their dwelling-houses levelled to the ground, their mulberry-trees and silk-worms, the sole sustenance of the people, cut down and destroyed. Thus, within a short space of time, both the Nestorians and Maronites became victims to a similar calamity. An old Egyptian tablet on Mount Lebanon was used by the French to commemorate the passage of the French army in 1860-1, at the time of the pacification of the Lebanon after the bitter and bloody quarrels of the Maronites and the Druses; and since that date the Lebanon has had a Christian governor, and has been on the whole peaceful and prosperous.

CHAPTER VIII.

The Fifth and Sixth Œcumenical Councils.

END of the Schism between Constantinople and Rome—Theodoric, King of Italy, and Pope John I.—Ephraim, Patriarch of Antioch—Justinian Emperor—His wife Theodora—Abolition of the Neo-Platonic Academy—Pope Agapetus I. at Constantinople—Memnas Patriarch—Origenistic controversy in Lavra of St. Sabas—Theodore Ascidas—Edict of the Three Chapters—Silverius, Pope of Rome—The Exarchs at Ravenna—Vigilius Pope—His arrival at Constantinople—The Ὁμολογία Πίστεως—Eutychius, Patriarch of Constantinople—Fifth Œcumenical Council—Vacillating conduct of Vigilius—His character as described by Dr Dollinger—The Aphthardocetæ and Phthartolatræ—The Pandects—Institutes—And Novels—Building of the Church of St. Sophia—The Kingdom of Lombardy—John the Faster and the title of Œcumenical Patriarch—Pope Gregory the Great's attempt to "keep in check" the Patriarch of Constantinople—Power of the Emperors exercised over the Popes—Devastations of Chosroes II.—Heraclius Emperor—Birth of Mahomet—John the Almoner—Monothelitism—Honorius I. Pope—Sophronius, Patriarch of Jerusalem—The Ecthesis—The monk Maximus—The Type—The First Lateran Council—Pope Martin I. and the Emperor Constans II.—Sixth Œcumenical Council—Monothelitism condemned—Condemnation of Pope Honorius confirmed by Pope Leo II.—The Trullan Council.

THE Emperor Anastasius was succeeded by Justin I. (518—527), an illiterate Dacian peasant, sixty years of age, who had risen to the highest rank in the army, and who now, in the government of the Empire, availed himself of the talents and ability of his more capable nephew Justinian. The new Emperor was a man of inflexible orthodoxy, and no doubt had learnt experience from the stern lesson taught to his predecessor by Vitalian. He at once banished Severus, Julian of Halicarnassus, and the other Monophysite leaders, who took refuge in Alexandria, where every shade of Monophysitism was rampant, and which was too formidable a stronghold to be interfered with. The great event in Justin's reign was the termination of the schism between Constantinople and Rome. The persecution of the Orthodox Church by Anastasius, and the unflinching orthodoxy of the Popes, had immensely added to the prestige of Rome; and the help sought by and given to the Orthodox Church was one of the gradual steps by which Rome gained the ascendency over Constantinople. Persecuted in the East, and deposed simply for their orthodoxy and their adherence to the Council of Chalcedon, the Eastern Prelates sought the protection of the Bishops of Rome; and, but for the arrogant claims of the Popes for the erasure of the name of Acacius from the Diptychs, there is no doubt there would have been at that time an overwhelming secession from the Eastern to the Western Church.

Anastasius II. (496—498), the successor of Gelasius in the See of Rome, was a man of gentler character than his predecessor, and he committed a mortal offence in the eyes of his Church in deviating from the conduct of Gelasius by sending two Bishops to Constantinople to propose that the name of Acacius should be left on the Diptychs as the means of effecting peace. But his Pontificate was of too short a duration to effect the purpose, animosity, which pursued him during his life-time, did not cease with his death, and Dante describes his suffering in hell the torments inflicted on one who had deviated from the right path [a].

On the death of Pope Anastasius there was a double election to the Papacy, Laurence being chosen by the party who favoured the conciliatory policy of Anastasius, Symmachus by the intolerant party. The matter was referred to the Arian King Theodoric, who decided in favour of Symmachus, and he was in consequence elected Pope (498—514). The Emperor Anastasius had favoured the cause of his rival; between Emperor and Pope there was in consequence but little love; they mutually accused each other of Manichæism, which at that time was synonymous with heresy in general; and under two such opponents the healing of the schism was doomed to failure.

On the death of Timothy, who was a violent persecutor of the orthodox Christians, John II. (517—520), surnamed of Cappadocia, became Patriarch of Constantinople, and Hor-

[a] Inf. XI. 819, quoted in Smith's Dict.

misdas (514—523) succeeded Symmachus as Pope of Rome. The Emperor Anastasius, when hard pressed by Vitalian, sought a reconciliation with Hormisdas. But the Pope, imposing upon the Emperor's necessities, demanded the erasure from the Diptychs not only of the name of Acacius, but of other Patriarchs who had died out of Communion with Rome; and required such concessions to the supremacy of Rome that (A.D. 517) the Emperor broke off all negotiations, contrasting the haughty pretensions of the Pope with the forgiving spirit of Christ.

Justin and Justinian, as soon as the former became Emperor, entered upon fresh negotiations with Hormisdas, who acted under the authority of the Arian King, Theodoric, with the view to putting an end to the schism. On March 28, 519, a reconciliation was effected at Constantinople, and the schism ended, but on the condition that not only the name of Acacius, but also those of Favritta, Euphemius, Macedonius, and Timothy, as well as of the Emperors Zeno and Anastasius, should be removed from the Diptychs. Still the Patriarch John, unwilling to acknowledge any superiority of Rome over the Patriarchate of Constantinople, obtained from Justin the title of Œcumenical Patriarch, a title given by the civil power, and therefore of neither greater or less importance than that previously given to the See of Rome by Valentinian III. Hormisdas, elated with his victory over the See of Constantinople, styled Justin a second Hezekiah, but the concession made by the Emperor to the Pope formed an unfortunate precedent, and through it the thin end of the wedge of Rome's afterclaims of superiority over the Patriarchs of Constantinople was inserted.

On the expulsion of Severus, Paul, a Presbyter of Constantinople, was appointed Patriarch of Antioch (519—521), and he rigorously enforced the Council of Chalcedon. But the Antiochenes, still persisting in holding that Council in disfavour, accused him first of Nestorianism, and afterwards brought various other accusations, which made his position so intolerable that he obtained permission to resign the Patriarchate, in which he was succeeded by Euphrasius (521—526).

Justin, in his determination to establish orthodoxy in the East, issued, A.D. 523, an edict, ordering Manichæans (i.e. heretics generally) to leave the Empire under pain of death; and Pagans and Jews were forbidden to hold civil or military offices. An exception to the rule was made in the case of Goths and other foreign soldiers (*federati milites*) who were serving in the armies of the Empire.

Epiphanius, the successor of John, was at the time Patriarch of Constantinople (520—535), and an abettor of the Emperor in his intolerant measures. Hormisdas was succeeded in the See of Rome by John I. (522—526). Theodoric, King of Italy, was as relentless an enemy against Paganism as Justin, and under him Paganism almost entirely disappeared from the Western dominions. But though himself an Arian, he had observed toleration towards the Catholics, and expected Justin to be equally tolerant towards Arians, and he now threatened that if toleration was not accorded to Arians in the East, to retaliate on the Catholics in the West. The Popes had professed it to be derogatory to their dignity to attend the Œcumenical Councils of the Church. But the immunity which the Roman Church enjoyed through its remoteness from the seat of government was now rudely broken. In 524 Theodoric despatched Pope John on a mission to Constantinople to obtain the revocation of the edict against Arians and other heretics, and the restoration of the Churches which had been given up to the Catholics. John was received with great honour at Constantinople, and the Patriarch Epiphanius yielded him precedence in his Cathedral Church on Easter-day; but, either on account of the honour accorded him, or because he failed in obtaining terms for the Arians, John was on his return to Italy thrown into prison at Ravenna, where he died shortly afterwards, to be venerated by succeeding generations as Saint and Martyr of the Roman Church.

The Fifth and Sixth Œcumenical Councils. 283

On the death of John, Theodoric, though an Arian, took a step which must have been peculiarly galling to the Catholics, and himself, without waiting for the election by the clergy and people, appointed Felix IV. as Pope (526—530), and the appointment was afterwards acquiesced in by the clergy and the Senate of Rome.

In 526, the city of Antioch was nearly entirely destroyed by a series of earthquakes, in one of which the Patriarch Euphrasius lost his life, and Count Ephraim, who held a high position in the Emperor's service, was sent by him to superintend the reconstruction of the city. Ephraim forbade the terrified inhabitants to leave the city, and ordered them to inscribe over their gates the words, "May Christ be with us," and the earthquake ceasing, the grateful citizens unanimously chose him as their Patriarch (527—545); Antioch, in memory of the miracle, assuming the title of Theopolis—*the City of God*. The orthodox Patriarch showed himself a champion against Severus and the Acephali, and wrote several treatises in favour of the Council of Chalcedon.

In 527, Justin associated with himself in the Empire his nephew Justinian, who on his death, which occurred in the same year, became sole Emperor (527—565). In civil and military matters, the reign of Justinian was one of great glory. But with an overweening confidence in his own abilities, he thought himself a theologian, and unmindful that the Patriarchs were the proper governors of the Church, and with a mind utterly unfitted to grasp subtle points of doctrine, he thought to remodel the Church in such a manner as to comprehend both the orthodox and unorthodox parties. Himself a waverer in religion, at first a supporter of the Council of Chalcedon and opponent of the Monophysites, he went on in his self-confidence, till he made shipwreck of his faith, and ended his days by himself becoming a Monophysite. But whether Orthodox or Monophysite, he was throughout a persecutor, and his long reign was a momentous one to its close.

At the commencement of it he admitted Theodora, a woman of immoral character, whom he had made his wife, to a share of the government. She, as far as she had any religion at all, was a Monophysite, under the influence of Severus, the deposed Patriarch of Antioch, and Anthemius, Bishop of Trebizond, the latter of whom was on the death of Euphemius, A.D 635, translated through her influence to the Patriarchate of Constantinople.

Against Pagans Justinian was equally as severe as his predecessor. In 529, he issued an edict abolishing the Neo-Platonic Academy at Athens, where the philosophers, who, though themselves not open professors of the heathen deities, preserved Paganism alive by teaching it as an esoteric religion. Damasius, so called from his being a native of Damascus, the Head of the Academy, with six of his colleagues fled to Ctesiphon, and placed themselves under the protection of Chosroes or Nushirvan, the powerful King of Persia, at whose court they found a friendly welcome. But finding the religion of Zoroaster still less to their minds than Christianity, they returned to the Roman Empire, where they were allowed, through the intercession of Chosroes, to live unmolested, although not in Athens; and on the further condition of their not attempting to proselytize the Christians. Thenceforward the Pagan religion died out from the Eastern dominions of the Empire.

Theodoric, King of Italy, having died A.D. 526, Justinian availed himself of the confusion that ensued for the reconquest of Italy. Theodoric was succeeded by his grandson, Athalaric, the son of his daughter, Amasalunta, and when he, after a reign of eight years, fell a victim to his vices, Theodohad, the nephew of Theodoric, succeeded to the kingdom, and sent Amasalunta into exile on an island on the Lake Bolsona, where she was shortly afterwards found strangled in her bath. The dissensions in the royal family consequent on the murder of Amasalunta gave Justinian a plea for invading Italy, and to ward off the invasion, Theodohad, following the example set by Theodoric, despatched Pope Agapetus I. (535—536) to Constantinople, who, accompanied by his Archdeacon, Vigilius, arrived there on February 2, 536. The Pope at once refused to hold Communion with the Patriarch Anthemius on the ground that the latter was a Monophysite, and had been, contrary to the Nicene Canon, translated from one Diocese to another. Justinian first threatened the Pope; "I came hither," said Agapetus, "in my old age, expecting to find a religious and Christian Emperor, but I find a second Diocletian." The Emperor was so struck with respect and admiration of the unflinching fortitude of the Pope, that he authorized a Synod to meet at Constantinople, over which the Pope presided; Anthemius being convicted of Monophysitism was deposed, and Memnas (536—552), President of a Hospice at Constantinople, appointed in his place and consecrated by the Pope.

Agapetus died in April at Constantinople. By another Synod at Constantinople in May and June, convened by Justinian and presided over by Memnas, Anthemius was convicted of Eutychianism, and together with Severus, Peter of Apamea, and an excommunicated Eutychian monk, named Zoaras (all of whom were living at Constantinople under the patronage of the Empress), were anathematized. The sentence pronounced against Anthemius, being confirmed by the Emperor on August 6, he was sent into banishment. In this Synod, Memnas publicly claimed for the Patriarch of Constantinople the title of Œcumenical Patriarch, the cause of future disputes between the Sees of Rome and Constantinople.

At this time there were also living at Constantinople, in high favour with the Empress, two monks of Palestine, named Domitian and Theodore Ascidas, who with Eutychian combined Origenist views. In the early part of the century the controversy which had taken place in Palestine in the time of St. Jerome, with regard to the writings of Origen, was renewed in the Lavra of which St Sabas was at the head, and excited the alarm of Peter, the Patriarch of Jerusalem (524—544). At the request of Peter, St. Sabas, at the time 94 years of age, went in 530 to Constantinople to, amongst other matters, request Justinian to expel the two Origenist monks. The Emperor received him with the greatest reverence, lodged him in his palace and asked his blessing, and promised to grant all he asked; but St. Sabas died the next year, before any steps could be taken by the Emperor The monks who in the lifetime of St. Sabas had dissembled their opinions, now that the restraint was removed, and the weak and timid Peter was ill-qualified to stand in the gap, openly asserted them, and widely diffused Origenism through the monasteries. The two monks, who still continued to reside in Constantinople, gained such an influence over the Emperor, that, in 537, Theodore Ascidas was appointed Archbishop of the Cappadocian Cæsarea, and Domitian Bishop of Ancyra in Galatia, both of them continuing to reside in Constantinople.

Under their influence the number of Origenists so greatly increased in the East, that Peter induced Pelagius, afterwards (555—560) Pope of Rome, who was at the time resident in Jerusalem, to go with four monks to Constantinople in order to obtain from the Emperor a sentence of condemnation against Origen. Pelagius and his monks obtained from the Emperor the desired condemnation, and Justinian, always ready to pose as a theologian, addressed to Memnas a rescript, confuting the writings of Origen, and requiring the Patriarchs of the East to convene Synods for the same purpose. In 543 Origen was condemned in a Synod under the Patriarch Ephraim at Antioch, and also by Zoilus, Patriarch of Alexandria (542—551); and a Synod of Bishops resident at Constantinople (σύνοδος ἐνδημοῦσα), under Memnas, issued in the same year fifteen anathemas, which were subscribed by Theodore Ascidas and Domitian, against Origen and his doctrines.

Theodore Ascidas, however, although he had subscribed the anathemas, continued to favour the Origenists, who, under his wing, became dominant in Palestine, so that, on the death of Peter, Macarius, an Origenist, was appointed his successor. But this election not being confirmed by Justinian, Macarius was deposed, and Eustochius (544—556), who held an office in the Church of Alexandria, but was at the time resident in Constantinople, appointed in his place.

It was probably with the view of engaging the Emperor on a different matter, and so removing from himself the suspicion of Origenism, that Theodore Ascidas in concert with Domitian stirred up the controversy of the "Three Chapters" (τρία κεφάλαια). By the Three Chapters were meant the writings of three deceased Bishops, Theodore of Mopsuestia, Theodoret, and Ibas. The controversy kindled a flame in the Church which it took long to extinguish, and it was said of it that it filled more volumes than it deserved lines.

Theodore Ascidas, himself a Monophysite, knew that it was Justinian's wish to reconcile the Acephali to the Church. He persuaded him into the belief that the Monophysites were not opposed to the Council of Chalcedon itself, but to the writings of the three Bishops, which they considered of a Nestorian character, although Theodore of Mopsuestia was dead before the Council was held, whilst Theodoret and Ibas had at the Council anathematized Nestorianism and been pronounced by it to be orthodox. He told the Emperor that if the Council could be cleared of having defended them, the Monophysites would no longer reject it, and thus could be won over to the Orthodox Church. Justinian, falling into the trap laid for him, issued (probably A.D. 544) the Edict of the Three Chapters, in which, without impugning the Council itself, he condemned the writings of the three Bishops; the edict he sent to the Patriarchs and Bishops for their signatures, with an intimation, in case of refusal, of their deposition. Memnas signed it reluctantly; and, mindful of the recently healed schism between Constantinople and Rome, insisted on the condition that if it was not approved by the Pope his signature would be revoked. The other three Patriarchs also, Zoilus of Alexandria,

Ephraim of Antioch, and Eustochius of Jerusalem, signed under the fear of deposition, and the majority of the Eastern Bishops followed their example. But not so the Bishops of the West, who, being for the most part ignorant of the Greek language, knew little about the condemned writings, and regarded Justinian's Edict as a direct attack on the Council of Chalcedon.

The intercession of Pope Agapetus was unsuccessful in turning Justinian from the invasion of Italy. His great General Belisarius having, A.D. 534, destroyed the Vandal dominion in Africa, and in the following year recovered Sicily and Naples from the Ostrogoths, in December, 536, marched on Rome. In all the dominions thus recovered to the Empire, Justinian ordered the laws against Arians and other heretics to be enforced, and orthodoxy established. Sixty years had elapsed since Odoacer had conquered Rome, but from the first, the Gothic rule had been disliked by the Romans, who, although they had generally been left in possession of their ecclesiastical as well as their civil laws and institutions, never acquiesced in their dependence on their Arian conquerors, but turned their eyes to the Emperors in the East as their legitimate sovereigns.

On the death of Pope Agapetus, the election of Silverius (536—537), son of the late Pope Hormisdas, was supposed to have been brought about by simony, and forced on the Roman Church by the Arian King Theodotus. The approach of Belisarius was welcomed by the Romans, and, by the advice of the Pope and Senate, the gates of Rome were thrown open to the Imperial troops. Theodotus having been shortly before deposed, was now murdered by his successor, Vitiges, whom Belisarius conquered and took captive to Constantinople. Ildibald, the next King (539—541), was assassinated and succeeded by Evaric, who was also in his turn after five months murdered and succeeded by Totila; who, in 546, regained all the conquests made by Belisarius, and threatened to reduce Rome into a pasture for cattle. Under him the Kingdom of the Arian Goths was once again established on a strong footing in Italy. But in 552, Totila was killed in battle by Narses, the successor of Belisarius, and with him perished for ever the race and the name of the Ostrogoths. Italy was recovered to the Eastern Emperor, and thenceforward, for nearly two hundred years, the Greek possessions in Italy were governed by Exarchs living at Ravenna, of whom Narses was the first. The Romans were now nominally subject to the Exarchs as vicegerents of the Emperors living at Constantinople, but in reality they looked on the Popes not only as their religious but political chiefs.

The taking of Rome by Belisarius seemed to the Empress Theodora to offer the opportunity of reinstating Anthemius and establishing Monophysitism. She had, by the bribe of succession to the Papacy, brought over to her Monophysite views Vigilius, the Archdeacon of Agapetus, he promising, on becoming Pope, to disavow the Council of Chalcedon and to favour the Monophysites. But the difficulty was how to get rid of Silverius, who, whatever else he was, was orthodox, and whose orthodoxy formed a barrier to herself and Vigilius. Antonina, the wife of Belisarius, who ruled her husband much in the same way as she herself ruled Justinian, was the confidante of the Empress. Acting under the influence of his wife, Belisarius seized the Pope who had befriended him, by whose aid he had gained possession of Rome. After attempting in vain to persuade him to accede to the wishes of the Empress, to condemn the Council of Chalcedon, and to recognize Anthemius, whom his predecessor had deposed, as Patriarch, Antonina accused him with having betrayed Rome to the Goths; the end was that Silverius, stripped of the pallium and arrayed in the dress of a simple monk, was banished to Patara, and Vigilius, by order of Belisarius, on payment of two hundred pounds in gold, elected in his place.

The Emperor, when he learnt what had happened, and how he had been outwitted by the Empress, ordered the return of Silverius to Rome, with the promise that, if the accusations brought against him proved unfounded, he should be reinstated in the Papacy. But means were taken to intercept his return; by order of Belisarius he was given up to Vigilius, and banished to the island of Palmaria in the Tuscan Sea, where, but by what means was never discovered, he died in the following year.

Soon after he became Pope, Vigilius wrote to the Monophysite Bishops, Anthemius and Severus, expressing his agreement with them; and to the Empress he wrote, condemning, in accordance with his stipulation, the Tome of Pope Leo, and anathematizing Diodorus of Tarsus, Theodore of Mopsuestia, and Theodoret. He also wrote to Justinian and Memnas, accepting the Tome of Leo and the Council of Chalcedon, and condemning Anthemius, Severus, and the Monophysites.

The Emperor ordered the Pope to appear at Constantinople. Loaded with imprecations and assailed by the populace with stones as the murderer of Silverius, Vigilius, in obedience to the Emperor's order, arrived at Constantinople in 547, where he at once found himself in a pitiful dilemma between the Emperor and Empress, who were hopelessly at variance; to both of whom he had pledged himself, professing to the Emperor that he was orthodox, to the Empress that he was a Monophysite.

He at first refused to condemn the Three Chapters, or even to communicate with Memnas. But by the death, in the following year, of the Empress Theodora, he was delivered from his embarrassment; at Easter he issued a document called the *Judicatum*, agreeing with the Emperor's Edict and condemning the Three Chapters without disparaging the Council of Chalcedon. Thus he thought to satisfy all parties, the Easterns by condemning the Three Chapters, the Westerns by not including in his condemnation the Council of Chalcedon. But he only added to his difficulties. Two Roman Deacons and his own nephew, who had accompanied him to Constantinople, renouncing

The Fifth and Sixth Œcumenical Councils. 291

communion with him, returned to Rome; the Bishops of Illyricum and Dalmatia in the Synod of Illyricum, A.D 549, condemned the *Judicatum*, and those of North Africa formally excommunicated the Pope. He now withdrew the *Judicatum*, throwing the blame on the Empress, of whose intentions he pleaded with the Westerns that he had acted in ignorance.

In 551, Justinian issued a Second Edict, styed the ʽΟμολογία Πίστεως, against the Three Chapters, and called upon Vigilius to subscribe it; but Vigilius firmly refused to do so. Zoilus, Patriarch of Alexandria, was the only Eastern Bishop who stood by him, and he was in consequence deposed, and Apollinarius appointed in his place. Vigilius, finding himself beset with difficulties, fled for refuge first to the Church of St. Sergius in Constantinople, and afterwards to that of St. Euphemia in Chalcedon, where he remained nearly a year, returning at length under the safe conduct of the Emperor to Constantinople at the end of 552.

In that year, Memnas, Patriarch of Constantinople, died, and was succeeded by Eutychius (552—582)[a]. Justinian now determined to call a General Council, and on May 5, 553, the Fifth Œcumenical Council, the second of Constantinople, met under the Presidency of Eutychius. The Council was attended by Apollinarius of Alexandria, Domnus of Antioch, and 165 Eastern Bishops ; Eustochius, Patriarch of Jerusalem, was represented by three legates. Vigilius and about twenty Western Bishops who were in Constantinople, although twice waited on by a deputation of the three Patriarchs and twenty Metropolitans, refused to attend. The Pope, however, sent to Justinian a document entitled *Constitutum*, in which he condemned the Three Chapters, but without naming the authors, on the ground that it was unlawful to anathematize the dead. The Council proceeded by order of Justinian and held Eight Sessions,

---

For twelve years (565—577) Eutychius lived in banishment, John Scholasticus being intruded into the Patriarchate by Justinian.

extending to June 2. In the first Session a letter from the Emperor was read, setting forth how his orthodox predecessors had convened all the Œcumenical Synods,—Constantine, that of the 318 Fathers at Nice; Theodosius, of the 150 at Constantinople; Theodosius, the younger, the Synod of Ephesus; the Emperor Marcian, that of Chalcedon. But divisions having arisen since the last Council, he had summoned the Council to the capital to give judgment on "the Three impious Chapters." Vigilius, the Pope of Old Rome, he said had come to Constantinople, had repeatedly anathematized them in writing, and he had lately anathematized them in his *Judicatum* The Pope had previously desired that a Synod should be assembled, but now he had altered his views, and although he had several times commanded him to do so, he had refused to attend. He asked them to consider, as to Theodore of Mopsuestia, the absurd assertion that no one is to be anathematized after his death; to consider also the writings of Theodoret, and the supposed Letter of Ibas, in which the Incarnation of the Word is denied, the expression "God-bearer" and the holy Synod of Ephesus rejected, Cyril called a heretic, and Theodore and Nestorius defended and praised. In the 4th, 5th, and 6th Sessions the Three Chapters were examined, and precedents were found in Ecclesiastical history for anathematizing persons who had died in the Communion of the Church. The Emperor sent to the 7th Session the writings of Vigilius, in which he had condemned the Three Chapters, and ordered the Synod to continue, without regard to the Pope, and to remove his name from the Diptychs. In the 8th Session, sentence, in accordance with the will of the Emperor, was delivered; anathemas were pronounced against both the writings and person of Theodore, and against the writings, but not the person, of Theodoret and Ibas.

The vacillating Pope once more turned round, and under fear of banishment assented to and confirmed the decrees of the Council. At length, after a seven years' absence, he was allowed by Justinian to return to Rome, but he died on the road.

Other Popes fell into heresy and repented, but charity can scarcely find a good word for Vigilius. He at least three times, says Dean Milman, yielded and then desperately resisted Justinian; three times condemned the Three Chapters and three times recanted the condemnation. But in case the judgment of an Anglican may be called in question, we will hear what his own Church has to say of him. The late Dr. Döllinger, perhaps the most learned theologian of the day, says [b], "Perhaps a just judgment, which was the consequence of his iniquitous seizure of the Pontificate, weighed heavily upon him, deprived him of light and strength from above, till he was tossed to and fro, like a helmless bark, in this tempestuous commotion." That, between Constantinople and Syracuse, where he died, he may have seen the error of his ways awakens the Christian's hope, and no one will withhold from him the pious wish, *Requiescat in pace.*

He was succeeded by Pelagius I. (555—560), who accepted the decrees of the Fifth Œcumenical Council, and the condemnation of the Three Chapters But in the West, where they were vigorously defended, troubles and schism arose [c]; whilst in the East the Acephali remained as estranged as ever. In the West the Council was eventually accepted as Œcumenical, and Pope Gregory the Great ranked it with the four preceding Councils [d].

In the last years of his life, Justinian, who had passed his long reign in oppressing now Pagans, now Monophysites, and latterly the Orthodox party, fell into the worst form of the Monophysite heresy. Alexandria, whither Severus and Julian of Halicarnassus had, after being expelled from their Sees, repaired, continued to be the abiding stronghold of the heresy. But soon a violent dispute arose between the two as to the corruptibility of our Lord's

---

[b] Hist. of the Church, II. 187.
[c] Epistles of St. Gregory the Great, IV., XVI., XXIV.
[d] Mansi.

Human Body before the Resurrection; Severus maintaining that before the Resurrection the Body of Christ was, but after it ceased to be, corruptible, i.e. subject to corporal affections and changes; Julian, that it was not so subject, and therefore was not ordinary Flesh. The followers of the latter were called Aphthardocetæ (ἀφθαρδοκῆται, believers in only *an apparent body*), those of the former, Phthartolatræ (φθαρτόλατραι, believers in the *corruptible*). Justinian, whose old age was not satiated with his theological despotism, issued, in 563, an edict declaring the Apthardocetic doctrine to be the correct one, and sent it to the Patriarchs for subscription under pain of deposition. But the edict of the Emperor in favour of a doctrine which approximated to Docetism was everywhere opposed.

In vain Eutychius of Constantinople disproved the doctrine from Scripture; he was arrested by a band of soldiers when celebrating the Holy Eucharist, deposed and exiled, and John, surnamed Scholasticus, a man more eminent as a lawyer at Antioch than as an ecclesiastic, was appointed to the Patriarchate (565—577). Anastasius, called, from his having once been a monk of Mount Sinai, Sinaita, the holy Patriarch of Antioch (561—593), the successor of Domnus in the See, was threatened. He wrote a letter to the monks in Syria, who had applied to him for advice, " that our Blessed Saviour's Body was absolutely liable to corruption; that this was the opinion of the Holy Fathers as well as of the Apostles themselves, and therefore he exhorted them with the utmost earnestness to undergo all extremities rather than suffer a doctrine so well grounded to be wrested from them e." Further persecution of the Orthodox was however stayed by the death of Justinian, who had exceeded 80 years of age, A.D. 565.

The legislation, of which Justinian was the author, was of too extensive a character, even as concerns the Church, to be more than barely mentioned in a work of this kind. It is comprised in three works, the Code published in 529,

'Evag Scholast., B. IV.

The Fifth and Sixth Œcumenical Councils. 295

the Pandects in 533, and the Institutes about the same time, whilst after his death were published the Novels. These works, in which the most minute points of Church discipline, the relations of the Bishops to their clergy, and the regulation of Monasteries form a conspicuous part, remain a permanent memorial of his reign.

Justinian was the founder of the style of Architecture called, from the ancient city on the ruins of which Constantinople are built, the Byzantine, the distinctive features of which are the Greek Cross and the Cupola. This style, he being Emperor of the West as well as of the East, was introduced into Italy. The Greeks, with their usual conservatism, have always adhered to their Byzantine model; but in the West, Church Architecture was progressive under the different features of Byzantine, Romanesque, Norman, and Gothic. The Romanesque was really only a Roman development of the Byzantine style, and Gothic Architecture grew out of the Romanesque, so that the Western is indebted to the Eastern Church for its Church Architecture.

In the versatility of his genius he aspired to being himself an architect, and adorned Constantinople and other cities in his dominions with stately churches, monasteries, hospitals, and other magnificent edifices; but the work was effected with money raised by the oppression and impoverishing taxation of the people. The great Church of Edessa, supposed to have been the earliest Christian Church in the world, and built in great magnificence, on the model of the Jewish Temple, by St. Thaddæus at the expense of King Abgarus, having been destroyed by an inundation, Justinian rebuilt in such splendour, that the Arabians regarded it as one of the four wonders of the world [f].

Most magnificent of all his works was the Church of St. Sophia at Constantinople. The original Church, built by Constantine, having been destroyed by fire, and another

---

[f] The others were the Pharos at Alexandria, the bridge over the river Sarrgia in Mesopotamia, and the Mahometan temple at Damascus —Etheridge.

built to take its place, having suffered a similar fate in the insurrection, known as that of the Nika, in January, 532, Justinian determined to erect on the site another Church more magnificent than any in existence, and in order to avoid similar calamities to build it entirely of stone and marble. For the work he employed the two most famous architects of the day, Anthemius of Tralles, and Isidore of Miletus. Artists were collected from all parts of the world, and some ten thousand workmen engaged, Justinian himself being constantly present and superintending the work. It was commenced on February 23, 532, and Consecrated on December 26, 537. The cost amounted to £320,000 in gold, a sum equivalent to about thirteen million of our money. Having thus built one of the wonders of the world, he exclaimed, with pardonable pride, νενίκηκα σὲ Σολομών (*I have conquered thee, O Solomon*). When this Church was, before twenty years, partially destroyed by an earthquake, he caused it to be restored; and after a second Consecration in December, 561, it was re-opened, mainly as the structure stands in the present day, the model of every subsequent stage of Byzantine art. For its services Justinian made provision for 60 Priests, 100 Deacons, besides 40 Deaconesses, 90 sub-Deacons, 110 Readers, 25 Singers, and 100 Ostiarians or door-keepers.

The Church also of the Holy Apostles at Constantinople, in which the reliques of SS. Andrew, Luke and Timothy were believed to be deposited, having been originally built of wood, Justinian rebuilt in marble.

To a Scythian by birth, although a monk of the West, Dionysius, surnamed Exiguus, who lived in the time of Justinian, we owe the adoption of the Vulgar Era, i.e. the custom of dating events from the Birth of Christ. But in his calculation it is now known that he placed the Birth of the Saviour four years too late.

The whole of Italy had, by Justinian's great Generals, Belisarius and Narses, been recovered to the Empire, the greater part of it, however, to be lost under his three successors, Justin II. (565—578), Tiberius II. (sole Emperor 578—582), and Maurice (582—602). So oppressive was the government of Narses, the first Exarch of Ravenna, that the Romans complained to the Emperor Justin that Gothic servitude had been more tolerable than the government of the Exarch, and Narses was superseded by Longinus. Narses, in revenge for this act of ingratitude, called in the Lombards, a German people holding the Arian form of doctrine, who, A.D. 568, only three years after Justinian's death, began, under their King Alboin, to pour into Italy, the North of which they conquered, founding the Kingdom which after them was called Lombardy. In 573 Alboin was murdered; still the Lombards continued their conquests, and, A D. 584, under their King Antharis, they founded the Duchies of Spoleto and Benevento in the South. The Eastern Empire still held an uncertain sovereignty over the rest of Italy, including Rome and Ravenna, a large part of the South, as well as the islands of Sicily, Sardinia and Corsica. Italy was thus divided into two unequal parts, the larger under the Arian Lombards, with Pavia for its capital, the smaller part under the Exarchs of the Greek Emperors, with its capital at Ravenna.

On the death of John Scholasticus, A.D. 577, Eutychius was restored to the Patriarchate of Constantinople, which he held till his death in 582. Towards the end of his life he fell into an Origenist error with respect to the nature of man's body after the Resurrection, but was convinced and reclaimed to orthodoxy by Gregory, the future Pope, who was at the time residing in Constantinople as the Nuncio of Pope Pelagius II., and he is commemorated as a Saint in the Greek Church.

His successor in the Patriarchate was John the Faster (582 —595). In 588 John summoned a Council at Constantinople to enquire into a charge of a very foul nature which had been brought against Gregory, the intruded Patriarch of Antioch (569—594). Anastasius Sinaita, threatened by Justinian for opposing his Aphthardocetic edict, was *actually* deposed by Justin II., and Gregory appointed in his place. Gregory is described as a singularly holy man, possessing almost every excellence of mind and person, and in his trial before the Council he received a triumphant acquittal. On his death, which occurred in 594, the deposed Patriarch Anastasius was restored.

The Council is rendered famous in Church history from the incident of the Patriarch, John the Faster, having assembled it under the name of the Œcumenical Patriarch. The term œcumenical (οἰκουμένη) the Greeks understood as comprising all the dominions of the Emperor, West as well as East; the Patriarch of Constantinople, therefore, in calling himself Œcumenical Patriarch, claimed supremacy over the whole Christian Church [g]. The term was no new one; not only did the Patriarchs of Constantinople often call themselves by it, but it is also applied to them by the Emperor Justinian in his Code and Novels. It was perhaps natural for an Emperor to magnify his own Patriarchate; he also styles the Church of Constantinople the "head and mother" of Churches; but it shows at least that no recognized supremacy attached to the See of Rome.

Pelagius II., at the time Pope of Rome (578—590), was highly indignant at the claim made by John, refused to recognize the acts of the Council (except so far as the acquittal of Gregory of Antioch went), and forbade his nuncio, Laurence, to hold communion with the Patriarch of Constantinople.

Pelagius was succeeded by Gregory I. (590—604), the Great, under whom the controversy was renewed. Gregory resented the assumption of the title even more strongly than his predecessor, as it seemed to him to signify that not only the Patriarchs of the East, but also the Pope of Rome, were mere representatives of the Patriarch of Constantinople. He stigmatized in different Letters the title as haughty, blasphemous, a diabolical usurpation, dishonourable to the whole Church; and he compares the Patriarch John to

[g] Phillimore's Internat. Law, II. 449.

Lucifer, in the desire of the latter to exalt himself above the Angels.

The Letters of Gregory, one of the greatest of the Popes, are the best commentary on the relative position of the Eastern and Western Churches at that time. The Papacy had for more than two centuries been advancing pretensions which Gregory himself, although he called himself, as his successors, whose distinguishing virtue has certainly not been that of humility, have done, by the humble title of *servus servorum Dei*, was as willing as any to magnify. The Patriarch of Constantinople had been recognized by the Second Œcumenical Council as Head of the Eastern, on the same ground as the Pope of Rome was the recognized Head of the Western Church. For some time after that Council, the Patriarchs of Alexandria resented and contested the pre-eminence of Constantinople, but by degrees the latter established their position, which was afterwards fully recognized by the Council of Chalcedon. What Gregory not unreasonably resented was that the Patriarchs of Constantinople, who had lately shown themselves so subservient to the Emperors, should claim superiority over the whole, the Western as well as the Eastern, Church. A Letter (*Epist. VIII.*) from Gregory to Isaac, Patriarch of Jerusalem (600—609), shows that not only the Church of Jerusalem, but the Eastern Church generally, was sunk deep in corruption and simony. But the Patriarchate of Constantinople was at the time, notwithstanding adverse circumstances, in the zenith of its prosperity; whereas, under the arms of the Lombards and the despotism of the Greeks, Rome at the close of the Sixth Century sunk to the lowest depths of her depression[h]. The Patriarch of Constantinople was elated with the same pride which, since the Eastern Church was overwhelmed by the Saracens, the Crusaders, and the Turks, has characterized, in its prosperity, the See of Rome.

That a contest for supremacy was going on between the two Sees, and that Gregory was trying to keep the Patriarch

[h] Gibbon, VIII 158.

of Constantinople "in check," we learn from one of his letters (*Epist. XII.*) to John, Bishop of Syracuse. He had been informed, he says, that people *murmured* at the Pope's imitating the usages of the Church of Constantinople; "How can he be arranging," he asks, "so as *to keep the Constantinopolitan Church in check*, if he is following her usage?" Gregory denies imitating the Greeks, and his point is that his adopting Greek usages was not in imitation of the Greeks, but a return to primitive usage. He here unintentionally plays into the hands of the Greeks, who always maintain that their Church is more primitive and catholic than the Roman. "Wherein then," he asks, "are we following the Greeks?" So important does the Pope consider the matter that he requests; "Let your charity . . . . proceed to the Church of Catania, or hold a Conference in the Church of Syracuse with respect to the murmuring *as though for a different purpose* (that sounds like a pious fraud), and so not desist from instructing them. For, *as to what they say* about the Church of Constantinople, who can doubt that it is subject to the Apostolic See, as both the most pious Lord the Emperor and our brother the Bishop of that city continually acknowledge?" There is perhaps more weight in what *people say* than in what a man says about himself; and so far from the Bishop of Constantinople admitting his subjection to the Papal See, we find him at the very time claiming to be *the Œcumenical Patriarch.*

That Gregory had an honest aversion to the title of Œcumenical Patriarch, by whomsoever claimed, we have in his own words. That the Patriarch of Alexandria, the successor to Theophilus and Cyril, would prefer an Œcumenical Patriarch in the West to one set over himself in the East, can easily be understood, and he addressed Gregory as *Universal* Pope. But in his reply[1] Gregory entreated him never more to address him by that "haughty title." But again to the Patriarchs of Alexandria and Antioch he wrote[2],

---

[1] Epist. VIII. 30. [2] Ibid. V. 43.

that in the Council of Chalcedon the title was offered to one of his own predecessors, but that none of them would use so *profane* a title. Gregory's ignorance of the Greek language may account for this error, as there is no reason for believing that the Council ever offered to the Bishop of Rome that title, and if it had, we may rest assured that the Pope would have accepted it. He tells them that John of Constantinople in assuming it was guilty of a *diabolical usurpation*. To the Emperor Maurice he wrote [k], "I confidently affirm that whosoever styles himself Universal Bishop is, by his pride, the precursor of Antichrist (*Antichristum præcurrit quia superbiendo se cæteris præponit.*) To the Patriarchs he wrote that there is only one Apostolic See, which was established on the Prince of the Apostles, whose "name implies a rock;" yet "that See is in three places, in Rome, where he died, in Alexandria, where it was founded by St. Mark, and in Antioch, where he lived seven years. These three, therefore, are only one See, and on that sit three Bishops, who are but one in Him, Who said, I am in My Father and you in Me, and I in you." In the end the Patriarchs of Alexandria and Antioch attached little importance to the representations of Gregory, and treated the matter with indifference; whilst the Emperor Maurice connived at, if he did not actually sanction, the assumption of the title by the Patriarch of Constantinople. Gregory shortly afterwards wrote a letter to St. Eulogius, Patriarch of Constantinople, which cannot fail to be of great interest to Englishmen, announcing the success of the Roman mission under St. Augustine, and that at the preceding Christmas 10,000 Angles had been baptized.

The Pontificate of Gregory the Great was a turning-point, and under him the See of Rome began to acquire a political, which added materially to the advancement of its spiritual, precedence. In the discharge of his ecclesiastical duties Gregory was one of the best, some would say the very best, of the Popes of Rome; but the force of circumstances

[k] Epist. VII. 33.

compelled him to be a Statesman as well as a Churchman. Gibbon styles him the Father of his Country; and of the benefits which he conferred on his country the Church of Rome reaped the benefit and appropriated the honour; and in him we get a glimpse of the mediæval Papacy.

Of all the Arian conquerors of the Empire, the Lombards were the most cruel and the least civilized, the ferocity of their character being scarcely at all mitigated by their profession of Christianity. So miserable and wide-spread was the havoc and desolation which they caused that the Italian people believed not only that the end of all things was at hand, but that it had actually commenced. They were threatening Rome itself. Plague, which carried off his predecessor Pelagius, and famine devastated the city; to such an extent were the clergy demoralized and the Church disorganized that Gregory compared it to an old and rotten ship violently shaken by the winds[1]. No help was forthcoming from the Exarch and none from the Emperor, the latter of whom was concerned nearer home in wars with the Persians, Avars, and Slavs. Such were some of the misfortunes which circumvented the Roman Empire when Gregory, by the unanimous voice of Senate, clergy and people, was summoned to the Pontificate. He wrote to the Emperor Maurice, who had up to that time been his personal friend and of whose eldest son he was Godfather, imploring him not to confirm the election; his letter was intercepted and Gregory was forced to yield.

As a Christian Bishop he preferred the salutary offices of peace; but the sword of the enemy was suspended over Rome, whose misfortunes at once involved him alike in the business of peace and war. He awoke the Emperor from a long slumber and exposed the guilt and incapacity of the Exarch; in the crisis of danger he named the tribunes and directed the operations of the Imperial troops, and "presumed to save the country without the consent of the Emperor and Exarch[m]." The Patrimony of Peter, extending

[1] Epist. I. 44.   [m] Gibbon, VIII. 170.

throughout all Italy and the Isles, gave him the authority of a powerful secular Prince far beyond the Roman Duchy, compared with which the rank of the Exarch was insignificant. He was the first of the Popes to assume an independent attitude, and although he showed no wish to sever his connection with the Roman Empire, behaved as if he considered the Emperor as his suzerain rather than his immediate ruler.

The Lombards treated him as an independent political power. When, A.D. 594, Romanus, the Exarch, was at war with the Lombard Duke, Agilulf, Gregory by his own authority made peace with the latter; Romanus complained to the Emperor, but Maurice was too much occupied in his own troubles to interfere further than with a strong reprimand. When a few years afterwards Agilulf was again at war with the Exarch, and was threatening Rome, it was the Pope and not the Exarch who concluded peace, and purchased the withdrawal of the Lombard forces with the treasures of the Church.

Such political influence as Gregory gained is dangerous to any subject, especially to an ecclesiastic. A Pope, in the modern sense of the word, Gregory never was, but his Pontificate threw a halo over the Papacy, and enabled his successors to assert a pre-eminence from which their rivals at Constantinople, ever under the watchful eyes of the Emperors, were debarred.

It can scarcely be a matter of surprise that the relations between the Emperor and Gregory, after the latter was chosen Pope, became strained. In 592, Maurice interfered with the Pope in a matter affecting the latter's jurisdiction. Hadrian, Bishop of a small See in Thessaly, having been on various charges deposed by his Metropolitan, the Bishop of Larissa, appealed to Gregory, who reversed the judgment and ordered the Metropolitan to reinstate him. The Metropolitan thereupon appealed to Maurice, who disregarding the judgment of Gregory, ordered the case to be reheard by the Bishop of Corinth, by whom the sentence of Gregory was set aside, and a reconciliation effected between Hadrian and his Metropolitan. Again, in 593, Maurice issued an edict forbidding soldiers, on the completion of their service, to become monks; Gregory acknowledged that it was his duty to submit, but denounced it as a flagrant act of impiety by which the Emperor imperilled his soul.

Stronger proof it would be difficult to adduce of the fact that the Emperors claimed and exercised the same power over the Popes of Rome as over the Patriarchs of Constantinople. Gregory in one of his Letters (*Epist. XXIV.*) to Romanus (*defensor*, guardian, that is, of the patrimony of Peter), expresses his intention of "sending the Pallium to our brother and fellow-Bishop, Syagrius," of Autun, "*inasmuch as the disposition of our most serene Lord the Emperor is favourable*," which indicates that the Emperor's consent was necessary for sending the Pall to a See which had not previously enjoyed the dignity [n].

In 602, Maurice, an Emperor distinguished by many estimable qualities, was murdered at Constantinople by a vulgar and deformed centurion named Phocas, who was then elected Emperor (602—608) by the soldiers. Phocas, who had before murdered Maurice's five sons, now inaugurated his reign by the murder of his wife, Constantina, daughter of the late Emperor Tiberius II., and her three daughters. If Maurice's treatment explains, it does not palliate, the conduct of Gregory, and his obsequiousness to the tyrant Phocas has left an indelible stain on his otherwise stainless life. He hailed with pleasure his accession, addressed him in terms of adulation, and placed portraits of the Emperor and his wife (a woman of little better character than himself) in his private chapel.

John the Faster died A.D. 596. Another event recorded of his Episcopate is the discovery of the seamless robe of our Lord, laid up in a marble chest at Zafed, which is

---

[n] It may be mentioned that the Bishop of Autun (Augustodunum) was one of the Bishops whom Gregory gave Augustine commendatory letters to on his way to England.—Epist. VI.

supposed to signify Jaffa. It was conveyed by the three Patriarchs, John of Constantinople, Gregory of Antioch, and John IV. of Jerusalem (574—596), accompanied by a large number of Bishops, and deposited in the chest in which it was found in the same Church as the true Cross at Jerusalem.

John the Faster was succeeded by Cyriacus (596—606). Phocas well understood that it was to his interest to favour the See of Rome over that of Constantinople. Cyriacus offended Phocas by affording protection to the wife and daughters of Maurice. Notwithstanding the remonstrances of Gregory, he retained the title of Œcumenical Patriarch. St. Eulogius, Patriarch of Alexandria, wrote to Gregory mentioning his having refused the title to Cyriacus "as you ordered me." "I pray you," replies Gregory, "to use the word *ordered* no more; I know who I am and who you are; my brother by position, my father in character; I ordered nothing, I only advised." Gregory died A.D. 604, and after the short Pontificate of Sabinianus (604—606), Boniface III. (February—November, 607) was Pope for less than a year. During his short Pontificate he succeeded in obtaining an edict from Phocas, that Rome was the head of all Churches, and that the Bishop of Rome should alone hold the title of Œcumenical Patriarch. Boniface did not hesitate to accept from a tyrant like Phocas the title which Gregory had denounced as blasphemous, profane, and diabolical. The edict, however, of such an Emperor could have little validity, and cannot be thought of value or importance, and it was soon restored to, and still continues to be held by, the Patriarchs of Constantinople.

Scarcely had Phocas ascended the throne than Chosroes II., King of Persia (590—628), declared war against him. Chosroes having being supplanted in the kingdom, found an asylum in the Roman Empire, and owed a debt of gratitude to Maurice for his restoration to the throne. On the pretence of avenging the death of his benefactor he began a disastrous war against the Empire, which lasted for more

than twenty years, and it appeared at one time that the
Roman Empire would succumb to Persia. Isaac, Patriarch
of Jerusalem, was succeeded by Zacharias. Zacharias complained of the corrupt state of the Patriarchate. Though his
predecessor, Isaac, had been orthodox, yet in his time simoniacal practices prevailed to such an extent that bribery
was the only road to Ordination and preferment; and
frequent strifes marred the peace of the Holy City[o]. These
evils Pope Gregory in his letter exhorts Isaac to remove.
But a terrible avenger was now at hand. Scarcely had
Zacharias entered upon his Episcopate (609—614; 628—
633), when Amida, Edessa, and Aleppo fell under the
Persian arms. Phocas' reign was a continued series of
cruelties and oppression; every province in the Empire
was in rebellion; and he did nothing to stem the invasion.
Accused before Heraclius, the Exarch of Africa, of the
crimes and misgovernment of eight years he was, after
suffering every kind of insult and torture, dethroned and
beheaded.

Heraclius, proclaimed by the common voice of the senate,
clergy and people, was crowned Emperor (610—641) by
Sergius, the recently consecrated Patriarch of Constantinople (610—638). The commencement of Heraclius' reign
synchronizes with the commencement of one of the greatest
events in the history of the world, that of Mahomet's mission.
For some time the new Emperor did nothing to stem the
advance of the Persians, who were still carrying all before
them. In 611 Antioch, in 614 Damascus fell. The disastrous condition of the Empire inspired the Jews with the
hope that the Advent of the long expected Messiah and
their own deliverance was at hand. Chosroes, with an army
recruited by 26,000 Jews, having reduced Galilee and the
region beyond Jordan, effected, A.D. 614, apparently without
a struggle, the conquest of Jerusalem. The Holy Places
were defiled; the Church of Gethsemane and that erected by
Helena on Mount Olivet were the first to be burnt; then

[o] Williams' Holy City, I. 300.

The Fifth and Sixth Œcumenical Councils. 307

the Basilica of Constantine, the Churches of Calvary and the Holy Sepulchre were demolished; and the greater part of the city was destroyed. Sacred vessels without number and other treasures accumulated in the Churches, together with the Patriarch Zacharias, and the True Cross, and an immense number of captives, were carried away to Persia; and the massacre of 90,000 Christians is imputed to the Jews and Arabs.

Fugitives from Palestine, amongst them the monk Sophronius, the future Patriarch of Jerusalem, sought a refuge from the Persians in Egypt. John, afterwards called from his piety and charity the Almoner, was at the time, in succession to St Eulogius, the Orthodox Patriarch of Alexandria (609—616). Men of every rank and station, Bishops and clergy, nobles and common people, threw themselves upon his hospitality, without which they must have perished. The Orthodox Church of Alexandria was at the time immensely rich, its resources amounting to £400,000 in gold. These funds, when other sources failed, he applied to furnishing the refugees with the absolute necessaries of life. He collected £10,000 more from the liberality of the faithful. Every day, through the Archimandrite Modestus, he at his own expense fed 7,500 poor; he established hospitals, himself ministering day and night to the wants of the sick and dying, and he sent large sums to Jerusalem for the redemption of captives and rebuilding the Churches. A story is told how that, when in the moment of his dire distress, a rich merchant of Alexandria offered him a large supply of corn and a hundred and eight pounds of gold, if he would relax some point of the Canon Law in his favour, the Patriarch told him that God, Who multiplied the five loaves, could multiply the two measures of corn which alone remained to him. Immediately a message was brought that two Church ships had almost at that moment arrived laden with corn from Sicily. Gibbon sneers[p] that his bounties always were dictated by superstition, or

[p] VIII. 363.

benevolence, or policy; but he is forced to admit that in his Will he could boast that he left behind him no more than the third part of the smallest of the silver coins. During his Patriarchate the rivalry between the Orthodox and Copts was laid aside, and after his death he was, by both communities alike, commemorated as a Saint.

The Persians having firmly established themselves in Syria, soon advanced into Egypt. Here they were now welcomed as deliverers by the native or Coptic population, who, in their hatred of the Orthodox Church, were ready to throw off the Byzantine yoke. In 616, Alexandria fell, and the holy Patriarch John was forced to fly to his native land of Cyprus, where, A.D. 620, he died, and where his Feast is still observed with peculiar solemnity[q]. For ten years the Persians were masters of Egypt, the granary of the East, so that the Roman Empire in the East was threatened with famine. In 617, they took Chalcedon, and threatened Constantinople, and so imminent was the danger that Heraclius thought to make Carthage the capital of the Roman Empire.

The loss of the Holy Cross produced a state little short of despair in the Eastern Church; Chosroes was believed to be Antichrist, and the end of the world to be at hand. The fate of Christendom seemed to lie in the hands of the Emperor. The Churches of Constantinople, under the Patriarch Sergius, now nobly came to the rescue, melting down their treasures and their gold and silver ornaments as a loan to the impoverished exchequer, *to be repaid* after the Persians were conquered and the Holy Places recovered. In a series of brilliant campaigns between 620—628, Heraclius turned the tide of victory, recovered the lost provinces, and penetrated Persia itself. One of his victories was gained on the site of Nineveh. By a crowning victory, A.D. 628, the Persian power was completely defeated, and Chosroes slain; the Holy Cross was recovered, and in the

[q] From St. John the Almoner, the Order of Hospitallers, in the first instance, derived their name.—Neale's Alexandria, II. 59.

The Fifth and Sixth Œcumenical Councils. 309

following year restored to the Holy Sepulchre, carried back by the Patriarch Zacharias, Heraclius himself going on a pilgrimage for the purpose to Jerusalem. Almost at the very time Heraclius was returning in triumph over the Persians to Jerusalem, Mahometanism was beginning its attacks on the Eastern Church.

Modestus, who had acted as Vicar and Coadjutor of Zacharias, succeeded him in the Patriarchate (633—634). "In him a second Bezaleel or Zerubbabel arose; he had the satisfaction of seeing the Churches of Calvary, the Resurrection, the Holy Cross, and the Assumption raised from their ruins, and the Holy City again became an object of attraction to Christian pilgrims[r]."

With the great event in the reign of Heraclius, the rise of Mahometanism, the controversies of the Eastern Church are intimately connected. Monothelitism was the corollary of Monophysitism; if our Saviour had only one Nature, He could only have had one Will ($\mu \acute{o}\nu o\nu$ $\theta \acute{e}\lambda \eta \mu a$); and the holders of the doctrine were called Monotheletes, or, as they are commonly known, Monothelites. And yet Theodore, Bishop of Pharan in Arabia, who is generally held to have been the originator of the doctrine, taught that though our Saviour had only one Will, He had two Natures, the Divine alone operating in Both. The heresy was held by Sergius, Patriarch of Constantinople, and, reluctantly at first, by Cyrus, Bishop of Phasis in Colchis, whom Heraclius, himself a holder of the doctrine, appointed to the Patriarchate of Alexandria; and by Honorius I., Pope of Rome (625—638). On the other hand it found a strong opponent in Sophronius, of whom mention has been made above, who was, A.D. 634, consecrated to the Patriarchate of Jerusalem (634—637).

The idea of the One Will had been instilled into the mind of the Emperor during his expeditions against the Persians, by Athanasius, the Monophysite Patriarch of Antioch; and the Emperor having conquered his enemies

[r] Williams' Holy City, I. 304

in the other Provinces of the Empire, seized upon it as a means of reconciling the Copts of Egypt. Sergius, Patriarch of Constantinople, and Cyrus, at the time Bishop of Phasis, were brought over to his view by the Emperor. Sergius was induced to believe that a common point of agreement could be found in the acknowledgment of the One Will, which was tantamount to the acknowledgment of One Nature, and a practical abnegation of the Council of Chalcedon. It was thought that the Monophysites might be thus reconciled; as to the feelings of the Orthodox they troubled themselves but little. In 630, Cyrus was rewarded with the Patriarchate of Alexandria (630—641), in succession to George the Orthodox, Benjamin being the Monophysite, Patriarch. A basis of agreement was formulated in a Council at Alexandria, A.D. 633, in which nine articles were drawn up, eight of which were orthodox, but the seventh, affirming that the same Will or energy produced the Divine and Human actions of our Lord " by one Theandric operation [s]," had the effect of bringing many thousand Monophysites to the Church.

Sophronius, who had been the intimate friend of John the Almoner, having been forced by the advance of the Persians to leave Alexandria, followed him to Cyprus, and after John's death visited Rome, and, about A.D. 620, Palestine. Happening to be now again in Alexandria, he stood forward as the champion of Orthodoxy against Monothelitism, and throwing himself at the feet of the Patriarch implored him, with tears in his eyes, not to countenance such an Apollinarian heresy. Finding that his entreaties made no impression upon Cyrus, he proceeded to Constantinople to plead the cause of Orthodoxy with Sergius. Sergius, who had received a letter from Cyrus, with which he was much delighted, announcing the re-union, complained of Sophronius' opposition, and Sophronius, finding his remonstrances unavailing, went to Palestine.

Modestus dying shortly after his appointment to the

---

[s] Τόν αὐτὸν ῞Ενα Χριστὸν καὶ Υἱὸν ἐνεργοῦντα . . μιᾷ Θεανδρικῇ ἐνεργείᾳ.

The Fifth and Sixth Œcumenical Councils. 311

Patriarchate of Jerusalem, Sophronius was, much against his will, appointed to succeed him. About this time Honorius I., Pope of Rome (625—638), was brought into the controversy. Sergius, alarmed at the appointment of Sophronius, sought to enlist the Pope on his side against the Orthodox Patriarch, and both he and Sophronius wrote to Honorius. It was hard on the Pope that he should be mixed up in a controversy not of his seeking, and in the subtleties of Eastern Theology for which his Western mind was little adapted. If the Pope was the head of the whole Church and infallible, it was of course proper that he should be consulted, and his judgment, whatever the character of the religious dispute, could not be wrong. But the Popes of Rome in those days never dreamt of Papal infallibility, and Honorius gave his opinion as a simple-minded, honest, but not very intellectual, Bishop, in the cause of peace. The doctrine which Sergius advocated had brought back many thousand opponents to the Church. Honorius wrote two letters to Sergius (both of which were ordered to be burnt by the Sixth Œcumenical Council), in which he approved of what Sergius and Cyrus had done, and agreed that there was only One Will in Christ; in his answer to Sophronius he enjoined silence on the subject of the Two Wills or Energies. Sophronius, overwhelmed with the troubles which at that time arose from the Saracens, and resulted in the fall of Jerusalem, took little further part in the controversy, and did not long survive. After his death in 637, the Patriarchate was vacant for twenty-nine years. Unfortunately Honorius (and he was not the first of the Popes to do so) fell into a dire heresy; he had, perhaps in an unguarded moment, given his opinion in the charitable hope of healing the long-standing troubles of the Eastern Church, of which perhaps he, on maturer reflection, repented. It is a proof against the modern doctrine of Papal Infallibility. But for this one error in judgment he has been handed down to all time as an arch-heretic, anathematized by Councils of the Church as well as by succeeding Popes.

Sergius, dying A.D. 638, was succeeded in the Patriarchate of Constantinople by Pyrrhus, (638—641 ; again, 654—655), a Monothelite, Archimandrite of the monastery of Chrysopolis (Scutari), in which he was succeeded by Maximus, a man of noble birth, a learned theologian and friend of Sophronius. In 639 Heraclius issued a document expressing the opinions of Sergius, and probably drawn up by him, called the Ecthesis ("Ἔκθεσις τῆς Πίστεως). It prohibited alike the teaching of the One or Two Energies, the former appearing to destroy the Two Natures, the latter to imply two contrary Wills. At the same time it asserted that the acknowledgment of only one Will was agreeable to the Catholic Faith. It was an effort after ecclesiastical comprehension at the expense of Catholic truth; and instead of healing, only made confusion worse confounded.

In 638, Pope Honorius died, and, after the short Pontificate of Severinus, was succeeded by John IV. (640—642), who together with his predecessor protested against the Ecthesis. Heraclius wrote to the new Pope, disclaiming, now that Sergius was dead, responsibility for the Ecthesis, which he attributed to Sergius. John charitably defended Honorius, whom his successors anathematized. In February, 641, Heraclius died, and in September his grandson, Constans II. (641—668), became Emperor. In the same year Cyrus died; in October, Pyrrhus, after a popular tumult in Constantinople, abdicated, and was succeeded by Paul (641—654), a Monothelite and favourer of the Ecthesis. John IV., Pope of Rome, was succeeded by Theodore I. (642—649), as the name implies, a Greek.

In 645, the Monk Maximus, finding that Pyrrhus, the deposed Patriarch of Constantinople, was propagating his opinions in Africa, left his monastery and held, in the presence of the African Bishops and the Prefect of the Province, a public discussion with him, with the result that Pyrrhus was for a time convinced of his error and went to Rome, where he was received into communion by Theodore. But reverting soon afterwards to his former opinions he was excommunicated by the Pope, who had previously excommunicated his successor, Paul, the sentence being written in the consecrated Wine of the Eucharist.

In 648 the Emperor Constans, by the advice of Paul, put forth a new document, composed by the latter, called the Type (Τύπος τῆς Πίστεως), advocating neither side of the controversy, but forbidding all disputes, and the mention of the One or Two Natures in the Person of Christ.

In 649, Theodore was succeeded in the Papacy by Martin I. (649—654), who equally with his predecessor was opposed to the Type. In the year of his accession he held the First Lateran Council, attended by one hundred and five Bishops from Italy, Sardinia, Sicily and Western Africa, and many other clergy, and also by Maximus; it condemned the expression "One Theandric Operation;" denounced Theodore of Pharan, Cyrus, Patriarch of Alexandria, Macedonius, who had been Consecrated and intruded into the Patriarchate of Antioch by Sergius; Sergius, Pyrrhus and Paul, Patriarchs of Constantinople; together with "the most impious Ecthesis and the most impious Type."

Pope Martin sent the Acts of the Council to the Emperor. Constans received the proceedings of the Council with the greatest indignation, and, in 653, the aged Pope was seized at Rome by the Exarch Calliopas, acting under orders of the Emperor, and carried off, suffering much cruelty on the way, as a common criminal, to Constantinople. After being detained there a prisoner six weeks and exposed, even in the Imperial palace and in the presence of the Emperor, to much cruel treatment, he was saved from execution only through the intercession of the Patriarch Paul; he was then banished to Cherson in the Crimea, where, deprived of the barest necessaries of life, but still bearing his treatment with great fortitude and resignation, he died in the following year. The Emperor went to apprize Paul, who was then lying on his deathbed. Paul, overwhelmed with grief at the event, died in the same year. Pyrrhus was then reinstated, and on his death, which happened a few months afterwards,

Peter, another Monothelite, was appointed to the Patriarchate.

In 655, Maximus, the monk, was arrested in Rome and taken a prisoner to Constantinople, and refusing to subscribe the Type, was banished to Thrace. In 662 he was recalled to Constantinople, and again ordered to subscribe, and on his second refusal and his refusing to communicate with the Patriarch Peter, he was, in a Synod under Peter, after being cruelly flogged, and his tongue and right hand cut off, again ordered into banishment, in which he, as zealous a champion for Orthodoxy as SS. Athanasius, Cyril, or Sophronius, died in the same year, from the effects of his treatment, a Confessor to the faith.

The persecutions were sanctioned by the Emperor, who now gave fuller vent than before to his vices and cruelties; but these, and the execution of his own brother, provoked the detestation of his Eastern subjects, and in 668 he was himself at the age of 38, after a reign of 27 years, assassinated by an officer of his own household at Syracuse.

Constans II. was succeeded by his son, Constantine IV. (668—685), surnamed Pogonatus (*the bearded*), an orthodox Emperor. The Monothelite controversy still continuing, the Emperor determined to summon an Œcumenical Council to Constantinople, with the view of determining the right faith, and reconciling the Eastern and Western Churches. The Emperor wrote to the Pope of Rome inviting him to send his legates to the Council, and Agatho (678—682) readily sent two Bishops and a Deacon to represent him. The See of Constantinople had since the deaths of Paul and Pyrrhus been alternately held by orthodox and Monophysite Patriarchs. Peter (655—666), a Monothelite, was succeeded by three orthodox Prelates, Thomas (666—669), John V. (669—674), and Constantine I. (674—676). Then followed two Monothelites, Theodore (676—dep. 678; restored 684—687), and during his interrupted Episcopate, George I. (678—684). The Emperor wrote to the Patriarch George, "the most blessed Archbishop and Œcu-

The Fifth and Sixth Œcumenical Councils. 315

menical Patriarch" (μακαριωτάτῳ ἀρχιεπισκόπῳ καὶ οἰκουμενικῷ πατριάρχῃ), bidding him summon the Metropolitans and Bishops under his jurisdiction, and to request Macarius, the Patriarch of Antioch, a staunch Monothelite, also to summon his. No mention was made of the Patriarchs of Alexandria and Jerusalem, those cities being in the hands of Saracens; Macarius was from the same cause resident in Constantinople.

The Third Council of Constantinople, or the Sixth Œcumenical Council, met on March 7, 680, in the room of the Imperial Palace, called from its vaulted roof Trullus, whence the Council is sometimes called the First Trullan Council, and was attended by about two hundred Bishops. Whenever the Emperor was present, as he was in the first eleven and the last Sessions, he himself presided. The Council was attended by George, the Patriarch of Constantinople, and Macarius of Antioch; the Pope of Rome and the Patriarchs of Alexandria and Jerusalem were represented by their legates.

Eighteen Sessions were held. In the First, the papal legates attacked the Monothelite doctrines as novelties; George and Macarius on the other hand contended that they were not novelties, but consonant with the Œcumenical Councils and the Fathers, and with the teaching of Paul, Pyrrhus and Peter, successive Patriarchs of Constantinople, with that of Cyrus, Patriarch of Alexandria, and Honorius, Pope of Rome. In the three next Sessions the Acts of the preceding Councils, the writings of the Fathers, and two dogmatical epistles written by Pope Agatho were read. In the Fifth and Sixth, Macarius presented extracts from the Fathers in favour of Monothelitism, which the Council pronounced, and he himself afterwards confessed, to be spurious. In Session VII., the Papal legates adduced testimony from the Fathers, and the testimony of Pope Agatho, in favour of Two Wills, and the Council, at the request of George, sanctioned the insertion of Vigilius' name upon the Diptychs.

Macarius was then called upon to make his defence, and although he admitted the genuineness of the documents adduced against him, and that his own extracts had for his own purpose been mutilated by him, he adhered to the One Will, and was in the Ninth Session sentenced to deposition.

In Session XIII. the Council pronounced both the letter of Sergius and that of Honorius to be heterodox, and anathematized the maintainers of the One Will, and with them they combined Honorius; "Together with these we anathematize and condemn to be cast out from the holy Catholic Church of God, Honorius, who was Pope of Old Rome, because we find that through his writings to Sergius he followed his mind in all respects and confirmed his impious dogmas."

In Session XIV., May 5, 681, Theophanes, who had been appointed to succeed Macarius, took his seat. In Session XVI., when the Council was about to pronounce its final anathemas, George of Constantinople proposed that the names of his predecessors, Sergius, Pyrrhus, and Paul, should be omitted from the anathemas, but was outvoted. His own return to orthodoxy was however recognized, and the Synod exclaimed: "Many years to the Roman Pope Agatho, to the Patriarch George of Constantinople, and to the Patriarch Theophanes of Antioch[t]."

The last Session of the Council was held on Sept. 16, 681, and its decrees were subscribed by the Emperor and one hundred and sixty Bishops. Macarius, who remained firm to the end and withstood all inducements and the offer of restoration to the Patriarchate, with several leading Monothelites, were exiled to Rome as a place where they were likely to be converted from their errors. The Council anathematized Sergius, Pyrrhus, Paul, Peter, Theodore of Pharan, and Honorius. It decided that, following the five Œcumenical Synods and great Fathers, there were in the Saviour Two Natural Wills operating without division,

[t] George is commemorated in the Greek Church on Aug 18.

The Fifth and Sixth Œcumenical Councils. 317

change, antagonism, or confusion (ἀδιαιρέτως, ἀτρέπτως, ἀμερίστως, ἀσυγχύτως); that the Human Will could not come into collision with the Divine Will, to which it was in all things subject.

The Council drew up a Synodal Letter to Pope Agatho, but before the legates left Constantinople intelligence of his death arrived; whereupon the Emperor sent the Letter by the hands of the Pope's chief legate, the Bishop of Porto (who himself afterwards became Pope as John V.), to his successor Leo II. (682—683). In his answer to the Emperor the Pope confirmed the decrees of the Council and the condemnation of Honorius. Pope Leo is spoken of in the highest terms, as being endowed with great eloquence, profound knowledge of the Scriptures, and erudition in both the Greek and Latin languages. His condemnation of Honorius is expressed in the plainest language;—" Pariter anathematizamus novi erroris inventores, i.e. Theodorum Pharanitanum, Episcopum Cyrum Alexandrinum, Sergium, Pyrrhum, Paulum, Petrum, Constantinopolitinæ Ecclesiæ subsessores magis quam præsules; necnon et Honorium, qui hanc Apostilicam Ecclesiam non Apostolicæ traditionis doctrinâ lustravit, sed profundâ proditione immaculatam fidem subvertere conatus est; et omnes qui in suo errore perfuncti sunt." Of Macarius, who had been exiled to Rome, the Pope says that he had tried to lead him into the right path but that he had remained stubborn. The anathema pronounced by the Council (and Pope Leo on Honorius, succeeding Popes for three hundred years repeated.

The Emperor Constantine Pogonatus was succeeded by his son Justinian II. (685—711), called Rhinometus (ῥινοτμητός, *slit-nosed*), who was sixteen years of age. The character of the new Emperor bore a marked resemblance to that of his grandfather, Constans, and it cannot be supposed that the conduct of such a man would be strongly influenced by religious convictions. Justinian, as the sequel will show, had little reverence for his own Patriarch, but at the same time he had no intention that the Patriarchate of Constantinople should be overshadowed by that of Rome. In the late controversies the Popes had exhibited a consistent orthodoxy in marked contrast to the Eastern Patriarchs. Pope Agatho had triumphed in the late Œcumenical Council as the champion of orthodoxy; whereas four of the recent Patriarchs of Constantinople had been anathematized by it for heresy; the reigning Patriarch had only been reclaimed to orthodoxy by the Council; and Macarius of Antioch had been deposed by it and sent into exile to Rome.

To restore the balance, and to give the triumph to Constantinople over Rome, was Justinian's object in summoning, A D. 691, to Constantinople, the Council which, being held in the same room as the Sixth Council, is known as the Trullan Council, and, as being supplementary to the Fifth and Sixth Councils, is also called the Quinsext Council (σύνοδος πενθέκτη). Since those Councils were concerned with dogmatical questions, no disciplinary Canons had been enacted; the Trullan Council is therefore considered by the Greek Church to be a continuous and supplementary Council, and the Canons enacted in it to be the Canons of the Sixth Œcumenical Council. It was presided over by Paul III., the successor of George in the Patriarchate of Constantinople. It was attended by all the Eastern Patriarchs, Peter of Alexandria, George of Antioch, and Anastasius of Jerusalem; whether the Pope of Rome, Sergius I. (687—701), was represented by his legates is uncertain; and its Canons were subscribed by two hundred and thirteen Bishops.

It passed one hundred and two Canons. Canon I. declared the adherence of the Council to the six Œcumenical Councils, and confirmed the anathema pronounced against Honorius. Canon II. declared all the eighty-five Apostolical Canons to be binding, an evident hit against Rome, which only accepted the first fifty; but it rejected the Apostolical Constitutions. Canons VI. and XIII. were opposed to the Roman Church with regard to the marriage of the clergy. The latter of these two Canons remarks on the different rule between the Churches. "In the Roman

The Fifth and Sixth Œcumenical Councils. 319

Church," it says, "those who wished to be ordained to the Diaconate or Presbyterate must have no further intercourse with their wives. We, however, in accordance with the Apostolic Canons allow them to continue in marriage. If any one seeks to dissolve such marriages, he shall be deposed, and the cleric who under pretence of religion dismisses his wife shall be excommunicated." Canon XXXVI.; "Renewing the decrees of the Second and Fourth Œcumenical Synods, we decide that the See of Constantinople shall enjoy equal rights (τά ἴσα πρεσβεῖα) with those of Old Rome, shall be highly regarded in ecclesiastical matters as that is, and be second after it. After Constantinople comes the See of Alexandria, then Antioch, and next Jerusalem." Canon LV. ; "At Rome they fast every Saturday in Lent. This is contrary to the Sixty-sixth Apostolical Canon, and may not be done. Any one who does so will, if a cleric, be deposed, if a layman, excommunicated." Canon LXVII. forbade the partaking of the blood of animals, which, though condemned by Scripture, was not considered in the Latin Church to be permanently binding. A cleric who offends was to be deposed, a layman to be excommunicated. Canon LXXXII. forbade representations of our Saviour under the form of a Lamb, and only allowed them in Human Form. These Canons were evidently directed against the Western Church.

We must notice one other Canon, LII., which enacted that "on all days in Lent except Saturdays, Sundays, and the Annunciation of the Virgin, only the Liturgy of the Presanctified should be used."

These Canons were signed first by the Emperor and the Eastern Patriarchs, then, in all, by 211 Eastern Bishops. All the Canons were received in the Greek Church, but several of them were naturally objected to by the Roman Church; but they met with a general acceptance in the Second Council of Nice, and Gratian reckons the Trullan Council as a continuation of the Sixth General Council.

CHAPTER IX.

The Saracenic Conquests.

CHARACTER of Mahomet—Simplicity of his teaching—Islam—The Hegira—The battles of Beder and Ohud—Mahomet's Letters to Chosroes and Heraclius—His conquest of Arabia—Commencement of the invasion of the Persian and Roman Empires—Death of Mahomet—His successors, Abu-Bekr, Oman, Othman, Ali—The Shiites and Sonnites—The Ommiad dynasty—Fall of Persia—Fall of Bozra, Damascus, Heliopolis, Emesa—Capitulation of Jerusalem—The Mosque of Omar—Death of the Patriarch Sophronius—Syria conquered—The Copts of Egypt favour the Saracens—Egypt betrayed by the Governor of Memphis—Fall of Alexandria—Of Carthage—The Patriarchates of Alexandria, Antioch, and Jerusalem subject to the Turks—Conquest of Spain—Scinde conquered but recovered—Defeat of the Saracens before Constantinople—Fall of the Ommiad under the Abbaside dynasty—The Ommiad Emirate at Cordova—The Caliphate of Bagdad—Haroun al Raschid—The Fatimite Caliphate—Al Hakim—Saladin.

WHILST the Christians were quarrelling amongst themselves, and the heads of Eastern and Western Christendom were struggling for pre-eminence, a new religion was rising up on the earth, destined not only to ruin the Eastern Church, but to influence the history of the whole world for more than twelve hundred years. The rise and progress of Mahometanism, the greatest and most permanent scourge with which it has ever pleased God to visit the world, was from the first regarded as a just and righteous chastisement on the corruption and schisms of the Church. A united Christendom might have nipped it in its bud, but a united Christendom no longer existed. For two hundred years Rome and Constantinople had been engaged in a struggle for pre-eminence; and whilst the Western Church enjoyed comparative immunity, persecution by the Emperors rent the Eastern Church asunder, so that it fell an easy victim to the dreadful scourge which has ever since afflicted it.

The propagation of Mahometanism, says Paley, "is the only event in the history of the Christian race which admits of comparison with the propagation of Christianity." The birth of Mahomet "was placed in the most degenerate and disorderly period of the Persians, the Romans, and the barbarians of Europe; the Empires of Trajan, or even Constantine or Charlemagne, would have repelled the assaults of the naked Saracens, and the torrent of fanaticism might have been obscurely lost in the sands of Arabia [a]." When Mahomet commenced his career, the two prominent powers of the world were the Empires of Rome and Persia; within a few years after his death Persia was entirely subdued, and Rome was shorn of its Oriental provinces.

The fatherland of Mahometanism was Arabia, a country hitherto little developed, without influence beyond its own boundaries, and from which a foe to Christianity might have been least expected. Its only cities of any importance were Mecca and Medina, in the former of which was the Kaaba, built, according to Arabian tradition, by Abraham, to which the Arabians paid the deepest reverence. In that city, with its three hundred and sixty idols, Mahomet was born, A.D. 569, in the reign of Justin II., of the noble tribe of the Koreish, the hereditary guardians of the Kaaba. Being early left an orphan and in straitened circumstances, he became, when eight years old, the servant of a rich widow at Mecca, named Khadijah, and grew up a thoroughly illiterate man, able neither to read nor write. At twenty-four years of age, through his marriage with Khadijah, he was raised to affluence and importance, and to her, a woman fifteen years older than himself, he remained faithful till her death, and by her he became the father of six children, all of whom, except the youngest, a daughter named Fatima, died young.

As to his character and the character of the religion which he founded, there is a great difference of opinion; at one time no words were strong enough to denounce him as an impostor, even the Antichrist; in the present day the opinion of some has veered round to an opposite ex-

[a] Gibbon, IX. 360.

treme. The worship which he inculcated of the one God, and the certainty of future retribution, was at least an improvement on the polytheism of the Arabians which it superseded ; and he may have been at first an enthusiast, with a tendency to monomania in the belief that he received his revelations from the Archangel Gabriel. These revelations, mere odds and ends, were put together by his successor Abu-bekr, but, as they were burnt by his third successor Othman, who put forth a version of his own, the Koran, as we know it now, is not Mahomet's at all. But, if he was at first an honest enthusiast, be became, after the death of Khadijah, either an impostor or a maniac ; for it is, of course, impossible to believe that the Angel Gabriel revealed to him that, whilst his followers were restricted to four, he might take to himself as many wives as he chose.

A distinction must be drawn between Mahomet and the religion which he founded If Mahomet was an impostor, Mahometanism, a religion which, scarcely a century after his death, reigned supreme over Arabia, Syria, Persia, Egypt, the whole of Northern Africa, as far as Spain, cannot briefly be dismissed as nothing but an imposition. It does not come within our province to describe what Islam did for the world from the Ninth to the Thirteenth Century, or the part it took in the development of art and science during the " dark Ages ; " but the rapid progress in its propagation must, we think, be attributed to the simplicity of its teaching. Its starting-point was the fundamental principle of Christianity, " There is one God," and this paved the way for its equally simple, though false, concomitant, " Mahomet is his prophet." This was the whole simple faith on which Mahometanism was built up, " There is only one God, and Mahomet is his prophet." Christ could not be God, because " God is not begotten ; " so it was part of the doctrine that Jesus was only the Apostle of the one God, and that He was superseded by Mahomet. Christians were being perplexed by subtle points of theology, with Creeds and Councils, and as to whether there were One or Two Natures, One or Two Wills in Christ, points which, if perplexing to Christians, would be more so to the minds of Barbarians. Mahometanism had the advantage of its simplicity, and this was the secret of its success.

Mahomet preached the simple doctrine of one God; but instead of removing the evils which beset the East, he perpetuated and sanctioned by his own example the worst of all, polygamy. After the death of Khadijah he took to himself seventeen wives, and was not over-scrupulous in the means of getting them. His faithful slave Zeid had a beautiful wife; a fresh dispensation was vouchsafed to the prophet; Zeid divorced her, and Mahomet added her to his Harem.

One month in every year he had been accustomed to withdraw from the world, and to seek in the cavern of a mountain near Mecca a solitary retirement for meditation. It was not till A.D. 609, when he was in his fortieth year, that he announced himself an Apostle of God, and began his mission in his native Mecca. It was directed against the polytheism of the Arabs, and in behalf of the restoration of the Monotheistic worship of the prophets who had preceded him, Abraham, Moses, and Jesus. Of the Gospel he spoke with reverence; Jesus was born miraculously in the Flesh and was the greatest of the Teachers sent from Heaven. Of the Virgin Mary he spoke respectfully, but in his ignorance of the Bible he identified her with Miriam, the sister of Moses and Aaron. That Jesus was the Son of God he not only denied, but he denied also that Mahometans needed an Atonement; he believed that Jesus worked miracles, he believed in His Resurrection and Ascension, in His second Advent, in His triumph over Antichrist, and in a Millennium; but he did not believe the Saviour's Crucifixion; though the Jews boasted that they had put Him to death, it was not Jesus, but some one like Him, who was substituted in His place. He himself was a prophet as superior to Christ as Christ was to Moses, and he was sent to reveal a more perfect religion than either. The doctrine of the Trinity he rejected as tritheism. He never aspired to work miracles, but rested his mission on the bare assertion that God had revealed Himself to him.

Like the Jews he accepted the rite of Circumcision; but as the Jews, the descendants of Isaac, the child of promise, practised it on the eighth day, so the Arabs, the descendants of Ishmael, the son of the handmaid, circumcised their sons on their thirteenth year, the age at which their progenitor Ishmael was circumcised[b]. His faith Mahomet called Islam (from which the word Moslem is derived), or resignation to the Will of God. To support his cause he produced what he professed to be a divine revelation made to him by the Angel Gabriel, it was made to him as a whole, but communicated by him to his followers in pieces, which were afterwards collected, as mentioned above, into the book called in the Arabic language, Al Koran (*The Book*). It speaks of the Bible as the Word of God, and mentions with approval many leading events in the Old and New Testaments; but for the Koran Mahomet claimed a higher authority than for the Bible. To the One God the Koran bears noble testimony; and on the Bible Mahomet professed to ground the watchword which has ever since been the invariable profession of Islam, "There is no God but one, and Mahomet is His prophet."

By slow degrees he made a few converts; first in time were his wife Khadijah, his friend, and one of his future fathers-in-law, Abu-Bekr, his own cousin Ali, Othman his secretary, his slave Zeid, and a few others. In three years he had only made fourteen, and in seven years' about one hundred disciples. In 619, Khadijah died. But so strong was the opposition which he raised up amongst the families of his own tribe, the Koreish, that in July, 622, he was forced to fly, accompanied by Abu-Bekr, to Medina, a city about two hundred miles from Mecca, which he reached

---

[b] Dollinger, Hist of the Church, II 91.

in sixteen days; and from that year, known as the Hegira, the Mahometans date the commencement of their era[c].

From that time the character of his mission underwent a change; as his spiritual exhortations had been rejected, he turned from persuasion to the sword; it was the duty of Islam, he told his followers, to wage carnal war against the unbelievers; "The sword," he said, "is the Key of Heaven and Hell; whosoever falls in battle his sins are forgiven at the day of judgment, . . . the loss of his limbs shall be supplied by the wings of Angels and Cherubim." It was the assurance of Heaven as their reward that induced them to bear the danger of battle, and to observe the rigid precepts of the Koran.

In January, 624, the Saracens, as his followers were called, gained over the Koreish the battle of Beder; his victory he attributed to divine aid; the second battle, in the same year, at Ohud, six miles from Medina, his followers lost. Thenceforward no toleration was to be allowed, and the rule was adopted which has been part of the religion of the Mahometans ever since; the Koran, Tribute, or the Sword. Therein lies the upas-tree of Mahometanism, and the reason that it has been a curse to the world for more than twelve hundred years.

Mahomet now determined to spread his religion over the Persian and Roman Empires. He sent to Chosroes, King of Persia, at the time when the latter was at the height of his power, inviting him to embrace Islam, and when Chosroes indignantly tore his letter in pieces, Mahomet exclaimed, "Thus will God tear the Kingdom of Chosroes." In 628 Heraclius, as we have seen, completed the conquest of Persia. When on his triumphal return from the Persian war the Roman Emperor was at Emesa, he received the ambassador of Mahomet with so great respect that the Arabians founded on the circumstance the secret conversion of Heraclius to their faith.

After remaining seven years at Medina, where he was

[c] This era was commenced under the second Caliph, Omar.

treated with great honour, and his mission met with success, he attacked and took Mecca, which he re-entered as a conqueror, and destroyed the three hundred and sixty idols of the Kaaba. The conquest of Mecca determined the fate of Arabia; those who had been his principal adversaries were now converted to his faith; Mahometanism became the language of the country, and Mecca the capital of Islam.

The conquest of Arabia effected, Mahomet next determined to attack the two greatest powers of the world, the Persian and Roman Empires, which, he well knew, were so exhausted by their long wars that they could offer but a feeble resistance to an enthusiastic enemy like the Saracens. The Persian Empire never recovered the blow inflicted on it by Heraclius; with Chosroes the glory of the Sassanidæ ended; in the course of four years (628—632) no fewer than nine sovereigns were put up and deposed, and at the time of the Saracenic invasions the Persian throne was occupied by a female.

In the Western part of the Roman Empire the Goths had gained possession of Spain. In the East the religious controversies added to the weakness of the Empire; there was there a large number of the subjects of Heraclius, who, although one and all they regarded Mahomet as Antichrist, and stigmatized his followers as infidels, were ready to welcome the Arabs as friends and deliverers.

Such was the condition of the Persian and Roman Empires when, A.D. 632, the invasion of both was undertaken by the Saracens. In June of that year, Mahomet, in his sixty-third year, died at Medina, where he was buried, and for a short time the expedition was suspended, the army of the Saracens, from a feeling of respect, halting at the gates of Medina.

The successors of Mahomet, called Caliphs (*successors*), were both temporal and spiritual rulers. No sooner was Mahomet dead than a schism arose as to his successor. The only survivor of the Prophet's family was his daughter

Fatima, who was married to her cousin Ali, and some of Mahomet's followers looked upon Ali as the rightful successor. Abu-Bekr, the aged father of Mahomet's wife, Ayesha, who was ultimately chosen, only survived Mahomet two years. He by his Will left the Caliphate to Omar (634—644), who being assassinated by a Persian slave, was succeeded by Othman (644—655), Mahomet's former secretary. He, too, was murdered in a religious tumult of the Faithful, and Ali, the husband of Fatima, then succeeded to the Caliphate (655—680). But not even then did their quarrels and schisms end. Two rival parties arose, the Shiites, who held the divine right of Ali as husband of Mahomet's daughter, and the Sonnites, holding the right of popular election, and acknowledging the order of succession of the first four Caliphs, Abu-Bekr, Omar, Othman and Ali, but regarding with less favour that of Ali. The religious antagonism has lasted to the present day, the Sonnite, which is considered the orthodox party, comprising the Turks, Tartars, and Indians, branding the Shiites, to whom Persia belongs, as sectaries.

The first four Caliphs were all friends or kinsmen of Mahomet. Ali, the fourth Caliph, added to the title, hitherto born by the Caliphs, of Prophet, that of Vicar of God. His reign was one continued succession of civil wars, and he, too, fell by the hand of an assassin, leaving a son named Hassan. The crafty Moawiyah, the son of a man who had been Mahomet's greatest enemy, managed to get appointed Caliph (655—680), murdered Hassan, and founded the dynasty of the Ommiads, so called from the house of Ommiyah to which he belonged; and removed the seat of the Caliphate from Medina to Damascus.

Having given the above short account of the early Caliphs, and the transference of the Caliphate to the Ommiad dynasty, we will now narrate briefly the success that attended the early arms of the Saracens.

The war with Persia ended, A.D. 651, in the destruction of the Persian monarchy; the long dynasty of the Sassanidæ came to an end; Yesdigird, the last native king, defeated near Bagdad, fled to the mountains, where he was murdered; the ancient religion was annihilated, and Persia became a Mahometan country.

The invasion of Syria commenced in the same year as that of Persia. In Syria, as has been before said, Greek and Roman civilization had never taken firm root; the mass of the people still spoke their old language and professed a religion alien to that of the Orthodox Church; the Greeks they regarded as their national enemies, in whose battles they were forced to fight, against whom, as conquerors, their national feelings revolted. This accounts for the easy manner in which the Syrian cities fell before the Saracens.

The enthusiasm of the Saracens superseded and took the place of military tactics. The Imperial armies, deprived of the leadership of Heraclius, who was at the time suffering from the effects of a severe illness, seem to have been paralyzed with the suddenness and impetuosity of the attacks, and Syria was conquered in six years. In 633 Bozra, betrayed by the treachery and apostasy of the Roman governor, fell; in 634 Damascus, the capital of Syria; in 635 Heliopolis and Emesa; and in 637, after a siege of a few months, Jerusalem fell. Sophronius the Patriarch refused to treat with any but the Caliph Omar; a messenger was despatched to Medina, and Omar appeared in person. He fixed his headquarters at a village named Jabit, where he negotiated with a deputation of Christians the capitulation of the Holy City; and the preliminaries being arranged, the Caliph was met at the gates of the city by the Patriarch. Sophronius was compelled to point out the Holy Places and the site of the Temple; "Verily," he said, "this is the abomination of desolation, spoken of by Daniel the Prophet, standing in the Holy Place." The magnificent Mosque now to be seen at Jerusalem, although not the same as that originally built, perpetuates the name of Omar, the second Caliph, its first Moslem conqueror. By the treaty of capitulation peace and protection were secured for the Christians, and the terms

The Saracenic Conquests.   329

were faithfully observed by Omar's successors; but thenceforward Jerusalem became almost as much an object of religious attraction to the Mahometan devotee as to the Christian pilgrims [d]. In the same year the holy Patriarch, having lived just long enough to see his Patriarchate fall under the hands of the Infidels, ended his troubled life, and for sixty years afterwards the See of Jerusalem was left without a Bishop. In the year after his death Aleppo and Antioch were captured by the Saracens, and thus fell a second Patriarchate.

From Jerusalem and Antioch the Saracens marched on Phœnicia. Tripoli and Tyre were betrayed to them. Cæsarea, the capital of Syria, next surrendered without a blow, the citizens soliciting pardon by their payment of two hundred thousand pieces of gold; and the remaining cities of the province followed the example of the capital. Thus Syria was conquered. Except for a short time, during the Crusades, the Holy Places have ever since remained in the hands of the Infidels, Christianity being thenceforth tolerated as an appendage to Mahometanism. No outward sign of Christianity was permitted to offend the susceptibilities of Mussulmans, no Cross to be exhibited on the Churches; no bells to summon the Christian worshippers to Church; the monasteries were allowed to stand, but only on the condition of their affording to Mahometans the same hospitality, free from payment, which they gave to Christians.

The conquest of Syria effected, the Saracens under Amrou, in the same year (638), invaded Egypt. Here, again, the same schism as in Syria existed amongst the Christians, and Amrou found the province divided into two hostile parties; one the Orthodox Greek party, whom the native inhabitants considered as intruders into the country, and stigmatized as Melchites, or Imperialists, the followers of the religion of the Emperors and of the Council of Chalcedon; the other, the natives, bearing the common

[d] Williams' Holy City, I. 319.

name of Copts, who followed the religion of the Monophysites or Jacobites. The former held all the highest ranks in the Court, and civil and military tribunates; whilst the Copts, who formed the bulk of the people (and amongst them the majority of Bishops and Priests), groaning under the severe burdens of the State and oppression, were the merchants, artificers, and husbandmen. Between these two communities so bitter was the hatred that they never coalesced nor intermarried; constant murders were committed by the one upon the other; and now we find the Copts preferring submission to infidels who entirely denied the Divinity of their Saviour, as the means of avenging themselves on their fellow-Christians who differed from them only as to the One or Two Natures in our Lord.

The Greeks fought bravely, but owing to the treachery of the Copts, Egypt, like Syria, fell an easy prey to the Saracens. The Governor of Memphis told the Saracenic General that they desired to have no communion with the Greeks either in this world or in the next; that they abjured the Byzantine tyrant, the Council of Chalcedon, and the Melchite slaves. The siege of Alexandria lasted fourteen months; then, after the Saracens had lost 23,000 men, the capital of Egypt capitulated. Many Churches, and amongst them St. Mark's, in which reposed the relics of the Evangelist, were burnt. Amrou was asked to spare the famous library founded by the Ptolemies; he answered that he must learn the Caliph's pleasure. Omar is said to have answered (but the whole story has been doubted), that if the books were in accordance with the Koran they were superfluous, if contrary to it, pernicious, in either case they must be destroyed. The books, the priceless treasure of the learning of ancient Greece, were said to have been used for heating the public baths of Alexandria.

In Africa, which had been more thoroughly brought under Roman influence than Syria and Egypt, the Saracens met with a longer and more stubborn resistance. Their invasions commenced, A.D. 647, under the Caliph Othman, but

Carthage, which held the Orthodox faith, was not taken till A D. 698, nor the whole country conquered till 709. But Carthage also, the Metropolis of Africa, fell; the country of SS. Cyprian and Augustine was lost to Christianity, and from no part of the Empire were all traces of Roman dominion so effectually swept away as from Africa.

Thus the Patriarchates of Alexandria, Antioch, and Jerusalem were reduced to little beyond a name, and the Roman Empire in the East was confined to Constantinople. In 711 the Arabs, with the Moors who had embraced Mahometanism, invited into Spain by Count Julian, the Governor of Ceuta, whose daughter Roderic, the Gothic King of Spain, had dishonoured, landed, under their General Tarik, on the rock which came to be called after him Gebel el Tarik (*the rock of Tarik*), modernized into Gibraltar; and on July 7, defeated Roderic near Xeres, who is supposed in his flight to have been drowned in the waters of the Guadalquiver. The conquest of the whole of Spain, except the inaccessible district of Asturias, was effected in about three years; thus the kingdom of the Goths, after it had existed there for 300 years, came to an end. The Saracens conquered also for a time the South of Gaul, and threatened to stall their horses in St. Peter's at Rome. This, however, was their furthest advance in Western Europe; they were soon driven back across the Alps by Charles Martel's victory at Tours; and thus Gaul, and perhaps Rome and Britain, were saved from the civil and religious yoke of Islam.

The same year which witnessed the overthrow of Roderic witnessed also the conquest of Scinde and the first Mahometan settlement in India. Scinde, however, was lost to them, A.D. 750, in a national revolt of the Rajpoots, and the conquest of India was not effected by the Mahometans till the close of the Tenth Century, when they invaded Hindoostan, and the whole of India, after a time, became subjected to Mahometan rule. But before the walls of Constantinople the Saracens met with a crushing defeat. A saying attributed to Mahomet, that the sins of the first soldiers who besieged the capital of the Cæsars should be forgiven, animated the Caliph Moawiyah to lay siege to Constantinople. The old spirit of the Romans was now rekindled through the recent disasters in Syria and Egypt; the walls of the city were defended by an army of unanimous and well disciplined troops; the Saracens were dismayed and terrified by the lately discovered Greek fire which was poured upon them; in vain the siege was renewed in six successive summers (669—675); and after the loss of 30,000 men they were obliged to retire, and to purchase peace by payment of an annual tribute.

A similar but even worse result attended another attack (716—718) of Constantinople by the Saracens under their Caliph Walid. The Saracenic fleet, recruited by the "invincible force" of the navies of Egypt and Syria, was said to have amounted to 18,000 vessels, so that, in the language of the Greeks, the Bosphorus was overshadowed by a moving forest. Again the Greek fire fought on the side of the Greeks; famine, disease, and shipwreck caused havoc amongst the Saracens. A report that the Franks, the unknown nation of the Latin world, were arming in defence of the Christian cause, so alarmed them, that after thirteen months the siege was abandoned, and their fleet had been so repeatedly damaged by fire and tempest, that only five ships returned to Alexandria to relate the tale of their almost incredible disaster[e].

As yet the whole Saracenic power had been held together under one Caliph. But simultaneous with the re-conquest of Scinde was the fall of the Ommiad dynasty, of which Merwin II. (744—750) was the fourteenth, and the last of the Caliphs at Damascus. In the latter year the Ommiads were overthrown and driven out by the descendants of Abbas, the uncle of Mahomet; and Abdul Abbas, seated on the throne of Damascus, founded the dynasty of the Abbasides, the second Caliph of which dynasty, Ali Mansur,

[e] Gibbon, X. 14.

removed, A.D. 768, the seat of the Caliphate to the newly-founded city of Bagdad. The fall of the Ommiads led to the dismemberment of the Saracenic Empire. For a Prince of the Ommiad family, the young Abdarahman, eluding the vengeance of the conquerors, fled from Syria into Spain, where the Moslems refused to recognize the Abbassides; and there he founded the equally brilliant dynasty of the Ommiad Emirate, and afterwards Caliphate, of Cordova. Thus there were now two rival Caliphs, each giving himself out as the rightful Caliph, the one at Bagdad, where it ruled from A.D. 750—1258, when the last Abbasside was taken and put to death by one of the descendants of Ghengis Khan; the other at Cordova, where it reigned about two hundred and fifty years. After the restoration of the Western Empire the rival Caliphs were the friends or enemies of the rival Emperors, the Caliphs of Cordova being the natural enemies of the neighbouring Western Empire, and those of Bagdad of the neighbouring Eastern Empire. The most famous of the Abbasside Caliphs was the fifth, Haroun al Raschid (786—809), the hero of the Arabian Nights, the contemporary of Charlemagne, under whom the Caliphate of Bagdad reached its greatest height of glory. After his time it gradually declined.

When once the spell of union was broken, other provinces followed the example set them; the two Caliphates became split up, and several Mahometan powers arose, professing only a nominal adherence to the Caliphs at Cordova or Bagdad. In the Ninth Century independent Saracen States arose in Crete and Sicily, which to that time had belonged to the Eastern Empire. In the Tenth Century the Fatimites, pretending to be descendants of Mahomet's daughter Fatima, having founded Algiers, Tripoli, and Tunis, subsequently gained possession of Egypt, where they established, A.D. 969, a Caliphate at Cairo, which continued under eleven Caliphs. The most famous or infamous of the Fatimite Caliphs was the third, Al Hakim (996—1020), the destroyer of the Church of the Resurrection in Jerusalem. The reason assigned by him was the fraud practised with respect to the miraculous fire at Easter; but he also destined to destruction a thousand other Churches in which no such deception was practised. He afterwards gave himself out to be God, and, strange to say, he relaxed his cruelties against the Christians and allowed them to rebuild their Churches [f]. The Dynasty was overthrown, A.D. 1171, by the great Saladin, who, as "lord of Egypt," founded a new dynasty; but he transferred the Egyptian Caliphate to Bagdad, and the name of the Abbasside Caliph, the true Commander of the Faithful, instead of that of the Fatimite Caliph, again appeared in the public prayers. Yet notwithstanding all its divisions, Mahometanism went on increasing until, A D. 1453, the Crescent displaced the Cross on the dome of St. Sophia's at Constantinople.

[f] Freeman's Saracens, p. 113.

CHAPTER X.

The Seventh Œcumenical Council.

THE Iconoclastic controversy—Simplicity of worship in the primitive Church—Gradual introduction of pictures and images—Reaction against images—The Emperor Leo, the Isaurian—His defeat of the Saracens—His edicts against the Images—Germanus, Patriarch of Constantinople—Hostility to Leo in Italy—Gregory II , Pope of Rome—Luitbrand, King of the Lombards—Provinces withdrawn by Leo from the Pope and placed under the Patriarch of Constantinople—St John Damascene—Greek Hymnologists—Pope Gregory III —Charles Martel's victory at Tours—Constantine Copronymus, Emperor—Pipin the Little—Iconoclastic Council at Constantinople, A D 754—Pipin and Copronymus—The Patrimony of Peter—The Empress Irene—Tarasius appointed Patriarch of Constantinople—Irene summons the Seventh General Council—The Council decides in favour of the Images—The Council not properly Œcumenical—Opposed in the West under Charlemagne—Charlemagne destroys the Lombard Kingdom — The Caroline Books—Council of Frankfort—Adoptionism—Council of Paris—Theodora Studita—Irene deposed—Revival of the Western Empire —Rise of the Bulgarians—The Iconoclastic Controversy ended by the Empress Theodora—"Η Κυριακὴ τῆς 'Ορθοδοξίας—Character of the Icons in the Greek Church—The Paulicians.

OF all the controversies which have agitated the Christian Church, the Iconoclastic is perhaps the most remarkable and one of the most important in its results It was, says Dean Milman, not a mere controversy but an actual war of one part of Christendom against the other; it began A.D. 726, and lasted for a century and a half; it excited the worst passions of human nature, and it shook the Church to its very centre. It was an era-making event; not only did it cause the revolt of Italy, but it prepared the way for Pipin and Charlemagne, and so for the temporal power of the Popes, and the restoration of the Western Empire.

The primitive Church was partly composed of Hebrew converts to whom images would have seemed a violation of the Second Commandment, partly of converts from heathendom who held in abomination the idols of the religion which they had abandoned. For these reasons the services of the primitive Church were marked with extreme simplicity, Gradually Christian symbols such as we find in the catacombs—the Cross, the Lamb, the Good Shepherd, the Dove, the Fish, the Anchor, were adopted, but pictures in Churches were reprobated by the Thirty-sixth Canon of the Council of Illiberis (Elvira) in Spain, perhaps A D. 324 (" placuit picturas in Ecclesiâ esse non debere "). When in the time of Constantine Christians were able, without fear from the heathen, to devote their wealth to building and adorning their Churches, and embellishing the Church-Services, a change commenced. As time went on, magnificent and richly endowed Churches were erected; and the same religious motives which led people to build and endow Churches led them to adorn them with costly ornaments and to advance the ritual. Not only such reasonable representations as the Cross and the emblems of our Salvation; not only pictures, which may be called the books of the poor and ignorant; but representations of the Apostles and Martyrs, not in pictures and mosaics but in statues, were introduced, so that before the end of the Fourth Century St. Augustine of Hippo speaks of people in his time being *adorers* of images. By degrees a miraculous power—especially was this the case in the East—came to be attributed to them; the worship of such images in the Greek Church is avowed and defended by an ecclesiastical writer, Leontius, Bishop of Neapolis in Cyprus, who flourished in the last years of the Sixth Century; whilst his contemporary, St. Gregory the Great, had to deprecate the adoration of images. The adoration of relics and the invocation of Saints led to the full development of the adoration of the images representing those Saints; in the middle of the Seventh Century a Mahometan Prince, the son of the Caliph Omar, ordered the removal of all pictures from the Christian Churches within his dominions. There is no doubt that the adoration of pictures and images grew to such a height, both in the Eastern and Western Churches, as was opposed to every Christian principle, and came very near the violation of the Second Commandment.

A reaction against images set in under the Monothelite Emperor, Philippicus, and the Monothelite John, whom he intruded into the Patriarchate of Constantinople. By John's advice, the Emperor, A D. 712, ordered a picture representing the Sixth General Council, to which they were both opposed, to be removed from the Cathedral of St. Sophia at Constantinople, and he also issued an order for the removal of similar representations in Rome. Constantine I., the Pope, so far from complying with the order, denounced in a Council the Emperor as an apostate, and refused to allow his name to be mentioned in the Mass.

Leo III. (716—741), a native of Isauria, a brave but rough and uneducated soldier, raised to the Imperial throne by the suffrage of the army, founded the Isaurian dynasty of the Roman Emperors. The affection which the army bore to him and to the successors of his dynasty forms an important element in the great Iconoclastic struggle on which we are now entering. When Leo came to the throne the Saracens were carrying everything before them; and though, owing to his Iconoclastic measures, he lost the greater part of Italy which still remained to the Empire, yet it was mainly owing to him that the Saracens were driven away from Constantinople. This defeat of the Saracens by Leo deserves to be ranked with that afterwards gained over them in the battle of Tours by Charles Martel; it is, says Professor Freeman[a], one of the greatest events in this world's history, for had Constantinople been taken by the Mahometans before the nations of Western Europe had grown up, it would seem as if the Christian religion and European civilization must have been swept away from the earth.

Leo soon began to turn his mind from military to ecclesiastical matters; and, thinking it an inherent part of the Imperial office to coerce the consciences of his subjects, he, in the sixth year of his reign, ordered the Jews and Montanists to conform to the Orthodox Church. For the first ten years he abided by the prevailing ritual of the

[a] General Sketch, p. 126.

Greek Church; but, a Monophysite by extraction, he had learnt in his native home amongst the Isaurian mountains a simpler faith than that which he found prevalent at Constantinople; and before he became Emperor he had been brought into contact with the Mahometans, who taunted the Christians with idolatry. In A D. 726, and again in 730, he issued edicts against the images [b]. He was at first contented with the removal of pictures and images from public places, but he at once met with a firm opponent in the aged Patriarch, Germanus. When, probably after the second edict, an Imperial officer further proceeded to hew in pieces the figure of our Saviour over the Brazen Gate (perhaps that of the palace) at Constantinople, the women of the city pulled down the ladder on which he was mounted, and he was beaten to death by the clubs of the enraged citizens. The Emperor sent soldiers to appease the riot, and a terrible massacre ensued; but the images were everywhere removed and the walls of the Churches whitewashed Nor were the riots confined to Constantinople. Many of the image-worshippers had taken refuge in the monasteries, where the monks were the staunch defenders of the images. The people of Greece and the Cyclades, instigated by the monks, rose in rebellion, denouncing the enemy of Christ, of His Mother, and of the Saints. They proclaimed as Emperor one Cosmas, and equipped a fleet against Constantinople, the fleet was destroyed by the newly-invented Greek fire, and the leaders were either killed in battle, or afterwards, together with the usurper, executed.

The Patriarch Germanus and Pope Gregory II. of Rome (715—731) were for once united. In Italy, the edicts of the Emperor excited even greater hostility than in the East, and the Italians vowed to die in defence of their images. More than a century had intervened between Gregory I and Gregory II. In the time of the former, the two Patriarchs of Rome and Constantinople were, says Gibbon, nearly

[b] The chronology of events at this period is given so differently, that we must state the events without placing them under the years in which they occurred

equal in rank and jurisdiction. But in the interval a marked change had taken place in their position. In the great controversies which intervened, whilst there was one organized Church in the West there were several disorganized Churches in the East; the Popes were growing more and more independent, and only awaited an opportunity for shaking off their subjection to the Emperor. This was given to them by the Iconoclastic Controversy, and was fraught with important consequences to Christendom. Gregory wrote two letters to his nominal sovereign, Leo, defending the images, telling him that Christians and unbelievers alike were scandalized with his impiety; accusing him of such ignorance that, if he entered their school-room, the very children would throw their tablets at his head ($\tau\grave{\alpha}\varsigma$ $\pi\iota\nu\alpha\kappa\acute{\iota}\delta\alpha\varsigma$ $\alpha\grave{\upsilon}\tau\hat{\omega}\nu$ $\epsilon\grave{\iota}\varsigma$ $\tau\grave{\eta}\nu$ $\kappa\epsilon\phi\alpha\lambda\grave{\eta}\nu$ $\sigma o\hat{\upsilon}$ $\rho\acute{\iota}\psi o \upsilon \sigma \iota \nu$). Civil rulers, he told him, had power over the body, to the Church belonged the more powerful weapon of excommunication. Do you not know, he asked, that the Popes are the bond of union, the mediators of peace between East and West? The Emperor might, he tells him, threaten to carry off the Pope a prisoner, like the Emperor Constans did his predecessor Martin, but he could easily retire twenty-four miles into Campania, whither the Emperor might as well try to follow the wind.

Riots occurred in Ravenna, the residence of the Exarch, and in the provinces. The Lombards, who, as we have seen, conquered the North of Italy, and founded Lombardy, had been, A.D. 599, converted from Arianism to the Catholic Church, through St. Gregory the Great and their Queen Theodelinda, the latter of whom succeeded in converting her husband, Agilulf or Aistulf; but they still continued to be feared at Rome, and were always a thorn in the side of the Popes. Luitbrand, the reigning Sovereign and the most powerful of all their Kings, professed to favour the images, and in his zeal for orthodoxy availed himself of the opportunity, which he had long sought, of invading and gaining possession of the Pentapolis and Ravenna, the

Catholics of the Exarchate welcoming him as their deliverer. Ravenna was, however, speedily recovered by the Venetians, who, at the request of the patriotic Pope, now came to the help of the Emperor. The Pope thus gained a moral victory for himself, but a substantial, if temporary, victory for the Emperor. But Leo could not forget nor forgive the Pope's former opposition; he now confiscated the patrimony of the Pope in Sicily and Calabria, withdrawing those provinces, as well as Eastern Illyricum, from his jurisdiction, and placing them under that of Constantinople.

This was a severe blow to the Papacy. Illyricum had undergone many vicissitudes. The Gospel had been preached in that country by St. Paul (Rom. xv. 19), and it was early placed under the See of Rome. It was in the Metropolis of Thessalonica, which, with Ephesus, occupied a position second only to the Patriarchal Sees, and embraced the whole of Greece. Gratian, A.D. 379, annexed it to the Eastern Empire, and the transference was confirmed by a rescript of Theodosius the Younger, which placed it under the jurisdiction of Constantinople. Pope Boniface I, however, prevailing with the Emperor Honorius to interfere, the statute was abrogated and a return to the old arrangement made. Nor was this interfered with by the Council of Chalcedon, which, though it greatly added to the jurisdiction of Constantinople, gave the Patriarch no authority over Illyricum. Under Justinian, Illyricum was divided into two parts, Eastern and Western, in the former of which the Greek, in the latter the Latin, language was spoken. The action of the Iconoclastic Emperor in separating Eastern Illyricum from Rome, and placing it under the jurisdiction of Constantinople, added another serious cause, of which more will be heard further on, of difference between East and West.

Paul the Exarch was sent by the Emperor from Ravenna to coerce the Pope into obedience to the Iconoclastic measures, and even to seize him; but he was safe under the protection of the Lombards. Paul was excommunicated by the Pope; the Italians broke in pieces a statue of the Emperor, and renounced their allegiance; and Paul, in attempting to enforce the Emperor's edict, was killed in a tumult at Ravenna. His successor Eutychius met with little better success, and was likewise excommunicated. The election of the Popes had hitherto required the confirmation of the Exarchs; but the manner in which Gregory defied both Exarch and Emperor shows how far the See of Rome had advanced towards completely throwing off the yoke of the Eastern Empire.

The Lombards had always a hankering after Rome, which they regarded as the key which would open to them the possession of the whole of Italy, and in 729, Luitbrand, forsaking the Pope, joined the Imperial forces, and appeared before the walls of Rome. The Pope repairing at the head of his clergy, the Cross borne before them, to the camp of the Lombard King, succeeded in convincing him that he was on the point of committing a mortal sin, and urged him to repentance; Luitbrand was thus from an enemy turned into a friend; treating the Pope with the deepest reverence, and entering Rome in his company, he divested himself of his crown, and laid his sword on the altar of St. Peter, and signed a treaty of peace in which the Imperialists were obliged to acquiesce.

Far different was the power which the Emperor was able to exert over his own Patriarch, resident under his eye at Constantinople. In 730, Germanus, more than ninety years of age, worn out with the long struggle, much to the delight of the Emperor, resigned the Patriarchate and retired to an estate of his own, Anastasius (731—754), the Emperor's secretary and an Iconoclast, with whom Pope Gregory refused to communicate, succeeding him.

Equal to Pope Gregory as the intrepid defender of the images and their ablest literary defender, was St. John Damascene, the most learned of the Greek writers of his time. John, called in Arabic Mansur, but generally known, from his native place Damascus, as St. John Damascene, was born of Christian parents towards the end of the Seventh Century, and received his education from a learned Greek monk, named Cosmas, who having been made a prisoner of war by the Saracens, and put up for sale at Damascus, was ransomed by John's father, Sergius. On the death of his father, John was appointed by the Caliph to succeed him as Governor or Vizier of Damascus. When the Emperor Leo issued his second edict, although he well knew that the Caliph was in favour of the Iconoclasts, John Damascene boldly entered the list against them, and through an able pamphlet which he wrote he at once enlisted the clergy, but especially the monks, in favour of the Images, and became the acknowledged leader of the party. The immunity which John enjoyed as a resident at Damascus, and a subject of the Saracenic Kingdom, determined Leo to resort to treachery. John, under an accusation of treacherous designs against the Mahometans, was sentenced to have his right hand cut off, and the sentence was executed; but the story goes that on the same night the hand was miraculously restored by the Virgin Mary, and that the Caliph, thus convinced of his innocence, ordered him to be re-instated in his office.

However that may be, John, wearied with the world and the world's honours, retired, in company of Cosmas, into the Lavra of St. Sabas in the wilderness of Engedi, which was also in the territory of the Saracens. There he was ordained Priest; and through the remainder of the reign of Leo and the whole of that of his successor continued to prosecute his studies, and to advocate the cause of the Images; leaving the Lavra only once for the purpose of kindling opposition to the Iconoclastic measures of the Emperor Constantine, dying probably in the same year as that Emperor (A.D. 755).

Cosmas, the slave, ransomed by St. John Damascene's father, lived to become Bishop of Mazuma. The Lavra of St. Sabas sheltered about the same time three of the most famous Greek hymnologists whose verses have come

The Seventh Œcumenical Council. 343

down to us, St. John Damascene, his brother's son, Stephen, and St. Cosmas. We have already mentioned St Anatolius, Patriarch of Constantinople, as the first in order of time of the Greek hymn-writers of whom we have any record. Another was St. Andrew, a native of Damascus, and Archbishop of Crete, to whom the Church owes the Sacramental Hymn, "O the mystery passing wonder," and the Hymn translated by Dr. Neale to be found in Hymns Ancient and Modern, "Christian, dost thou see them?" Andrew was deputed by Theodore, Patriarch of Jerusalem, to attend the Sixth Œcumenical Council, and is famous in the Greek Church as the author of the *Great Canon* sung on the Thursday before Palm Sunday, known as the Feast τοῦ μεγάλου κανόνος.

The compilation Hymns Ancient and Modern is so familiar to English Church people, that it may be of interest to mention the hymns which are attributed to the three contemporary monks of St. Sabas, all, we believe, translated by Dr. Neale. St. John Damascene was the writer of the Hymns commencing, "The day of Resurrection," and "Come, ye faithful, raise the strain;" Stephen, "Art thou weary, art thou languid;" whilst to St Cosmas are attributed the Hymn commencing, "In days of old on Sinai;" and another, not included in that work, "The choirs of ransomed Israel."

Gregory II., dying A.D. 731, was succeeded by Gregory III. (731—741), a Pope equally as zealous as his predecessor in the cause of the Images. The election of the new Pope had still to be confirmed by the Emperor, and not before his sanction arrived was Gregory Consecrated. At the very commencement of his Patriarchate he, in a Council attended by ninety-eight Bishops, at Rome, anathematized all those (and the Emperor was included in the number) who attacked the traditions of the Church and the Images of the Saints. The Pontificate of Gregory III. was one of great importance in the future relation of the Greek and Roman Churches, and indeed in the history of the world. Not only was Germany brought into subjection to the See of Rome by the missionary labours of the English Winfred, better known as St. Boniface; but the seeds sown by Pope Gregory II. were watered, which led to the severance of the Roman See from the Eastern Emperor; to the great increase, if not the foundation, of the patrimony of Peter; and the restoration of the Western Empire. Gregory III. was the last Pope for whose Consecration the authority of an Eastern Emperor was either asked or required.

In 732, Charles Martel gained the victory over the Saracens in the battle of Tours, which may be reckoned as one of the great battles of the world; a battle which, had it resulted otherwise than it did, would probably have changed the whole subsequent history of Christendom. After that, it was little likely that the Pipin family would rest contented with the humble pageant of Mayors of the Palace, which they had hitherto borne, to the puppet Kings of France. Charles Martel was thenceforward the champion of the Faith in the West. It is true he was not scrupulous in using the property of the Church, nor in his manner of appropriating the revenues of its most lucrative Bishoprics, in order to maintain the efficiency of his army. But the Pope saw in the Pipin family the rising power of the day. Though the political importance of the Papacy had grown immensely under the Iconoclastic troubles, the Pope was still sorely pressed by the Lombard Kingdom. Twice, once in A.D. 739, and again in 740, Gregory applied for assistance to Charles Martel, who received the Pope's ambassadors with the greatest reverence; but both he and the Pope died shortly afterwards (A.D. 741), and although the ice was broken, nothing further was at present effected.

In the same year the Emperor Leo III. died, and was succeeded by his son, Constantine V. (741—775), to whom the insulting nickname of Copronymus was given by his enemies. Constantine had, A.D. 733, married Irene, daughter of the Khan of the Khazars; she is described as a pious Princess, and, although she swore at her marriage that she would renounce them, was a secret favourer of the images, of which the Emperor was even a stronger opponent than his father. Of Constantine's character it is difficult to form a just estimate, for whilst his enemies attribute to him every kind of vice and stigmatize him as an atheist, the Iconoclasts praise his virtue. No doubt his vices as well as his virtues have, through religious zeal, been exaggerated; though gifted with military ability he was certainly a violent and cruel man; but, perhaps, the fact that his tomb was violated and his remains burnt by one of his successors, the orthodox drunkard Michael, may throw some light on the matter. Iconoclastic fanaticism became hereditary in the Isaurian family, and it was exercised probably as much, if not more, from an arbitrary zeal for a paramount power over the Church, as from religious principles. At any rate during his reign the persecution of the Iconoclasts, and particularly of the monks, continued and increased.

Shortly after the commencement of his reign, Artavasdes, who married his sister Anna, headed a rebellion of the orthodox party, whom, by advocating the images and their erection in the Churches, he had gained over to his side. He was crowned by the previously Iconoclastic Patriarch, Anastasius, who had now become a worshipper of the images and denounced the Emperor as a Nestorian and a denier of the Godhead of Christ. Constantine, however, was enabled in two years to recover the throne; the orthodox Bishop of Gangra, who had taken part in the rebellion, was beheaded, and Artavasdes with his two sons, having had their eyes put out, were immured in a monastery. The unworthy Patriarch Anastasius, deprived of his eyes, and seated upon an ass, his head turned towards the tail (a similar story, however, is told of Constantine, his successor in the Patriarchate), having been thus ignominiously paraded through the city, was afterwards, in mockery, allowed to hold the Patriarchate till his death, A.D. 754.

At the time that Constantinople was in the hands of the usurper, Artavasdes, the Lombards under Luitbrand were again threatening Rome. Zacharias (741—754) succeeded Gregory III. as Pope ; Pipin, surnamed the Little, succeeding his father, Charles Martel, as Mayor of the Palace. In 749 Agilulf became King of the Lombards, and on him the Pope so far prevailed as to prevent the Exarchate of Ravenna becoming part of the Lombard Kingdom. Stephen II, the successor of Zacharias, dying before his consecration, was succeeded by Stephen III. (752—757); and Agilulf soon broke the treaty made with Zacharias, took Ravenna and threatened Rome. The Pope having in vain implored the Emperor Constantine to send troops to recover the Exarchate, travelled to Paris to solicit the aid of Pipin; and there, in July, A.D. 754, in the Church of St. Denys, he anointed Pipin (who had already, two years before, been crowned by the English Boniface, the Archbishop of Mayence), together with his two sons, one of whom was the future Charlemagne, as Kings of France, Chilperic, the last King of the line of Clovis, being relegated to a monastery. Pipin in return promised the Pope the aid he sought.

The Emperor, who concerned himself but little about these events which were going on in the Western part of the Empire, summoned, in February, 754, a Council, which sat six months, in the suburbs of Constantinople. No Patriarch was present, the See of Constantinople was vacant by the death of Anastasius ; Stephen III. of Rome refused to attend ; the Patriarchates of Alexandria, Antioch, and Jerusalem were in the hands of the Saracens. The Council was attended by 338 Bishops, under the presidency of Theodosius, Archbishop of Ephesus, an Iconoclast; and occasionally under the Bishop of Perga. The last of its sessions was held in the Emperor's palace at Constantinople on August 8, at which the Emperor himself was present. On August 27 the decree of the Council was subscribed by the Emperor and Constantine, who had now been translated from the Bishopric of Sylæum to the Patriarchate of Constantinople. The Council declared its adherence to the Six General Councils ; it pronounced those who depicted an

The Seventh Œcumenical Council. 347

Image of Christ to be either Monophysites or Nestorians, and those who depicted images of the Virgin, Apostles, Prophets, or Martyrs, imitators of the heathen worship of images. In Christ Two Natures were united; no picture, therefore, or statue, it declared, can depict Him as He is, and His only proper representation was the Holy Eucharist. It disproved the view of the Image-worshippers from Scripture and the Fathers, and anathematized and condemned to severe punishments all that used them. Holy vessels and vestments, and all that was dedicated to Divine Service, it allowed to remain adorned, as before, with figures. Several anathemas were added, under which were included St. Germanus, the late Patriarch of Constantinople, George (as to whose personality there is much doubt), and Mansur (St. John Damascene).

As a consequence of the Council, images were everywhere removed from the Churches; but a violent opposition was headed by the monks The troubles, which beset Italy, now for a time engaged the Emperor, and delayed the execution of the decrees of the Council. Pipin, in the performance of his promise to Stephen, not only saved Rome from the Lombards during two invasions, one in the year of the Council, the other in the following year, but he forced Agilulf to give up the Pentapolis and the Exarchate of Ravenna, which he bestowed on the Papacy. To the ambassadors, whom Constantine sent requesting him to restore the lands to the Empire, Pipin replied; "The Franks had not shed their blood for the Greeks, but for St Peter and the salvation of their souls, and he would not for all the gold in the world take back the promise which he had made to the Roman Church." The ambassadors took with them, as a present to Pipin, an organ, the first, it is said, which was ever imported into the West.

Thus, as is generally believed, commenced what is known as the Patrimony of Peter; thus was laid the foundation of Rome's temporal power; and the Popes took their place amongst the Sovereigns of the world. The contest for supremacy between the Sees of Constantinople and Rome was thenceforward carried on on different and unequal lines.

In 766 the Emperor Constantine set himself to the complete extirpation of Iconolatry, with a view to which he exacted an oath against the images from all his subjects. His chief opponents being the monks, he determined to eradicate monasticism. That the monks, in their opposition, went beyond the limits of discretion, and the bounds of duty, thus increasing his wrath, seems not to be denied. They denounced him as a second Mahomet, and all the Iconoclasts as atheists and blasphemers. The vengeance the Emperor took was terrible. The monastic societies were dissolved; their lands and cattle confiscated, the monasteries converted into taverns, barracks, or stables. The profession of monasticism was proscribed; the monks were forced to assume secular attire, and the Consecrated virgins to marry. The Iconoclastic Patriarch, who had himself been once a monk, was compelled to swear from the pulpit by the Holy Cross, not only never to be a worshipper of images, but to abjure the monastic vow. Offending the Emperor shortly afterwards, he was deposed and banished, but was brought back again to Constantinople; and after being subjected to even more brutal treatment than his predecessor, was beheaded; Nicetas, a man of Slavic and servile birth, and a eunuch (and from this last circumstance canonically ineligible), reading the sentence and succeeding him in the Patriarchate.

In the Western part of the Empire the images were regarded with mixed feelings. The Popes were wholly in favour of them. Constantine wrote to Pipin the Little, with the view of enlisting the sympathy of the Franks in his Iconoclastic proceedings. Pipin answered that he could do nothing without the consent of the Bishops and nobles of the Kingdom. Paul I. (757—767) was at the time Pope of Rome, and to him Pipin wrote declaring his continued adherence to the Roman See; but he himself summoned, A.D. 767, the Council of Gentilly near Paris. The Acts of the Council have been lost, and we have no information with respect to it. But the fact of its being convened by Pipin, whilst it shows the independence which has always characterized the Gallican Church, seems to point to the same opposition to image-worship on the part of Pipin which characterized his successors Charlemagne and Louis the Pious, and a disposition on his part to meet the wishes of the Emperor rather than those of the Pope.

Constantine died A.D. 775, and was succeeded by his son, Leo IV., 775—780, surnamed Khazarus, a name derived from his mother's nationality. The laws against images were allowed to exist, but as the Emperor was a man of religious and gentle character, he, although no favourer of the images, inclined to toleration, and during his reign the Church and State enjoyed a respite, and the monks were allowed to return to their monasteries. The Emperor's wife, like his mother, named Irene, was an Athenian of great beauty, who with orthodoxy combined a cruel and intriguing, as well as an abandoned and profligate, character. At her marriage she had been compelled by the Emperor Constantine to abandon their veneration, with which she had been familiar at Athens, and was during the lifetime of Leo only a secret favourer of images. The support of such a woman as Irene was enough to disparage any cause, but on the death of Leo, as has been stated, although on insufficient authority, by poison administered by Irene, a great change in the Iconoclastic controversy ensued. Her son Constantine VI. (Porphyrogenitus, so called from the purple chamber in which he was born), a boy ten years of age, now became Emperor (780—797); and Irene, who was appointed guardian, at once resolved to bring the triumph of the Iconoclasts to an end, towards which she took the first step by issuing an edict for the toleration of both parties. On the death of Nicetas, A.D. 780, whilst the Emperor Leo was still living, Paul IV., on binding himself by an oath not to restore the images, was elected to succeed him in the Patriarchate of Constantinople. In 784 Paul, smitten by remorse of conscience on account of the oath which he had taken, laid down his Patriarchal office, and retired, for the purpose of doing penance, into a monastery; and on his death-bed recommended that a General Council should be held as the only means of terminating the Iconoclastic troubles and healing the schism in the Church.

Irene, in order to have a Patriarch favourable to her views, appointed her secretary Tarasius (784—806), as yet a layman, to succeed Paul. He at first pleaded his unfitness; but, inasmuch as the three Eastern Patriarchs, as well as the Pope of Rome, were all in favour of the images, he thought his acceptance would be a favourable opportunity for healing the schism by which the Church of Constantinople was divided, not only from the West but also from the East. He was accordingly Ordained and Consecrated to the Patriarchate, making it a condition that a General Council should be called for restoring the unity of the Church. He at once renewed Communion with the Eastern Patriarchs, and wrote to them, as well as to Pope Hadrian (772—795), requesting their co-operation in assembling the Council. Irene also determined that the Council should be one of such importance as to nullify the acts of the previous Council of Constantinople; and she likewise wrote to the Pope announcing her intention, and requesting that he would attend either in person or by learned representatives.

The Council first met in August, 786, at Constantinople. But the Imperial Guards, who still held the memory of the Iconoclastic Emperor Constantine in honour, assuming a menacing attitude, Irene, having first replaced them by others more favourable to her views, arranged for the Council to be transferred to Nice, the seat of the first General Council; and the Second Council of Nice met on September 24 of the following year.

Between that date and October 23 the Council held eight sessions. Although Tarasius actually took the lead, the most honourable place was accorded to the two Papal legates. There were also present two monks of Palestine,

The Seventh Œcumenical Council.   351

John and Thomas, who represented themselves as legates of the Eastern Patriarchs; Politian of Alexandria and Theodore of Antioch, owing to their subjection to the Saracens, not being able to attend, whilst the See of Jerusalem was vacant. With the exception of the two Papal legates, those present were members of the Greek Church. Nicephorus, afterwards Patriarch, was secretary. At the very commencement of the sittings a number of Prelates who had taken part with the Iconoclasts, recanted, and were absolved by Tarasius. Many of the Greek Bishops, under the existing prevalence of simony, had purchased their Sees, and, as might be expected in such men, were not over-scrupulous; and now, under Court influence, were ready to change their opinions rather than forfeit their revenues.

The case of those Bishops having been considered in the first three Sessions, they were allowed to retain their Sees. In Session IV., passages in support of the images were adduced from the Scriptures and the Fathers, and the late Iconoclastic Council was condemned. In Session V. it was decreed that images should everywhere be restored, and before them prayers should be offered. In Session VI. the assumptions of the Pseudo-Synod were exposed and refuted, and it was shown that many passages quoted in it from the Fathers were spurious or distorted. Session VII. declared that the Council neither intended to add to, nor to take from, the Six Œcumenical Councils; the Creeds of Nice and Constantinople were repeated, and anathemas against several heretics, including Pope Honorius, were pronounced.

At this Session the decree of the Council was drawn up. It enacted that, together with the venerable and life-giving Cross, Images of our Lord, His Mother, the Angels, and the Saints should be set up, whether in colours, or mosaics, or any other material; that they might be depicted on sacred vessels, on vestments, the walls and tablets of Churches; in houses and by the road-side; the oftener they were looked on, the more would people be stirred up in remembrance of the originals; that adoration including kissing (ἀσπασμὸν καὶ τιμητικὴν προσκύνησιν), should be paid to them, but not worship (λατρεία), which belongs exclusively to God (οὐκ ἀληθινὴν λατρείαν ἢ πρέπει μόνῃ τῇ Θείᾳ φύσει). Incense and lights were to be burnt in their honour. Whoever does reverence (προσκυνεῖ) to an image does reverence to the person whom it represents. The opponents of the images were anathematized (τῷ μὴ ἀσπαζομένῳ τὰς ἁγίας εἰκόνας ἀνάθεμα); Bishops and clergy who objected to them were to be deposed. In Session VIII. the decree drawn up in the Seventh Session was read in the presence of Irene and the Emperor, and agreed to; "this we believe, this we all think; this is the faith of the Apostles, of the Fathers, and of the Orthodox;" and the anathema pronounced in the Seventh Session was repeated.

The decrees were signed by three hundred and ten Bishops, and twenty-two Canons were passed, a few only of which require notice. Canon I. decreed that the clergy must observe the holy Canons, and recognize as such the Apostolical Canons and those of the six Œcumenical Councils. It thus accepted, like the Trullan Council, all the Apostolical Canons. Canon III. pronounced invalid the election of clerics by the secular power; and decreed that a Bishop must be elected by Bishops, according to the Fourth Nicene Canon. Canons IV. and V. were directed against the prevalent evil of simony, in accordance with the Thirtieth Apostolical Canon and the Second of Chalcedon. Canon VI. enacted that, agreeably to Canon VI. of the Sixth Œcumenical Synod (by which is meant the Trullan Council), a provincial Synod should be held every year. Canon VII. decreed that, whereas under the Iconoclasts, Churches had been Consecrated without relics, they must be placed in them with the customary prayers, and that no Bishops should in future Consecrate Churches without relics. Canon XIII. decreed that ecclesiastical buildings and monasteries, which in the late unhappy times had been converted into private dwellings, were to be restored. By

Canon XVIII. women were forbidden to reside in Bishops' houses or in monasteries. By Canon XX. double monasteries were forbidden; and a monk might not converse with a female relative in the monastery, except in the presence of the Hegumen. Canon XXI. forbade monks and nuns to go from one convent to another.

The Second Council of Nice was the last of the Councils that can lay any claim to the title of œcumenical, for it was the last of the Councils previous to the schism of the Eastern and Western Churches, which has for a thousand years rendered the assembling of such a Council impracticable. The Council was recognized both in the East and generally in the West as an œcumenical Council, and for a time effected a better understanding between the Sees of Rome and Constantinople. But it had no greater claim to be called œcumenical than the Iconoclastic Council of A.D. 754; neither of the three Patriarchs, of Alexandria, Antioch, and Jerusalem, was present, and it is questionable whether they were even invited to it; the two monks, John and Thomas, had received no legation from them; nor was the Western Church fairly represented; nor were its decrees ever universally received in the Catholic Church; and had a Council of the Western Church been convened, it probably would have condemned them, even though they were supported by Pope Hadrian.

The images or Icons ($εἰκόνες$), as they are called, of the Greek Church are not, it must be remarked, sculptured images, but flat pictures or mosaics; not even the Crucifix is sanctioned; and herein consists the difference between the Greek and Roman Churches, in the latter of which both pictures and statues are allowed, and venerated with equal honour.

Pope Hadrian accepted the decrees of the Council, and went further than the East in allowing not only painted, but sculptured, Icons, and Italy followed the example of the Pope. Hadrian sent a copy of the decrees to Charles, better known as Charlemagne, who in 768 succeeded his father Pipin, and on the death of his brother Carloman, A D. 771, became sole King of the Franks. To Charlemagne the Pope was deeply indebted. The defeat of the Lombards by Pipin had only a temporary effect; they again threatened Rome, and, in 773, Pope Hadrian applied to Charlemagne for assistance, who, in the following year utterly defeated in battle the Lombard King Desiderius, and consigned him to a monastery. Thus the Lombard Kingdom of Italy, after it had lasted more than two hundred years, came to an end. Charlemagne was in the same year crowned King of Lombardy, and the King of the Franks became, except in the South, which the Emperor still held, King of Italy. What Pipin commenced, Charlemagne completed; he ratified the former grant made to the Papacy, and increased the Patrimony of Peter with a large part of the territory which he conquered from the Lombards.

But Charlemagne was no blind follower of the Pope With regard to the Second Council of Nice he took up an intermediate position, opposed alike to that of the Pope and to that of the Iconoclasts. The treatise known as the Caroline Books, a work in which the English Alcuin is supposed to have had a hand, published, A.D. 790, in Charlemagne's name, shows as strong an opposition on his part to the fanaticism of the Iconoclasts in the pseudo-Council of 754, as to the superstition of the image-worshippers in the Second Council of Nice. Charlemagne sent a copy of the Caroline Books to Hadrian, which the latter acknowledged in a long letter. The Pope brought forward the opinions of former Popes and of Roman Councils, which decreed an anathema on those who refused "to venerate the Images of Christ, His Mother, and the Saints, in accordance with the testimony of the holy Fathers." He reminded Charlemagne how much his success was due to the See of St. Peter (he forgot to mention how greatly the See of St Peter was indebted to Charlemagne and his father Pipin), and he does not forget to remind him of the provinces taken from the Roman See by Leo the Isaurian. Those provinces, he tells him he would, if Charlemagne approved, admonish the Eastern Emperor to restore, and if he refused he would declare him a *heretic;* not on account of the Nicene Council which had rightly restored image-worship, but for his refusal to surrender the provinces; a somewhat strange application of the word heretic.

But the Pope made no impression on Charlemagne, and wishing, for political reasons, to stand well with the Franks, did not press the matter further.

Instead of accepting the decrees of the Second Nicene Council which the Pope had sent him, Charlemagne summoned, eight years afterwards (A.D. 794), the Council of Frankfort, which Du Pin says was attended by three hundred Bishops from France, Italy, and Germany, and, it is supposed, from England; as well as by two Bishops as representatives of the Pope. In this Council the heresy known as Adoptionism was condemned. Adoptionism, which taught that Christ as to His Divinity was the Son of God, but in His Human Nature was adopted into Sonship, unlike the other heresies as to the Nature of our Lord, which arose in the East, was a Western heresy, and owed its origin to two Spanish Prelates in the latter end of the Eighth Century, Elipand, Archbishop of Toledo, and Felix, Bishop of Urgel. In the Council of Frankfort the principle of the Caroline Books was upheld, and the decrees of the late Council of Nice repudiated, images might be retained in Churches as memorials and ornaments, but the worship of images, under any form, was condemned [e].

The Council of Paris, held A.D. 824, was an echo of the Council of Frankfort, and not only condemned image-worship, but the Pope himself. It is evident that a strong feeling against the images prevailed in the West, nor was the Second Council of Nice till two Centuries later recognized in the Frankish Church; so that for such reasons

[e] " In Ecclesiis memoriæ et ornamenti causa retineri posse, omnem vero cultum et adorationem penitus esse abrogandam "

it may be doubted whether the Second Council of Nice can rightly be considered an Œcumenical Council.

By the Council, Iconoclasm received a blow from which it never recovered, but it was far from extinguished. In the East the controversy continued with varied results under the next five Emperors, one Emperor approving, another condemning, the decrees of the Council. Irene had, by a bad education, corrupted the mind of the young Emperor. She may have felt that the traditional policy of the Isaurians would, as soon as he attained his majority, turn her son against the images. The young Emperor had been betrothed to a daughter of Charlemagne; but when Charlemagne declared against the Second Council of Nice, Irene broke off the contract, and married him against his will to an Armenian Princess, whom, in January, 795, he divorced, and in September of the same year took another wife, one of Irene's maids of honour, named Theodota. For this act he was excommunicated by the famous Iconolatrist monk, Theodore Studita, who was in consequence banished by the Emperor to Thessalonica. Irene contrived to gain the military over to her side, and a conspiracy was formed against the Emperor, with the result that, whilst he was asleep in the porphyry-room in which he was born, his eyes were put out by the emissaries of his unnatural mother. Irene then reigned alone for five years (797—802), after which she herself, in a conspiracy headed by her secretary, Nicephorus, was dethroned, and banished to the Island of Lemnos, where she was forced to gain a scanty subsistence by the labour of her own hands. A few months afterwards her wicked life was terminated; her orthodoxy, instead of her wickedness, was taken into account, and she was canonized in the Greek Church as an orthodox Saint.

Meanwhile, Pope Hadrian I. was succeeded by Leo III. (795—816). The government of the Empire by a woman, and one of Irene's character, gave the Pope the pretext for shaking off the subjection to the Eastern Emperors. Some serious accusations having been brought against the

Pope, Charlemagne determined himself to enquire into them at Rome; and, greeted on the way by the acclamation common in the Middle Ages, " Blessed is he that cometh in the Name of the Lord," arrived in Rome towards Christmas, A.D. 799. The Pope and his accusers were brought face to face before a Synod, presided over by Charlemagne, with the result that the latter were condemned and banished, and the Pope, having publicly taken the canonical oath of purgation, was acquitted. The temporal ruler had acquitted and reinstated the spiritual head of Western Christendom.

On Christmas Day, Charlemagne, dressed in the habit of a Roman Patrician, attended Mass in St. Peter's at Rome. Suddenly, as if moved by a heavenly impulse, the grateful Pope, in imitation of the Coronation of the Emperors by the Patriarchs of Constantinople, placed upon the head of the kneeling King a golden crown. It was an act of rebellion on the part of the Pope against the Eastern Empress, but the Iconoclastic troubles had paved the way; ever since the reign of Leo the Isaurian, the Romans had been in a state of smothered revolt against the Empire, and were only prevented by fear of the Lombards from breaking out into open rebellion. Charlemagne affected surprise, but probably it was only at the suddenness of the event, or perhaps, as has been surmised by Eginhard, from his desire to maintain friendly relations with the Eastern Empire. Irene, although her overthrow was imminent, was still popular with a large class of her subjects, and Charlemagne even, on political grounds, contemplated a matrimonial alliance with her. But the Pope could not have ventured on so important an undertaking without there being some tacit understanding between the two principal actors. The King's feeling with regard to the suddenness of the proceeding soon gave way to one of satisfaction, when he saw that there had been a preconcerted arrangement, and that the Pope was acting as the mouth-piece of the people; the dome of St. Peter's resounded with the joyful acclamations of the multitude within and outside the Church; "Long life and victory to the most pious Augustus, crowned by God, the great and pacific Emperor."

The new Emperor of the West, far from resting satisfied with this act of rebellion on the part of the Pope, strove to set himself right with the East, through means of a union between the two Empires. We cannot imagine that Charlemagne with his experience of three wives, one of whom he had divorced, could have been so enamoured of a woman of Irene's character as to desire, from personal motives, a matrimonial alliance with her. Still, in the autumn of 802, an Embassy from Clarlemagne, proposing the union of the Western and the Eastern Empires through a marriage between himself and Irene, arrived at Constantinople; Gibbon [d] suggests that the story may have been invented by her enemies to charge her with the guilt of betraying the Church and State to the Western power. In October of the same year occurred the revolution that sent Irene into banishment, and the negotiation necessarily came to an end.

Thenceforward there were again two Empires, one in the West, the other in the East, each styling itself the Roman Empire; the spiritual status of East and West continued the same as before, the former being under the Patriarch of Constantinople, the latter under the Pope of Rome. It need scarcely be said that the revival of the Western Empire, effected by the instrumentality of the Pope, was of the highest consequence to the Papacy. But it accentuated the differences between the two Sees. The memory of what Italy had suffered from the Iconoclastic Emperors, and the continued retention by the Eastern Patriarch of the provinces which had been severed from Rome, rankled in the minds of the Popes; other causes of difference soon arose, and the final separation of the two was only a matter of time.

Irene was succeeded by her rebellious secretary, Nicephorus I. (802—811). The new Emperor had little sympathy with the Iconolatrists, and was a favourer of the Isaurian

[d] IX 197

dynasty, the traditional opponents of the images. On the death of Tarasius, A.D. 806, he appointed a Patriarch named, like himself, Nicephorus, and a layman. He forbade him from corresponding with the Pope, whom he regarded as the Pope of Charlemagne, and therefore his own enemy; and, whilst he granted general toleration to the Iconolatrists, he severely persecuted the monks, who opposed the appointment of Nicephorus on the ground of his being a layman, and a man who had stabled his horses in their monasteries. But his reign was troubled by wars abroad and rebellion at home. The Caliph Haroun al Raschid (*the Just*), the famous hero of the Arabian Nights, compelled him to sign an ignominious treaty on the terms of payment of a large annual tribute to the Saracens. In 809, we begin to hear of inroads of the Bulgarians, by whom he was, A.D. 811, slain in battle, his head being exposed on a spear and his skull converted into a drinking-cup, often to be replenished, says Gibbon [e], in their feasts of victory. Stauracius his son, who succeeded him, soon afterwards died of a wound which he had received in the same battle. After the victory the Bulgarians carried their devastations as far as Hadrianople, taking the Bishop and a large number of Christians, captive. We shall find this savage nation softened before the end of the century by intercourse with the Greeks, and converted to Christianity by the Greek Church. The next Emperor, Michael I. (812—813), Rhangabe, who owed his elevation to his marriage with Procopia, the daughter of Nicephorus, was a favourer of the images; he was supposed to be too much under the influence of Priests, and a man of too peaceful a character to be of service against the Bulgarians; a mutiny occurred amongst the troops, and the Emperor was deposed, to end his life in a monastery.

Leo V. (813—820), the Armenian, for whom his religious inconsistency gained the title of Chameleon, was then elected Emperor by the soldiers, the friends of the Iconoclasts; and he inflicted such a defeat on the Bulgarians as prevented

[e] X 200.

them for fifty years from troubling the Empire. Leo, in a Synod of Constantinople, A.D. 815, rescinded the Nicene decrees which had been allowed to remain under his two predecessors, and ordered pictures and images to be removed from all the Churches. Nicephorus the Patriarch, the opponent of his iconoclastic measures, he caused to be deposed and confined in a monastery, in which he died, A.D. 828; Theodotus, a layman opposed to the images, being appointed to succeed him. Leo met with a strenuous opponent in Theodore, who had been recalled from exile and appointed by Irene Abbot of Studium, where he raised the number of monks from twelve to one thousand; he was now again banished to Smyrna.

A conspiracy was formed against the Emperor, and Leo, when on Christmas-day, A.D. 820, he was attending Mass in his own Chapel, was, at the time that the Eucharist hymn was being sung, assassinated; he was succeeded by Michael (820—829), surnamed Balbus, or the *Stammerer*, a native of Amorium in Phrygia. In 821 the new Emperor liberated Theodore Studita from banishment. In a letter to Louis the Pious, King of France, he advocated the retention of images as a means of instruction (*pro scripturâ*), but that they should be raised to such a height from the ground as to prevent a superstitious reverence being paid to them. He proclaimed a toleration for all his subjects, but, by refusing to give them a preference which they expected over the Iconoclasts, he incurred the wrath of those who, since the Council of Nice, must be called the orthodox party. One of his opponents was that sturdy champion of orthodoxy, Theodore Studita, who was in consequence again sent into banishment, and, after wandering about from place to place, died on the island of St. Trypho on November 11, 826, the day of his death being still commemorated in the Greek Church.

In the reign of Michael the Stammerer, the islands of Crete and Sicily were subdued by the Saracens, whose successes at this time were so rapid that, says Gibbon, but for their divisions and the rivalry of the Caliphates, Italy must have fallen a prey to the Empire of the Prophet [f]. Michael having died a natural death, the first ruler of the Empire for fifty years, says Mr. Oman [g], who had done so, was succeeded by his son Theophilus (829—842), a man of learning, and in other respects a just and tolerant Emperor, but a bigoted Iconoclast, and almost as cruel a persecutor of the orthodox party as Copronymus had been. His education he owed to John, who being one of the most learned men of the day was styled the Grammarian, like himself an Iconoclast, whom he appointed to the Patriarchate of Constantinople (832—842).

On the death of the Emperor Theophilus, the long and weary contest between the Iconolatrists and Iconoclasts was destined to come to an end in the permanent victory of the image-worshippers. His widow, Theodora, who was appointed regent during the minority of their son Michael III. (842—867), a boy three or four years of age when his father died, was as enthusiastic in favour of the images as Theophilus had been against them. The character of the new Emperor is delineated in the unenviable title which attached to him, that of *the Drunkard*. Theodora at once determined to restore the images, and having deposed John, the Iconoclast Patriarch of Constantinople, she appointed in his place Methodius, a supporter of the orthodox party, from whom she obtained for her husband, to whom she had been sincerely attached, Absolution for his iconoclastic delinquencies. In 842 she convened a Council at Constantinople, in which the decrees of the Second Council of Nice were re-affirmed, and the images restored to the Churches of the capital; and to commemorate the event a solemn Festival (ἡ Κυριακὴ τῆς Ὀρθοδοξίας), which is still observed in the Greek Church, was instituted. The final victory being thus obtained, Theodora caused the body of Theodore Studita, together with that of the Patriarch Nicephorus,

---

[f] X 57.   [g] Story of the Nations, p 208.

and of other Iconolatrists who had been banished for their faith, to be translated to the capital.

Under Theodora, who was not a persecutor of the Iconoclasts, a compromise between the two parties was effected, and the custom, which has ever since obtained in the Greek Church, was adopted. Statues, as bearing too great a resemblance to heathen worship, gave place to Icons, and paintings or mosaics became the characteristic of the Greek, as opposed to the statues of the Western, Church.

During the regency of Theodora a violent persecution of the unhappy Paulicians occurred. Their heresy was a reaction from the accretion, especially in the veneration of Saints, of images, and relics, which had grown up around the Gospel; and, so far as they asserted the right of the laity to a free use of the Scriptures, they may be regarded as the Protestants of the Greek Church, the precursors of the Albigences in the West. But it was a mutilated and distorted Protestantism. The worship, of which Constantine, a native of Armenia, is thought to have been the founder, seems to have been a revival, with a strict mysticism, of the dualistic teaching of the Gnostics, that there are two Gods, one the Demiurge, or the God of the Old Testament, the other the God whom they worshipped, the God of the New Testament and of the spiritual world.

Constantine is said to have been converted from Manichæism through means of a copy of the Gospels, and of the Epistles of St. Paul, which was put into his hands by a Deacon returning from captivity under the Saracens in Syria. This accounts for their great reverence for St. Paul, from whom the sect derived its name [h], and for their calling themselves after his disciples, Constantine being named Silvanus, others, Timothy, Titus, Epaphroditus, Tychicus. The two Epistles of St. Peter, whom they regarded as the opponent of St. Paul, they rejected; also the Apocalypse, and, like the Gnostics, the Old Testament. The charge, brought against

---

[h] Others, however, attribute it to Paul, a native of Samaria, in the Fourth Century

them by the Greeks of being Manichæans, they denied, and professed the greatest horror of Manes, and of the writings of Manichæans and kindred sects. The name of Christians they exclusively confined to themselves, calling all others Romans; they held heterodox opinions as to the Human Nature of Christ, the perpetual Virginity of His Mother, and rejected the Sacraments.

From the first they were treated with the greatest cruelty. Constantine, their reputed founder, was stoned to death, A.D. 684, by order of the Emperor, Constantine Pogonatus. Simeon, the official who was sent to execute the judgment, himself afterwards, renouncing his civil honours, joined the sect of which, assuming the name of Titus, he became the leader; he, too, A.D. 690, under a charge of Manichæism, was burnt by order of Justinian II. That, through their opposition to images they should incur the wrath of the Iconolatrists is not more than might be expected; but we might expect to find that the Iconoclasts would tolerate a sect, which, even if it held erroneous doctrines, was opposed, like themselves, to image-worship. Yet, for one hundred and fifty years, if we except the short reign of Nicephorus I., they were the victims of every Emperor, Iconolatrists and Iconoclasts alike. Their persecution culminated during the regency of the rigidly orthodox Theodora, who thought to exterminate the heresy; and under her, A.D. 844, many thousand Paulicians in Western Armenia are said to have perished under the hand of the executioner. Their remnant, revolting from the Eastern Empire, joined the Saracens, who welcomed them as allies, and with their help they again and again resisted and overcame the Imperial forces, and ravaged the Byzantine provinces. When at last the well-disciplined forces of Basil the Macedonian, A.D. 871, prevailed, and their political power was annihilated, they, in alliance with the Saracens, still continued to infest the borders of the Empire, and so prepared the way for the Turks, and the triumph of the Crescent over the Cross.

CHAPTER XI.

The Culminating Schism of the Greek and Roman Churches.

ST. IGNATIUS, Patriarch of Constantinople — The Emperor Michael the Drunkard and Cæsar Bardas—Ignatius deposed and Photius appointed—Both apply to Pope Nicolas I.—The Forged Decretals—Acted upon by Nicolas—The Conversion of the Teutonic nations primarily attributable to the Greek Church—Ulfilas—The Slavs converted by the Greek Church—Cyril and Methodius—Conversion of the Khazars—Of Bulgaria—The latter proselytized by Rome but returns to the Greek Church—Conversion of Moravia—Of Bohemia—Of Poland—Poland subjected to Rome—Ruric, Grand Prince of Russia—Seeds of Christianity sown in Russia—Early antagonism between Russia and Constantinople—Photius and Pope Nicolas I.—Four Synods at Constantinople—Photius excommunicated by Nicolas—His Encyclical against the Roman See—He excommunicates the Pope—Revolution at Constantinople—Photius deposed and Ignatius reinstated—Basil the Macedonian, Emperor—Death of Ignatius and restoration of Photius—His restoration ratified by Council of Constantinople, which condemns the Filioque Clause—Approval of the Council by Pope John VIII —Deposition and death of Photius—Photius excommunicated by nine Popes — Pope Formosus — Leo the Philosopher, and Nicolas Mysticus, Patriarch of Constantinople—Patriarchate of Bulgaria—Eutychius, the historian, Patriarch of Alexandria — Theophylact, Patriarch of Constantinople—The Emperors Nicephorus Phocas and John Zimisces—The Emperor Basil II., Bulgaroktonos—The Ottos, Western Emperors—Corrupt state of the Roman Church—Zoe and Theodora, Empresses—Leo IX., Pope—Michael Cerularius, Patriarch of Constantinople—His controversy with Leo—The schism consummated—The difference as to leavened or unleavened bread in the Eucharist—Conversion of Russia—Olga—Conversion of the Grand Prince Vladimir—The Bishopric of Kiev—Michael the Syrian, first Bishop of Kiev—Boris and Gleb, Russian Martyrs—Yaroslav, Grand Prince of Russia—The Russian system of Appanages.

METHODIUS having held the Patriarchate of Constantinople for four years, was succeeded by Ignatius (846—857 ; and again, 867—877). Born of an illustrious and noble family, his mother Procopia being a daughter of the Emperor Nicephorus, and his father Michael Rhangabe, he, in the revolution which dethroned his father, had taken refuge from the jealousy of Leo the Armenian in a monastery, where he exchanged his name Nicetas for the religious name Ignatius, and from whence, being a favourer of the images, and a man of holy character, he was summoned by Theodora to assume the Patriarchate.

On Advent Sunday, A.D. 857, a day on which it was customary for high officials to receive the Holy Communion from the Patriarch, Ignatius refused to administer it to Bardas, the brother of Theodora, a man whose notoriously immoral life laid him open to the censures of the Church. Bardas had gained a complete ascendency over the mind of the Emperor Michael, the Drunkard, which he determined to employ for the ruin both of the Patriarch and his patroness Theodora. He prevailed on the Emperor to consign her and her daughters to a monastery, and when Ignatius opposed the scheme, he also was sent into banishment to the island of Terebinthus.

Bardas, knowing that the people would resent the deposition of so holy and beloved a Patriarch as Ignatius, by way of appeasing their indignation, obtained the appointment of Photius (857—867, and again, 877—886) to the Patriarchate. Photius, like his predecessors Tarasius and Nicephorus, was a layman, a scion of a distinguished family, chief secretary to the Emperor, and a nephew of the late Patriarch Tarasius. He was, moreover, a man of unblemished character, reputed the most learned theologian of his time, and, like Ignatius, a favourer of the images. He accepted with reluctance the office vacated by the deposition of the rightful holder, a man whom he revered, and conferred upon him by such unworthy patrons as Michael and Bardas. The different Orders of the Ministry he received at the hands of Gregory, Archbishop of Syracuse, who, having been driven from his See by the Saracens, happened to be at the time in Constantinople. This was a very sore point with Nicolas I., who was in the next year appointed Pope of Rome (858—867). Not only had Gregory been Bishop of a Diocese which had been taken from Rome and conferred on Constantinople by Leo the Isaurian, but he was also under the ban of Rome. His Consecration, therefore, of Photius was regarded by the

Pope as an insult to the Papal See, and to the deposition of Ignatius, and the Consecration in his place of Photius, is to be ascribed the penultimate stage in the schism between East and West.

Ignatius naturally complained of the unjust treatment which he had received, and two parties arose in Constantinople, the followers of Ignatius excommunicating Photius as a usurper, and those of Photius, a man of somewhat irascible temper, excommunicating the followers of the gentler Ignatius. The low debauchee, Michael, laughed at both parties; Ignatius he styled the Patriarch of the people, Photius, the Patriarch of Bardas, whilst the Imperial buffoon Bardas he styled his own Patriarch. Ignatius, the rightful head of the Greek Church, suffering under unjust treatment, sought the help of the head of the Western Church. Photius announced, as was usual, his election to Pope Nicolas, informing him at the same time that the Emperor, Bishops, and Clergy had forced on him, against his own will, the unwelcome burden; he was also desirous of having on his side an ally so influential as the Pope of Rome.

It is necessary to state that, since the time of Charlemagne, and the restoration of the Western Empire, the See of Rome had received an immense leverage through a forged compilation, known as the pseudo-Isidore Decretals. It was the work of an impostor styling himself Isidorus Mercator [a], purporting to be the work of St. Isidore, Bishop of Seville (595—636); the word *peccator* (*sinner*) was a title under which Bishops of that time designated themselves, and the slip of *mercator* for *peccator* was in itself sufficient to expose the imposture. There was nothing in the early history of the Church to warrant the pretensions of the See of Rome, or the jurisdiction of the Popes over the other Patriarchs, and one object of the document was to make the Pope the universal Bishop of the Church. It is now allowed by Roman Catholics themselves to be a forgery, but to it the Popes for a long time appealed as genuine.

[a] The Preface commences ' Isidorus Mercator."

In the time of Pope Nicolas I. the imposture had not been fully exposed; but, innocent though he might have been of its character, he was the first Pope to receive it as genuine, and to act upon it. Under Nicolas the Forged Decretals began to do their work, and the full theory of papal claims to develope itself; he carried the papal pretensions to a greater height than any of his predecessors; he declared the judgment of Rome to be the "Voice of God;" and he took advantage of the Photian schism to impose his authority on the See of Constantinople.

Whilst Rome was, through the generosity of the Pipin family, rising to a political, and through it to an ecclesiastical, ascendency, the Greek Church may well claim a great spiritual triumph in the conversion of the Slavic nations, of which this may be a convenient place to give some account.

The conversion of the Teutonic nations to Christianity is generally attributed to the Latin Church. But even here its meed of praise must not be withheld from the Greek Church. Ulfilas, the Apostle of the Goths, was a Greek Bishop of Cappadocian descent, and exercised his ministry in Mœsia and Dacia, the latter of which countries comprised the modern Moldavia and Wallachia. Theophilus, the Bishop of the Goths who attended the Council of Nice, A.D. 325, was, there is no reason to doubt, an orthodox Bishop, and he was the predecessor of, and perhaps ordained, Ulfilas. Ulfilas, when he signed the Creed of Rimini, A.D. 359, thought himself orthodox, but his orthodoxy was of a vague and indistinct character, and when he was on a visit at the Court of the Emperor Valens, to induce him to allow the Visigoths to pass from Dacia into Roman territory, he became confirmed in Arianism. Over both Visigoths and Ostrogoths, Ulfilas exercised an unbounded influence; from the former Arianism passed to the latter, and the preference of the Vandals and Burgundians for its doctrines was stimulated by their hatred of the Romans. His translation of the Scriptures into their language, the oldest

Teutonic writing in existence, "the parent, so to speak, of all the Teutonic versions of the Scriptures [b]," was of the highest importance. By Ulfilas the whole Gothic nation was converted, but it was to the Arian form of Christianity; and after his death, which occurred at Constantinople, A.D. 480, his work was continued by the Latin Church, which converted the Teutonic nations from Arianism to Catholicism.

The Greek Church converted the Slavs from Paganism to Orthodoxy. It need scarcely be remarked that the word *slave* imparts to modern minds a very different sense to the word from which it has its derivation. "The word slave got the sense of bondman because of the great number of bond-men of Slavic birth who were at one time spread over Europe [c]." The word Slav is now universally allowed to be derived from *slovo*, and means the man who speaks intelligibly, as opposed to the Germans whom Russians style *neemets*, the *dumb* men.

The conversion of the Slavs was due to two brothers of the Greek Church, Constantine a native of Thessalonica, who is better known by his monastic name of Cyril, on account of his learning, called the Philosopher, and Methodius. The first of the Slavic nations converted to Christianity were the Khazars, a people dwelling in the neighbourhood of the Crimea, the daughter of whose Khan, as we have seen, the Emperor Constantine V. took as his wife. In A.D. 850, messengers from the Khazars arrived at the Court of the Emperor Michael entreating him to send some well-instructed (*eruditum*) missionary amongst them, and accordingly Cyril was chosen, and by his means the country was converted to Christianity, and parmanently attached to the See of Constantinople.

The conversion of Bulgaria, about the same time, is due to Cyril in connection with his brother Methodius. The seeds of Christianity had probably been already sown in the country by Bishops and Christians whom the Bulgarians had

[b] Stanley's Eastern Church, p. 346.   [c] Freeman's General Sketch, p. 15.

taken captive in battle at Adrianople. In one of the many wars between Bulgaria and the Eastern Empire, the sister of the Bulgarian Tsar, Bogoris or Boris, had been taken prisoner to Constantinople, where, in her long captivity of thirty-eight years, she was fully instructed in the Christian faith, the principles of which, after her liberation and return to Bulgaria, she succeeded in instilling into the mind of the Tsar. At her suggestion Cyril, fresh from the conversion of the Khazars, and Methodius were sent by the Empress-regent Theodora into the country, where they preached with such success that Boris was led to favour their teaching. The country being visited by a severe famine, the Tsar, having first sought in vain the help of the heathen gods, determined to invoke the God of the Christians. His prayers meeting with the desired result, he, with the chief men of his country, received, A.D. 864, Baptism from Photius, Patriarch of Constantinople, the Emperor Michael, whose name he took in exchange for his own, standing Godfather; the people followed his example, and Photius wrote to the royal convert, "his illustrious and beloved son," a letter containing the Creed of the Greek Church, with the omission of the Filioque Clause.

Two years afterwards, whether because he feared that the influence of the Greek clergy endangered his political independence, and in order to weaken it through a Latin counterpoise; or whether because Latin missionaries had instilled into his mind, especially in regard to the omission of the Filioque, a doubt of Greek orthodoxy; or perhaps because he had in the meantime learnt more thoroughly to appreciate the character of his Godfather, Michael the Drunkard; Boris or Michael, as he was now called, seems to have had misgivings as to his Greek Baptism, and to have applied to Louis the German and to Pope Nicolas for Latin instruction.

The Pope eagerly seized the opportunity for asserting the supremacy of his own See, and sent two Bishops, one of whom was Formosus, Bishop of Porto, the future Pope, to preach the Gospel in Bulgaria, with a long letter dwelling on no less than 106 points condemnatory of the Greek teaching, and thus prevailed with the Bulgarians to sever their connection with the mother-church of Constantinople, and to accept the Roman mission. In answer to the question of the Bulgarians as to how many Patriarchs there were, the Pope told them there were only three, those of Rome, Alexandria, and Antioch, and of the last two Alexandria was chief The Bishops of Jerusalem and Constantinople, although called Patriarchs, were not of equal authority with the others; Constantinople was not of Apostolical foundation, nor recognized by the greatest of the councils, that of Nice, and its Bishop was only called a Patriarch, because it was New Rome, by royal favour.

As to the addition of the Filioque to the Creed, he omitted to tell them that it did not occur in the Nicene Creed; nor did he tell them, that the See of Constantinople was not recognized by the Council for the reason that Constantinople did not then exist Nicolas was here, as Mr. Ffoulkes, once a member of the Roman Catholic Church, mentions [d], straining a point against a rival, and arguing as one Patriarc in opposition to another. The Bulgarians were so charmed with the last speaker, the missioner Formosus, that the accepted the Latin Church, expelling the Greek clergy and other foreigners from their dominions, and requested that Formosus might be consecrated as Archbishop of Bulgaria Formosus, however, was not a *persona grata* at Rome, and the request was refused by the Pope.

The Emperor, Patriarch, and people of Constantinople were all as one man in holding that Bulgaria, since it was indebted for its conversion to Constantinople, owed allegiance to that See and not to Rome. The Bulgarian Tsar Michael, being perhaps disappointed with the refusal Nicolas to raise Bulgaria to the rank of a Metropolitan See, sent to the Eastern Emperor requesting that a Council might be held to decide to which Patriarchate Bulgar

---

[d] Christendom's Divisions, Part II 11.

belonged. The matter was accordingly brought before the Council of 869, and settled, under the protest of the Papal legates, in favour of Constantinople. The Bulgarians thereupon threw off their short allegiance to Rome and returned to the Greek Church; Ignatius, when he was restored to the Patriarchate of Constantinople, sent a Greek Archbishop and Greek Priests into Bulgaria, and the Roman clergy were in their turn driven out of the country. In vain Pope John VIII. (872—882) remonstrated with the Tsar of Bulgaria, warning him not to follow the Greeks, who were filled with heresy and sure to contaminate his people. In vain he threatened Ignatius that, unless within thirty days the Greek clergy and Bishops should quit Bulgaria, he would be excommunicated, and if he remained obdurate would be deprived of the Patriarchate "which you owe to our favour." Ignatius died on October 23, 877, before the threat was fulminated, and the Pope had to deal with Photius, a Patriarch as determined as he was himself. Constantinople thus gained the victory, but the sore rankled in the mind of the Popes, for Bulgaria was within the area that had once been subject to the Archbishop of Thessalonica, and therefore within the Roman Patriarchate, and this was a further cause which led to the final schism

About the same time as Bulgaria, Moravia received the Gospel through Cyril and Methodius.

The two Apostles of the Slavs, soon after the middle of the Ninth Century, had, for the use of the people in their native town of Thessalonica, translated passages from the Gospels, Acts, and Epistles News of this translation into their own tongue seems to have reached the Slavs of Moravia; and, A.D. 863, at the request of the Grand Duke Vratislav, who had lately freed the country from the Franks, the Emperor Michael, acting by the advice of Photius, sent the two brothers as missionaries into Moravia. Through the translation of the Bible, and by preaching to the people and conducting services in their own language, whilst the Latins used in their services the Latin language, they soon won the people to the Greek Church. The opposition of the Latin clergy to the use of the Slavic language induced the missionaries to consult the Pope, and they accordingly accepted the invitation of Pope Nicolas I. to visit him at Rome. The two brothers are said to have conveyed with them to Rome the relics of St. Clement, which were then buried in the Church of San Clemente. On their arrival they found that Pope Nicolas was dead, but they met with an honourable reception from his successor, Hadrian II., who conceded to them the use of the Slavic Liturgy. At Rome, Cyril took the cowl of a monk, and there died, A.D. 869.

After the death of Cyril, Methodius continued the translation of the Bible, and according to the witness of a contemporary, translated all the Canonical Books out of the Greek language, and thus completed the first Slavic Bible[e]. At Rome he was consecrated Archbishop of Moravia and Pannonia, and in that capacity re-entered on his labours. Having again, through his use of the Slavic language in Moravia, where a German mission from Saltzburg had lately been settled, incurred the wrath of the German Bishops, he was on this ground, and on that of the Greek doctrine of the Procession of the Holy Ghost, accused, in 880, of heresy to Pope John VIII., the successor of Hadrian. Presenting himself before the Pope at Rome, he again established his orthodoxy and was confirmed in his Archiepiscopal rights, with permission to use the Slavic language in the services of the Church, the Pope declaring that God had made other languages besides the Hebrew, the Greek and the Latin, but on the condition that the Gospel and Epistle should first be read in Latin and afterwards in Slavic.

A serious misunderstanding, however, arose between him and the Moravian Duke Sviatopolk, the successor of Vratislav, and persecution from the German clergy, who found a supporter in Pope Stephen V., followed him to his death,

---

[e] See Church Quarterly Review, October, 1895

A D. 885. After his death, under a general persecution of the Slavic Priests, the Metropolitan See of Moravia was kept vacant for 14 years, until it was restored in 899 by Pope John IX. In 908 the Moravian Kingdom was overthrown by the Bohemians and Magyars, and the followers of Methodius fled from the country to Bulgaria; and when the Church of Moravia again appears on the page of history it was subject to the Bishops of Bohemia. The Magyars or Hungarians, it may here be mentioned, were first converted to Christianity, in the middle of the Tenth Century, from Constantinople; but the connection with the Greek Church was soon broken off in favour of Latin Christianity.

The Czechs or Bohemians owed their Christianity to their political connection with Moravia. Vratislav's nephew and successor, Sviatopolk (870—894), married in 871 a sister of the Bohemian Prince Borsivoi, afterwards the sainted Ludmila, and they both in the same year received Baptism from Methodius. But in spite of the pious efforts of Ludmila and those of her two sons, who became Princes of Bohemia, one the bearer of a name even less euphonious than his father's, Spytihnev, who died A D. 912, the other, Vratislav, who died in 928, heathenism held its own in Bohemia. Ludmila, who outlived them both, took especial care in the education of her grandson, Wenzeslaus, a Prince who inherited her saintliness, and in his reign (928—936) Churches were built in every city in the realm, and the Gospel was firmly established in Bohemia. The peaceable disposition of Wenzeslaus was little suited to cope with the fierce barbarian nobles, and he was killed in a conspiracy headed by his pagan brother Boleslav, surnamed the Cruel; but he remained the object of veneration to the people, and became the titular Saint of Bohemia. Under Boleslav the Cruel and his successor, Boleslav the Pious (967—999), Christianity underwent several vicissitudes, till the Bohemian Church was organized under a Bishopric at Prague, founded about A.D. 970. The people long continued to adhere to their Slavic ritual, notwithstanding the opposition of the German clergy, who always tried to abolish it. The latter were at last successful, one of the conditions imposed by Pope John XIII., when the Bishopric of Prague was founded, being, that the service should be conducted "non secundum ritus aut sectas Bulgariæ gentes, vel Russiæ, vel Slavoniæ linguæ," but according to the Latin Ritual.

The Germans continued to persecute the deceased Methodius, and the Roman Church seems strangely to have confounded the Slavs with the Arian Goths. It speaks of "Gothicas literas a quodam Methodio hæretico inventas," and Methodius is spoken of as having been "divino judicio, repentinâ morte damnatus." When the Slavs, after a Synod, appealed to Pope Alexander II. (1061—1073) for the repeal of the obnoxious disavowal of their language, they were told that it could not be granted "propter Arianos hujusmodi literaturæ inventores." Still the struggle for their Slavic service continued between the Slavs and Latins, and in 1080 Gregory VII. (Hildebrand) wrote a violent letter to Vratislav, Duke of Bohemia, and utterly prohibited its use. In some parts of Bohemia, however, the vernacular language held its ground, and one convent in Prague continues to use it in the present day[f]. The Wends, another Slavic nation, were converted, partially at the end of the Tenth Century, and completely in the middle of the Twelfth Century, by German settlers.

From Bohemia Christianity spread amongst the kindred tribes of Poland. Poland passes from the domain of legend into that of history in the reign of its Duke, Mieczyslav I. (962—992). In order to obtain in marriage the hand of Dambrowka, daughter of Boleslav, Duke of Bohemia, he was, A.D. 965, induced to abandon Paganism and embrace Christianity; and many of his courtiers followed his example. But his compulsory suppression of Paganism, and enforcement, under the guidance of Adalbert, Archbishop of Prague,

[f] Giesler, II p 458.

of the Canons of the Christian Church on an uninstructed people, met with such an obstinate resistance, that Christianity for some time made little progress. So long as Poland was a mere fief of the German Empire, it had a single Bishopric of Posen. The Emperor, Otto III., A.D. 1000, freed its Church from the jurisdiction of Magdeburg, and gave it an Archiepiscopal See of its own, and made Poland an independent Kingdom. But for some time such a state of anarchy prevailed as threatened the very existence of Christianity. In the reign of Casimir I. (1034—1058), who, from being a monk in a Benedictine Monastery, was raised to the throne, an impulse was given to Christianity, and the Church gained a firm footing. But Casimir swept away whatever traces remained of Greek Christianity, and Poland was brought into subjection to the See of Rome.

Thus of the two great Slavic nations, Poland and Russia, which for centuries were engaged in a death-struggle, not only for political but Ecclesiastical ascendency, the former belonged to the Latin Church. The conversion of Russia to Christianity is wholly attributable to the Greek Church. At the time when the Roman Church had fallen to its deepest degradation, and the Papacy was the prey of profligacy and wickedness, then it was that the Eastern Church gave birth to its mightiest progeny.

Photius, the Patriarch of Constantinople, writing, A.D. 866, against the pretensions of Rome, speaks of the conversion of Russia by Eastern missionaries as an accomplished fact. During his Patriarchate, and in the reign of Basil the Macedonian, the seeds of Christianity were first sown in Russia. In A.D. 862, when the land was harassed by enemies on its frontiers as well as by a band of Scandinavian pirates at sea, Ruric, the chieftain of the band, was invited into Russia by the inhabitants of Novgorod to establish order and assume the government. "Our land is large and rich," he was told, "but in it there is no order, do thou come and rule over us." Ruric thereupon assumed the rank of Grand Prince, making Novgorod his capital; thus he was the founder of the Russian monarchy, and from him dates the commencement which developed into the great Russian Empire. The word Novgorod signifies New Town, and implies the existence of the older Town, Kiev, on the Dnieper, which Askold and Dir, two of Ruric's companions, proceeding southwards, conquered.

Before long the new Russian power entered into commercial relations with Constantinople, and began at once to cast longing eyes on its wealth; and, in 866, a naval expedition under Askold and Dir sailed down the Dnieper and appeared under the very walls of Constantinople. Thus early did the antagonism between Russia and Constantinople commence. Tradition relates how that the capital was only saved by a miracle, how the alarmed citizens were relieved from their fears by the action of the Patriarch, probably Photius, throwing the robes of the Mother of God into the sea. Suddenly a storm arose, in which the vessels of the heathen were wrecked; the victory was ascribed to the Mother of God, and the two leaders, Askold and Dir, struck with awe, recognizing the hand of God, became the first-fruits of Christianity to the Russian people. After their return home, they sowed the seeds of Christianity in Kiev; there a Christian Church was built and a Bishop sent by Ignatius, then Patriarch of Constantinople; and Christianity, if it did not at that time take deep root in the country, yet, probably kept alive through the Russian merchants in their commercial relations with Constantinople, never afterwards died out.

We must now revert to the contest between the Patriarch Photius and the Pope of Rome. Photius had, as we have seen, announced his election to Pope Nicolas. The Emperor also wrote to the Pope requesting him to send legates to Constantinople to assist him in the task of restoring union and discipline. Nicolas seized the opportunity to judge, and, as he thought, humble, his rival Patriarch, and on receiving the letter he entered into a correspondence with the Emperor Michael. He began by demanding the restoration of the provinces of which the Papacy had been deprived by Leo the Isaurian, and that the Archbishop of Syracuse should receive Consecration from Rome. He protested against the deposition of Ignatius without the Pope being consulted; and at the same time wrote to Photius that his legates would enquire into, and report to him, as to the validity of his hurried Ordination.

Of the Pope's request with regard to the restoration of the provinces the Emperor took no notice; but, indignant at the tone of the letters of the Pope, he treated his legates as insubordinate subjects, and for a time imprisoned them. Four important Synods between this time and A.D. 879 were held at Constantinople. The first was summoned by the Emperor in 862, and Ignatius was advised by the Pope to attend. Nicolas was represented by his two legates, Rodvald, Bishop of Porto, and Zacharias, Bishop of Anagni; the Council was attended by three hundred and eighteen Bishops, the same number which was present at the First Council of Nice. The legates were told, amongst other instructions, to deal with the matter of the Images. It was afterwards said at Rome that the legates were bribed. The Synod confirmed the deposition of Ignatius, the Papal legates acquiescing in the sentence, but, by way of propitiating the Pope, condemned Iconoclasm. Ignatius, cruelly beaten and rendered, by his long sufferings and starvation, unconscious of what he did, traced the sign of the Cross in subscription of his own condemnation; and Photius was confirmed in the Patriarchate.

A terrible earthquake, for forty days together after the Council devastating Constantinople, alarmed the Emperor and Bardas, the terrified citizens accounting it a just retribution for the persecution of Ignatius. Ignatius in consequence obtained his liberty, and drew up a petition to the Pope, which, after it was signed by ten Metropolitans, fifteen Bishops, and a large number of Priests and monks, was conveyed to Rome by Theognostes, an Abbot of Constantinople.

The acts of the late Council were also sent to the Pope, together with a long letter from Photius, who wrote as the Pope's equal, ignored the Forged Decretals, and defended his appointment to the See of Constantinople by the similar cases of some of his own predecessors, as well as by that of St. Ambrose, the famous Bishop of Milan.

The Pope, after the return of the legates and the receipt of the letter of Photius, disowned the part they had taken in the Council, and declared that he had given no instructions for the deposition of Ignatius or for the appointment of Photius. In letters to the Emperor and Photius he took the highest ground ever yet taken by a Pope, declared Ignatius to be the rightful Patriarch of Constantinople, and the appointment of Photius, whom he addressed as a layman, to be uncanonical. In a Synod at Rome, A.D. 862, he declared Photius deposed, annulled his Orders, and threatened him with excommunication. He sent a third letter addressed to the Patriarchs of Alexandria, Antioch, and Jerusalem, and to their Metropolitans and Bishops, condemning the action of the legates, and commanding them by the *Apostolical authority* to agree with him with regard to Ignatius and Photius.

In a second Council at Rome, in the following year, Nicolas excommunicated his own legates for the part they had taken in the late Council, and pronounced anathemas against Photius and his Consecrator, Gregory, and restored Ignatius; "We, through the power committed to us by our Lord through St. Peter, restore our brother Ignatius to the See and all the honours of the Patriarchate."

The Emperor and Photius treated the anathema with indifference, and Photius continued to hold the See. The former wrote a violent letter to the Pope, stating that when he invited him to send legates to the Council of Constantinople, he had never intended to admit him as a judge in the affairs of the Eastern Church; he threw in his teeth his ignorance of the Greek language, and spoke of the Latin language, in which the Pope wrote, as a "barbarous jargon." The Pope sent his reply in 866, by the same messenger, and charged the Emperor with disrespect to God's Church, and to himself who derived his authority from St. Peter. He advised him to cease calling himself Emperor of the Romans, and warned him of the fate of former Emperors, Nero, Diocletian, and Constantius, who had persecuted the Church.

In 866 Cæsar Bardas was, at the instigation of the Emperor, assassinated on the charge of conspiring against the throne.

The ill-feeling which the Pope's action caused at Constantinople was increased through the Bulgarians, at this time, breaking away from the Eastern and joining the Western Church. In the second of the Councils held at Constantinople, A.D. 867, Photius drew up a famous Encyclical containing eight articles against the See of Rome; (1) the observance of Saturday as a Fast; (2) the partaking of milk and cheese during Lent; (3) the enforced celibacy of the clergy; (4) the restriction of Chrism to Bishops; (5) the double Procession of the Holy Ghost; (6) the promotion of Deacons to the Episcopate, (7) the Consecration of a Lamb according to the Jewish custom, (8) the shaving of their beards by the clergy. A sentence of excommunication was pronounced against the Pope, and its decrees were signed by the Cæsar, Basil the Macedonian, whom the Emperor had admitted as his colleague, the three Eastern Patriarchs, and nearly one thousand Bishops and Abbots.

So long as Photius enjoyed the favour of the Court he was safe. But in the same year in which the Council was held, a revolution occurred in the Palace at Constantinople, followed by a revolution in the Church. Basil, the Macedonian, is said to have been originally the Emperor's groom, who, through his practical ability, had risen to the post of Chamberlain, and, after the execution of Bardas, was invested with the Imperial title. His antecedents had been far from respectable, and he had been the friend and companion of the Emperor in his drunken bouts and revels. But after the death of Bardas, the profligacy and intemperance of Michael reached such a height that even Basil had endeavoured in some measure to restrain his debaucheries. Unwilling to submit to the restraint, Michael, when in a fit of intoxication, gave orders for the assassination of his colleague, and Basil, feeling that it was with him a matter of life or death, compassed his murder. With Michael ended the Isaurian dynasty; Basil became sole Emperor (867—886), and the founder of the Macedonian, the longest and most important, dynasty of the Eastern Empire.

Basil I. (the Macedonian) showed himself as arbitrary in the treatment of the Eastern Church, as Michael and Bardas had been in the deposition of Ignatius. Photius did not hesitate to condemn the execution of Bardas and the murder of Michael; he was in consequence deposed, and Ignatius reinstated in the Patriarchate. Pope Nicolas died in the same year and was succeeded by Hadrian II. (867—872), who in a Council at Rome, in the year of his election, confirmed the deposition of Photius, annulling the Orders conferred by him, and requested Basil to confirm the decision of the Roman Council by a Council at Constantinople.

The Emperor, who was now in accord with the Pope, summoned to Constantinople, A D. 869, the third of the Councils above alluded to. Two Roman Bishops attended as representatives of the Pope; the Patriarchs of Alexandria, Antioch, and Jerusalem sent their representatives; everything, as might be expected, was decided in favour of the Emperor and the Pope; the restoration of Ignatius was confirmed, Photius anathematized and degraded, and his Ordinations annulled; the sentence of condemnation being written in the Sacramental Wine. Thus the victory of Rome was for a time consummated, and this Council, although, owing to the absence of a large party of Bishops who adhered to Photius, it was attended only by one hundred and two Bishops, the Roman Church calls the Eighth General Council.

The Pope, relying on the compliancy of Basil, thought the time favourable for the recovery of the provinces alienated by Leo III., and for the confirmation of his supremacy over the Bulgarian Church. But Bulgaria had now returned to its first allegiance to the Patriarch of Constantinople, and Ignatius, no less than Photius before him, the Emperor, and the Greek Church generally, were alike opposed to the Papal claims.

Photius now being in his turn in exile, where for several years he languished without company and without books, Ignatius was, till his death on Oct. 23rd, A.D. 877, left in peaceful possession of the Patriarchate. Notwithstanding the posthumous maledictions pronounced against him by Pope John VIII. (872—882), Ignatius is Canonized by the Roman Church.

The majority of the Eastern Bishops were in favour of the restoration of Photius, and Basil, who had formerly entrusted to him the education of his sons, now finding that it was the only means of restoring unity to the Eastern Church, recalled him to the Patriarchate. Italy being at this time much threatened by the Saracens, Pope John VIII. had reason for obliging the Emperor, and he approved his restoration. He wrote to Photius condemning in the strongest language the addition of the Filioque to the Creed; "Non solum hoc non dicimus, sed etiam eos, quo principio hoc dicere *suâ insaniâ ausi sunt, quasi transgressores Divini verbi condemnamus, sicut theologiæ Christi Domini eversores, et Apostolorum et reliquorum sanctorum Patrum, qui synodicè convenientes sanctum symbolum nobis tradiderunt* [g]."

Photius, being under excommunication by the previous Council, another Council was necessary to exonerate him. The fourth of the Synods of Constantinople sat from November, 879, to March, 880. It was attended by three hundred and eighteen Bishops, by two legates sent by Pope John, by representatives of the other Patriarchs, and was presided over by Photius. Photius successfully defended his

[g] Labb. Concil.

position; the Council confirmed his restoration; the Papal legates ratified all that Basil and Photius demanded, and joined in anathematizing the previous Council The Roman claims on Bulgaria were remanded to the Emperor. The addition of the Filioque clause was, with the consent of the legates, condemned, and if any should dare to tamper with the Creed, deprivation in the case of clergy, excommunication in that of lay people, was to be the punishment. Pope John at the time acquiesced in the decision of the Council; "The Pope acknowledged the usurper, the monster of wickedness, the persecutor, the heretic, him who had desired to assert the co-equality, the supremacy, of Constantinople, as the legitimate Patriarch [h]."

Photius did not long enjoy the Patriarchal dignity. Basil was succeeded by his son, Leo VI. (886—912), who was dignified by the title of Philosopher. Photius was again ejected, not on Ecclesiastical grounds, but in order that the Emperor might appoint his own brother, Stephen, a youth eighteen years of age, who had been a pupil of Photius. John VIII. having met a violent death at the hands of assassins, Stephen V., after the short Pontificates of Marinus I. and Hadrian III., was elected Pope (885—891). To sanction his unrighteous proceeding, the Emperor Leo wrote to Stephen through Stylianus, Archbishop of Neo-Cæsarea, addressing him as "*sanctissimo et beatissimo Stephano,*" and giving him the title, which previously belonged to the Patriarchs of Constantinople, "*œcumenico Papæ.*" The result was that Stephen remained Patriarch of Contantinople. Pope Stephen V. was succeeded by the unhappy Formosus (891—896), who, notwithstanding that he had been, when Bishop of Porto, excommunicated by John VIII., was elected Pope. His election to the Papacy was in direct opposition to the Canon of the Great Nicene Council which forbade the translation of Bishops. Yet we find him, although Photius had been undoubtedly Conse-

[h] Milman's Latin Christianity, II. 357.

crated by a Bishop, who, even if no longer Archbishop of Syracuse, was a real Bishop, and although he had been distinctly recognized by John VIII., insisting that clergy ordained by Photius should only be admitted to Communion as laymen.

It is evident that in the eyes of the Pope the grievance was, not the translation of Photius, but his Consecration by the Archbishop of Syracuse. Formosus paid dearly for what, we fear, must be called this act of hypocrisy. Formosus is said to have been the first Pope who was translated from another See to the Papacy. His immediate successor, Boniface VI., was a man of such profligate character that Baronius does not acknowledge him as a Pope. The next Pope, Stephen VI. (896—897), a man of equally profligate character, declared Formosus to have been no Pope at all; rescinded in a Synod all his Ordinations, and exhumed him from the grave; and after having cut off the three fingers used in benediction, caused his mutilated body to be cast into the Tiber. John IX. (898—900), rescinded in a Synod all the decrees against Formosus; so that one Pope in Synod condemned Formosus and his Ordinations, and another Pope in Synod cleared his memory.

Photius, the most learned man of his time, died, A.D. 891, in exile in a convent. He was excommunicated, says Finlay, by *nine Popes of Rome;* what kind of men some of those Popes were, we have seen, and no man, even to the present day, has been the subject of more unfounded accusations from the Roman Church than Photius. It is pleasant to find that, in all the vicissitudes of their fortunes, neither Ignatius nor Photius lost their esteem for each other. By the death of Photius, the schism of more than 30 years' standing was apparently healed; between that great Patriarch and the accession of Michael Cerularius, A.D. 1043, the next Patriarch of whom there is much of importance to be related, seventeen Patriarchs of Constantinople and thirty-seven Popes of Rome intervened, between whom uninterrupted, if not sincere, Communion was kept up.

At the commencement of the next century a breach between Church and State, which led to a schism at Constantinople, occurred, owing to a fourth marriage contracted, A.D. 901, by Leo the Philosopher with his concubine Zoe. Although under him a law condemning third marriages, had been passed, he himself took a fourth wife. The Patriarch Nicolas Mysticus had in the Cathedral of St. Sophia baptized with the ceremonial of a legitimate Prince his illegitimate son by Zoe, the future Emperor, Constantine VII., on the promise of the Emperor that he would separate from her; notwithstanding which, he afterwards married her. The Patriarch Nicolas refusing, as contrary to the laws of the Greek Church, to celebrate the marriage, and degrading the Priest who performed the ceremony, Leo drove him into exile, and appointed in his place Euthemius, who approved the marriage on the ground of expediency. Thus the Church of Constantinople was split up into two factions. A Synod at Constantinople, in 906, sanctioned the marriage and confirmed the banishment of Nicolas; that the Emperor obtained a dispensation from the infamous Pope Sergius III. is without foundation.

Leo VI. was succeeded by his son Constantine VII., Porphyrogenitus (912—958), a boy seven years of age, at first under the guardianship of his father's brother, Alexander, who reigned as Emperor-regent (912—913). Alexander reinstated Nicolas, and Euthemius was banished. No sooner, however, was Nicolas reinstated than, following the servile spirit, too often observable in Eastern Patriarchs, of modelling their consciences on the wills of the Emperors, he recognized the action of Euthemius with regard to the fourth marriage of Leo, as done to avoid scandal to the Church.

After the death of Alexander the regency remained under the Emperor's mother, Zoe, a woman of frivolous character, whose consequent unpopularity led to the appointment of Romanus I. (Lecapenus), as joint Emperor (919—944), and he was crowned by the restored Patriarch, Nicolas. A Synod of Constantinople under Romanus condemned the

Synod of 906, and pronounced a fourth marriage to be unlawful.

Though the Bulgarians continued to follow the doctrine and ritual of the Greek Church, the Tsar Simon, the son and successor of Boris or Michael, determined to have a Patriarch of his own. Having, A.D. 923, conquered Romanus in battle, he stipulated, in the terms of treaty, for the acknowledgment of Bulgaria as a separate Patriarchate, and that the Patriarch should be placed on a level with the Patriarch of Constantinople; nor when, A.D. 970, the Emperor John Zimisces conquered Bulgaria, could he, or his successors, annihilate the ecclesiastical independence of Bulgaria.

On the death, A.D. 925, of the Patriarch Nicolas, Stephen, a eunuch, was translated from the Archbishopric of Amasia to succeed him; and he, after a Patriarchate of three years, was succeeded by Tryphon, who held the Patriarchate as *locum tenens* for Theophylact, a youth sixteen years of age, the son of the Emperor Romanus. The election of Theophylact received the confirmation of Pope John XI. (931—936), the son of the infamous Sergius III., whom Baronius styles an apostate rather than an Apostle. With Pope Sergius the so-called Roman Pornocracy commenced, and, in 933, Theophylact was Consecrated Patriarch of Constantinople by his equally infamous son, John XI. That a profligate Patriarch like Theophylact sought, and a Pope of Rome of the character of John XI. seized the opportunity of conferring on him, the Pall, is only mentioned to be dismissed with scorn.

In the same year as Theophylact, Eutychius, the historian, or rather annalist, of the Alexandrine Church, was Consecrated Patriarch of Alexandria. We have before[1] had occasion to quote his authority as to the mode of election to the Alexandrine Episcopate; his history was highly thought of in his day, and to him the Church is indebted for almost all of the little that is known of the

[1] p. 113.

Orthodox Church in Egypt[j]. He is often adduced by Presbyterians as a staple authority for their form of Church government; nor can his testimony be dismissed on the sole ground of its lateness, for similar testimony is afforded by St. Jerome (345—420). Objections to Episcopacy have, we think, been satisfactorily refuted, but such passages as those adduced from Jerome and Eutychius teach at least one lesson, viz., to be charitable in dealing with those who differ from us, and who believe their opinions to be as scriptural (for on the Bible the test of every doctrine must be grounded), as we do our own.

Theophylact, the Patriarch, lived, says Finlay, like a debauched young Prince; spent his time in hunting, sold ecclesiastical preferments to raise money for his pleasures, defiled St. Sophia with profane songs and indecent ceremonies, and converted its services into musical festivities. Whilst celebrating Mass in the Cathedral, a page brought him word that his favourite mare had foaled, the young Patriarch abruptly ended the service, and, throwing off his Ecclesiastical vestments, rushed from the Cathedral, and when he found that all was going on favourably, returned thither to join the procession. After a Patriarchate of twenty-five years he was killed, A D. 956, by the accident of his horse dashing him against a wall, and was succeeded by Polyeuktes.

The Emperor Constantine was succeeded by his son Romanus II. (959—963), whose wife Theophano, a beautiful woman of low birth, was the object of many serious accusations, and amongst other crimes was accused of poisoning her husband. Romanus dying unexpectedly at the early age of twenty-four, left two young sons by Theophano, both of whom became Emperors, Basil II. (963—1025), known as Bulgaroktonos, or *Slayer of the Bulgarians*, and Constantine VIII. (1025—1028); as well as two daughters, Theophano, who became the wife of the Western

---

[j] Neale's Alexandria, II 182.

Emperor, Otto II., and Anne, the wife of Vladimir, Grand Prince of Russia.

Basil, who at the time of his accession was seven years of age, had, for the first twelve years of his reign, for his colleague, first, Nicephorus Phocas (963—969), and then John Zimisces (969—976); after whose deaths he was sole Emperor till his death, A.D. 1025. During the period between his accession and his death, the Eastern Empire reached its greatest height of power since the division of the Empire, and gained back many of the provinces which had been lost to the Saracens.

Though the Mahometan power had been considerably weakened by the division of the Bagdad and Cordova Caliphates, yet in the Ninth Century the four greatest powers of the world continued to be the Eastern and Western Roman Empires, and the Caliphates of Bagdad and Cordova. During that century the Saracens continued their conquests, and, A D 823, during the reign of Michael the Stammerer, took from the Greeks the islands of Sicily and Crete. But they became further weakened by continued divisions, and the rise of new Mahometan powers and Emirates, owning little more than a nominal allegiance to their Caliph, so that they could no longer meet the Emperors on equal terms; and the Eastern Empire availed itself of the weakened state of the Caliphate of Bagdad, to recover many of its lost provinces. This was affected by the three Emperors, Nicephorus Phocas, John Zimisces, and Basil II.

Nicephorus Phocas, through his second marriage with Theophano, the widow of the Emperor Romanus, became the guardian of his two sons, Basil and Constantine. Nicephorus, says Gibbon [k], had "the double merit of a hero and a saint;" but he adds that his religion, his hair cloth next to his skin, his fasts and his almsgiving, were a cloak to his ambition by which he imposed upon the holy Patriarch. The opinion of the historian does not appear to

[k] IX 68.

be borne out by facts. Polyeuktes, after he had performed the ceremony of his marriage with Theophano, had occasion to prohibit Nicephorus from entering the Cathedral of St. Sophia. The reason for the prohibition is differently given According to one account Nicephorus refused to submit to the penance which the Greek Church imposes on second marriages; according to another, and more probable account, it was on the ground of a rumour that he was Godfather to one of the children of his wife; and when the rumour was dissipated by the denial of the Priest who had administered the Baptism, the prohibition was removed.

Nicephorus had already, in the reign of Romanus II., distinguished himself as a General by recovering from the Saracens, A D. 961, Crete, and taking its Emir captive to Constantinople; and in the following year, Hierapolis and Aleppo, the latter of which cities was the capital of another Emir. After he himself became Emperor he continued his conquests, by taking, in 965, Cyprus, in 968 he invaded Syria and recovered Antioch (which had been in the hands of the Saracens for three hundred and thirty years), Hierapolis, Apamea, and Emesa; and threatened Bagdad.

Returning in the following year to Constantinople, the good old Emperor was murdered by his wife Theophano, and one of her numerous lovers, John Zimisces, who had distinguished himself in the Syrian war; the last words of the dying Emperor being, " Grant me mercy, O God !"

John Zimisces, who was then proclaimed joint-Emperor, disappointed the infamous Theophano by refusing to marry her, consigning her instead to a monastery. The intrepid Patriarch at first refused to crown him; but the public indignation being appeased by the exile of Theophano, and Zimisces having exonerated himself by throwing the blame on his accomplice, he at length consented; the guilt of Zimisces was forgotten in his virtues; the profusion of his charities, and the gentleness of his character charmed all who approached him.

The Patriarch Polyeuktes, dying three months after the coronation of Zimisces, was succeeded in the Patriarchate by a monk of Mount Olympus, named Basilius; he being banished to a monastery by Zimisces was succeeded by Antonius, Abbot of Studium.

The greater part of the reign of Zimisces was passed in war; of his great victory over the Russians we shall have occasion to speak in another chapter; he was equally successful against the Saracens, and he advanced the boundaries of the Eastern Empire to Amida and Edessa. "By his double triumph over the Russians and the Saracens, he derived the title of Saviour of the Empire and Conqueror of the East[1]."

On his death, not without suspicion of poison, Basil II, now twenty years of age, entered on his full inheritance, and completed the work of Nicephorus Phocas and John Zimisces; and his reign was the culminating point of Byzantine greatness. His life was a strange mixture of war and religion. The conflict between him and Samuel, Tsar of Bulgaria, having lasted thirty-five years, only ended in the complete defeat and death of the latter in 1014. Four years later the last fortress of the Kingdom surrendered to Basil. To atone for the sins of his youth, he, when thirty years of age, took a vow of chastity, and always afterwards, under his Imperial robes in the palace, and under his armour on the field of battle, wore the sackcloth garb of a monk Yet he was guilty of great cruelty, and his victory over the Bulgarians and his inhuman treatment of his prisoners gained for him his title of Bulgaroktonos.

Basil next turned his arms against the Saracens. The Caliphate of Bagdad had become further weakened by the establishment of the Dynasty of the Fatimites at Cairo, he extended the conquests made by his predecessors, and, says Professor Freeman, besides being the slayer of the Bulgarians, he was "a considerable slayer of the Saracens also[m]." But his annexation to the Eastern Empire of the

[1] Gibbon, IX. 67.   [m] History and Conquests of the Saracens, p. 125.

Christian Kingdom of Armenia was a doubtful expedient, for it destroyed a useful bulwark against future inroads of the Mussulmans. Basil died just when he was on the point of sending an expedition to recover Sicily, which had been in the hands of the Saracens since the reign of Michael the Stammerer.

The ascetic Basil, disfigured though his reign was by cruelty, interested himself in Church matters, and in the last year of his reign a remarkable effort was made to effect a closer union between the Eastern and the Western Churches. His sister, the talented Theophano, was, as we have seen, married to Otto II., the Western Emperor. The Western Empire had been transferred to the German nation in the person of Otto I., crowned, A D. 962, Emperor, at Rome, by Pope John XII. (whom he in the next year deposed), the Emperor binding himself on his part to protect the Holy See, and the citizens swearing that they would elect no Pope without the Imperial consent. The Kingdom of Italy was thus united with the Kingdom of Germany; whoever was elected King of Germany had the right (and he alone) to be crowned, at Milan, King of Italy, and, at Rome, Emperor, the Emperors generally not residing in Rome or Italy but in Germany.

Otto I. was the second restorer of the Western Empire, and when, through the profligate Popes of the Tenth Century, the Papacy was brought to the very verge of ruin, he revived and virtually saved it. He was succeeded by his son, Otto II. (973—983), the husband of Theophano, who exercised a strong influence over the Western Empire[n]; when her husband died, leaving a young son only five years of age, Otto III. (983—1002), she governed the Empire during his minority, and it was through her that when, A.D. 997, Pope Gregory V. was driven out from Rome, a Greek subject of the Eastern Empire, John XVI. (997—998), was appointed Anti-Pope.

The Eastern and Western Empires were thus brought

[n] She introduced, Finlay says, the Byzantine style of painting in Germany.

into a close connection, and Basil not unnaturally desired a closer union than that which existed between the two Churches. The Tuscan family, under which the Papacy had so long groaned before the time of the Ottos, had again acquired an ascendency in Rome, and an unprincipled member of that family, John XIX. (1024—1033), occupied the Papal throne. In the last year of his reign, a singular attempt was made by Basil and Eustathius, Patriarch of Constantinople, to gain, by a large bribe, the Pope's consent that the Patriarch of Constantinople should be acknowledged Œcumenical Patriarch of the East, as the Pope of Rome was of the West. The avaricious Pope caught at the bait; but, the affair being prematurely revealed, all Italy naturally resented the treachery of the Pope. The Pope was brought to his senses by a zealous Abbot, William of Dijon, who boldly charged him with the abandonment of the rights of St. Peter, and he was obliged to resign the project. But the attempt only increased the ill-feeling between East and West, and, though the final schism was postponed for thirty years, was the beginning of the end.

Under the unworthy successors of Basil the decline of the Eastern Empire commenced. He was followed by his brother, Constantine VIII. (1025—1028), a mere man of pleasure, who left three daughters, Eudocia, who retired into a convent, Zoe, and Theodora. Romanus III. (Argyrus) married, when she was forty-eight years of age, Zoe, the second daughter, and succeeded as Emperor (1028—1034). Constantine had wished Romanus to marry his youngest daughter, Theodora, but she had scruples about going through the form of marriage with a man who had already a wife living; Zoe, less scrupulous, threatened him with blindness and death in case he should refuse her hand. Thenceforward Theodora was an object of jealousy to the Empress Zoe, and also of suspicion to Romanus, who accused her of conspiring against the throne; and she was in consequence consigned to a monastery. Romanus, now entirely under the hands of Zoe, lived long enough to see several towns in Syria recaptured by the Saracens, and died from the effects of slow poison, supposed to have been administered by Zoe. Zoe had fallen in love with Michael, a handsome Paphlagonian money-lender, who had taken service in the Imperial household; and on the same night that she became a widow, she became his wife. Michael was proclaimed Emperor as Michael IV., the Paphlagonian (1034—1042), the Patriarch Alexius (1025—1043) being forced to perform both the marriage and coronation services. Various conspiracies were at once formed against the low-born Emperor by the chief men in Constantinople, amongst whom was one Michael Cerularius, who, in order to escape the punishment inflicted on his fellow-conspirators, assumed the garb of a monk.

Michael, seized with remorse and despair on account of his previous criminal intercourse, and subsequent marriage, with the scandalous Zoe, spent the remainder of his life in acts of penance, and, being from the first a hopeless invalid, died in his thirty-sixth year. His nephew, Michael V., through the influence of Zoe, was appointed to succeed him (1042). He soon threw off all disguise; expelled the Patriarch Alexius, who had offended him, and compelled Zoe to retire into a monastery. This ungrateful conduct to his benefactress so disgusted the people of Constantinople that, after a meeting held in St. Sophia's, Zoe was brought back, and proclaimed by the Senate and people joint Empress with Theodora; and Michael, having had his eyes put out, was consigned to a monastery.

Zoe and Theodora disagreeing, the union only lasted two months. Thereupon Zoe, now sixty-two years of age, took to herself a third husband, "an old debauchee who had been her lover thirty years before[o]," whom her former husband, Michael, had banished to Mitylene. Constantine IX., Monomachus, thus became Emperor (1042—1054), and the Patriarch Alexius, now restored to his See, refusing to celebrate the marriage as a violation of the Canons of the Church, the ceremony was performed by an ordinary

[o] Oman's Story of the Nations.

Priest. Constantine, as a salve to his conscience, built Churches and completed the Church of the Holy Sepulchre at Jerusalem. But his worthless character, says Finlay, his public parade of his vices, and the profligacy of Zoe, typify the moral degradation to which the Eastern Empire had at this time fallen.

Such was the state of the Eastern Empire when, on the death of Alexius, A.D. 1043, the aforesaid hot-headed Michael Cerularius was appointed to the Patriarchate of Constantinople (1043—1059), in which he showed himself as restless an agitator in ecclesiastical, as he had before been in political, matters.

One hundred and fifty-two years had elapsed since the death of Photius, and for that period, although little intercourse had been kept up between the two Churches, there was comparative peace. Since the time of Photius the Roman Church had been brought to the verge of ruin. We have seen how Formosus, one of the Popes who persecuted Photius, had himself been uncanonically appointed to the Papacy, and the savage cruelty to which he had been subjected by his successor. A schism in the Roman Church had arisen between the supporters and the opponents of Formosus, and whilst one Pope revoked the Orders conferred by him, another, John IX. (898—900), in a Synod at Rome, rescinded the decrees of his predecessor, and reinstated those who had been Ordained by him. This does not look like Papal Infallibility. But we need not wade through the disgraceful history of the Popes of the Tenth Century [p], the most revolting profanation of religion in the whole history of Christendom, so that it was commonly said amongst Christians that the end of the world was at hand. A better state of things was introduced by the German Emperors, and several German Popes in succession redeemed the Papacy from its corruption. But again the Papacy fell back, till at one and the same time

---

[p] It may be dismissed in the words of Baronius, "homines monstruosi, vitâ turpissimi, moribus perditissimi, usquequaque fœdissimi."

three deeply simoniacal Popes ("three devils," Canon Robertson, quoting from a writer of that century, says they were called), occupied the Papal chair.

A German, the Emperor Henry III., again came to the rescue, and in the Synod of Sutri, A.D. 1046, deposed all three Popes, and himself appointed Suidgar, Bishop of Bamberg, who took the title of Clement II. (1046—1047). With Clement began a series of able Popes; after him followed Poppo, Bishop of Brixen, who took the title of Damasus II.; and when he died shortly afterwards, the Emperor chose his own cousin Bruno, Bishop of Toul, a man of saintly character and with a high reputation for learning, who, after he had been duly elected by the clergy and people of Rome, ascended the Papal throne as Leo IX. (1049—1054).

In January, 1054, St. Leo (for he has been canonized by the Church) wrote to Cerularius, "Archbishop of Constantinople," as "his honoured brother." Since the time of Photius, the Greek Church, although outwardly in communion with it, had grown more distrustful than ever of the orthodoxy of the Latin Church, especially was this the case with regard to the addition of the Filioque Clause to the Creed. But the two Churches agreed to differ; there were Greek Churches and monasteries in Rome, and Latin Churches and monasteries in Constantinople, at this very time, in a correspondence between Leo and Peter, Patriarch of Antioch, whilst the latter condemned the addition of the Filioque to the Creed, and Leo declared that he was ready to die in defence of it, the Pope spoke of the faith of the Patriarch of Antioch as sound and Catholic (*sanam et Catholicam*) [q].

An important point of divergence was the matter of Bulgaria, which still rankled in the breasts of the Popes. That this was not absent from the mind of Leo is evident from a letter which he wrote to the Emperor Constantine, in which he urges the same claim which, in the time of

---

[q] See Ffoulkes' Christendom's Divisions, II p. 55, *note*.

Photius, his predecessor Nicolas had made on the Emperor Michael. Another point of divergence was the claim to supremacy which, increased by the Pseudo-Isidore Decretals, the Popes, even in the depths of corruption of the Tenth Century, continued to put forward. This claim the Patriarchs of Constantinople had ever studiously denied The superiority of Greek culture and learning always predisposed the Greek Church to look down upon the Latins; and now a feeling of disgust at the great abyss into which the Papal See had lately fallen (although, as Mosheim says[r], few examples of piety were conspicuous at the time in the Greek Church), may to a certain extent explain, although it does not justify, the over-bearing conduct of Cerularius, which brought about the final rupture between East and West

Cerularius, in agreement with Leo of Achrida, which had lately been made the Metropolitan See of Bulgaria, addressed, styling himself "*universalis Patriarcha Novæ Romæ,*" a letter full of invective against the Latin Church, to John, Bishop of Trani in Apulia, which country had been from the time of Leo the Isaurian subject to the Greek Church, the jurisdiction over which was viewed with jealousy by the Popes of Rome; and this letter he desired to be communicated to Pope Leo and the Frankish clergy and laity. The points complained of were the Roman Fasts on Saturdays in Lent; the use of unleavened bread, or Azyms, in the Holy Eucharist; the eating of things strangled and of blood, in violation of the decree of the Council of Jerusalem (Acts xv); and not singing the Hallelujah during Lent[s]. Whilst he claimed that the Greek Church followed the teaching of SS. Peter, Paul, the Apostles, and Christ, and the Catholic Church, the Latin usages he stigmatized as relics of Judaism[t]; those

---

[r] II. 471

[s] "Item Alleluia in Quadragesima non psallitis, sed semel in Paschâ tantummodo"

[t] "Azyma et Sabbata ipsi custodire a Moyse jussi sunt, nostrum vero Pascha est Christus"

who used them were neither wholly Christians nor Jews, but a mixture of the two; "they were like the leopard whose hairs are neither black nor white." The word which the Latins call *panis* the Greeks call ἄρτος, the meaning of the latter word being something *raised;* unleavened bread, thereore, the Greeks considered no bread at all, and the Latin Eucharist to be no Eucharist.

Cerularius also closed the Latin Churches and monasteries in Constantinople.

A copy of the letter fell into the hands of Cardinal Humbert, at the time resident at Trani, who translated it into Latin and sent it to the Pope. The letter caused much indignation and astonishment at Rome, for the Greeks had been long acquainted with the Latin usages, and it appeared that Cerularius by bringing them forward on that occasion was seeking a quarrel. The Pope sent to Constantinople three legates, Humbert himself, a man as self-willed and obstinate as Cerularius, the Archbishop of Amalfi, and Frederic of Lorraine, Cardinal Archdeacon of Rome, who afterwards became Pope as Stephen IX. (1057—1058).

The Pope's case was at first presented in more conciliatory language than that used by Cerularius; but it soon became evident that it was a contest for supremacy on both sides, and the Pope, to establish his own supremacy, did not hesitate to ground it on the Forged Decretals. He wrote that both inside and outside Rome there were many Greek monasteries and Churches, none of which had been interfered with, nor prohibited from following the customs of their forefathers; so far from this being the case, the Greeks had been advised to observe them; for uses differing according to time and place were no hindrance to salvation; it was faith working by love which recommends believers to God. He complained of the assumption of the title of Œcumenical by the Patriarchs of Constantinople; of their endeavouring to subject to themselves the Patriarchs of Alexandria and Antioch; of the Greeks re-baptizing converts from the Latin Church; of their permitting their clergy to marry; and of their not allowing the Procession of the Holy Ghost from the Son. Ever since their first utterance, the Pseudo-Isidore Decretals had been used to give supremacy to the Popes of Rome over the Patriarch of Constantinople; and as his predecessor, Nicholas I., had appealed to them in the case of Photius, so now Leo adduced them as genuine, and a crushing rejoinder to the claim of the Patriarch of Constantinople over Trani [u].

It cannot be imagined that a man of Leo's saintly character would have applied to them as genuine, if he had believed them, what every one in the present day knows them to be, a forgery and an imposition; but it is evident that the Popes had for two hundred and fifty years, however innocently, been, in order to establish their supremacy, trading on a forgery.

Cardinal Humbert brought one remarkable accusation against the Greek Church which it is difficult to account for, except that it arose from an ignorance of Church history. He accused the Greeks with the expungement of the Filioque Clause from the Creed. That Clause was absent from the Creed of Nice and Constantinople, and was first inserted by the Spanish Church in the Synod of Toledo, A.D. 589. From Spain its conveyance into France was easy, and, about sixty years before the time of Charlemagne, Æneas, Bishop of Paris, wrote, "Every Church in France uses it in that form." In the present instance both Pope Leo and Cardinal Humbert were Frenchmen, and perhaps an ignorance of history explains, although it does not excuse, the mistake.

The conduct of the profligate Emperor, Constantine, was throughout the controversy marked with double dealing. It was with him a matter of policy to stand on good terms with the Pope, whom he wished to have on his side against the Normans, who were beginning to make conquests in the Eastern Empire; and he accordingly lodged the Papal

[u] Ffoulkes, II. 47, and *note*.

legates in the Imperial Palace, where Cerularius declined to visit them. Humbert then sought out the Patriarch, in whose presence he assumed an arrogant tone, and managed to put himself as much in the wrong as Cerularius had been before; so that Cerularius in a letter to Peter, Patriarch of Antioch, complained that Humbert, refusing even to discuss the points of difference, insisted on an unconditional surrender. The Papal legates excommunicated all those who refused to obey the Apostolical See to which "the special care of all the Churches belongs." Cerularius, supported by the people, refused to give way; and finally, on July 16th, A D. 1054, and therefore after Pope Leo was dead, the Legates left a writ of excommunication on the Altar of St. Sophia [v], and departed, shaking off the dust from their feet.

The Emperor allowed the legates to excommunicate the Patriarch, and lavished presents on them at their departure. Cerularius, in a Council at Constantinople, retorted with an excommunication on the Church of Rome No sooner had the legates departed and were out of sight and hearing, than the Emperor ordered the writ of anathema to be burnt, and approved of Cerularius convening the Synod which excommunicated the excommunicators.

The Patriarchs of Alexandria and Antioch made common cause with the Patriarch of Constantinople. That there were faults on both sides; that the Eastern Church was wrong in making such a comparatively unimportant matter, as the difference between leavened and unleavened bread, a crucial test; and that the Western Church had no right to make, in the teeth of an Œcumenical Council, an unauthorized addition to the Creed; may be admitted. But the Eastern and Western Churches had weathered more formidable storms before; but for the arbitrary act of Humbert, to have employed whom as his legate was, if we omit the use he made of the Forged Decretals, the Pope's principal fault, the difficulty might have been surmounted.

[v] "Sint Anathema Maranatha .... cum omnibus hæreticis, immo cum diabolo et angelis ejus, nisi resipuerint, Amen, Amen, Amen."

of the Greek and Roman Churches. 399

The schism was the culminating result of the long contest for supremacy between the Patriarchs of Constantinople and the Popes of Rome. The former, although they were less arrogant than Cerularius, were at that time fully as resolute in their claims for supremacy as the Popes are in the present day. To such a height of presumption did Cerularius attain, that, as he did not possess the immunity which distance afforded to the Western Patriarch, he exposed himself to the civic jurisdiction. "I made him Emperor and I can unmake him," said Cerularius, when the Emperor Isaac I. (1057—1059), the first of the dynasty of the Comneni, tried to curb his haughty aspirations. The Emperor determined to depose him, but to depose openly, in Constantinople itself, the head of the Greek Church was a dangerous venture. When Cerularius was outside the walls of the city, he was seized by the soldiers, and carried off to Proconnesus, where his death saved the Emperor further trouble, and Constantine Leichudes, as yet a layman, was appointed his successor.

The final act was the act of Rome; the English Church was unconnected with it, nor has there ever been a formal schism between the Greek and Anglican Churches. When, A.D. 1066, only twelve years, therefore, after the writ of excommunication was left by Humbert on the Altar of St. Sophia, the Norman William ascended the throne of England, he refused the demand of Pope Gregory VII. for supremacy, on the ground that England knew no such right belonging to the Pope, "I do not find that my predecessors have professed it to yours." The Roman Church cut itself off alone, not only from the See of Constantinople, but from Sees older than itself, those of Antioch and Alexandria; from the Greek Church, which produced the greatest Saints whom the Church reveres;—Ignatius, Polycarp, Justin Martyr, Clemens Alexandrinus, Gregory Thaumaturgus, Athanasius, Cyprian, Chrysostom, Basil the Great, the two Gregories, Nazianzen and of Nyssa, and numberless other Saints and Martyrs.

A few words may be said as to the bread used in the Holy Eucharist. It may be taken for granted that the Last Supper which our Saviour eat with His disciples was the Mosaic Passover, for He Himself told them, "with desire have I desired to eat this Passover with you;" and since on that day leaven was forbidden, that He used unleavened bread. The weight of evidence leads to the conviction that, in very early times, Latins as well as Greeks used leavened bread, probably against the Ebionite doctrine, that works of the Mosaic Law were binding upon all Christians. About the Ninth Century the Latin Church adopted the use of unleavened bread, which, in the next two centuries, it was led to believe had been the Apostolical use; whilst the Greek Church, in its universally conservative spirit, never varied from its original practise.

Since the division between East and West (writes Dr. Neale), Ecclesiastical history is almost entirely confined to writers of the Roman Communion, and as they interested themselves but little about what they considered a schismatical body, little is heard about the Eastern Church. An exception must, however, be made with regard to the Church of Russia, whose conversion was completed by the Greek Church shortly before the schism commenced, its Church, although Russia had to go through the fiery trial of affliction and well-nigh political extinction, rose by degrees to the place which it now holds as, although nominally under the Primacy of Constantinople, practically the head of the Orthodox Greek Church.

After the death of Ruric, which occurred A.D. 879, Oleg was, during the minority of Ruric's infant son, Igor, appointed regent of Russia; but he continued to govern the kingdom (879—913) till his own death. In 882 he subdued Smolensk, and having slain in battle Askold and Dir, added Kiev to his dominions. Continuing the national antipathy to Constantinople, he, A D. 904, in the reign of Leo the Philosopher, appeared, with an army of 80,000 men, before its walls; and after he had devastated the country and committed fearful acts of licentiousness and atrocity, Constantinople being only saved by a humiliating treaty, he returned, laden with rich spoils and trophies, in triumph to Kiev. On his death, Igor, Ruric's son, at the time forty years of age, who had married Olga, a Scandinavian lady of great beauty, succeeded to his inheritance, and reigned from 913—945. In 941 he, too, marched against Constantinople; but, after he had ravaged the neighbouring towns with a wanton ferocity, exceeding even that of Oleg, torturing, impaling, and otherwise maltreating the miserable inhabitants, the unoffending Priests being the special objects of his cruelty, his immense army was annihilated by the newly-invented Greek fire, and scarcely a third part, with Igor himself, eluding the vigilance of the Greeks, effected their escape home. In 945 he was slain, as some say, in battle, and others, on account of his cruelty, by his own subjects; whereupon Olga, who was surnamed in her life-time the Wise, and after her death venerated as a Saint, administered the kingdom till A.D. 955, during the minority of her son Sviatoslav (945—972).

The seeds of Christianity had, as we have seen, been already sown in Russia, and about A.D 910, a Christian church existed at Kiev; but it would seem that Christianity was little more than kept from dying out, and had little influence on the people.

In 955, the year in which she resigned the regency, Olga went on a voyage to Constantinople, with the sole object of obtaining a knowledge of the true God, of whom she had probably heard through the little Christian community at Kiev. At Constantinople, after having been instructed in the faith of the Greek Church, and living in fasting, prayer, and almsgiving, she, together with her retinue, was baptized by the Patriarch Polyeuktes, the Patriarch dismissing her with his blessing; "Blessed art thou amongst Russian women; from generation to generation the Russian people shall call thee blessed." The Eastern Emperor, Constantine Porphyrogenitus, in order to show his respect for the new Northern power, and his joy for the conversion of the royal convert to the Greek Church, stood Godfather at her Baptism ; and Olga, in remembrance of the first Christian Emperor, Constantine, changed her name for that of his mother Helena From Constantinople she took with her a Greek Priest, named Gregory, and exerted her influence to spread Christianity in Russia.

Her son, Sviatoslav, a staunch adherent of the Pagan worship, during his long absences in his wars, confided to Olga the regency of the kingdom, and although he himself refused to abandon his god Perun, allowed her to instil her own impressions into the minds of his people. It was owing to her influence that he abstained from persecuting Christianity, and that her grandson Vladimir was brought up in the doctrines of the Orthodox Church. Olga died A.D. 967, at the age of 85, and is canonized as a Saint in the Russian Church. She was enthusiastic in spreading Christianity, and the monk-historian, Nestor of Kiev (1056—1114), who stands in somewhat the same relation to the Russian as the Venerable Bede does to the English Church, calls her "the morning star which precedes the sun, the twilight, the dawn which heralds the full day." But it must be confessed that her practice little tallied with her sacred profession ; she was vindictive, treacherous, and cruel. Her faults may be attributed to the savage temper of the time, but a Saint, in a non-ecclesiastical sense, she, like many others who are dignified with that title, was far from being.

Sviatoslav, A.D. 972, in a battle for the possession of Bulgaria with the Eastern Emperor, John Zimisces, suffered a disastrous defeat ; and in the same year, in his retreat from Bulgaria to Russia, was killed by the Pechenegs, a tribe dwelling to the east of the Dnieper ; his skull being turned by the Prince of the country into a drinking-cup, bearing the inscription, that whilst attempting to seize the property of others, he lost his own. To the same use the skull of the Eastern Emperor, Nicephorus I., was turned by the

Bulgarian Tsar, and in it the Slavic Princes of the Court pledged him when he celebrated his triumph.

Sviatoslav was succeeded by his eldest son Yaropolk, who ruled at Kiev; but he, having killed in battle his brother Oleg, was himself, A.D. 980, treacherously assassinated by his half-brother Vladimir, Prince of Novgorod, who then succeeded as Veliki-Kniaz, or Grand Prince. Vladimir added Red Russia to his dominions.

In his adventurous and stormy career, and amidst the deep sins of his early life, Vladimir had forgotten all the instructions which Olga had instilled into him, and even offered up Christian Martyrs to his pagan gods. After his return to Kiev, elated by a victory which he had gained over a neighbouring tribe, he determined to offer as a thank-offering a human sacrifice, and in this manner died two Varangians, who had embraced Christianity, Feodor and his son Ivan, who have ever since been honoured as Saints and Martyrs of the Russian Church.

But all the while the instructions of Olga were doing their silent work, and it became gradually evident that Vladimir was at heart no pagan. His mind was on the move; in vain Mahometans and Jews tried to bring him over to their faith; next came a Latin mission from Germany; but Olga had enlisted his affections for the Greek and not the Roman Church. A philosopher from Greece, a monk named Constantine, by the simple eloquence of enthusiasm, impressed on him the falseness of Paganism, the redemption of the world by the Saviour, and a future retribution of good and evil. He loaded the philosopher with presents and dismissed him. But although he was seriously moved, a struggle still went on within him; so he resolved to despatch messengers from Kiev to examine the various religious systems of the world. They visited Mussulman and Roman Churches; but when they arrived at Constantinople, and the Patriarch himself celebrated the Eucharist in the Church of St. Sophia, with all the magnificence of the Greek ritual, so forcibly were they struck with the splendour of the ceremonial, and so persuaded of the truth of the Orthodox faith, that they were already Christians in heart. "When we stood in the Temple," they said, "we did not know whether we were not in Heaven, for there is nothing like it on earth. There in truth God has His dealing with men, and we can never forget the beauty we saw there, nor can we any longer abide in heathenism."

The Boyars then, who formed (after the Princes) the first nobility in Russia, impressed on Vladimir the religion of the Greek Church as the best, on the ground that otherwise his grandmother Olga, "who was the wisest of women," would not have embraced it. Vladimir's doubts as to the truth of Christianity were now entirely removed, but for a time he still hesitated to receive Baptism. Having embarked with his warriors on an expedition against Cherson, a city in the Crimea, subject to the Greek Emperor, he vowed that if he were successful in battle, he would be baptized. Having gained possession of the city, he, elated with his victory, determined to cement his conquest by a matrimonial alliance with the Byzantine Court; and sent to demand in marriage the hand of the Princess Anna, the Christian sister of the Emperor, Basil II., accompanying the demand with a threat that a refusal would be followed by an attack on Constantinople. To the condition required by the Greek Emperor that he should receive Baptism, he replied that he had long examined and conceived a love for the Greek Law. The Princess, for the good of the Church, consented to the marriage with the barbarian, and, attended by a body of Greek clergy, arrived at Cherson; and there, A.D. 988, in the Church of the Panagia, the Most Holy Mother of God, the Baptism of Vladimir (who took the name of Basil), and his marriage, were on one and the same day celebrated by the Bishop of Cherson.

In Cherson he built a Church, which he dedicated to St. Basil, and on his return to Kiev, accompanied by Bishops and Priests, amongst whom was a Syrian Priest named Michael, he caused his twelve sons to be baptized. Paganism was abolished; Perun, the god of Thunder, the principal of the Russian idols, was thrown into the Dnieper; the Court, and the Boyars, and the great multitude of the people flocked to the river, and in it received, as a nation, Baptism from the Greek Bishops and Priests. "On that day," says the Chronicler Nestor, "the Heavens and the earth rejoiced."

The sweeping assertion made by Le Roy Beaulieu, and Rambaud, that the people of Russia, without being previously prepared to receive the new faith, accepted Christianity by order of Vladimir, is not borne out by facts Even before the time of Ruric, in the commercial intercourse of the Russian Slavs with Constantinople, they must have heard of Christianity; about the time of Ruric, a Christian Church was built at Kiev; and, in addition, there was the influence of Olga, and Vladimir's Christian wife, Anna. A better explanation is given by M. Boissard[x], that the Evangelists of Russia acted as servants of the Cross, claiming supremacy for none but Christ, and preaching to the people the Word of God in their own language.

From Kiev, Christianity spread into the provinces. After his conversion, Vladimir's character was completely changed. Like Oswald with the holy Aidan (a sight which the Venerable Bede describes as "beautiful"), he accompanied the Bishops in their missionary work throughout the country, schools were established and organized, with Greek teachers from Constantinople set over them, Greek and Latin taught, and the principles of the Orthodox Church inculcated. Vladimir built several Churches, for which he employed Greek architects; he built of stone the cathedral Church of Kiev, endowing it with the tenth part of all his revenues, and dedicating it, doubtless after the Church of his conversion at Cherson, to the Most Holy Virgin; and appointed Michael the Syrian Bishop of Kiev. Michael founded Churches in Rostov and Novgorod, but died before the completion of the Cathedral of Kiev. He was succeeded by Leontius, a Greek by birth, sent over by the Patriarch

[x] L'Eglise de Russie.

of Constantinople; by Leontius the Cathedral was consecrated, and the Sees of Novgorod, Rostov, Chernigov, and Belgorod established. The third Bishop was Ivan (or John)

Thus the Russian Church was firmly established, and with Christianity civilization dawned on Russia, and Russia, which had been before sunk in gross ignorance and material paganism, was brought into intercourse with the other Kingdoms of Christendom. Vladimir, "equal to the Apostles," as the people called him, and Canonized as a Saint in the Russian Church, died A.D. 1015, and was buried by Ivan in the Cathedral of Kiev. There also his wife Anna, who predeceased him, was buried, and thither the bones of St. Olga were translated.

Thus the Russian was entirely the child of the Greek Church. The liturgical language employed by the Greek missionaries was the language of Cyril and Methodius, and the "old Slavic" language is still used in the Russian Church in the present day. Ever since its first foundation, although the Roman Church has made several abortive attempts to separate it from its first love, it has firmly adhered to the doctrine and discipline of the Orthodox Church, of which it is in the present day, under the ultimate supremacy of the Patriarch of Constantinople, the leading representative.

After the death of Vladimir, Kiev, the capital of his dominions, was seized by his nephew Sviatoslav (1016—1019), who signalized his short reign by the murder of the two sons of Vladimir, Boris and Gleb, whom the Russian Church reckons amongst its Saints. He was, A.D. 1019, driven out by another son of Vladimir, Yaroslav I., who had succeeded his father in Novgorod, and now, till A.D. 1054, held the whole Kingdom under his sole government at Kiev Yaroslav was not only a theologian but also a legislator. He continued the work begun by his father, building churches, monasteries and schools, and in the schools of Vladimir and Yaroslav, the Bible, translated by Cyril and Methodius, formed, as we learn from the Chronicler

Nestor, an important feature in the teaching. The Pechersky monastery at Kiev, founded by Yaroslav, was the birthplace of Russian literature and a training-school for the clergy. The piety of Vladimir and Yaroslav penetrated the national life, and to them is attributable much of the piety and learning which, till all learning and knowledge was swept away by the terrible Mogul invasions, combined to characterize Russia. Well stored with works of the Greek Church, Yaroslav caused many of them to be translated into the Russian language and circulated through his dominions; through him the Nomo-Canon was translated from the Greek; and to him Russia was indebted for its first written code of laws, the Russkaya Pravda.

In order to clearly understand the ecclesiastical no less than the civil history of Russia, it is necessary to draw attention to, what primarily belongs to the political history of the country, the fatal system, initiated by Ruric but more completely carried out by Vladimir, of parcelling their hereditary fiefs amongst their numerous illegitimate offspring. Thus were created independent Appanages, having absolute sovereignty within their own dominions, with only a nominal subjection to the Grand Prince, from whose control we shall find them revolting, and even assuming that title to themselves. Russia, convulsed and thrown into disorder through their conflicts, was subjected to the attacks of foreign enemies, whom they did not scruple to join as allies against those of the same flesh and blood as themselves. These feuds led to the dismemberment of Russia, and the fearful calamities inflicted on it by the Moguls.

CHAPTER XII.

The Schism widened by the Crusades.

RISE of the Seljuk Turks—Battle of Manzikert—Capture of Jerusalem—Pilgrims maltreated by the Seljuks—Alexius I, Emperor—Peter the Hermit and Simeon, Patriarch of Constantinople—Pope Urban II —Councils of Piacenza and Clermont—Council of Bari—The first Crusade under Godfrey de Bouillon—Jerusalem taken—Latin Kingdom and Patriarchate set up—The Knights Hospitallers and Templars—Godfrey de Bouillon succeeded by Baldwin I., Baldwin II , Fulk of Anjou, Baldwin III.—Signal failure of Second Crusade—Kings of Jerusalem, Almeric, Baldwin IV., Guy de Lusignan—Battle of Tiberias—Jerusalem taken by Saladin—Third Crusade —Cyprus taken by Richard Cœur de Lion—Acre taken by Crusaders—Jerusalem not recovered—The Fourth Crusade—The Crusaders capture Constantinople—Their cruelty and profanity—Latin Kingdom of Constantinople—Baldwin first King—A Venetian Patriarch intruded—Innocent III. sanctions the Kingdom and Patriarch—Fourth Lateran Council—Fifth Crusade—Jerusalem recovered by Frederic II of Germany—Crowned King of Jerusalem—Sixth, an English Crusade—Jerusalem again taken by the Mahometans--St Louis, King of France—Seventh Crusade under him—Antioch taken by the Mahometans—Eighth Crusade under St. Louis—His death—Fall of Acre—End of Crusades—Baldwin II , Latin King—The Greek Empires of Nice and Trebizond—Theodore Lascaris, Emperor of Nice—Nice the centre of Orthodoxy—John Ducas Vatatces, second Emperor at Nice—Attempts at union of Greek and Latin Churches—Theodore II., third Emperor—John IV., fourth Emperor—Michael Palæologus appointed joint Emperor—Latin Patriarchs of Constantinople;—(1) Morosini, (2) Gervasius, (3) Matthias; (4) Simeon; (5) Nicolas; (6) Pantaleon.

THE schism between the Eastern and Western Churches, deplorable under any circumstances, was specially so at the time when it occurred, a time when a united Christendom was specially required. The year 1048, six years before the commencement of the schism, was the date of the entrance of the Turks into the annals of Ecclesiastical history. No race has ever thrown so dark a page on the history of Christendom as the Turks. Goths, Vandals, English, Lombards, Danes, have all been converted to Christianity, but the Turks from the first to the present day have been its persistent and unmitigated foes.

The dynasty of the Turks, of whom we have to deal in this chapter, is not that of the Ottomans, of whom we have in the present day such painful reminders, but their immediate predecessors, the Seljuks. Their founder Seljuk in the last years of the Tenth Century, having quarrelled with his native Prince, retired from Turkestan to Samarcand, embraced Mahometanism, the religion which his father had adopted, and having wrested the power from the first Turkish dynasty, the Gaznevids, lost his life, at the age of 107, in battle against Pagans.

The Seljuks inherited all that was bad, and rejected whatever there was of good, in the Mahometan faith, of which they became the champions, the entrance, A.D 1048, of Togrel Beg (1037—1063), son of Michael and grandson of Seljuk, into Persia, inaugurated the undying enmity of the Turks to Christianity. Four hundred years from that date their successors, the Ottomans, took Constantinople, put an end to the Eastern Empire, and inflicted a blow on the Greek Church from which it has never since recovered.

Togrel, whilst he wallowed in sensuality, inherited all the Mahometan fanaticism of his grandfather Seljuk, and of his father Michael, the latter surnamed, from his having fallen in battle against the Pagans, the Martyr. In A.D. 1050 he penetrated to Bagdad, and thenceforward took the first place amongst Mahometan Princes, ruling in Persia as a spiritual no less than a temporal monarch, a sort of mock Pope, Cardinal Newman styles him. At Kazem the Caliph of Bagdad, to whom he was able to render valuable services, conferred on him the title of the "Pillar of Religion," and under him the Turkish wars of the Crescent against the Cross commenced; the Saracens had persecuted the Christians, but, as compared with Togrel, they were like lambs; 130,000 Christians slain in battle was the holocaust which he offered to the false Prophet.

The next Sultan in the Seljuk line was Togrel's nephew, Alp Arslan (1063—1073), who received from the Caliph the title of Azzadin, or "Protector of Religion." Having added to the conquests of his predecessor, he, in the battle of Manzikert, A.D. 1071, defeated and took prisoner the

Eastern Emperor, Romanus IV. (Diogenes); and it is said that he, although Gibbon doubts the story[a], who was generally a merciful victor, placed his foot, in the established usage of his nation, on the neck of the fallen Emperor, afterwards giving him his liberty on the payment of a heavy ransom. The result of the battle of Manzikert was the loss to the Eastern Empire of nearly all its provinces in Asia, and the extermination of the greater part of the Christian population; whilst by the capitulation in the same year of Bari to Roger, the younger brother of Robert Guiscard, and the future conqueror of Sicily, the Eastern Empire in Italy came to an end.

Alp Arslan, at a time when he flattered himself that "the earth trembled under his feet," died by the hand of an assassin, and was succeeded by his son, Malek Shah (1073—1092), who subdued Syria, took Jerusalem, in 1076, and obtained from the Caliph the title of "Commander of the Faithful;" he also demanded of the Greek Emperor, Alexius, the hand of his daughter in marriage. The capture of Jerusalem by Malek Shah was the immediate cause of the Crusades, and it was in his time that the great troubles in Jerusalem began, which led to the preaching of Peter the Hermit and the First Crusade.

The Crusades owe their origin to the Christian pilgrimages from the Western Empire to the Holy Land, which, since the days of Constantine and the discovery of the Holy Cross by Helena, to the time of the Saracenic conquests, had become frequent. For the four hundred years since A.D. 637, when it fell under the arms of the Saracens, Jerusalem had been subject to the Caliphs of Bagdad. The Saracens, instead of opposing, favoured the Western pilgrimages, and viewed the pilgrims with sympathy, as people engaged in a pious work. The Caliph Aaron sent to Charlemagne, "*en signe*," says Fleury, "*de la liberté de pèlerinage*," the keys of the Holy Land; even Mussulmans themselves, he adds, took part in the pilgrimages to

[a] X 359.

Jerusalem, which they called "*la maison sainte, et l'ont en singuliere veneration;*" and the Christians were allowed to visit unmolested the scenes of their Saviour's Life and Death. A reasonable tax was imposed upon them, and, in return, food and accommodation was supplied on the road, and a comfortable hospice greeted them on their arrival. This continued till the Seljuk Turks gained posession of Jerusalem, after which a system of persecution set in. Rich pilgrims were robbed, and the poor so oppressed, that many succumbed to death on the way; or, if they arrived at Jerusalem, were so worn out with their sufferings as to be unable to perform their devotions.

The pilgrims, a large proportion of whom were French, returned to Europe with pitiful accounts of the robberies and ill treatment to which they had been subjected, and a cry for vengeance arose throughout Europe But the nations of the West, as also the Greek Emperors, were too much engaged in contests amongst themselves, or in the defence of their own territories, to engage in a distant war for the recovery of the Holy Land The Emperor, Michael VII. (Ducas) (1067—1078), entered into communication with the Papal See, ostensibly with the object of the re-union of the Churches, but principally in the hope of obtaining help against the Turks. The schism was only twenty years old, and the Pope of Rome, Gregory VII (Hildebrand), still entertained hopes that it might be healed He wrote to, the young King of the Romans, Henry IV., that the Church of Constantinople, although it differed from the Western Church in the Procession of the Holy Ghost, yet wished for agreement with it; and that the Greeks desired on the question the decision of the Roman See.

The Pope, desirous of meeting the wishes of the Emperor, published an Encyclical, setting forth that the Pagans had arisen against the Eastern Empire, were laying waste the whole country to the very walls of Constantinople, and offered to put himself at the head of an army of 50,000 Christians to go out to meet them. Gregory's avowed object was to heal the schism between the Eastern and Western Churches; but, although he was also willing to help the Greek Emperor against the Saracens, and to enlist Henry IV. in the cause, it was evident that his principal thought was the establishment of the supremacy of the Roman See. Soon afterwards the Pope's hands were tied by his own quarrels with the King of the Romans. In 1075 he threatened to excommunicate Philip, the King of France, from which he was only diverted by the same cause, his quarrels with Henry IV. Not confining his anathemas to the West, he, A.D. 1078, made an impolitic attack on the independence of the Greek Church, by excommunicating the Eastern Emperor, Nicephorus III (1078—1081); thus he estranged the Greeks, as he had the Latins, from the cause which he advocated. In 1084 he was driven away from Rome, and in the next year died in exile; thus the hope of Western help was for a time laid aside.

Meanwhile a new dynasty in the Eastern Empire arose under Alexius I. (Comnenus) (1081—1118), an able Prince, the father of the historian Anna Comnena; under whom the Eastern Empire began to recover itself, and everything favoured a common enterprise on the part of the Christians. The sufferings of the Christians in the East were again brought before the Western nations by Victor III. (1086—1087), who succeeded Gregory VII.; he, however, was only Pope for a few months, and his promise of forgiveness of sins to those who would take arms against the Turks had not time to take effect. But no sooner did his successor, Urban II. (1088—1099), enter upon his pontificate, although during the whole time Rome was troubled by, and the larger part of it occupied by, an Anti-Pope, than his sympathy was enlisted in the East by the Emperor Alexius. Alexius, having first invited Urban to Constantinople to discuss the schism between the two Churches, next solicited him to enlist the sympathy of the German Princes against the Seljuk infidels. Peter the Hermit, a native of Amiens, himself an eye-witness of the sufferings of the Pilgrims, took counsel with Simeon the Patriarch of Jerusalem. The Patriarch informed him that no help could be expected from the Greeks, who could scarcely defend themselves, and had within a few years lost more than half their Empire; that the sins of the people were so great that God would not hear their prayers, and that all their hopes lay in the Latins He gave him a letter to Pope Urban, whom Peter on his return to Europe sought out, representing to him the miserable condition of Jerusalem, and the persecutions suffered by the Christians.

Urban, whose sympathy was by such means wholly enlisted in the cause, held, A.D. 1095, a Council at Piacenza. Envoys sent by Alexius pleaded before it the miseries which beset the East and threatened Constantinople, and the certainty of further danger which, if the Turks were left a free hand, would follow in the Western Empire. The good will of the West was obtained, and the cause of a Crusade initiated. From Italy, the Pope, himself a Frenchman, crossed the Alps into France, and in the same year held the famous Council of Clermont in Auvergne, attended by his court of Cardinals, thirteen Archbishops, two hundred and twenty-five Bishops, and four hundred mitred Abbots. "As you value your souls," he said, "rush quickly to the defence of the Eastern Church. It is from her the glad tidings of your salvation emanated; she dropped into your mouths the heavenly milk upon which you feed; she passed on the inestimable dogmas of the Gospels for you to imbibe." The Saviour, he told them, would be their Leader; the penance due for their sins would be remitted, and absolution secured; sufferings they would endure, but death would be to them a blessed Martyrdom.

It may here be mentioned in passing, that, A.D. 1098, Urban, with the view of reconciling the Greek and Latin differences with regard to the Procession of the Holy Ghost, held the Council of Bari. Bari, the last town in Apulia which had been left to the Greeks, was captured A.D. 1071, by Robert Guiscard, whom Pope Nicolas II., and after him Gregory VII., bound by an oath of allegiance to the Roman Church. In that Council, Anselm, Archbishop of Canterbury, whom the Pope greeted as Pope and Patriarch of another world, a man of greater theological learning than Urban, took the principal part. Anselm, in defending, on historical grounds, the Filioque clause, had a difficult task to perform ; he must have known that it was an addition made by the Latin Church, and that it had been imported into the Creed against the judgment of a Pope ; could he have believed that it originally stood in the Creed, and that it had been expunged, as Humbert pleaded against Cerularius, by the Greeks? However that may have been, he, in the opinion of the Council, successfully vindicated the double Procession, and thus gained the victory for the Latin Church.

To the appeal made by Pope Urban in the Council of Clermont, a unanimous shout of *God wills it* was raised, the religious enthusiasm quickly spread over Europe ; and August 15, 1096, was fixed upon for the departure of the Crusade to the Holy Land.

There are two points of view, an Eastern and a Western one, from which the Crusades may be regarded. We have to regard them as they affected the Greek Church, and to the Greeks they were an unmitigated calamity. They professed to be Holy Wars, to deliver the Holy Land from the oppression of the Turks. Some of them were mere filibustering expeditions, composed, under incompetent leaders, of undisciplined troops, the scum of the population of Europe. Although to the Papacy they were a deeply politic movement, there is no reason to doubt that the Popes started them with the best of motives, viz., the rescue of the Holy Places from the Infidels. But they soon degenerated into a Latinizing movement, and in the East they were from the first regarded by the Emperors and the people alike with suspicion. Many pious enthusiasts no doubt joined them from true love and reverence of their Saviour, and many from a sincere, but mistaken, idea of making atonement for a misspent life, and the delusive promise offered by the Popes of an eternal reward. But the Crusaders carried on the wars like savages, rather than like Christians, and from fighting against the Turks they turned to fighting against the Eastern Christians. After the first Crusade, they set up the feeble Latin Kingdom in Palestine During the Fourth they burnt and sacked Constantinople with greater wantonness and rapacity than the Saracens had ever shown in their hour of victory ; and they established a Latin Patriarch and Latin Emperor. The only really noble characters of the Crusades were the Sultan Saladin and the saintly Louis of France. The leaders quarrelled amongst themselves, and they failed to effect the object for which they were promoted.

After the Crusades were ended the Eastern Emperors and Greek Patriarchs re-asserted themselves, but it was only a feeble imitation of what they were before. The Crusades have left an indelible stain on the memory of one of the greatest of the Popes ; but through them the long contest for supremacy between the Patriarchs of Constantinople and the Popes resulted in favour of Rome. It could scarcely have been otherwise. A new mode of salvation, of which the Pope was the author, and in which the people thoroughly believed, was invented. The Pope was placed on a higher pedestal than earthly Kings and potentates. He had the direction of the armies of Christendom , he could impose a Crusade for their souls' health on Kings and Emperors ; and through him the greatest criminals could obtain forgiveness by taking the Cross of the Crusader. But we are anticipating.

The regular army of Crusaders started on the appointed day under the command of Godfrey de Bouillon, Duke of Lorraine. When the Emperor, Henry IV., took Rome, and Pope Gregory VII. was forced to take refuge in the Castle of St. Angelo, Godfrey had distinguished himself in the army of the Emperor, and was the first to scale the walls of Rome. Soon afterwards a serious illness brought the conviction to his mind that he had fought against the Church, and he formed the resolution, which he now carried out, of going on a pilgrimage to the Holy Land in atonement for his sin. Other leaders who served under Godfrey were his brother Baldwin, Raymond, Count of Toulouse, Robert, Duke of Normandy, eldest son of William the Conqueror, and Robert, Count of Flanders. These were followed by Bohemund, Duke of Apulia and Calabria, eldest son of Robert Guiscard, attended by a body of Normans, and by his cousin Tancred. From the fact that most of those who took part in the Crusades were French-speaking people, the Eastern nations have ever since called *all* the people of Western Europe, Franks.

No sooner had the Crusaders, having pillaged the lands on the way, entered Constantinople, than the long-standing suspicion and enmity of the Greeks towards the Latins revived. Violent quarrels ensued between the chiefs and the Emperor Alexius; they were, however, for a time ended by their swearing allegiance, the Emperor engaging to assist them to recover the Holy Sepulchre, but viewing with pleasure their departure to the opposite shore of the Bosphorus. In June, 1097, the Crusaders took Nice, the capital of the Sultan of Roum; the Turks being driven away from the neighbourhood of Constantinople, the Sultan establishing a new capital at Cogni (Iconium). This was eminently gratifying to the Emperor; but thenceforward his interest flagged, and he seems to have forgotten his zeal for the Holy Land, and even to have made a secret treaty with the Turks by permitting them to erect a Mosque in Constantinople. In the following year the Crusaders took Edessa, where a Latin Principality under Godfrey's brother Baldwin was established. They next besieged the Syrian Antioch. There, in the Church of St. Peter, is said to have been discovered the Holy Lance which had pierced the Saviour's side. After a siege of seven months the city was betrayed to them, and made a Principality for Bohemund, who bound himself to the Emperor Alexius that the Patriarch should not be chosen from the Latin but from the Greek Church. This agreement the Latins soon forgot, and in two years the Greek Patriarch was made to give place to the chaplain of Adhemar, Bishop of Puy, who had accompanied the Crusade as representative of the Pope [b].

In May, 1099, the Crusaders set out from Antioch, and after much suffering and loss of life on their part, and a terrible massacre of the Moslems, Jerusalem was taken by them on July 15th. The capture was effected at three o'clock in the afternoon of Friday, the day and hour of the Saviour's Death. The Holy Sepulchre was recovered, and the Kingdom of Jerusalem, with a nominal dependence on the Emperor, established. Simeon the Patriarch dying in the same month, Paschal II., who had succeeded Urban as Pope, appointed a Latin Patriarch, Daimbert, Archbishop of Pisa, and Latin clergy, who usurped their jurisdiction and revenue, in place of the Greeks. Godfrey de Bouillon, being by the unanimous vote of the army elected King, was invested in the Kingdom by the new Patriarch; but refusing to wear a crown of gold in the city where the Saviour had worn a Crown of thorns, contented himself with the title of Defender and Baron of the Holy Sepulchre.

The Latin Kingdom comprised little more than the city of Jerusalem, and Jaffa (the ancient Joppa), with a few neighbouring towns, whilst the country in general was under the Mahometans. It consisted of a troop of adventurers, without any principle of cohesion, and was weakly from the first, containing in itself the seeds of its own dissolution. The appointment by the Pope of Rome of Latin Patriarchs at Antioch and Jerusalem was an act of treachery to the Greek Church. The strength of the Latin Kingdom lay mainly in the Military Orders, the two principal of which were the Knights Templars, so called from their residence near the Temple, who converted the Mosque of Omar into their Church, and were the Guardians of the Holy Sepulchre;

---

[b] "Hoc pacti conventi caput . minime observatum fuit a Latinis."— Le Quien, III. 787

and the Knights Hospitallers, or Knights of St. John, a name which they took after St. John the Almoner, Patriarch of Alexandria, and whose special office it was to attend the sick pilgrims who visited the Holy Land. These Orders consisted of Knights who devoted themselves to fight in defence of the Holy Land against the Mahometans. They were bound by the monastic vows of chastity, poverty, and obedience, and were a kind of sacred militia, half military, half monastic, the Templars being distinguished by a white dress with a red cross, whilst the Hospitallers wore a black dress with a white cross; and they were granted plenary Indulgence by the Popes. Soon many of the clergy joined their ranks, so that they themselves were able to administer the rites of the Church. Popes vied with each other in conferring privileges upon them, and Innocent III. relieved them from Episcopal jurisdiction, even from that of the Patriarch of Jerusalem, and rendered them amenable to the Pope only. Being thus exempted from Episcopal control, they became in time societies antagonistic to the clergy, without fear of censure or excommunication from Bishops or Patriarchs; whilst from the first they were the persecutors of the Orthodox Church. For a time they observed the rule of their Order, and did good service by fighting bravely against the infidels. But by degrees, both Orders, but especially the Templars, amassed great wealth, and with wealth followed the usual abuses; they evaded the Rule of their Order, and showed a spirit of insubordination against the military authorities, thwarted their plans, and stood aloof from campaigns at their own will. The two Orders quarrelled with each other. Holding social intercourse with the Mahometans, they lost their original antipathy to them, and became tainted, not only with their vices, but their doctrines, and forgot that the Mahometans and not the Christians were their enemies. We will sum up their character in the words of Fleury;—" Peu après leur installation ils abusaient de leurs privileges, les étendant a l'infini, méprisant les evêques dont ils etaient exempts, et n'obeissant au Pape même qu'autant qu'il leur plaisait Ils ne gardaient point les traites avec les infideles, et quelquefois s'entendaient avec eux pour trahir les Chretiens, plusieurs menaient une vie corrompué et scandaleuse.... Les faits dont les Templiers furent accusés sont si atroces qu'on ne peut les lire sans horreur, et on a peine les croire, quoique prouvés par des procédures authentiques."

The first Crusade was the only one attended by any degree of success, and, such as it was, the Christians of the Latin Kingdom had difficulty in holding their own against the Mussulmans.

Godfrey, dying a few days within a year after his appointment, was succeeded by his brother, Baldwin I. (1100—1118), Prince of Edessa. Next followed his cousin, Baldwin II. (1118—1131), and after him his son-in-law, Fulk, Count of Anjou (1131—1144), who was succeeded by his son, Baldwin III. (1144—1162), a boy 13 years of age, during whose reign the second Crusade was undertaken.

Most of the Crusaders having, after the capture of Jerusalem, returned to England, the Mahometans set themselves to harass the Christians of the Latin Kingdom; in 1146 they took Edessa, and the Christians again applied to the West for help. A second Crusade was accordingly preached the next year by St. Bernard, the celebrated Abbot of Clairvaux, the most influential person in Christendom of his time, who induced Conrad the German Emperor and Louis VII., King of France, to join the expedition, of which they in vain entreated Bernard to assume the conduct. Eugenius III. (1145—1153), the Pope of Rome, whilst he renewed all the promises made by Urban at the Council of Clermont, warned the Crusaders against the vices of their predecessors, which had brought disaster and disgrace on the arms of Christendom [c]. But in this respect, neither this, nor any of the following Crusades, seems to have learnt experience from the first Crusade; nor did they make their calculations with a view to the difficulties before them;

' Cox's Crusades, p. 86.

their forces were wholly inadequate, and they rushed headlong, as Gibbon puts it, down the precipice that was open before them.

Quarrels between the Greek Emperor, Manuel I., and Conrad, who had married sisters, ensued. Manuel and Louis were at first on better terms; but the French army receiving no assistance from Manuel, and the latter having concluded a truce with the Turkish Sultan of Cogni, a French Bishop advocated, as a preliminary to their advance to the Holy Land, an attack on the Greeks of Constantinople. This was not effected during the second Crusade; but nothing except a miserable loss of life occurred; and after a siege of Damascus, which, owing to the treachery of the Barons of Palestine, who were bribed by the Turks, was unsuccessful, the leaders, in 1149, with the scanty remnant of their fores, returned to Europe, and not even the venerable name of Bernard was able to shelter him from blame and obloquy.

To Baldwin III. succeeded in the Kingdom of Jerusalem his brother Almeric (1162—1173), next followed Almeric's son, Baldwin IV. (1173—1186), a leper; and then, in 1186, Guy de Lusignan, the husband of Baldwin's sister Sibylla, by right of his wife, became King. Under him the Latin Kingdom of Jerusalem, after it had lasted eighty-seven years, came to an end.

In the reign of Almeric the Latin Kingdom had become embroiled in the contests between the Fatimite Caliph of Egypt and Noureddin, who ruled as Sultan of Aleppo under the Caliph of Bagdad. The Latins espousing the cause of the former, Noureddin inflicted a disastrous defeat upon them near Antioch (A.D. 1163). One of his Generals was the famous Saladin, who, A.D. 1171, suppressed the Fatimite Caliphate and made himself master of Egypt, and, after the death of Noureddin in 1173, master of Syria.

Saladin, now the greatest Mahometan Prince of the time, having in the battle of Tiberias, A.D 1187, defeated Guy, and made him prisoner, laid siege to Jerusalem. Fourteen days sufficed for his object; the Latins melted down the golden ornaments of the Churches to provide the sinews of war; the Greeks within the city were in league with the enemy; and on October 3, 1187, Jerusalem, after the loss of 30,000 men, again fell into the hands of the infidels; the Cross which had been placed on the summit of the Mosque of Omar was pulled down, the Mosque purified and re-dedicated to the Moslem worship, and the Christian Churches were converted into Mosques. Two hundred and fifty Hospitallers died at the hands of the executioner Martyrs to their faith. A third Crusade for the recovery of Jerusalem was preached, A.D. 1189, and Frederic Barbarossa, Emperor of Germany, started in command of it for the Holy Land. Henry II., King of England, took the Cross of a Crusader, but died before he could set out.

The Greek Empire was in a very demoralized condition and was verging on its decline. The Emperor, Manuel I. (1143—1180), was succeeded by his son Alexius II. (1180—1183), a boy thirteen years of age, but who had already married Agnes, daughter of Louis VII., King of France. After two years he was murdered by Andronicus I. (Comnenos), the grandson of Alexius I. The Greek Church appears to have been in an equally corrupt state with the Empire, and few people at the time acknowledged the restraints of religion. Andronicus I. was, says Mr. Oman[d], an unscrupulous ruffian and a consummate hypocrite, who won his way to the throne by professions of piety and austere virtue. He had attempted the murder of the Emperor Manuel and twice deserted to the Turks. The murderer, who found no difficulty in inducing the Greek clergy to grant him absolution, was consecrated Emperor (1183—1185) by Basilios Camateros, intruded into the See of Constantinople in the place of the Patriarch Theodosius, who had been deposed for refusing to truckle to the vices of the Emperor.

[d] Story of the Nations, p. 272.

Chapter XII.

Andronicus himself, after having his eyes put out and subjected to every form of indignity, was eventually murdered and succeeded by Isaac II. (Angelus; 1185—1195; and again, 1203—1204). Andronicus was the last of the male branch of the Comneni, and Isaac II., the first Emperor of the family of Angelus, was a descendant of the female branch through Theodora, daughter of Alexius I. The reign of the two Angeli, Isaac II. and his brother Alexius III., which cover the period 1185—1204, may be pronounced the most despicable and disgraceful in the whole annals of the Eastern Empire.

When Jerusalem fell under the arms of Saladin, Isaac II. was Emperor. The German Emperor Barbarossa, who had served under his uncle Conrad and gained experience during the second Crusade, wished to avoid any collision with the Byzantine government, and even asked permission of Isaac to pass through his territories. Isaac, who possessed the habitual Greek hostility to the Latins, threw every obstacle in his way, blocking the passes and stopping the supplies. Frederic was in consequence compelled to make war upon him, and received substantial assistance from the Armenians of Philippopolis, who in their hereditary hatred to the Greeks, welcomed the Latins, and aided the Western Emperor, besides giving him useful information as to the state of the Eastern Empire and the movement of the troops. So deep-rooted was Isaac's hostility that he addressed a letter to Saladin boasting that he had done everything to arrest the advance of the Crusaders [e]. But by a victory gained by Barbarossa over the Turks at Cogni, Isaac was so alarmed that he sent envoys soliciting peace at any price.

The deliverance of the Holy Land under a numerous and well-disciplined army, led by a General experienced, like Barbarossa, in Eastern warfare, was hopefully expected, when death suddenly ended his career, the great Emperor being drowned, A.D. 1190, while crossing or bathing in the

[e] Finlay, III 235, *note*

Cnidus, a narrow river of Cilicia. In the summer of that year Richard Cœur de Lion of England and Philip Augustus of France started by sea for the Holy Land.

In 1191, whilst Richard was on his outward journey, two of his ships were wrecked on the coast of Cyprus, where Isaac Comnenos, a relative of the Emperor Manuel I., having stirred up a rebellion, and defeated a fleet despatched against him by the Emperor Isaac, reigned under the title of Emperor of the Romans. The ship, which contained Richard's betrothed wife, Berengaria of Navarre, having been, during the storm, refused admission into the harbour, Richard landed with his troops, defeated the Greeks and occupied Cyprus, the sovereignty of which he transferred to Guy de Lusignan, who, by the death of his wife, had lost his title to the Kingdom of Jerusalem; and Guy founded a dynasty of Frank kings in Cyprus "From that time to the present day," says Finlay, " the Greeks of Cyprus have suffered every misery that can be inflicted by foreign masters, and the island, which at the time of the conquest by Richard was the richest and most populous in the Mediterranean, is now almost uncultivated and very thinly inhabited." Most of the Greek families emigrated from the island, their place being taken by Latin families from the Kingdom of Jerusalem. The Cyprian Church was Latinized; Guy made the French language the language of the government, Latin becoming the language of the Church. Latin Bishops and Clergy were put in possession of the rich endowments of the Church; toleration, however, was allowed to the Greeks, who, although deprived of their property, remained under the jurisdiction of their own Bishop; whilst Armenians, Nestorians, and Copts were allowed to build Churches[f]. The history of Cyprus ceased till the present time to be connected with the history of the Greeks.

Acre, a city about seventy miles distant from Jerusalem, which had, in consequence of the battle of Tiberias, yielded to Saladin, was, after a siege of nearly two years (1189—

[f] Finlay, IV 74.

1191), in which it suffered enormous losses through famine, the climate, and the sword, taken by the Crusaders, and Acre thenceforward became the Metropolis of the Latin Christians and the residence of the titular King and Patriarch of Jerusalem.

The Crusading leaders, jealous of each other, quarrelled amongst themselves. Philip Augustus, jealous of Richard, returned to France. Richard offended Leopold of Austria, by pulling down the Austrian banner from the battlements of Acre; and, on another occasion, so wounded his pride, by the seasonable, but unroyal, application of his fist, that the Duke returned in wrath to Austria.

Richard Cœur de Lion continued in Palestine a year longer, and defeated Saladin in several battles, taking Jaffa and Cæsarea. But in vain Richard demanded of Saladin the restitution of Palestine and the Holy Cross, Jerusalem was left in the hands of the infidels; all that he could obtain for the Christians was the suspension of hostilities for three years and eight months; that pilgrims should enjoy liberty and security, and that the Holy Sepulchre should be open to them without payment or tribute.

Readers of English history need not to be reminded how the treachery of Richard's brother John recalled him from Palestine; how he was shipwrecked at Trieste and made prisoner by Leopold of Austria, by whom he was delivered to the Emperor, Henry VI., of Germany, and only released on the promised payment of a heavy ransom, for which hostages were left as a security.

After his defeat by Richard, Saladin took up his abode at Damascus, where he died, full of honour, in March, 1193, in the fifty-sixth year of his age and the twenty-first of his reign. The last act of the great Sultan was to order his winding-sheet, in place of a standard, to be carried through every street in the city, to signify the instability of human greatness; whilst he left alms to be distributed in equal proportions between Christians, Jews, and Mahometans.

After the third Crusade the state of Palestine grew even worse than before. The sons of Saladin quarrelled amongst themselves, and the government became broken up into the rival dynasties of Egypt, Damascus, and Aleppo. Saladin's soldiers supported his brother Saphadim, by whom, on the expiration, in 1197, of the truce made with Saladin, Jaffa was taken, twenty thousand Christians being put to death. The Crusaders began to experience treachery in their own camp; rumours abounded of the Templars holding treasonable correspondence with the Mahometans, who made many converts from the Order instituted for the defence of the Holy Land.

In the following year Innocent III., under whom the Papal See reached the zenith of its power, and advanced far beyond anything claimed for it even by the Forged Decretals, became Pope of Rome (1198—1216). The Pope was now no longer contented with being the successor of St. Peter, but claimed to be the Vicar of Jesus Christ [g].

The lust of conquest, engendered by the fatal gift of patrimony conferred by Pipin and Charlemagne, led the Pope to imagine that he might augment it by the acquisition of Constantinople. It was impossible for the Greeks not to despise a Church which sheltered itself under the shallow pretence of Innocent; "You see," he says, "that the time has come when, the golden calves being destroyed, Israel should return to Judah, and Samaria be converted to Jerusalem [h];" that the breach between the two Churches should not be widened; and that the East could any longer doubt that the Crusades were schemes for the aggrandisement of the Papacy, rather than for the defence of the Holy Land.

The fourth Crusade was preached through France and Flanders by Fulk, a parish Priest of Neuilly, near Paris, and was undertaken at the instance of Pope Innocent. It

[g] "Quamvis simus Apostolorum principis successores, non tamen ejus aut alicujus Apostoli aut hominis, sed Ipsius sumus Vicarii, Jesu Christi."

[h] "Tempus advenisse videtis in quo, destructis, vitulis aureis, Israel vertatur ad Judam, et ad Hierosolumam Samaria convertatur."

did nothing for the Holy Land, and degenerated into a Crusade for the conquest of the Eastern Empire, and the subjugation of the Greek Church. The Crusade was in its inception far from popular in Europe. Rumours of the rapacity of the Papal Curia, and that the money raised for Crusades was diverted to other uses, were spread and credited. But appeals for help from the Patriarchs of Antioch and Jerusalem became more and more urgent; Innocent applied to the clergy and laity of Europe; the people he requested to contribute liberally to the best of their power, whilst the clergy were to contribute a fourth part of their revenues, with the assurance that it would be in safe keeping under the custody of Rome.

At last, A.D. 1201, several Barons of Europe, amongst the chief of whom were Baldwin, Count of Flanders, and Boniface of Montferrat, determined to set out on a Crusade Apprehensive of the long and dangerous journey through Asia, and fearing the hostility of the Greeks, they determined to proceed by sea; but the difficulty was how to procure sufficient transports. They applied to Venice, which with Genoa and Pisa were, at that time, the greatest naval powers in Europe. The Doge Eurico Dandolo, ninety years of age, who had been deprived of his sight by the Emperor Manuel Comnenos, readily granted their request, on the understanding that whatever conquests were made should be equally divided between the Barons and the Venetians. The Crusaders, having assembled in Venice in October, 1202, set sail, to the number of 200,000, the old Doge himself, who had taken the vows of a Crusader in St. Mark's, Venice, accompanying them, under Boniface of Montferrat, who was invested with the Cross of a pilgrim.

A change of purpose suddenly occurred. Dandolo prevailed with the Crusaders to assist him in recovering Zara in Dalmatia, which had been seized by the King of Hungary; and the Pope in vain threatened them with excommunication if they attacked a city, which belonged to a King who had taken the Cross of a Crusader.

No sooner was Zara taken after a siege of six days, than the Doge again turned aside the object of the expedition. The Eastern Emperor, Isaac Angelus, had been blinded and imprisoned in a dungeon at Constantinople by his brother, who usurped the throne under the title of Alexius III. The Greeks willingly transferred their allegiance from a tyrant whose vices they knew, to a new tyrant whose vices they had not as yet discovered. Isaac's young son, Alexius, managing to effect, on board a Pisan vessel, his own escape to Venice from imprisonment, strove to induce the Crusaders to aid him in the restoration of his father to the throne. The Franks he endeavoured to gain over by the promise that, as soon as his father was restored to the throne, he would subjugate the Greek Church to the obedience of the Pope. With the Venetians he had little difficulty, as they were desirous of an opportunity for paying off a grudge against the Greeks, on account of help given by them to their rivals, the Genoese. The young Alexius was profuse in his promises to pay the cost of the proposed expedition.

Differences arose between the Franks and the Venetians. The former, having run the risk of excommunication once, were unwilling to risk it a second time. But Dandolo and the Venetians, who owned no allegiance to the Pope, knew no such scruples; and they prevailed. The Franks, although many of them left the camp, refusing to stain their hands with the blood of their fellow-Christians, accepted the proposal of the young Alexius; probably they had a shrewd suspicion that their success, and the establishment of a Latin Church at Constantinople, would, as afterwards proved to be the case, please and satisfy the Pope. Thus the fourth Crusade was, from Syria, diverted to Constantinople, and instead of being turned against the infidels, was turned against the Eastern Christians.

In the summer of A.D. 1203, the Crusaders appeared in the neighbourhood of Constantinople. By this time the Greeks had seen enough of their usurping Emperor, and, as no one was desirous of espousing his cause, Alexius III., taking with him whatever jewels and treasures he could lay hands on, fled from Constantinople. In July the Crusaders entered Constantinople in triumph, the blind Emperor, so old and imbecile as scarcely to understand what was going on, was restored to the throne, his son Alexius being crowned in St. Sophia's, as his colleague, with the title of Alexius IV. The youg Alexius was an idle and dissipated tyrant, who proved himself as incapable as his father or his uncle, of governing. In order to carry out part of his bargain with the Crusaders, whose help he required to keep him on his insecure throne, he persuaded his father to acknowledge the supremacy of the Pope, and even wrote to the Pope to that effect; but he mistook the feelings of the Greeks, who regarded him as a traitor to their faith, and he became an object of contempt alike to Greeks and Latins.

The misfortunes of the inhabitants were increased by a fire which ravaged Constantinople; and their indignation was still further excited, when the emissaries of Alexius, in order to carry out his bargain with the Latins, proceeded to strip the Cathedral, the Churches, and the monasteries, of their gold and silver plate, and ornaments The people rose in rebellion and found a leader in Alexius Ducas, surnamed, from his shaggy eyebrows, Murtzuphlus (the *beetle-browed*); the old Emperor died of fright; the young Emperor, under assurance that he was being conveyed to a place of safety from enemies who were seeking his life, was thrown into a dungeon, where he was strangled by the hands of Murtzuphlus, who ascended the throne as Alexius V. (Ducas) in 1204.

It was soon evident that the government could not carry out the pecuniary engagement on which the Crusaders insisted; the Crusaders therefore declared war against the Empire, and, in April, 1204, commenced their attack on Constantinople. Murtzuphlus, finding it impossible to infuse a warlike spirit into the cowardly citizens, to whom the Imperial government had become hateful, fled fiom the capital. The Greek clergy alone stood in the gap and advocated resistance. Theodore Lascaris, the son-in-law of Alexius III., was, at their instance, chosen Emperor; but meeting with no better success he, too, found it necessary to fly from Constantinople to Nice. The conduct of the champions of the Cross in their hour of victory formed a sad contrast with that of the Mussulmans under Saladin, when the latter conquered Jerusalem. Never was victory more cruelly abused. In vain the unhappy citizens implored the mercy of their victors; two thousand Greeks were ruthlessly murdered, and sacrilege and plunder, even though it was Holy Week, prevailed everywhere. No restraint was exercised, no mercy, for religion, for age or sex, was shown. The Churches were profaned with sacrilegious ceremonies, the Priests maltreated, the ritual of the Greek Church ridiculed, and the vessels of the Altar turned into drinking-cups for drunken orgies. The monuments of religion were destroyed or defaced; the precious shrines, the receptacles of the holy relics of Saints and Martyrs, ransacked; the sacred plate, golden crowns, candelabra of precious stones, Crosses, rich Altar-cloths, and jewelled ornaments were seized; mules and horses being driven through the Churches to cart away the sacred treasures. An abandoned female who had accompanied the Crusaders, seated, in shameless dress, on the Patriarchal throne, sang ribald songs, and danced before the very Altar in the Cathedral of St. Sophia. Amongst the immense amount of spoil carried away were the four bronze horses which now adorn the Piazza of St. Mark in Venice, and the picture of the Holy Virgin, said to have been painted by St. Luke. Baldwin, the future Emperor, declared that the riches of Constantinople at the time equalled the accumulated wealth of Western Europe[1].

Before these horrors were perpetrated, the Franks and Venetians had settled between themselves the plan for destroying the Greek, and establishing a Latin, Empire and

---

[1] Finlay, III 274

a Latin Patriarch, the Emperor to be chosen from one nation, the Patriarch from the other.

The Bishop of Soissons announced to the assembled chiefs the result of the election. Baldwin, Count of Flanders, was chosen Emperor (1204—1205) by the Franks. Murtzuphlus, the late Emperor, being made prisoner by the Crusaders, was tried for the murder of Alexius, condemned, and executed, by being hurled from the Theodosian column in one of the squares of Constantinople. The Patriarch, John Camateros, stripped of his Patriarchal robes and seated upon an ass, was driven from the city, and Thomaso Morosini, one of their own countrymen, was intruded by the Venetians into the Patriarchate.

Such were the tender mercies of the Latin Crusaders to the Greek Church, so long the bulwark of Christendom against the Saracens; and to the fourth Crusade are to be attributed all the subsequent evils and degradations of the Eastern Empire, of the Orthodox Church, and the Greek nation. Constantinople and the Eastern Empire it despoiled beyond the possibility of recovery, and prepared an easy victory for the Turks. No blacker stain of hypocrisy, cruelty, and rapacity disfigures the annals of the Christian Church. Pope Innocent III., in some respects the greatest of all the Popes, at first endeavoured to prevent the Crusade from deviating from its proper purpose; but his subsequent conduct does not entitle him to the same meed of praise; he took advantage of the cruel and unmerited injustice inflicted on the Patriarch and the Greek Church, to extend his own power. The Crusade had, by force of arms, conquered the Greek Church, and the conduct of the Crusaders in St. Sophia's was not surpassed during the reign of terror by the revolutionists in Notre Dame at Paris. Innocent himself complained of the foul deeds, too foul to be described, which disgraced the name of Christians[k], yet he took the new Latin Empire under his pro-

---

[k] "Nec religioni, nec ætati, nec sexui pepercerunt, sed fornicationes, adul-

tection; he had passed sentence of excommunication on the Venetians when they had refused to obey him; but now that they had got all they wanted, and had no reason for disobeying him any longer, he withdrew the sentence. John Camateros, the Patriarch of Constantinople, was still living; but the Venetians would have a 'Patriarch of their own, nor would they accept one appointed by the Pope. Without consulting Innocent's wishes or approval, they insisted on Morosini, a Venetian sub-deacon; and in January, 1205, the Pope sanctioned the election, and took the intruded Patriarch under his special patronage; with his own hands he Ordained him Deacon, and, within a week, Priest and Bishop, and invested him with the Pall, insisting that he should recognize the supremacy of the Pope of Rome. Innocent violated every Canon of the Catholic Church, which regulated the election and deposition of Bishops, and forbade two Bishops to exist in the same city.

The consequence of the Pope's action was, and still is, that the Greek Church spurns the idea of returning to union with the Roman Church; and for such works of darkness, as marked the fourth Crusade, it abhorred the Latins as "dogs." Innocent himself wrote, " How is it possible that the Greeks should ever return to unity when they have been treated in such a manner that they regard the Latins as dogs?" Why did he not ask the question, How could they return after the schismatical dealings of the Pope?

But the Latins were far from conquering the whole Eastern Empire. Rival dynasties were established in Epirus, Nice, and Trebizond, the last two under Princes with the title of Emperors. The Latin Empire in the East lasted for fifty-seven years (1204—1261); but the Emperor of Romania, as he was styled, could never subdue the spirit of his Greek subjects, and the Latin Empire, from the first moment of its existence, was feeble and had unfailing signs of decay and destruction. In its very first year the

teria, et incestus in oculis omnium exercentes, non solum maritas et virgines Deo dicatas exposuerunt spurcitiis garcionum"

Latins suffered a disastrous defeat near Adrianople, from the Tsar of Bulgaria, their army cut to pieces, the Emperor Baldwin taken captive, and put to death in prison. He was succeeded by his brother, Henry of Flanders (1205—1216).

Pope Innocent found the Greeks more difficult to rule than he had imagined, and thoroughly misunderstood the character of the Greek Church. The Roman Church has never doubted that the Greeks are Catholics, but Innocent dealt with the Greek Bishops and Priests as ministers of a false faith. The Crusaders, says Sir George Cox[1], had come to a Christian land which boasted Churches of a more venerable antiquity than Milan, Ravenna, or even Rome itself; to a land where the ritual of the Church had taken root while Christianity was in its cradle. This Church-honoured civilization the Latins thought that they could crush.

The population with which Innocent had to deal consisted of two distinct classes, Greeks and Latins, and there were constant disputes between the Greek and Latin clergy Over the Latin Patriarchs the Emperors of Romania exercised the same rights as the Byzantine Emperors had exercised over the Greek Patriarchs; and the Greek clergy would admit of no controlling power in the Pope different to what they had been accustomed to under their own Patriarchs and Emperors. Innocent, finding it impossible to coerce the Greeks into conformity, bribed them into acquiescence by sanctioning the celebration of divine service in their own language. But many regarded this as an insidious means of drawing them from their allegiance to the Orthodox Church, and were more incensed than ever against the Latins. They complained of the Pope's presumptuous claims; of his dictating, according to his own pleasure, or rather commanding, in matters belonging to the Church; of Rome, instead of a mother, being a *step-mother* (*de matre noverca facta*); so that instead of sons they might more

Crusades p. 163

properly be called slaves, so heavy was the yoke imposed upon their necks; that the schism was occasioned "*a tyrannide vestræ oppressionis, et exactionum Romanæ Ecclesiæ;*" and that they were obliged to act as Paul acted to Peter[m].

There were also constant frictions and contentions between the Franks and Venetians. The Venetians opposed the Patriarchs as being too submissive to the Popes, and tried to induce them to appoint Venetian Bishops. The Franks never cordially acquiesced in a Venetian Patriarch, and insisted on the appointment of French Bishops, the Popes had to interfere to preserve the peace between them; and one of the first acts of Morosini was to excommunicate half of the clergy of the Empire.

Eleven years after the establishment of the Latin Empire, Innocent assembled the Fourth Lateran Council, as stated in his Bull, for the recovery of the Holy Land and the reformation of the Church. The Council was attended by two rival claimants of the Latin Patriarchate of Constantinople, and the Patriarch of Jerusalem. How calamitous was the schism between Greeks and Latins in the East may be learnt from the complaint made by the Romans before the Council, that the Greeks treated the Altars where the Latins had celebrated as polluted, and rebaptized those who had received Latin baptism[n]. Nor need we, although heretical baptism is recognized both by the Greek and Latin Churches, wonder at the indignation felt by the Greeks. The Popes not only treated them as heretics, but worse than Mahometans. In the contests which took place between the Latin Emperors at Constantinople and the Greek Emperors at Nice, the Latins allied themselves with the Mahometans. Henry of Flanders boasted of his alliance with the Turks against Orthodox Greeks as an honourable one; yet the Popes, who considered Mahometans less

[m] Matthew Paris

[n] "Si quando sacerdotes Latini super eorum celebrassent altaria, non prius ibi sacrificare volebant quam ea, tanquam per hoc inquinata, lavassent. Baptizatos etiam à Latinis, et ipsi Græci rebaptizare ausu temerario præsumebant."

dangerous to their supremacy than Greeks, made the contests between Greeks and Latins holy wars, and granted *Indulgences* to the latter in their attacks on the Greek heretics.

All civil dignities and offices were at first conferred on the Latins. But the Latin Emperor, having to deal with the superior culture of the Greek landed proprietors, soon found it necessary to leave the civil and municipal administration in their hands. He had also to contend with the Greeks of the lower classes, the artificers and agriculturists. So that not only Ecclesiastical but civil affairs also were thrown into utter confusion, and it required all the firmness of Henry of Flanders to avoid open quarrels between Church and State [o].

Henry, in default of male heirs of the Counts of Flanders, was succeeded by Peter of Courtenay (1217—1219), who had married his sister Yolande, and was crowned by Pope Honorius III. (1216—1227), the successor of Innocent. By Yolande he became the father of the last Latin Emperor, Baldwin II.

In the fifth Crusade, Frederic II., Emperor of Germany (1220—1250), was the principal actor. His life doubtless was not faultless, but he was a man endowed with every princely virtue, and of such varied accomplishments that he was styled the *Wonder of the World*. "That excellent Prince," says Hallam, "was perhaps the most eminent pattern of unswerving probity and Christian strictness of conscience that ever held the sceptre of any country." Pope Honorius III., a man of mild and gentle character, urged upon him, at his Coronation, the fulfilment of a vow, which he had previously made, to go on a Crusade for the rescue of the Holy Sepulchre. "Never did Pope love Emperor as he loved his son Frederic," were the words of Honorius [p]. But political exigencies at home, and subsequent illness, for a time prevented the Emperor from ful-

---

[o] Finlay, IV. 101   [p] Cox's Crusades, 185.

filling his vow. The whole of the Pontificate of Gregory IX. (1227—1241), a man of vulgar and violent temper, the successor of Honorius, was taken up in quarrels and in excommunicating the Emperor. Twice he excommunicated him because he could not fulfil his vow and go to the Holy Land; and then, when he fulfilled it and went, he excommunicated him a third time and deposed him. "What means this arrogant and daring Pope" (*quo spiritu vel ausu temerario*), asked Louis IX., the saintly King of France (1226—1270), "to disinherit a King who has no superior, not even an equal, in Christendom!"

In 1229 the Emperor arrived in Palestine, took the field against the infidels, and succeeded in making, with the Sultan Kamel, an advantageous truce for ten years, by which not only Jerusalem, but Lydda, Bethlehem, Nazareth, Tyre and Sidon were restored to the Christians. But the persecution of the Pope still followed him. He had, A.D. 1225, married Iolante, daughter of John de Brienne, the titular King, who transferred to him as his dowry the barren title of King of Jerusalem. When he entered Jerusalem he found the Holy Sepulchre closed against him. The Bishops stood aloof; the Latin Patriarch refused to crown him; whereupon he himself took the crown from the High Altar in the Church of the Holy Sepulchre, and placed it on his own head. Having gained more for the Christians than had been done since the first Crusade, he returned to Europe to find himself again placed under the bann of excommunication by the Pope.

The Sixth was an English Crusade, which left England, A.D. 1240, under Richard, Earl of Cornwall, brother of King Henry III., and William Longsword, son of the Earl of Salisbury. They succeeded in obtaining from the Sultan even more favourable terms than had been granted to the Emperor Frederic; and Palestine was once again in the hands of the Christians. But at a time when the strength of Christendom was divided; when the East was broken up into two rival Empires; when the West was distracted by the quarrels of the Popes and the Hohenstaufens, it was impossible for the Christians to defend themselves.

Peace was broken, A.D 1243, by the irruption of the barbarous hordes of Mahometan Corasmians, who, flying from the Moguls, a tribe as barbarous as themselves, entered and sacked Jerusalem. Under their savage onslaughts Jerusalem was abandoned by its garrison; the Grand-Masters of the Templars and Hospitallers were slain in battle, and the military Orders almost exterminated; the Christian Churches and the Holy Sepulchre were violated; thousands of pilgrims, decoyed from the city, were subjected to a cruel and indiscriminate slaughter, surpassing even what had been suffered from Turks and Saracens. Thus the Holy City was again taken by the Mahometans and has never been recovered; and although the German Emperors continued to style themselves Kings of Jerusalem, Frederic was really the last Christian King who reigned.

Not the Pope of Rome, but the opponent of Popes, the pious, saintly, and ascetic Louis IX.[q], was at that time the acknowledged representative of Christendom. Pope Innocent IV. (1243—1254) continued the persecution of the German Emperor, Frederic II.; but he, too, met with an opponent in St. Louis, and not finding Rome a safe place of residence, sought, A.D. 1244, an asylum, which was denied him in England, at Lyons. In the next year St. Louis, when lying, as was supposed, on his death-bed, vowed that if he recovered he would lead a Crusade to the Holy Land. His peaceful and gentle character fitted him for the life of a monk, rather than that of the leader of armies, for which he lacked every necessary quality. Circumstances, for three years, prevented him from carrying out his vow; but, on August 27th, 1248, having taken the Cross of a Crusader from the Archbishop of Paris, he started, with the seventh Crusade, for Cyprus, the appointed place of the meeting. After spending nine months on that island, the Crusaders

---

[q] He was canonized by the Church of Rome twenty-eight years after his death.

set out for Egypt and took Damietta. But everything—the newly-invented Greek fire, famine, pestilence—seemed to conspire against them and committed terrible havoc amongst their troops. The fortune of war turned against them, and they suffered a total defeat; the Count of Artois, the King's brother, was killed in battle; Louis himself was captured and imprisoned at Missourat near Cairo. The noble traits of his character enlisted the admiration of the Sultan Turah Shah; and eventually, by payment of an immense ransom, he effected the release of himself and his barons, and after having concluded a truce for ten years, and having made a pilgrimage to Nazareth, he was recalled to France (A.D. 1254) by the death of his mother.

The infidels continued to extend their conquests in Syria, and in 1268 Antioch fell. The vow of the Crusader was still upon him, and the King, nothing daunted with the failure of the former Crusade, started, in July, 1270, on a second expedition to the Holy Land. No sooner had the army encamped at Tunis than the plague broke out, and on August 25 the saintly King, having first witnessed his son Tristan (*the child of his sorrow*) carried off by the fatal epidemic, followed him to the grave.

In the same year Prince Edward joined the Crusade, but returned to England, in 1274, as King Edward I. Acre, whither the Hospitallers and Templars had, after the fall of Jerusalem, transferred their head-quarters, was then the sole possession left to the Christians It is described as having become a sink of iniquity, whither the scum of the Crusaders had conglomerated, so that it was said to be better in the hands of the Mahometans, than to continue to disgrace the name of Christians. Acre was in 1291 taken by the Mahometans. The Patriarch contrived to escape. The Crusades, although the embers for some time smouldered on, had come to an end; the Christian Kingdom of Jerusalem terminated, and the Holy Places are to this day in the possession of the Turks.

The Crusades were a miserable failure, the only gainers

from them were the Popes of Rome; to the Greeks they were scarcely a less cause of terror than the attacks of the Turks. They had, however, one unexpected result; the power of the Seljuk Turks received a check, and the conquest of Constantinople by the infidels was delayed for one hundred and sixty-two years.

Meanwhile, whilst the Latin Empire of Constantinople was, under the Emperor Baldwin II. (1228—1261), growing weaker and weaker, the Greeks continued under their Emperors their independence and their orthodox worship, and far from despairing of their rights, kept a watchful eye on their lawful heritage. Nor was their enforced absence from Constantinople without its corresponding advantages, for it kept them free from the luxuries and dissoluteness into which the capital of the Latin Empire sunk.

Of the independent Greek thrones the principal were the Empires of Nice and Trebizond, and it is with the former, of which Theodore Lascaris was Emperor, that we are chiefly concerned. Fortunately for Lascaris, the violent conduct of Pelagius, the Papal legate at Constantinople, in persecuting those who refused to acknowledge the Pope's supremacy, so disgusted the Orthodox Greeks, that whatever remained there of the aristocracy and wealth, as well as most of the distinguished clergy and monks, followed him to Nice. The Orthodox Patriarch, John Camateros, being unwilling to resume the office, Michael Autorianus was appointed to the Patriarchate (1206—1212); by him Theodore was crowned Emperor (1204—1222); and Nice was recognized by the Greek Bishops and Clergy as the centre of Eastern Orthodoxy.

Theodore addressed a Letter to Pope Innocent III., proposing, as a basis of agreement, that the Latins should retain the European, and the Greeks the Asiatic, dominions of the Byzantine Empire. The Pope in his reply, written A.D. 1208, denied him the title of Emperor, required him to acknowledge himself the vassal of the Latin Empire,

The Schism widened by the Crusades. 439

and to assume the Cross for the recovery of Palestine. Forgetful of his own former condemnation of the Fourth Crusade, he told the Emperor that the Greek Church had "rent asunder the seamless robe of Christ," and was suffering under the righteous hand of God, who had employed the Latins to punish their iniquity.

To Theodore, John III. (Ducas Vatatces), his son-in-law, succeeded as Emperor (1222—1254); an able and pious Prince, under whom the Greek Empire continued to flourish. Notwithstanding the rebuff administered to Theodore, he, in the hope of recovering his lost dominions, entered into negotiations with Pope Gregory IX. for the re-union of the Greek and Latin Churches. In consequence of a communication which he received from Vatatces through the Patriarch Germanus, the Pope sent to Nice, A.D. 1233, two Dominican and two Franciscan monks to discuss points of agreement. The envoys were received with great honour, and the Emperor assembled a Council at Nymphæum. No sooner had they got to work, than both Greeks and Latins brought forward mutual accusations and invectives. The Latins complained of the Greeks condemning the Latin Azyms; of their purifying their Altars after Latin Celebrations; rebaptizing Latins; and of their erasure of the Pope's name from the Diptychs. The Patriarch met the charges with a counter accusation, viz., the desecration by the Latins of Greek Churches and Altars and vessels after the conquest of Constantinople. The charge of erasing the Pope's name he met with the question, "Why has the Pope erased my name?"

That was not a favourable commencement. But the two chief points of discussion were the Azyms and the double Procession. When the Emperor suggested that the Pope should meet the Greek Church half-way, and a *via media* be adopted, he was met with the stereotyped *non possumus*, and the Latin monks insisted that the Pope could not yield one iota. The Emperor himself overlooked the fact that he would have to reckon with the Greek Church, which has always, both before and afterwards, given a more stringent *non possumus* against the resort to the *via media* than the Latins.

As to the matter of leavened or unleavened bread, the Latin envoys were willing that the Greeks should be left to their own use, so long as they burnt all books which condemned the Latin practice. On the Emperor remarking that that was "no form of peace," nothing further was done and no agreement arrived at; the monks returned home, after a very pleasant visit at Nice, charmed with the hospitality shown them by the Emperor.

Several subsequent attempts at re-union made by Vatatces were all grounded on the condition that the Greek Empire at Constantinople should be re-established, the Latin Patriarchs, except the Patriarch of Antioch, who might continue till his death, be removed, and the Greek Patriarchs restored.

Theodore II (1254—1259), the successor of his father Vatatces, was, after a short reign, succeeded by his son, John IV. (1259—1261), a boy eight years of age, under the tutorship of Arsenius, who had been appointed as a layman to the Patriarchate, and in one week went through the different Orders of the Ministry. The events that follow do not reflect credit on the Greek clergy. "Neither law, honour, nor morality," says Finlay[r], "were then predominant in the Greek mind." Michael Palæologus, an able General, but an unprincipled and ambitious demagogue, soon contrived to gain the Bishops over to his side, and to get himself appointed joint-Emperor, the Patriarch at first refusing, but eventually yielding, and performing the ceremony of coronation.

Nor was the state of the Latin Patriarchate any better. Between Morosini the first and Pantaleon the last Patriarch, four others intervened. After the death of Morosini, two opposing candidates, one of whom was the Metropolitan of Heraclea, presented themselves, and such violent quarrels

[r] III. 335.

occurred amongst the Latins, that Pope Innocent, in the Lateran Council of 1215, put both aside, and, not till the Patriarchate had been vacant four years, appointed Gervasius. On his death, in 1220, another quarrel ensued [s], and Pope Honorius appointed Matthias Bishop of Aquila. The conduct of Matthias was so scandalous as to call down the reproof from Honorius that he made himself a cause of offence to many (*factus est multis offendiculum*). Simeon, the next Patriarch, was appointed by Gregory IX under similar circumstances as those which led to the appointment of Gervasius. The Latin Patriarchate grew weaker and weaker, till Nicolas, the immediate predecessor of Pantaleon, wrote to Pope Gregory IX. that the number of his suffragans had dwindled down from thirty to three, that he himself was brought to the greatest straits, and had not enough to live upon [t]. During the Episcopate of Pantaleon, Alexander IV. was Pope (1254—1261); but it was the time when Italy was distracted with the dissensions of the Guelphs and Ghibillines, and the Pope was too much occupied in his own conflicts with the Hohenstaufens to interfere.

[s] "Clerus Constantinopolitanus consentire non potuit"—Le Quien, I. 801
[t] "Nec sibi remansit unde valeat sustentari."—Ibid., III. 800—807.

CHAPTER XIII.

Intrigues of the Palæologi with Rome, and Fall of Constantinople.

END of the Latin Empire of Constantinople—Michael Palæologus, Emperor—Restoration of the Orthodox Church—Michael's submission to Pope Urban IV.—Battle of Benevento—Creed of Clement IV.—Second Council of Lyons—Great indignation at Constantinople—Four Patriarchs of Constantinople at one time—The Sicilian Vespers—The Pope excommunicates Michael—Andronicus II, Emperor—Eight Patriarchs during the reign—Rise of the Ottoman Turks—The Knights Hospitallers gain possession of Rhodes—Suppression of the Templars—Fall of the Seven Churches of Asia—Andronicus II. deposed by his grandson, Andronicus III —Othman succeeded by Orkhan—The tribute of Christian children—Barlaam and the Pope—The Hesychasts—John V., Emperor—The Emir does homage to the Pope—The battle of Kossova—Manuel II, Emperor—Battle of Nicopolis—Battle of Angora—The Council of Pisa—Of Constance—Communion in both Kinds forbidden—Council of Basle—Of Ferrara—Of Florence—John VI in fear of the Sultan Murad submits to the Pope—The Eastern Patriarchs threaten to excommunicate the Emperor—Battle of Varna—Constantine XI., Emperor—Mahomet II., Sultan—Constantine subscribes the Florentine Union—The Greek Clergy generally and the laity repudiate it—Constantinople taken by the Turks—Noble endeavour of Pope Pius II to promote a Crusade—His death at Ancona—Mahomet favours the Orthodox Church—Effect of the conquest on the Greek Church—Pius II's Letter to Mahomet—Further conquests of Mahomet II—Mahomet succeeded by Bajazet II —Selim, Sultan—He captures Rhodes—Knights Hospitallers fly to Malta—Battle of Lepanto.

MICHAEL PALÆOLOGUS, having defeated the allied armies of the Emperor, Baldwin II., expelled the Latins, and twenty days afterwards, on August 14, 1261, entered Constantinople in triumph, where, in the Cathedral of St. Sophia, the ceremony of his coronation was repeated by the Patriarch Arsenius. Thus the Latin Empire of Romania came to an end, and the Roman Empire, weakened and crippled by the Crusades, was re-established at Constantinople. But nothing short of being sole Emperor would satisfy Michael; he soon threw off the mask, and, having on Christmas Day, 1261, put out the eyes of the boy-Emperor, John IV., he cast him into a dungeon, where he pined away thirty years of his miserable life. Thus was founded the last and most ignoble dynasty of the Roman Empire in the East. The family of the Palæologi, with the exception of the last and only noble one of the dynasty, caring for little beyond their own interests and nothing for their subjects, continued to reign till Constantinople was, A.D. 1453, captured by the Ottoman Turks. This period is known as that of the Greek, in distinction to that of the Byzantine, Empire, of which it was a feeble imitation, shrunk to the narrowest limits, and marked by a general decay; whilst the Emperors who ruled over it were men fitted to destroy rather than support an exhausted Empire. The Empire of Trebizond still continued its independence; but the Empire of the Palæologi boasted the proud title of Roman; and they styled themselves Emperors of the Romans.

The closing years of the Eastern Empire were overclouded with internal dissensions, with the advance of the Ottomans, and the servile submission of the Emperors to the Popes, in which last respect they found themselves in opposition to the Greek Church. The friendly or hostile attitude of the Palæologi towards the Popes was determined by the measure of their prosperity or adversity. When threatened by domestic or foreign enemies they looked to the West for help, which could only be obtained through the profession of obedience to the Popes; when the danger was averted, and they found themselves in collision with their Orthodox subjects, who refused to accept Western help at the expense of their Church, they were as eager to reject, as they had before been to seek, the alliance. It was the case of the sick man who repents in illness and on recovery shakes off his repentance.

The Orthodox Church was now again restored, and its ascendency was characterized by even more than its former hatred of the Latins. But it had degenerated and lost its influence. It was eminently conservative and Orthodox; well skilled in ecclesiastical formulas and religious doctrines; enthusiastic in defence of the Church against the Popes, and, when its orthodoxy was endangered, against the Emperors, to whom, however, when anything else was involved, it yielded a blind subservience. So long as it was allowed to preserve its orthodoxy intact, it concerned itself but little with the mal-administration of the civil government, with the evils of which the clergy became frequently tainted; whilst avarice and simony were rife amongst them. The clergy themselves were often blind leaders of the blind, torpid, and exerting no influence in averting the calamities which were too surely coming upon the Empire and the Church.

For his last crime, of intentional murder, although most of the Prelates were desirous of screening him, the Emperor Michael was interdicted from Communion by the Patriarch Arsenius. For a time Michael, finding it to his interest to stand well with the Orthodox Church, submitted to the censure; but when Arsenius refused to remove it, he was banished to Pioconnesus, and a Synod convened by the Emperor excommunicated the Patriarch. After the Patriarchate had been vacant a year, Michael, in June, 1266, appointed Germanus, Metropolitan of Adrianople, who reluctantly accepted the appointment, his acceptance being generally condemned on the ground that he was translated from another Diocese. So strong was the opposition, that, in December of the same year, Germanus resigned, Joseph, the Emperor's Confessor, being intruded into the Patriarchate. But a long-standing schism between the followers of Arsenius and Joseph was effected in the Orthodox Church.

Meanwhile, Michael, being a usurper and, at any rate in will, a murderer, apprehensive of the vengeance of his subjects, and smarting under the excommunication of the rightful Patriarch, found it expedient to have the Pope as his ally. Urban IV. (1261—1264), a Frenchman by birth, who was at the time Pope, had been Patriarch of Jerusalem under the Latin Empire. The circumstance that he had been a schismatic, Michael, in the correspondence on which he entered in 1262, overlooked. Urban wrote to him, rejoicing that God had put it into the heart of so great a Prince (he does not recognize him as the Emperor), to bring back the Greek Church to the Church of Rome, the daughter to the mother, the member to the head ; but he passed unnoticed the crime for which his own Patriarch had excommunicated him.

The Emperor despatched two monks to Rome with strong professions of obedience, but pointing out the great evils that had resulted to Christendom through the Latin Empire. Urban answered that all the evils which beset the Eastern Church were owing to its disobedience to Rome, and that, if Michael would return to the bosom of the Roman Church, he would afford him the support which he sorely needed to keep him on his throne. The Pope sent to Constantinople two Franciscan monks to arrange terms of union, and to absolve all the Greeks who were willing to return to Roman allegiance. Again he made no mention of Michael's crime. The Emperor replied that he had already been fully instructed in the Latin faith by the Bishop of Cortona, that he found it in all respects in harmony with that of the Greek Church, and that he would take all means in his power to bring the Greek Church into the obedience of the Pope.

Urban IV. was succeeded by another Frenchman, Clement IV. (1265—1268). The Popes, as we have already seen, were the hereditary enemies of the Hohenstaufen Emperors of Germany. The great Emperor, Frederic II, had died excommunicated by Pope Innocent IV. ; but so far from the enmity of the Popes to the Hohenstaufens ceasing with his death, they would be contented with nothing short of the extermination of the whole family Frederic had been not only Emperor of Germany, but King of Sicily. Urban took upon himself to confer that kingdom, much against the will of his brother Louis IX., King of France, on Charles of Anjou, proclaimed a Crusade against

Frederic's son Manfred, who had since A D. 1258 been King of Sicily; and in January, 1256, Charles was crowned King at Rome. In February of the same year he defeated and slew Manfred in the battle of Benevento.

The Latin Empire of Constantinople had, before its final fall, been brought to the direst straits through the levity and extravagance of the Emperors. Baldwin II., the last Latin Emperor, had married Charles of Anjou's daughter. To such a miserable plight had Baldwin been reduced, that, after begging succour from the Courts of Europe, he was even driven to demolishing houses in Constantinople for winter fuel, and tearing off the copper roof of his palace to sell to the Venetians, with whom he left his son in pawn. After he was driven from Constantinople by Michael Palæologus, he, together with the ex-Patriarch Pantaleon, sought an asylum in Rome. In Baldwin's marriage with the daughter of Charles of Anjou, combined with the Papal hatred of the Hohenstaufens, lay the key of the arrangements between the Popes and the Emperor Michael.

After the battle of Benevento, Charles signed, in the Pope's private apartments in that city, a treaty with his son-in-law Baldwin, by which he engaged himself to assist him in the recovery of the Eastern dominions. The young Conradin, grandson of the Emperor Frederic, having entered Naples, with the view to recovering his lawful dominions, was met by the excommunication of the Pope; and, being defeated in battle and made prisoner by Charles, he, the last of the Hohenstaufens, was, on August 23, 1268, miserably executed on the scaffold, if not by the suggestion, at any rate with the connivance of, the Pope.

Michael, owing to Baldwin's alliance, and the success of Charles in the battle of Benevento, stood more than ever in need of the Pope's assistance, and his attention was turned from the schism which was still going on at Constantinople about Arsenius, to Charles of Anjou. The battle of Benevento decided the action of the Pope in his dealings with Michael; and Charles of Anjou, the favourite of the French Popes, pulled the strings, by which the puppet Emperor of the East was made to obey their behests.

Clement IV. well understood the position of Michael, and seeing that he was ready to subscribe anything which he demanded, seized the opportunity of imposing the very hardest conditions. Clement, " in virtue of the supreme primacy and authority enjoyed by the Popes of Rome over the whole Catholic Church . . . ., together with the fulness of power derived from Christ Himself by blessed Peter, whose successor the Roman Pontiff is," thought to impose on the Eastern Church a new Creed, based on no Councils, but simply by his own authority, not only with regard to the double Procession, but Penance, Purgatory, the Azyms, and Matrimony. The Greek Church never thought of entertaining such interference on the part of the Pope, still, to the end of the Pontificate of Clement, the Emperor continued the negotiations.

After the death of Clement on November 29, 1268, when the Papacy had been, owing to the dissensions of the Cardinals, vacant for three years, Theobald, Archdeacon of Liége, was summoned from Acre, whither he had gone on the Crusade, to fill the Papal throne, and became Pope under the title of Gregory X. (1271—1275). He left the East with the pious ejaculation of the Psalmist, " If I forget thee, O Jerusalem, let my right hand forget her cunning."

The new Pope, a man of gentler character than his predecessors, having been an eye-witness of the calamities of the Christians in the East, desired to promote a peaceful Crusade as the means of reconciling the Eastern and Western Churches. Michael tried, by renewed promises of obedience, to detach the new Pope from Charles of Anjou. Gregory, understanding the advantage of having the assistance of the Greek Emperor in his projected Crusade, promised to persuade Charles to abandon his attack on the Eastern Empire; but at the same time he insisted upon Michael's accepting the Creed of his predecessor, and holding at Constantinople a Council to promote the union of the Churches.

The Council was accordingly held, the Emperor, in order to enforce the articles of union, resorting to severe persecution; but rather than commit such an act of apostasy many families emigrated to Thessaly and Trebizond; and two of the stoutest opponents to the union were the Patriarch Joseph, whom Michael himself had nominated, and Veccus, the Keeper of the Records, the latter of whom was consequently imprisoned.

In May, 1274, the Pope convened the Second Council of Lyons, one of the objects being to effect the union of the Churches. On June 24 the Greek envoys, consisting of the ex-Patriarch Germanus, some nobles and a few Greek Bishops and clergy, arrived. The Emperor requested that the Greek Church should have the liberty of using the Nicene Creed in the form in which it had existed before the schism of the Churches, and their other rites "qui non sunt extra supradictam fidem," i.e. the Creed of Clement. Gregory appears to have taken no notice of the request, and the First Canon of the Council enacted, "We profess that the Holy Spirit proceeds eternally from the Father and the Son; this is the teaching of the Holy Roman Church, the mother and mistress of all the faithful, and is the true and unchangeable teaching of Latin and Greek alike." At the Council the Imperial envoys conceded everything, the Latin doctrines and usages, and the primacy of the Pope. The Pope celebrated Mass, and after the Nicene Creed, with the addition of the Filioque, had been sung in Latin by the Latins, it was repeated in Greek by the Greeks.

On the return of the envoys, the greatest indignation was manifested at Constantinople. But in the meantime, Veccus, whilst in prison, had, under strong pressure, been induced to acknowledge the Papal claims. The Patriarch Joseph was now deposed by the Emperor, and Veccus intruded into the Patriarchate, and in the public services the Pope was declared to be "supreme Pontiff of the Apostolic Church and œcumenical Pope."

So that there were now four Patriarchs of Constantinople,

the canonical Patriarch Arsenius, and the three intruded Patriarchs, Germanus, Joseph and Veccus, the last of whom, though Michael visited his opponents with imprisonment and many acts of fearful cruelty, had only a few adherents.

By a series of intrigues, Michael had gained all he sought, and by his submission to the Popes a foreign war, at the cost of troubles at home, by which his throne was constantly endangered, was averted.

As to the Procession of the Holy Ghost, even Michael would not give way; and Veccus was fully convinced no Greeks would allow any tampering with the Creed. At this time there was a rapid succession in the Papacy. Innocent V., the successor of Gregory, was Pope for only five months; his successor, Hadrian V., for less than a month; John XXI. for eight months; and Nicolas III. from 1277—1280 In vain they all insisted that in the matter of the Creed no difference should be allowed; but that all must follow the Roman practice Nicolas refused to allow Charles of Anjou to attack the Greek Empire, and sent four nuncios to Constantinople to complete the Union. But before the nuncios arrived a quarrel between the Emperor and Veccus had taken place, the latter advocating the double Procession of the Holy Ghost, whilst the Emperor with difficulty prevented the Greek clergy from rising in open rebellion.

The next Pope, Simon de Brie, who succeeded as Martin IV. (1281—1285), was a Frenchman, and did all in his power to promote the cause of Charles of Anjou, and of the French, in Sicily. On March 30th, 1282, occurred the massacre known as the Sicilian Vespers; in which the French throughout the length and breadth of Sicily were indiscriminately slaughtered, till it was supposed not one Frenchman in the whole country was left alive. Thus came to an end the hated dynasty of the House of Anjou in Sicily. So long as the sword of Charles of Anjou hung suspended over his head, Michael was ready to forfeit the affection of his subjects, in order to gain the help of the Pope; after the Sicilian Vespers he began to breathe the air of freedom. Martin now saw that the whole transaction had been throughout a mere political movement, and that the Popes had been hoodwinked by the Emperor. His first act was to excommunicate Michael, "the favourer of heresies and schismatics;" Michael avenging himself by ordering the Pope's name to be omitted in the public services. Thus ended this attempt to bring the Greek Church under the supremacy of the Pope. The Union of the Churches in a Latin Council; the acceptance by a few Greeks of the Latin Creed, and the Pope's supremacy, under pressure put upon them to meet the political exigencies of an unscrupulous usurper, was speedily ignored, and the attachment of the Greeks to their Orthodox Church never wavered.

Michael died on December 11 of the year of the Sicilian Vespers, and was succeeded by his son, Andronicus II. (1282—1328), the Elder. To the perfidy and cruelty of his father the character of the son added cowardice and superstition. Andronicus, like so many Emperors before him, unduly interested himself in ecclesiastical matters; so that no Bishops could succeed in working with him, and were in consequence being always deposed. Finding it to his interest to support the Orthodox Church, though he had himself written to the Pope professing his acquiescence in the Latin union, he at once set himself to neutralize the effects of his father's double-dealing. So strong was the feeling in Constantinople against his father's memory that he allowed his funeral to be conducted without the customary honours, and forced his mother to abjure the union. The intruded Patriarch Veccus being deposed and committed to prison, where he spent the last fourteen years of his life, and Arsenius, the rightful Patriarch, having died in 1274, Joseph was now restored to the Patriarchate Laymen who had favoured the Union were by a Synod in Constantinople subjected to penance, Bishops and clergy to suspension, and on January 2, 1283, the Cathedral of St. Sophia, in which the objectionable words in the Creed had been recited, underwent purification, and a solemn recantation was effected.

On the death, in the same year, of the Patriarch Joseph, Gregory II., who, a native of Cyprus and born of Latin parents, had supported the Union, but on the deposition of Veccus joined the Orthodox Church, was appointed to succeed him. The Arsenian schism was now continued under the leadership of Andronicus, Archbishop of Sardis and Confessor to the Emperor, who aimed at succeeding Gregory in the Patriarchate. Andronicus, who was a Unionist, was, on an accusation of political intrigue, deposed from his See. In 1289 the Patriarch Gregory was also, on a charge of heresy in regard to the double Procession, deposed, Athanasius I., a hermit of rigid principles, being appointed his successor. But the reforms which he introduced were of too rigid a character for the times, and offended both the Bishops and monks, the former of whom he ordered to return to their Dioceses, and the latter to their monasteries. Nor was his reforming spirit more to the taste of the Court and nobles[a]; to them the weak Emperor now yielded, and the Patriarch was, after four years, forced to resign. John XII., an Archimandrite, was next appointed (1294—1304), but finding a refractory spirit existing amongst the Bishops, he went back to his monastery; and when afterwards he was desirous of resuming the Patriarchate, a sentence of deposition was passed against him. Athanasius was then restored; but his reforming tendencies rendered him more hateful than ever to the Bishops, and, after eight years, he yielded to circumstances and resigned the Patriarchate.

Niphon I., Metropolitan of Cyzicus, was the next Patriarch (1313—1314), and under him the long Arsenian schism came to an end. Niphon, siding with the Emperor and the Arsenians, caused the bones of Arsenius to be translated to

"Quum sese rebus temporalibus vehementius unimisceret, civibus quoque invisus factus."—Le Quien, I. 290

the Cathedral of St. Sophia, and ordered the suspension of the clergy who had taken part against him. Niphon being after one year deposed for simony and sacrilege, John Glykys, under the title of John XIII., was the next Patriarch (1316—1320). He being a man of infirm health, "ordered by his physician to eat meat," resigned on the ground of his infirmities.

Gerasimus, "a deaf and ignorant old monk [b]," altogether under the thumb of the Emperor, was Patriarch for only one year (1320—1321). At this time commenced the disputes which continued, with interruptions, to the end of the reign, between Andronicus the Elder and his grandson, Andronicus the Younger; in consequence of which the Patriarchate was, on the death of Gerasimus, kept vacant for more than two and a half years, after which a disreputable old monk of Mount Athos, named Isaiah (1323—1333), whom the Emperor expected to find as docile as Gerasimus, was appointed. Isaiah, the last of the eight Patriarchs of Constantinople in the reign of the Elder Andronicus, not proving his pliant tool in the civil war with his nephew, was deposed and consigned to a monastery.

In the reign of Andronicus the Elder, the Ottoman Turks first enter the page of Ecclesiastical history. In the early years of the Fourteenth Century the dynasty of the Seljuk Turks came to an end, and the Ottomans took their place. They derive their name from their leader Osman or Othman, a soldier of fortune in the service of the last of the Seljuks. Inheriting some small power from his father Ertogrul, who held office in the Seljuk family; inheriting also from him his Mahometan fanaticism, Othman, at first little more than a shepherd and a free-booter, and then leader of a nomad horde, crossing, A.D. 1299, the Greek frontier, invaded Nicomedia and the Asiatic possessions of the Empire. On the death, in 1307, of Aladdin, the last

---

[b] "Vir simplex, literarum nescius, surdaster, ad imperatoris obsequia plus quam idoneus."—Le Quien, I. 296.

and Fall of Constantinople. 453

Sultan of the Seljuk line, Othman became sovereign, under the title of Emir, of a new dynasty of Turks.

The servitude of Rhodes was, says Gibbon, delayed about two centuries by the establishment of the Knights Hospitallers, or the Knights of St John of Jerusalem[c]. After the fall of Acre they migrated first to Cyprus, but despairing of rendering any effectual aid to Jerusalem against the growing power of the Ottomans, they obtained from Pope Clement V. permission to turn their arms against the Greeks. The Pope praised their Christian zeal, and the Knights, under pretext of a Crusade, collected a force, with which, in 1310, they defeated the troops of Andronicus and gained possession of Rhodes, where they set up an independent kingdom, which was long the bulwark of Christian Europe against the Ottoman power[d]. The Templars were less fortunate. Their wealth excited the covetousness of Philip the Fair, King of France. Inveigled by him into France, after being subjected to fearful privations and cruelties, they were suppressed in the Council of Vienne, A.D. 1312, by Pope Clement V., a Frenchman, who presided as a mere tool in the hands of the French King.

About A.D. 1312, the fall of six out of *the Seven Churches of Asia* was effected under two of Othman's chieftains, Sarukham and Aidin. The elder Andronicus could not well avail himself of the usual resort of the Palæologi in their difficulties, the Pope of Rome; "in his last distress pride was his safeguard; he could not in his old age, with any decency, retract the orthodox profession of his youth[e]." So no help was forthcoming from the West. Of the seven Churches addressed by St. John from Patmos, two only, Smyrna and Philadelphia, were spoken of without blame; to them, alone, promises were made without threat or warnings. Of those two, the *candlestick* has not been removed; they alone of the seven Churches remain in the present day, erect amidst the surrounding ruins. The most flourishing is Smyrna, containing the tomb of St. Polycarp,

[e] XI. 438.   [d] Finlay, III. 409.   [c] Gibbon, XII. 66.

and the See of a Metropolitan. Philadelphia, called by the Turks Ali-Shahir (*the fair city*), still retains the form of a city, and, being the road traversed by the Persian caravans, enjoys a considerable trade. It is inhabited by many Greeks, and, wrote Sir Paul Ricaut, contained twelve Churches, of which the principal was that of St. Mary; although, alas! the Church dedicated to St. John has been converted into a dunghill [f].

But of all the others the *candlestick* has been removed, and most of them are a mere heap of ruins. Ephesus, once the seat of a Metropolitan and ranking next to the Patriarchates, is said by travellers not to contain one Christian family; the stately building of St John's Church has been converted into a Mosque, and, says Gibbon, the Temple of Diana and the Church of Mary (meaning thereby the Blessed Mother of our Lord), alike elude the search of travellers.

Laodicea, once the mother of sixteen Bishoprics, so overwhelmed by earthquakes that scarcely one stone remains upon another, its very name forgotten, not so much as inhabited by shepherds, is the abode of wolves and foxes.

Sardis, once the seat of the wealthy Crœsus, though ancient pillars and ruins still rear their heads, is a miserable village, inhabited only by shepherds, living in their low and humble cottages.

Pergamus, seated on a lofty hill overlooking a fruitful valley watered by the Caicus, is described as possessing a soil so fertile, that, if cultivated, it might prove one of the most fruitful gardens of the world. But Mahometanism rules without a rival, and the inhabitants, abhorring all kinds of labour, prefer to gain their livelihood by robbery and violence.

Of Thyatira, the very site is a matter of conjecture, and in the Mosques, in the place which is supposed to represent it, the god of Mahomet is invoked without a rival [g].

---

[f] Ricaut's Present State of the Greek Church.
[g] Palmer's Dissertations on the Orthodox Communion.

Alone of the Seven, Philadelphia survived for a time the fall, under Othman's Generals, of its sister Churches, and for some years longer maintained its independence of the Turks as the last Christian stronghold in Asia, but it, too, eventually fell under the arms of the Emir, Murad I., or, as some think, of his son, the Sultan Bajazet.

The quarrels and civil war between the Elder and Younger Andronicus were especially unfortunate, as occurring at a time when the Eastern Empire was going to ruin, and when a united Empire, against the attacks of the Turks and other enemies, was most required They ended in the capture of Constantinople in 1328, the deposition of Andronicus II., and the proclamation by the soldiers, as sole Emperor, of Andronicus III. (1328—1341). Isaac was then restored to the Patriarchate, which he held till his death, A.D 1333.

There were few to regret the fall of the Elder Andronicus, who, in February, 1332, ended, as the monk Antony, his life in a monastery. At the time of his death the Empire was only two-thirds of the size that it had been at his accession [h].

Othman, the Turkish Emir, died A D. 1326, having lived long enough to hear on his death-bed of the fall of Prusa, after a siege of ten years, under the Turkish arms, and was succeeded by his son Orkhan (1326—1360), who threw off the nominal subjection to the Sultan of Cogni, and was the real founder of the Ottoman Empire, with Prusa as its capital. What, more than anything, contributed to the spread of the Ottoman power, was the fiendish institution by Orkhan of the tribute of Christian children. Thus was formed the famous corps of Janissaries, or *new soldiers*. The strongest and most promising boys were, at ages between six and nine years, torn away from their families, cut off from every Christian tie, and educated so as to know no other than the Mahometan faith, to abjure which, afterwards, subjected them to the punishment of renegades, certain death They were trained in the profession of arms to

[h] Story of the Nations, p 320

fight against enemies of the same Christian birth as themselves, and grew up to be the best soldiers in the Turkish armies, from whom their Generals and Governors were selected. So that the conquest of Eastern Christendom was really effected through soldiers born of Christian parents; when in 1687 the tribute of Christian children ceased, the Turkish power declined, but the corps of Janissaries continued till it was abolished by Sultan Mahmoud, A D. 1826. Orkhan, by the capture of Nicomedia in 1327, and in 1330 of Nice, the seat of the Greek Empire and the cradle of Orthodoxy under the Latin Empire, completed the conquest of Bithynia. Thus the Ottoman power was firmly established in Asia Minor, the Empire of Andronicus III. being limited to little beyond the walls of Constantinople on the European, and Chalcedon on the Asiatic, shore of the Bosphorus.

In the year of his becoming sole Emperor, Andronicus III. took a second wife, Anne, sister of the Duke of Savoy ; and, as his marriage with a Roman Catholic inclined him favourably to her Communion, he had not the same restraints as his grandfather from applying to the Pope for help. In 1309 had commenced the period which is known as the Babylonish captivity of the Roman Church, during which the Popes sat, not at Rome, but at Avignon. From the time of Michael Palæologus to the death of Andronicus II., there had been little intercourse between the Eastern and Western Churches. In 1333 Andronicus III., actuated by fear of the advancing Turks, sent, through two Dominican monks who were returning from the East, a message to Avignon to seek assistance from Pope John XXII. (1316— 1334). The Pope despatched two Bishops to Constantinople to remind the Emperor of the great evils which, since the schism, had befallen the Greeks, and of the great advantages which would accrue to them if they returned to union, acknowledged the primacy of the Pope, and the faith of the Roman Church. But the Greeks would have nothing to do with them. They were fully convinced of the rightfulness of their own Church, remembered the Creed of Clement IV., and how the Popes had served the Emperor Michael. They may also well have imagined that, if the Popes could do so little for them whilst they were in Rome, they could do still less now they were at Avignon. So the negotiations came to nothing, the wily Greeks demanding that the Popes should first give the assistance asked, as some proof of the advantage to be derived from a Roman alliance.

In 1337, Pope Benedict XII. (1334—1342) re-opened with Andronicus the matter of the proposed re-union. In 1339, Barlaam, a monk of the monastery of St. Saviour at Constantinople, who, though born and educated in Calabria in the Latin Church, was a strong opponent of Romanism, was sent by Andronicus to Avignon to procure assistance against the Turks, on the condition of re-union, which was to be effected by a General Council to decide the points of dispute between the Eastern and Western Churches. Barlaam told the Pope that the Emperor desired re-union, but that he was obliged to consult his own dignity and the prejudices of the Greeks. The Greek Church, he said, reverenced the General Councils, but reprobated the arbitrary decrees of the Council of Lyons. The Empire, he told him, was endangered by the Turks, and required assistance. He proposed that a Latin legate should be sent to Constantinople to prepare a universal Council, which the Patriarchs of Constantinople, Alexandria, Antioch, and Jerusalem should be invited to attend. The Turks, he said, were the common enemies of the Christian name. The Greeks had been alienated by a long series of oppression and wrong; and, even if certain differences of faith or ceremonies were unalterable, needed to be reconciled by some act of brotherly love, and some effectual succour; and the legate must be accompanied, or preceded, by an army of Franks to expel the infidels, and open the way to the Holy Sepulchre.

The Pope objected to a Council on the ground that the

Procession of the Holy Ghost had been decided by holy Fathers, and the great Councils, which a Pope could not call in question. When Barlaam asked whether the Greek Church might not be left at liberty to hold its own belief as to the Procession, he was told that the Pope could listen to no terms but unconditional surrender, for that a two-fold faith was impossible. The Pope returned an offensive answer to "the persons who styled themselves the Patriarchs of the Eastern Churches." This attempt at re-union was as futile as former ones had been, the plain truth being that the Pope, himself an exile at Avignon, had not the means adequate to the occasion.

Shortly before his mission to Avignon, Barlaam had, when on a visit to Mount Athos, come in contact with the Hesychasts (ἡσυχία, *quietness*) or Quietists, a school which had lately sprung up amongst the monks of that famous monastery. They held the strange opinion that the soul had its seat in the umbilical region, by the intent contemplation of which, and after long abstinence, they could discern the Light which appeared at the Transfiguration to the Apostles on Mount Tabor. This notion, which was supported, on the side of the monks, by Gregory Palamas, afterwards Archbishop of Thessalonica, was ridiculed by Barlaam. A controversy between the Palamites and Barlaamites was the consequence, which, after having lasted five years, was decided in a Council at Constantinople, A.D. 1341, in favour of the Hesychasts, and in the establishment of the doctrine of the Uncreated Light of Mount Tabor. Barlaam ended in returning to the Latin Church, and became a Bishop in his native country; and the mystics of Mount Athos were, amidst the troubles of the waning Greek Empire, dispersed.

Andronicus III. was succeeded by his son, John V. (1341—1391), a boy nine years of age, under the guardianship of his mother, Anne of Savoy, John Cantacuzene, who had been Prime Minister under Andronicus, continuing to hold that office. Nothing could more plainly show the degradation to which the Eastern Empire had fallen, than the marriage, in 1346, of Cantacuzene's daughter, Theodora, with Orkhan, the Turkish Emir. Cantacuzene was an aspirant to the throne, to enable him to obtain which, he called in the aid of Orkhan, giving him, as the price of the alliance, his daughter in marriage ; and the marriage, as the means of effecting peace, received the assent of the Byzantine government. In 1347 Cantacuzene was recognized as co-regent in the Empire, if Empire, now extending little beyond the walls of Constantinople, it could be called. In the same month the young Emperor, then fifteen years of age, married Helena, a girl thirteen years of age, another of Cantacuzene's daughters. Thus one Emperor was father-in-law, the other brother-in-law, of the Mahometan Emir. A hollow truce was thus patched up between the two Emperors, and Cantacuzene reigned with John V. for seven years (1347—1354). At this period the Greek Church had fallen into the same state of anarchy as prevailed in the State ; John Cantacuzene, who was a heretic, and the Empress Anne, who was a Roman Catholic, quarrelled with the Orthodox Bishops, and protected the enemies of the Church.

The accession of Cantacuzene did not, as was expected, put an end to the invasions of the Turks, and his own position was insecure. In 1342 Clement VI. (1342—1352) succeeded to the Papacy at Avignon. The new Pope was, unlike his predecessor, in favour of a Council, and also of organizing a Crusade against the Turks. In 1348 Cantacuzene opened negotiations with the Pope, and two Bishops were sent from Avignon for the purpose of effecting a union between the Churches and arranging for a Crusade. Cantacuzene disclaimed the action of Michael Palæologus, declared that the schism between the Churches had been caused by the pride and overbearing conduct of the Latins, and that the Greeks would never be bound by anything short of a free and universal Council. The Pope assented to the proposed plan, there was nothing, he said, that he desired more than the union of the Churches, but the death of the Pope, and the compulsory abdication, two years afterwards, of Cantacuzene, who had throughout his whole career been the evil genius of the Emperor, to end his days as a monk on Mount Athos, put an end to the negotiations.

In A D. 1356 Suleiman, the son of Orkhan, seized Callipolis in the Thracian Chersonese, thus effecting the first permanent settlement of the Ottomans in Europe. In 1358 Suleiman was killed through a fall from his horse, and Orkhan dying, after a reign of more than thirty-three years, in 1360, his son Amurath, or Murad I., succeeded to the Ottoman Emirate.

The next year Murad with his army crossed the Hellespont and occupied Adrianople, which he made the European capital of the Ottoman Empire, and Constantinople itself was now at his mercy. The increasing power and near proximity of Murad so alarmed the Emperor John that, acting on the advice of his Roman mother, Anne of Savoy, he determined to seek the assistance of the Pope, and in October, 1369, visited the Court of Rome in person.

Urban V. (1362—1370) had in the previous year moved back the Papal chair from Avignon to Rome. The Emperor met with a magnificent reception; but his vanity was lost in his distress, and he was profuse in empty sounds and formal submission[1]. On the Sunday following his arrival, whilst the Pope, in the midst of his Cardinals, was seated on his throne in St. Peter's, the Emperor, having previously recited the Creed of Clement IV. and acknowledged the supremacy of the Pope, did homage; and, after High Mass was concluded, held the bridle of the Pope's mule, and was entertained at a sumptuous banquet in the Vatican.

But it was the action of the Emperor alone; and, although the Pope wrote to the Greeks a letter full of the praises of their Emperor, and exhorting them to follow his example they were little likely to be led by a profligate Emperor, whom they had before despised, who had now made himself the vassal of the Pope. His alliance with Rome availed

---

[1] Gibbon, XII. 75.

him little; the assistance which he wanted against the Turks was not forthcoming; and, on his homeward journey, he was at Venice arrested by some money-lenders for a large debt which he had incurred at exorbitant usury. His eldest son, Andronicus, whom he had left regent at Constantinople, but who employed the time in plotting against his father, pretended that he could not raise the money required for his release; but his second son, Manuel, succeeding in doing so, John returned in 1370, covered with disgrace, to Constantinople.

The Emperor John dragged on his long and dishonoured reign till A D 1391. In 1389 the Emir Murad, after having gained the great victory of Kossova over the confederate armies of Bosnia, Servia, Bulgaria, and Wallachia, died, stabbed by the hand of a Servian noble; and was succeeded by his son, Bajazet I. (1389—1402), surnamed, from the rapidity of his movements, Ilderim (*the Thunderbolt*), who exchanged the humbler title of Emir, hitherto borne by the Ottoman Princes, for that of Sultan.

John, having disinherited his eldest son, Andronicus, whom he had before blinded on a charge of conspiracy, was succeeded by his son, Manuel II. (1391—1425). The period between A D 1378—1417 was that of the great Schism in the Roman Church, when there were two Popes, one residing at Rome, the other at Avignon; no one knowing which was the rightful Pope; each anathematizing the followers of the other; so that the whole of Western Christendom was under the ban of one Pope or the other. At such a time the Popes were generally too much engaged in their own dissensions to divert their attention to the affairs of the Eastern Church.

The victory of Kossova left Bajazet a free hand, and the capture of Constantinople appeared imminent. Elated with the victory, he threatened to invade Germany and Italy, to stable his horses in St. Peter's at Rome, and to feed them on its Altar. In A.D. 1394, Pope Boniface IX. (1389—1404), notwithstanding the schism in the Roman Church, proclaimed a Crusade against the Turks. He complained in his Bull of the massacres and slavery inflicted by the Ottomans on the Eastern Christians, and that the jealousies and wars of the Western Princes prevented them from making common cause against the infidels. Germany and France responded to his call, but with an unfortunate result. In the fatal battle of Nicopolis in September, 1396, the Christians, led by Sigismund, King of Hungary, suffered, at the hands of Bajazet and the Christian tributaries whom he forced to fight under his banner, a disastrous defeat, and by far the greater part of the army was either slain in battle, or drowned in the waters of the Danube.

In A D. 1400 the Emperor Manuel started on a visit to the principal nations of Europe, under the hope of obtaining assistance against the Turks. Amongst other countries he visited England, where he received a small gift of money from King Henry IV ; but his visit to Europe met with no further success. The Papacy was still distracted by the great Schism, so that, not knowing which was the rightful Pope, and which to apply to, he applied to neither. His visit to Italy coincided with the institution of the Jubilee, A.D. 1400, at Rome by Benedict III.; the Pope was offended at the Emperor's neglect, accused him of irreverence to an Icon, and exhorted the Princes of Italy to reject and abandon the obstinate schismatic.

Now that the Turks were threatening, not only Constantinople, but Rome itself, and an Eastern Emperor could pass through Italy without even visiting the Papal city, the Pope must have lamented the unwise part taken by his predecessors, in depressing the Orthodox Greek Church and the Eastern Empire. He must have felt that but for the Fourth Crusade, and the weakening by the Latin Empire of the Eastern Empire of Constantinople, the Turks would have been driven away from Europe. We no longer hear him speaking of the merited retribution of the Greeks, but of the Turks, as the common enemies of all who bore the Name of Christ.

At the moment when the fall of Constantinople seemed to be imminent, and that of Western Christendom likely to follow; when the Emperor Manuel had entered into a treaty with Bajazet, allowing him to erect a Mosque in Constantinople; an unexpected event favoured the Greeks, and the remnant of the Eastern Empire received an unexpected reprieve. In A D. 1400, Bajazet suffered, on the plains of Angora in Asia Minor, a disastrous defeat at the hands of Timour, or Tamerlane (a Prince of the same Mogul race as Ghengis Khan), like himself a Mahometan, who had in 1369, after a series of victories, seated himself upon the throne of Samarcand; and Bajazet himself was taken prisoner. No such blow, ever before or afterwards, fell on any Ottoman Prince. The Ottoman power, almost annihilated at Angora, was as unequal as Manuel to continue the contest; and the Fall of Constantinople was delayed for fifty years. It appeared at the time that the Ottoman power had received a blow from which it could never recover. That would have been the time for a Crusade, had the Princes of the West, who were distracted by their own quarrels, and by the great schism of the Roman Church, and dispirited by the defeat of Nicopolis, been able to coalesce, Christendom might for ever have been delivered from the tyranny of the Ottomans That the Ottoman power ever recovered from the utter destruction of the field of Angora is, says Professor Freeman, without a parallel in Eastern history[1].

Timour, the terror of the whole world, Christians, Mahometans (except those of his own Shiah sect), and heathens, died A.D. 1405, his victorious career cut short before time was left him to invade Europe.

Bajazet dying in captivity, his sons fought for the remains of his Empire, which, in ten years, was again united under the youngest of the family, Mahomet I. His power was, however, still too weak for him to think of further conquests, and he lived on amiable terms with the Eastern

[1] Freeman's Conquests of the Saracens, p 181

Emperor, dying, A.D. 1421, at the age of thirty-two, to be succeeded by his son Murad II. (1421—1451).

The Western Councils which were held in the first half of the Fifteenth Century, although convened for the purpose of healing the schism which still continued in the Church of Rome, materially affected the Eastern Church. The summoning, by the Roman Cardinals, of the Council of Pisa, A.D 1409, was a recognition of the fact, that Patriarchs and Popes were subordinate to the Councils of the Church. It was attended by the Patriarchs of Alexandria, Antioch, and Jerusalem, as well as by twenty-six Roman Cardinals, twelve Archbishops, and one hundred and eighty Bishops, either in person or by proxy ; the sentence of the Council, by which both the reigning Popes were deposed as notorious schismatics and heretics, being pronounced by the Patriarch of Alexandria [k].

The Council of Constance (1414—1418), attended by representatives of all the Western kingdoms ; by twenty-six Princes and one hundred and fifty Counts ; by five Patriarchs, twenty-four Cardinals, ninety-one Bishops, and six hundred Abbots and Doctors ; having deposed the Pope, John XXIII., as a heretic and simoniac, a fortnight afterwards passed the decree forbidding Communion in both Kinds. The decree was passed when there was a papal interregnum, John XXIII having been deposed on May 29, 1415, and his successor, Martin V., not appointed till November 21, 1417.

The forty years' schism in the Roman Church was healed through the election by the Council of Pope Martin (1417—1431). It declared, in two Sessions, that a General Council lawfully assembled (*legitimè congregata*) "in the Holy Spirit," and representing the Catholic Church, derives its power directly from Christ, and that to it every one, of whatever rank or dignity, even the Pope (*etiam si papalis existat*), owes obedience, and that he, unless he comes to his senses (*nisi resipuerit*), is subject to punishment.

[k] Milman's Latin Christianity, V. 458.

In 1422 Pope Martin sent envoys to the Emperor Manuel to point out to him what a great advantage the disunion of Christendom was to the Turks, and how much more ready the Latins would be to help the Greeks, if the Eastern and Western Churches were united. The Emperor did not view the matter in the same light as the Pope. He advised his son, John Palæologus, to play off the Turks against the Pope, and the Pope against the Turks; that he might threaten the Turks with the re-union of East and West; that he might even assent to the principle of a Council; but that the actual assembling of one would be undesirable for the Greeks. Neither Latins nor Greeks, he told him, would recede from their position; the former were too proud, the latter stubborn; an attempt at re-union, whilst it would only confirm the schism, would leave the Greeks more hopeless for the future, and more than ever at the mercy of the barbarians.

On the day fixed for the audience of the Pope's legates, October 3, 1422, Manuel was seized with the paralysis from which he never recovered. His son John, it would appear, had himself already sent envoys to Rome on the subject of re-union He now gave the Pope's messengers an interview, with the result that the latter, on October 23, laid before the Patriarch, and a large assemblage of Greeks and Latins, the Pope's Encyclical It stated how the Pope had heard that the Greeks spoke of the Latins as dogs, and how serious danger threatened the former of becoming the slaves of the Turks. Envoys from the East, it said, had assured the Pope of an honest desire on the part both of Emperor and Patriarch of re-union; of their willingness to embrace the faith and obey the Church of Rome; and of their wish for a General Council. He himself (the Pope) advocated a Council, to which he promised to send his legates, not to dispute about the faith, but that Greeks and Latins might confer together with the view to an agreement; and as soon as that was arrived at, the Greeks might rely on Western assistance. To this John replied that his envoys had gone beyond their instructions, but that he was ready to abide by the decisions of a General Council, assembled on the principle of the Seven General Councils, by means of which the union might be effected; and a suitable place of meeting would be Constantinople. Constantinople was objectionable to the Pope, and no envoys were sent thither.

The Emperor Manuel, three years afterwards, ended his life in a monastery, and was succeeded by his son, John VI. (1425—1448)[1], who acted against his father's advice. The reduced extent and revenues of the Eastern Empire, the diminution of its population in contrast with the rapid increase of the Turks, the threatening aspect of the Sultan Murad, and the inadequate defences of the capital, convinced the temporizing Emperor that, without aid from the West, there was little prospect of his being able to defend his position, and that his only hope lay in acknowledging, at any price, the Pope's supremacy.

After a Council at Pavia, A D. 1423, and another, in the following year, at Siena, at neither of which anything of importance was effected, Pope Martin V. summoned a Council to meet, A.D. 1431, at Basle, and nominated Cardinal Julian Cæsarini as his legate; but in February of that year, before the Council met, Martin died.

He was succeeded in March by the Cardinal Bishop of Siena, who took the title of Eugenius IV. (1431—1439). The Council of Basle, one of the objects of which was the re-union of East and West, held its first Session on December 14 of the year of the Pope's election, and continued its Sessions from 1431—1443. But as Pope Eugenius feared that the same opposition to the Papacy, which had prevailed at Constance, would be renewed at Basle, he from the first did all in his power to discredit the Council, and issued a Bull for its transference to Bologna, on the pretext that the Greek Emperor desired that the Council, if not held at Constantinople, should be held in that city, as more easily accessible. The President of the Council, Cardinal

---

[1] Or, if Cantacuzene is reckoned under his name John, John VII.

Julian Cæsarini, made a firm stand against the Pope's suggestion, and expressed his preference for the reform of the Western Church to the re-union of East and West, the old song, as he called it, which had run on for three centuries without any result.

The Basle Fathers, supported by the Emperor Sigismund, continued their sittings, and ordered the Pope to appear before them; in December, 1433, Eugenius signified his tardy approval of the Council by sending to it his deputies. Various decrees passed by the Council were little to the Pope's liking, such as, on June 26th, 1434, the ratification of the decrees of the Council of Constance; on June 9, 1435, the abolition of Annates; on March 25, 1436, of Papal Reservations and Provisions. On July 31, 1437, the Council issued a peremptory order to the Pope to appear in person within sixty days.

Such measures led the Pope to issue a document ordering the transference of the Council to Ferrara. Thereupon the Basle Council, on Oct 1, 1437, pronounced the Pope contumacious, and on October 12 declared his order for the transference of the Council invalid. In January of the following year the Council suspended the Pope. Already, on January 8, the Pope had opened the Council of Ferrara, which the Council of Basle immediately excommunicated, the Pope responding, on February 15, with a counter-sentence of excommunication.

Thus there was again a schism in the Roman Church, and the Councils of Basle and Ferrara were at open war. Both invited the Emperor, John VI., to attend, and offered to pay all expenses of the Greeks; and both sent their vessels to Constantinople to bring off the Emperor. The Emperor, who was ready to bargain with the highest bidder, cared little which Council he attended. The vessels of the Pope won the race, and conveyed away the Emperor, the Patriarch Joseph II., and many Bishops, Archimandrites, and Clergy. An earthquake (an evil omen), just as they were leaving it, shook Constantinople. Visiting Venice on the way, where they were received with much pomp and magnificence, and saw in St. Mark's many trophies which had been taken from Constantinople after the fourth Crusade, the Emperor and the larger part of the envoys arrived at Ferrara, the Patriarch, who was old and travelled more slowly, reaching it later. The Patriarch, who had undertaken at Constantinople to have no dealings, except as his equal, with the Pope, found that not even the Cardinals met him, as they had met the Emperor; and was astonished that the first thing required of him was that he should kiss the Pope's feet[m]. This, however, was going too far; "Did the other Apostles," he asked, "kiss St. Peter's feet?" and he threatened to return home. Still, whilst the Emperor fared sumptuously, and passed his time pleasantly in hunting in the neighbourhood of Ferrara, every kind of indignity was heaped upon the Patriarch, nor was it till after several days that the Pope granted him an audience, which, as neither could speak the language of the other, had to be conducted through an interpreter.

The Emperor appeared before the Council of Ferrara accompanied by the Patriarch Joseph, and Bessarion, Archbishop of Nice in Bithynia, the latter of whom was in favour of the union and took a prominent part in the debates; the Patriarchs of Alexandria, Antioch, and Jerusalem, were represented by their legates, Russia was represented by Isidore, Metropolitan of Kiev.

After the second Session, the Pope was represented by Julian Cæsarini, who had now transferred his allegiance from the Council of Basle to the Pope's Council. We need not enter into the dissensions at the Council between the Latins and Greeks, for in the fifth Session the Pope, on the pretext of the plague having broken out at Ferrara, announced his intention of transferring it to Florence, where a far more important Council was held. The Greeks, especially Mark of Ephesus, objected to the transference,

[m] When this custom originated we have not been able to discover.

which they regarded as a plan for bringing the Council more under the control of the Pope.

At the Council of Florence, in 1439, the chief speakers were, on the part of the Latins, Julian Cæsarini, of the Greeks, Isidore, Bessarion, and Mark of Ephesus. The four principal points of discussion, which had already been raised at Ferrara, were (1) the Procession of the Holy Ghost; (2) the use of leavened and unleavened Bread; (3) the nature of Purgatory; (4) the Pope's supremacy. The doctrine of Purgatory had been fully debated at Ferrara. The Latins contended for a purgatorial fire, the Greeks that Purgatory is a state of gloom and darkness, and exclusion from the Divine Presence. The chief and longest debate was on the Procession of the Holy Ghost; Bessarion contended that the difference between the two Churches was not one of doctrine but of expression; that the Greek ἐκ Πατρὸς δι' Υἱοῦ was essentially the same as the Latin *ex Patre Filioque;* whilst Mark of Ephesus declared all holders of the double Procession to be heretics and schismatics.

The Twenty-fifth and last Session was held on March 24. The Pope and the Emperor were resolved on the Union. The Emperor declared that suffrages belonged only to Bishops and Archimandrites. Very much the same occurred as occurred at the Council of Rimini. The Greek Bishops were intimidated, they had been kept in close confinement, with barely sufficient food to keep them from starvation; their own resources were exhausted, and they saw no hope of their being replenished, so long as they opposed the Pope and Emperor; so at length they all gave way except Mark of Ephesus, who, with the Emperor's brother Demetrius, to avoid witnessing the Union effected, retired to Venice. So important a Bishop was Mark that Eugenius exclaimed, "without him all our labours are lost!" A compromise was effected; each Church was left at liberty to use leavened or unleavened bread; but the Latins got all they desired. The addition of the Filioque clause to the Creed, and the other points were conceded by the Greeks;

the supremacy of the Pope, as successor of St Peter and Vicar of Christ, was acknowledged, some vague reservations of the privileges and rights of the Patriarch of Constantinople being allowed; and the treaty of Union, by which the Pope guaranteed the aid required, was subscribed. The Patriarch Joseph, who had all through supported the Union, died on June 9; whether he signed the decree or not, is uncertain. A solemn service followed in the Duomo, the Te Deum was chanted in Greek; the Mass celebrated in Latin; the Creed sung with the addition of the Filioque; and the Emperor and Greek clergy sailed away to Constantinople.

Meanwhile, on May 25, 1439, the Fathers, assembled in the Council of Basle, deposed the Pope[n], and in November elected in his place Amadeus, Duke of Savoy, who had resigned his crown to assume the cowl of a monk, and now took the title of Pope Felix V. (1439—1449). So that at the time the Union was ratified there was no Pope, for the Pope had been canonically deposed, and the continuation of the Council of Florence, whilst the Council of Basle, canonically summoned by Pope Martin V., was sitting, was a schismatical act. And when it is remembered that the Council of Basle was summoned by a Pope, and that it was attended by Roman Cardinals, no other conclusion can be arrived at, from the scant reverence shown throughout to Pope Eugenius, and his ultimate deposition by the Council, than that it altogether negatives the modern doctrine of Papal Infallibility.

Bessarion went, after the Council, to Rome, and he, together with Isidore, who afterwards followed him thither, were created Cardinals, the former being appointed Bishop of Tusculum. He was afterwards put in competition for the Papacy, and, but for his being a Greek and "wearing a beard," would probably have been elected.

No sooner had the Emperor and Bishops, on their return from Florence, set foot in Constantinople, than the flimsy

---

[n] "Simoniacum, perjurum, pertinacem hæreticum, dilapidatorem jurium et bonorum Ecclesiæ.

fabric of the Union melted into air. The Emperor and all who signed the Union were received with a storm of indignation as traitors, contact with them avoided, and the Churches emptied as soon as they entered them. Mark of Ephesus was the hero of the day. The Emperor, in fear of the Sultan, still hoping for Western help, stood firm, and appointed to the vacant Patriarchate Metrophanes, a Unionist, Metropolitan of Cyzicus. Metrophanes the people branded as Μητροφόνος, the slayer of their mother-Church, and refused to enter St. Sophia's at his Consecration; his Suffragans, treating him as a heretic, would not acknowledge him as Patriarch. The Bishops who had subscribed the Union, several of whom were Latins holding Greek Sees, now joined the popular side against the Emperor, declared that their consent had been extorted by force, and publicly retracted their subscription. Nor was the schism confirmed to the Greeks. The Russian, which at that time comprised the larger part of the Orthodox Church [o], abjured the Union. The three other Eastern Patriarchs, in a Synod at Jerusalem, A.D. 1443, with one voice condemned it [p], and threatened to excommunicate the Emperor and all who adhered to it, denouncing Metrophanes as a heretic, and cancelling his Ordinations. The Emperor's brother, Demetrius, raised the standard of Orthodoxy in rebellion, and claimed the throne; but the Greeks thought one Palæologus as bad as another, and refused to make a change.

Thus ended the last united effort of a Council to heal the schism between the Eastern and Western Churches. In a few years all signs of the Union were obliterated. Its only permanent results were to intensify the hatred of the Greeks against the Latins, and to make them indifferent as to the fate of the expiring Empire, so that it was commonly said that Greeks would prefer to see the

---

Mouraviev, p. 77.
[p] " Sancitum Florentiæ unionem execrabant."—Le Quien, I. 1268.

Crescent of the Turks, rather than the tiara of the Pope, in the Churches of Constantinople.

Nowhere in the West was the supposed re-union of Christendom more thankfully and joyfully received than in England. Letters conveying words of encouragement and welcome were delivered by envoys of King Henry VI. to the Patriarch and the Emperor during the deliberations at Florence; the King, after its consummation, addressed to the Pope a letter expressive of joy and satisfaction; and ordered public thanksgivings, with processions, litanies, and prayers, in all parts of his dominions q.

After the return of the Greeks to Constantinople, the Pope, not unmindful of his engagement to the Emperor, but also having reason to apprehend an invasion of Italy by the Turks, fitted out an expedition to proceed to the East, under Cardinal Julian Cæsarini. The Sultan Murad had lately suffered a defeat from the famous Commander of the Hungarian armies, Hunyades, with whom he signed a Treaty, highly favourable to the Christians, for ten years. By that treaty, Servia, which had after the battle of Kossova fallen to the Turks, recovered its independence, and Wallachia was ceded to the King of Hungary. The Treaty was ratified by the most solemn oaths, by the Christians on the Gospels, by the Mahometans on the Koran. Notwithstanding this, the Cardinal persuaded the Hungarians, and their young King Ladislaus, that they might break their oath; Christ's Vicar on earth, he told them, was the Roman Pontiff, without whose sanction they could neither promise nor perform; and in his name he absolved them from its performance. Gibbon, with reason, says, the Turks might well retort the epithet of infidel upon the Christians r.

A fresh expedition was sanctioned by Cæsarini, and the character of a Crusade (*a holy war!*) imposed upon it the Turks were nearer the truth, when they branded it as

---

q Bekynton's Letters as quoted by Williams, "The Orthodox Church in the East."   r XII. 159

an act of perjury. The young Ladislaus, under whom the Kingdoms of Hungary and Poland were now united, advanced without delay into the Ottoman dominions. The hostile armies met, on November 10, 1444, on the field of Varna; a copy of the treaty, "the monument of Christian perfidy [s]," was displayed by the Turks on the field of battle; the result of which was that ten thousand Christians fell, Cardinal Cæsarini and his victim, the young Ladislaus, being found amongst the slain.

John VI. was, on his death, A D. 1448, succeeded, with the consent of the Sultan Murad (for the acknowledged supremacy of the Sultan preceded the fall of the Eastern Empire), by his brother, Constantine XI., Dragases, (1448—1453), the last and the best of the Palæologi, at the time 54 years of age. Constantine was crowned at Sparta, where he was residing at the time of his brother's death, and refused, from fear of the continued disputes between the Orthodox and the Unionist parties, a second Coronation in St. Sophia's.

The Sultan Murad II. was, after a reign of thirty years, succeeded by his son, Mahomet II. (1451—1481), twenty-one years of age.

The great aim of Mahomet's ambition was the conquest of Constantinople. We are not concerned with his ability as a strategist, but the opposition which he encountered, in the defence of their capital, from the Greeks, would not alone warrant the character of being one of the ablest Generals in ancient or modern times, which is sometimes given him. When the Sultan appeared before the walls of Constantinople, it was at once evident to the Emperor that the half-hearted Greeks, even with the advantage of its almost impregnable fortresses, would be unequal to its defence. He complained that he was surrounded by men whom he could neither love nor trust. The late Emperor in the last years of his life, finding little result from the Latin alliance, had renounced the Florentine Union. Poli-

[s] Gibbon, XII. 162.

tical circumstances regulated to the end the religious thermometer of the consciences of the Palæologi. Constantine's last hope was reposed in the assistance of the Western powers. He, too, now applied to the Pope of Rome, professing his obedience, and expressing his willingness to accept the union of the Churches under whatever conditions the Pope might impose. Nicolas V. (1447—1455), a liberal patron of the Renaissance, the successor of Eugenius IV., was then Pope. He appears to have placed no confidence in the success of the Greeks, but to have foreseen the fall of Constantinople; he was, moreover, offended with the failure of the Florentine Union, and the return of John VI. to Orthodoxy. He now sent to Constantinople Cardinal Isidore, the former Metropolitan of Kiev, the most objectionable legate he could have selected, who he thought would, being a Greek, be acceptable to the Emperor; and before him Constantine professed himself a member of the Roman Church, and subscribed the former Union. On Dec 12, 1452, Isidore celebrated, in the presence of the Emperor and Court, Mass according to the rites of the Latin Church, in the Cathedral of St. Sophia; and there the Union of the Churches was proclaimed. The Greeks were now placed in the dilemma of submission to Rome, by which alone Western help could be obtained, or submission to the Ottomans. The Court, and some of the higher clergy, advocated the former, but to the Greeks generally the Union was more hateful than ever; the secular clergy, almost with one voice, as well the monks, the nuns, and the laity, repudiated it. So soon as the service commenced, the congregation, with one accord, left the Cathedral as a place polluted. Everywhere the Unionists were branded with sacrificing their Church, with preferring the interest of their bodies to the good of their souls, and of insulting God to serve the Pope. The clergy bound themselves by a vow, that, under penalty of forfeiting their Orders, they would never be united to the Church of Rome; the laity declared that they would rather see, in the streets of Constantinople, a Sultan's turban than a Cardinal's hat.

However favourable the Pope might have been to the Greeks, Western help was not available at the crisis. The nations of Western Christendom were indifferent to their cause; some were occupied in their own affairs, and too weak to afford help; others regarded the ruin of the Eastern Empire as inevitable; and Constantinople had fallen, before the fleets of Genoa and Venice were able to sail from their harbours.

To describe the skill with which the siege was conducted by the Turks, and the pusillanimity of the Greeks, who had little heart in fighting under the banner of an heretical Emperor, is beyond our province. Amidst the many melancholy reflexions which centre round the fall of Constantinople, one of the saddest of all is, that it was mainly effected by Greeks, by the corps of Janissaries, formed from the kidnapped children of Christian parents; by soldiers fighting against Christians of the same blood as themselves.

On May 29, 1453, Constantinople fell. The Emperor, having previously received the Holy Eucharist in St. Sophia's, and asked the forgiveness of all whom he might have offended, died the death of a hero, his body being found by the Janissaries, sword in hand, amidst a heap of slain; his head was cut off and sent round the city as a sign of victory.

In order to pay his unwilling soldiers, Constantine had been forced, poor though they were in comparison with their richness and splendour previously to the Fourth Crusade to despoil the Churches; whatever of the plate and vestments of the Churches remained was divided amongst the conquerors. A Turk is always a Turk, and doubtless many acts of rapacity and cruelty were committed, many thousands of both sexes taken captive and sold into slavery, many Churches and monasteries plundered. But Mahometans might well plead the example set them by Christians;

and all accounts agree, that no such acts of blasphemy and desecration of Churches, as those which disgraced the Latins in the Fourth Crusade, were committed by the Turks, and the conduct of the infidels stands a favourable comparison with the wanton destruction and desecration of the Crusaders.

No sooner had the city fallen than the panic-stricken and before disunited, citizens were at one again; and St. Sophia's was crowded with worshippers from every part of the city, of every age, sex, and station. Isidore, in his terror and despair, was barely able to make his escape from the city in disguise. The Sultan, Mahomet, allowed the Greeks to choose their own Patriarch, and George Scholasticus, who had favoured the Florentine Union, but, influenced by Mark of Ephesus, afterwards rejected it, was elected under his monastic name of Gennadius, and consecrated by the Metropolitan of Heraclea, the Sultan continuing the custom of the Emperors in delivering the crozier into his hand. The Patriarchal palace was occupied by the Sultan, the Patriarch taking up his residence in the Monastery of the Apostles.

Thus, fourteen years after the abortive Council of Florence, Constantinople fell into the hands of the Infidels, and the Patriarch of New Rome, the ancient rival of Old Rome, was humbled. The Cathedral of St Sophia, the Metropolitan Church of the East, the noblest Christian Temple in the world, built to commemorate the Wisdom of God, the Second Person in the Blessed Trinity, was converted into a Mahometan Mosque, the Crescent taking the place of the Cross on the summit of its dome. The Church of the Holy Apostles, which was believed once to have contained the relics of SS. Andrew, Luke and Timothy, was at first granted by the Sultan to Gennadius, but the grant was soon revoked; it too was converted into the Mosque which still bears the name of Mahomet. About forty other Churches were in like manner converted into Mosques, Mahomet allowing the Greek Church to celebrate its rites in the remainder

Constantinople became the capital of the Turkish Empire, and the Turks a leading power in Europe. Having taken the capital of the Eastern Empire, the Sultan looked forward to a time when he should be able to carry his armies into Italy. Now that danger threatened Rome also, the Pope must have felt that, but for the action of his predecessors, the common enemies of all that bear the Name of Christ would have been driven out from Europe. Some Romans still continued to speak of the fall of Constantinople as the judgment of Heaven; but horror reigned in Rome at the thought of an infidel taking the place of a Christian, Church, and feelings of sorrow and compassion arose for an erring sister, or perhaps daughter, in her bitter distress. The reigning Pope, the pious and learned Nicolas V., in vain, four months after its fall, issued a Bull proclaiming a Crusade, and offering the usual Indulgences to all who should take part in it. His successor, Calixtus III., vowed by every means within his power[t] to attack the Turks, the most cruel enemies of Christianity. The next Pope, Pius II., called, A.D. 1459, a Council of Christian Princes to Mantua; and in the following year Bessarion was sent on a fruitless mission to Germany, only to lament the lack of the zeal, which he had hoped to find amongst Christians[u]. To the end of his life the Pope continued his pious efforts; he enlisted in the cause the Venetians, who were anxious for their possessions of Crete and Corfu; and, although suffering from a fever, and warned by his years that he required rest, himself started to join their fleet at Ancona. In vain the aged Doge, Christofero Moro, pleaded his old age as an excuse for not joining the Crusade; the Venetians told him, that if he would not embark willingly, they would force him to do so. The Pope told them that, though he could not take part in their battles, he would be present, and stretch out his arms,

---

[t] "Bello, interdictis, excecrationibus, et quibuscunque rebus potero"
[u] "Non est apud Christianos religionis cura quam credidimus"

like Moses, in prayer; but at Ancona, on August 15, 1464, he died, as was supposed, from a broken heart. His successor, Paul II., a man of vulgar show, who prided himself on his handsome face, and was with difficulty dissuaded by his Cardinals from assuming the title of Formosus; a man who began life as a merchant, and ended it by overeating himself at supper, was little likely to trouble himself about a Crusade. Under his three successors (1471—1503), the last of whom, Alexander VI., accomplished the feat of surpassing all his predecessors in wickedness, the dark Ages seem to have returned, and the Papacy fell again into the lowest depths of degradation.

That the Church of England felt sympathy for the Eastern Church in its distress may be gathered from one of the Collects of Good Friday, composed in the Primacy of Archbishop Bourchier (1454—1486) for the conversion of Jews, Turks, Infidels, and heretics. But when it became noised in England that a Pope's envoys were collecting money for a Crusade, the government, which had been long suffering under Papal exactions, forbade any public fund being raised for the purpose. The day of Crusades was over, and the Princes of Europe had learnt to regard them as a means of enriching the Popes.

Of the 100,000 inhabitants of Constantinople, about 40,000 are supposed to have perished in the siege. The Greek aristocracy was either then, or immediately afterwards, annihilated. But it was the policy of Mahomet to favour the Orthodox Church, although it did not present itself in favourable colours to the eyes of Mahometans. The divisions between the Orthodox and Separatist Communities, and the religious controversies between Greeks and Latins, were not without their effect; could those be Christians in heart who were always fighting amongst themselves? There is reason for believing that the Orthodox Church was, at the time, in a very corrupt state, and that the Mahometans were morally, as they certainly were intellectually, superior to the Greeks. The outward observances were patent to the eye, but the

Mahometans, whilst they considered the worship idolatrous, doubted the sincerity of their inward convictions. The conduct of Pope Eugenius IV, in persuading Ladislaus to break his oath with his father, Murad, could not have presented the Christian Church in a favourable light to the mind of Mahomet.

But under him the Orthodox Church met with toleration. Mahomet was a statesman as well as a warrior, and his conduct to the Church was guided by interested and political motives. It is the opinion of some that he was desirous of keeping alive the schism between East and West; and that, as he proposed to carry his arms into the West, he showed favour to the Orthodox Church in the hope of making it a barrier against Roman pretensions. He knew that the Patriarch exerted a strong influence, and he determined not to lower the ancient Greek Hierarchy. The Greek Bishops took the place of the old aristocracy, and Gennadius was regarded as the head of the Greek population; the Greek Prelates, says Finlay, acted as a kind of Ottoman Prefects over the Orthodox population. But after the reconstruction of the Orthodox Church, Mahomet claimed the same rights over it as had previously been exercised by the Emperors. He allowed the Greeks to elect their own Patriarchs, but kept in his own hands their confirmation, which virtually meant, their appointment and deposition.

The Patriarchs of Alexandria, Antioch, and Jerusalem, elected by the suffrages of the Bishops, were generally those most distinguished amongst the clergy for their piety and learning, and, when elected, were, owing to their poverty and insignificance, little thought of by the Turks, and being out of sight were generally out of mind. But the Patriarchate of Constantinople was an office of great dignity, and, under Mahomet's successors, was often obtained by the highest bidder, rather than from merit or ecclesiastical attainment. The appointment came to be a source of great profit to the Sultan, and often of great trouble and scandal to the Church. The object being to obtain as much money as possible, the more unfit the candidate, the more acceptable was he to the Sultan; for his unfitness would render him unacceptable to the Greeks, and the Vizier was always ready to listen to the most frivolous reasons for his deposition, as the appointment of another Patriarch in his place would bring more money into the Sultan's pocket. Such has been no uncommon occurrence in the history of the Greek Church under the Ottomans; as the present narrative proceeds, we shall find one, and him the greatest, of the Patriarchs of Constantinople, Cyril Lucar, five times appointed and five times deposed. Between the taking of Constantinople and A.D. 1710, the year to which his authority extended, Mr. Appleyard says that sixty Prelates presided over the See, nearly all of whom died in exile or by violence.

Even in cases where the Patriarchate had been obtained by the most open and profligate corruption, the Canons of the Church could not be enforced, because it was to the advantage of the Turks to encourage it, and the temporal power would not allow the Spiritual to take proceedings against it. Hence the Patriarchs of Constantinople were led to bow down to the Sultans and Viziers, whose servile instruments, in order to retain the Patriarchal throne, they often became; and, living in the vicinity of the Court, and being under the very eyes of the secular power, they were exposed to temptations from which the other Patriarchs were comparatively free.

The contests between the higher clergy, and the simony practised in order to obtain the coveted honour of the Patriarchate, involved the Episcopate in obloquy, and, as compared with the lower Orders of the Church, in popular disesteem. And this feeling extended to the monasteries and to the Kaloirs, from whom the Bishops were chosen. Hence arose the greater respect in which the Secular are held over the Regular clergy, in the Greek Church, and the confiding reverence which the people display in the injunctions and censures of their Parish Priests, who are taken, not like the Bishops from the monasteries, but from the masses of the people, with whom they are allied by, almost compulsory, marriage, and social ties.

But when simony was rife in the highest Order, what could be expected in the lower Orders of the clergy? There is reason for believing that a better state of things is now setting in, but the Secular clergy were long steeped in ignorance, just able to go through the services, without even understanding the idiom in which they were written. Hence arose the absence of sermons and catechizing which still prevails generally in the Greek Church, and the perfunctory dulness of the services, unrelieved as it is by instrumental music; the shell was preserved but the kernel lost[x]. Many of the clergy led licentious lives, one of their principal vices being that of intemperance; we need not place implicit confidence in all we hear from travellers, and may believe that a higher morality now exists, but there is reason to fear that intemperance still extensively prevails.

The fall of the Eastern Empire, and the low state to which the persecuted Greek Church fell, and from which it is little less than a miracle that it should now be recovering, is a chapter of dishonour and disgrace in the history of Western Europe. Pope Pius II., the Pope who, as we have seen, devoted his life to the prosecution of a Turkish war, lamented the discordant state of Western Christendom. "What eloquence," he said "could unite so many hostile and conflicting Powers under one standard? ... If a small army enlisted in a holy war, they must be overthrown by the infidels, if a large one, it would be overthrown by its own confusion." He wrote, in 1461, a long letter to Mahomet himself[y], explaining the character of the Christian Faith, and urging him to be Baptized; in which case, instead of proclaiming a Crusade against the Turks, he would make use of their assistance in restoring the Greek Church. But the successors of Pius have, only in a

[x] It must be mentioned that the above does not include the Russian Church.
[y] Dean Waddington, Present State of the Greek and Oriental Church, p. 152, styles it "that most memorable monument of arrogance and piety."

lesser degree than the Mahometans, been the persistent enemies of the Greek Church. Instead of sympathizing with its affliction, they have laboured to make the Greeks renounce their own Patriarchs, and acknowledge the supremacy of Rome. That they met with some measure of success, we have evidence in the fact that, between 1453—1599, no less than thirteen of the Patriarchs of Constantinople professed the faith and authority of the Roman Church. Large numbers of Greek refugees, driven away from Constantinople by the Turks, fled into foreign lands, where they founded Churches of their own under the name of Uniat Greeks, in which they retained all the essentials of the Greek Church, its doctrines and its Liturgy, but were induced to acknowledge the supremacy, not of their canonical Patriarch, but of the Pope of Rome. But, ever since the fall of Constantinople, the great mass of the Greek people have resisted to the present day all bribes and temptation to forsake their Church, and have stood firm to Orthodoxy, says Professor Freeman, rather than forsake their faith, they have lived for two, for four, for five hundred years, in a state of abiding Martyrdom.

Soon after the fall of Constantinople, the remaining fragments of the Eastern Empire gradually succumbed to the Turks. In 1459, Servia, and six years later Bosnia, and then Albania, were conquered. One little strip of territory to the South of Servia and Bosnia, called Montenegro, or the *Black Mountain*, remained unconquered, and under the succession of its warrior Bishops, although sorely harassed by the Turks, preserved, and continues to the present day to maintain, its independence. What part Montenegro will play in the Eastern problem, and the history of the Greek Church, it is difficult to conjecture. It is considered in Russia a *point d'appui* for the whole Servian element, and being the one Servian stronghold that has always maintained the Orthodox Faith, it has enlisted the sincere and long-standing friendship of Russia[z]. In 1461, Trebizond, the

[z] St Petersburg Gazette, as quoted in the Times, June 2, 1898.

last remaining seat of the Eastern Empire, and, before Mahomet II's death, the Morea and nearly the whole of Greece was subjugated by him. The year before his death, his troops took Otranto in Southern Italy; by the siege and sack of the city a thrill of consternation was diffused through Western Europe; had this place been kept, Italy might have fallen, as well as Greece. Pope Sixtus IV. was already preparing to fly beyond the Alps, when, in the next year (A.D. 1481), Mahomet II. died, in the fifty-first year of his age, and Otranto was recovered from the Turks by Naples.

We will carry on the history of the Ottoman Empire a few years longer, till it reached the summit of its power, and its furthest conquests from the Greek Church. Under Mahomet's son, Bajazet II. (1481—1512), a man of peaceful character, who lived in apprehension of danger from his rebellious brother Zizim, no important conquests were effected by the Turks. Bajazet, being deposed, was succeeded by his son, Selim I. (1512—1520), *the Inflexible*. With him the toleration granted by Mahomet II. did not find favour, and he did his best to put down Christianity altogether. Selim took upon himself the title and the authority of the Caliphs, and from his time to the present day, the Sultans have exercised a spiritual as well as a temporal supremacy. In systematic bloodthirstiness, whether towards Christians or heretical Mahometans (for he belonged to the Sonnite or orthodox sect), Selim outdid all his predecessors[a]. With the view of extirpating Christianity, he gave orders for the conversion or the massacre of all Christians in his dominions, and that every Christian Church should be turned into a Mahometan Mosque; but from these acts he was, by the advice of his Divan, diverted. Still, with the view of preventing Christian Churches from vying with the Mosques, he ordered those built of stone to be confiscated, and only wooden ones to be left to the Greeks, an order which continued in force under his successors, and could only be

[a] Freeman's Ottoman Power, p. 126.

evaded by a pecuniary payment. Selim's arms were principally directed against Mahometan enemies, and under him Palestine and Egypt were added to the Ottoman dominions. Thus the Holy Sepulchre came into the hands of the Ottomans; a guard of Turkish soldiers is to the present day stationed there (for the, alas! necessary, purpose of keeping peace between the Christians who flock to it); and to the infidel police a tribute must be paid, before a Christian is allowed to enter the sacred enclosure which contains the Sepulchre of his Lord.

Selim was succeeded by his son, Suleiman, or Solomon (1520—1566), *the Magnificent,* and, as his reign marks its height, so from it may be dated the commencement of the decline of the Ottoman power. In the first year of his reign he invaded Hungary, where he received valuable assistance through the dissensions of the Catholics and Protestants, and inflicted on it a blow from which it has never recovered. In the same year he took Belgrade, and in a second invasion of Hungary, in 1526, he captured Buda. Between those two invasions he, A.D. 1522, besieged Rhodes, which belonged to the Knights Hospitallers of St. John. After a siege of six months, the Crescent was victorious over the Cross; the few surviving Knights, under their Grand Master, Villiers de l'Isle Adam, left Rhodes, and eventually received from the Emperor Charles V. the Island of Malta, where they were known as the Knights of Malta, and became the formidable opponents of the Turks in the Mediterranean. In 1565, a large fleet, conveying on board the best of the Turkish soldiers under the command of Suleiman's ablest General, suffered a disastrous defeat, and a loss of 25,000 men, in attempting to capture Malta from the Hospitallers.

Suleiman was succeeded by his son, Selim II. (1566—1574), *the Drunkard.* In 1571, Don John of Austria, in alliance with the Venetians, inflicted a serious defeat on the Turks in the battle of Lepanto, in the Corinthian Gulf but in the same year the Island of Cyprus, whither Selim was attracted by the wines of the country, was taken from the Venetians by the Turks The battle of Lepanto was the turning-point in the career of the Ottomans.

Since the fall of the Eastern Empire, the history of the four great Patriarchates, of Constantinople, Alexandria, Antioch, and Jerusalem, has generally been little more than a string of names and a series of persecutions. The Patriarch of Constantinople still continues to be the recognized head of the Orthodox Greek Church; but its dignity and importance henceforward centres round the Church of Russia, under which, it may be hoped, it will some day regain its ancient prestige and influence in Christ's vineyard.

CHAPTER XIV.

The Making of Russia.

THE Russian Metropolitans—Monasticism—The Appanages—The Mogul invasions—Influence of the Church—Interference of Rome—Vladimir Monomachus—St Niphont—Foundation of Moscow—The Principality of Suzdal—Conversion of Livonia—The Knights of the Sword—The Prince of Galich and Pope Innocent III.—Prosperous state of the Church at the commencement of the Mogul invasions—Genghis Khan—Batou—Fall of Kiev—The Golden Horde—Alexander Nevski—Cyril II, Metropolitan—The See of Sarai—Transference of the Metropolitan See to Vladimir—Ivan (Khalita), Grand Prince—St Peter, Metropolitan—Transference of the Metropolitan See to Moscow—St Sergius—St. Alexis, Metropolitan—Dmitri Donskoi, Grand Prince—Isidore, Metropolitan—The Council of Florence—Ivan III, Grand Prince—The "Builder of Russia"—Conversion of Lithuania—Union of Lithuania and Poland—Marriage of Ivan III. with the heiress of the Palæologi—Pope Alexander VI and the Russian Church—Fall of Novgorod—Archbishop Bassian—Fall of the Golden Horde—The Strigolniks—Zosimus, Metropolitan—End of the Appanages—Review of the Liturgical Books—Ivan, the Terrible—Macarius, Metropolitan—Anastasia Romanov—Ivan, the first Tsar of Russia—"Book of the Hundred Chapters"—The Reign of Terror—The Opreechniks—Ivan's impiety—Martyrdom of the Metropolitan, St Philip—Massacre of the Novgorodians—Ivan and the Jesuit Possevin—Feodor, Tsar—Boris Godonov—Murder of Feodor's half-brother, Dmitri.

THE earliest See of the Metropolitans of Russia was at Kiev. The first three Metropolitans probably bore the simple title of Bishops, for Theopemptus (1037—1051), the fourth in order, is the first whom the Chronicler Nestor designates Metropolitan. As his name (Θεὸς πεμπτός, *sent by God*) implies, he was a Greek, and was sent to Russia by Alexius, the predecessor of Michael Cerularius in the Patriarchate of Constantinople; and so long as the Metropolitans resided in Kiev, they were generally Greeks, chosen and Consecrated by the Patriarchs of Constantinople. Their election the Patriarchs tried to keep in their own hands; but this the Grand Princes resented, sometimes sending back the Metropolitan who had been Consecrated by the Patriarch, and commissioning the Russian Bishops to Consecrate the Metropolitan themselves.

Theopemptus dying at a time when Russia had lately been at war with the Greeks, his successor, Hilarion (1051—1072), a monk from the famous monastery of Kiev, was chosen by Yaroslav I., and Consecrated Metropolitan in a Synod of Russian Bishops; but this infringement of the discipline of the Greek Church was rectified by his election being afterwards confirmed by Cerularius.

Although, before his time, several small monasteries already existed in Kiev, Hilarion is the reputed founder of Russian monasticism, which was planned on that of the monks of Mount Athos, and was under the strict Rule observed in the monastery of Studium, near Constantinople.

Yaroslav I. (*the Great*) was succeeded by his son Isiaslav I. (1054—1078), in whose reign the fatal consequences of the Appanages began to show themselves. During the period of the Appanages, the chief Principalities were those of Kiev, Smolensk, Chernigov, Suzdal (with its capital, Vladimir); and the Republics of Novgorod and Pskov. From his reign to A.D. 1238, the year of the commencement of the Mogul invasions, the civil historians of Russia lament that, except the uninteresting quarrels of the appanaged Princes, there is next to nothing to record. Still the history of the Russian Church at the time has a peculiar interest; for not only was the Church the successful mediator in the quarrels of the Princes, but to its Metropolitans and Bishops Russia owes, if not its salvation, at any rate its preservation and coherence during, and after, those stormy times.

The exact opposite happened in Russia to what happened in the West, with regard to the Roman Catholic branch of the Christian Church. When, in the Tenth Century, the Roman Church was, through the profligacy of the Popes, brought to the verge of ruin, it was the civil power and the German Emperors that saved it; when Russia was, first through the Appanages, and afterwards by the Moguls, brought to a similar state, it was the Russian Church that rescued the Nation.

There was at the time no central government in the State;

for, though the Grand Prince, residing first at Kiev, and afterwards at Vladimir, was nominally the Head of the Russian Princes, his authority was not powerful enough to keep the other Princes in subjection. When all was confusion in the State, and there were many contending Princes, there was in the Church one Metropolitan, and in the Church there was union; and, says Mouraviev[a], "from the time that the Moguls invaded the country, Russia had cause to be thankful to the Church, to remember with devout gratitude all the holy defenders of her youth, especially and above all, Cyril, Peter, Alexis, Cyprian, and Jonah."

During the unhappy period of the Appanages, whilst the number of new Sees which were erected is an evidence of its flourishing condition, the Russian Church was presided over by a body of singularly able and exemplary Metropolitans; the duty of peacemakers became a recognized part of their office; and the consideration which they enjoyed was the one link which bound together the whole nation[b]. From there being one Metropolitan, the Grand Princes conceived the idea of national unity; the appanaged Princes learnt to lay aside their contentions; the rising Empire settled down under one head, and the Grand Prince of Moscow grew into the Tsar of Russia, the ruler of the ninth part of the Globe.

The reign of Isiaslav is memorable for the first attempt made by Rome on the independence of the Russian Church. At a time when Russia was exposed not only to the feuds between Isiaslav and his brethren, but also to an invasion of Boleslas, the King of Poland, George, the Metropolitan, does not appear to have been equal to the occasion, and fled in terror to Constantinople. Isiaslav, deprived of his throne, sought, in 1075, the interposition of Pope Gregory VII. (Hildebrand); the Pope caught at the oppor-

[a] p 31.
[b] The same was the case in England, and affords one of the many parallel cases between the English and Russian Churches. Whilst the Kings of the so-called Heptarchy were contesting for supremacy there was one Archbishop, and the unity of the Church paved the way to the unity of the State

tunity of severing Russia from the Greek Church; offered military aid, on the condition that Russia would become a fief of Rome; and promised to confer the throne, after Isiaslav's death, on his son, *dono sancti Petri*. Isiaslav, however, succeeding, without the Pope's help, in regaining his throne, the negotiations came to an end.

Isiaslav was succeeded by his brother, Ysevolod (1078—1093), who married a Greek Princess, the daughter of the Emperor Constantine Monomachus. On his death the people requested his son, Vladimir Monomachus, to ascend the throne But, according to the law regulating the Russian succession, the throne did not devolve upon the son of Ysevolod, but went back to Isiaslav's son, Sviatopolk (1093—1113). To this arrangement Vladimir raised no objection; Sviatopolk's father, he said, was older than his father, and reigned first at Kiev. When, in the reign of Sviatopolk, Russia was desolated by civil wars, and the Princes were threatening the Grand Prince under the walls of Kiev, the Metropolitan Nicolas presented himself before them as peacemaker; "We beseech thee, O Prince, thee and thy brethren, that ye will not be so unnatural as to ruin your own country of Russia; know that, if you fight amongst yourselves, the unbelievers will rejoice, and will take away from us our land, which your fathers and grandfathers won by great toil and labour[c]."

On Sviatopolk's death the universal voice of the people urged on Vladimir his acceptance of the throne; he had been through the two preceding reigns the mainstay of the country; and now, in the perils that beset Russia, he yielded to the prayers of the people, and reluctantly accepted the Grand Princedom. Russia, by the marriage of the Grand Prince with Gytha, daughter of our English King Harold, slain in the battle of Senlac, was for the first time brought into connection with England. During a period of twelve years (1113—1125), Vladimir II (Monomachus) found an able fellow-labourer in the Metropolitan

[c] Mouravlev, p 30.

Nicephorus. Nicephorus sent him the 101st Psalm as a compendious instruction in his duties, with an exhortation to learn it by heart, to meditate, and to fashion upon it his government [d]. The two worked together as "models of Christian virtue, the one on the kingly, the other on the Episcopal throne [e]," and the latter succeeded in suppressing the civil wars, and uniting the Princes of the Appanages in a common cause.

The importance of Kiev at this time may be estimated by the number and splendour of its Churches and Chapels. But under the Metropolitan Nicetas (1124—1126), Kiev was visited by a terrible fire which laid the city in ruins, and nearly all its Churches, the number of which Nestor places at seven hundred, but Gibbon, with three hundred, is probably nearer the mark, were destroyed. Shortly before this conflagration, Monomachus had founded in Suzdal the city after him called Vladimir, which afterwards became the capital of Russia, and the See of the Metropolitan, until, in its turn, it had to give place to Moscow.

After the death of Monomachus, the glory of Kiev waned. The old state of anarchy revived; new and independent Principalities were founded; in the course of thirty-two years no fewer than eleven Princes mounted the throne of Kiev; the capital, left to the rapacity of the Princes, declined and fell into insignificance, and the Grand Princedom was reduced to little beyond the walls of the city.

Still, in the midst of this dismemberment of Russia, the Church and the confession of the Orthodox Faith throughout the Kingdom continued to be the one bond of union. The Metropolitans, who still resided at Kiev, drew thither the attention and respect of the whole of Russia. We read that the Bishops in their Dioceses and the Hegumens from the monasteries, going backwards and forwards between the opposing camps, served as mediators and peacemakers. One sign of the influence of the Russian Church at this time was the great increase in the number of monasteries,

---

[d] Palmer's Orthodox Communion, p 95.   [e] Ibid, p 31

the Princes, whilst at war amongst themselves, never forgot their Church ; and many of them founded and built monasteries, where, wearied out by the continual strife and turmoil of the world, they themselves often ended their troubled lives.

But the disorders of the civil government were leaving their marks on the Church, and on society. After Vladimir Monomachus, three of his sons in succession followed on the throne of Kiev, of whom the third was, in 1139, deposed. Soon afterwards Igor II., Prince of Suzdal, gained the supremacy, seized Kiev, and took possession of the throne. A fortnight afterwards he was expelled and forced to receive the tonsure at Kiev ; nor did the sacred character of a monk secure him from being torn in pieces, in a subsequent riot at Kiev, by the party of his opponent.

The disastrous contentions of the Princes bring us about this time into contact with a prominent name, that of St. Niphont, Bishop of the powerful Principality of Novgorod. The Metropolitan Michael, having in vain tried, by the threat of an interdict, to quell the feuds between the Principalities of Novgorod and Suzdal, wearied out with his troubles, retired to Constantinople. On his death, the Grand Prince Isiaslav II., resenting the Metropolitan's abandonment of his See, determined not to have another Greek Metropolitan ; and, the Patriarchate of Constantinople being at the time vacant, he convened a Synod of Russian Bishops, who resolved to take the election in their own hands, the only voice raised against it being that of Niphont. Clement, a monk of Smolensk, was accordingly elected, the Bishop of Chernigov proposing that, as a substitute for the Patriarch of Constantinople, the hand of St. Clement of Rome, whose remains had been translated to Kiev by Vladimir, should be laid upon his head.

Niphont, in consequence of his opposition to the wishes of Isiaslav and the Russian Bishops, was for a time committed to the Pechersky Monastery. But, on the dethronement of Isiaslav, he was recalled by Yury Dolgorouki, his successor on the throne of Kiev, and sent to Luke Chrysoberges, the newly-elected Patriarch of Constantinople, with the request that he would Consecrate another Metropolitan in the place of Clement. Constantine, Bishop of Chernigov, who was in consequence Consecrated, condemned in a Synod the acts of Isiaslav and Clement, suspending the clergy who had been Ordained by the latter. Before the new Metropolitan arrived, Niphont died and was buried in the catacombs of Kiev, his name being afterwards added to the catalogue of Russian Saints as the "Defender of Russia [f]."

After another revolution, Misteslav, the son of Isiaslav, became Grand Prince at Kiev, and by him Constantine, on account of the part which he had taken against his father, was deposed and forced to return to his former See of Chernigov, and, whilst he was still living, another Metropolitan, Theodore, was Consecrated by the Patriarch Luke. So that there were now, at one and the same time, three Metropolitans of Kiev.

Yury Dolgorouki, who, A D. 1155, recovered the Grand Princedom which he held till his death in 1157, did much towards the improvement and extension of his own patrimony of Suzdal, and was also the founder of Moscow. After his death, confusion, if possible, worse confounded, ensued at Kiev, which, whilst the power of Suzdal went on increasing, became the prey of a rapid succession of Princes. In 1169 Andrew Bobolupski, Prince of Suzdal, a son of Yury, gained, through a coalition of Princes, the Grand Princedom Believing that its throne at Kiev was the cause of all the calamities which beset Russia, he determined to strike at the root of the evil, and after a three days' siege took Kiev and reduced it to a fief. "To their eternal shame," says the Russian Historian Karamsin, "the victors forgot that they too were Russians. During three days not only the houses, but the monasteries and Churches, and the temple of St. Sophia, were given over to pillage The precious images, the sacerdotal ornaments, the books and the bells were all taken away[g]"

Thus fell the Holy city of Kiev; in 1170, the Grand Prince

---

[f] Mouraviev, p 31.   [g] Rambaud's Hist of Russia, I 110.

Andrew made Vladimir the capital of his Princedom, and Novgorod for a time acknowledged his supremacy. The centre of Russia was now changed to Suzdal, Andrew greatly enlarged and strengthened its capital, Vladimir, and transferred to the *Church of the Mother of God*, which he built for its reception, the miraculous *image of the Virgin*, the work, it was supposed, of St. Luke, brought from Constantinople. The Princes of Kiev still retained the title of Grand Princes, but it was a barren honour, and they were appointed and displaced at the will of the Princes of Vladimir. Andrew in vain attempted to induce the Patriarch of Constantinople to allow the Metropolitan See to be transferred to Vladimir; he only so far consented that, for the future, the Bishops of Rostov should have their residential See at Vladimir, the Primates continued to be styled Metropolitans of Kiev.

Andrew, now chief amongst the Princes of Russia, was a pious Prince, and sought the friendship of the Bishops, whom he felt to be the most powerful force in the land. But, in trying to make himself an autocratic Prince, he signally failed, Prince after Prince revolted from him, Kiev and Novgorod again asserted their independence, and, in 1174, he was assassinated by his Boyars. After his death the work of disintegration was renewed; fresh Appanages were created, and the dismemberment of Russia was complete. The Sees of Rostov and Vladimir were, only for a short time, united. The two Princes quarrelling, not being content to have one Bishop in common, applied to Matthew, the Metropolitan of Kiev (1201—1205), for a resident Bishop, and Matthew, to oblige both parties, erected a new Metropolitan See for Vladimir[h].

In the last years of the twelfth century, the Gospel was, amidst scenes of revolting cruelty and bloodshed, introduced by Latin missionaries amongst the barbarous people of Livonia, a Russian province on the Baltic. Meinhard, an Augustinian monk, sent as missionary by the Archbishop of Bremen, was, in 1186, Consecrated by Pope Urban III.

[h] Mouraviev, p 41.

first Bishop of Livonia, and in the country he built a Church, enclosing it with a fortress. The Livonians, or Livs, fearing, as proved to be the case, that the mission had designs on their national independence, lent a deaf ear to the Gospel; whereupon the Pope proclaimed against them a Crusade. Berthold, Abbot of Lucca, appointed their second Bishop, marched into the province with a powerful army, "preached the Gospel sword in hand, proving its truth by blows instead of arguments[1]," and, A.D. 1198, perished in battle. One of the first acts of Pope Innocent III. was to proclaim another Crusade against the unhappy people, and Albert of Buxhevden (1198—1229), third Bishop of the See, continued the same method of military conversion that had been adopted by his predecessor. In 1200 he built the town of Riga, which became the Episcopal See of Livonia; and in the following year, by direction of Innocent, established the Order of the Knights of the Sword (*Ordo Militum Ensiferorum*), to whom he gave the Rule of the Templars, and the right of wearing a white mantle, with a red Cross on their shoulders. They were to enjoy the lordship of all the lands they could conquer, subject to the Bishop of Livonia, and were commissioned to drag over the Livonians into Christianity and Baptism [k].

The time was favourable to the Knights of the Sword. Russia, distracted with contentions, the weakness of the neighbouring Princes of Polotsk, and the intestine quarrels of Novgorod, was hindered from watching over its own interests. The Livonians, after having in vain implored the help of the Princes of Polotsk, suffered, A.D. 1206, a disastrous defeat at Riga, the alternative offered them being Baptism and obedience, or fire and the sword[1]. The end was that the unhappy people, cruelly oppressed and exhausted, unable to stand firm against persecution, were forced into Baptism; their lands and possessions, under circumstances of great cruelty and violence, were torn from them, and the conquered country was divided into fiefs, the Knights

---

Mosheim, Cent. XII.   [k] Ibid.   [1] Rambaud, I. 148.

of the Sword and the Bishops dividing the spoil, and quarrelling over their respective rights.

No sooner was the Latin Kingdom established in Constantinople, than Latin legates sought an opportunity for extending their influence over Russia. Roman (1188—1205), the Grand Prince of Galich in Red Russia (for after the fall of Kiev several of the Princes assumed that before unique title), was one of the most powerful, although one of the cruellest over his enemies, of all the Princes. The Russian Chroniclers, whilst they represent him as a redoubtable hero, " savage as a wild cat, sweeping down on his enemies like an eagle," praise him as " walking in the ways of God, exterminating the heathen, and a very lion against the infidels." To this powerful Prince, Pope Innocent III. sent, offering him the protection of the Apostolic Sword. " Has the Pope a sword like this ? " pointing to his own, he proudly asked the papal legate. But in 1205, in a battle on the borders of the Vistula, he was defeated and slain by the Poles, and a Latin Archbishopric set up in Galich. Roman was succeeded by his young son, Daniel, under whom Red Russia was a prey to civil wars ; in 1218 Galich was stormed and taken by Mistislav " the Brave," Prince of Novgorod, by whom the Roman clergy were driven out of the country. But Novgorod was at the time itself contending with the Knights of the Sword, and being thus unable to offer any permanent assistance, the Romanists re-established themselves at Galich. The Russian people, however, during the Latin Kingdom, remained faithful to the Greek Church, and when there was no longer a Patriarch of the Orthodox Church in Constantinople, Cyril I., who, A.D. 1205, succeeded Matthew as Metropolitan, was Consecrated not, as usual, at Constantinople, but by the Greek Patriarch resident at Nice.

In the first quarter of the Thirteenth Century, at the time when Russia, worn out with the incessant strife of the Princes, and tired of war, was desirous of rest and peace, a calamity, unparalleled since the invasion of the

Saracens, from the Moguls, or Tartars, befel Europe. The Russian Chroniclers speak of the disasters which befel their country, as a just punishment for the sins of the people. The invasions commenced at a time when the Russian Church, notwithstanding the conflicts of the Princes, was in a highly prosperous condition. From the days of Vladimir and Yaroslav, the education of the Russian people had been held of paramount importance, and, under Greek teachers sent from Constantinople, had rapidly advanced; schools had been established and organized, by means of which civilization was spread, and the Christian faith widely diffused. Evidence of great activity existing was shown in the circulation of the Bible, the whole or a large portion of which had been translated into the Slavic language by Cyril and Methodius; and we find the Metropolitans and Bishops insisting on the importance of the Bible, as the basis of instruction and morals. By the terrible devastations of the Moguls, all these hopeful signs were swept away, and all attempts to spread knowledge and civilization arrested The early promise of intellectual life and literary development was blasted, most of the translations of Cyril and Methodius were destroyed, and the work had to be done over again. But for the Moguls, Russia, instead of loosing all that it had acquired and the advantages it possessed, instead of being the last, would have been one of the first, of European nations in the race of civilization.

The Moguls first began to rise to power under Genghis Khan (1206—1227), who having succeeded in uniting the Mogul race, declared that, just as there was one sun in the heavens, so there ought to be one Emperor on earth.

In 1221 Genghis, taking advantage of the dissensions of its Princes, fell upon the disunited and enfeebled Russia. Had the country been united, it is supposed that it would easily have succeeded in repelling the invasions; as it was, its disunion, and the absence of all means of political concentration, rendered it an easy prey to its enemies.

In 1224 the Russians, in a sanguinary battle on the banks of the river Kalka, in the southern part of the country, suffered a terrible defeat, hardly a tenth part of their army making good their escape; the Grand Princes of Kiev and of Chernigov fell, the Prince of Galich escaping to his capital to end his troubled life in a monastery. Of a sudden the Moguls unexpectedly stopped and returned to their Asiatic homes in quest of new adventures. Thus a breathing-time was allowed to Russia, and the land, as far as the Moguls were concerned, was for thirteen years left in peace. Instead of profiting and utilizing the time in preparing against future invasion, the Princes, though warned by famine, plague and pestilence, forgot the Moguls and the rude lesson which they had learnt, and reverted to their old quarrels for supremacy.

In 1237 the Moguls returned, under Batou, the grandson of Genghis; for two hundred and forty years (1237—1477) the land groaned under their oppression, and it seems almost miraculous that Christianity should have survived in Russia The work of the Church was impeded in the sad havoc of the times; but the more the people suffered, the stronger did their attachment to their Church become; and, in their despair of any human help, they betook themselves to outward acts of contrition and of penance. The Princes, though quarrelling amongst themselves, drew to their Church; and although it is undoubtedly true that they led lives of sensuality, yet, in order to appease their Priests, they liberally distributed alms; many assumed the life and obligations of monks; and many founded monasteries, as a salve for their consciences and in atonement for their sins. This discipline does not give a high idea of the spirituality of their religion, but unfortunately it is true; so that it was said that more monasteries were built and endowed in Russia during the Mogul invasions, than in any other period of its history.

The zeal for building monasteries the Bishops and Metropolitans encouraged, the latter sometimes founding monasteries themselves, so that in Russia they became a more prominent feature, even than in other countries of the Greek Communion; in fact so greatly did the monasteries increase in number, and such vast domains and wealth did they acquire, that they became injurious to the State. The civil government of Russia, as has been the case in other countries, availed itself of the plea for legislation, and we consequently find a system of confiscation of their lands and wealth adopted [m].

This devotional spirit the Moguls found it to their interest to encourage, and viewed without resentment the growing influence of the Russian Church. The monasteries they protected, and forbade their own people to molest them; on the Orthodox Church they conferred munificent grants, and exempted the clergy from taxation and tribute. Whilst the Grand Prince himself was obliged, in order to be invested in his Princedom, to go on a long and dangerous journey, and humbly do obeisance before the principal Khan at Kaptshak, the Khans, hoping to make the Church their ally against the Princes, treated the Metropolitans and Bishops with the utmost reverence. But the opposite result was effected, and the Russian Church, so far from being propitiated, viewed with disgust the favour of the infidels. The Metropolitans and Bishops and Clergy understood how that a united Russia, the elevation of the Grand Princedom and the concentration of the supreme control, were the only means of driving the Moguls out of Russia; for this they watched the opportunity, and for this the Church educated the State.

The Moguls under Batou commenced their ravages in 1237. In that year the Capital of Bulgaria, the ancient enemy of Russia, was burnt, its inhabitants being given to the sword. The first Principality in Russian territory to suffer was that of Riazan, her Princes, Oleg and Theodore, falling in battle; Suzdal and Rostov followed; Moscow was burnt; the Grand Principality of Vladimir reduced to ashes,

---

[m] This system, once commenced, was carried out to its full extent in the Eighteenth Century by Peter I., Peter III, and Catherine II

and the Grand Prince Yury II. killed; the people, who sought refuge in the Cathedral, where the Bishop Metrophanes, standing in their midst, commended their souls to God, being to a man piteously massacred. Suddenly, when they arrived within sixty miles of Novgorod, the Moguls, for what reason is not known, after having destroyed fourteen fortified cities, besides a large number of scattered towns and villages, stopped short, as on the former occasion they had stopped short on the banks of the Dnieper. Thus Novgorod, although its neighbour Tver was sacked, escaped, the amazed citizens attributing their deliverance to the intercession of the Saints and the prayers of the Church.

Again in 1240 Batou appeared, and in that year Kiev, the "Mother of Russia," was besieged. The destruction of Vladimir warned the people of Kiev of the fate which awaited them, and every Church was converted into a fortress. So struck were the Moguls with the grandeur of the city, that they offered to spare it, if it would capitulate; after a heroic defence it was subdued, its Cathedral and monastery and noble Churches were reduced to ruins, and the citizens either slain or led away into captivity. The Russian Church was at this time presided over by Joseph, the successor of Cyril I., and he is supposed to have perished in the general conflagration.

From this time forward Russia was a Mogul province; and in 1242 Batou settled himself on the banks of the Volga, and built the city of Sarai; there he established the Empire of the Mogul Khans, or the Golden Horde, whither the Princes were obliged to bring in person their tribute, and do homage, and to purchase from the Khans the right of governing their Principalities.

Yury II. was succeeded in the Grand Princedom of Vladimir by his brother Yaroslav II. (1238—1246), after whose death one of his sons, Andrew (1246—1256), was confirmed in the title of Grand Prince by Batou, whilst another son, Alexander, reigned at Novgorod. Under the latter a new gleam of hope dawned on the country, and he, the famous Alexander Nevski, with his grandson Dmitri Donskoi, are the two principal figures during the period of the national debasement.

The Novgorodians having opposed the Livonian Knights of the Sword, the indefatigable enemies of Orthodoxy, Pope Gregory IX., the arrogant Pope who persecuted the great German Emperor, Frederic II, and drew upon himself the censure of St. Louis of France[n], proclaimed against them a Crusade with the promise of plenary indulgence. Alexander, nothing daunted, feeling that he was fighting for the Orthodox Church, opposed the Western with an Eastern Crusade. Having first received in the Church of St. Sophia the benediction of the Archbishop Spiridion, he set out against the army of Scandinavian and Western Crusaders, and won the brilliant victory on the Neva, which gained for him the surname of Nevski. Novgorod was the only Principality which had preserved its independence from the Moguls; yet Nevski was obliged, like the other Grand Princes, to go to Sarai and do homage to the Khan. He, who united in his character the virtues of the greatest General and Statesman since the commencement of the invasions, well knew that a Fabian policy was the only one that had a chance of success, and he taught his rebellious Novgorodians that, in view of the immense hordes of the Moguls, present resistance was madness.

For ten years after the death of Joseph, Russia was, owing to its troubles, left without a Metropolitan. Pope Innocent, conscious of the oppressed state of the country, and the difficulty of the Russian Church in procuring a Metropolitan, whilst the Orthodox Greek Patriarch continued to reside at Nice, took advantage of the vacancy of the See, but, learning how the attempts of his predecessor to coerce Russia by force of arms had been defeated by Nevski, he had resort to more peaceful measures. He sent to David, Prince of Galich, a present of a royal Crown, with

---

[n] See p 435

a proposal for a union of the Churches, and a Crusade against the Moguls. Had the Prince of Galich entertained the Pope's proposal of a Crusade, he would have defeated all the plans of Nevski, and probably have completed the ruin of Russia. With regard to the union of the Churches, David held that that could only be effected by an Œcumenical Council.

In 1250, Cyril II., a Russian, was elected Metropolitan, and Consecrated by Manuel, the Greek Patriarch, at Nice. Cyril, who was Metropolitan for thirty years (1250—1280), was one of the many able Metropolitans who presided over the Russian Church during the Mogul invasions. His Episcopate extended over the reigns of Alexander Nevski, and of his brothers Yaroslav III. and Basil I., in all of whom he found able assistants. The ravages of the Moguls, and the hard necessities of war, had been attended with serious consequences to the Russian Church; and when Cyril became Metropolitan, the number of its Dioceses was reduced from eighteen to five. Going about from one city to another, he threw into the desolated Churches renewed life, and restored the discipline which in these troublous times had been sadly relaxed. In compliance with the request of Yaroslav, who had once been Prince of Tver, he established a See in that city. By the threat of an interdict he awed the turbulent citizens of Novgorod, which had now, owing to its commerce, grown into a powerful State, into obedience to the Grand Prince. He improved the Nomo-Canon; and in 1274 held a Council at Vladimir, with the object of restoring the ceremonial, and rooting out the simony which had become prevalent in the Church. Batou having established the Golden Horde at Sarai, Cyril, knowing that it must necessarily become the meeting-point of the Russian Princes, made the capital of the Khans a Diocesan See, and appointed Metrophanes its first Bishop. So far were the Khans from showing opposition to the Russian Church, or resenting the appointment of a Christian Bishop, that Mangou Temir, who succeeded Batou, appointed Theophanes, the successor of Metrophanes, his envoy to the Patriarch of Constantinople.

St. Alexander Nevski was the staunch defender of Orthodoxy. In 1251, Pope Innocent IV., acting on false information, sent to him by two cardinals a Bull, as *to a devoted son of the Church*, assuring him that his father Yaroslav had, on his death-bed, expressed a desire to submit himself to the Church of Rome [o]. With regard to this assertion it would be rash to hazard an opinion ; what is certain is, that Alexander Nevski is a Canonized Saint of the Russian Church, and that a splendid monastery outside St. Petersburg was erected to his memory by Peter the Great. When, in 1256, the reigning Prince of Kiev left the Orthodox, to join the Roman Catholic, Communion, and acknowledged in his Principality the supremacy of the Pope, he so offended the Khan that he transferred to Alexander Nevski the territory and Principality of Kiev. When the intelligence of Nevski's death was brought to the Metropolitan, at the time that he was celebrating Mass, Cyril, turning to the people, exclaimed, " Know, my people, that the sun of Russia is set." Under such a brave soldier and prudent statesman as Nevski, Russia bade fair to emulate its former glory ; but the jealousy of the superior character of the Grand Prince was a bar to his conferring on the country the advantages for which his ability qualified him. After his death, the Princes, whose disunion it was the policy of the Khans to promote, still preferred the misery and degradation to which their common country was subjected by the Moguls, rather than lay aside their rivalries, and acknowledge the Grand Prince set over them.

For two years after the death of Cyril II., the Russian Church, owing to the deposition, by the Emperor Michael Palæologus, of Joseph, the Patriarch of Constantinople, and the intrusion of Veccus [p], refusing to have any relations with the Latin Patriarch, remained without a Metropolitan. After the death of Michael, the deposition of Veccus, and

[o] Rambaud, I. 167.   [p] See p. 448.

the restoration of Joseph, Maximus, a Greek, was elected Metropolitan, and Consecrated by Joseph. Maximus, who held the Primacy for twenty-two years (1282—1304), followed in the footsteps of his predecessor, enforcing discipline in the Church, and reconciling the Princes; the latter task arising out of the contentions of two of the sons of Alexander Nevski, Dmitri and Andrew, which brought new swarms of Moguls into the country. Finding the Southern parts in complete ruin, and Kiev ill-suited for the Metropolitan, Maximus transferred the Metropolitan See to Vladimir; and there his successor, St. Peter, for a time continued it, although the Princes were still styled Metropolitans of "Kiev and All Russia."

The transference of the Metropolitan See from Kiev, first to Vladimir, and afterwards to Moscow, marks an important era in the history of the Russian Church; thenceforward, although its dependence on the Patriarch of Constantinople continued, the Metropolitans were generally Russians, elected by the clergy, and confirmed in their office by the Sovereign.

During the Thirteenth Century, Moscow was an obscure and insignificant village of Suzdal, and continued so till the time of Daniel, son of Alexander Nevski, whose Appanage it was, and who considerably increased and raised it to importance. Daniel, dying A.D. 1303, was succeeded in turn by his two brothers, Yury III., (1303—1326), and Ivan. Yury strengthened his position, as Grand Prince of Moscow, by marriage with a Mogul Princess, the sister of Usbek, the reigning Khan (1313—1343). Having by a false accusation of the murder of his wife, the Khan's sister, compassed the death of Michael, the Grand Prince of Tver (he has been Canonized as a Saint and Martyr), Yury was himself assassinated by Michael's son, Dmitri. Ivan (1328—1341), surnamed Kalita (*the purse*), the brother and successor of Yury, was Grand Prince both of Vladimir and Moscow; he did all in his power to raise and embellish the latter Principality, so that, though Vladimir continued to be the nominal Moscow became under him the real, Capital of Russia.

St. Peter, a native of Volhynia, Consecrated at Constantinople Metropolitan (1308—1328) by the Patriarch Athanasius, had, like his predecessor Maximus, his See at Vladimir. Although, under Usbek, the Moguls at the Horde were converted to Mahometanism, the Khan still continued to favour the Orthodox Church. St. Peter, presenting himself before Usbek at the Horde, obtained from him the decree;— "Let no one injure the Catholic Church [q], the Metropolitan Peter, the Archimandrites or the Popes in Russia ; let them be free from all tax and tribute, for all this belongs to God, and these people by their prayers preserve us ..... let the Metropolitans pray with a true heart and without fear, for us and for our children ..... whosoever shall dare to speak evil of the Russian faith, whosoever shall injure any Church, monastery or Chapel, let him be put to death [r]."

The object which Ivan had in view during his reign was to subject all the Princes to himself, and to unite the whole of Russia under his government; he first proposed to Peter to transfer the Metropolitan See from Vladimir to Moscow. Peter, seeing that Moscow had become practically the seat of government, realized the inconvenience which would result from the Metropolitan residing in the South ; he lent a ready ear to the proposal, having made it a condition that Ivan should build, to the glory of the Blessed Virgin, the Church of the Assumption. To Peter is to be ascribed the building of that Church, in which the successors of Ivan, no longer mere Princes of Moscow, but the Tsars of all the Russias, have since his time been crowned.

Ivan, with consummate ability, played the Princes against the Moguls, and the Moguls against the Princes , and the Metropolitans were again the pioneers. Feeling that the unity of the Principalities, under a single ruler, would be

---

[q] Mr. Blackmore, in his notes on Mouraviev, explains that the word *Sobornuyou* is that by which the Slavic nations expressed the word Καθολικός in the Creed   [r] Mouraviev, p. 53.

more beneficial to the Church than a number of conflicting authorities, Theognostes (1328—1353), a Greek by birth, the successor of St. Peter, together with the Russian clergy, heartily co-operated with Ivan, the example of the clergy was soon followed by the Boyars and Princes; the Metropolitan was made arbitrator in their quarrels; the head of the clergy was identified with the paramount civil authority, and Church and State in Russia became united. The Princes, watching their opportunity, adopted the policy of bowing down to the Horde when it was strong, and attacking it when it was weak. And at the very time when the Princes were becoming united, the Moguls became disunited; the Golden Horde, the prey of civil war, began to be split up into several Hordes or Khanates, which, by their sanguinary conflicts, undermined the supreme authority, and resulted in making the Khanate no longer formidable, and eventually in the abolition of the Horde of Sarai.

Simeon (1341—1353), surnamed, from the haughtiness with which he treated the Russian Princes, Gordii or *the Proud*, succeeded his father, Ivan, whose policy he continued, assuming the title of the Grand Kniaz, or Prince, of all the Russias. In his reign the holy hermit, St. Sergius, a native of Rostov, the bearer of a name dear to every Russian heart, founded, in the woods near Moscow, the Troitsa (*Trinity*) monastery, the richest and most venerated of all the religious houses in Russia. Owing to its great wealth, it was thought advisable to fortify it with ramparts; it was consequently surrounded by a thick wall, 1,500 yards in length, with a triple row of embrasures, flanked by nine towers, and its dimensions and strength may be estimated from the fact, that it was able to accommodate all the Muscovites who flocked into it, during the French invasion of 1812. Simeon having been, together with the Metropolitan Theognostes, and Basil, Archbishop of Novgorod, carried off by the Black Plague, which was then devastating Europe, was succeeded by his brother, Ivan II. (1353—1359).

St. Alexis (1353—1377), a scion of a noble Russian family,

succeeded Theognostes as Metropolitan; and, says Mouraviev, during his Primacy of twenty-four years, he took the helm of the Empire. Ivan II.'s "kindly and guileless disposition might have unfitted him for the stormy post which he held, had there not been at his side the keen-eyed and strong-willed Metropolitan of Moscow, Alexis [s]." When, under the pacific rule of Ivan II., Russia fell back into its former anarchy, Alexis was at that time the salvation of the country; and when, after the death of Ivan, the Grand Princedom was threatened by the house of Suzdal, it was Alexis who saved the supremacy of Moscow.

The policy of Ivan I., if suspended under Ivan II., was resumed by the son of the latter, Dmitri (1362—1389), whose object was, whilst he united the Princes, to strengthen, at their expense, the Boyars. The long reigns of Dmitri and his two successors, during which they were ably seconded by the Metropolitans, greatly conduced to the ascendency of the Grand Princedom. Dmitri, having thrice repulsed the Lithuanians, who ravaged the country up to the very walls of Constantinople; and having successfully contended against the Princes of Suzdal, Riazan and Tver, set himself to gain the Boyars on his side; and then to induce the Princes to coalesce; with the view of an attack on the common foe of their Church and State.

To Alexis, who died A.D. 1377, the magnificent monasteries of the Choudov within the Kremlin and the Pechersky owe their foundation, and he, together with Peter, is reckoned amongst the Saints of the Russian Church. His successor was Cyprian (1377—1410). In 1380 Dmitri, having first attended Mass in the Troitsa monastery, and received the blessing of the saintly Sergius (1315—1392) [t], who promised him that, with the aid of the Mother of God, he would win the battle, he set out, at the head of the united Princes and an army of 150,000 men, and gained over Mamai, the successor of Usbek, the splendid victory on

---

[s] Ralston's Early Russian History, p 95.   [t] Canonized 1428.

the banks of the Don, from which the name of Donskoi was given him.

The victory of the Don, the first defeat of the Moguls, was of the greatest importance to Russia ; it did not accomplish, but it was the forerunner of, the expulsion of the Moguls from the country. Notwithstanding this great victory, the Princes, jealous of Dmitri and of the rising power of Moscow, refused to serve under him, and in two years the Moguls returned under Toktamish, who had dethroned Mamai Dmitri, abandoned by the Princes, retired from Moscow, which, betrayed by the Prince of Riazan, the Moguls burnt to the ground, despoiling the Churches, and massacring every citizen who fell into their hands.

Dmitri Donskoi, on his death, in A.D. 1389, was succeeded by his son Basil III. (1389—1425). It was in the early part of his reign that Timour or Tamerlane, a Prince of the same race as the enemies of Russia, was making his religious zeal an excuse for overwhelming the whole world, Christians and the Sonnite, or orthodox Mahometans, alike. He had, in the battle of Angora, defeated and taken captive the Ottoman Sultan Bajazet[u], when, by his death A.D. 1405, his career was cut short and his dominion broken up ; he was thus prevented from crossing into Europe, and adding to the Mogul forces in their attacks on Russia.

Basil III. was succeeded by his son Basil IV. (1425—1462), a boy ten years of age Cyprian was succeeded as Metropolitan by Photius (1410—1432), after whose death the See was vacant for seven years. The Grand Prince Basil then summoned a Synod, which elected Jonah, Bishop of Riazan, who was sent to Constantinople for institution by the Patriarch Joseph. But he found that Isidore, Bishop of Illyria, had been already Consecrated by the Patriarch, and Isidore became Metropolitan. It was at this time that the Eastern Emperor, John Palæologus, being threatened by the Turks, was seeking the aid of the Western powers, and on Jan. 8, 1438, Pope Eugenius IV. opened the Council

[u] See p. 463.

of Ferrara. Isidore, who was a friend of the Pope and in favour of the union of the Eastern and Western Churches, suggested to Basil that, as the Sovereigns and Primates both of the East and West were assembled to confer on the faith of the Church, it was only fitting that Russia also should be represented Basil reluctantly consented, beseeching him to stand fast in the Orthodox faith, and he directed the Bishop of Suzdal to accompany him to Ferrara. Mention has been already made in a former chapter how the Council was transferred to Florence, where the Pope gained everything he wished ; how the Union of the Churches was decreed, all the Bishops (except Mark of Ephesus) assenting to it, and to the supremacy of the Pope. Amongst the subscribers to the Union was Isidore.

Isidore, rewarded with the title of Cardinal Legate of the Apostolic See, returned in triumph to Russia, bringing friendly letters from the Pope to the Grand Prince. But the Russian Church was as opposed, as the other branches of the Greek Church, to the Union of Florence. Basil received him with the greatest indignation, rebuking him as a false Bishop and a traitor to the cause of Orthodoxy, the Boyars and people with one voice rejected the supremacy of the Pope, and the addition of the Filioque to the Creed ; and Isidore was consigned to the Choudov monastery [v]. Contriving to escape thence, he fled to Rome, where he was received with much honour, and was sent, as we have seen in the previous chapter, to Constantinople, where the Union met with violent opposition. There he was safe, so long as the Palæologi were Emperors, on the fall of the Eastern Empire, he with difficulty escaped to Rome, at which safe distance he styled himself Patriarch of Constantinople, dying with that barren title, A.D. 1463. It is deserving of note how anxious Rome has always been to detach the Russian from the Orthodox Church, and how uniformly unsuccessful (and when we come to the return

[v] "Universâ Orientali Ecclesiâ pactam Florentiæ unionem detestante."— Le Quien, I 1268.

of the Uniats by millions to the Russian Church, it may almost be said, ludicrous) have been its endeavours.

St. Jonah (1448—1462), the successor of Isidore, was, in consequence of the troublous state of the East preceding the fall of Constantinople, consecrated Metropolitan in a Synod of Russian Bishops. After the " comparatively insignificant reign of the two Basils [w]," Ivan III., the son of the last Basil, became Grand Prince of Moscow. Twenty-two years of age at his accession he reigned more than forty-three years (1462—1505) ; under him the consolidation of the Empire was effected, and Russia was emancipated from the Mogul supremacy. Thus he acquired the title of " Builder of Russia," and was the founder of Russia's greatness, but his cruelty gained for him another title afterwards, still more deservedly, and to all ages, borne by his grandson, Ivan IV., that of the "*Terrible.*" In the reign of Ivan III. we first hear of that terrible scourge, the knout, and that an Archimandrite and some nobles were *publicly knouted* for the forgery of a Will.

At the time that Ivan entered on the Grand Princedom, Poland had attained the position of the great power of Eastern Europe ; and as that country, together with its neighbour Lithuania, plays so important a part in the history of the Russian Church, we may here give some account of the Church in those countries.

Of Poland, which, like Russia, was a member of the Slavic family, somewhat has been already said, and it has been explained how Russia and Poland came to belong, the former to the Greek, the latter to the Latin, Church.

Lithuania first emerges from legend in the time of its King, Mindovg, who lived in the time of Alexander Nevski. Under Mindovg, the Lithuanians, at that time worshippers of Perkun, like the Perun of the early Russians, the God of Thunder, made their first serious attempt against Russia. Mindovg knowing that Russia was enfeebled through the

---

[w] Morfill's Russia, p 50.

Moguls, expected to find it an easy conquest; but hearing that at its head was the powerful Alexander, who, besides the victory which gained him the title of Nevski, had been victorious over the Sword-Bearers, and being at the time threatened by the Knights of Livonia, he bethought himself of the plan of turning Christian, and submitting to the Pope, thinking that the Livonians would hail as an ally an opponent of the Orthodox Church. He accordingly applied to Pope Innocent IV., and, together with his wife, received Baptism in the Roman Church; but soon afterwards, when he no longer required the Pope's aid, he renounced Christianity, and re-introduced Paganism into his dominions. He began his reign by murdering his brothers and his sons, and exterminating the Princes who opposed his rule; he ended it by being himself, in 1263, assassinated by one of the Princes whose wife he had abducted, and after his death Lithuania, under the contests of his descendants and the Princes, fell back into its former state of anarchy and barbarism.

The real founder of the Lithuanian power was Gedymin (1315—1340), who, taking advantage of the disastrous condition of Russia, in 1320 seized several of its Western provinces and gained possession of Kiev, which was destined to remain for four hundred years in the hands of strangers. Although he authorized Greek Churches to be built in his dominions, and allowed his sons to embrace the Orthodox faith, Gedymin himself lived and died a pagan. His son Olgerd (1345—1377) governed a united kingdom and extended his conquests in Russia; but in Volhynia he found successful opponents in the Poles, who oppressed the Orthodox, and introduced the Roman Catholic faith into the country, converting the Greek into Latin Churches.

Olgerd thereupon sought the alliance of Simeon the Proud, and, whilst still a pagan, married an Orthodox Princess of Tver. Under her influence, he, together with many of his nobles and other subjects, accepted Christianity from the Greek Church; and before his death his Capital, Vilna, contained thirty Christian Churches[x], and the bulk of the people remained for many years adherents of the Greek Church[y].

Olgerd was succeeded by his son Jagiello (1377—1434). Lithuania was under the Ecclesiastical jurisdiction of Moscow, and it seemed at the time that the victors would be absorbed by the vanquished, and become Russified by their conquest[z]. An unexpected event turned the course of history. The Crown of Poland had, on the death without male heirs of Louis the Great, who combined the Kingdom of Hungary with that of Poland, devolved on his beautiful daughter Jadwiga (1384—1389), whom Jagiello sought in marriage, but who refused to marry him on the double ground, that she had another suitor, and that he was a schismatic of the Greek Church. The religious difficulty was surmounted by Jagiello's adandoning the Greek and adopting, at Cracow, the Latin faith; and whatever other scruples Jadwiga had were set aside by the Polish Diet compelling her to marry him, with the view of uniting the Polish and Lithuanian Crowns. As soon as the bride and bridegroom arrived at Vilna, Jagiello, who at his marriage had taken the name Ladislaus, gave orders that his subjects should adopt the form of worship of his wife, and a large number of still Pagan Lithuanians underwent compulsory Baptism into the Roman Church.

Lithuania was thus annexed to Poland; the Capital was transferred to Cracow; and the Jagiello dynasty continued to reign in Poland from 1386—1572. The union of its Polish and Lithuanian foes impeded the development of Russia, but Lithuania felt that, through the union, it had forfeited its independence, so that it was never cordial, and there were constant dissensions and even wars between them. Those wars were not without advantage to Russia, to whose existence their united forces might have been fatal. We are accustomed in the present day to think of the Russians

[x] Ralston, p. 119. [y] Morfill's Poland, p. 15
[z] Rambaud, I 186.

as the oppressors of the Poles, and find it difficult to realize a time when the Poles were the oppressors of the Russians. Yet so it was, and we shall find further on that, in the troubles which preceded the present Roman dynasty, Russia was even forced for a time to accept a Polish Tsar. But the Roman Catholic religion had been rendered especially hateful to the Orthodox Christians of Lithuania, in their fierce wars with the Knights of Livonia; by far the greater part of the people refused to abandon the Greek Church[a]; and under the Jagiello dynasty the Orthodox Christians in Lithuania, as well as in Poland, were generally left, without molestation, to follow their own faith.

In 1392 Jagiello ceded Lithuania, with the title of Grand Prince, to his cousin Vitoft (1392—1430), a member of the Roman Church, under whom a lamentable schism occurred in the Russian Orthodox Church. Though Jagiello had renounced the allegiance of the Greek Church, and Vitoft also was a Romanist, no outward rupture occurred during the life-time of the Metropolitan, Cyprian, who was much respected and beloved by both; but on his death, in 1410, and the election of Photius, the schism broke out. Vitoft, no longer subject to the restraint, summoned a Synod of Bishops to Novgorod, to whom he represented the difficulties arising to the Church of Lithuania, through the Metropolitan being resident at Moscow, and advocated the appointment of a second Metropolitan at Kiev for Western Russia. The Bishops, although for some time they resisted, were eventually intimidated; and Gregory, a native of Bulgaria, was elected Metropolitan and sent for Consecration to Constantinople.

This arrangement being objected to by the Metropolitan Photius, Joseph, the Patriarch of Constantinople, rejected the petition of the Synod as a violation of the unity of the Russian Church, and refused to perform the act of Consecration. Thereupon Vitoft convoked to Novgorod another Synod of the Bishops, whom he compelled to con-

---

[a] It was in a town of Lithuania in which the Uniat movement, of which further mention will be made in the next Chapter, was effected

secrate Gregory as Metropolitan of Kiev and All Russia. Gregory himself, who was strongly attached to the Orthodox Church, long stood out against the arrangement, and endeavoured, although in vain, to lead Vitoft to Orthodoxy; but Russia had thenceforward two Metropolitans, one at Moscow, the other at Kiev.

In 1418 Gregory was, with nineteen suffragan Bishops, sent by Vitoft to the Council of Constance, to congratulate Martin on his election as Pope, and to seek re-union with the Latin Church. But it was simply the act of the Romanist Grand Prince Vitoft; the deputies were in no sense representatives of the Greek Church, and went to Constance against the will of the Patriarch of Constantinople, as well as of the Metropolitan of Moscow.

Under Vitoft, Lithuania gained the height of its power; after his death it waned, and the country underwent several vicissitudes of government, till, in 1501, it was definitely placed under the Polish Crown, as the Grand Duchy of Lithuania.

We must now return to Russia and its Grand Prince, Ivan III. It was predicted by Euphemius, Archbishop of Novgorod, at Ivan's birth, that he would be an illustrious Prince, but "Woe," he said, "to Novgorod; Novgorod will fall at his feet and will never rise again." Early in his reign Russia was brought into close connection with the Eastern Church. On the fall of Constantinople, the Patriarch Joseph determined to seek an asylum in Russia, but died on his journey. In 1472, Ivan married Sophia, daughter of Thomas, the brother of the last two Palæologi, and heiress of the Greek Emperors. After the fall of the Eastern Empire, Thomas took up his residence in Rome, where his daughter was educated in the principles of the Council of Florence. The marriage was brought about by Pope Paul II., acting under the advice of Cardinal Bessarion, who after the Council had joined the Roman Church.

The Roman Church had, at the Council of Florence, signally failed to bring the Russian Church into its obedience. The Pope would without difficulty have foreseen that in Russia a Third Rome was arising, destined to supersede, and take the place of, the Old Rome in the councils of the Eastern Church. The marriage of a Roman Catholic Princess, the heiress of the Palæologi, with the Grand Duke of Moscow, was, on the part of the Pope, a smart stroke of policy; but it was a deeper and more successful one on the part of Ivan. He, too, foreseeing the time when the Third Rome might succeed to the place of the Second Rome, immediately after his marriage, added the two-headed Eagle, the symbol of the Imperial power, which is still borne by the Tsars, to the arms of Russia; thus designing to show himself the heir of the Emperors of Constantinople, and of the Roman Cæsars. The importance of the marriage cannot be overrated. Moscow succeeded to Constantinople, as the Second Rome had succeeded to Old Rome; it became virtually the Capital of Orthodoxy, its champion in withstanding Islam, and protecting the Greek Church from the effects of 1453.

The Pope of Rome brought about the marriage, partly in the hope of promoting a Crusade against the Turks, chiefly in the expectation that a Byzantine Princess of the Roman Church would bring Russia under the obedience of the Popes. But no sooner had Sophia arrived in Russia than she became a convert to Orthodoxy; and her conversion may well be claimed as a triumph by the Greek Church. She went to Russia attended by a number of Greek emigrants, who took with them from Constantinople the rich collection of valuable MSS, which became the nucleus of the present Library of the Patriarchs, she did much towards restoring the learning which had suffered under the Moguls; over Ivan she exerted a paramount influence; and encouraged the people to shake off the yoke of the Moguls, which she bore with less composure than Russians, whom their long servitude had habituated to it.

We have noticed elsewhere [b] the death of Ladislaus, King of Poland and Hungary, on the field of Varna, A.D. 1444.

[b] See p. 473.

He was, after a short interregnum, succeeded on the throne of Poland by his brother, Casimir IV (1447—1492). Casimir at his death left Poland to his eldest son, John Albert (1492—1501), and Lithuania to his second son, Alexander. A short war, which was popular in Russia, from its desire to shake off the yoke which the Latin had imposed on the Orthodox Church, had been concluded in 1494, between Russia and Poland. Ivan, wishing to cultivate the friendship of Poland, determined to cement it by the marriage of his daughter Helena with Alexander, the brother of the Polish King But, so far from cementing peace, the marriage was the cause of a fresh war. The Princess, the daughter of Sophia, was a staunch member of the Greek, whilst Alexander belonged to the Roman, Church. By the treaty made in October, 1494, it was agreed that Helena was to have her own attendants, to follow her own religion, and a Chapel for the Greek services was to be built in the Palace at Vilna; and she received strict injunctions from Ivan never to enter a Latin Church. On these terms the marriage was celebrated in January, 1495

At that time Alexander VI., who possesses the character of being the wickedest of the number, was Pope of Rome. A contrast, much to the advantage of the former, might be drawn between the Spiritual Heads of the Eastern and Western Communions at this time. It does not appear to have occurred to Alexander, that the opinion of a Pope, who was scandalizing Christendom with his crimes, was worth very little. The Pope urged upon the Prince the violation of God's command, "Whom God has joined together let not man put asunder," he insisted that either the Prince must renounce his wife, or that the wife must renounce the Greek Church Both Ivan and Sophia were strongly opposed to their daughter's renunciation of the Orthodox faith. Ivan also had reason to complain that she was forced, contrary to the agreement at her marriage, to violate her conscience, that the services of the Orthodox Church had to be abandoned, her Orthodox servants replaced by those of the Roman Communion, that the Orthodox Metropolitan of Kiev had been murdered, and a Latin intruded into his See. A quarrel between Ivan and his son-in-law, followed by a war in 1500, was the consequence of the Pope's unrighteous interference; and the Poles, notwithstanding the alliance of the Sword-bearers, were defeated and cut to pieces in the battle of Vedrocka.

In 1501, Alexander (1501—1506) succeeded his brother as King of Poland. Helena effected a reconciliation between her father and husband, and in March, 1503, a truce for six years was agreed to, on the condition, on which Ivan insisted, viz., that his daughter's faith should not be tampered with. Pope Julius II, whose military propensities scandalized Christendom only in a less degree than the lives of his three predecessors, directed the papal thunders against the perplexed King[c], who, however, refused to abandon his wife, and, notwithstanding the action of two Popes, lived in complete harmony with her till his death.

Ivan III. succeeded during his reign in reconciling, and subjecting the Princes to his control. Still there remained the two independent Republics of Novgorod and Pskov; and these he determined to bring into subjection. Novgorod wavered between Russia and Poland, between allegiance to the Metropolitan of Moscow and the Metropolitan of Kiev, and the Republic was rent asunder with anarchy. Gerontius, the Metropolitan of Moscow, the Bishops, and the Boyars, urged Ivan to proclaim a holy war against Lithuania and the allies of the Pope; and in 1478 Novgorod fell. Theophilus, the Archbishop, interceded for the lives of the inhabitants; their lives were spared, but thousands of them were driven into exile, and their goods confiscated; whilst the great bell, which had been accustomed to summon its Vetché, or Common Council, was carried off to Moscow. Theophilus, who was a strict adherent of Orthodoxy, had already, by refusing to receive Consecration at Kiev, and seeking it from the Metropolitan of Moscow, offended the

[c] Morfill's Poland, p. 64.

Novgorodians; he now for some cause or another offended Ivan, and was forced to end his days in the Choudov Monastery.

Pskov survived for a time, but it too fell under Ivan's son and successor; and its bells were taken off to Moscow.

Ivan, after the fall of Novgorod, turned his attention to the Horde, which had now become split up into three rival Khanates, those of Sarai, Kazan, and the Crimea. In alliance with the Moguls of the Crimea, he first subdued the Khanate of Kazan. Secured against Kazan and the Crimea, he next determined entirely to throw off the Mogul yoke, and made war against the Golden Horde at Sarai. It had been the custom, whenever the ambassadors of the Horde visited Moscow, for the Princes to fall on their knees to receive the orders of the Khan. Ivan, urged on by his wife Sophia, the proud daughter of a Palæologus, now refused to comply with the degrading custom. When the Khan Akmet sent his messengers to receive the tribute, he openly rebelled, and, it is said, put all to death except one, whose life was spared to convey the intelligence to the Horde. It does not come within our province to describe minutely the victory of Russia, in 1480, nor to enquire into the character of Ivan, whether, as some say, he was a coward, or whether, from motives of prudence, he counselled delay. His resolution, however, appears for a time to have faltered, perhaps he was unwilling to stake the fortunes of Russia on a single battle. Murmurs and indignation met him on all sides. Archbishop Bassian of Rostov rebuked his cowardice with stinging words; "Dost thou fear death; thou too must die like others ... give me thy warriors, and, old as I am, I will not turn my back upon the Tartars." The Metropolitan of Moscow reminded him how "the good Shepherd lays down His life for the sheep." Akmet had expected help from the Lithuanians; but they were kept at bay by Ivan's ally, the Khan of the Crimea. We will sum up the unheroic manner in which Russia at last shook off the Mogul yoke in the words of M. Rambaud[d];—"An inexplicable panic seized the two armies; Russians and Moguls both fled when no man pursued. The Khan never stopped till he reached the Horde, and Akmet was put to death by his own soldiers."

The Khanate of Kazan had fallen. The Golden Horde at Sarai attacked by the Khans of the Crimea, survived its defeat by the Russians but a short time; and although the Moguls still continued to trouble Russia, Sarai was, in 1502, reduced to ruins.

In the reign of Ivan III. a heresy arose, which has ever since left its mark on the Church of Russia.

In 1491, Zosimus, a name of unfortunate omen[e], Archimandrite of the Simonov Monastery, was, without the consent of the Synod being obtained, elected successor to the Metropolitan Gerontius About twenty years previously a Judaizing sect, styled Strigolniks, had made their appearance, under a Jew named Zacharias, at Novgorod, purporting to found their creed on a cabalistic writing which they said God, at the Creation of the World, had delivered to Adam, and from which Solomon derived his wisdom and the Prophets their foreknowledge. They cast odium on the Virgin Mary and on the Saints, and taught that the Advent of the Messiah was yet to come. They seduced to their opinions two Priests of Novgorod, Alexis and Dionysius, the former of whom, in his zeal for the Jewish dispensation, went so far as to exchange his own name for that of Abraham, and his wife's for Sarah. They thought to engraft their doctrines on those of the Orthodox Church, and gained a large following in Novgorod and Pskov; they deceived the Metropolitan Zosimus, and, for a time, Ivan, the latter of whom brought the two Priests to Moscow, and raised them to high positions in the Church.

In time the sect attained such a height of power and influence, that the politic Ivan, feeling that danger to the Church involved danger to the Throne, determined to extirpate the heresy. Yielding to the earnest solicitations of the

---

[d] Vol. I. 239.   [e] See p 202

Orthodox, he summoned a synod to Moscow, in which the Strigolniks were condemned, the offending Priests, though still screened by Zosimus, anathematized and committed to prison, and their goods confiscated. Zosimus was himself, after a time, although on another charge, that of intemperance, deposed, and forced into a monastery; but it was not before the corrupt teaching had done much harm, and given rise to many blasphemous opinions and practices. Ivan himself appointed, as successor to Zosimus, Simeon, Hegumen of the Troitsa Lavra, thus claiming the same rights over the Church as he had succeeded in exercising over the State.

Ivan the Great died in 1505, having almost, although not entirely, eradicated the Appanages, and converted Russia from a congeries of feeble and disabled States into a united Kingdom. The reign of his son and successor, Basil V. (1505—1533), was a continuation of his father's policy, which he carried out with an even more despotic will, not allowing the least opposition to himself, nor did his subjects show any disposition to oppose him.

On the death of his brother-in-law, Alexander, King of Poland, Basil in vain tried to induce the nobles of Lithuania and Poland to elect him as his successor. Having in 1510 reduced Pskov, the last of the Republics, to submission, Basil, in 1514, wrested from Sigismund I. (1507—1548), Alexander's successor, the important city of Smolensk, a city which for one hundred and ten years had been held by its Lithuanian conquerors. In 1517 he destroyed the independence of Riazan, which was one of the few Appanages to which Ivan III. had conceded some share of separate authority[f]; and, before his death, the Appanages completely came to an end.

After having been for twenty years married to his wife Salmone, Basil, without any cause of complaint, except that she had borne him no successor to the throne, obtained, uncanonically, a dispensation from the Metropolitan Daniel (1522—1539), enabling him to take another wife,

[f] Rambaud, p 138

and Salmone, protesting against her cruel treatment, was forced to take the veil. Basil then married a noble Lithuanian lady, Helena Glinsky; but, for this weak compliance of the Primate, Russia paid dearly, for the fruit of the second marriage was Ivan IV., *the Terrible.*

In the reign of Basil V. it was found necessary to make a review of the Liturgical books of the Russian Church, into which copyists had introduced many novelties and interpolations These changes the people held in the deepest reverence, on the ground of their supposed antiquity; and the more unintelligible they were, the greater was their sanctity, as containing mysteries which were believed to have been derived from the great Fathers of the Church. But so flagrant were the errors, that the Metropolitan Barlaam impressed on Basil the need of a revision. Basil, who is described as a pious Prince, who reverenced the traditions of the Orthodox Church, acting under the advice of the Metropolitan, requested, in 1518, Theoleptus, Patriarch of Constantinople, to send to Moscow some learned Greek monk to arrange the valuable collection of Greek MSS., which had been brought into Russia by his mother Sophia, and to revise the Church Service-books. Maximus, a monk of Mount Athos, was accordingly selected for the task; he had spent much of his early life at Florence at the time that Savonarola was preaching there; his teaching and example he took as his guide, and after Savonarola's tragic end, sought a refuge from the world amidst the monks of Mount Athos.

Maximus found in the Kremlin at Moscow so large a number of MSS., as led him to aver that, neither in Greece nor in Italy, had he ever seen so large a collection. He now took up his residence in the Choudov Monastery, with the task assigned him, of revising and correcting upwards of twenty folio volumes in the Palace Library, translating and commenting on the Psalter, and correcting the Liturgical books; a task which engaged him nine years.

Barlaam having resigned the Metropolitan See in order

to end his life in his former, the Simonov, monastery, was succeeded by Daniel, to whom we have referred above, an old-fashioned, ignorant Hegumen, who was jealous of the learning and influence of Maximus. Owing to the blind deference paid to the old books, Maximus also encountered from the clergy and the people, but more particularly the Strigolniks, violent persecution, being accused of interpolating, instead of correcting, the books. Having completed the task assigned him he desired to return to Mount Athos. But in denouncing, with the fortitude of Savonarola, the vices that prevailed at Moscow, he made enemies of Basil and the Boyars; the Metropolitan Daniel took part against him, and the Church, on account of the changes he had effected in the ritual, denounced him as a heretic. Basil had at first supported him; but when Maximus boldly opposed his putting away his lawful wife and taking to himself another, the Grand Prince delivered him over to his enemies; and, being condemned in a Synod for heresy and a wrong translation of the Liturgical books, he was consigned, in 1527, first to a monastery at Tver and afterwards to the Troitsa monastery.

Four years after his marriage with Helena Glinsky, Basil, having first received the tonsure of a monk, died after a reign of twenty-seven years, leaving a consolidated Empire to his son Ivan, a boy three years of age.

The young Prince was left in the hands of his mother, a woman of indifferent character, and unfitted for the regency; the country was consequently plunged into anarchy, the evils of which were increased by the licentiousness of the Court. After her death, supposed to have been caused by poison administered by them, in 1538, the Boyars took upon themselves the guardianship of the throne. Under Ivan III. they had risen to great power and influence, and they now succeeded to the unruliness of the Princes. The Kingdom was rent asunder by their turbulence and quarrels; the Metropolitan Daniel, as well as his successor, Joasaph (1539—1542), were without trial or conviction, by their arbitrary sentence, deposed, and ended their days in monasteries.

Left to the guidance of such unprincipled guardians, the young Prince, together with his feeble-minded brother, Yury, was subjected to great privation and cruelty; as he himself afterwards wrote, "treated like the children of beggars, ill-clothed and hungry" The Boyars themselves intrigued for the supreme power; the Grand Prince was deliberately reared in ignorance, his education neglected, his faults connived at, and all that was bad in his nature encouraged, in the hope that when he obtained his majority, he might be found incapable of governing.

Macarius, the Metropolitan (1542—1564), was a wise counsellor. But the tares had been sown in a soil naturally harsh and cruel, and delighting in fiendish amusements; so that, notwithstanding the endeavours of the Primate to eradicate them, they grew stronger with his years, and ripened into the thick harvest of unparalleled horrors and impiety, which have handed him down to all time as Ivan the Terrible.

His character is a problem difficult to be explained. His inhuman love of bloodshed for its own sake; delighting in the torture of wild animals, throwing cats from the summit of his palace; worrying the human victims of his wrath to death by dogs; letting loose wild bears on groups of innocent and unsuspecting people, as they were passing under his windows; such are some of the traits which meet us in his history, and which might lead us to dispose of him as a madman. But in his madness there was method. At every period of his life we find a strange mixture, acts of religion combined with cruelty and murder; we find him observing and reverencing the external forms of the Church; ringing the bells for Matins at three o'clock in the morning; attending Church services of seven hours' duration; praying with such fervour that the marks of his prostration were to be observed on his forehead; then rushing off to the dungeons to gloat over the agonies of the tortured prisoners, claiming for himself a reverence scarcely second to that due to God, sinning and repenting and then falling into greater sins than ever, till he became a master of vice and sacrilege, and even then again he is seen showing some short glimpses of better things, and at last ending his life, by receiving the tonsure of a monk. Such horrors we might pass by, except that they bring him in contact with the Church, or rather the Church in contact with him.

After a minority of cruelty and bloodshed, he was, in January, 1547, at the age of eighteen, crowned Grand Prince by the Metropolitan Macarius in the Cathedral of the Assumption, when he was the first of the Grand Princes to assume the title of Tsar. Through his grandmother, Sophia, he was connected with the Emperors of Byzantium, and Joasaph, Patriarch of Constantinople, sent him a Letter with his blessing, "as the last scion of the ancient Imperial house." The Letter was subscribed by thirty-six Metropolitans, Archbishops and Bishops of the Eastern Church; the Second Rome thus recognizing the heir of Moscow, the Third Rome. Shortly afterwards he married the virtuous Anastasia Romanov, to whom the present dynasty of Russia owes its descent. In the same year occurred a fire, which consumed a large part of Moscow, and in which 1,700 people perished. The influence of his wife, the terror caused by the conflagration, and a simultaneous insurrection of the people, in which his own life was endangered, brought for a time conviction to his conscience, and a desire to amend his life; and his good resolutions were strengthened by Silvester, a holy Priest of Novgorod, whom he had taken as his Confessor. This was the happiest period of his reign, and an era of success to Russia.

Ivan now professed a zeal for the discipline and constitutions of the Church, and, in order to remedy the errors which had crept into the performance of divine service, and to correct the irregular lives of the clergy, he, by the advice of Macarius, summoned, A D. 1551, a Synod of Bishops, the Hundred-Chapter Synod, to Moscow. There he professed repentance for his early sins; he implored the Bishops to enlighten and instruct him in the way of Godliness; exhorted them to establish Orthodoxy; promised to help them in correcting what was amiss, and in confirming what was right; and if he should ever oppose them, bade them not to hold their peace, but openly to rebuke him.

One result of the Synod was the publication of the "Book of the Hundred Chapters," which prescribed, amongst other matters, rules as to the discipline and ceremonies of the Church, such as the monastic state, the morals of the clergy, the eradication of superstition, the property of the Church, and the much needed reformation of the Service Books. The revision of the Books had, as we have seen, been lately undertaken in the reign of his father Basil. The Council of 1551 ordered a further revision; such, however, was the ignorance of the clergy, that no important corrections were made, and the undertaking, so far from doing good, only stirred up the enemies of the Church, who turned the ignorance of the clergy into a weapon against it.

The good results of the reformation in the Tsar's character were shown by the prosperity of the State and of the Church, in the conquest of Kazan, in the conversion of the family of the Khan, and the establishment of a Diocese at Kazan; in the introduction, under the patronage of the Tsar and the Metropolitan Macarius, of printing into Russia; the annexation of Siberia, to which country Ivan sent Bishops and Priests; the foundation of Archangel, and the introduction of a better system of laws into the Kingdom. Everything seemed to prosper with Ivan; the birth of his son Dmitri, and after his premature death, the birth of his other sons, Ivan and Feodor, secured in his family the succession to the throne.

Nor was the Tsar unmindful of the source from which this prosperity of the Church and nation was derived. When, on his triumphal entry into Moscow, after his victory at

Kazan, the Metropolitan Macarius and the clergy went out to meet him; Ivan humbly prostrated himself, and in his speech attributed his victories to the prayers of the Prelate; and as a lasting memorial of his gratitude to God, built the most magnificent of the Churches in Moscow, which was Consecrated under the name of the *Protection of the Holy Virgin.* If he had died at that time, his name would have been handed down to posterity as that of a wise and good Monarch.

Contrast this with the later period of his reign; the Russians conquered by the Poles, under Stephen Batory; expelled from Livonia; Polotsk lost; all Moscow, except the Kremlin, reduced to ashes by the Khan of the Crimea.

So long as his pious wife, Anastasia Romanov, lived, the amendment in the Tsar's life continued, but by her death, in 1560, and his subsequent marriage with Mary, a Circassian Princess, a woman of a very different character, all restraint was removed; his evil genius re-asserted itself, and the series of horrors ensued. In forming an estimate of his character, we must judge him, and whatever allowance is possible afforded him, in the light of the Sixteenth Century; nor must we forget the characters of Henry VIII., and of Catherine de Medici, the Inquisition, and St. Bartholomew's Day.

Athanasius (1564—1565) succeeded Macarius as Metropolitan of Moscow. The Tsar, pretending that he was impeded by the Metropolitan in his work for the good of the people, and that it was impossible to carry on the government at Moscow; having first ordered Athanasius to celebrate Mass in the Church of the Assumption, where he prayed with much devotion, and received his blessing, left the city and took up his residence in the neighbouring fortress of Alexandrovskoe. But the people clamoured for his return; they declared that the Tsar was given them by God Himself, and compared his throne to the Throne of Heaven; they complained that, exposed to their enemies, they were, without the Tsar, as sheep without the shepherd;

and appointed a deputation of Prelates and Boyars to seek him out, who, humbly prostrating themselves before him, implored him, in the name of the Orthodox Church, to return. After a show of resistance, and having exacted a promise that he was not to be interfered with, but that his opponents should be left to his mercy, he yielded to their entreaties and returned to Moscow.

Soon after his return the reign of terror commenced The gentle and timid Metropolitan, who was wholly unable to cope with the evils which beset the Church, he deposed and drove out from Moscow. In 1568 he instituted, as a bodyguard, a select Legion, called Opreechniks, consisting, professedly of men of noble birth, but really of 6,000 villainous youths of the lowest class, whose duty it was to act as spies and informers, and to massacre all persons opposed to the Tsar. From the bloodthirsty acts which they committed they were called by the people Kromieshniks, a word which may perhaps be best rendered in English, *Black-Guards* [g].

The Palace which he built at Alexandrovskoe, and which, in preference to Moscow, he still made his residence, he converted into a monastery, with cells and a magnificent Chapel. There he and his mock-monks donned gorgeous vestments, mimicked the services of the Orthodox Church, and the observances of monastic life, inflicting on themselves severe tortures; Ivan himself, as a salve to his conscience, underwent rigid penance, and wrote to other monasteries, rebuking the neglect of their Rules, and remonstrating with them for their slothfulness and the laxity of their discipline.

Hearing of the holy life of Philip, a man of noble family, Hegumen of the Solovetsky monastery, he summoned him, on the ground of needing his spiritual advice, to his presence. With bitter tears the old man, foreseeing too surely the fate that awaited him, quitted his peaceful retirement, and, notwithstanding his entreaties, the Tsar forced him to accept the Metropolitan See.

A holier Prelate than St. Philip the Church does not

---

[g] See Mouraviev, *note*, p 387

number among its Saints and Martyrs. The fleeting fit of conscience which induced Ivan to hunt up for Metropolitan one of Philip's saintly character, it is difficult to explain. The Metropolitan was soon brought into conflict with the Tsar and his Opreechniks. Ivan, in company of a number of these men, dressed in the peculiar garment of their Order, entered on a Sunday the Church of the Assumption at Moscow, and sought in vain the blessing of the Metropolitan. This was the first scene in the fatal drama which ensued; the Metropolitan remonstrated with the Tsar, and his remonstrance cost him his life. Ivan, beside himself with rage, was with difficulty for a time restrained from laying violent hands on him, but shortly afterwards threw off all restraint. Two unworthy Prelates, those of Suzdal and Riazan, the creatures of Ivan, found a false witness, who trumped up an accusation against the Metropolitan. In vain he, every act of whose holy life belied the accusation, asked leave to return to his peaceful monastery. The Tsar's wrath was not to be thus appeased; the censure had been pronounced in public, the vengeance must be public also. In the midst of the Liturgy, whilst Philip was celebrating before the Altar, the Opreechniks rushed into the Church, tore the robes off his back, and dragged him off, almost naked, to prison; the one word he spoke was "Pray;" the next day the sentence of deposition was pronounced against him. He was first confined in the Monastery of St. Nicolas, but was soon afterwards conducted, under a strong guard, to the Monastery of Tver. Thither the fanatic Tsar sent his Minister, Skuratov, to ask his blessing. Philip well understood what that meant; the only words he spoke were, " Perform thy mission;" and he was smothered in his cell, "suffering for the truth like another John the Baptist [h]."

Cyril III., formerly Hegumen of the Novinsky Monastery in Moscow, and Antony, Archbishop of Polotsk, the Metropolitans of Moscow during the greater part of the latter

[h] Mouraviev, p 118.

days of Ivan's rule, passed as insignificant Prelates, mere tools of the Tsar, and left no mark on the Russian Church.

But in 1569, during the Primacy of Cyril III., a terrible massacre occurred at Novgorod. Ivan, at war with Sigismund, King of Poland, accused the people of Novgorod of a project, which only existed in the imagination of his Ministers, for admitting his enemy into their city. The Tsar, having first attended divine service in the Cathedral at Novgorod, afterwards partook of a banquet in the Palace of the Archbishop Pimen. At a given signal the Opreechniks rushed in, seized and threw into prison the Archbishop, and a general massacre, lasting over five weeks, of the innocent inhabitants followed; the wealthiest and best of the citizens were slaughtered; the monasteries ransacked; more than 500 clergy perished; and, at one time, 60,000 bodies lay unburied in the streets of Novgorod. The massacre was followed by a famine and pestilence, which carried off most of the survivors, and from the effects of its desolation the ancient capital of Ruric never recovered. At the same time that Ivan was plundering some monasteries, he was devoutly enriching others and building Churches; whilst the river Volkov was running red with human blood, he asked for the thanksgiving of the Church for his victories, and himself prayed for his victims, "Remember, O Lord, the souls of Thy servants, to the number of 1,505 persons, Novgorodians[1]."

Ivan next went to Pskov with the intention of massacring the whole population, as he had done at Novgorod. The trembling inhabitants, having passed the night in prayer, went forth and threw themselves, imploring mercy, at his feet, offering him bread and salt. A mad hermit, Nicolas of Pskov, made him a more appropriate offering, a piece of raw meat; it was the season of Lent; "I am a Chris-

---

[1] Rambaud, I 285. M. Rambaud states that to this day any slight disturbance of the soil near one of the churches of Novgorod manifests heaps of human victims, and mentions a current belief that, in the severest winter, the Volkov in the vicinity of the slaughter never freezes.

tian," said the Tsar, "and do not eat flesh during the Great Fast." "Thou doest worse," replied the hermit, "thou eatest man's flesh;" and he threatened him with the vengeance of Heaven if he touched the hair of a child's head in the city. Just then the sound of the Church-bells summoning the people to Matins struck the Tsar's ears. Pskov was saved. Ivan, as superstitious as he was brutal, trembled and hastened away to Moscow, only to find that the Khan of the Crimea had burnt his Capital, the Metropolitan Cyril barely escaping, and that the Poles, and Swedes, and Lithuanians were ravaging Russia.

After that he had murdered a Metropolitan, it can scarcely be imagined that Ivan would trouble himself to seek the sanction of a Synod of Bishops before contracting a third marriage, still less that the Bishops would grant it. But such was the case; the Bishops sanctioned the uncanonical marriage, imposing only the slight penance which was imposed on the contractors of a second marriage, without a word of reproof for the murder of St. Philip, the Tsar's sacrilege, and the fearful bloodshed with which he deluged Russia. This subservience of the Russian Bishops may to some extent be accounted for by the fact that the Metropolitan Cyril had died, and his successor had not been appointed. In the number of his wives Ivan ultimately outdid Henry VIII.; he could boast of seven, and is said to have courted our Queen Elizabeth, whether or not he sought the polygamous sanction of the Bishops, we are not able to affirm. But we find another Synod, presided over by Cyril's successor, Antony, equally compliant to the Tsar; it not only prohibited the monasteries from acquiring landed property, but compelled them to surrender to the Tsar the property bestowed on them by his predecessors.

We may pass over Ivan's application, when his mind was haunted by a revolution of the Boyars, and deprivation of his throne, to Queen Elizabeth (the first instance of a Russian Prince being drawn into direct contact with the West), for an asylum in England. But when Stephen Batory, King of

Poland, was carrying all before him, we find him imploring the mediation of the Pope, and holding out hopes of his conversion to Romanism. Pope Gregory XIII., in consequence, sent to Moscow the Jesuit Antony Possevin, for the purpose of mediating between Russia and Poland, and inducing Ivan to accept the Florentine Union. Possevin was more successful in the political, than in the religious, part of his mission; he succeeded in obtaining from Batory favourable terms of peace; but the wily Jesuit met his match in the Tsar. As soon as the armistice was signed, Antony urged the Union Ivan, now that he had obtained all that he wanted, inveighed, to Possevin's face, against the ambition of the Popes, and told him plainly that the Jesuits would never convert Russia; and against his back, he called him "a wolf," and refused to allow the Romans to erect Churches in his dominions. The mission, however, of Possevin, although a failure in Moscow, left its traces in Lithuania, and paved the way to the introduction of the Unia.

The Tsar attained the climax of his crimes by the murder, in 1581, during one of his fits of frenzy, of his eldest and favourite son, Ivan. The dying Tsarevitch, clasping the hands of his father, told him that he died an obedient son and faithful subject But this last act brought despair to his conscience, and his remaining days, haunted with the shades of the many men whom he had murdered, were embittered with remorse. He ordered prayers to be offered in the Russian Churches for the souls of his victims, and sent rich gifts, for the good of his own soul, to the monasteries of Mounts Sinai and Athos, and to the Holy Sepulchre. In March, 1584, the fiftieth year of his life, being seized with a fatal illness, he, shortly before his death, sent for the Metropolitan Dionysius, from whom he received the tonsure; and Ivan the Terrible died the monk Jonah.

Ivan left two sons; Feodor, by his first wife, Anastasia Romanov, a man of pious but weak character, at the time 27 years of age, and Dmitri, by his seventh wife. The new Tsar, Feodor, inherited the gentle traits of his mother's character, and was more fitted for the life of a recluse than of a monarch; the young Dmitri, on the other hand, inherited the savage temper of his father, like him delighting in the torturing of domestic animals. The real power fell into the hands of the Boyars, chief amongst whom were Nikita Romanov, the brother of the Tsar's mother, and Boris Godonov, the unscrupulous brother of his wife, Irene.

Between the Tsar Feodor and the aspirations of Boris, into whose hands, after the death of Nikita Romanov, the government passed, one heir of the family of Ruric, Dmitri, an important name in the coming annals of Russia, alone existed. Dmitri was sent for his education to Ouglich, on the Volga, where he was, at the age of eight years, as was supposed by the instigation of Boris, murdered.

CHAPTER XV.

The Three Romes.

JOACHIM V., Patriarch of Antioch, at Moscow—Jeremias, Patriarch of Constantinople, at Moscow—Job, first Patriarch of Moscow—The Third Rome succeeds to the Patriarchate vacated by Old Rome—Approved by the Eastern Patriarchs—Correspondence of the Patriarch Jeremias with the Lutherans—Diet of Lublin—The Jesuits—Establishment of the Unia—Constantine, Prince of Ostrog—Boris Godonov—"The Period of Troubles"—The false Dmitris—Hermogenes, Patriarch of Moscow—Philaret, Patriarch—Cyril Lucar—His Correspondence with Archbishops Abbot and Laud--The *Confession* attributed to him—His persecution—And murder—Intercourse between the Greek and Anglican Churches—Synod of Jassy—Peter Mogila—His 'Ορθόδοξος 'Ομολογία--The Patriarch Nicon—Revision of the Service-Books—Hostility to Nicon—The Starovierts—Nicon deprived and banished—The Settlement at Vetka—Death of Nicon—His character—The Synod of Bethlehem—Renewed intercourse between the Greek and Anglican Churches—Proposed Greek College at Oxford

IN the reign of Feodor (1584—1598), the Russian Primacy was raised into a Patriarchate. The Russian clergy reasonably complained of their being subject to a Patriarch, who was himself a subject of the Infidels. It was found that, whilst the Patriarchate of Constantinople was hampered in its action through the oppression of the Turks, one, and that a comparatively small Russian Diocese, had a more populous jurisdiction than the three Patriarchates, of Alexandria, Antioch, and Jerusalem, taken together.

In the Greek Church the number of five Patriarchates, as defined by the Œcumenical Councils, was regarded as something almost sacred, and the violation of the principle was looked upon as a violation of the unity of the Church. But it was contended that the Old Rome, through the schism in the Eleventh Century, had apostatised from the Catholic Church, and that a Patriarchate of the "Third Rome" was required to fill up the place thus vacated.

Joachim V., Patriarch of Antioch, having lately arrived in Moscow in quest of alms, Boris Godonov, who, hated though he was by the people, had contrived to get the clergy on his side, prevailed on the Tsar that the visit of the Patriarch afforded a favourable opportunity for raising the Metropolitan See of Moscow to a Patriarchate.

The Metropolitan Dionysius, a man who from his learning was styled Grammaticus, not seeming to Boris likely to favour his ambitious scheme, was deposed, the compliant clergy raising no voice against the proceeding, and ended his days in the monastery of Novgorod, and Job, Archbishop of Rostov, as being of a more yielding temper, was raised to the Metropolitan throne. The matter of the Patriarchate was brought before Joachim, who promised to consult his brother Patriarchs of the Eastern Church; and in the following year a Greek refugee brought intelligence to Moscow, that the Patriarchs of Constantinople and Antioch had invited the other Patriarchs to Constantinople to discuss the matter.

We must for a moment advert to the troubles which at this time beset the Eastern Church. The Church of Constantinople was suffering persecution from the Sultan Murad III. Jeremias, the successor of Metrophanes, after having been twice deposed, had again recovered the Patriarchal See. But, A.D. 1584, Theoleptus, sister's son of Metrophanes, bribed the Sultan, with an offer of 2,000 pieces of gold over and above the usual price, to make him Patriarch; in vain Jeremias reminded the Sultan of the Firmans issued by his predecessors ever since the taking of Constantinople, Theoleptus was intruded into the Patriarchate, and Jeremias banished, and for five years imprisoned in Rhodes. Theoleptus, however, was in his turn deposed; the Sultan plundered the property of the Church, destroyed the cells of the *religious*, and substituted a Mosque for the Patriarchal Church. After that, he reinstated Jeremias, and ordered him to rebuild a Patriarchal Church, and the cells of the *religious*, in another part of Constantinople. Everything in the Patriarchal treasury having been plundered by the Turks, the Patriarch having no other means of carrying out the

Sultan's order, determined, with the consent of his Synod, and the permission of the Sultan, to visit Moscow in search of alms. In June, 1588, when Job was Metropolitan of Moscow, he arrived at Smolensk (such an event as a Patriarch of Constantinople visiting Russia, the Tsar informed his Boyars, had never before occurred), whence he, "as by the Grace of God Archbishop of Constantinople, which is New Rome, and Patriarch of the whole Universe," wrote to the Tsar that he had been before desirous of visiting Russia, but that his country was so suffering under troubles and persecutions, he himself having been thrown into prison by the unbelievers, that he had hitherto been prevented. He now asked permission to visit the Tsar at Moscow. The permission being readily accorded, the Patriarch, seated upon an ass, made his entry into the Kremlin, where he was received with great magnificence; the Tsar, vested in his Royal robes, being seated on a throne of great richness, his crown on his head, and a richly-carved sceptre in his hands; whilst the Boyars and great Lords of his court, magnificently attired, stood around him. The Patriarch gave his blessing to the Monarch, signing on his head the Holy Cross, and presented him, amongst other relics, with a golden Panagia, containing pieces of the True Cross, of the Robes of our Saviour and of the Mother of God, as well as with the Spear, the Reed, the Sponge, the Crown of thorns, parts of the instruments of our Lord's Passion. After this the treasurer conferred upon the Patriarch valuable presents from the Tsar, provision being made for his accommodation at Vladimir.

Still the Tsar had in his mind some scruples as to the rights of the Metropolitan Job, and the Patriarch, after having been detained in Moscow for several weeks without anything being settled, announced his desire to return to Constantinople. The Tsar thereupon, through Godonov, announced to him his desire for a Russian Patriarchate; and proposed that, as Jeremias had informed him of the persecution under which he suffered, he should himself become

Patriarch of the ancient throne of Vladimir and Great Russia. that Job should continue Metropolitan of Moscow, for, as he was a man of holy and irreproachable life, it would be wrong to remove him, and inexpedient to replace him by a Greek, with whom the Tsar could not converse on spiritual matters except through an interpreter.

But the Patriarch could not accede to such terms, nor recognize the possibility of his living so far as Vladimir was from the Patriarchal See. The Tsar then requested him to appoint Job Patriarch of Vladimir (in the same manner that he appointed the Patriarchs of *Alexandria* and *Jerusalem*), but on the condition that the Patriarchs of Russia might afterwards be appointed through their own Synod.

The proposed arrangement could not have recommended itself to the Head of the Orthodox Church. The political importance lately acquired by Russia must have foreshadowed to him the increasing importance to a Russian Patriarch, and have excited fear that, in time, he would not be contented with any but the first place amongst the Patriarchs. But what could he do? Money, as the condition of his retaining his Patriarchate, was required; so he made a virtue of necessity and concurred in the Tsar's suggestion. Old Rome, he said, had fallen away through the Apollinarian heresy (a vague reference probably to the double Procession), and New Rome was in possession of the Infidels. It was only right, therefore, that, as Russia surpassed all other countries in piety, and its Orthodox Sovereign was everywhere regarded as a pattern of a Christian King, the Tsar's wish should be granted. He consented that there should be a Patriarch for Russia, and that the Patriarch should be appointed by Russian Metropolitans; but with the proviso that notice of the election should be given to the Œcumenical Patriarch, the same notice being given to the Patriarch, who was to have his See at Moscow, of the election of the other Patriarchs.

On January 19, 1589, a Synod of the Russian Bishops assembled at Moscow submitted, through the Patriarch

Jeremias, three names to the Tsar, who selected the Metropolitan Job; and on January 23, in the Church of the most Immaculate Mother of God, Jeremias, assisted by the assembled Bishops, Consecrated Job as the first Patriarch, repeating the whole office for the Consecration of a Bishop, "it being rightly thought," says Mouraviev, "that a double portion of Grace was necessary to fulfil the duty of his high calling." The new Patriarch then, blessing the city, and Godonov himself holding the bridle of his horse, rode round the walls of Moscow.

On Jan. 30, Job, with the blessing of the Œcumenical Patriarch, raised the two Bishops who had been put into nomination with him, Alexander of Novgorod and Barlaam of Rostov, to the rank of Metropolitans. Two other Metropolitan Sees were at the same time erected; the Archimandrites were raised to the rank of Metropolitans; several Bishoprics were raised to Archbishoprics, and new Sees were founded. Russia had now a Patriarch at Moscow, and four Metropolitan Sees, viz., those of Novgorod, Rostov, Kasan, and the combined See of Astrachan and Krutich.

The Third Rome thus, in the eyes of the Greek Church, succeeded to the Patriarchate vacated by Old Rome, the number of the Patriarchates, as it had been ever since the time of the Seven General Councils, being still limited to five. If the marriage of Ivan III. with the heiress of the Greek Emperors was of importance, and foreshadowed the time when Russia may occupy the place of the Byzantine Emperors; the institution of the Patriarchate of Moscow was of a parallel importance, as foreshadowing the time when the Russian Church, now placed on an equality with the other Patriarchates, may become the recognized Head of the Orthodox Greek Church.

In the spring the Œcumenical Patriarch, having received magnificent presents from the Tsar and the pious Tsaritza, Irene, left Russia, promising soon to send Letters from an Œcumenical Council, to be assembled at Constantinople, confirmatory of the Russian Patriarchate. He had proceeded no further than Smolensk when he was overtaken by messengers conveying, towards the repairs required by the Sultan, a present from the Tsar of a thousand roubles [a], as also with a letter to Murad, his "brother and good friend," asking the same protection, which former Sultans had granted to the Patriarchs, for the Patriarch Jeremias.

A year after the departure of Jeremias, Dionysius, Metropolitan of Bulgaria, brought to Moscow a document signed, at the Synod of Constantinople, by the three Patriarchs (Silvester, Patriarch of Alexandria, having died, his successor Meletius had not yet been appointed), Jeremias of Constantinople, Joachim of Antioch, and Sophronius of Jerusalem, as well as by forty-two Eastern Metropolitans, nineteen Archbishops, and twenty Bishops. The Moscow Patriarchate was confirmed in the place of the Roman Bishop who had fallen away ; the Patriarch of Moscow acknowledged as their brother, and assigned the fifth place, next to the Patriarch of Jerusalem. Feodor was disappointed in his desire for the third place, next after the Patriarchs of Constantinople and Alexandria, to the latter of whom he was ready to allow a precedence, on account of his title of *Œcumenical Judge*.

Notwithstanding this disappointment, the Tsar dismissed the Envoy Dionysius, with bountiful alms towards the erection of the Church which was to replace that taken from the Christians by the Sultan

It was during the Patriarchate of Jeremias that an interesting, although ineffectual, correspondence was carried on between the Greek Church and the Lutheran Reformers. As early as 1559 Melanchthon wrote a letter, enclosing a Greek copy of the Augsburg Confession, to the Patriarch Joasaph ; but, says Mosheim, the Lutherans were disappointed, for the Patriarch did not even vouchsafe an answer to it. But, A.D. 1576, the Tubingen divines re-opened the correspondence in a letter to Jeremias, " nor did they leave unemployed any means to gain over this Prelate to their

---

[a] A rouble being about 4*s.* 6*d*

Communion [b]." They declared that the Augsburg Confession, without any innovation, taught the same faith as the Holy Apostles and Prophets, and as that defined by the Œcumenical Councils [c]. The answers of the Patriarch Jeremias to the Lutheran divines form the earliest modern doctrinal authority of the Eastern Church, which the Orthodox Church values, as breathing the genuine spirit of the faith They bear the same relation to the Lutherans, that the XVIII. Articles of the Synod of Bethlehem, of which mention will be made further on in this chapter, do to the Calvinists. They were also put forth before the Eastern Church was brought under Western influence, and are therefore free from the spirit of Latinism, which is observable in later authoritative documents of the Greek Church. The Patriarch's answers were written in a spirit of benevolence and cordiality; but in terms which showed the impossibility of the union so much desired by the Protestants. The whole strain of his letters showed an inviolable attachment in the Greeks to the opinions and institutions of their ancestors [d].

Soon after the constitution of the Russian Church was thus settled under its Patriarch Job, danger on the side of Poland and Lithuania threatened it, in consequence of the election of Sigismund III. (1587—1632), son of the King of Sweden, to the throne of Poland. Poland, as we have before seen, belonged to the Roman Catholic Communion. The Reformation had exerted a strong influence on Poland, which, at that time, like the other nations of the North, broke away from the Roman See. The reign of Sigismund I. (1506—1548) of Poland nearly coincides with that of Henry VIII of England, and covers the most important period of the Reformation. But long before his reign a reforming spirit had shown itself in Poland. The Polish Nobles, who were present at the Council of Constance, indignantly protested against the violation of the "safe conduct" granted to Huss by the German Emperor Sigismund;

---

[b] Mosheim, IV. 235   [c] Le Quien, III 327   [d] Mosheim, ibid.

and after Huss' death, his doctrines were widely circulated and eagerly embraced in the country. Sigismund I kept aloof from the differences which distracted Western Europe, allowing his subjects perfect freedom in religion,

He was succeeded by his son, Sigismund II. (Augustus) (1548—1572), whose first wife was a daughter of the German Emperor, Ferdinand I ; whilst the family of his second wife was strongly Protestant, in favour of the Reformation. In the violent struggles for ascendency between the Roman Catholics and the Dissidents (under which latter title Protestants and members of the Orthodox Church were included), which took place in Poland, Sigismund, evidently a man of weak character, played an inconsistent part. He was himself in favour of the doctrines of the Reformers, and, whilst he enjoined the Bishops to put down heresy, he allowed Calvin to dedicate to him one of his works, and Luther his Bible [e]. In his reign, the first Protestant Bible in the Polish language was published (A.D. 1563), the Polish Nobles adopted the Reformation, and the clergy took to themselves wives. One of the Protestant teachers, whom Archbishop Cranmer imported into England, was from Poland, John à Lasco, to whose spiritual care Bishop Ridley entrusted the foreign communities in London.

In Lithuania also, the Reformation found many adherents. In 1569, at the Diet of Lublin in Little Poland, a closer political union between Lithuania and Poland was effected; but the union, principally on account of the difference in religion of the two countries, Lithuania belonging to the Orthodox, and Poland, principally, to the Roman Catholic Church, was never at any time cordial. Soon after the institution of their Order, the Jesuits were introduced into Poland by Stanislaus Hosen, a native of Cracow, who was appointed by Pope Pius IV. Cardinal Bishop of Ermeland. He obtained from Lainitz, the successor of Ignatius Loyola in the Generalship of the Order, Jesuit recruits for the complete recovery of Poland to the Roman

[e] Morfill's Poland, p. 88.

Catholic Church, and from that time the Roman religion regained a firm ascendency in the country.

Notwithstanding the massacre of St. Bartholomew's Day in 1572, Henry of Valois (1574—1575) was elected to succeed Sigismund II., Ivan the Terrible being an opposing candidate. Soon afterwards, however, Henry, by the death of his brother, Charles IX., became King of France, in consequence of which he left Poland for that country, where, in 1589, he was assassinated; and Stephen Batory (1576—1586), Voivode of Transylvania, and a Protestant, succeeded to the throne of Poland. As the means of obtaining in marriage the hand of the Princess Anna, the last of the line of Jagiello, he was induced by the Jesuits to join the Church of Rome. Batory and his wife, though they were munificent benefactors of the Jesuits, who in their reign swarmed into Poland, were tolerant rulers and averse to persecution. At the head of the Jesuits were Possevin, whom we have seen employed by the Pope as mediator between Batory and Ivan the Terrible, and Peter Skarga, the latter of whom, when in Rome, in 1568, had joined the Society of Jesus, and whom Batory now appointed his Chaplain. The one thought of these leaders was to bring the Orthodox Church into subjection to Rome. Schools, colleges, and a convent (over which Skarga was placed) were built by them, and the Jesuits took deep root, not only in Poland and Lithuania, but amongst the aristocracy of the adjacent parts of Russia.

With the death of Batory, says Mr. Morfill[f], many historians consider (and they are justified in their opinion) that the decadence of Poland began. Three candidates presented themselves for the vacant throne, Maximilian of Austria, Sigismund, son of John, King of Sweden, and, by the advice of Boris Godonov, who wished to combine the two great Slavic nations, the Russian Tsar Feodor. To the election of the Tsar his Orthodoxy was an objection; and Sigismund, who had been educated by the Jesuits in the

[f] Poland, p 110.

strictest ways of Romanism, and was a bigotted partizan of the Church of Rome, living to receive the title, in which he gloried, of King of the Jesuits, was elected, as Sigismund III.

Soon after Luther's rupture with Rome, Romanism had been abolished, and the Reformation introduced by one of Luther's disciples into Sweden, in the reign of Gustavus Vasa. But in the reign of his son, John III. (1568—1592), the Jesuits, under Antony Possevin, gained for a short time a footing in the country. On the death of John, the Swedes reluctantly accepted as their King, his son Sigismund, who was at that time King of Poland. Sigismund, both on account of his religious opinions, and because his father John had tried to enforce Romanism on his Swedish subjects, was thoroughly disliked in Sweden, the Swedes, however, accepted him, on the pledge to allow them religious liberty made at his coronation. In 1593, the Swedish deputies assembled at Upsala, together with the clergy and chief ministers of State, signed a resolution that the faith of the Augsburg Confession should alone be acknowledged in the Fatherland, and when Sigismund revoked the resolution of Upsala, they, in 1598, raised an army, defeated the troops which he brought from Poland, and elected to the throne his uncle Charles, son of the great Gustavus Vasa, and expelled the Jesuits from Sweden. Thus short-lived was the Jesuit domination in Sweden.

The Jesuits found in Sigismund III., the recently elected King of Poland, a zealous patron, and they hoped to meet with better success for the Union of Florence in Russia, than they had found under Ivan IV. Sigismund, although he was bound, by the terms agreed on at Lublin, to protect the Orthodox Greek Church, used all the influence and seductions of the throne to convert the Orthodox nobility in the neighbouring country of Russia, and little by little the nobles yielded to the influence of the Court. Thus a breach was effected between the aristocracy and the masses of the people, the latter being profoundly attached to the Orthodox Greek Church. The King filled the

Lithuanian Sees with great Princes, proud of their riches and possessions, and wholly indifferent to theological questions; so that the people found themselves abandoned, not only by their natural compatriots, but even their own Bishops Orthodox clergy were subjected to incessant persecutions, and both private and public influence was brought to bear in order to induce them to abandon the Greek, and join the Roman, Church. The few Orthodox Prelates were placed in a difficult position; as defenders of Orthodoxy they brought upon themselves the enmity of the Government, whilst by the Orthodox masses, because they were unable to protect their flocks and afford them the assistance which they needed, they were accused of lukewarmness. Hence arose a relaxation of discipline, and even of morals, amongst the clergy.

Onesiphorus, at this time Metropolitan of Kiev, was a weak Prelate, and moreover, though otherwise a man of irreproachable life, had been, contrary to the Canons of the Church, twice married.

The Patriarch Jeremias, on his homeward journey from Moscow, visited the Southern and Western part of Russia, which was at that time still in his Patriarchate; and, on the ground of the irregularity of his having been twice married, deposed Onesiphorus. At the same time, through his ignorance of the unorthodox spirit which was gaining ground, he, by his own authority, appointed in his place Michael Ragoza, who was recommended to him by the Lithuanian nobles, and gave it in charge to the new Metropolitan to convoke a Synod for the reform of the Church. Ragoza seems to have been an honest but weak, and (under the arguments which Skarga and the Jesuits brought to bear upon him) a vacillating, Prelate.

One of the several irregularly Consecrated Bishops was Cyril Terlecki, Bishop of Luck, in Volhynia, who had not only been twice married, but was also a man of notoriously profligate life; but, deceived by his hypocritical assurances, the Patriarch at his visitation allowed him to retain his See.

Terlecki, dreading a reforming Synod, by which he well knew his profligacy and hypocrisies would be exposed, prevailed with Ragoza not to convoke one Having been imprisoned by the civil Governor of Luck, a convert to Romanism, he attributed it to his being a Bishop of the Orthodox Church ; and, seeing no other means of preserving his Episcopal revenues, conceived the idea of a Union on the basis of his acknowledging the supremacy of the Pope, but retaining the doctrines and ritual of the Greek, with the Roman, Church.

The Patriarch, finding, on a second visit, that Ragoza had not summoned the Council, and that the misdemeanours of Terlecki were too glaring to admit of doubt, as he could no longer trust Ragoza, committed, by his Letters, the task of summoning the Council to Meletius, Bishop of the neighbouring See of Vladimir in Volhynia [g]. But the crafty Terlecki, who was as averse as before, and for the same reasons, to a Council, made a friendly visit to Meletius and abstracted the Patriarchal Letters ; and on the death of Meletius, which happened shortly afterwards, prevailed upon Ragoza to Consecrate to the See of Vladimir, a man of no better character than himself, Ignatius Pociej, who, as he well knew, held the same views as himself regarding the Orthodox Church. Terlecki and Pociej were the two authors, in 1595, of the Unia, in which they were soon joined by Ragoza.

In that year the two Volhynian Bishops, furnished with letters from King Sigismund, applied, professedly in the name of all the Russian Churches, to Pope Clement VIII., seeking reconciliation with the Roman Church, and offering their submission and obedience to the Pope ; but only on their own terms ; viz. the reservation of the doctrine and practice of the Orthodox Church as to the Filioque clause, and the marriage of the clergy. Union on these terms was eagerly caught at by Rome, Pope Clement returning public thanks for its completion ; and, although only three

[g] Not to be confounded with the Vladimir founded by Vladimir II

Prelates advocated it, was ratified by a Synod held by the dissidents in 1596, and authorized by Sigismund, at Brzesc in Lithuania. The Unia was "received," says Ustrialov[h], "with the universal murmurs of the Russian people, as a criminal act." Religious confraternities at Lemberg, Vilna and Luck were formed against it. Gideon Balaban Bishop of Lemberg, and Constantine, Prince of Ostrog in Volhynia, the Palatine of Kiev, the leaders of the opponents of the Unia, were determined to stand by the faith of their fathers, and the supremacy of the Patriarch of Constantinople. To Prince Constantine, a man venerable with one hundred years, the Russian Church was already indebted, not only for the establishment of several schools in Ostrog and Kiev, but for the first edition, printed in Russia, A.D. 1581, in the Slavic language, of the Old and New Testaments; a work for which he called to his aid learned Greek Professors, and, at great labour and expense, collected MSS from the monasteries, and from Moscow, and even Constantinople

The Prince of Ostrog and the Orthodox party were summoned to attend the dissident Synod at Brzesc, but, instead of attending it, they themselves held a counter Synod, and one much more numerously attended, of the Orthodox, at the same place, to which were sent two Exarchs, Nicephorus and Cyril Lucar, by the Patriarch of Constantinople. The Synod refused to accept the terms of the Unia, and passed an anathema on the apostates from the Orthodox Church. The Uniats retaliated with an anathema against the Orthodox. Cyril Lucar barely escaped with his life, whilst Nicephorus was actually seized and strangled. But the "attempt in favour of Rome failed piteously, the people everywhere declaring against them[i]." Bishop Pociej was assassinated by the citizens at Vilna. At Vitepsk riots occurred, in which Jehoshaphat, the Uniat Archbishop of Polotsk, who had severely persecuted the

[h] Reign of the Emperor Nicolai I., p. 100.
[i] Rambaud, I 391

Orthodox, was stabbed and his body thrown into the river[k]. The renegade Ragoza was succeeded by another Uniat, Routski; but in 1632 that robust champion of Orthodoxy, Peter Mogila, was appointed Metropolitan of Kiev.

Thus the Church of Western Russia became broken up into two parts, the Orthodox and the Uniats. No further changes were at first effected, and the Uniats had few adherents But the Polish government soon took measures for the more rapid propagation of the Unia, and a violent and long-lasting persecution of the Orthodox clergy set in. Their Bishops were prevented from holding intercourse with their clergy, their Priests dared not show themselves in public, not even to bury their dead; their monasteries were emptied, the monks expelled; their Churches were farmed to Jews; "In Vilna," says Mouraviev, "the Orthodox Churches were converted into inns .... in Mensk the Church lands were given to a Mahometan morgue." Horrible atrocities were perpetrated; "Many Priests," says Dr. Neale, "were baked and roasted alive, or torn in pieces by iron instruments." The stipulation made with the Uniats by Rome was violated; their ancient Liturgies were mutilated, or their use forbidden. The Jesuits, under pretext of being Uniat Monks, overcame the mind and conscience of the Lithuano-Russian nobility, establishing schools for the well-born youth, and insinuating themselves into the families of the great, so that, in one century, the XVIIth, "all the nobility of Western Russia were Uniats, although the greater part of them subsequently went over to the Roman Catholic religion. Of the remaining classes, the clergy and the inhabitants of the towns and villages, one half preserved the faith of their ancestors, the other joined the schism. .... Inimical to each other, both parties were equally persecuted and hunted down by the Roman Catholics, were deprived of civil rights, and were about to sink in a harassing struggle with implacable fanati-

[k] Jehoshaphat, says Mouraviev, was added by the Romans to their list of martyrs.

cism¹." Thus, with the religious bigotry of Sigismund III., began the reign of intolerance and persecution of the various sects of religion, which was the immediate cause of Poland's fall.

The Unia continued for nearly 250 years, and it was the pitfall by which Cyril Lucar ᵐ was overwhelmed. We shall, in another chapter, come to the time when the Uniats, not merely in thousands, but in millions, returned to the Orthodox Church; but the end of the movement, and the readiness with which the Uniats returned, in their millions, to the Orthodox Church, can only be appreciated through an understanding of the commencement of the movement. It was a political movement, brought about at the time when Roman Catholic Poland had a political importance far superior to that of Orthodox Russia. So that, when, on the first partition of Poland, all of the Western region which had been wrested from it reverted to the sceptre of Catharine II., the Uniats, so soon as they gained toleration, and had liberty to follow the dictates of their own consciences, especially in Volhynia and Podolia, reverted in shoals to the Orthodox Church. And, as they had all along held at heart its doctrines, and only professed the supremacy of the Pope of Rome, all that was required of them was that they should abjure the supremacy of the Pope and acknowledge our Saviour Jesus Christ to be the sole Head of the Church.

With the death of Feodor, on June 1, 1598, the dynasty of Ruric, after having lasted six centuries, came to an end; on the 15th of the same month his widow Irene retired into a convent. At the suggestion of the Boyars and by request of the Patriarch Job, under whose presidency the government had, during the interregnum, been conducted, Boris Godonov, the brother of Irene, with feigned reluctance, accepted the throne, and was crowned by the Patriarch in the Cathedral of the Assumption, on Sept. 1

---

¹ Ustrialov. This last sentence refers to the time when, after the first partition of Poland under Catharine II, the first return of the Uniats to the Orthodox Church took place.   ᵐ See p 551.

1599. The Romanovs (the family of Anastasia, the first wife of Ivan IV.) he treated with much harshness and cruelty; Feodor, the eldest member of it, was forced to become a monk, and took the name of Philaret, and his wife Marpha to assume the veil; whilst their young son Michael, destined to become Tsar, was placed in confinement.

Boris, having committed his young son Feodor to the care of the Patriarch, died suddenly in 1605. Although the reign of Boris had not been unattended with glory, the first years of the XVIIth Century were a period of great anxiety to Russia. From 1601—1604 a frightful famine devastated the land, and, soon after his death, what is known as "the Period of Troubles" followed.

For a short time Feodor, the son of Boris, was Tsar, and to him the Boyars took the oath of allegiance. The first false Dmitri (for there were other impostors of the name), who had been educated at the Jesuit College in Livonia, was soon palmed off on the Russians as the real Dmitri, who, it was pretended, had not been murdered[n]. He advanced in triumph to Moscow, and to him the fickle Boyars now swore allegiance. He at once set himself to fulfil promises which he had made to the Jesuits, built for them a magnificent Church at Moscow, and wrote to Pope Paul V., announcing his intention of bringing the Russian nation over to the Roman Church. Whilst the Patriarch Job was celebrating the Liturgy in the Cathedral of the Assumption, a band of miscreants rushed into the Church and stripped him of his pontifical robes. The intrepid Patriarch, standing before the Icon of the Virgin, said with a strong voice; "Here before this Icon was I Consecrated to this office; I now see that misery is coming on the Kingdom, and that fraud and heresy are to triumph. Oh! Mother of God, do thou protect Orthodoxy[o]." Ignatius, Bishop of Riazan, a friend of the Pretender, was intruded into the Patriarchate. The young Tsar and his mother were put to death. This was the beginning of the

[n] See p 531.   [o] Mouraviev, p 150.

Troubles. The false Dmitri, however, set the Romanovs at liberty, and the monk Philaret was Consecrated Metropolitan of Rostov. After Dmitri had occupied the throne for a year and a half, an insurrection of the people broke out; he was himself assassinated, and the Jesuits were driven from Russia.

We need only briefly touch upon the political chaos which ensued during this troublous period, when, at one time, there was danger of the Russian and Polish Crowns being consolidated under a Polish Prince. At first Sigismund tried to be Tsar himself, and many of the Boyars, who were at the time sunk in the deepest sensuality, were ready to acknowledge him; they even wrote a letter begging him to make his entry into Moscow. The Patriarch Job, dying in 1606, was succeeded by Hermogenes, Metropolitan of Kazan. The new Patriarch, who had already been a Confessor under the false Dmitri, refused to sign the letter, and had the support of the people, more patriotic than the Boyars. But the Poles were assisted by the Germans; Philaret, Metropolitan of Rostov, was arrested, and sent a prisoner to Marienburg in Prussia.

The Polish King, unable to get the Russian throne for himself, next desired it for his son, Ladislaus, who was actually appointed, and without the consent of the nation being asked, acknowledged Tsar by the Council of Boyars. Russia was now on the verge of ruin. Bands of brigands and highwaymen pillaged the country, and devastated the Churches; famine ensued, and men were actually driven to eat human flesh [p]. The Strigolniks seized the opportunity, by corrupting the minds of the common people, to create disaffection towards the Church. The Lutheran Swedes were now in Novgorod, the Roman Catholic Poles in Moscow. So perilous did the state of the Russian Church appear that the Christians of Palestine, hearing that their Orthodox brethren were being persecuted, met together at the Sepul-

---

[p] Rambaud, I 366.

The Three Romes. 549

chre of our Lord, and despatched Theophanes, Patriarch of Jerusalem, into Russia [q].

Whilst confusion everywhere else prevailed, the Orthodox Church of Russia remained firm and consolidated, and the fidelity of the people to their Church unshaken. The clergy knew that a Polish Prince on the throne meant the introduction of Romanism into Russia. The Patriarch Hermogenes, throwing himself into the breach, organized an army of the citizens, bestowing his blessing on all who enrolled themselves on behalf of their country. But before the forces could be concentrated, all Moscow, except the Kremlin and the parts occupied by the Poles, was burnt; and the Patriarch was committed to prison.

The Church, after many acts of heroism and Martyrdom were performed, brought the nation to a sense of its danger and duty, and saved Russia [r]. The common people, who had long been sensible of their obligations to the Church, now reposed on it all their hopes; and the Boyars, persuaded by Dionysius, the Archimandrite of the Troitsa Monastery, came to see things in the same light, and to act in unison for the Fatherland. The nation was again one; and a three days' Fast throughout the land was enjoined, and rigidly observed. The people, headed by the clergy, rose in a body; and in August, 1612, the Bishops and monks and clergy, with the Holy Icons borne before them, marched with the army upon Moscow, and the Poles, reduced to the greatest straits of suffering and famine, were driven from the country. The Russian Bishops, headed by the Archimandrite Dionysius, and attended by the clergy with their Crosses and Icons, entered the Kremlin, the Archbishop

---

[q] It was this Theophanes (see *infra*) who took part in the Council of Constantinople in 1638 on the affairs of Cyril Lucar, together with Metrophanes of Alexandria. Le Quien, III. 519.

[r] His meed of praise, however, must not be withheld from the famous butcher who put himself at the head of the movement, and declared that he "would fight for the Orthodox faith," and exhorted the people to spare no sacrifice (himself setting the example) of their lands and goods, to save the Empire.

of Archangel coming out to meet them, bearing in his hands the venerated picture of the Virgin. The *Period of the Troubles* was ended, the King of Poland, who little thought to find the feeling against Romanism so strong, offered, when it was too late, that his son should conform to the Orthodox Greek Church.

Just as it was the Church which preserved Russia in those terrible years of usurpation and anarchy, and saved it from dissolution, so, after order was restored, it was the Church which led to the establishment of the Romanov dynasty on the throne.

The most influential man of the time in Russia was Philaret, the venerable Metropolitan of Rostov, and head of the Romanov family. As he himself was debarred from the Tsardom, the General Assembly of Bishops, Boyars, and delegates of the people, in 1613 unanimously elected as Tsar his son, Michael Romanov, a youth 15 years of age, recommended by the virtues of his father, the latter being still a prisoner at Marienburg. The Pseudo-Patriarch managed to escape to Poland; Hermogenes, the rightful Patriarch, died from starvation in prison; Philaret was released from his captivity, and, in 1620, was through Theophanes, Patriarch of Jerusalem, who was then in Moscow, translated to the Patriarchal See. "Thus," says Mouraviev, "was brought about an event remarkable in the annals of the world, which in no country nor in any time has been repeated, of a father as Patriarch and his son as Sovereign, governing together in the Kingdom."

Michael reigned, but Philaret, under the title of Veliki Hossoudar, virtually ruled, and to his high character and abilities Russia is indebted, for the tranquillity which set in with the Romanov dynasty. The great Patriarch, having raised the Primatial See of Russia to a greater height of dignity and influence than it ever possessed before, died A.D. 1633, and was succeeded by Joasaph, the Archbishop of Pskov.

The Unia brings into prominence the name of the greatest

Patriarch that, since the taking of Constantinople, adorned the Greek Church, Cyril Lucar (1572—1638). Cyril was a native of Candia in the Island of Crete At a time when the neighbouring nations were suffering under persecution from the Turks, Crete, which was not as yet taken by them, was subject to the mild rule of the Venetians, who, although they belonged to the Roman Church, allowed their Cretan subjects the free exercise of their religion. To this toleration Cyril Lucar owed his education in the Orthodox faith, and his being carefully guarded against Roman influence.

At the age of ten years he was sent by his parents to Alexandria, on a visit to his relative, Meletius Pega, like himself a native of Candia, who, having in his early life studied in Italy, brought away from that country a settled dislike of, and a strong prejudice against, the Roman Church and its usages. Returning for a time from Alexandria to Candia, Cyril was next sent to complete his education at Venice and Padua, in the University of which latter place he had for his tutor Maximus, a strong opponent of Rome, who became afterwards Bishop of Cerigo, an island also in the dominions of the Venetians. Under such teaching, Cyril was confirmed in his dislike of the Roman, and his preference for the Greek, Church.

After he had completed his education, his anti-Roman views were further strengthened during a tour through various parts of Western Christendom, in which, especially in Germany and Switzerland, he gained an insight into the Reformed faith, and imbibed an attachment and sympathy for Protestant and Calvinistic doctrines. His prejudice against Roman doctrine was thus further increased, he was led to think lightly of the differences between the Greeks and the Reformers, and he conceived the idea of remodelling the Greek Church on the principles of the latter. Having finished his travels, he again took up his residence in Alexandria, where he was, in 1595, Ordained by Meletius, who had in the meantime become Patriarch of Alexandria, and by him he was appointed Archimandrite of a convent [s].

In consequence of the Unia which had lately been effected in Western Russia, Meletius wrote a letter, denying the universal supremacy of the Popes of Rome, to Sigismund III., King of Poland. This letter he entrusted to Cyril Lucar and Nicephorus; of the former of whom he spoke in terms of high commendation to the king; of the fate which befell Nicephorus we have already heard. On reaching his destination, Cyril, from prudential motives, suppressed the letter, and was accused of himself writing a letter (which, however, was generally supposed to be a forgery), to the Bishop of Lowenberg, professing his allegiance to the Roman Catholic Church. However this may be, Cyril himself afterwards confessed that he was at one time favourably inclined to Romanism, and the accusation, which was brought against him by Peter Skarga, of writing the letter may have had some foundation. On the conversion from Romanism of Antonio di Dominis, Bishop of Spalatro, who was one of the Consecrators of Archbishop Laud, Cyril wrote him a letter, in which he states that he had himself once a leaning towards Romanism, but that, on comparing the doctrines of the Reformers with those of the Greek and Roman Churches, he had a preference for many of the former, where they differed from those of the two latter Churches. His Roman tendencies must have been short-lived, for his opposition to the Unia was the cause of his being deprived of his situation as Ruler of the Greek seminary at Ostrog, and of his expulsion from Poland in 1600.

In 1602 he returned to Alexandria, to find Meletius on the point of death, and in the same year was himself appointed his successor; and from that time the reformation of the Greek Church was the great object of his life.

[s] During the absence of Jeremias in Moscow, which we have before noticed, Meletius governed the Patriarchate of Constantinople. Le Quien says, I. 329, " vices quoque gerebat Joachim Antiocheni et Sophronii Hierosolymitini."

The Greek Church has always had a fossilized aversion to change; boasting that it follows the doctrines and practices of the Apostolic Church, it believes that it has no need of reform; and in the then existing relations of the Greek and Roman Churches to each other, and of the former to the Turks, the fate of a reformer could have been foretold with certainty. The Sultan regarded the Orthodox Church in his dominions from a purely monetary point of view; the average value to him of the appointment and re-appointment of the Patriarch of Constantinople was 60,000 dollars; so that the oftener a Patriarch was deposed and restored, and another Patriarch intruded into his place, the better for the Sultan.

The Jesuits, the special body-guards of the Popes, taking advantage of the oppressed state of the Greek Church, left no stone unturned to bring it into subjection to Rome. Particularly zealous in his endeavours to the same effect was Urban VIII. At the commencement of the great schism between the two Churches, the Latins accused the Greeks, as the Greeks accused the Latins, of heresy. Since the Council of Florence, the Church of Rome was willing to lay aside the charge of heresy, if only the Greek Church would acknowledge the Pope's supremacy. The Greek Church, on the contrary, adhered to its conviction that the Latins were both heretics and schismatics. Several erudite works in the interest of the Roman Church had lately been published, to show that little more than a verbal difference existed between the two Churches, and that the desired union could be effected by allowing the Eastern Church to maintain its own peculiar usages and doctrines. This insidious plan of the Unia Cyril set himself to oppose, whilst he was contemplating his reform of the Greek Church on the principles of the Western Reformation The Orthodox Greeks, whilst they hated the Unia, at the same time feared lest, through any suspicion of Protestantism attaching to their Church, the number of the Uniats might be increased. The Jesuits, therefore, who hated Cyril for his opposition to the Unia, and were afterwards foiled in their endeavour to bring him over to the Roman Church, assailed him to the Greeks on the ground of Protestantism.

The Turks were utterly callous to the differences between the two Churches, although of the two the Sultan would have preferred his own Patriarch to a Pope of Rome. With the connivance of the French Ambassador at Constantinople, the Jesuits concocted a perfectly unfounded accusation of Cyril's political disaffection to the Turkish government. This being so ludicrous, that even the Vizier dismissed it with contempt, they brought the last and most terrible accusation of all, one of exciting disaffection to the Mahometan religion.

Cyril Lucar was five times deposed from the Patriarchate of Constantinople; the Roman party found the money required for the appointment of the Pseudo-Patriarchs, and there can be little doubt that, as the Greek Church was too impoverished to find it, England, which had been drawn to the side of justice by its Ambassador at Constantinople, Sir Thomas Lowe, furnished money towards Cyril's restorations. The fatal termination of these schemes will be seen further on. That Cyril was an honest enquirer after truth, there is no reason to doubt; that he was only a lukewarm believer in Orthodoxy, and that the Greeks had much reason to be apprehensive of his teaching, is evident from the Calvinistic spirit which resulted from it, and to a certain extent tinged the doctrine of that champion of Orthodoxy, Peter Mogila. Cyril himself professed to be opposed to Calvinism, and to be an admirer of the Orthodox doctrine:—" The Greek Church," he said, " is contented with the faith which she learnt from the Apostles and our own forefathers. In it she perseveres even unto death. She never takes away, never adds, never changes; she always remains the same, always keeps and preserves untainted, Orthodoxy." But the Orthodox faith he thought could be combined with the doctrines of Calvin.

So many conflicting opinions exist as to the character

and teaching of the great Patriarch, that it seemed advisable to preface his tenure of the Patriarchates of Alexandria and Constantinople with the above explanation. At Alexandria he found the people steeped in ignorance; holding, as the Greeks always do, the office of the Priesthood in the highest reverence; yielding their clergy blind obedience, and contented to leave their personal religion in their hands; whilst the clergy he found scarcely less ignorant than their flocks. It was his experience at Alexandria that impressed upon him the necessity of a reformation, with a view to which he sent young men to study theology in Switzerland, Holland, and Germany.

The business of his Patriarchate took him, in 1612, to Constantinople, and on the deposition by the Sultan, in the same year, of the Patriarch Neophytus, a large party of Metropolitans and Bishops desired that he should be his successor. But a powerful, because richer, faction under the Jesuits supported the cause of Timothy, Metropolitan of Patras, who was a favourer of the Unia; Timothy was elected, and obtained the confirmation of the Vizier. The new Patriarch being actuated by no kindly feeling towards him, Cyril retired for a time to Wallachia; and finding on his return to Constantinople the same temper still existing, he thought it prudent to seek a refuge amongst the monks of Mount Athos.

On the death of Timothy in 1621, Cyril, to the great dismay of the Pope and Jesuits, as well as of the Latinizing Priests and Kaloirs, received the approbation of the Vizier, and was translated to the Patriarchate of Constantinople. In the following month, Sir Thomas Lowe, who, together with the Ambassador for Holland, nobly espoused the cause of Cyril, arrived as English Ambassador to the Porte.

Cyril's intimacy with the English and Dutch ambassadors laid him open to the malice of the French ambassador and the Jesuits, who found a pliant tool in Gregory, Metropolitan of Amasia, called from his misfortune Monophthalmos (*the one-eyed*), "who had submitted to the Pope [t]." Cyril was first accused of heresy; when this charge was met by a sentence of excommunication passed on Gregory by the Patriarch, four Archbishops, and the clergy of Constantinople, he was next accused to the Vizier of treasonable designs, and was, within a year of his appointment, banished to Rhodes. Gregory then purchased the Patriarchate for 20,000 dollars, but being unable to find the money, was within three months banished, and suffered death by strangulation (ἐπνίγη). Anthimus, Metropolitan of Adrianople, was the next purchaser, but he was so obnoxious to the Greeks, that, after a few days, he too was deposed. By the intervention of Sir Thomas Lowe, who had received advice from England, Cyril was then restored to the Patriarchate, which he continued to hold for eight years.

In June, 1627, a Greek Kaloir, named Metaxa, whom Cyril had sent to London to learn the art of printing, imported from England a printing-press, and set up at Constantinople as a printer, with the permission of the Vizier, and under the protection of the English Ambassador. The printing-press at once caused a great sensation; the Jesuits and French Ambassador, fearing that it would be used for the publication of anti-Roman books, denounced it as a dangerous invention, and Cyril was accused to the Vizier of employing it for political purposes. Metaxa was charged with being a heretic and an infidel, and, in danger of his life, took refuge in the English Ambassador's house, the printing-press being seized and confiscated.

At this time Cyril wrote his celebrated *Confession of Faith*, written as a defence of himself against the aspersions of the Jesuits, who accused him with introducing novel doctrines into the Greek Church. The work which, in consequence of the seizure of the printing-press, could not be published in Constantinople, was brought out in 1630 in Latin, at Geneva. An answer to it [u] was published in the next year

---

[t] Smith's Account, p 254.
[u] *Censura Confessionis Fidei, seu potius Perfidiæ Calvinanæ*

under the influence of the Jesuits. After about eighteen months Cyril Lucar, by the payment of another large sum, was restored [y].

In 1638 Sultan Murad IV. declared war against the Persians for the recovery of Bagdad, which had fallen into their hands, and, together with the Vizier, who was friendly to Cyril, had left Constantinople for the seat of war. Cyril's enemies, taking advantage of the Vizier's absence, represented to the Turkish government that Cyril was too influential a person to be left in Constantinople, for that he might stir up the Greeks and Janissaries into rebellion. The Sultan, alarmed by this groundless representation, sent to Constantinople an order for his strangulation; and on June 27 of that year, Cyril, inveigled into a ship on the pretence that he was being taken into banishment, was strangled on board, if not actually by, at least at the instigation of, the Jesuits. His body was thrown into the sea, and being found and brought to land by some fishermen, was long denied Christian burial; till at length some friends, secretly at night, laid it at rest in one of the secluded islands in the Bay of Nicomedia.

Such was the end of the Great Patriarch. We may not sympathise with his views, but he fell a victim to religious bigotry, which every Christian man and woman must abhor; and if any member of the Church ever deserved the title of Saint and Martyr, it is Cyril Lucar[z] His history has a peculiar interest for members of the Anglican Church, between which and the Greek Church, a feeling of cordiality has always existed. Since the abortive attempt at the Council of Florence, in which, as we have seen, Henry VIth of England greatly interested himself, no further intercourse, as far as is known, for some time took place between the two Churches. Constantinople was taken by the Turks

---

[y] "Cyrillus Berrhœensis locum occupavit, qui post annos duos (Χρόνοις δύο) denuo ejectus"—Le Quien, I. 333

[z] We need scarcely say that of such a great man a different account is given by his enemies, the chief of whom, Allatius, is altogether undeserving of credit.

in 1453. The period between 1455—1485 was taken up by the Wars of the Roses, and was one of the most calamitous periods in the annals of English History. The Popes had at last succeeded in imposing their yoke on the Anglican Church. Pope Martin V. inaugurated the system of appointing in England residentiary Cardinals, thus superseding even the Archbishop of Canterbury. The Anglican Church was for a time Romanized, and its nationality destroyed; and the Church and nation had little time, in their own distress, to devote to their suffering fellow-Christians in the East. Next came the Reformation, in which the Church was fully occupied in asserting its old independence of Rome, and then the troublous times of the Rebellion, the overthrow of the Church, and the reign of Puritanism.

From such causes, relations between the Greek and Anglican Churches were necessarily suspended. But nothing has ever occurred which, rightly understood, could constitute a breach between the two. Intercourse was renewed under Cyril Lucar. King James I., sympathizing with the oppressed Greek Church, offered to its members an education free of expense in England. Cyril took advantage of the offer to send over, in 1616, a young Greek named Metrophanes Critopulus, to complete his education in this country, with a commendatory letter to Archbishop Abbot. The intercourse was kept up under King Charles I.; Cyril corresponded with Laud, and in 1628 he sent to King Charles I. that priceless treasure, the *Codex Alexandrinus*, now to be found in the British Museum.

Metrophanes found a friend in Abbot, who sent him, according to Antony Wood, to Baliol College, Oxford (whether he signed the XXXIX. Articles we are not told); kept him free of expense for six years, and set him up with a valuable library. Abbot, however, to the surprise of Cyril, did not eventually form a good opinion of Metrophanes, who seems to have fallen into bad company; the Archbishop sent him £10, hoping thus to get rid of him altogether. This, however, was no easy matter, and the Archbishop wrote to Sir Thomas Lowe at Constantinople complaining that he had, subsequently, more than once made his appearance. When at length he left England, Metrophanes studied in the German Universities, ending his education at Helmstad. Here was published, A.D. 1625, a *Confession of the Faith of the Orthodox Greek Church*, of which he was alleged by the Lutherans to be the author; which, whilst it contained no essentially distinctive doctrine of the Greek, and was opposed to the Roman, Church, was written in a spirit favourable to the views of the Reformers. Luthero-Calvinist there seems little doubt that he was, and he was thought by some to be the author of the *Confession*, which the Lutherans put forth of their faith, claiming for it that it was the faith of the Orthodox Church. But he seems to have turned out better than Abbot expected, if at least he is to be identified with the Metrophanes who became Bishop of Memphis, and eventually Patriarch of Alexandria, in which latter capacity he took part in the Synod of Constantinople of 1638. That the friend of Cyril Lucar and the Patriarch of Alexandria are one and the same person, is the opinion of Mr. Smith, as stated in his work, *De Græcæ Ecclesiæ hodieno Statu*, published in 1676. Although he was said to have obtained the Patriarchate by Lutheran gold, yet at his death he left the reputation of a pious, learned and orthodox Prelate [a].

Cyril of Berrhœa succeeded Cyril Lucar in the Patriarchate of Constantinople. In 1638, the year of his election, he summoned a Synod, which took it for granted that the Confession was the work of Cyril Lucar, and anathematized both the Book and Cyril, as its author; and Metrophanes, now Patriarch of Alexandria, subscribed the anathema. If he is the same as Critopulus, he not only showed himself deeply ungrateful to his former benefactor, but he must also have greatly changed from his previous views, for

---

[a] Le Quien, II. 508, doubts the identity; "Metrophanem Patriarcham confundi, jure ne an injuriâ, cum Metrophane illo Critopulo, qui Protestantium è grege fuit."

we find him joining the Council in a sweeping condemnation of Calvinistic and Lutheran doctrines. Under Cyril of Berrhœa, the union of the Greek and Latin Churches, on the terms of submission to Rome, seemed imminent; in the next year, however, he was deposed and anathematized, one of the charges brought against him being, that, by falsely accusing him to the Turks, he had borne a share in the murder of Cyril Lucar. He was then banished to Tunis, and met, by order of the Sultan Murad, the same fate which befel his predecessor. Parthenius I., Metropolitan of Adrianople, succeeded him [b] "After this period," says Mosheim [c], "the Roman Pontiffs desisted from their attempts upon the Greek Church, no favourable opportunity being offered them of deposing the Patriarchs, or gaining them over to the Romish Communion."

In a second Synod, held in 1642 under Parthenius, in Constantinople, the Confession, together with Calvinism, was condemned, but Cyril was not charged with being its author, nor condemned by name. The author of the Confession was unjustly condemned as holding the double Procession of the Holy Ghost, for the Confession distinctly speaks of τὸ πνεῦμα Ἅγιον ἐκ τοῦ Πατρὸς δι' Υἱοῦ προερχόμενον And this is the teaching of St. John Damascene as to the Procession of the Holy Ghost The Holy Ghost proceeds from the Father as the Beginning (ἀρχή), Cause (αἰτία), Source (πηγή), He cannot proceed out of the Son (ἐκ τοῦ Υἱοῦ), because there is in the Godhead One Beginning, One Cause; but He is called the Spirit of the Son (πνεῦμα Υἱοῦ), and proceeds through the Son (δι' Υἱοῦ).

In 1642 the famous Synod of Jassy, in Moldavia, was held under Parthenius By it the Confession was condemned and also the author, but the work is only spoken of as attributed to Cyril Lucar, not as certainly his. This Synod, at which Peter Mogila, Metropolitan of Kiev, was present,

---

[b] "Parthenio sedente," says Le Quien, I. 336, "celebrata synodus est, in quâ vox Μετουσίωσις ad Transubstantionem Eucharisticam significandam approbata fuit"   [c] Vol V 250.

is famous rather for the sanction which it gave to his *Confession*, than for its condemnation of the *Confession* attributed to Cyril Lucar.

Peter Mogila, a member of a noble family in Moldavia, having in his early years distinguished himself as a soldier, afterwards embraced the monastic life, first as a simple monk, and afterwards as Archimandrite, of the Pechersky monastery. In 1632 he was elected by the Orthodox party Metropolitan of Kiev, and confirmed in the appointment by Cyril Lucar, the then Patriarch of Constantinople. It was at the time when the Western part of Russia was under the influence of the Unia, and a hostile spirit towards the Orthodox Church prevailed. But Mogila never forgot that he was an old soldier, and was ready to meet force by force; and when a Uniat monastery in his diocese mutinied against his authority, he marched at the head of the troops and defeated the rebels.

The rough soldier, who had received a theological education in the Sorbonne at Paris, afterwards distinguished himself in the field of literature; he became a shining light and a bulwark of Orthodoxy in the Greek Church. His chief production was that referred to in the Introduction of this Work, Ὀρθόδοξος ὁμολογία τῆς Καθολικῆς καί Ἀποστολικῆς Ἐκκλησίας τῆς ἀνατολικῆς.

The Tsar Michael dying, A.D. 1645, was succeeded by his son, Alexis (1645—1676). Dr Samuel Collins, who was Court Physician at Moscow for eight years, thus speaks of the new Tsar [d],—" He never misses Divine service. .... On Fasts he frequents midnight Prayer, standing four, five, or six hours together, and prostrating himself on the ground, sometimes a thousand times, and on great Festivals fifteen hundred. .... No monk is more observant of Canonical hours than he is of Fasts." The principal Ecclesiastical events of his reign centre round Nicon, the Patriarch of

[d] History of the Present State of Russia Dr Collins, Fellow of King's College, Cambridge, and incorporated at Oxford as Fellow of New College, published his book in 1671.

Moscow, who, through his influence over the Tsar, may be said to have, for a time, ruled the State, no less than the Church, of Russia. Nicon was, like Cyril Lucar, a reformer; and through his reforms he, the most famous of the Patriarchs of Moscow, met with a fate scarcely less disastrous than that of the great Patriarch of Constantinople.

Born near Novgorod, the son of very humble parents, Nicon entered on a noviciate in the Jeltovodsky monastery; but at his father's request he, without taking the vows of a monk, left the monastery, married, and was Ordained at Moscow. After ten years of married life, and having lost all their children, he and his wife resolved to embrace the monastic life, and Nicon became a monk in a desolate Lavra in the North of Russia, and after seeking a still more distant solitude, eventually settled down as Hegumen at Novgorod. From Novgorod, he in 1649, in quest of alms for his monastery, visited Moscow, where he made the acquaintance of the gentle and religious, but, as his after life showed, the weak and stubborn Alexis. The Tsar was so pleased with what he saw and heard of his character, that he received him with much friendship and reverence, followed his spiritual counsels, appointed him Archimandrite of the Novospasky monastery, and soon afterwards Metropolitan of Novgorod; Nicon being Consecrated by Paisius, Patriarch of Jerusalem, who, also in want of alms, had lately arrived at Moscow.

Nicon at once effected a much needed reformation not only in the lives of the clergy and laity, but also in the services and singing in the Churches of his Diocese. The alterations gained for him anything but good will from Joseph, the aged and old-fashioned Patriarch of Moscow, and were also objectionable to many of the equally old-fashioned Priests. He was regarded as a despiser of Russian antiquity; they complained of his desiring a thorough conformation of the Russian Church with that of Constantinople, which they maintained (no doubt in allusion to Cyril Lucar) had in some respects abandoned its primitive orthodoxy. During the several visits he paid from Novgorod to Moscow, Nicon further increased his influence over Alexis, no less in spiritual than in civil matters. At the request of the Tsar, who thought thus to gain absolution for his ancestor, John the Terrible, he translated the remains of the Martyr St. Philip to the Church of the Assumption at Moscow, "To-day," says Beaulieu, "the silver shrine of the Sainted Bishop occupies one of the four angles of the Cathedral in Moscow (the place of honour, after the Eastern custom), and the Russian sovereigns come to kiss the relics of the old Tsar's victim."

Scarcely had the translation of the Saint's remains been effected, than, in 1653, the Patriarchal throne of Moscow, vacant through the death of Joseph, was offered to Nicon. He knew that he possessed the affection of the Tsar, but he knew equally well that the Boyars bore him no love; and he only, and with reluctance, accepted the Patriarchate, after having extorted a promise from the government and the Boyars, that they would conscientiously obey him as their Ecclesiastical ruler in spiritual matters.

In order to understand the troubles which arose in the Patriarchate of Nicon, a knowledge of the state of the Russian Church is necessary. During the centuries that Russia suffered under the Moguls, when all learning was swept away, the clergy had given up the study of Greek, and even forgotten what little they before knew of the old Slavic language, into which their Scriptures were translated, and in which their Liturgies were celebrated. They had also become very remiss in their duties. We need not credit all the accounts we read, such as that the clergy generally were accustomed to live unmarried with women; that the men stood in Church with their hats on, and that it was the ordinary custom for the congregation to talk, laugh, and quarrel, during the Services[e]. But there is no doubt that great irregularity prevailed. The Churches stood

[e] Stepniak's Russian Peasantry.

empty at great solemnities, the higher clergy sometimes did not celebrate the Liturgy for months together; the lower clergy were addicted to drinking, and many of them to even worse living; and preaching was altogether disused, except when an occasional sermon was preached by the Patriarch.

Probably no Service-books needed so thorough a revision as those of the Russian, and indeed of the Eastern Church generally, if in the present day, in Russia, they still require revision, it is probably because no one, with the knowledge of the fate of Nicon and Maximus[1], would be hazardous enough to undertake the task. Notwithstanding the revisions made by the latter, many errors still continued to exist, on account of the revision having been cut short by the cruel treatment which he received. Ivan the Terrible introduced into Moscow the printing-press, but the prejudice against corrections hampered its use. The task was resumed with no better success under the Patriarch Job, in the reign of Feodor; and again, in the reign of Michael, by the advice of Theophanes, Patriarch of Jerusalem, who was then in Moscow, the revision was entrusted to Dionysius, Archimandrite of the Troitsa monastery; but it only exposed him to the censure of the ignorant, and led to his being committed to prison.

Though the work could not have been a promising one to Nicon, he at once resolved to resume it where it had been left unfinished by Maximus. The Tsar assembled, in 1654, a Synod to Moscow, at which he himself presided, to consider the matter. It was attended by Nicon, by four Metropolitans, five Archbishops, eleven Archimandrites, and thirteen Protopopes. Nicon pointed out that, during the calamitous times of the East, when all communication between Russia and Constantinople was cut off, many errors and discrepancies, as well as interpolations, at variance with the ancient Greek and Slavic copies, had, through the ignorance of copyists and printers, crept into the Service-books; and that the present books widely differed from

[1] See p 521.

those which had been in use under SS. Athanasius, Basil, Gregory, Chrysostom, and John Damascene, as well as the other Fathers of the Greek Church. A revision was accordingly determined on. It was agreed in the Synod that the old Greek and Slavic books should be taken as a guide by those to whom the revision should be entrusted, so that the primitive use of the Church might be followed, and the Tsar wrote to the Patriarch of Constantinople, asking him to solicit the co-operation and advice of the other Eastern Patriarchs.

In accordance with the request of the Tsar, a Synod of Greek Bishops, convened under Paisius, Patriarch of Constantinople, confirmed the decision of the Synod of Moscow Paisius wrote to Nicon, recommending the maintenance of the Orthodox text of the Greek and Slavic languages, he advised, in order that there might be one common authoritative form, that, whilst not one word should be taken from or added to the Nicene Creed, the Orthodox Confession of Peter Mogila should be adopted, as a correct and accurate statement of the doctrine of the Eastern Church. At the same time he gave him the salutary advice, which it will be found that Nicon did not follow, to observe moderation and indulgence for the feelings of those who differed, not in essential but external matters

To assist him in the revision, Nicon invited monks from Constantinople and Mount Athos, and collected from all parts Greek and Slavic manuscripts, about five hundred Greek manuscripts were sent from Mount Athos, many of them some seven hundred years old, whilst the Patriarchs themselves contributed a large number of others of a similar antiquity. The Slavic and Greek versions were compared, with the result that many mistakes and interpolations were expunged. In 1655, Nicon summoned another Synod to Moscow, in which the acts of the former Synod were confirmed, and the revision was approved. The "Old" Books were called in, and "New" Books at once adopted, their use being made obligatory everywhere in the Russian

Church; Nicon, forgetful of the advice of the Patriarch of Constantinople, was recklessly regardless of the feelings and long-standing prejudices of the people.

The revision, as far as it went, was good, but it was not sufficient to restore the purity of the texts; whether, under more favourable circumstances, it would have advanced further, we have no means of judging; another revision is still needed, and has been proposed; but, in the light of former experience, the undertaking would not hold out much encouragement.

The revision, whilst from the higher and the less ignorant part of the Secular clergy it met with a general approval, was loudly denounced by an overwhelming majority of the lower and more ignorant; as well as by the monks, from whom their old Service-books had been forcibly taken away. The opposing party mistook the interpolations and mistakes which encumbered the old books, as if they had been part of the original text, and were something sacred. The ignorant part of the laity were naturally influenced by the ignorance of the Priests; and the hand that had dared to tamper with the sacred books was declared to be sacrilegious. Monks, Priests, Deacons, denounced the corrections as concessions, either to Protestantism, or Romanism. Nicon was a Lutheran, a Calvinist, a Romanist; but they were all at one in agreeing that he was the enemy of the Orthodox Church, and had introduced a new religion. They found allies in several of the Bishops, who objected to the revision, on the ground that religion, not only in its essence, but also in secondary matters, was unchangeable; that the Church had become Babylon, and the Patriarch was a forerunner of Antichrist.

At the same time the political influence of Nicon, exercised through the affection and confidence of the Tsar, excited the jealousy of the Boyars, and also of the Tsaritsa, who resented his power over her husband. Not only had the Tsar made him Godfather to his children, but, during his absence from Moscow in two campaigns against the

Poles, he entrusted him, over the heads of the Boyars, with the regency of the Council; and it was during his regency that Kiev and the Ukraine were brought back under the Russian dominion. Such power as Nicon held was a dangerous possession for any subject, more especially an Ecclesiastic.

Nicon further enraged some Boyars by ordering the Latin Icons, which they had brought home with them after the Polish wars, and also some organs which, in imitation of the Latins, they had erected in their private houses, to be burnt, as inconsistent with Greek Orthodoxy.

Still, so long as Nicon possessed the confidence and protection of the Tsar, he was able to bear up against the ill-feeling of the clergy and the enmity of the Boyars. Into the means by which the Boyars effected the estrangement between the Tsar and the Patriarch, it is not necessary to enquire; nor indeed was the cause of the estrangement ever known.

It may be that they instilled into the mind of Alexis the conviction, which his able son, Peter the Great, grasped with greater firmness, that the Patriarchate of Moscow had reached a height incompatible with the well-being of the State. From the first the Patriarchs of Moscow, although they often consulted on Ecclesiastical matters the Patriarch of Constantinople, the Head of the Orthodox Church, were practically independent of him. They were chosen (although in this respect Nicon was an exception), from the noblest and richest families in the land, and became the possessors of such extensive domains as almost equalled those of the Tsars, whom, even in civil matters of national importance, they could, and often did, oppose. They held, next to the Tsar, the highest rank in Russia, so that, not from any direct act of the legislature, but from the ever-increasing respect of the people for their office, not even war could be declared nor peace concluded without their consent. No wonder that they grew haughty and overbearing, and embarked on enterprises alien from their office, of which they claimed that nothing short of an Œcumenical Council, which, whilst the East was in subjection to the Turks, was impossible, could deprive them. The Patriarchate of Moscow under Nicon reached its zenith, and such power in an Ecclesiastic, who had offended them on private grounds, the Boyars might have represented to the Tsar as a public danger. At any rate, after the return of Alexis, the Boyars took advantage of a time when Nicon was absent from Moscow, to make the Tsar their ally against the Patriarch.

Nicon, now that he had to encounter the wrath of the Tsar and the hostility of the Boyars, thought it prudent to retire from the Patriarchate, and solemnly announced his intention in the Cathedral of Moscow. Leaving his crozier in the Church, and assuming the dress of a Kaloir, he retired to Vosresenk, where he was building a monastery to be called the New Jerusalem, with a Church after the model, which he had procured from Palestine, of that of the Holy Sepulchre. His abandonment of the Patriarchate was afterwards brought against him by the Boyars as a State crime, and many false accusations, one of even anathematizing the Tsar, were laid to his charge.

Returning after a time to Moscow, from his self-imposed retirement, he thought to resume his former position; but, finding the feeling too strong against him, he soon offered to resign the Patriarchate altogether, and consented to the appointment of a new Patriarch in his place. To the Patriarch of Constantinople he wrote denying all the charges which were brought against him, defending his conduct from the first days of his Episcopate, and enumerating the injuries inflicted upon him. This Letter being intercepted formed against him a fresh ground of accusation.

After the struggle had lasted eight years, and there was practically no Patriarch, the Tsar, who could no longer allow such scandalous disorder to continue, wrote to the four Patriarchs, requesting them to appoint a court of Metropolitans to inquire into the charges which were brought against Nicon. A Synod, in which two Patriarchs, Paisius of Alexandria and Macarius of Antioch, were present, was consequently held in Moscow, in 1666; and in January of the following year the sentence, to which the two absent Patriarchs assented, was pronounced, in the presence of the Tsar, that Nicon should be deposed from the Patriarchate and degraded, and do penance in a monastery for the remainder of his life, as a common Kaloir. By this Synod, it may be mentioned, Siberia, where an Archbishopric had been founded by the Tsar Michael, was, together with the Archiepiscopal See of Riazan, raised to Metropolitan rank; Astrachan was made a separate Metropolate, and several new Archbishoprics and Bishoprics were created.

A schism with regard to the Service books had long prevailed, but the Synod of 1666, presided over by two Patriarchs, rent the Russian Church in twain. With glaring inconsistency it condemned Nicon, but approved the revision, and anathematized its opponents. The opposition of the Staroviertsi, or "Old Believers," was by no means lessened by the fact that the revision was approved by the Eastern Patriarchs. They maintained that Greek and Syrian Bishops, as they knew nothing of the Slavic language, had no right to pronounce a judgment on Slavic books. Bearing in mind the schism of the Uniats, they got into their heads the idea that it was a subtle attempt of the Pope of Rome to subject the Russian Church to his obedience. One Bishop alone, Paul of Colonna, had previously sided with them, but he, having been first degraded by Nicon, was afterwards, by order of a Council, consigned to a convent, in which he died, without Consecrating any Bishop as his successor. But now the opposition to Nicon's reforms was headed by a Priest of Moscow, named Nicetas, who took the lead of the Strigolniks; a rebellion in Moscow, in 1672, was the consequence, and Nicetas and the ringleaders of the party were condemned by the civil power, and executed. No sooner was he got rid of, than two Priests, Cosma and Stephen, headed a schism of the

Starobredski; but, warned by the fate of Nicetas, they abandoned Moscow and founded a settlement at a place called Staradubofsk, in the Ukraine, on the borders of Poland; and soon afterwards another settlement, sixty miles distant, at Vetka.

Nicon, in the year of the Synod which condemned him, went into banishment, in which he was treated with much cruelty, the half-penitent Tsar mitigating it as far as was in his power. Alexis died in 1676, asking, when on the point of death, Nicon's forgiveness and Absolution. The former (although his answer did not reach Moscow till after the Tsar's death), Nicon granted; the public wrong, he said, was beyond his power to remit.

Nicon lived on in his monastic imprisonment under three Patriarchs, Joasaph II., who succeeded him in 1667, Pitirim, who became Patriarch in 1672, and Joachim (1673—1690), the last but one of the Patriarchs of Moscow.

Alexis was succeeded by his young son, Feodor II., the Godson of Nicon, who bore an equal love and reverence, with his weak-minded father, for the deposed Patriarch. Feodor, in 1681, gave an order for the liberation of Nicon, with permission to return to his convent of the New Jerusalem, the building of which had been suspended during his imprisonment. Nicon was accordingly released, but on his homeward journey he died.

The schism, which grew out of the revision of the Service-books, was primarily due to the jealousy of the Boyars of the increasing influence of the Patriarchate, to the ignorance of the clergy, and, in a lesser degree, to the ignorance of the laity. Nicon was a reformer when reform was much needed, but when all members of society were too ignorant to appreciate his learning, or too worldly-minded to understand his motives. He has been called the Thomas Becket of Russian Orthodoxy. He stands out as one of the few Patriarchs in the Greek Church, and the only Patriarch in the Russian Church, who persevered, even to deprivation, in upholding the rights of the Spiritual against the temporal Head of the Church. We are generally wont to look to the Western, rather than to the Eastern Church, for such a Prelate as Nicon. To him the Priesthood was higher than Royalty. The Tsar was by the Church anointed with the power to rule ; that a Patriarch should derive authority through the Tsar, was to him a fearful blasphemy. Between his opponents and panegyrists it is difficult to arrive at the just estimate of his character. In the conflict between Church and State he fared the worst, and posterity condemns the vanquished, he was the victim of a weak and vacillating Tsar, who stood by him when all was well, and would have stood by him to the last, if Nicon had been on the winning side.

But this was not all. The conflict which led to his deposition was not merely a personal one between himself and the Tsar ; it was the commencement of a conflict between Church and State in Russia, and determined the action of Peter the Great. The Patriarchate of Moscow, if under Nicon it reached its zenith, contained the seeds of its own dissolution. Peter never forgot nor forgave the conflict in which the Patriarch was engaged with his father. The defeat of Nicon not only weakened the Russian Church, but paved the way for the abolition of the Patriarchate of Moscow, and to consequences, political and Ecclesiastical, of which Russia has not probably seen the end.

Whilst Nicon was the greatest Patriarch that presided over the Russian Church, he was certainly an injudicious man ; stiff, unsympathetic, and probably of a domineering and obstinate disposition. The Patriarch of Constantinople seems to have understood his character, when he gave him the advice, useful at all times, but especially in introducing reforms or changes, to have respect, in non-spiritual matters, to long-existing prejudices. By the changes which he hastily made, he sacrificed the real good which might have been effected by the revision of the Service-books. The Russian people were in the habit of crossing themselves with two fingers, whilst the other Greeks crossed themselves with three; a difference also in the manner of signing the Cross prevailed between Russian and the other Greek Priests. The Russians celebrated Mass with seven Prosphers, the other Greeks with five. Whilst the Greeks sang the Hallelujah three times, the Russians sang it only twice. Nicon did not even contend that in such trivialities any doctrine was involved, and these customs were fondly cherished by the Russians; yet, in such matters, he thought it worth while to insist on the exact conformity of the Russians with the other parts of the Greek Church. How deeply the people cherished their customs may be judged, not only from their resistance to their Patriarch, "but it was for these trifles that thousands of people, both men and women, preferred to encounter death and tortures, rather than abandon them [g]."

Such was the result of Nicon's reforms. The doctrinal reforms, attempted by Cyril Lucar (to whom we must for a time recur), left their mark on the Greek, and to some extent on the Latin, Church. Teachers of Calvinism propagated in the East their doctrines, for which they claimed his authority. In the Gallican Church, about thirty years after the Synod at Jassy, a controversy, with regard to Transubstantiation, occurred, between the Calvinists under John Claude, and the Roman Catholics under the Jansenist Arnaud, a doctor of the Sorbonne; the former maintaining that it was a modern doctrine, the latter that it was received in the Church of the earliest ages; both claiming to be in agreement with the Greek Church. The controversy is supposed to have been the occasion of the famous Synod of Bethlehem, held in the year of his accession, under Dositheus, Patriarch of Jerusalem (1672—1715); said to have been convened, under the influence of M. de Nointel, the French Ambassador at Constantinople, to refute the doctrines of Calvin and to favour Latinism [h].

[g] Stepniak's Russian Peasantry.
[h] See The Present State of the Greek Church, by Dr Covil, who was at the time residing in Constantinople

If Cyril Lucar leaned towards Calvinism, Dositheus leaned towards Latinism. The Synod condemned the *Confession*, but clearly asserted that it was not the work of Cyril, but a Protestant forgery, palmed on him to give it a show of authority. It thus sought to clear the See of Constantinople from heterodoxy, and only blamed Cyril on the ground that he had not, as Patriarch, condemned and anathematized the heresy. It went far beyond the *Confession* of Peter Mogila, and the Council of Jassy, and gave its authority, with *accidents* as well as *substance*, to the full doctrine of Transubstantiation.

The subjects of the Eighteen Articles of Bethlehem were:—

1. The Trinity, and the Procession of the Holy Ghost from the Father.
2. The Holy Scriptures given by God, to be firmly believed as the Church has interpreted them.
3. Predestination and Reprobation.
4. The Origin of Sin in the world.
5. The Inscrutability of Divine Providence.
6. Original and actual Sin.
7. The Incarnation
8. The sole Mediation of Christ and the Intercession of Saints and Angels.
9. Justification by Faith working by Love.
10. Christ's Headship of the Church, and the necessity of Episcopacy.
11. The faithful alone members of the Church.
12. The Church, instructed by the Holy Ghost through the holy Fathers and Doctors, ruled by the Œcumenical Synods, and therefore infallible.
13. Good works testify to the efficacy of faith.
14. Free-will and preventing Grace.
15. The Sacraments, seven in number, not bare signs but instruments of Divine Grace.
16. Infant baptism necessary, and may be performed by lay persons in case of necessity.

17. Μετουσίωσις (*Transubstantiation*).
18. The intermediate state after death.

With regard to Art. XVIII., it has been before said that the Greek Church does not hold the Roman doctrine of Purgatory. The Doctrine is expressed: "We believe the souls of the deceased are either in rest or in torment; because immediately they have left their bodies they are carried to the place of joy, or of sorrow and lamentation, although they yet receive not the completion of their happiness or damnation." This will only be at the general Resurrection. Such as have begun in life their repentance for sins by which they have defiled themselves, but have not brought forth works meet for repentance, are carried to Hades, where they are relieved by prayers and alms of the faithful, particularly by the unbloody Sacrifice, and eventually "freed from their pains before the general Resurrection, and universal Judgment."

We have, in a former part of this chapter, alluded to the renewed intercourse between the Orthodox Greek and Anglican Churches, in the reigns of James I. and Charles I. That the Greek Church was not insensible to the troubles which, at the rebellion, beset the English Church and nation, is shown by the earnest remonstrance it addressed to the English government on the murder of Charles I [1] The intercourse was auspiciously continued by the English, and reciprocated by the Greek, Church. After the Rebellion, Dr. Isaac Basire, a Clergyman of considerable importance in the English Church, Chaplain to Morton Bishop of Durham, and to the King, Prebendary of Durham, and Archdeacon of Northumberland (of which appointments he was deprived at the Rebellion), went to the Morea. It was no small mark of the confidence of the Greek Metropolitan of Achaia, that he importuned Dr. Basire, on two occasions, to preach to his assembled suffragans and clergy. He then went into Palestine, where he was received with much honour by the Patriarch Paisius, of Jerusalem, who expressed to him his

---

[1] Williams' Orthodoxy of the East in Eighteenth Century, p x.

desire of Communion with the old Church of England, and gave him, as he says, "his Bull or Patriarchal seal in blank (which is their way of credence), besides many other respects [k]." Whilst acting at Constantinople as Chaplain to the English residents, he availed himself of the opportunities of spreading amongst the Greeks the Catholic doctrines of our Church, and gained the hearty approbation of the four Patriarchs to our Church Catechism.

The intercourse was kept up by a succession of singularly able English Chaplains at Constantinople, beginning in 1668 with Mr. Thomas Smith, an eminent Fellow of Magdalen College, Oxford, of which appointment he was deprived at the Revolution; his successor, Dr. Covel, Fellow and (1688—1722) Master of Christ's College, Cambridge, and Chancellor of York Cathedral, and the next Chaplain, Edward Browne. Of these the first published in 1676, under the sanction of the Bishop of Oxford, a work entitled *De Græcæ Ecclesiæ hodieno Statu*." and, 1680, an English translation of the same work, which he dedicated to Compton, Bishop of London [l]. When Covel was Chaplain at Constantinople he, at the request of Sancroft, Dean of St. Paul's, afterwards Archbishop of Canterbury, and of Pearson, Master of Trinity. College, Cambridge, afterwards Bishop of Chester, the famous author of *An Exposition of the Creed*, examined into the doctrine of the Real Presence as held by the Greek Church; and, shortly before his death, published a valuable folio volume entitled, *Some Account of the Greek Church*.

In 1661 Sir Paul Ricaut went as Secretary to the English Embassy at Constantinople, and there wrote, A D 1670, his *State of the Ottoman Empire*. He was afterwards Consul at Smyrna, where, by the command of King Charles II., he composed his work, *The Present State of the Greek and Armenian Churches*.

---

[k] Williams, ibid xi

[l] Several statements in Mr. Smith's book, it is right to say, the Greek Church entirely denies.

The last movement in the Seventeenth Century, in connexion with the Greek Church, was a plan for the education at Oxford of twenty Greek youths, in the College now called Worcester, to which it was proposed to give the name of Greek College. Dr. Woodroffe, Canon of Christ Church, who was appointed Head of the College, wrote in March, 1694, in his own name and that of Compton, Bishop of London, the Metropolitan of the transmarine possessions of England, to Callinicus, Patriarch of Constantinople, that "lovers of Greece" in England wished to make this return for what they had received from that country in education, and "the Evangelical Word and Wisdom of God." Five young men were to be sent over every year to take the place of five who would be sent back to their own country. They were to be supplied for five years with rooms, board, clothes, and medicines, in addition to education, free of charge. In 1705, the College, partly through the irregularities of the Grecians themselves, and partly owing to agents who tried to gain them over to the Roman Church, came to an end. It was regarded with jealousy at Rome; the King of France, Louis XIV., bribed them, with greater advantages, to a College at Paris; a rival seminary was also established at Halle in Saxony; and the Greek Church forbade the students to go to Oxford [m].

The proposer of the Greek College, it may be mentioned, was Joseph Georgirenes, Metropolitan of Samos, who, having been driven from his See through the tyranny of the Turks, was at the time resident in London, for whom was built, in 1677, in the then aristocratic quarter of Soho, the first Greek Church erected in England.

Compton, Bishop of London (1675—1713), was much interested in the cause of the Greek Church. Tenison, Archbishop of Canterbury (1694—1715), was also at first favourably disposed to the Greeks; and when the Archbishop of Philippopolis was staying in England, and had received,

[m] *Fragmenta Varia* from the Lambeth Library in Union Review, 1863.

in 1701, the degree of D.D. at Oxford, he was recommended by him to the good offices at Cambridge of Dr. Covel, who was then Master of Christ's College. But Covel, when in Constantinople, had formed an unfavourable opinion, which he instilled into the mind of Tenison, of the Greek Church. "The irregular life of certain Priests and laymen of the Eastern Church, living in London," which the Greek Church at Constantinople itself censured [n], rendered them undesirable residents in England; and two hundred Pounds were obtained from Queen Anne, to induce them to leave the country. The Archbishop of Philippopolis, with tears in his eyes, in vain besought Robinson, who had succeeded Compton in the See of London, that they might be allowed to remain; he was plainly told that, if they did not leave with, they would have to leave without, the money.

[n] Ibid.

CHAPTER XVI.

The Holy Governing Synod.

THE brothers Lichoudi—Union of Kiev under the Patriarch of Moscow—Peter the Great, Tsar—Adrian, the last Patriarch of Moscow—Foundation of Petersburg—Peter appoints an Exarch as Guardian of the Church—Murder of the Tsarevitch—The Spiritual Regulation—Appointment of the Holy Governing Synod—Approval of the Eastern Patriarchs—Not Erastian—Composition of the Synod—Its authority—The English Non-jurors and the Greek Church—The Non-jurors and the Holy Governing Synod—Proposal of the Gallican for union with the Russian Church—The Staroviertsi and Peter's reforms—The Raskol—The Strigolniks—The Popofsky and Bez - Popofsky — Plato, Metropolitan of Moscow — The Raskol under Catharine II, Paul, and Alexander I — Under Nicolas I. — Under Alexander II —Massacre of Thorn—Divisions of Poland—Contrast between Roman Catholic Poland and Orthodox Russia.

ON the death of the Tsar Feodor, A.D. 1682, Russia was thrown into a state of faction and disorder. Ivan, born A.D. 1668, the brother of Feodor, and, by right of primogeniture, Tsar, was, by reason of his imbecility, set aside for his brother Peter, a boy ten years of age, who was by the Patriarch Joachim, acting in concert with the Boyars, proclaimed Tsar under the regency of his mother Natalia. This arrangement, however, was opposed by his half-sister Sophia, who was unwilling that her own brother Ivan should be supplanted by the family of her stepmother; she therefore fomented a sedition of the Streltsi, the flower of the Russian army; and, after many valuable lives were lost and that of the Patriarch endangered, a proclamation was issued that Ivan and Peter should reign as joint Emperors under her regency, and they were crowned in July, 1682. This was a triumph for Sophia, for, as one of the Tsars was imbecile, and the other a mere child, the government of the country was left entirely in her hands. But Sophia was a favourer of the reforms of Nicon, and the

Streltsi were "Old Believers," so that there was in the country little unanimity.

Political disagreements led to evil consequences to the Church, and gave rise to various sects of fanatics, who were opposed, not only to the Orthodox Church, but also to each other. One such sect declared that, since the Patriarchate of Nicon, the Grace of the Priesthood had been lost and the reign of Antichrist had commenced. Other fanatics, the followers of two Priests who had been banished in the time of Nicon, solemnly burnt themselves alive by whole families, fancying by such voluntary Martyrdom to ensure Heaven.

A new Heresy, "incorrectly taught," says Mouraviev[a], "according to the Romish traditions, concerning the time of the Transubstantiation of the Holy Gifts," was introduced into Russia from the West. A certain Silvester Medvedev, the superior of a monastery, taught that the change of Substance in the Eucharist was not effected at the Consecration by the Priest, but through the words themselves, " Take eat . . . . drink." The heresy was refuted by two brothers named Lichoudi, sent into Russia by the Eastern Patriarchs; and Silvester, having been condemned in a Synod of Russian Bishops under Joachim, was degraded from his office. The Orthodoxy of the Lichoudi, which was appreciated by Joachim, subjected them after his death to much persecution from the Latinizing party, and to a long imprisonment; one of them, Joannicus, died, A D. 1701, shortly after their release, the other, Sophronicus, surviving him to make a valuable revision of the Slavic text of the Bible.

Another difficulty arose about the same time. For more than two and a half centuries, ever since the time of Vitoft, Kiev and the Church of Little or Western Russia, had been disunited from the See of Moscow, and two distinct Churches, holding the same doctrines, had existed in the Empire. The Metropolitans of Kiev claimed independence of the Patriarchs of Moscow, and did all they could, in which they

[a] p. 252.

were supported by the Unia, to maintain the sole jurisdiction of the Patriarch of Constantinople. But when, by a treaty signed with Poland at Moscow in 1686, the possession of Kiev was confirmed to Russia, the two Primates despatched ambassadors to Constantinople with a request that the Patriarch would likewise, for the better defence and protection of the Russian Church from the Unia, confirm the spiritual dependence of Kiev upon Moscow. To this two Patriarchs, Dionysius of Constantinople and Dositheus of Jerusalem, readily acceded, and decreed by letters patent the union of Kiev and Little Russia with the Church of Great Russia and the Patriarchate of Moscow. The Polish Government, however, notwithstanding the lately declared treaty, averse to the Ecclesiastical connexion with Moscow, extirpated all the Orthodox Sees in the Polish provinces; and the Uniat Archbishop of Polotsk, assuming the title of Metropolitan of Kiev and all Russia, appointed by degrees Uniat, in all the Sees previously occupied by the Orthodox, Bishops [b].

In 1689 a second revolt of the Streltsi broke out, and a second struggle for the throne took place between Sophia and Peter, the latter having the moral support of the Patriarch Joachim. Peter, compelled to take refuge in the Troitsa Monastery, was, after four days, enabled to re-enter Moscow in triumph, and Sophia was committed for the remainder of her life to a monastery. Thus Peter, who was then seventeen years of age, and is described as a giant no less in stature than in mind, but whose education had been wholly neglected, became virtually sole ruler. In that year he married his first wife, Eudoxia. Ivan died in 1696, leaving three daughters, one of whom, Anne, married the Duke of Courland, and afterwards reigned as Tsaritza (1730—1740).

Peter now, by the death of Ivan, actually sole Tsar (1696—1725), in 1697 started on his first European journey, visiting Germany and Holland, and spending three months

[b] Mouraviev, p. 254.

in England, where he worked for some time as a common labourer in the Dockyard at Deptford, and received the honorary degree of D.C.L. at Oxford. He left England in April, 1698, taking with him artificers and engineers; he then visited Austria, whence he was recalled to Russia by a formidable rebellion of the Streltsi, to find it, on his arrival at Moscow, on September 4, already quelled by General Gordon, a Scotchman, who early in life had joined the Muscovite standard, and attained his rank in its service. The Tsaritza Eudoxia, who was accused of complicity in the rebellion, was divorced by Peter, and confined in a convent.

His travels in Europe gave the key-note to Peter's government, both civil and Ecclesiastical; and the former almost as much as the latter has left its mark and influence on the Russian Church to the present day. The latter abolished the Patriarchate; both together perpetuated the Raskol, the name under which dissent of all kinds in Russia is included. In his foreign travels he imbibed an admiration for the religious tenets of Germany and Holland, and became tainted with Protestantism and Calvinism, which showed themselves in his Ecclesiastical reforms. If his father, Alexis, instead of being misled by the Boyars, had continued his unabated confidence in Nicon, and entrusted to him the guardianship, as he had before made him the Godfather, of his sons, the education of Peter, instead of being thoroughly neglected, would have been in the hands of the Church. Nor would Peter, when he came to the throne, have found, as he did, the Church trampled down and made the tool of the Boyars, which furnished him with his excuse for abolishing the Patriarchate of Moscow.

The Patriarch Joachim, having died in 1690, was succeeded by Adrian (1690—1700), the aged Metropolitan of Riazan. The feeble Prelate, though possessed of many virtues, was thoroughly out of harmony with the times and the creative genius of Peter, and penetrated with the anti-reforming spirit which has always characterized the

Greek Church. When Peter came to the throne, the Church of Russia was as corrupt as the Church of Rome had been before the Othos. Owing to the disorder which had arisen out of the revision of the Service-books, followed by the military and civil troubles at the commencement of his reign, an Ecclesiastical as well as civil reformation was required. The aged Patriarch outlived his powers, and in his last days the duties of the Patriarchate had to be administered by a Vicar, Triphyllius, Metropolitan of Sarai.

On his return to Moscow, Peter determined to reform Russia on the European system. Whatever estimate may be formed of Nicon, there can be no question that the Patriarchate under him had attained an excessive, and even dangerous, height. Peter felt that two swords and two commensurate authorities in the same State were incompatible, and that the regulation of the external matters of Religion should proceed from the Sovereign. Himself the great grandson of a Patriarch, he knew that whilst the Tsar Michael reigned, the Patriarch really governed; he remembered also how the last days of his father, Alexis, had been embittered by contentions with Nicon. He believed that the Church of Russia was the natural foe of innovations; that it was too powerful and must be weakened; and that this government of the Church by many was better than the government by one; so, on the death of Adrian, he determined to abolish the Patriarchate. It does not appear to have occurred to him that the same arguments against one Patriarch were equally applicable to the autocratical government of one Tsar.

In 1703 he founded Petersburg. Peter was no lover of monks; but, knowing the reverence in which the Russians held their monasteries, he translated thither from Vladimir the remains of St. Alexander Nevski, and round his shrine a vast monastery soon sprung up, rivalling in grandeur those of the Troitsa and the Pechersky.

In abolishing the Patriarchate he proceeded cautiously, first teaching Russia how to do without it, with a view to which he appointed a substitute under the title of Exarch. To aid him in the civil and military reforms which he effected, he had employed foreigners. As he could not well follow the same course in his Ecclesiastical reforms, he employed Russians educated in the Academy of Kiev, as more in touch with his Western ideas; and on them he bestowed nearly all the Ecclesiastical dignities. The Churches of Great and Little Russia were now united, and Kiev was the intellectual centre of the whole Empire. Barlaam, the Metropolitan of Kiev, was a zealous promoter of education. Its academy was presided over by Theophanes Procopovich, a man of profound learning, both secular and Ecclesiastical. In the schools of Little Russia were educated two distinguished men, St. Dmitri and Stephen Javorski, whom Peter brought from Kiev to Moscow; the former, whom he made Metropolitan of Siberia, completed a work entrusted to him by Barlaam, which had been begun by Peter Mogila, the *Lives of the Greek and Russian Saints;* the latter he first made Metropolitan of Riazan, and now appointed, as guardian of the Patriarchate, Exarch. Theophanes Procopovich he appointed to the Archbishopric of Pskov.

After having, in 1718, completed his reform in the various departments of the State, he set himself to the reform of the Church. It must be mentioned, in passing, that in that year he perpetrated the crime which, if his many other acts of cruelty and sensuality are forgotten, has left an indelible stain on his memory. By his first wife, Eudoxia, he had one son, the Tsarevitch Alexis. He seems to have grown up an indolent and narrow-minded man, and, like his mother, an opponent of Peter's reforms. He had been forced, much against his will, to marry the Princess Charlotte of Brunswick, who was treated by him with much cruelty, and died leaving a son, who afterwards became Tsar under the title of Peter II. Peter the Great could not have increased the affection of the Tsarevitch by divorcing his mother Eudoxia, and marrying, in 1712, his low-born wife Martha, the future Tsaritsa Catharine I., a woman of bad character, and without any pretension to refinement or good looks. By a Ukase signed on February 2, 1718, Alexis was disinherited; and in the same year, by a tribunal of the highest officers of the State, was, as the centre of a conspiracy against the throne, sentenced to death, and two days afterwards met with a violent death in prison, as was supposed under the torture of the knout[c].

As to the nationality of Martha opinions differ, but she was probably a Lutheran servant-girl, taken captive by the Russians in 1702 in the Swedish war. In 1703 she, under the name of Catharine, joined the Russian Church, and after being the Tsar's mistress, became his wife. In 1717 she earned the gratitude of the Tsar through a successful ruse, by which she extricated the Russian army from a Turkish disaster; and it was this which determined Peter to appoint her his successor to the throne.

Peter observing "great irregularity and defects" in the Spiritual Order, thought it his duty, "after the example of religious Kings in the Old and New Testaments," to regulate this also, lest "when the great Judge should demand an account of the trust committed to us," he should be unable to give an answer. Considering the burden too onerous for one person, he abolished the Exarchate; and on January 25, 1721, in a full assembly of the most eminent clergy, he, by his own authority, appointed an Ecclesiastical College, which afterwards took the title of the Holy Governing Synod. To Theophanes Procopovich, Archbishop of Pskov, he entrusted the task of drawing up a "Spiritual Regulation" for the guidance of the new college.

A wave of Luthero-Calvinism was passing over the land, the result of the teaching of German and other foreigners whom Peter had introduced into Russia[d]; who, by their assertion of the right of private judgment, had excited great irreverence amongst members of the Russian Church, and caused much trouble to Stephen Javorski. To counteract such views and in defence of the Orthodox Church, Stephen

[c] Rambaud, II 62. [d] Mouraviev, p. 271.

had written a work entitled *The Rock of Faith*. Theophanes had already, when Ruler of the Academy of Kiev, exhibited Lutheran tendencies; and his promotion to the Archbishopric of Pskov was viewed by the Exarch, who was acquainted with his views, with feelings of dismay, and drew from him a pastoral rebuke. This, however, Theophanes disregarded, and continued to inculcate the same views after he became Archbishop. His being selected by Peter to draw up the Spiritual Regulation was an arbitrary act on the part of the Tsar. Theophanes, however, whatever his religious opinions, was a zealous promoter of learning, and was not only the author of the Spiritual Regulation, but also of a Catechism, which received the authority of the Russian Synod, and likewise of the Answer to the Fathers of the Sorbonne in Paris, of which mention will be made further on in this chapter.

The Spiritual Regulation, after being drawn up by Theophanes, and several corrections made by Peter, was, on February 23, signed by the Tsar, by the Nobles, both Spiritual and temporal, and, in a later meeting in Moscow, by the Archimandrites and Hegumens of the principal monasteries; in all ninety-five persons. In the following year an Appendix was drawn up, likewise by Theophanes, and subscribed in a similar manner. The Regulation sets forth the reasons which induced Peter to abolish the Patriarchate. It states that a Council is better suited than a single individual to arrange matters; that, being under the direction of the Tsar, there could be no intrigues nor rebellion, whereas the vulgar, not discerning the difference between the spiritual and temporal governments, are apt to be dazzled by the dignity of the chief Prelate, and to think him equal with the Emperor. The members of the Council, who were appointed by the Tsar himself, were required to swear that they would act in all things conformably to the Rules and Canons of the Spiritual Regulation; would be his faithful followers, and acknowledge that the Tsar is "the Supreme Head of the Spiritual

College." The Spiritual Regulation has been accepted by every Bishop of the Orthodox Church of Russia since the time of Peter.

The Holy Governing Synod (the title given to the new Council), and the Senate, both of which have their seats in Petersburg, are now the two bodies through which the laws, Ecclesiastical and civil, are administered in the Russian Empire. The Synod at first consisted of twelve members, principally Bishops, Archimandrites, and Protopopes. At the Head was, and always was to be, a layman, denominated the Chief Procurator, to represent and act in the name of the Tsar, by whom all the decrees of the Synod must be approved, before becoming law. Stephen Javorski was appointed the first Vice-Procurator, an office which he continued to hold till his death, two years afterwards.

The Synod is dignified by the name Sobor, the same word that is applied to the Œcumenical Councils, and was inserted in the Prayers and Ectænias of the Russian Church, in all places where the Patriarch of Moscow had been previously mentioned. By way of giving it an appearance of Ecclesiastical authority, Peter first submitted it to the Russian Bishops, and afterwards, "that the unity of the Catholic Church might not be violated [e]," wrote to Jeremias, Patriarch of Constantinople, giving him notice of its institution; this was at least a recognition of the Patriarch as the Head of the Greek Church. What could the Patriarchs, oppressed as they were with poverty, and often requiring pecuniary help from Russia, and by their subjection to the Turks, do against the determination of the powerful Tsar? Peter knew that he could rely on their compliance; they connived at the change; and on September 23, 1723, the Patriarch of Constantinople wrote to signify his own approval, and his consent was soon followed by that of the other Patriarchs. In their Letters legitimizing the Holy Synod, the Patriarchs "exhorted and enjoined the Church of Russia to hold and preserve inviolably the

[e] Mouraviev, p 285.

customs and canons of the Seven Œcumenical Councils, and all besides that the Holy Eastern Church acknowledges and preserves, as well as the XVIII. Articles of the Synod of Bethlehem," and of this document every Church in Russia is expected to have a copy [f].

The abolition of the Russian Patriarchate was perhaps the most arbitrary abuse of power which a secular monarch ever imposed on the Church, and the claim of Peter to appoint the members of the Synod was an almost equally arbitrary act. Yet, from the Russian Bishops, Peter did not meet with the least opposition, not only did they not oppose his reforms, but not a voice was raised, not a pen, except in adulation of the Tsar, was dipped in ink. The lower clergy were powerless; they in vain remonstrated, in vain protested, against the abolition of the Patriarchate. To their remonstrances Peter lent a deaf ear; he knew he could rely on the Russian Bishops and the Eastern Patriarchs; and he only assented so far as to abolish it first, and to consult the Patriarchs afterwards.

The abolition of the Patriarchate affected the external discipline of the Russian Church, it did not touch, still less destroy, Russian Orthodoxy. It was an arbitrary act on the part of the Tsar, but it was not of the Erastian character with which its Roman opponents charge it. Rome, having failed in all its attempts against the Russian Church, now tries to depreciate and misrepresent it. One means is by charging it with Erastianism. The Tsar claims no rights over the Russian, which he does not exercise over the Roman, Church in his dominions. In 1847, an agreement was drawn up between Rome and Russia, as to the appointment of Roman Catholic Bishops. All direct communication between Rome and Roman Catholic Bishops in Russia was forbidden, and could only be carried on through the Department of Foreign Affairs at Petersburg; Roman Catholic Bishops are nominated by the Tsar, the Pope ratifying the appointment, if he approves of the

[f] Palmer's Visit to the Church of Russia.

nominee [g]. Nothing has ever occurred in Orthodox Russia equalling the Law passed, by three hundred and eighty-four to one hundred and seventy-two votes, in 1887, in the Chambers of Catholic France, rendering Priests liable to Military Service. And if in Russia, as in England, the civil upholds, in its just rights, the Ecclesiastical authority, so did Rome call to its aid the terrors of the Inquisition.

It must be borne in mind that, in the eyes of Russians, even of the Raskol, the Tsar enjoys a quasi-Sacerdotal character; he is "the anointed of the Lord," appointed by God Himself, and thus put above the level of other mortals; he has received a kind of Ordination, which fits him for the accomplishment of his mission. We will take a leap over one hundred and seventy years, and learn the sentiments of the Russians in our own times, as expressed in an address presented, on the occasion of his escape from assassination in March, 1887, to the Tsar Alexander II.:— "The Law of the Lord teaches us that Sovereigns are appointed and Consecrated by God Himself. He it is that invests them with sceptre and supreme power, for He governs men, and delegates His power at His pleasure. . . . The Sovereign is the *image of God on earth.*"

At the inauguration of the Holy Synod, Peter is reported to have used the words, "I am your Patriarch [h]." For the meaning of this we must turn to the Orthodox Catechism, in which the Tsar is described as "the chief guardian and protector of the Church." "Submit yourselves to every ordinance of man for the Lord's sake," is the Gospel precept. Peter himself wrote to the Patriarch of Constantinople, that God will call Princes to account for the care they have taken of His Church. If a Tsar like Paul (1796—1801), the successor of Catharine II., arrogated to himself an absurd power over the Church, it was an unconstitutional claim, the act of a lunatic, as Paul probably was. Peter the Great never tried to modify any dogma, nor interfered in

[g] Phillimore's International Law, II. 411.
[h] Tondini, The Pope of Rome and the Eastern Popes, p. 106.

any way, except in what he considered the *external* arrangements of the Church. In such matters alone, the Tsar claims to be Head of the Russian Church, even to appointing the members of the Synod.

In Russia the Church is a check on the Tsar, rather than the Tsar on the Church. The Tsar, even if he wished to interfere in doctrinal matters, would be restrained for fear of shocking popular feeling; he knows that he has to deal with a religious people, and that he must respect the traditions of the Orthodox Church. The Tsar, a high Russian dignitary told Mr. Palmer[j], is the Governor of a mighty Empire, but to interfere in the internal matters of the Church was more than his throne is worth. A distinguished Roman Ecclesiastic said to Mr. Athelstan Riley; "I suppose that if the Tsar were converted to Catholicism," meaning Romanism, "the whole country would follow his example." "On the contrary," was the reply, "it was very much more likely that the Tsar would lose his throne[k]." No Russian of the Orthodox Church, no Orthodox Greek, believes that a temporal sovereign, except in external matters, is head of the Church; there is only one head under Christ, and that is an Œcumenical Council[l]. Under the Tsar Alexander III., a project was set on foot for such a Council, with a view to the re-union of Christendom, but the time and the public feeling was not ripe for it, and it had to be abandoned as impracticable. It is true that the Tsars have plundered the Church. Peter the Great plundered it; Peter III., who despised the Icons, and was really a Lutheran, plundered it more; and Catharine II., in 1672, whilst she pretended to favour Orthodoxy, completed the spoliation. But in that respect the East has differed little from the West.

---

[j] Palmer's Visit to the Russian Church.

[k] Address on "Our Relations with the Eastern Church," 1897.

[l] M Beaulieu admits (III. 167) that there is nothing in the authorized documents of the Russian Church comparable with, or so humiliating as, the Chapter "On Duties towards Emperors" in the Catechism of Napoleon I.

The Orthodox States which have resulted from the dismemberment of Turkey—Greece, Roumania, Servia—have all followed the example of Russia in instituting a Synod to act, under the Sovereign, in Ecclesiastical matters, the head, if little more than nominal, being the Patriarch of Constantinople; but in such matters nothing is decided without the Synod. So that, in theory at any rate, given the abolition of the Patriarchate and the impossibility of assembling an Œcumenical Council, the plan of a Synod may be taken to be as good a one as can be devised; at any rate an Ecclesiastical Senate is less liable to error than the authority of a single man.

The number of the Holy Governing Synod was originally twelve, but in the present day is not limited; and it is almost wholly comprised of Bishops, some of whom are elected for a time, some permanently. In the latter category are the ex-officio members, the Metropolitans of Kiev, of Moscow, and of the combined Sees of Petersburg and Novgorod; and the Exarch of Georgia; amongst the former are Archbishops, Bishops, and Archimandrites, these last to represent the Monastic or Black Clergy. There are also two Secular or White Clergy, one being the Tsar's Confessor, the other the Chief Chaplain of the Army and Navy. At one end of the table where the members sit, is a Cross and the Book of the Gospels; at the other the throne of the Tsar, who only claims the same right as was possessed by the Roman Emperors, who summoned all the Œcumenical Councils. The Tsar is generally represented by the Chief Procurator (*Ober-Procurator*), who is a layman, the intermediate between the Tsar and the Synod; on purely Ecclesiastical and doctrinal questions he has no voice; but without him, no act of the Synod is valid. In the election of Bishops each member of the Synod is, by the Spiritual Regulation, required to write down the name of the person whom he recommends, and when two or three are agreed upon, the names are to be presented to the Tsar, who determines which is to be elected. But as a matter of fact the Tsar reserves the right of setting aside both candidates, and often himself nominates whomsoever he thinks proper, and him the Synod is compelled to elect.

In the Russian Empire there are about seventy Dioceses, and all Prelates are subject to the Synod. The Bishops chosen to sit on the Synod are always able men; the three Metropolitans of Moscow in the present century, Plato, Philaret, and Macarius, will bear comparison with any Western Bishops; nor are those of Petersburg far behind. And of the Russian Episcopate it may be said that it has long been free from simony, which unfortunately, in consequence of its subjection to the Turks, cannot be said of the Greek Church generally.

Subordinate to the Holy Synod is the Consistorial Court of each Diocese. Subordinate again to the Consistorial are the Courts called Cantoirs. Appeals lie from the Cantoirs, first to the Consistorial Court, next to the Bishops themselves, and finally to the Synod, which, through the Chief Procurator, is accountable to the Tsar. The highest classes of monasteries, the Lavra and the Stauropegia, are immediately subject to the Synod; whilst the lower monasteries are subject to the Bishop in whose Diocese they are situated. This different treatment of the higher and lower monasteries is owing to the circumstance that from the former the chief Ecclesiastical dignitaries are generally chosen.

We have in the last chapter alluded to the friendly intercourse existing, during the Seventeenth Century, between the Greek and Anglican Churches; we will now mention an interesting correspondence which took place, during the reign of Peter the Great, between a small section of the Anglican, and the Greek Churches. But before doing so it will be necessary to say a few words as to the circumstances which gave rise to the correspondence.

On Feb 1, 1690, six English Prelates, together with about four hundred clergy, refusing to take the oaths to the new government of William III. and Mary (whence they were called Non-jurors), were deprived of their appointments.

Of the Prelates, the most considerable were Sancroft, Archbishop of Canterbury, and Ken, Bishop of Bath and Wells; whilst of the Second Order of Clergy we need only mention, for the present purpose, Hickes, Dean of Worcester, Kettlewell, Spinckes, Wagstaffe, and Jeremy Collier, the historian. In 1694, Hickes and Wagstaffe were Consecrated by the Non-juring Bishops, the former Suffragan Bishop of Thetford; the latter of Ipswich. On the death of King James, A.D. 1701, there was no longer reason for the continuation of the schism, and it might have been expected that it would have terminated. Such, however, was not the case. In 1710, Hickes' Diocesan, Lloyd, Bishop of Norwich, one of the Non-juring Prelates, died; Ken died in 1711, Wagstaffe in 1712.

By the death of Ken the first generation of Non-juring Bishops came to an end, and as Hickes' commission as Suffragan terminated at the death of his Diocesan, it might have been expected that the Non-juring Episcopate had died a natural death. But Hickes determined to continue it, and as three Bishops are required for the Consecration of a Bishop, he had recourse to the Scotch Church, and by the aid of two Scotch Bishops, Campbell and Gadderer, he, A.D. 1713, Consecrated Jeremy Collier, Samuel Hawes, and Nathaniel Spinckes. Hickes died in 1715, and in the following year two more Bishops, Gandy and Brett, were Consecrated. Thus a second generation of Non-jurors arose in England.

Arsenius, Archbishop of Thebais, had, in 1713, arrived in England for the purpose of collecting alms for the oppressed Greek Church in Alexandria. On the resignation of Gerasimus, the aged Patriarch of Alexandria, to end his days on Mount Athos, the people elected the Archbishop of Lybia as his successor; but the Archbishop of Sinai having, by means of money, secured the favour of the Sultan, Arsenius was sent to England to seek pecuniary assistance from the English Church[m]. The Greeks, we know, were good beggars; but their preference, in

---

[m] See Williams' Orthodox Church, p. xxvii.

their distress, for the Church of England may be taken as significant of the sympathy existing between the two Churches[n]. The Non-jurors seized the occasion of his presence in London to open, in July, 1716, negotiations with a view to a union of their portion of the Anglican with the Greek Church One of them professed ignorance of the doctrines and ritual of the Greek Church; another considered that the Greek Church was more bigoted and corrupt than the Roman; but eventually Collier, Campbell and Spinckes drew up proposals (which Spinckes translated into Greek) to be conveyed by Arsenius to the Eastern Patriarchs.

In the same year Wake succeeded Tenison as Archbishop of Canterbury. We are not here concerned with the question whether the original schism was or was not justifiable; its continuation after the cause of it was removed, was certainly an error of judgment. It is with the dealings of the Non-jurors with the Orthodox Greek Church that we are concerned; with regard to which they assumed a position to which they were not entitled, and misrepresented both themselves and their Church to the Eastern Patriarchs. The knowledge which they possessed of the early Fathers, of Church history, of ancient Liturgies, and Ritual, eminently fitted them for the task. But they styled themselves the Catholic Remnant of the British Churches, one of them (Collier) signing himself, as if there had been no Archbishopric of Canterbury, Primus Anglo-Britanniæ Episcopus; and there is no doubt that the Patriarchs were deceived into the idea that they were corresponding with deputed representatives of the Church of England.

The position which they assumed and the arguments which they employed were not such as would be adopted in the present day, to promote the cause of union. They magnified difficulties and differences which either do not really exist, or were such as could easily be reconciled; and (to mention only one point) the arrogance

[n] Dr Covel says Arsenius came here to intrude himself, and put what he could get into his pocket.

with which they claimed a precedence for the Patriarch of Jerusalem over the other Patriarchs, showed an ignorance of Greek character which courted failure.

Nor was it a time when the Orthodox Greek Church was in a position to be favourably represented. The higher Clergy had, under the oppression of the Turks, become corrupted, and simony extensively prevailed. Latinism had thrown a veil over, and obscured Greek Orthodoxy, and had recently received the sanction of the Synod of Bethlehem. The correspondence shows how the Patriarchs, frightened by the Confession attributed to Cyril Lucar, scented everywhere Lutheranism and Calvinism, thoroughly misunderstood the character of the English Church; and confounded the English with the foreign Reformation. Still, in view of future negotiations which may take place, when many of the same arguments will be used, we summarize it at greater length than our space can well afford.

The "Proposal for a Concordat betwixt the Orthodox and Catholic Remnant of the British Churches and the Catholic and Apostolical Oriental Church" consisted of three parts, the first containing twelve articles, which the Non-jurors proposed as the basis; the second of twelve points in which they agreed; the third of five points on which they said they could not at present so perfectly agree, with the Greek Church.

The principal articles in the basis of the Concordat were as follows,—

1. That the Church of Jerusalem be acknowledged as the true Mother of ecclesiastical unity, from which all other Churches are derived.

2. That a principality of order be in consequence allowed to it above all other Christian Bishops.

3. That the canonical rights and privileges of the Churches of Antioch, Alexandria and Constantinople be recognized.

4. That an equality of honour be given to the Patriarch of Constantinople and the Bishop of Rome.

5. That the Catholic Remnant of the British Churches

having first received their Christianity from the Church of Jerusalem, and holding the same Apostolic Faith and Creeds as the Eastern Church, the two Churches be reciprocally acknowledged as parts of the Catholic Church.

8. That the most ancient English Liturgy be restored, as more nearly approaching the manner of the Oriental Church, with additions and alterations as may be agreed upon, in order to render it still more conformable both to that and the primitive standard.

9. That several of the Homilies of St. Chrysostom and other Oriental Fathers be translated into English, and read in the Churches

10. That in public worship there be an express commemoration of the Bishop of Jerusalem, and that a prayer be offered up for him and the other Bishops, for the deliverance and restoration of the whole Oriental Church.

11. That the Orthodox Remnant be also on proper occasions publicly commemorated, and prayed for, by the Oriental Church.

Next follow the points of agreement, which, being points which all know to be held by the Church of England, it is not necessary to enumerate.

The five points of present disagreement were;—

1. Though they greatly revered the General Councils, yet they could not allow them the same authority as is due to the Sacred Text.

2. Though they call the Mother of our Lord, Blessed, and magnify the Grace of God which so highly exalted her, they were afraid of giving the glory of God to a creature, or to run into any extreme by unduly blessing or magnifying her.

3. As to Angels and Saints, they were jealous of detracting in the least from the Mediation of Jesus Christ, and therefore could not use a direct Invocation to any of them, the Blessed Virgin herself not excepted.

4. At the Holy Eucharist, though they believe that, through the Invocation of the Holy Spirit upon the elements, the faithful do verily and indeed receive the Body

and Blood of Christ, yet it was after a manner which flesh and blood cannot conceive; and, since there was no sufficient ground from Scripture or tradition to determine the manner of it, they were for leaving it indefinite and undetermined.

5. As to pictures; though there was no danger from them to the wise, yet, to prevent scandal to Jews and Mahometans, and the vulgar from being ensnared, they propose that the IXth Article of the Second Council of Nice, concerning the Worship of Images, be so explained by the wisdom of the Bishops and Patriarchs of the Eastern Church, as to make it inoffensive and to remove any possible scandal.

If a Concordat should, by some concession on both sides, be arrived at, they propose that a Church, to be called the Concordia, should be erected in London, under the jurisdiction of the Patriarch of Alexandria, where the English services of united British Catholics might be performed, as approved or licensed by that Patriarch, or representatives of the Oriental Church. They promise, on their part, to do their best that leave be given to a Greek Bishop to celebrate in the Cathedral of St. Paul's, according to the Greek rites; and propose that a common liturgy out of the ancient Greek liturgies, some passages being omitted, be compiled, which both the Greeks and united British Catholics might use.

These proposals were dated London, Aug. 18, 1716.

On Oct. 8, 1717, and therefore before the Holy Synod of Russia was established, they indited a letter to the Tsar, Peter the Great, stating that they had learnt from the Archimandrite, who had attended the Archbishop of Thebais in London, that he was pleased to encourage the union, and had offered to send the articles of the proposal to the four Eastern Patriarchs, and hoping that the undertaking would prosper in his hands.

The Patriarchs' Answer was dated April 12, 1718. It was a very lengthy and somewhat rambling composition, but we will endeavour to gather from it the salient points.

The Holy unspotted and immaculate Faith of the Holy and Orthodox Oriental Church, the faith of those who were formerly called Hellenes, but now Graicoi, and New Romans from New Rome, is the only true and uncorrupted faith, as may be shown by many demonstrative arguments. But it is not so with that of the Papists. How could they prove from the Holy Scriptures, which assert the contrary, the practice of giving to the faithful the Eucharist in one Kind only. They, as if they would be wiser than the Lord Himself, say that it is superfluous to give the Cup to the laity, because the Blood is contained in the Sacramental Body of the Lord; as if our Lord had not been aware of this when He said, "Drink ye *all* of it." Or how could they prove out of the Scriptures that the Pope is the Head of the Church, when St. Paul says that Christ is the Head? Or how, that the Spirit descends from the Son, when the Lord expressly says, "The Spirit of truth which proceeds from the Father?" They have added some things, as to the sacred Creed of the Second Œcumenical Council, and taken away others. They only act like all other heretics; but it is not so with the Greeks; the most pure faith of our Lord Jesus Christ continues only with the Catholic Apostolical Oriental Orthodox Church, and is by nobody else preserved unadulterated.

The Luthero-Calvinists, in order to make their own erroneous doctrines acceptable, had the assurance to belie the Orthodox Church, as if she held the same opinions with themselves. To this end they some time since made a Book entitled the *Confession of Faith* of the Orthodox Oriental Church, as if published by Cyril Lucar, the learned Patriarch of Constantinople; whereas he had not the least knowledge of it, but rather in private and public taught the very contrary to that fictitious Confession[o]. Therefore many amongst us, fired with divine zeal, wrote many books

---

[o] The Patriarchs, however, here confess that the Orthodox Greeks "called a Council and condemned Lucar upon this suspicion," whilst "they delivered over that forged book to anathema and the fire."

against the fictitious and false Confession of Lucar, and chiefly Dositheus, the celebrated Patriarch of Jerusalem, and Meletius, the ornament of divines, who confuted its articles, and broke and dissolved them like a spider's web. The more moderate amongst the Luthero-Calvinists next endeavoured to show that their false doctrines were the same as those of the Eastern Orthodox. To confute this falsehood an *Orthodox Confession* was published, from which every man may learn that the Orthodox Oriental Catholic and Apostolical Church has neither borrowed from the schismatical Papists, nor from the Luthero-Calvinists, but always preserves pure and uncorrupted the doctrines which from the beginning she has been taught by the Holy Scriptures, and has received from the Apostles and the Seven divine and holy Œcumenical Councils. When further contradictory statements were published, some asserting that the Orthodox Church agreed with the Luthero-Calvinists, others that it was in unison with the Papists, another short *Exposition of the Faith*, which, together with one more compendious and synodical, is appended to this Letter, was compiled by the Eastern Orthodox, and sent some time ago to the Luthero-Calvinists on their desiring to be informed what the true faith of the Oriental Church was. They then set themselves to answer the proposals of the Non-jurors.

The first five proposals are, they say, the same, because they relate to one point, namely, the order of the five Patriarchal thrones; and to them, therefore, they would give one answer.

Why should the order of the Patriarchal thrones be changed, to meet the wishes of the Remnant of Primitive Orthodoxy in Britain? The Oriental Church, the Immaculate Bride of the Lord, has never at any time admitted any novelty, nor will allow of any, but observes that saying, "Remove not the ancient landmarks which thy fathers have placed." They would seem to be wiser than those who placed the thrones in this order, as if they had acted rashly and unadvisedly; which God forbid.

Some time since the Pope of Rome, deceived by the malice of the devil, and falling into strange and novel doctrines, revolted from the unity of Holy Church, and was cut off, and is now like a shattered rag of a sail, the unity formerly consisted of five parts, four of these still continue in the same unity and agreement; but we behold him at a distance, tossed with constant waves and tempest, till he return to our Catholic, Apostolical, Oriental, Immaculate Faith from which he was cut off. Thus the Holy Church of Christ with us subsists on four pillars, the first in order being the Patriarch of Constantinople, the second the *Pope* of Alexandria, the third of Antioch, the fourth of Jerusalem; with these concur the other independent Archbishops, namely, the Archbishop of Muscovy, who is also Patriarch of all Russia, the Archbishop of Iberia (Georgia), the Archbishop of Cyprus (and others).

If those who are called the Remnant of Primitive Orthodoxy, out of any particular affection to the Holy and Apostolical Throne of Jerusalem, prefer and esteem it above the rest, there is no objection; only let them not despise the ancient order, nor accuse it of error, nor reject it. But, in that case, it is right and canonical that in Britain, as well as Jerusalem, they should mention him at the Altar by his canonical title, as their chief Shepherd and Patriarch. It is necessary that he should either immediately, or by deputation, Consecrate the British Bishops, no other Patriarch daring to Ordain in Britain or to enter upon his jurisdiction.

Having disposed of the first five Proposals, the Patriarchs next turn to the consideration of the others.

As to the eighth proposal, to reject the present English Liturgy as disagreeing with the Oriental Orthodox Liturgy, and to restore its ancient Liturgy, the answer is; that the Oriental Orthodox Church acknowledges but one Liturgy, that of St. James, the first Bishop of Jerusalem, afterwards, on account of its length, abbreviated by the great Father, Basil, Archbishop of Cæsarea, and after that again epitomised by John, the golden-tongued, Patriarch of Constantinople, which the Oriental Orthodox Church receives and uses everywhere. It is therefore right that the Remnant of primitive piety should, on proper days, officiate by the Liturgy of St. Basil, and daily by that of St. Chrysostom. As for the English Liturgy, they had neither seen nor read it, but they were suspicious of it (for many and various heresies, schisms, and sects have arisen in those parts); lest the heretics should have introduced into it any corruption or deviation from the right faith. It would therefore be necessary to receive it, and either to approve it as correct, or to reject it, or to alter it. But what occasion have those for any other Liturgy, who have the true and sincere one of the divine Father, Chrysostom, which is used in all the Churches of the Orthodox Greeks?

The ninth proposal they accept. An agreement with the tenth proposal shall be allowed and observed, on a mutual agreement in doctrine and discipline being effected; the same with regard to the eleventh proposal.

The Patriarchs turn to the part of the Proposals for a Concordat which expresses agreement with the Greek Church. The Non-jurors had stated that they agreed that the Holy Ghost is sent forth by the Son from the Father; and that, when they say in any of their Confessions that He proceedeth from the Son, they mean nothing more than what is, and always has been, confessed by the Orthodox Oriental Church; viz., that He proceedeth from the Father by the Son.

To this the Patriarchs reply, that they received no other Rule or Creed than that which was settled and most piously put forth by the First and Second Holy General Councils, in which it was decreed that the Holy Ghost proceeds from the Father. For the Creed says, "we believe in the Holy Ghost, the Lord, the Giver of Life, who proceedeth from the Father." Therefore they receive none who add the least syllable, either by word of insertion, commentary or explanation, to this Holy Creed, or take anything from it.

For the holy Fathers at that time anathematized all such as shall either take from, or add to it, any word or syllable. They could not allow it to be either publicly or privately read with the addition of the preposition διά or ἐκ; if any one has formerly inserted any word, let it be struck out, and let the Creed continue unaltered as it was at first written, and is to this day, after so many years, read and believed by the Greeks.

The Greek Church, they continue, believes in a two-fold Procession, the one natural, eternal, and before time, according to which the Holy Ghost proceeds from the Father alone. The other is temporal and outward; whereby the Holy Ghost proceeds, flows, or is sent, by the Son, or through the Son's Mediation, and so from the Son, for the sanctification of the creature. But this Πρόεσις, or Mission, they did not express like the Papists, who on account of the poverty of the Latin language, which is unable to express Πρόεσις, or Emission, by one word, and the Ἐκπόρευσις by another, have called them both *Processio;* which afterwards grew into an error, and makes them take the eternal Procession for that Πρόεσις which is temporal. And this is the reason for the false use of the Latins, which is contrary to the doctrines of our Lord and of the holy Fathers.

The Non-jurors had stated in their points of agreement a general agreement with the Greek Church, in regard to the Sacraments. The Patriarchs reply that they hold that the Holy Sacraments are seven in number, but two, Baptism and the Eucharist, exceed in necessity, and are such that without them no one can be saved. They hold that the Eucharist should be given in both Kinds, not under One, as the Papists wickedly administer it. The Sacrament of the Priesthood is one of the most necessary, for how shall Christians have the Sacrament of His Precious Body and Blood, if there be no Priest to consecrate and perform the sacred ministration? The other four, especially those of Chrism and Penance, are greatly profitable to salvation. Without Chrism (that being the seal of the Gift of the Holy

Spirit, which was imposed as necessary both by the ancient and present Church), none can be a perfect Christian. And since Baptism cannot be repeated, how can sin after Baptism be forgiven without repentance and Confession, and without a person endued with the power of binding and loosing?

As to the doctrine of a Purgatorial fire, the Greeks will by no means hear of it, it is a fiction and a doting fable, invented by the Papists for lucre, and to deceive the simple; and, in a word, has no existence but in the imagination.

The Patriarchs then turn to the Articles in which the British Remnant of Primitive Piety professed their disagreement. This disagreement was not to be wondered at; for they, being born and educated in the principles of the Luthero-Calvinists, and possessed of their prejudices, tenaciously adhere to them, like ivy to a tree. Paint of a deep colour sinking into a garment is almost indelible, and the garment will grow rotten and decayed, before the tincture can be washed off The British Remnant of Primitive Piety says (Article I.), that though they have a great reverence for the Canons of the ancient General Councils, they allow them not the same authority as is due to the Sacred Text. This Article can by no means be allowed by the Eastern Church, which receives the laws and Canons of the Seven ancient holy and sacred Councils, and the particular Synods held in the East (from the Apostolical age until the reign of Copronymus, in Constantinople), like the Holy Scriptures. But it by no means receives the rebellious Synods of heretics, such as that of the (Robber) Council of Ephesus, that of the Iconomachi, and those of the Papists; nor especially that Caiaphas-like Consistory at Florence. This last was a band of robbers, and not an assembly observing the form of the Apostolic Synod in Jerusalem, nor that of the first Seven holy General Councils; but one which had the Pope, at the same time, a criminal at the bar, and a judge upon the throne, giving sentence according to his own pleasure in a tyrannical and illegal manner.

As to the second point of disagreement; the Remnant say, though they call the Mother of our Lord, blessed, and magnify the Grace of God which so highly exalted her, yet they are afraid of giving the glory of God to a creature, or of running into any extreme, by blessing and magnifying her. The Greeks know how to make a distinction in worship, and they gave that of Latria to God only, and that of Dulia to the holy Apostles, Martyrs, and righteous and godly Fathers, honouring them as faithful servants and true friends of God. They worship our Lady the Virgin Mother of God with Hyperdulia, not as God, but as the Θεοτόκος and Mother of God; not with Latria, God forbid, that would be blasphemy. God alone they worship with Latria, and make her their intercessor with Him for post-baptismal sins, and hope, through her, to receive remission from Him.

As to the third point of disagreement with regard to the Invocation of Saints and Angels, the Patriarchs say that the above answer is sufficient. Though Christ is the only Mediator for our salvation, yet it is right and acceptable to God to honour His Saints, especially the God-bearing Virgin Mary, they mediate for our post-baptismal sins, and for our repentance (for they rejoice over one sinner that repenteth); and they intercede for our preservation and deliverance from temporal evils and misfortunes. "Set yourselves free," they say, "from the heavy bondage and the captivity of prejudice, and submit yourselves to those true doctrines which have been received from the beginning, and the traditions of the holy Fathers, and are not opposed to the Holy Scriptures."

The Patriarchs next advert to the fourth Proposition with regard to the Eucharist. "Can any pious person forbear trembling," they say, "to hear this blasphemy against the Holy Eucharist?" "To be against worshipping the Bread which is consecrated and changed into the Body of Christ, is to be against worshipping our Lord Jesus Christ Himself, our Maker and Saviour. For what else is the sacrificial Bread, after it is consecrated and transubstantiated by the access of the Holy Spirit?" "But if the consecrated Bread which we eat be not the very Body of Christ, and ought not as ye say to be worshipped, what else is it?" "Do you not regard our Lord when He said, 'This is My Body?'" "Our Lord did not say My Body is in, or under, or with this; but, This is My Body, showing them the Bread which lay in His hands." "The Shew-Bread of the Altar of the New Dispensation is changed into the Body of Christ, by the Invocation and access of the Holy Spirit, and by the Prayer and Blessing of the Priest in secret, the accidents only remaining immutable; the Bread ... no longer subsisting under those accidents, but being then the property of our Lord's Real Body." "We should say ... I believe that this is Thy Immaculate Body, having our eyes upon the Holy Bread; and that this is Thy precious Blood, looking upon the Holy Cup." If they read the Holy Fathers, they would find in all of them that the Shew-Bread is changed, transformed, converted, and transubstantiated into the very precious and unspotted Body of our Lord.

As to the fifth Proposition with regard to Pictures. The Patriarchs state, that in the Greek Church to honour the Saints, the Mother of God, and Christ our Saviour, by images and pictures, is an ancient piece of devotion, and is daily observed and piously practised by them. By such representations, every pious Christian is animated to the imitation of the Saints, and to a constant contempt even of death itself, for the sake of Christ and of Godliness. A picture is a kind of silent history, as history is a speaking picture. The Mahometans, to whom they were in bondage for their sins, do not reject, nor make objections to, pictures, but commend the practice of the Greeks, when they are brought to understand that it is not the Latria due to God which is given them. And what if others *are* offended at the worship of their mysteries? Are they therefore obliged to abstain from them? What could be more absurd? "It is impossible to repeal the Ninth Canon of the Second holy Council of Nice, as you desire; for it was well and rightly enacted, and in an assembly of many holy men, in the presence of the Holy Ghost, which inspired, illuminated, and directed them into the truth."

The proposal and promise that a Church to be called the Concordia should be built, and that it should be subject to the blessed Pope and Patriarch of Alexandria, they very much commend, and receive as determined wisely and by God's direction. As to what Liturgy will be most convenient and familiar for use, they think St. John Chrysostom's preferable to all others, for that is chiefly used by the Oriental Orthodox Christians all over the East. A union and agreement with all the Orthodox nations of the Eastern Church will be easier and more secure, when they everywhere hear and repeat the holy offices they have been used to from children. "We rejoice and leap for joy, and are exceedingly transported, when we see your eager desire to unite and agree with the pious Oriental Church, and we earnestly pray that your and our hope may have a good event, as by God's help we promise ourselves they will; and this we think sufficient for a sudden answer, such as the time will allow us to your proposals."

The answer of the Patriarchs, though dated April 12, 1718, did not arrive in England till November, 1721. Meanwhile, a schism, as to what were called the Usages, had sprung up in the ranks of the Non-jurors, one party, headed by Collier, advocating a return to the usages, sanctioned by the first English Prayer-Book of Edward VI., the other, headed by Spinckes, an adherence to the Prayer-Book of 1662. By the time the answer of the Patriarchs arrived, the interest of the non-Usagers seems to have flagged, and Spinckes retired from the movement. Each party Consecrated its own Bishops, and in 1722 Griffin was added to the number of the latter. This short digression was necessary, as we shall find Griffin amongst the signatories in the correspondence that followed.

The Non-jurors commence their reply, dated May 29, 1722, to the Patriarchs, with the announcement of their satisfaction that their Patriarchal Lordships refer the decision of their differences to the Scriptures and the primitive Church. They therefore have no uncomfortable prospect of a coalition, for the determining rule is equally received by the Oriental Churches and the Catholic Remainder. In the claims of the Patriarchs they can generally concur. But they conceive that the British Bishops may remain independent of all the Patriarchs.

They desire to observe, in general, that the suspicion of Luthero-Calvinism, entertained by the Catholic Oriental Church, is unfounded, for they openly declare that none of the distinguishing principles of either of those sects can be fairly charged against them.

As to the claim of the Patriarchs, that the seven General Councils possess equal authority with the Holy Scriptures, although they accept the first six, they could not advance so far as to believe the Fathers of those Councils to be equally inspired as the Prophets, Evangelists and Apostles; whilst with regard to the Second Council of Nice, they could not assent to the giving even the worship of Dulia to Angels or departed Saints.

With regard to the change of the Bread and Wine in the Holy Eucharist into the Body and Blood of our Saviour, nothing of the elements remaining, except the bare accidents, void of substance, they can by no means agree with their Lordships' doctrine; such a corporal Presence as they call transubstantiation, having no foundation in Scripture, and being by implication, and sometimes plainly, denied by the most celebrated Fathers of the primitive Church. It is true that our Blessed Saviour calls the Eucharistic Bread and Wine His Body and His Blood, but these words are not to be restrained to a literal sense, any more than when our Saviour calls Himself a Door, and a Vine.

Since they could not allow the Invocation of Saints and paying them religious worship, the argument applies still more forcibly against paying religious worship to their Images. The use of Images in Churches is not only lawful, but may be serviceable as a means of refreshing the memory and kindling the devotion of the people.

They then "suggest a temper and compromise" by which they hoped the union might be effected. If the Oriental Patriarchs, they say, would publicly and authoritatively declare that they were not bound to the Invocation of Saints and Angels, the worship of Images, or the Adoration of the Host, their objections would be removed. The Patriarchs should remember that Christianity is no gradual religion, but was perfect at the time of the death of the Evangelists and Apostles; and the earliest traditions were undoubtedly preferable, because the stream runs clearest towards the fountain-head. They hoped, therefore, that their Lordships' impartial consideration would be governed by the general usages and doctrine of the first four centuries (not excluding the fifth), rather than by any solemn decisions of the East in the Eighth Century, which were even then opposed by an equal authority in the West. Thus "the Orthodox Oriental Church and the Catholic Remnant in Britain might at last join in the solemnities of religion, and be much more intimately one fold under one Shepherd, Jesus Christ."

On May 30 the Non-jurors addressed a Letter to Arsenius, the Metropolitan of Thebais, acknowledging the encouragement which, through his means, the Tsar had accorded to the movement, which would "redound to the immortalizing the name" of his Imperial Majesty.

This Letter was signed by ;—

Archibaldus (Campbell) Scoto-Britanniæ Episcopus.
Jacobus (Gadderer) Scoto-Britanniæ Episcopus.
Jeremias (Collier) Primus Anglo-Britanniæ Episcopus.
Thomas (Brett) Anglo-Britanniæ Episcopus.

The Answer of the Patriarchs to this Letter was dated,

Constantinople, Anno Salutis 1723, in the month of September.

They acknowledge the zeal and piety of their correspondents, their religious benevolence, their diligence, and their readiness of disposition to a union of the Churches. But after the perusal of their second Letter the Patriarchs have nothing further to observe. The doctrines of the Eastern Church have been rightly defined by the Holy and Œcumenical Synods; it is neither lawful to add to nor to take from them; those who wish to join their Church must necessarily follow and submit to what has been so defined, "with sincerity and obedience, and without scruple or dispute." As for matters of custom and Ecclesiastical order, and for the form and discipline of administering the Sacraments, they could easily be settled when once the union is effected. For "a fuller and unanswerable testimony" they send them the Confession of the Orthodox Faith drawn up in the Synod of Bethlehem, A D 1672.

This Letter was signed, in a Synod, by ;—

Jeremias, Patriarch of Constantinople, the New Rome,

Athanasius, Patriarch of Antioch,

Chrysanthus, Patriarch of the most Holy City Jerusalem; and by as many as could be assembled of the Metropolitans, Bishops, and Clergy of the Orthodox Church.

Thus ended the correspondence. It was throughout, on the part of the Patriarchs, highly tinged with Latinism, and it ended in the exaltation of a local, to the level of an Œcumenical, Synod, and the adoption of that, as an indispensable basis of inter-communion. The Patriarchs thus assumed the same arbitrary authority of which they complain on the part of Rome, and which, in any future attempts at re-union, must be fatal.

Meanwhile a more hopeful correspondence was being carried on between the Non-jurors and the Church of Russia. As early as October 8, 1717, the Non-jurors, as we have seen, wrote to the Tsar Peter, thanking him for his encouragement of the proposed union, and begging its continuance. On

May 30, 1722, they wrote to the Holy Governing Synod of Russia, enclosing two copies of their Letter of May 29 to the Patriarchs, requesting them to forward one copy, which was in Greek, to the Patriarchs, and expressing their hope of their Lordships' countenance to second their endeavours. On the following day they wrote to Count Golovkin, the Chancellor of Russia, thanking him for his advocacy of the cause, and requesting his further countenance and assistance.

In February, 1723, the Holy Governing Synod wrote to the Non-jurors acknowledging their Letter of May 30, of the preceding year. They assure them that they received the Letter with great joy in the spirit, and also gave glory to Christ that the Non-jurors have at heart a desire for concord with the Oriental Church, and also for their expression of good-will and veneration towards the Synod. They tell them that they had forwarded their Letter to the Patriarchs, and promise their best assistance in so holy a negotiation. They had also, they write, acquainted the Tsar with the proceedings, who received them with much favour. The Tsar proposed that the Non-jurors should send to Russia two of their body to consult with them in the Name and Spirit of Christ, so that the opinions and arguments of both Churches might be considered and weighed, and it might be decided what could be yielded by one side or the other, and what for conscience-sake must be retained

On August 25, 1723, the Archbishop of Thebais wrote from Moscow to the Non-jurors, acquainting them that the Tsar and the Holy Synod had received their Letters, and their replies to the Patriarchs, with great joy, for that they thought nothing more desirable than the union of the Church of Christ; with a view to which they immediately sent their replies to the Patriarchs. He also informed them of the Tsar's wish that two of their brethren should be sent to Russia.

On February 2, 1724, the Holy Governing Synod wrote to the Non-jurors a second Letter, stating that, though a year ago they had given their Letter to the Protosyncellus (Πρῶτο, σύγγελος), his departure had till that time been delayed. They also send them the Letter of the Patriarchs dated September, 1723. They tell them that the Tsar still remained of the same opinion; they therefore renew the request that they would send over two of their brethren for a conference.

On July 13, 1724, the Non-jurors wrote to the Holy Synod, acknowledging their Letters, which made the prospect of a coalition "not unpromising." They regret that unforeseen circumstances prevented their sending two of their clergy that Summer, but they would do so, God willing, in the following Spring. At the same time they wrote to the Chancellor of Russia, acknowledging the Tsar's condescension, and his recommendation of a Conference for concerting measures of union. These two Letters, to the Holy Synod and the Chancellor, were signed as before by Archibaldus, Jeremias, and Thomas, but now Johannes (Griffin) appears in the fourth signature.

On March 8, 1725, intelligence arrived in England of the Tsar Peter's death, the Non-jurors wrote in consequence, on April 11, two Letters, one to the Holy Synod, the other to the Chancellor, expressing their regret, and the abeyance of the movement, till they should have learned their Lordships' pleasure, and also congratulating the Tsaritza, Catharine I., on her accession. On Sept. 16, the Chancellor Golovkin wrote to the Non-jurors, stating the necessity, under the circumstances, of some further delay; but that he would take the first opportunity of representing the union to Her Majesty, who, they might rest assured, would give it the same support as the late Tsar.

To send deputies to Russia, as had been proposed, would sorely have taxed the resources of the Non-jurors. But the whole affair was suddenly cut short by Archbishop Wake, who, in the same month, wrote to Chrysanthus, Patriarch of Jerusalem, exposing the nature of the Non-juring schism, and consequently the schismatical character of the movement of the Non-jurors, writing under the fictitious title of Metropolitan and Bishops of the Anglican Church. It is somewhat surprising that, as the movement had been going on for nine years, the Archbishop should only have heard of it, in the previous year, through one of his Presbyters, who was then resident at Constantinople. On the representation of the Archbishop, the movement collapsed. But the concluding words in the Letter, written by one of the greatest of the Archbishops of Canterbury, are, in view of future negotiations for union, important; "We, the true Bishops and Clergy of the Church of England, *as in every fundamental article we profess the same faith with you*, shall not cease, at least in spirit and effect (since otherwise owing to our distance from you we cannot), to hold Communion with you, and to pray for your peace and happiness [p]."

Shortly after the Non-jurors sent their proposals for a Concordat to the Patriarchs, a similar attempt, for a union between the Russian and Gallican Churches, was made in France. In 1717, Peter the Great visited Paris, and whilst there, the Academy of the Sorbonne presented him with a memorial mentioning the points of agreement between the two Churches, and proposing a union after the manner of the Uniats, the Greeks to continue to repeat the Creed with the omission of the double Procession of the Holy Ghost. The Sorbonne dwelt on the liberties of the Gallican Church; the Pope, they declared, had no right to a Primacy of jurisdiction, but only one of rank and honour, according to the testimony of the Fathers, his claim to infallibility they rejected, and held him to be amenable to Councils.

This memorial Peter, on his return home, submitted to Stephen Javorski, and an assembly of Russian Bishops. The answer of the Bishops, drawn up by Theophanes Procopovich, expressed the desire of the Russian Church for union, for which it constantly prayed in all its services; but it held that such a union could only be effected by

[p] Quoted, Williams' Orthodox Church, LVIII.

a common agreement between the whole of Eastern and Western Christendom.

The cordial feeling, with which the Russian Church greeted the proposed union of the Greek and Anglican Churches, stands in marked contrast with its thinly-veiled disfavour towards a union with the Roman Catholics of France. Failing with the Russian Church, the Fathers of the Sorbonne turned to the Anglican Church, as likely to be more favourable. The latter movement is outside the scope of this work, but it is not without instruction. In Orthodox Russia, the Holy Synod received the proposed union with the Church of England "with great joy in the spirit;" in Roman Catholic France, a union of the Anglican and Gallican Churches excited the fury of the Jesuits, and the chief author of it was threatened with the Bastile. But it left its mark on the Roman Church. The Pope, Clement XI., was so struck with admiration of Archbishop Wake, that he declared it was a pity he was not a member of the Roman Church! Four years later, Courayer, a learned Benedictine, and Canon of St. Geneviéve in Paris, declared that; "The validity of English Orders stands on the strongest evidence, has the most authenticated acts, the most uncontested facts to oppose to false .... mistaken reasonings." We commend such testimony to our brethren of the Greek Church, with the assurance, that a further knowledge of each other would remove an imaginary bar to the union of the Greek and Anglican Churches.

Ecclesiastical Dissent is a special characteristic of Russia, and is a curious, if not a ludicrous, feature in Russian life. No nation in Europe is so conservative as the Russian. Peter's reforms were of a varied character, some good, some bad, some indifferent; extending downwards, from the establishment of a new Capital and the extinction of the Patriarchate, to the minutest usages of daily life, and they created opposition amongst all classes of Russian Society. The computation of time, not as before from the foundation of the world, but, according to Western custom, from the Birth of Christ, the change in the commencement of the year from September 1 to January 1; the substitution of a Russian, for the Slavic, Alphabet; the introduction of Newspapers into Petersburg, the alteration in the dress of men; the withdrawal of the veil from the faces of women; the order that men's chins should be shaven; and the taxation of beards; these might be considered matters of purely civil or political arrangement. But strange to say, even by the Orthodox Church they were connected with the reforms of Nicon, many who were willing to accept Nicon's reforms, but to go no further, looked upon them as an attempt to revolutionize Russia, and regarded them as a religious grievance So that the reforms of Peter, through the converts who, in consequence of them, left the Orthodox Church, immensely increased the numbers of the Raskolniks (*Dissenters*).

To the Staroviertsi, or "Old believers," they were particularly odious, as a continuation of Nicon's reforms. Their rage against Nicon was, compared with what it was against Peter, mild. Nicon was the forerunner of Antichrist, Peter was Antichrist himself. It can easily be understood that a Tsar would desire to know, through a census, the strength of his Empire; the Staroviertsi held that God alone had the right to keep a register, and they instanced David's punishment. European civilization they excommunicated wholesale, tea, coffee, sugar, potatoes, tobacco, all were the inventions of Antichrist. The potato, and not the apple, was the forbidden fruit by which the Serpent beguiled Eve, for it was winter-time, and Eve could not have plucked an apple at that season. Brandy was better than tobacco, for is it not written, "Not that which goeth into the mouth defileth a man, but that which cometh out of the mouth, this defileth a man?" All the evil predictions of the Prophets, and the denunciation of the Revelation, were applied to the state of Russia. Even Peter's victories, after previous defeats, were attributed to the agency of the evil one. In the names of Peter and his successor, succeeding Raskolniks sought for the number of the Beast, and discovered the Apocalyptic 666. By spelling Russia, Russa, they identified her with Asser of the Bible, and applied to her the maledictions pronounced against Nineveh and Babylon [q]. Beards became the subject of legislation; to prove that, by cutting off the beards, the Image of God was not destroyed, Dmitri, Bishop of Rostov, wrote *A Treatise on the Image and Likeness of God in Man;* but it was to no purpose, the beards gained the victory.

The absurdities of the Raskolniks drew forth more than one work from the Russian Bishops; such as the *Signs of Antichrist* and the *Rock of Faith* from Stephen Javorski; the *Examination of the Raskolnikene Faith* by Dmitri; and the *Spiritual Sling* by Pitirim, Bishop of Nijni-Novgorod; the last of whom had been one of the community at Vetka, and was, on his return to Orthodoxy, expressly nominated by Peter to the Episcopate, as a fitting person to expose the errors of the Raskol.

Dissent in Russia, where it is not of a Jewish character, is, unlike its sister in England, in its ideal, *high Church.* The reform of the Service-books was the "fons et origo mali." It had its birth in a mistaken attachment to what it conceived to be Orthodoxy, and in an excessive attachment to forms and ritual; it was kept alive by ignorance and fanaticism; and it is owing to the reforms of Nicon and Peter, and to such frivolous reasons as we have mentioned, that Russia is honeycombed with dissent. The Strigolniks and the Judaizers were almost entirely superseded by the Raskolniks; and there are in the present day, in conservative Russia, almost as many different sects of Raskolniks as there are of dissenters in liberal England.

The Raskolniks had no scruples in coming out from the Orthodox Church, but they met with a dilemma on their very threshold. They must either get Priests from the old Church, which they condemned as Babylon, or they must

---

[q] Beaulieu's Empire of the Tsars, II 302.

go without an Apostolic Priesthood altogether. So they at once broke up into two sects, the Popofsky, who felt that they could only have the Sacraments through regularly ordained Priests; and the Bez-Popofsky, who also held that they must have Priests, but would not have them through the old Babylon. The former availed themselves of deserters from the Orthodox Church, "run-away Priests," as they were called, of however indifferent character it mattered not, so long as they abjured, or were abjured by, that Church The latter were forced to abrogate the Priesthood altogether, and to adopt a Presbyterian form of government, whilst they adhered to the forms and ritual of the Greek Church. But these "*No-Priests*" could, even from their own point of view, have no Sacraments except Baptism; not even Marriage, which in the Greek Church is held to be a Sacrament. So they resorted to all manner of shifts. The difficulty as to the Eucharist they imagined that they got over, by retaining some of the Bread and Wine which had been reserved for the Communion of the Sick, before the Orthodox Church had become Babylon; and, by perpetually mixing them with fresh bread and wine, they gave a salve to their consciences by the belief that they multiplied the originally Consecrated Oblations[r]. Thus the door was opened to innumerable sects of the Raskol, the number of which was placed in the last century at two hundred.

For a long time the Raskolniks were subjected to bitter persecution. But the reign of Catharine II. was theoretically marked (an exception must be made with regard to the plunder of the Orthodox Church), by a religious toleration, and under her the number of the Raskolniks immensely increased. In 1771 the Plague broke out in Moscow, and, during the months of July and August, the death-rate grew into a thousand a day. The alarmed citizens flocked to a favourite Image of the Mother of God

---

[r] Palmer's Dissertations on the Orthodox Communion.

in such numbers, that many were trampled under foot or suffocated A proposal of the Metropolitan, Ambrose, for the removal of the Image was the signal for a terrible insurrection. The Archbishop, they said, was an infidel, in depriving them of their protectress; if he had not had the streets fumigated, the plague would long since have ceased; he was in league with the Doctors to cause their deaths. The Raskolniks exclaimed against "the rule of women;" the Kremlin was threatened, the crowds were, by the muskets and cannons of the soldiers, with difficulty dispersed, but not before Ambrose was put to death, and his palace pillaged.

The plague gained for the Raskolniks, both the Popofsky and Bez-Popofsky, a recognized position in Russia. Their offer to establish a hospital and cemetery for their co religionists, at their own expense, was readily accepted by the grateful Government. Two magnificent cemeteries were erected; villages, tenanted by Raskolniks, sprang up around them; a Charter, to manage their own foundations, was granted by the Government to the founders; and the two Institutions have remained ever since, religious centres of the Raskolniks.

Their position being thus recognized by the State, they continued to flourish under Catharine II, Paul, and Alexander I. In 1800, Plato, the liberally-minded Metropolitan of Moscow, strove to recover them to the Church, by Ordaining men, chosen from their own body, to their Priesthood; allowing them to use their own liturgical books, and to observe the rites, in vogue before the time of Nicon. But it was too late; the attempt at reconciliation collapsed, and the schism continued. Money flowed in from all parts of Russia, till at length they became an asylum for the scum of society, military deserters, degraded Priests, and malefactors flying from justice, and were brought under the lash of the State. Their various attempts to obtain an Episcopate of their own at last, in 1846, in the reign of Nicolas I., succeeded, but not from the Orthodox Church of

Russia. In that year[s] they found a certain Greek named Ambrose, a former Bishop of Bosnia, who, having been deprived by the Patriarch of Constantinople, took up his residence in Austrian territory, on the confines of Russia, and Consecrated Bishops for the Raskolniks. But so many crimes were charged against them, that, under Nicolas, they received a blow from which they have never recovered; their buildings were seized, their property confiscated, and in their Churches Priests, sent by the Holy Synod, officiated.

Under Nicolas, the visits of the Raskol Bishops to their flocks had been, from the first, furtive and under disguise, and so they continued under Alexander II. But, under the tolerant system of Alexander III., they regained courage; and now they have within the Empire about fifteen Sees, which assume the titles of the Orthodox Sees, with Archbishops at Moscow and Kazan, the latter aspiring to be recognized as Metropolitan, if not Patriarch, of all Russia[t].

In the present day, the Raskol eats at the very vitals of the Orthodox Church in Russia. Whilst other methods to reconcile the Raskolniks have failed, a union between the Orthodox Greek and Anglican Churches might be the means of effecting it In separating from the Mother Church and appealing to antiquity, the Raskol did not lay aside the Orthodox prejudice, that the Church of Rome is schismatical, and, in its claim to Papal infallibility, protestant. They would thus far find a common stand-point with the Church of England, on the ground that the English Reformation was not the institution of a new Church, but an appeal, from the medievalism of Rome, to the verdict of undivided Christendom.

In the reign of Peter the Great, the dependence of Poland on Russia, and its consequent decadence, which was further accelerated by the oppression and cruelty of the Jesuits, commenced. The massacre, in 1724, of the Protestants at Thorn, and their subsequently legalized exclusion from all public offices, sent a thrill of horror and indignation through-

[s] Stepniak's Russian Peasantry.   [t] Beaulieu, III 367.

out Christendom. Russia took the side of toleration, and England in vain sent a memorial to the King of Poland, setting forth the various persecutions which Christians had undergone. In 1772 the first partition of Poland, between Russia, Austria, and Prussia, was effected; the second, between Russia and Prussia, in 1793; and, as Austria was excluded from it, a third partition between the three was made in 1795. Poland, as an independent nation, ceased to exist; in that year its King, Stanislaus Poniatowski, resigned the throne, and, in 1798, died broken-hearted at Petersburg. Such was the fate of religious bigotry, the result of the entrance of the Jesuits into Poland; whilst Russia, its Slavic rival of the Greek Church, with a population of some ninety million souls, rules over the ninth part of the Globe.

CHAPTER XVII.

Partial Recovery of the Greek Church.

DECLINE of the Ottoman Power—Treaty of Carlowitz—Decadence of Poland—Commencement of the Wars between Russia and Turkey—Peace of Passarowitz—Of Belgrade—Of Sistova—Catharine II, Tsaritza—Battle of Kagoul—Treaty of Kainardji—Georgia - Kara George—Treaty of Tilsit—Of Bucharest—Independence of Servia—War of Greek Independence—Ali Pasha of Joannina—Murder of the Patriarch Gregorios—The Holy Alliance—Treaty of Akerman—Canning, Prime Minister of England—Treaty of London—Battle of Navarino—Treaty of Adrianople—Greece, independent—Holy Synod of the Kingdom of Greece—Transfer of the Ionian Islands—Mahomet Ali—Return of the Uniats to the Russian Church—The Janissaries disbanded—Disputes about the Holy Sepulchre—Treaty of Paris—Montenegro—Treaty of San Stephano—Cyprus ceded to England—Treaty of Berlin—Bosnia and Herzegovina placed under Austria—Independence of Roumania established—Principality of Bulgaria—Baptism of Prince Boris—Battle of Tel-el-Kebir—English occupation of Egypt—Society for the Furtherance of Christianity in Egypt—The Mahdi Insurrection—Recovery of the Soudan and Khartoum—Turkish Evacuation of Crete.

FOR nearly four centuries and a half, the Patriarchal See of Constantinople has been in subjection to the Ottomans; for more than seven hundred and fifty years longer, the three other great Patriarchates of the East have, under their dominion, been little more than a name. "The Eastern Question" has been defined, as the question whether Russia will have Constantinople or not. Into the thorny region of politics, it is not our intention to enter; but there is one point on which all Christians agree, viz., that the Eastern Church could not be left indefinitely at the mercy of a nation, part of whose creed is to be intolerant, part of whose nature to be bloodthirsty.

The Battle of Lepanto, A.D. 1571 [a], is generally taken as the turning-point in the tide of Ottoman prosperity; since then, with the exception of Crete in 1669, it has made no important lasting conquests, and has gradually declined;

[a] See p. 485.

and, if at so early a date the "sick man" had not passed into a proverb, in the seventeenth century his early dissolution was expected.

The commencement of better times for the Greeks may be dated from the crushing defeat of the Turks under the walls of Vienna, in 1683, by the Polish General, John Sobieski. Encouraged by this disaster of Turkey, the Venetians, who had lately lost Crete, began, in 1684, under the Doge Francesco Morosini, the war which ended in their conquest of the Morea. By the Treaty of Carlowitz, in 1699, between the Sultan and the Tsar Peter the Great, which, as the consequence of that war, was brought about mainly by England, Turkey received one of the heaviest blows ever inflicted on it, a blow from which it never afterwards recovered. Turkey had to surrender to Austria all the territories, including Hungary, which, during two centuries, it had conquered from her, with Transylvania and part of Slavonia in addition, to surrender to Venice the Morea; the Ukraine, and part of Moldavia to the Poles; and Azov to Russia.

Its wars with the Christian nations of the West, Poland, whose days of greatness were now past, being almost the sole exception, continued throughout the eighteenth century; and in that century Turkey won back much that it had lost. But a new era had arisen upon it; the days when the laws and religion of Islam had been an appreciable quantity, in making peace with Christian powers, were at an end; the Peace of Carlowitz convinced the Turks, not only that they must treat for peace on equal terms, but that they must also forfeit territory to their Christian enemies.

The wars between Russia and Turkey had begun in the middle of the Seventeenth Century. Notwithstanding that an armistice for thirty years had been agreed upon in the Treaty of Carlowitz, another war broke out between them in 1709, and the two nations entered on that career of nine wars, which ended recently in the Treaty of Berlin. In the war of 1709—1711 the armies of the Tsar were defeated;

by the Treaty of Pruth in the latter year, Azov was restored to Turkey; and in 1715 the Venetians had to cede to it the Morea. A saviour arose to Europe in the person of the Emperor Charles VI, under whom the complete dissolution of the Ottoman Empire was expected, and men began to think that a Christian Emperor might again reign at Constantinople[b]. The Treaty of Passarowitz in Servia, signed in July, 1718, between his General, Prince Eugene, and the Vizier, confirmed to the Emperor the extensive conquests which that great General, in alliance with the Venetians, had acquired from the Turks By that Treaty, the small part of Hungary and Slavonia, which Turkey still continued to hold after the Treaty of Carlowitz, together with Belgrade, part of Bosnia, and the Western portion of Servia and Wallachia, were secured to the Emperor. Unfortunately, in the Treaty, Charles overlooked his allies, the Venetians, and the Turks were confirmed in the possession of the Morea. But all these conquests, the Emperor, deprived of the services of Eugene, again lost in an unsuccessful war, in 1737; and by the Peace of Belgrade, in 1739, Belgrade, Servia, Bosnia and Wallachia were surrendered to the Turks. Between 1787—1791 there was again war between Austria and Turkey; in 1789 Belgrade was again captured by Austria, but by the Peace of Sistova, in 1791, was again surrendered to the Turks. The Peace of Sistova ended the wars between the Austrians and the Turks, with the result that Hungary was freed from Turkey, but that Servia and Bosnia continued in its clutches.

Meanwhile wars between Russia and Turkey went on. The reign of Catharine II, a Prussian Princess, whose Baptismal name was Sophia Augusta, and who had qualified for the Russian throne by changing her Lutheran for the Orthodox faith, for the outward forms of which she showed a great regard, marks an important era in the history of Russia, and of the Greek Christians. In 1769, Russia defeated Turkey on the banks of the Dniester, in a war of

[b] Freeman's Ottoman Power, p. 157.

the latter's own seeking, and to the great joy of the Christian population, occupied Moldavia and Wallachia. In the following year, 15,000 Russians defeated, in the battle of Kagoul on the banks of the Pruth, 150,000 Turks. In 1771, Catharine excited the hopes of the Christians by sending a fleet to the Morea, and the Christian population, in consequence, revolted from Turkey. The Russian Admiral, however, deserting their cause to seek elsewhere further victories over the Turks, annihilated the Turkish fleet on the coast of Asia, and the fall of Constantinople itself appeared imminent; never were the Turks in greater straits, and nothing could have saved them, had not the appearance of the plague completely paralyzed their opponents. The Russian victories, and the previous victories of the Austrians, were of special value, for two reasons; one, because they taught the Christian subjects of the Porte, many of whom had fought in the armies of Austria and Russia, that Turkish armies were not invincible; the other, because they taught them that they had only to bide their time, trusting to their own strength and the righteousness of their cause, for freedom.

Of still more important consequence was the Treaty of Kainardji, which followed on the Turkish defeats, in 1774. Not only was Azof again restored to Russia, the Crimea rendered independent, and the Black Sea and the passage of the Dardanelles opened to her traffic, but the Treaty effected a great change in the condition of the Christians; the Danubian Principalities were indeed restored to the Turks, but the right to interfere on their behalf, and a kind of general protectorate of Russia over the Christian subjects of the Porte, was established. So that with the Treaty of Kainardji, a new chapter, in the emancipation of the Greek Church, opened.

In July, 1789, the French Revolution broke out; the ever-recurring wars between Russia and Turkey were consequently suspended, and at one time they were even allies. By the Treaty of Campo Formio in October, 1797, the

Ionian Islands were ceded to the French, but in the following year were, for a time, recovered by a Turco-Russian fleet.

We now come to our own century, during which the revolt of the Christian nations of the Greek Church from Turkey has been almost continuous.

In 1801, Georgia was annexed to Russia; and its Exarch, the Archbishop of Tiflis, is now *ex-officio* a member of the Holy Governing Synod of Russia.

Ever since Servia, where once (in the Fourteenth Century) the formidable Monarchy of St. Stephen Dushan ruled, had been given back to Turkey, the cruelties inflicted on it by the Janissaries and the Pashas, who were set over it, rendered its condition intolerable. At length the unhappy people could endure the tyranny no longer; and in 1801 an insurrection under Kara George (*Black George*), a rich pork-butcher of Belgrade [c], broke out, and the Janissaries were expelled from the country. So far the Sultan, Selim III., who had come to the throne in 1789, was disposed to help the Serbs, the Janissaries having long shewn a rebellious spirit against their Turkish rulers. But soon the Serbs broke with the Sultan, and succeeded in enlisting the aid of Russia, who insisted upon the rights given to it by the Treaty of Kainardji. Selim, it is said, received the claim made by Russia with tears of anger and humiliation [d]; it would be better, said the Turks, to be buried under the ruins of Constantinople, than to be bound by a Treaty which would annihilate the Ottoman Empire. By the help of Russia, Kara George, in 1806, captured Belgrade; but, through the intervention of the French Emperor Napoleon, Turkey was saved the loss of Moldavia and Wallachia.

By a secret clause in the Treaty of Tilsit, in 1807, between the French Emperor and the Tsar Alexander I., it was provided that all the Ottoman provinces in Europe except Constantinople and Roumelia, "should be withdrawn from the yoke and tyranny of the Turks."

[c] Rambaud, II 204.   [d] Creasy's Hist. of the Ottoman Turks, II. 360.

In 1807 Sultan Selim was murdered; and, after the murder of his successor, Mustapha III, Mahmoud II., styled by the Greeks "*the Butcher*," began his reign (1807—1839) at the age of twenty-five The threatening attitude of Napoleon made Russia desirous of having Turkey as an ally; a war which had, in 1810, broken out between the two countries, ended, in 1812, in the Treaty of Bucharest, in which an article was inserted for the independence of Servia, on payment of tribute to the Porte; whilst the Pruth and Lower Danube were defined as the boundary between the two Empires. By that treaty Turkey ceded to Russia Bessarabia, and a portion of Moldavia, Russia waiving her claim to all other territories which she had conquered.

The French invasion of Russia in that year revived the hopes of Turkey; Turkish garrisons re-occupied the Servian fortifications, and Kara George was obliged to escape into Austria; in 1813 Servia was reconquered by the Turks, and its condition became worse than ever, all the horrors usually resorted to by Turks, after the suppression of an insurrection, ensuing. Again the people, this time under the leadership of Milosh Obrenovich, flew to arms, and were again successful in obtaining their freedom; in 1815 Milosh was chosen Prince of Servia, his election being confirmed by a Hatti-Sheriff of the Sultan, and Kara George, on his return to Servia to claim his rights, was, at the instigation of Milosh, murdered. The independence of Servia, as a separate state, on payment of tribute, and with a slight dependence, such as the right of garrisoning some of its fortresses, was recognized by Mahmoud in the Convention of Akerman (1826), and was confirmed by the Treaty of Adrianople (1829).

The Servian Church under its early kings, whilst it acknowledged a general Primacy, though not the jurisdiction, of the Patriarchate of Constantinople, had existed as an independent Church, with its own Patriarch at Belgrade. In 1679, thirty thousand emigrant families from Servia established the See of Carlowitz. In 1765 the Servian Patriarchate was suppressed by the Turks; and Kara George re-established it at Carlowitz. In 1830 Servia declared its Church to be autocephalous; and when, in 1838, Belgrade became the Capital, the Metropolitan placed his See there, without, however, assuming the title of Patriarch. Milosh, who, in 1839, was forced to abdicate, was, in 1858, restored, with the Princely dignity made hereditary in his family; and on his death, which occurred two years afterwards, he was succeeded by his son, Michael III.

Whilst the war with Slavic Servia was going on, the War of Greek Independence broke out; and Mahmoud's engagements with Servia and Ali Pasha of Joannina determined the time of the outbreak. Ali was a native of Albania, a nation largely composed of zealous Orthodox Christians, but also with a large Mahometan element, to which latter Ali belonged. The Albanians, who were widely diffused over Greece, were intensely national, and Christians and Mahometans alike had often been in rebellion against Turkey. Ali was an unscrupulous and cruel savage, whose whole career was one of boldness and cunning; his one object in life was to weaken the Sultan, and to centralize all power in his own hands. Utterly devoid of all moral and religious principles he, in 1803, subdued, after a vigorous resistance, the Souliots, a Christian people in Albania; and, in return for the victory, the Sultan promoted him to the Governorship of Roumania. Himself a Mahometan, Ali kept his eyes open to every political change, and had discernment enough to understand that the tide had turned from the Crescent to the Cross; he broke out into open rebellion against the Sultan, and was in consequence, in 1820, deposed. Ali's opposition to the Sultan stirred up the spirit of the Greeks in Albania, and at the time of his death, before which the War of Greek Independence had broken out, he was actually in alliance with the Christians against the Turks [e]. He eventually, on an oath that his life should be spared, surrendered himself to the Sultan, but was, in February, 1822, executed.

[e] Freeman's Saracens, p. 177.

The time when one part of the Turkish forces was diverted against Servia, another against Ali, seemed to the Greeks to afford a favourable opportunity for their long contemplated outbreak. Since the fall of Constantinople, Greece, as a nation, had disappeared, and the glorious name of Hellenes had been swamped in that of Romans ('Ρωμαῖοι) [f]. But Greece had all along remained firm to the Orthodox Church, and the Church kept alive the national sentiment of independence. The idea had been fostered by the French Revolution, which recalled to their minds that they were not Romans, but Hellenes, the descendants of the ancient Greeks; "English liberty and American independence had struck chords that vibrated wherever civilization dwelt [g]." The gradual loss of their military superiority by the Turks, and the belief that Russia, the champion of Orthodoxy, was on the point of taking Constantinople, stimulated their hopes. Considerable disappointment was felt that so little had been done for them in the Council of Vienna; but the placing of the Ionian Islands under the protection of England, and the assertion by Servia of its independence, inspired the other Greeks with confidence, in asserting their own emancipation from the Turkish yoke.

The separate materials were brought into combination by means of a political Society, called the Philike Hetæria, founded, in 1814, at Odessa (itself the successor of a literary club called the Philomuse, founded in Athens in 1812); the several ramifications of which had laid, unknown to the Turks, the mine containing the seeds of the Revolution. The Hetærists were buoyed up with the hope of Russian aid, and the Society was believed to have the patronage of the Tsar Alexander. Its existence was also well known to the Greek Bishops and Metropolitans; yet, although they were assured that Russian assistance could be relied upon, they were averse to proceedings being carried on too hastily, and advocated delay. The Patriarch of Constantinople,

[f] Finlay, VI 97. [g] Ibid.

Gregorios, was also, before he had been elected to the Patriarchate, cognizant of an Orthodox conspiracy; but the knowledge had been conveyed to him through the Confessional; his only blame was that he had accepted the office, when he knew that Greek independence was in the air.

Matters, however, had been carried too far to be delayed by the cautious attitude of the Church; and, at the end of March, 1821, the first movement of the insurrection took place. On Easter Day, which in that year fell on April 22, the Patriarch Gregorios was, as an accessory to the rebellious scheme of the Hetæria, arrested at the Altar, and hanged in his Pontifical robes at the gate of his own Palace at Constantinople. After three days the body was cut down, and delivered by the Vizier to a rabble of Jews, the long-standing enemies of the Greeks, who dragged it through the streets and then threw it into the sea. Eugenius, Bishop of Pisidia, received from the Sultan investiture, as the successor of Gregorios. In the same year three Metropolitans and eight Bishops were put to death. Priests were murdered wholesale [h]. But it must be added that, in the wars of Greek Independence, Greeks and Turks were equally merciless to each other.

The Greeks were mistaken in their belief that Russia was ready to afford them material assistance. The Holy Alliance of 1815, of which the Tsar was a member, was opposed to free institutions and the liberty of the people, and was therefore naturally opposed to revolutionary principles, and Greek independence. The interest which the Tsar took in Greece was Ecclesiastical, and not political; he sympathized with Greek Orthodoxy, but that did not seem to him to imply the necessity of Greek nationality. On political grounds the independence of Greece was not consonant with the ideas of the Tsar; the time might come when the interests of the Slavic and non-

[h] Rambaud, II. 308. Gordon enumerates about twenty Bishops who were murdered or executed by the Turks in the early stage of the Revolution.

Slavic members of the Orthodox Church might clash, and conflicts between Russian and Greek interests arise on the Bosphorus. Greece, in the opinion of Greeks, was the heir of Constantinople, the seat of the Greek Emperors; whilst Russia, as the Third Rome, thought that the right of the Second Rome, from which she derived her Christianity, devolved upon her.

In July, 1821, however, the Tsar sent an ultimatum to the Sultan, demanding a cessation of the cruelties inflicted on the Christians; nor did he resume diplomatic relations with the Porte, till George Canning induced Russia and France to join England in establishing peace between Greece and Turkey. Amongst the Russian people there was from the first a strong desire to take up arms on behalf of those who belonged to the Orthodox Church, but this wish was not countenanced by the Tsar; and a fearful inundation that, shortly before the death of Alexander, devastated Petersburg, was looked upon by the people as a just chastisement for their culpable indifference to the Greeks.

In England the cause found many sympathisers, amongst whom the names of Lords Byron and Cochrane, Sir Richard Church, General Gordon, and Captain Hastings, were conspicuous. Especially dear to the Greeks is the name of Byron; but dear, beyond all, is that of George Canning. The British government, under Lord Liverpool, attributed the Greek revolt to Russian intrigues; before Canning took office in 1822, says Mr. Gladstone, "it viewed the rebellion with an evil eye, from jealousy to Russia [1];" "greater than any other power," says Finlay [2]; though several other European States preferred the success of the Sultan to the intermeddling of the Tsar. In the Parliament of 1822, Mr. Wilberforce lamented the want of combination of the leading powers, to drive the Turks out of Europe. In August, 1824, Greece entreated England to "take up the cause of Greek independence and frustrate the schemes

[1] Contemporary Review. III. 161.

of Russia;" and on December 1, Canning promised that England would mediate with the Sultan, "a friendly Sovereign who had given England no cause of complaint."

The Greek Insurrection was not confined to the country which, in the present day, is called Greece, but comprised Greeks in every part of the Turkish dominions, as well as Orthodox volunteers from Albania, Bulgaria, and Roumania; and so long as they were left to contend against the Turks alone, they were well able to maintain their cause, and their success was rapid. On December 12, 1822, Nauplia, the strongest fortress in the Morea, was taken by them. Their successes in that year established Greece as an independent State, with its own National Assembly; and it was then felt that Turkey could never reconquer it. In 1823, Canning, by the recognition of the Turkish blockade of the Greek ports, gave to the insurgents the character of belligerents. In 1824, Lord Byron, who had left England in 1816 never to return, arrived at Mesolonghi; his advocacy of the Greek cause was, however, connected with no important military event, for in the same year he died. In that year, Mahmoud had to humble himself by calling to his aid his rebellious vassal, Mahomet Ali, the Pasha of Egypt, who, biding the opportunity to establish his own independence, was now ready to fight for the Sultan against Christians; and, accordingly, sent his son Ibrahim, who conquered Crete in 1824, and in 1825 landed in the Morea. So great was its danger through the invasion of the Morea, that the Greek nation in 1825 "placed its liberty, independence, and political existence, under the protection of Great Britain." In 1826, the Turks captured Mesolonghi, and in 1827 Athens capitulated.

Meanwhile, in December, 1825, the Tsar Alexander, who had been sorely perplexed between the duties of Orthodoxy, and his despotic leanings, died, and was succeeded by his brother Nicolas; and the Holy Alliance came to an end. The new Tsar at once determined to exercise the protectorate of the Christians under the Treaty of Kainardji; and in March, 1826, presented an ultimatum to the Sultan, demanding the evacuation of the Danubian Principalities, which the latter had occupied, and the execution of the Treaty of Bucharest. The Sultan at first received the demand with indignation, but ultimately gave way; and on October 8, agreed to the Convention of Akerman; "to arrange the mode of execution of the Treaty of Bucharest which had not been executed by the Porte since the year 1821 . . . . . and to carry out the privileges which Moldavia, Wallachia, and Servia ought to enjoy under the protection (*sous l'influence tutelaire*) of Petersburg." Free passage was also allowed to Russian vessels from the Black Sea to the Mediterranean.

In that year Stratford Canning, with instructions to induce the Sultan to terminate the war, arrived at Constantinople; and in February of the next year, he, with the consent of the Greek National Assembly, treated with the Tsar for the independence, on payment of tribute, of Greece; but progress, when an agreement to that effect was on the point of being arranged, was suddenly stopped by the disunion of the Christian powers, and the Porte refused all mediation, or interference in the internal affairs of his Empire.

In April, 1827, George Canning became Prime Minister of England. In the same month, Capodistrias, a native of Corfu, who had been in the Russian service, was, through the influence of the Tsar, who wished to counteract the liberal policy of the two Cannings, elected President by the National Assembly, for seven years. Suddenly Russia was induced by George Canning to agree on a scheme for the liberation of Greece; and, on July 5 of that year, whilst Canning still lived, England, France, and Russia signed the Treaty of London, by which they bound themselves to compel Turkey by force to acknowledge Greek Independence, under the suzerainty of the Sultan, by payment of a fixed annual tribute. These terms the Greeks instantly accepted, but the Sultan again rejected all interference. In August, George Canning died. On October 20 was fought, be-

Partial Recovery of the Greek Church. 633

tween the three allied powers on the one side, and the Turks and Egyptians on the other, the battle of Navarino, in which the latter powers were defeated, and their fleets destroyed.

The Battle of Navarino, though it virtually settled the question of Greek Independence, only exasperated Mahmoud; and in December, the Ambassadors, finding their mediation fruitless, left Constantinople. George Canning was dead; Viscount Goderic was Prime Minister for less than five months; and the succeeding ministry of the Duke of Wellington lamented the destruction of the Turkish fleet. The Battle of Navarino was also far from satisfying the aspirations of the Tsar, who wished to occupy the Danubian Principalities. In April, 1828, Russia declared war against Turkey, and in August, 1829, its forces, though too weakened by the resistance of the Turks to reach Constantinople, gained possession of Adrianople, the second city of importance in the Turkish Empire. The Sultan, having no force sufficient to bar the further march of the Russians, yielding to the advice of England and France, signed, on September 14, 1829, the Treaty of Adrianople. The Sultan is said to have agreed to the Treaty, with tears in his eyes, and for weeks afterwards, utterly crushed in spirit, to have shut himself up in his palace at Therapia. The terms of the treaty were that Moldavia and Wallachia should be left under the suzerainty of the Porte, but that the Porte should not be allowed to retain in them any fortified post, nor any Mussulmans, except for mercantile purposes, reside in them; that they were to enjoy all privileges granted to them by former Treaties, and the free exercise of their religion. With respect to Servia, all the clauses of the Convention of Akerman were to be observed. By Article X., which related to the Greeks, all the stipulations of the Treaty of London of July, 1827, were to be carried out.

Both Servia and Greece were now free, and by a Protocol, signed on Feb. 3, 1830, the suzerainty of the Porte over the latter Kingdom was abolished. Thus its complete independence, although with a more restricted frontier than had been assigned by the Treaty of Adrianople, was declared; it was also arranged that the provisional Government of Capodistrias should be abolished, and that she should be governed by a King, not chosen from the families of any of the signatories of the Treaty of 1827. In the same month Prince Leopold, much to the disgust of Capodistrias, who expected it himself, accepted the Sovereignty; his election was received by the people with enthusiasm, and the Orthodox clergy were willing to accept a Sovereign, who, although a Protestant, was so eminently fitted for the post. In May of the same year, Leopold, although he at first accepted, refused the appointment, the reason which he assigned to King Charles of France being the restricted frontier, which he thought little consonant with the legitimate aspirations of the country. With his refusal passed away the hope of a brilliant future for Greece.

Greece now became the theatre of violence and civil war. Capodistrias, who still remained President, having, through his agency in the interests of Russia, and the jealousy of the leading men, become unpopular, his authority was undermined by open resistance; and on his refusal to make the reforms demanded of him, was, on October 9, 1831, assassinated; his brother Augustine being placed at the head of the provisional government. But, his authority being opposed by the insurrectionary Chiefs, Greece was practically without a government, and in a state of complete anarchy. The Courts of England, France, and Russia, which had taken Greece under their protection, as the only means of restoring tranquillity, resolved on a King to whom the Chiefs would yield obedience, which they refused to give to one of their own order. In February, 1832, the Crown was offered to, and accepted by, Prince Otho, a Roman Catholic, a thoroughly inexperienced youth, seventeen years of age, second son of the King of Bavaria. The King of Bavaria was authorized to appoint a regency during his

Partial Recovery of the Greek Church. 635

son's minority, and the succession to the throne was to devolve, in default of lawful heirs to Otho, on his younger brothers, and their lawful descendants by primogeniture, without regard to their religion. It is difficult to comprehend how Orthodox Russia, which well knew the antipathy always felt by the Greeks for the Roman Church, could consent to such an arrangement, or imagine that it could possibly answer. Greek Orthodoxy professes that the Greeks would rather be under the rule of Mahometans, than under the schism of the Latin Church; and it is with them a proverbial expression, that a heretic is worse than an infidel. It must be placed to Otho's credit that, when afterwards the nation clamoured for an Orthodox King, he never showed any inclination to secure the succession to his family, on the condition of a change of his religion.

In February, 1833, the young King was conveyed in an English frigate to his new Kingdom, where he was joyfully received by the people, as their deliverer from anarchy. The desire of the Greeks, however, for an Orthodox King only too surely paved the way for a new revolution.

The Church, though in temporal matters subject to a Roman Catholic King, remained, in doctrine and in ritual, in the same relation to the Patriarch of Constantinople, as the other branches of the Eastern Church. But its political independence was incompatible with an Ecclesiastical dependence on the Patriarch and Synod of Constantinople, the subjects of the Sultan with whom Greece had so lately been at war. The Church of the Kingdom of Greece seems to have been at the time in a very corrupt state. Finlay quotes, as the authority for his statements as to the venality of the higher Orders, and the general ignorance that prevailed amongst the clergy, a high Official in the Department of Ecclesiastical Affairs and Public Instruction (*un Grec temoin oculaire des faits qu'il reporte*). Simony was a general practice. The Bishops annulled marriages, cancelled Wills, and derived a considerable profit by trading in judicial business; giving decisions in most civil cases, and leaguing themselves with the Metropolitans, who were interested in the matter, against the establishment of proper Courts of Law. When Capodistrias deprived the Bishops of their jurisdiction in civil causes, except marriage and divorce, the mitred judge indignantly complained, that the Orthodox clergy were suffering a persecution similar to that under Pharaoh. Bigamy, and admission of minors to Holy Orders, were a source of gain to the Bishops. The fabrication of false certificates was a lucrative source of profit to the clergy, whose selfishness and corruption led them to resist the order, that Registers of Births, Marriages and Deaths should be kept in every Parish. To eradicate the prevalent evils from the gangrened members of the Priesthood would, it was said, be tantamount to amputating nearly the whole clerical body.

The Church of Greece had already in its services omitted the name of the Patriarch of Constantinople; and when the Patriarch and Synod remonstrated, Capodistrias told them, that the murder of the Patriarch Gregorios and the other Bishops rendered the return of liberated Greece to its former connection with a See, subject to the Sultan, impossible. On July 15, 1833, a national Synod (ἱερὰ σύνοδος τοῦ Βασιλείου τῆς Ἑλλάδος) met at Nauplia, the seat of government, to decide on the Ecclesiastical affairs of the Kingdom, and the reform of the Church[k]. In the Synod, a resolution, approved by all the Bishops, was passed on July 23rd, to the effect, that the Eastern Orthodox and Apostolic Church of Greece, whilst it preserves dogmatic unity with the Eastern Orthodox Churches, is dependent on no external authority, and spiritually owns no Head but the Founder of the Christian Church (τὸν Θεμελιωτὴν τῆς Χριστιάνης Πίστεως). In the external government of the Church (κατὰ τὸ διοικητικὸν μέρος) which belongs to the Crown, she acknowledges the King of Greece as her supreme head, as

---

[k] It was, says Dr. Neale, uncanonically assembled by the Minister of Worship and Education.

not being opposed to the Canons. A Holy Synod, after the model of the Russian Church, was to be established, as the highest Ecclesiastical authority, and to be entirely composed of Archbishops and Bishops, appointed by the King. A Royal Delegate was to be appointed to the Holy Synod, who, but without a vote, should attend every sitting, and countersign all the decisions, without which they should be void.

In its external government, the Church of the Kingdom is subject to the King, whilst its Spiritual administration is regulated by the Holy Synod of the Kingdom of Greece. This relation of the Spiritual and temporal Powers is the same that has obtained in the Church, ever since the days of Constantine; the government by the Holy Synod, as adopted in the Kingdom of Greece, was that adopted in Russia in the time of Peter the Great, and by other Greek Christians, as soon as they threw off the subjection of the Sultan. Although the Patriarchs had given their consent to the Holy Governing Synod of Russia, the Patriarch of Constantinople long refused to recognize the Synod of Greece; but negotiations, which had hitherto failed, were re-opened in 1850. In that year the Greek Ministry, at the instance of the Holy Synod, and in deference to the Œcumenical See, made a request to the Patriarch Anthimus, for its recognition. The Patriarch and Synod thereupon issued a Decretal, called *The Synodical Tome* (ὁ Συνοδικὸς Τόμος), which, whilst it recognized the independence of the Greek Church, was worded in so authoritative a tone, as to be derogatory to its national independence; requiring submission to an authority dependent on the Ottoman government, and putting forth, for the Patriarch of Constantinople, the same claims as those made by Rome, viz., as having received from God the Apostolical charge of all the Churches (τὴν Ἀποστολικὴν μέριμναν πασῶν τῶν Ἐκκλεσίων).

The Decretal was answered in a hostile volume, entitled *The Synodical Tome or regarding Truth* (ὁ Συνοδικὸς Τόμος ἢ περὶ Ἀληθείας), drawn up by an Archimandrite named Pharmacides. Two years were allowed to elapse before the Church of Greece accepted the terms of the Church of Constantinople. But in 1852 a law was adopted in the Greek Chambers, accepting the provisions of the Synodical Tome, but without mentioning the Tome itself; and embodying its conditions, one of which was that the Holy Synod should be presided over by the Metropolitan of Attica, instead of, as before, by a President appointed by the Crown.

It would appear that, two years later, an offer made by the Tsar Nicolas, to undertake the protectorate of the Greek Church, drew on him a rebuke from the Patriarch Anthimus. The Patriarch issued a letter in the name of the whole Orthodox Greek Church "against the schism calling itself Orthodoxy, which has transferred to St. Petersburg the Spiritual authority in religious matters[1]." It is an open secret, that between the Patriarchal See of Constantinople and the Holy Governing Synod of Russia, no great cordiality exists.

From the year of Otho's succession, Greece exercised little or no control over its own government, which was responsible to the King of Bavaria, the country receiving its guidance from Munich. It is not surprising, therefore, that, through an ignorance of its institutions, the country was badly governed.

In 1836 Otho married Amalia, a Protestant, daughter of the Grand Duke of Oldenberg, with whom, in the following year, he returned to Athens.

After 1838, native Greeks began to be appointed to the Prime Ministry; but, says Finlay, the Germans were so superior to the Greek Prime Ministers, that the Presidency was merely nominal; Otho, who thought that the Greek Kingdom was founded for his sole benefit, ruled, through means of his private Cabinet, as his own Prime Minister. The incapacity of the King and of the Rulers of Greece soon brought forth bitter fruit. Anarchy and insurrections, brigandage and piracy, prevailed; so that it

[1] Times, August 31, 1854.

Partial Recovery of the Greek Church. 639

was commonly believed that Greece was better off before, than since, her emancipation. Because Greece was a Kingdom, she must have a large army, the soldiers of which remained unpaid, and a navy, which was formed apparently for no other purpose except to rot [m].

The people clamoured for a Constitution, and Otho, to preserve his insecure throne, gave his tardy consent to the meeting of the National Assembly (November, 1843— March, 1844); and swore obedience to the new Constitution, one of the first Articles of which decreed, that the successor to the throne should be a member of the Orthodox Church. The Bavarians were dismissed from the government. The hopes entertained of the downfall of the Ottoman Empire, and its own succession to its European dominions, enlisted the Kingdom of Greece, in the Crimean War, on the side of Orthodox Russia against unorthodox France and England; and, regardless of international treaties, Greece thought it a favourable opportunity for the annexation of the coveted provinces of Thessaly and Epirus. This, for a time, rendered Otho, but particularly his wife Amalia, popular. The Greek Minister in London, Tricoupis, tried to deceive the English people with professions of neutrality; but after information received from Sir Thomas Wyse, its Minister at Athens, the English government, in April, 1854, warned Otho, that it would be obliged to enforce the engagement which placed him on the throne; the undisciplined Greek troops, which devastated Thessaly and Epirus, were easily driven away by the Turks, and the Greeks were obliged to abandon the Russian alliance.

The long expected Revolution in the Greek Kingdom came in 1862, at a time when the King and Queen were absent from Athens on a tour in the Morea. On October 22 of that year, the garrison of Athens revolted; little effort was made to uphold the Royal authority; and Otho's reign of more than thirty years, which secured neither order

[m] Finlay, VII. 127.

at home nor peace abroad, came to an end, and a provisional government was appointed.

Though Otho showed no signs of learning, in his reign an important work was done for education. In 1839, under strong opposition from the Court, the University of Athens was founded; the Court, says Finlay [n], slowly and sullenly yielded to the force of public opinion, and the Royal assent was eventually extorted, rather than given, to the measure. As to the private character of Otho, Mr. Masson, who was a Professor in the University of Athens, and had a knowledge of Greece extending over twenty years, speaks in the highest terms of praise; whilst both he and his wife were without a spark of bigotry.

What Greece needed was a Ruler of mature age, and a member of the Greek Church; yet the Hellenes, as they now called themselves, elected on March 23, 1863, another boy as King, Prince George, second son of the King of Denmark, and a Protestant; on the condition that his lawful heirs should embrace the faith of the Orthodox Greek Church.

By the Hellenic Constitution, granted in 1864, it was enacted;—Article I. The established religion of Greece is that of the Eastern Orthodox Church of Christ; and, though every other recognized religion is tolerated by law, interference with, or proselytizing from, the Established Church, is prohibited. . . . Article II. The Orthodox Church of Greece, "acknowledging for its Head the Lord Jesus Christ, is indissolubly united in doctrine with the great Church of Constantinople, and with every other Church of Christ holding the same doctrines; observing, as they invariably do, the holy Apostolic and Synodical Canons and holy Traditions."

The new King bound himself by oath, "in the name of the Holy Consubstantial and Indivisible Trinity, to maintain the Established religion of the Greeks." The members of the house of Representatives ($Βουλή$), if members of the

[n] VII. 132.

Partial Recovery of the Greek Church.

Greek Church, were required on entering on their office to swear in the same terms; if not members, to swear according to their own religious formula.

The Revolution of 1862 afforded an opportunity, of which the British Government availed itself, of transferring the Ionian Islands to Greece. By the Treaty of Tilsit, in 1807, Russia ceded the Ionian Islands to France; and though England conquered the other Islands, the French retained possession of Corfu until the peace of 1814. In 1815 the Ionian Republic was revived, and placed under the protectorate of England. The English occupation, however, was far from popular amongst the Greeks, and the English Government found all the means adopted for their improvement rejected. In 1858 Mr. Gladstone was sent to the Islands as Commissioner Extraordinary; but his return to England being, at the beginning of 1859, necessitated through his being a Member of Parliament, he was, in February of the following year, succeeded by Sir Henry Storks. After the Greek Revolution of 1862 broke out, the British Government promised the provisional Government of Greece that, if the King elected met its approval, measures would be taken for the restoration of the Islands to the Kingdom of Greece. The election of King George being approved, a Treaty was, on November 14, 1863, signed by the Five Great Powers, regulating the conditions of annexation, one of which was that King George's successors should be members of the Orthodox Greek Church. England also wished to give Thessaly and Epirus to Greece, but in view of reforms promised by Turkey in 1856, after the Crimean War, did not think it fair to press the proposal.

Much of what has been related above only indirectly comes within our province; but it is generally thought that, owing to the restriction of its territory and bad government, the Kingdom of Greece was from the first placed in a false position, and ambitious hopes were raised, which had their result in the abortive revolt of 1896, and the moral, as well as military, victory of the Turks.

Sultan Mahmoud had, as we have seen, in the early years of the War of Greek Independence, called to his aid his vassal Mahomet Ali, Pasha of Egypt, through whom he for a time stemmed the tide of the Greek Rebellion. In the break-up of the Turkish Empire Ali played an important part. Born in 1769, the same year as Napoleon I. and Wellington, this wonderful man is said to have begun life as a tobacconist; and to have raised himself, not only to the throne of Egypt, but, by the conquest of Syria, to such a position that, but for the intervention of the Western Powers, there seemed no obstacle to his supplanting the Ottomans on the throne of Constantinople, and in the leadership of the Faithful.

By the expulsion of the French in 1801, Egypt reverted to the Ottoman Empire; and in 1806 Ali was, on payment of tribute to the Sultan, appointed Pasha. In 1811 he put an end to the Mamaluke power in Egypt; and in 1820 annexed the Soudan, which remained nominally under the Egyptian Government till 1884 Ali, though he professed Islam, was wholly untrammelled with religion; his one object was to make himself Sovereign of Egypt, and, to obtain that object of his ambition, he was as ready to fight against the Turks, as he had been to fight for the Turks against the Christians. In 1830 the Sultan conferred on him the government of Crete.

After the annihilation of his fleet at Navarino, Ali constructed another; and, well knowing the thorough exhaustion and impotence of Turkey after the campaign of 1826 and 1827, he, in 1830, openly revolted; in the following year he instituted a kind of holy war, and his son Ibrahim wrested Syria from the Sultan. This act Mahmoud declared as one of treason against the Sovereign, and against the Prophet; Ali retaliated by stigmatizing the Sultan as an apostate from the faith of Mahomet. The Sultan in his emergency found a friend in the Tsar, and a Russian army and fleet were sent to Constantinople, which was thus prevented from falling into the hands of Ali. In return

Partial Recovery of the Greek Church. 643

for this timely aid, the grateful Sultan concluded with the Tsar the Treaty of Unkiar-Skelessi, which bound the Sultan to close the Bosphorus and Dardanelles against the fleets of all foreign powers [o]. Notwithstanding the discomfiture, Ali was, in 1833, confirmed by the Western Powers in the government of Syria, to be held in conjunction with the Pashalic of Egypt.

When, in 1838—1839, Ali was absent on a tour of inspection in the Soudan, Mahmoud thought the opportunity favourable for re-asserting his power in Egypt; his troops, however, although Mahmoud was dead before the news was made known, suffered, in June, 1839, a complete defeat. Ali's ambition, however, had carried him too far. In 1840, the combined fleets of England, Austria, and Turkey bombarded and took Acre, and restored Syria to Turkey; Ali had also to abandon Crete, and to content himself with the Pashalic of Egypt, which was made hereditary in his family, under the suzerainty of the Porte. Thus, mainly through the instrumentality of England, the Christians in Syria were again subjected to the Turks; they were taken "from a rule which was comparatively good, to be put under the worst rule of all; since then the Turk has had his way in Syria; he has done his Damascus massacres and the like [p]." Ali devoted himself with much energy to develope the resources of Egypt; schools were built and a library instituted, and the material prosperity of the country, although by the forced labours of the unfortunate peasants, was, during his reign, much advanced; and he would have been, in Syria, at least a better ruler than the Sultan.

In the reign of the Tsar Nicolas I, occurred one of the most remarkable events in the history of the Christian Church, the return of two million Uniats, at one and the same time, from the Roman, to the Orthodox Greek, Church. Two disreputable Bishops, from interested motives, and encouraged by the Roman Catholic King of Poland,

[o] Ustrialov's Nicolai I., p. 53.   [p] Freeman's Ottoman Power, p. 191.

had, as we have seen [q], introduced into the Church of Western Russia, the Unia; i.e., the system under which Christians were allowed by the Pope to follow the doctrines and ceremonies of the Greek Church, on condition of their abandoning the jurisdiction of their own Patriarch, and acknowledging his supremacy. After the partitions of Poland, in the reign of Catharine II., many thousand Uniats, being at liberty to follow the dictates of their own consciences, threw off the Roman allegiance and returned to their own Church. By the Congress of Vienna, in 1815, the Kingdom of Poland was formed, having a constitution of its own; and was placed, as a separate Kingdom, under the Russian Empire. In 1828, the Tsar Nicolas issued a Ukase, ordering that, for the Græco-Uniats in Russia, there should be established, under their Metropolitan, Josaphat Bulgak, a separate College, with the same jurisdiction over the affairs of their Communion, that the Holy Synod held over the Orthodox Church. In the Uniat Dioceses of Western Russia and Lithuania, were established Cathedral Chapters, Consistories, seminaries, and primary schools, as well as a Theological College at Polotsk; and abundant means for the maintenance of the clergy were supplied by the State.

But the long standing political feud between Russia and Poland was not eradicated; and, in 1830, Poland made its first unsuccessful attempt to shake off the Russian yoke, with the result that the revolt was, with great cruelty, put down, and in 1832 Poland became an integral part of the Russian Empire. Through such means as we have mentioned above, in the space of a few years, the Uniats, now freed from foreign interference, returned to their first principles; they frankly acknowledged that a number of innovations had crept into their Communion, and several changes been effected by the Uniat clergy set over them. On the death of the Metropolitan Josaphat, Joseph Siemasko, Bishop

---

[q] See p. 543.

of Lithuania, was appointed to succeed him in the headship of the Uniat College, which, on January 1, 1838, was placed under Count Pratasov, Chief Procurator of the Holy Synod.

In the Week of Orthodoxy, February, 1839, all the Greco-Uniat Bishops, together with the principal clergy, held a Synod at Polotsk, in which the following petition, to be presented to the Tsar, was drawn up;—" By the wresting from Russia in troublous times, of her Western provinces of Lithuania, and their annexation to Poland, the Russian Orthodox inhabitants were subjected to severe persecution, through the unwearied efforts of the Polish government, and the Court of Rome, to separate them from the Orthodox Catholic Eastern Church, and to unite them to the Western. Persons of the highest station, their rights being in every way circumscribed, were forced to embrace the Roman faith, which was novel to them . . . . citizen and peasant were alike forced from Communion with the Eastern Church, by means of the Union which was introduced at the close of the sixteenth century. From that time this people has been separated from its mother Russia . . . . and the Uniats experienced in its full sense all the bitterness of a foreign yoke. . . . . These reasons, and more especially anxieties for the external welfare of the flock confided to us, urge us, firmly convinced of the truth of the sacred Apostolic doctrines of the Orthodox Catholic Eastern Church, to fall at the feet of your majesty . . . . to permit them to be re-united to their ancestral Orthodox Church of all the Russias. In assurance with our conjoint agreement on this subject, we have the happiness of presenting a Council Act composed by us, the Bishops and ruling clergy of the Greco-Uniat Church in the city of Polotsk, together with the autographical declaration of thirteen hundred and five persons of the Greco-Uniat clergy, not present."

The Emperor ordered Count Pratasov to lay the Act and the Declarations before the most Holy Synod. The Synod resolved to receive the Bishops, Priests, and all the flock of the Greco-Uniat Church, into Communion of the Holy

Orthodox Catholic Eastern Church, and to present the Emperor a most humble report on the subject.

On March 25, the Festival of the Annunciation of the Blessed Virgin Mary, the report of the Synod received the ratification of his Majesty, in these words, "I thank God and accept [r]."

After hearing the consent of the Tsar read, on March 30, in a full assembly of the Synod, the Chief Procurator conducted the Lithuanian Bishop Joseph into the assembly. The Metropolitans of Novgorod and St. Petersburg (Seraphim) then announced the accomplishment of the re-union, and Philaret, the Metropolitan of Kiev and Galicia, read the synodical decree addressed to the re-united clergy. The name of the Greco-Uniat Ecclesiastical College was changed to that of the Lithuanian College of White Russia, the Lithuanian Bishop Joseph being appointed its President; and he was at the same time raised to the dignity of an Archbishop.

Thus the Russian Uniats returned to the Orthodox Greek Church. As the Uniats were, in doctrine, one with the Orthodox Church, and as the only point required of them, on their union with Rome, had been submission to the Pope, so now the only act of profession required of them was, "Our Lord Jesus Christ is the One True Head of the One True Church." The Pope, Gregory XVI. (1831—1846), issued, against the re-union, an ineffectual allocution; but the public opinion of Europe saw, in the return of the Uniats, a case of historical justice.

We have related the proceedings at considerable length, almost in the words of the Russian historian, in order to convey some idea of the cruel injustice which the Greek Christians have undergone from a Christian Church. The Jesuits, again in 1860, endeavoured to establish a Uniat Church in Bulgaria, and, in 1861, the Pope Consecrated Sokolski as Archbishop; but, in August of the latter year, he returned to the Orthdox Church. At the beginning of

---

[r] Ustrialov's Nicolai I., p. 106.

1875, fifty thousand Uniats, from forty-five Parishes in the Diocese of Seidlitz, in Poland, with twenty-six Priests, disagreeing with the late Vatican Decree, seceded from Rome, and were, by the Archbishop of Warsaw, admitted into the Orthodox Church; and later on in the same year, fifty-one Parishes at Zamoscié gave in their adherence to the Orthodox Church, and a former Uniat Priest was Consecrated Orthodox Bishop of Lublin.

In 1826 the Sultan Mahmoud disbanded the Janissaries, and, deprived of his best troops, the malady of the "sick man" entered on an acute stage. Servia, and soon afterwards Greece, having gained their independence, the emancipation of the other nations of the Greek Church could only be a matter of time. As the Creed of Europe is the Creed of Christ, and the Turkish Creed, the Koran, Tribute, or the Sword, meant death for the Christians, it was little likely, now that the Turks had lost their fighting pre-eminence, the nations of Europe would tolerate them for ever. But how was the emancipation to be effected? It might easily be brought about in one or other of three ways; either by a concerted Europe; or by the two nations which had the strongest political interests in the East, England and Russia; or by the natural protector of the Eastern Christians, Russia. We think that we are not straying beyond our province, in calling Russia the natural protector of the Greek Church, inasmuch as the Russian Church comprises a far larger number of Orthodox Christians, than the Patriarchates of Constantinople, Alexandria, Antioch and Jerusalem, put together. If there had been no Constantinople, no Eastern Question, no fear, real or imaginary, from Russia, there would be no doubt or difficulty in the matter. In the hope, however, of steering clear of politics, we will confine ourselves to little more than the bare statement of the progress in the recovery of the Greek Church. All Christians will rejoice in the deliverance from cruelty and oppression of fellow Christians; and people who believe that the Eastern Christians have sometimes shown themselves as blood-thirsty as the Turks, will admit that to be a reason, why they should be improved by the Christian Church, which they never will be, so long as they are subject to the Turks.

The immemorial struggles of Russia and France, at the Court of Constantinople, for the possession of the Holy Places at Jerusalem, came to a head in 1852, and brought Russia into the fray which led to the Crimean War [s].

Originally, by a treaty, early in the Sixteenth Century, between Francis I., King of France, and the then Sultan, the Holy Places were put under the protection of France. But the Greeks disputed the right, and were gradually supported in their claims by subsequent Firmans of the Porte; violent quarrels and conflicts, between the rival Churches in Palestine, were the consequence; and, by a Firman, in the Seventeenth Century, a key to the Holy Places at Jerusalem was granted to each of the Churches, the Orthodox Greek, the Armenian, and the Latin. Their quarrels still continuing, a Firman was issued by the Porte in 1757, that the Latins should be expelled, and the Holy Places should be put under the guardianship of the Greek monks. When, in 1808, the Holy Sepulchre was partly destroyed by fire, the Greeks obtained a Firman, allowing them to rebuild it; thus they acquired to themselves additional rights, which only led to renewed conflicts, and to such scandalous results, as to call forth, in 1819, the interference of the Russian and French Governments, as representing the Greek and Latin Churches. All hopes of arranging the matter were, however, prevented by the outbreak of the Greek Revolution.

Shortly after Napoleon III. became, in 1852, Emperor of the French, he thought fit to re-open the question, and put forward a claim which the Tsar resented, as an encroachment on his rights, as protector of the Eastern Christians [t].

[s] The present Prime Minister of England bluntly expressed it, that "England put her money on the wrong hoise."

[t] A French Bishop admitted that the Crimean War was undertaken, not to prevent the dismemberment of Turkey, but for the humiliation of the Greek, or, as he called it, the Photian, Church. Christian Remembrancer, January, 1857.

Partial Recovery of the Greek Church. 649

On February 28, 1853, Prince Menshikov arrived at the Porte, as Ambassador of Russia, but his demands were so haughtily made, that the Sultan rejected them; and on May 21 he left Constantinople. On May 31, Lord Clarendon wrote to the British Minister at Petersburg against the claims of Russia, stating that, however well disguised it might be, the fact remained, that a perpetual right to interfere with the internal affairs of Turkey would be conceded to Russia; and that 14,000,000 Greek subjects of the Porte would regard the Emperor of Russia as their sole protector; that their allegiance to the Sultan would be nominal.

On July 3, the Russian army crossed the Pruth, and, as a means of compelling the Sultan to yield, occupied Moldavia and Wallachia. On October 23, Turkey commenced hostilities. In March, 1854, France and England, and afterwards Sardinia, entered on the Crimean War, arising out of a professedly religious ground, on the side of a Mahometan, against a Christian, Ruler.

In March, 1855, the Tsar Nicolas died; and, soon after the accession of his son, Alexander II. (1855—1887), peace was made, and a Treaty arranged in the Congress of Paris, on February 25, 1856. Russia was deprived of the protectorate of the Greek Church; the Turk was admitted into the Council of European nations; "the independence and territorial integrity of the Ottoman Empire" were guaranteed; and the Sultan made promises of reform, which the best-meaning Sultan could not effect, even if he wished. Thus the work of a century and a half was undone; and the fruits of the policy of Peter I., Anne, Catharine, and Alexander I. were annihilated [u]. Though the Treaty deprived Russia of her protectorate of the Greek Church, it put nothing in her place; by abolishing interference in their behalf, it left the Eastern Christians to the promises and mercy of the Sultan.

The independence of Moldavia and Wallachia as two separate Principalities, was decreed, their future organization,

[u] Rambaud, II. 382.

as determined by the people themselves, was to be recognized by the contracting powers, and sanctioned by the Porte. Till 1858, they remained under separate Princes, but in the following year they elected the same Prince, Alexander Cusa; and since his deposition in 1866, the two Principalities, as the united Roumania, have been under a relative of the German Emperor, and are practically independent of the Porte[1].

One result of the war between France and Germany (1870—1871) was, that Russia refused to be bound any longer by the terms of the Treaty of Paris; and the prohibition was, in a Conference in London in 1871, removed, Russia assenting that no Power could liberate itself from its Treaty Engagements, without the consent of the other contracting Powers.

The Eastern Question was re-opened through an insurrection which broke out, in July, 1875, in the Slavic Province of Herzegovina, to which was added another, a few weeks later, in the adjacent Province of Bosnia. Russia declined to support the insurgents, but recommended the Porte to make concessions to the Christians. The insurgents, however, contended, that promises made by the Sultan would, like previous ones, be inoperative; nor when, in the early days of 1876, the promised reforms were embodied in a Note drawn up by the Austro-Hungarian Chancellor, Count Andrassy, and approved by all the Great Powers, did they meet with greater success. The repudiation, in the Autumn of 1875, by Turkey, of part of its national debt, created the belief in the early disruption of the Turkish Empire, and the result was to revive and strengthen the hopes of the insurgents.

The year 1876, therefore, opened inauspiciously for the Turks, nor did matters improve as the year advanced. On May 30 the Sultan, Abdul-Aziz, was deposed, and on June 4 he died (according to Turkish statements and as really seems to have been the case) by suicide, and his nephew, Murad V.,

---

[1] Freeman's Ottoman Power, p. 211.

reigned in his stead. These events were followed a fortnight later by the assassination of the Turkish Minister of War, and the Minister of Foreign Affairs. On June 23, intelligence reached England of massacres having occurred, in the previous month, in Bulgaria, which are fresh in the minds of the present generation, and which it is unnecessary, even if they were not too horrible, to describe. It was said at the time that such a feeling of horror and indignation had never been before known in England; the massacre was attributed in Turkey to the Bashi-Bazouks; but the feeling in England was increased by the fact, that the directors of the massacre had been promoted, decorated with the Order of the Medjidee, or otherwise rewarded. The English Government first thought lightly of the matter, but Lord Derby, the Foreign Secretary, asserted that, even if Russia declared war against Turkey, " it would be practically impossible to interfere on behalf of the Ottoman Empire."

The cruelties inflicted on their co-religionists stimulated the Principalities of Servia and Montenegro, which had been, from the first, covertly aiding the insurgents, into open rebellion; and on July 2, they simultaneously proclaimed war against Turkey. On July 4, the Archbishop of Belgrade addressed a Letter to the Archbishop of Canterbury, enclosing a Letter from the leading inhabitants of Bosnia and Herzegovina deploring the dreadful oppression which they suffered under the Ottoman yoke, and appealing to the Christian feelings of the English. It was the old story, a narrative so horrible and disgusting, that we must decline to commit it to these pages. The Archbishop returned a letter of commiseration and sympathy; he told the Archbishop of Belgrade that he had communicated the contents to Convocation, and assured him that the fleet, which the Government had despatched to Besika Bay, was for the defence of English subjects, and not in support of Turks.

The Christians of the brave little Principality of Czernagora or Montenegro, though constantly at war with Turkey, had never lost their independence. Of Slavic origin, the inhabitants of Montenegro (*Black Mountain*), or as they themselves call it, Czernagora, covering an area of about 1880 square miles to the South-east of Herzegovina, once formed part of the Servian Kingdom. But when the short-lived Empire of St. Stephen Dushan, after the Turkish victory of Kossova in 1389, came to an end, they, under their Vladika, who was at once their Bishop and their civil Ruler, maintained their independence. The Vladika, if not already in Orders, was obliged to be Ordained, and for some time received the Episcopate from the Orthodox Metropolitan of Carlowitz, in Austrian Servia; but, early in the present Century, when the country was drawn into closer connection with Russia, he received it from the Metropolitan of Moscow. The Vladika was not allowed to be a married man, and was succeeded in his office by a brother or some near relative. The last Prince Bishop was Peter II. (1830—1851), on whose death, his nephew Daniel was appointed to succeed him; but the two offices of Prince and Bishop were then divided, Daniel, in whose family the succession was, with the sanction of Russia, made hereditary, holding only the secular office.

In September, 1876, Sultan Murad was dethroned, and his younger brother, Abdul Hamid, elected in his place, who issued a Constitution for the Turkish Empire, and promised reforms. In the same month Servia proclaimed Prince Milan, King of Servia. At the end of October, Russia made a proposition, which had been before made by Mr. Gladstone, for an armistice, with the administrative autocracy of Bulgaria, Bosnia and Herzegovina; and, a few days later, presented an ultimatum that, unless the armistice was granted within forty-eight hours, she should break off diplomatic relations. At the Mansion House dinner, on November 9, the Prime Minister, Lord Beaconsfield, boasted of the military resources of England, and used language, which was thought to involve defiance to Russia and a threat of war; and the Tsar used at Moscow language of an equally defiant character. A Conference, however, of the Great Powers was arranged to be held at Constantinople, to which Lord Salisbury was appointed Special Ambassador, on the part of England. The Conference met at the end of the year, but all proposals of the Powers being rejected by Midhat Pasha, the Grand Vizier, it was dissolved on January 20, 1877, after a menacing speech to the Turks by General Ignatiev.

Peaceful measures were now exhausted, and shortly afterwards the Tsar issued a Circular that, with or without allies, he would force the Sultan to submit; and when the English Parliament met, in January, 1877, Lord Derby expressed a fear that a rupture seemed almost unavoidable. A few days afterwards General Ignatiev, having visited Berlin and Paris on the way, arrived in London. A Protocol, in the interest of peace, was drawn up, and approved by the Powers, the adhesion of England being given on the understanding that it would be withdrawn, if Russia declared war. Prince Gortchakov converted the Protocol into an ultimatum, and the Porte rejecting the terms, Russia, on April 24, formally declared war against Turkey. In March, Turkey had carried out one point recommended to it by the Conference, in making peace with Servia; but, in May, Roumania announced its independence, and declared war against Turkey.

We need not go through the military details of the war. Suffice it to say, that, by the fall of Kars on November 18, and of Plevna on December 18; Servia having declared war against Turkey; Greece putting forward its claims for Thessaly; and Russia having, on January 3, 1878, occupied Sophia, and advancing on Philippopolis and Adrianople, further resistance on the part of Turkey was impossible. The intervention of the Westerns was in vain sought; Russia refused to treat except immediately with Turkey; she had rejected the advice of the Powers at Constantinople; to engage in the war was an act of suicide on her part; and by her own act, she had killed the arrangement of 1856.

On March 3, the Treaty of San Stephano was signed;

the terms which principally concern us being, the cession of a large part of Armenia to Russia; the transference of Bessarabia by Roumania to Russia; the establishment of an autonymous Principality of Bulgaria; the complete independence, with an increase of territory, of Roumania, Servia, and Montenegro; privileges to Thessaly and Epirus; and the introduction of reforms into Bosnia and Herzegovina.

The Treaty of San Stephano was objected to in England. Lord Derby now resigned his place at the Foreign Office, in which he was succeeded by Lord Salisbury; who issued a State Paper, to the effect, that the Treaty of San Stephano, establishing the predominance of Russia over Turkey, was in contravention of the Treaty of 1856, and of the Conference of 1871; and that Russia and Turkey could not be left to settle the matters between themselves. To the position taken up by England, Russia demurred; and it was arranged, that a Congress of the signatory powers of 1856 and 1871 should be held in Berlin on June 13, and that the Prime Minister and Foreign Secretary should attend, on the part of Great Britain.

Meanwhile, on June 4, the English Government received from the Sultan the Island of Cyprus, on condition of its paying tribute to the Porte; England guaranteeing to protect the Sultan's dominions in Asia against Russian attacks; Turkey undertaking to introduce necessary reforms, subject to British approval; and to protect the Armenians from the Kurds and Circassians. How utterly Turkey has disregarded her part of the compact was evidenced in the fearful Armenian massacres of 1894, in which it has been computed that a hundred thousand lives were sacrificed.

But thus the Church of Cyprus, an autocephalous branch of the Orthodox Greek Church, came under British rule; the Orthodox Christians being subject to Sophronicus, the Archbishop of Nea-Justiniana and all Cyprus, resident in Nicosia, and those of the English Church being under the jurisdiction of the Anglican Bishop of Jerusalem.

The Church of England being thus brought into closer connection with the Island, the Cyprus Society was now formed, for assisting the Greek Bishops in the education of their clergy; the Rev. F. Spencer, the resident English Chaplain, being appointed H.M. Inspector of both Christian and Mahometan Schools. On the Cyprus Society coming to an end, the E.C.A. deputed, in 1893, the Rev. F. E. Brightman, of the Pusey House, Oxford, to proceed thither; and, agreeably to his Report, appointed, in 1895, the Rev. H. T. F. Duckworth as Assistant, for two years, to Mr. Spencer. Amongst his instructions were, one that he should recognize and uphold the jurisdiction of the Archbishop of Cyprus, and the Metropolitans of the Island; and another, that he should cultivate personal intercourse with the clergy and other members of the Eastern Church [y].

At the Congress of Berlin, Turkey was represented by two plenipotentiaries, one a Greek Christian, the other a German convert to Islam. The Treaty of Berlin, which was signed on July 3, 1878, and which Lord Beaconsfield, on his return to London, declared to an applauding crowd in Downing Street, brought "peace with honour," modified the Treaty of San Stephano; Bessarabia, Batoum, Ardahan, and Kars, were left in the hands of Russia; Bosnia and Herzegovina were placed under the protectorate of Austria; Roumania and Servia became independent; Montenegro was enlarged; and Bulgaria was divided into two provinces, separated by the Balkans; one erected into a Principality, paying tribute to the Porte, whilst a part, to be called Eastern Roumelia, was to be ruled by a Christian Governor, nominated by the Sultan. In 1885 Roumelia was, by its own population, annexed to Bulgaria, in the same manner as Moldavia and Wallachia had been before united in the Roumanian Kingdom. A proposal was also made recommending the Sultan to cede Thessaly and Epirus to Greece;

[y] Reports of the E.C.A., 1893, 1894, and 1895.

but the recommendation respecting Greece Turkey refused to carry out; all that the Ambassadors of Constantinople could extort from the Sultan, and that not before 1881, was almost all of Thessaly and the command of the Gulf of Arta; but she refused to abandon Epirus.

The Church of Roumania is now presided over by the Primate of all Roumania, whose See is at Bucharest, with the Holy Synod of Roumania; whilst there is a Metropolitan of Moldavia at Jassy. Bulgaria, in succession to Prince Alexander, elected Prince Ferdinand, a Roman Catholic, who, in 1889, became involved in a dispute with the Holy Synod through his encouraging a Roman Propaganda in Bulgaria, the element of a diplomatic quarrel with Russia. But the recent influence of Russia in Bulgaria is evidenced, by the Conversion of Prince Boris, the infant son of Ferdinand, from the Roman to the Greek Church.

In 1879 the Sultan, at the instance of France and England, issued a Firman, deposing Ismael Pasha, the Khedive, under whom Egypt had been brought to the verge of bankruptcy, and nominating as his successor his son Tewfik, under the dual control of England and France. The events that followed, the revolt of Arabi, and the Battle of Tel-el-Kebir, belong to secular rather than Ecclesiastical history. The Dual Control came to an end, and the English occupation, in 1882, followed, till such time as the Khedive could "stand alone;" and though Egypt remains nominally a province of the Ottoman Empire, England adheres to its resolution to occupy the country till the task which it has undertaken shall be fulfilled.

It was at once seen that the occupation would bring us into more intimate relation with the Copts, and that it was a call to the Church of England over the Churches of Africa. Mention has been already made in these pages of the formation of the *Association for the Furtherance of Christianity in Egypt*, with a view of affording assistance

Partial Recovery of the Greek Church. 657

to the Coptic Church[1]. Archbishop Benson, who accepted the Presidency of the Association, sent to the Orthodox Greek, and to the Coptic, Patriarchs, Letters of greeting, expressive of his desire to render the Christians of Egypt such assistance as they might think dersirable. When, in the Autumn of 1884, envoys to England from King John of Abyssinia, the Church of which country is in Communion with the Copts, were staying in London, a deputation from the Association which waited on them was assured that it would meet with a friendly welcome in Abyssinia.

Scarcely had the English occupation commenced, when troubles in the Soudan broke out under the Mahdi, a pretending Prophet of Islam, who, profiting by the insurrection of Arabi, took possession of the desert regions to the South of Khartoum. After a severe reverse suffered by the Egyptian troops, the English Government advised the Khedive not to attempt the re-conquest of the country. General Gordon, who had at one time put down a widespread rebellion in China, and had at another been Governor of the Soudan, where he had been renowned for his justice and kindness, as well as vigour, volunteered to go out, in the hope of saving Khartoum from the Mahdi. The sad events which followed, ending in the fall of Khartoum on January 28, 1885, and the death of General Gordon, the ideal of that type which all "who profess and call themselves Christians" delight to follow, are too familiar to the minds of the present generation, to need recapitulation. To his memory has been erected the Gordon College at Cairo, to carry on the work of the *Association for the Furtherance of Christianity in Egypt.* The untimely death, in 1892, of the Khedive Tewfik, and the succession of his son Abbas, a youth of eighteen years, rendered the abandonment of the country by the English, impossible; the revival of Egypt under the English control has all along continued unchecked.

In the first week of September, 1898, the Anglo-Egyptian

[1] p. 267.

army, by their brilliant victory over the Khalifa's Dervishes at Omdurman, destroyed the Mahdist power, and a Christian flag waved once more over Khartoum. As the Coptic Bishop of Khartoum still survives[a], there will be, it may be presumed, little difficulty in re-establishing the Christian Church; but, in honour of General Gordon, and as a means of remedying the thirteen years' check occasioned to civilization, the proposal of the Sirdar for the establishment of a Native Technical School at Khartoum, will probably be considered an appropriate memorial.

The latest event to be recorded in the recovery of the Eastern Church, is the withdrawal, in November, 1898, of the last Turkish troops from Crete. A murderous attack on the British forces was only characteristic, but it simplified matters, and led to peremptory demands on the part of the allied Admirals. What will be the ultimate destiny of Crete, it is not for us to forecast; but one thing is certain, viz., that it will be placed under a Christian Governor, and another branch of the Eastern Church be thus freed from Mahometan subjection.

"Eighteen millions of human beings," wrote Mr. Gladstone, "who a century ago, peopling a large part of the Turkish Empire, were subject to its at once paralyzing and degrading yoke, are now as free from it as if they were inhabitants of this Island; and Greece, Roumania, Servia, Montenegro, and Bulgaria stand before us as five living witnesses, that even in this world the reign of wrong is not eternal." Mahometan rule in Egypt, Cyprus, Eastern Armenia, and Crete, is also now at an end.

[a] Since this was printed, we learn that a Coptic Bishop of Khartoum, named Sarapanium, has been Consecrated. (Bishop of Salisbury on his visit to Jerusalem.)

CHAPTER XVIII.

The Greek Church in its present relation to Western Christendom.

THE Bull *Apostolicæ Curæ*—The Case of Bishop Gordon—Dr, Dollinger on English Orders — Opinion of the Bull in Russia — Opinion of Roman Catholics as to Papal Infallibility—Papal Encyclical of 1848—The Encyclical Answer of the Greek Patriarchs—Papal Letter of 1869—The Patriarchs of Constantinople and Alexandria refuse to receive it—The Papal Encyclical on the Unity of Christendom—" Answer of the Greek Church of Constantinople "—Agreement between the Greek and Anglican Churches—Need of better acquaintance with each other—Foundation of the Jerusalem Bishopric—Unfortunate results—Formation of the A.P U C. —Of the E.C.A —The object of Re-union with the Greek Church taken up in America—By Convocation—By the Lambeth Conferences—Archbishop Lycurgus in England—The Patriarch Gregory and Archbishop Tait —The XIXth. Article—The Procession—The Bonn Conference—Ninth Century of the Russian Church—Delegation of the present Bishop of London to Russia—The Archbishop of York in Russia—The Archbishop of Finland in England—The Revival of the Jerusalem Bishopric—Happy results of—Consecration of St. George's Church at Jerusalem—Reverend W. Palmer's Visit to the Eastern Church—The English Reformation— The Bible Societies in Russia—The Jesuits in Russia—The Metropolitans, Plato and Philaret—Progressive Character of the Slavic and Teutonic races—Importance of the friendly relations between the Russian and English Churches.

THE last year of the Nineteenth Century opens on a Christendom as disunited as when, A.D. 1054, Cardinal Humbert left the Papal writ of excommunication on the Altar of St. Sophia's at Constantinople. In one respect it may be said to be more disunited ; owing to the system of development adopted, since the schism, by the Church of Rome, the Western Church became split up into two parts, the Roman and the Anglican, the latter returning, at the Reformation, to the purer faith of the primitive Church. This disunion in the Western Church is, however, counterbalanced by the closer relations, bordering on re-union, which have been promoted between the Greek and Anglican Churches, and which are becoming every day strengthened, as the two Churches are brought into closer contact, and learn to understand each other better.

With the relations existing between the two branches of the Western Church, we are only here so far concerned, as may be necessary to counteract misunderstandings, and to establish, in the eyes of our Eastern brethren, the rightful position of the Anglican Church. In the several points which differentiate the Anglican from the Roman Church, the Greek Church also differs from the Roman. It has ever been the aim of the Church of Rome to misrepresent the Anglican, as it does the Greek, Church; to fasten on our formularies a false or inadequate meaning, and to depreciate our Orders. "The late Papal document," to quote the almost dying words of Archbishop Benson with reference to the Bull *Apostolicæ Curæ*, "exhibits ignorance of which their own scholars and critics are as well aware as we. Our Orders are in origin, continuity, matter, form, intention, and all that belongs to them, identical with those of Rome, except in one point of subjection to the Pope, on which point, at the Reformation, we deliberately resumed our ancient concurrence with the Catholic world. There is not a break anywhere in our Orders, Sacraments, Creeds, Scriptures, spiritual gifts, in all that compacts and frames the holiness of the One Catholic, Apostolic Church of all ages [a]."

The case of Anglican Orders, misrepresented by the Papal document alluded to by the Archbishop, is that of a Scotch Bishop, John Clement Gordon. Dissatisfied with his English Orders, "ejusmodi Ordinationem opinatus esse nullam," he supplicated Pope Clement XI. to annul them; "ut sanctitas vestra declarare dignetur hujusmodi Ordinationem esse illegitimam et nullam;" and adduced the *Nag's Head Fable* as an undoubted fact [b]. The Pope, having the very words put into his mouth, referred the question of English Orders to a *Congregation*, in agreement

[a] Letter of his son to the Times, October, 1896.
[b] Union Review, May, 1868.

with whose report he, on April 17, 1704, issued a decree that the petitioner "ab integro promoveatur;" and that he had not even received the Sacrament of Confirmation and must be confirmed.

The absurd Nag's Head Fable, invented sixty years after the event, received its death-blow from the Roman Catholic historian, Dr. Lingard. The full record of Archbishop Parker's Consecration, in 1559, which it assailed, is to be found in the Register of the Lambeth Library. The authority of Archbishop Benson, an Anglican Prelate, Roman Catholics may object to as prejudiced. We will give the opinion of the Roman Catholic Church itself. The late Dr. Dollinger, probably the most learned Canonist of his day, said; "If any one chooses to doubt the fact (of Parker's Consecration), one could as well doubt one hundred thousand facts..... Bossuet has acknowledged the validity of Parker's Consecration, and no critical historian can doubt it. *The Orders of the Roman Church could be disputed with more reason*[c]." Mr. Wakeman, in his excellent *History of the Church of England*[d], says; "In quite recent times a school has formed itself in France, including the distinguished names of the Abbé Duchesne, one of the most eminent living ecclesiastical historians, and Monsignor Gaspari, the Professor of Canon Law at Paris; which ... has arrived at the conclusion that the validity of English Orders cannot be denied." The Bull *Apostolicæ Curæ* has been demolished by the two English Archbishops; it could do no harm, for Anglicans understand the character of their Orders much better than a Pope; it has strengthened the allegiance of wavering Anglicans to their Church; and will help on the union between the Greek and Anglican Churches. The recognition, in the present day, of our Orders by the Pope, is impossible, for, if he were to pronounce them valid, he would bring upon himself a hornet's nest from the Cardinals; and expose the schismatical character of the Roman hierarchy in England.

[c] Conference at Bonn, 1874.   [d] p 328.

It may be well, however, to learn what the Russian Church thinks of the Bull. One of the principal Russian Church Newspapers[e] says, " It very soon became evident that this stroke of policy (i.e. of the Pope) had not only not obtained its object, but that it had produced exactly the opposite effect. . . . The conscience of the whole of English Society was raised to indignation, at the attitude which the Pope had assumed towards them. . . . Everybody has realized . . . that any union which is either possible, or necessary, for the English Church to effect with a Church based on strong organic principles, can only be a union with the Orthodox East; which has never definitely declared against English Ordinations, and with which the English Church has always found it more easy to confer, than with Rome, in the insolence and self-conceit in her own infallibility. And as a matter of fact, amongst the Anglicans, a movement towards approximation with the Orthodox Church of the East has already started."

We will devote this Chapter to the consideration of the existing relations, firstly between the Greek and Roman, and then between the Greek and Anglican, Churches.

The supremacy is the essence of the whole Roman system; take away the assertion of St. Peter's supremacy, and the Pope's equal power as his successor, and the Roman Church is Roman and imperial no longer[f]. The Greek, like the Anglican, Church, asks, that the Roman Church shall first prove that Peter was ever Bishop of Rome; which it cannot do, because it is an historical impossibility that he could have been. Peter's Roman Episcopate and the Pope's Infallibility stand or fall together. Learned Roman Catholics, writing before the Vatican Council, speak against both. Dr. Dollinger (to refer to him once more) says, that for the first three centuries, history gives nothing more than a Primacy to Rome; Ellendorf, that the true inference to be drawn from history is, that St. Peter never saw Rome,

---

[e] The Tzerkovny Viestnik (*Church Messenger*) of Jan. 2, 1897 (O S.), as given in the Church Times.   [f] Hussey's Rise of the Papal Power.

much less was ever Bishop of Rome [g]. Alban Butler, who from the age of eight years was educated in the Roman College of Douay, and died, in 1773, President of the College of St. Omar, wrote [h]; "The learned Bossuet and many others, especially the School of Sorbonne, have written warmly against that opinion" (Papal Infallibility). "It is the Infallibility of the whole Church, whether assembled in a General Council, or dispersed over the whole world, of which they speak in controversial disputations.... The Infallibility of the Pope is never found in our Creed."

It is on the Pope's Supremacy, through a right derived from St. Peter, that the Roman Church grounds its claims over the Greek Church. Soon after the fall of Constantinople, Pius II., in his famous letter to the Sultan Mahomet, promised that if he would embrace Christianity, he would, by his Apostolical authority, confer on him the legitimate sovereignty of the lands which he had conquered from the Greeks; and use him as the instrument of establishing Papal Supremacy over those countries, "which usurp the rights of the Roman Church, and lift up themselves against their mother."

The figment of Papal Supremacy is the barrier which stops the way of reunion. Shortly before the Papal Aggression in England, Pius IX., soon after he became Pope, in an Encyclical, dated January 6, 1848, made a similar attempt on the Eastern Church. It was in modern Greek, written with the old thread-bare arguments; it did not even speak of the Eastern Prelates as Bishops, but as "excelling others in Ecclesiastical dignities." The Pope, he said, "must speak words of peace and affection to the Easterns, who indeed serve Christ, but are aliens from the holy throne of the Apostle Peter;" "scattered sheep into pathless and rough ways;" he exhorted them to return without further delay into the unity of the Church, "for their eternal life;" "we lay on you no other burden, except

---

[g] Ist Petrus in Rome und Bishof der Romischen Kirche gewesen.
[h] Letters on the History of the Popes.

the necessary things, that in writing to us you agree with us in the confession of the true faith, which the Catholic Church guards and teaches, and that ye maintain Communion with the holy throne of Peter;" he added that he "will help all such *Ecclesiastics*, as return to the Roman faith, in their respective ranks;" and concluded with a prayer to the Mother of God, the holy Martyrs, Apostles, and Fathers of the Church, that the prayer of his dearest wishes, the return of the Eastern Church, may be brought to pass.

The Encyclical was full of mistakes, which the Eastern Patriarchs were not backward in seizing on, and exposing. St. Ignatius was spoken of as Bishop of *Alexandria*, and the Œcumenical Council of *Chalcedon* was called the Council of *Carthage ;* "another proof," says the Pope, "is exhibited in the Council of Carthage, in the year 451."

The Encyclical irritated the Patriarchs, and not without reason, to the last degree. It was not a proposal for the union of the Churches, but of submission of the one to the other; it also contained exhortations to individual Bishops, to disavow their own Church, and to acknowledge the claims, and join the Church, of Rome. An answer was returned in an "Encyclical Epistle of the one Holy Catholic and Apostolic Church to the Orthodox everywhere," signed by the four Patriarchs, Anthimus of Constantinople, Hierotheus of Alexandria, Methodius of Antioch, and Cyril of Jerusalem. It commenced with the assertion that the Greek Church preserved the faith pure and undefiled, as at first. Of heresies which spread over the whole world, Arianism was one, and, at the present time, the Papacy is another; the former had long since died away, the latter would no less surely fall, "and the loud voice of Heaven shall say, 'It is cast down.'" (Rev. xii. 10). It next entered into the differences between the Eastern and Western Churches; the Western, it said, neither know the truth, nor care to learn it. Notwithstanding this, "the Papal power has not ceased to deal despitefully with the peaceful Church of

God ;" sending its so-called missionaries ; "compassing sea and land to make a proselyte, to deceive one of the Orthodox ; " it then spoke of countless other things which " the demon of innovation dictated to those darers of all things, the Schoolmen of the Middle Ages."

Another Answer to the Papal Encyclical was published by Constantius, an ex-Patriarch of Constantinople, who, owing to Turkish oppression, was living in exile from his See, and was at the time Archimandrite of the Monastery of Mount Sinai. So fully was the Papal Encyclical exposed, that it was ordered to be recalled ; and so sedulously was the order obeyed by the Pope's emissaries, that it is doubtful "whether a copy of it could be procured now by love or money, throughout the very parts in which it was originally circulated[1]."

On October 5, 1869, a Letter from Pope Pius IX. was delivered to Gregory VI., Patriarch of Constantinople, inviting him to the Vatican Council, which was to assemble at the end of the year. The Easterns were adjured by the Pope to come to the Council, as their predecessors were to the Councils of Lyons and Florence ; but to those Councils the Patriarchs were invited under their respective titles ; by Pius IX., all Prelates of the Eastern Church were comprehended in the same category. The Letter was tied with gold cord, and enclosed in a morocco case. The Patriarch told the envoys that the contents were already known to him through the Papers ; since the Pope would not deviate from his position, neither " by Divine Grace would he deviate from his ; " and he ordered the Letter to lie unopened on the desk. Two reasons which he gave were, that there is no Bishop supreme over the whole Church, except the Lord ; and that no Patriarch speaking ex-Cathedrâ is infallible, for that infallibility belongs alone to Œcumenical Councils, "when they are in accordance with Scripture and the Apostolical tradition."

A similar invitation to the Council was, on February 16,

[1] Christian Remembrancer, Vol. XXII.

1870, conveyed to the Patriarch Elect of Alexandria, by the Roman Catholic Patriarch of that See, whom the Pope employed as his Plenipotentiary. The Orthodox Patriarch said, that the Orthodox Eastern Church always fervently prays for the union of Christ's Churches. To the Papal Brief there were numerous objections, chiefly on three grounds ;—(1) Although it was universally known that the Œcumenical Councils conceded to the Pope of Rome a precedence of honour, the Brief claimed a Sovereign power, thus abolishing the equality of the Churches of God ; (2) it proclaimed that salvation was confined exclusively to Rome; (3) the Council was summoned to meet on the Feast of the Immaculate Conception, a dogma wholly unknown to the Church. When the Papal Plenipotentiary stated that the Pope was the successor of St. Peter, the head and Sovereign of the Church, the Patriarch told him that the Church taught that Christ was its sole Head. The envoy then stated that Mark was Consecrated Bishop of Alexandria by Peter ; and that Athanasius had resorted to Rome as the Court of Appeal. To this the Orthodox Patriarch objected, that Antioch might rather boast of being the first of the Patriarchs, because there Peter was first Bishop ; and that Athanasius only had recourse to Rome, when persecuted by the Arians, in the same manner as the Patriarchs were accustomed to appeal to each other, for brotherly succour. He, like the Patriarch of Constantinople, refused to receive the document, which the envoy took back with him unopened.

The other Orthodox Bishops returned similar replies to the Pope's invitation.

A Papal Encyclical on the Unity of Christendom was, on St. Peter's Day, 1894, issued, "To our venerable brethren the Patriarchs, Primates, Archbishops, and other Ordinaries, in peace and Communion with the Apostolic See." It stated that, "By the Will of its Founder, it is necessary that the Church should be one in all lands, and at all times." As He willed that His kingdom should be visible, Christ designated a Vicegerent on earth in the place of Peter, to be inherited in perpetuity by Peter's successors. Consequently, the Roman Pontiffs who succeed him in the Roman Episcopate, receive their supreme power in the Church *jure divino*, which is declared fully by the General Councils. The Pope has always undoubtedly exercised the office of ratifying, or rejecting, the decrees of Councils. Leo the Great rescinded the Acts of the Conciliabulum at Ephesus. Damasus rejected those at Rimini. The Twenty-eighth Canon of the Council of Chalcedon [k], by the very fact that it lacks the assent and approval of the Apostolic See, is admitted by all to be worthless." The incorrectness of these statements has been already pointed out in this work.

A study of the "Answer of the Great Church of Constantinople to the Papal Encyclical on Union," signed by the Patriarch Anthimus and twelve Metropolitans and Bishops, would well repay those who desire to understand the true character and position of the Orthodox Church [1].

The Answer, whilst it speaks of its desire for union, says:—" The Orthodox Eastern Church justly glories in Christ, as being the Church of the Seven Œcumenical Councils, and the first nine Centuries of Christianity; and therefore the one holy, Catholic and Apostolic Church of Christ, "the pillar and ground of the truth; but the present Roman Church is the Church of innovation, of the falsifications of the writings of the Church Fathers, and of the misinterpretation of Holy Scriptures, and of the decrees of the Holy Councils." It calls upon the Westerns, "to prove from the teaching of the Holy Fathers, and the divinely assembled Œcumenical Councils, that the Orthodox Roman Church, which was throughout the West, ever, before the Ninth Century, read the Creed with the addition; or used unleavened bread; or accepted the doctrine of a pur-

---

[k] Leo XIII in this respect is better acquainted with the name of the Council than his predecessor

[1] A correct English Translation by the Very Reverend Eustathius Metallinos has been published, at the expense of the Orthodox Greek Community in Manchester.

gatorial fire ; or sprinkling instead of Baptism ; or the Immaculate Conception of the ever-Virgin ; or the temporal power; or the infallibility and absolutism of the Bishop of Rome."

"Certainly Pope Leo XIII. is not ignorant that his orthodox predecessor and namesake, the defender of Orthodoxy, Leo III., in the year 809, denounced synodically this anti-evangelical and utterly lawless addition, "and from the Son" (*filioque*) ; and engraved on two silver plates, in Greek and Latin, the holy Creed of the first and second Œcumenical Councils, entire and without addition ; having written moreover, "These words I, Leo, have set down for love, and as a safeguard of the Orthodox Faith."

The Answer disproves Papal Supremacy and Infallibility ; "Our Lord Jesus Christ alone is the eternal Prince, and immortal Head of the Church," for "He is the Head of the Body; the Church." "The Church of Rome was chiefly founded, not by Peter, whose Apostolic action at Rome is totally unknown to history, but by the heaven-caught Apostle of the Gentiles, Paul, through his disciples, whose Apostolic ministry in Rome is known to all." "The divine Fathers, honouring the Bishop of Rome, only as the Bishop of the Capital city of the Empire, gave him the honorary prerogative of Presidency, considering him simply as the Bishop first in order, that is, first amongst equals; which prerogative they also assigned afterwards to the Bishop of Constantinople, when that city became the Capital of the Roman Empire, as the twenty-eighth Canon of the Fourth Œcumenical Council, of Chalcedon, bears witness." "There is no hint given, in any Canon, or by any of the Fathers, that the Bishop of Rome alone has ever been Prince of the universal Church, and the infallible judge of the Bishops of the other independent and self-governing Churches, or the successor of the Apostle Peter, and the Vicar of Jesus Christ on earth." "The first of these claims of a papal absolutism were scattered abroad in the pseudo-Clementines . . . and in the, so-called, pseudo-Isidorian decrees, which are a farrago of spurious and forged royal decrees, and letters of ancient bishops of Rome."

"These facts we recall with sorrow of heart, inasmuch as the Papal Church, though she now acknowledges the spuriousness and the forged character of those decrees, on which her exclusive claims are grounded, not only stubbornly refuses to come back to the Canons and decrees of the Œcumenical Councils ; but, even in the expiring years of the Nineteenth Century, has widened the existing gulf, by officially proclaiming, to the astonishment of the Christian world, that the Bishop of Rome is even infallible. The Orthodox Eastern and Catholic Church of Christ, with the exception of the Son and Word of God, Who was ineffably made Man, knows no one that was infallible on earth. Even the Apostle Peter, whose successor the Pope thinks himself to be, thrice denied the Lord, and was twice rebuked by the Apostle Paul, as not walking uprightly, according to the truths of the Gospel. Afterwards, the Pope Liberius, in the Fourth Century, subscribed an Arian confession ; and likewise Zosimus, in the Fifth Century, approved an heretical confession, denying Original sin. Vigilius, in the Sixth Century, was condemned for wrong opinions, in the Fifth Council, and Honorius, having fallen into the Monothelite heresy, was condemned, in the Seventh Century, by the Sixth Œcumenical Council, as a heretic, and the Popes who succeeded him acknowledged and accepted his condemnation."

The Letter complains of the proselytising habit of the Papal Church, which "began, to our general astonishment and perplexity, to lay traps for the consciences of the more simple Orthodox Christians, by means of deceitful workers, transformed into Apostles of Christ ; sending into the East clerics, with the dress and head-covering of Orthodox Priests, inventing also divers other artful means to obtain her proselytising objects."

When the Pope says that "a kindly relation and mutual sympathy was brought about, between the Slavic tribes and the Pontiffs of the Roman Church," the Encyclical hints at ignorance of history on the part of the Pope. It speaks of the persecution suffered by the Slavs from the Latins, "with the official co-operation of the Bishops of Rome, as doing little honour (ἤκιστα τιμῶντα) to the holiness of the Episcopal dignity. But, notwithstanding all this despiteful treatment, the Orthodox Slavic Churches, the beloved daughters of the Orthodox East, and especially the great and glorious Church of divinely preserved Russia . . . . . have kept, and will keep, till the end of the ages, the Orthodox faith, and stand forth conspicuous testimonies of the liberty that is in Christ."

Such are the existing relations between the Orthodox Greek and Roman Churches. The Roman Church refuses to return to union, not because the Greek Church is heretical, but because it will not acknowledge the Pope's Supremacy and Infallibility; the Greek Church will not accept union with Rome, not only because it denies that the Pope is successor of St. Peter, but because it also holds that the Roman Church has engrafted on primitive faith new and uncatholic doctrines; and is heretical.

The late Mr. Ffoulkes, Vicar of the University Church at Oxford, wrote, when a member of the Roman Church, in a Letter to the late Cardinal Manning; "I feel it my imperative duty to state that . . . . though the re-union of Christendom, which has been the dream of my life, seems coming in the distance, it cannot be, that it ought not to be, till material guarantees have been secured, that Rome shall never again be what she has been, and to some extent, still is; so irresistible to my mind are the evidences that it is her conduct, more than anything else, which has divided Christendom." And again, "I am deeply convinced now, after reading Ecclesiastical history again, as a Roman Catholic, that, if ever there was a justifiable revolt from authority, it was the revolt we call the Reformation [m]." In a criticism on Mr. Ffoulkes' Letter, a prominent member

[m] The Church's Creed and the Crown's Creed.

of the Roman Church put forth the dilemma, that one must either accept the Pope as a legitimate monarch of the Church, or reject him as Anti-Christ.

From the relations between Constantinople and Rome, we will now turn to those existing between the Greek and Anglican Churches. The starting-point between the two latter Churches is theoretically the same; both deny the supremacy of the Pope, as successor to St. Peter; both reject the development of Church doctrine; both ground their faith on the Bible and the Primitive Church. De Guettée, Priest and Doctor in Theology of the Orthodox Church of Russia, thus writes[n]; "The doctrine of the Anglican Church is nearer to that of the Orthodox Church, than the doctrine of the Roman Church. To be completely in accord with the Russian Church, the Anglican Church should reconcile the contradictory statements in her official Books, and declare more distinctly; (1) That there exists a divine teaching transmitted orally by the Apostles; (2) that the oral teaching is preserved infallibly in the Church; (3) that it is to be ascertained by the constant testimony of the Apostolical Churches (i.e. the Greek Churches), which have remained unchanged from the first ages."

The first requisite is, that the two Churches should become better acquainted with each other; intercourse has created mutual sympathy; and recent events represent a spirit of love, and a desire to be at one, between the two Churches, which a fuller understanding can only increase. The Greeks invite our clergy into the Sanctuary during the celebration of their Liturgy; they treat our Bishops as they do their own; they admit the validity of our Orders, and hold that marriages performed by English Priests are valid. They bury our dead, when no English clergyman is present; they frequently ask members of our Church to stand sponsors for their children; they themselves stand sponsors for English children, according to the English

---

[n] Exposition de la Doctrine de l'Eglise Catholique Orthodoxe.

Prayer Book, and promise that they shall be brought up in the faith of the English Church.

The first instance of renewed intercourse between the Greek and Anglican Churches, in this Century, the foundation, in 1841, of an Anglican Bishopric at Jerusalem, to which the Lutheran King of Prussia and the Crown of England were alternately to appoint, presented our Church in a false light to the Greek Church; nor was it more favourably received in England. That the English Church should combine with the Lutheran Church of Prussia, was reasonably objected to, and alienated many pious Anglicans from their own Church; Dr. Alexander, a converted Jew, was Consecrated the first Bishop, after whom followed Bishops Gobat and Barclay; but the mission was so conducted, that by petty aggression on their jurisdiction, it excited the indignation and contempt of the Eastern Prelates; and the Bishopric was in consequence suppressed.

But unfortunate as it was in its results, the Jerusalem Bishopric was designed, as an embassy of good will to the Greek Church, in which the large-hearted Archbishop of Canterbury, Dr. Howley, took a warm interest. The duties of the Bishop were to be confined to English and German Protestants, and the Jewish converts that might be made. He was "to establish and maintain, as far as in him lies, relations of Christian charity with other Churches represented at Jerusalem, and in particular with the Orthodox Greek Church; taking care that the Church of England does not wish to disturb, or divide, or interfere with them, but that she is ready, in the spirit of Christian love, to render them such offices of friendship, as they may be willing to receive [o]."

The Archbishop appointed, as Chaplain to the first Bishop, that staunch Catholic and Grecophil, the Reverend George Williams, Fellow of King's College, Cambridge [p]; and the Bishop went out with commendatory Letters from the Archbishop of Canterbury; "Our hearty desire is to renew that

[o] 5 Vict. VI. 1.   [p] Williams' Orthodox Church of the East, XLIII.

amicable intercourse with the ancient Churches of the East, which has been suspended for ages, and which, if restored, may have the effect, with the blessing of God, of putting an end to divisions which have brought the most grievous calamities to the Church of Christ."

The repeated desire for the re-union of Christendom led to combined action, in the formation, in 1857, of the Association for Promoting the Unity of Christianity. Its object was simply to pray for re-union; Pope Pius IX. at first gave it his blessing, and it soon numbered many Easterns, as well as twelve hundred Roman Catholics. Cardinal Wiseman also, till his death, approved of it, but Dr. Manning and the Ultramontanes obtained a Papal Rescript against it. Notwithstanding this, few Roman Catholics left, and more continued to join the Association.

This was followed, in 1863, by the foundation of the Eastern Church Association, the Archimandrite, Constantine Stratulia, attending the preliminary meeting, and being appointed one of the Standing Committee; and in 1865, the Metropolitan of Servia and the Bishop of Schabatz enlisted themselves as members. The objects of the latter Association are; (1) To give information as to the state and position of the Eastern Christians. (2) To make known to the Christians of the East the doctrines and principles of the Anglican Church. (3) To take advantage of opportunities for intercourse with the Orthodox Church, and also for friendly intercourse with the other ancient Churches of the East. (4) To assist as far as possible the Bishops of the Orthodox Church in their efforts to promote the spiritual welfare and the education of their flocks.

The object of re-union was taken up in America; in October, 1862, a Committee of the General Convention of the American Church was appointed, "to consider the expediency of opening connection with the Russo-Greek Church." This was followed, in 1863, by a petition of the Lower to the Upper House of the Convocation of Canterbury; "Your petitioners have learned with much interest that in the recent Synod or Convention of the Bishops and Clergy of the Northern States of America, certain steps were taken with a view to promote inter-communion between the Russo-Greek Church and the Anglican Communion. Your petitioners believe that the present time may be more favourable than former times have been for efforts in that direction. They therefore pray your honourable House to bring about such inter-communion."

The matter was accordingly brought before the Upper House by the Bishop of Oxford (Wilberforce), and a Committee was appointed, in view " to such Ecclesiastical intercommunion with the Orthodox East, as should enable the laity and clergy of either Church to join in the Sacraments and offices of the other, without forfeiting the Communion of their own Church." In the first Report of the Committee, February, 1864, it was recommended, that the overtures proposed by the American Church should be extended to the Eastern Patriarchs. At one meeting of the Committee two Archpriests, Popov and Vassiliev, Chaplains of the Russian Embassies of London and Paris, attended, and gave the most cordial assurance of their co-operation. Friendly visits were made to Russia; and the Holy Governing Synod expressed its willingness "to co-operate in any measures having for their object the restoration of unity."

A still more important attempt at inter-communion was made in the first Lambeth Conference, in 1867. The Archbishop of Canterbury, in his opening address, commended as a subject to the assembled Bishops, the best way of promoting the Unity of Christendom; and a resolution was passed, that "his Grace the Archbishop of Canterbury be requested to convey to the Church in Russia an expression of the sympathy of the Anglican Communion, at the loss it has sustained by the death of his Eminence Philaret, the venerable Metropolitan of Moscow."

The third Lambeth Conference, of 1888, spoke hopefully of re-union with the East; in respect of the Separatist Communities it frankly admitted much that is good in them; and it put forward a reasonable minimum as a basis of future agreement, consisting of four clauses; (1) the Scriptures as the ultimate standard of appeal; (2) the Apostles' and Nicene Creeds; (3) the two great Sacraments; (4) the historic Episcopate. The Encyclical Letter stated; "the Conference has expressed its earnest desire to conform and improve the friendly relations which now exist, between the Churches of the East, and the Anglican Communion. . . . We reflect with thankfulness that there exist no bars, such as are presented to Communion with the Latins, by the formulated sanction of the infallibility of the Church residing in the supreme Pontiff; by the doctrine of the Immaculate Conception; and by other dogmas, imposed by the decrees of Papal Councils. The Church of Rome has always treated her Eastern sister wrongfully. She intrudes her Bishops into the ancient Dioceses, and keeps up a system of active proselytism. . . . It behoves us of the Anglican Communion to take care that we do not offend in like manner."

In the Lambeth Conference of 1897 (whilst the Roman Catholic Church was ignored under the unity of the Church), by Resolution 36, "The two English Archbishops, with the Bishop of London, were requested to act as a Committee, with power to add to their number, to confer with the authorities of the Eastern Church with a view to their obtaining a clearer understanding, and of establishing closer relations." "The Committee of the Conference expressed the hopeful belief, in regard to the Eastern Church, that our differences are either matters of unauthorized individual opinion, or capable of explanation and adjustment." The Encyclical Letter stated; "on the Unity of the Church our Committee has not been able to propose any resolutions, which would bind us to immediate future action."

Acts of what may be called Ecclesiastical comity, between the Greek and Anglican Churches, have of late years become so frequent, that we can only mention a few of an official character, which plainly indicate an inclination for closer intercourse on both sides. Lycurgus, Archbishop of Syros, Tenos, and Melos, before concluding, in 1870, his visit to England, wrote to Archbishop Tait; "I am now departing for Constantinople, and will there announce by word of mouth and by letter, to our most Holy and Œcumenical Patriarch, and to all the august Prelates in the East, and above all to the Most Blessed Patriarch of Jerusalem, my own Spiritual Father .... the many things, pleasing and acceptable to God, which I have seen and heard in this country. And for the time to come I will never shrink from labouring to the utmost of my power to bring about the harmony of the Churches."

On April 20, Gregory, the Patriarch of Constantinople, wrote to the Archbishop of Canterbury, that Lycurgus had told him at length "all the good things that were said of our unworthy self, both by your Holiness, whom we highly regard in Christ," and, amongst others, "by the most eminent and distinguished Lords, Gladstone and Redlik Kanınk" (Lord Stratford de Redclyffe); and he heard with pleasure "the ardent and lofty reverence and sympathy towards this Holy and Orthodox Eastern Church. These things straighten, smooth, and prepare beforehand, the ways and paths of the Spiritual Unity of the faithful everywhere .... who are as branches growing together on the one tree planted by Heaven, and watered by God, as inseparable members of the one Christbearing body, the Church."

The Archbishop sent, with his answer to the Patriarch, an English Prayer-book, adding a request for the burial of Englishmen who died within the Patriarchate. The Patriarch returned his answer on October 8 of the same year; "Be it known to your much desired Holiness that, even if we had not been expressly exhorted and requested by any of the venerable Bishops, we would have of ourselves granted every permission to bury English strangers within our cemeteries, at the request of their relations, well knowing that 'the Earth is the Lord's and the fulness thereof.' This we will much rather permit for the future, from consideration of your Holiness, beloved of God, and in recompense, as is meet, of the tribute of brotherly kindness." As to the Prayer-book, the Patriarch said that he had examined it to discover how far it inclines to, or diverges from, Catholic teaching, and confirms the statement of the Preface, that "it contains nothing contrary to the Word of God and to sound doctrine." The Patriarch naturally turned to the XXXIX. Articles. The points to which His Holiness demurred were; the Procession of the Holy Ghost; the Divine Eucharist; the number of Sacraments; Tradition; the number of Œcumenical Councils; the relation between the Church on Earth and the Church in Heaven; the honour to be paid to Saints; and Article XIX. "These statements," he adds, "throw us into suspense, so that we doubt what we are to judge of the rules of Anglican Orthodoxy."

This is a long indictment; the Patriarch probably read the XXXIX. Articles, without studying the Prayer-book itself; but even on the XXXIX. Articles, properly understood, the Church of England is ready to take its stand; and we believe that, without the sacrifice of any principle, the difficulties, as the two Churches become better acquainted, might be explained and surmounted. We must confine ourselves to two of the Patriarch's strictures. With regard to Article XIX., it probably did not refer to the Orthodox Greek Church at all, but to the separatist Communions of Alexandria, Antioch, and Jerusalem, which fell into the Nestorian and Monophysite heresies. If it meant to include the Orthodox Patriarchates in the same condemnation as the Church of Rome, it surely would not have omitted to name the Church of Constantinople.

As to the Procession of the Holy Ghost, we have already quoted the words of St. John Damascene. The Greek Church holds a twofold Procession, one Eternal, by which the Holy Ghost "proceedeth from the Father;" the other

temporal, in which He manifests Himself by the Son ;—
"whom I will send to you from the Father" (John xv. 26).
On the doctrine there is no difference, although the Greek
Church at present believes there is, between the Greek and
Anglican Churches; the latter of which, equally with the
Greek Church, disclaims two Principles (ἀρχαί), or Causes
(αἰτίαι), in the Holy Trinity [q].

As to original insertion of the Filioque claim into the
Nicene Creed, although it was never adopted in the East,
it was made before the schism between East and West took
place; and, as there is no difference between the two
Churches in point of doctrine, its removal now would be as
unadvisable as it is impossible. But since, in the abstract
question of the addition, the Eastern Church is right and
the Western wrong, perhaps an explanatory note, such as
that recommended to Convocation by the Royal Commissioners on the Prayer-book in September, 1689, might meet
the difficulty; "It is humbly submitted to the Convocation,
whether a note ought not here to be added with relation to
the Greek Church, in order to our maintaining Catholic
Communion."

With regard to the Procession of the Holy Ghost, the
Conference of Old Catholics at Bonn, under the Presidency
of Dr. Dollinger, in 1875, has shown how a reasonable
solution of the difficulty may be effected. After the publication of the Vatican Decree of Papal Infallibility, a party
of Old Catholics, including some of the most learned Theologians of the Roman Catholic Church, arose, who felt it
their duty "to cling to the Old Catholic Faith, as laid down
in Holy Scripture and traditions, and to the old Catholic
forms of Divine Service . . . . . and to reject the dogmas
proclaimed in the Pontificate of Pius IX., as contrary to the
doctrines of the Church." They, in consequence, incurred
excommunication.

[q] A clear Exposition of the subject is to be found in *Dogmatic Theology
of the Orthodox Eastern Church*, by Antonius, Archimandrite, and Rector
of the University of Kiev, pp. 119—123.

One result of the Old Catholic movement was, to bring the Greek and Anglican Churches into contact; to vindicate, by unprejudiced testimony, the validity of our Orders and Sacramental doctrine; and to open negotiations which, since the abortive Union at Florence, which was no union at all, have been in abeyance.

At the Bonn Conference twenty Orthodox Greeks were present, and Archbishop Lycurgus took a prominent part; two Archbishops from Roumania attended it; two Archimandrites, as representatives of the Patriarch of Constantinople; an Archimandrite from Belgrade; an Archpriest from Petersburg; and five Professors of Theology, from Petersburg, Dalmatia, Kiev and Athens. A Russian Professor expressed the longing of the Russian Church for closer contact with the Western Brethren. A chief matter of debate was the Procession of the Holy Ghost; it was agreed that a Union might be effected;

(1.) By the acceptance of the Œcumenical Creeds, and the dogmatic decisions of the ancient undivided Church.

(2.) By the acknowledgment that the addition of the Filioque was not made in a regular manner.

(3.) By the setting forth of the doctrine of the Holy Ghost, as taught by the Fathers of the undivided Church.

(4.) By the rejection of any kind of expression, by which two Principles or two Causes in the Trinity could be supposed to be held.

The Conference was attended by more than fifty members of the Anglican Communion, amongst them the Bishop of Gibraltar, the Dean of Chester, and Canon Liddon. The Eastern Church Association, in the same year, addressed a Petition to the Convocations of Canterbury and York, expressing its satisfaction with the Bonn Conference, and praying them to promote friendly relations, and closer intercourse, with the Orthodox Church of the East.

In June, 1870, the Holy Synod of the Kingdom of Greece wrote to Archbishop Tait, that, in gratitude for the honour paid to Archbishop Lycurgus, it had directed its clergy, by Encyclical Letters, to show brotherly kindness in all things to members of the Anglican Church ; and to bury, and offer prayers for the souls of, those who died where there was no Anglican Priest. The Archbishop, in his answer in September, said; "During the eighteen months we have had our present office, we have received letters of brotherly love from several of the most distinguished of your branch of the Catholic Church, and amongst others the Most Holy Patriarch of Constantinople." He stated his opinion, that the Church of England does not sanction prayers for the dead.

In 1886, the Rev. George Williams, carrying with him commendatory Letters from the Archbishop of Canterbury and other English Bishops, went to the East ; and in several interviews with the Patriarchs of Constantinople, Antioch, and Jerusalem, found that, in every case, the idea of inter-communion was received with cordial approbation, and an earnest desire was everywhere expressed for opportunities of more frequent intercourse. The Metropolitan of Chios and other Prelates publicly expressed their opinion, that delegates should be appointed on both sides, to discuss the points of difference ; and the Patriarch of Antioch expressed a desire, that an English Professor should be appointed to his High School on Mount Lebanon, so that the differences might be explained.

The congratulatory letter of the Archbishop of Canterbury, in 1888, to the Metropolitan of Kiev, on the ninth centenary of the Russian Church, profoundly stirred the hearts of our Orthodox brethren in Russia. "The Russian and the Anglican Church," the Archbishop wrote, "have common foes. Alike we have to guard our independence against that Papal aggressiveness, which claims to subordinate all the Churches of Christ to the See of Rome. . . . But the weapons of our warfare are not carnal, and by mutual sympathy, and prayers that we may be one ἐν τοῖς δέσμοις τοῦ Εὐαγγελλίου, we shall encourage each to promote the salvation of all men." The Metropolitan, in his answer, wrote; "I entirely agree that the Russian and

English Churches have the common foe of which you speak .... and that we ought, together with you, to contend against them .... but for this it is indispensable, that your and our Churches should enter into a more complete spiritual union with one another. Our Church sincerely desires such a union." Mr. Birkbeck, who conveyed the Archbishop's Letter to Kiev, relates how that the *Tablet* asserted, that the Metropolitan of Kiev had taken no notice of the Archbishop's Letter; it would be difficult to find more friendly language than that of the Metropolitan, whose death, which occurred shortly afterwards, prevented further correspondence.

The delegation, in 1896, by the Church of England, of the present Bishop of London, with the approval of the Queen, to the Coronation, and sacred anointing with Chrism, of the Tsar, and the special honour accorded him in Russia, is an addition of another link to the chain which is slowly, but surely, being forged to unite the Russian and Anglican Churches. Expression was given in the letter, written by the Archbishop of Canterbury, to Palladius, Metropolitan of Petersburg and Ladoga, and President of the Holy Governing Synod of Russia, which speaks, " of the truly deep and sympathetic reverence which the Church of England entertains towards the throne and person of the Emperor, and towards the Orthodox Church of Russia." This was followed, in April, 1897, by a visit of the Archbishop of York to Russia. The latter was private and unofficial; but the union of the Greek and Anglican Churches became in Russia a common topic of conversation; and an Article in the Moscow *Gazette* expressed the hope, that the understanding between the Churches would lead to more friendly feelings between the English and Russian peoples.

That this friendly intercourse between the Churches was appreciated by the Russian Government, was evidenced by the delegation of an eminent scholar and divine, and a member of the Holy Governing Synod, Antonius, Archbishop of Finland, accompanied by a General of the Russian army, to the Queen's Jubilee, in 1897. He came in a twofold capacity, sent with the authority of the Tsar, as representative of the Russian nation, and of the Holy Governing Synod, as representative of the Russian Church. His arrival was accordingly greeted by a deputation, with an English Officer of the Tsar's own regiment, whose address to the Archbishop concluded ; "We pray the Great Head of the Church to bestow his Benediction upon the most religious and gracious Emperor, Nicolas Alexandrovich, and upon his most religious Consort, the Empress Alexandra Theodorovna, the illustrious granddaughter of our most Gracious Sovereign ; and to vouchsafe to draw our two Communions together, to the honour of His Holy Name, and the furtherance of the salvation of souls ; " and the Archbishop, in his reply, said, that his prayer would be "for the closer intercourse and union of the Church."

What Russia now thinks of the relations existing between hers and the Anglican Church, may be learnt from the *Official Journal of the Petersburg Ecclesiastical Academy*, after the return home of the Archbishop of Finland [r]. "It will be sufficient," it says, "to point to those very recent events, in which has been expressed a mutual approximation, and inter-communion, of the two greatest representatives of Eastern and Western Christianity, the Orthodox Russian and the English Churches. It is evident to all, that an entirely new dawn of mutual understanding and respect was arising in the relations of the two Churches. . . . . It is so important that Russia should have been personally visited by such learned and highly enlightened Bishops, as the Archbishop of York and the Bishop of London ; and that England should have been visited and studied by, the no less learned and highly enlightened Russian Bishop, and Member of the Holy Synod, Archbishop Antonius of Finland ; who has brought back with him a strong personal conviction that, in the English nation,

---

[r] Extracted from Church Times, July 30, 1897.

there is secreted a profound feeling of sympathy for the Orthodox Russian Church."

The revival, in 1885, of the Jerusalem Bishopric, when the relations between the Greek and Anglican Churches had been established on a securer basis, was free from the former objections, and has been attended with the happiest results. The Greek Church had learnt, in the interval, to understand and appreciate the position and motives of the Church of England; that its mission to the East, so far from a desire to proselytize from, and weaken, is to help and strengthen, the Orthodox Church; to cultivate cordial relations with the Patriarch of Jerusalem, and the other Patriarchs, and with members of the Greek Church generally, there and in other parts of the East. The Bishopric was revived with the approval, or rather at the request, of the Patriarch of Jerusalem, who expressed to Archbishop Benson, his desire for a nearer approach to the union of the two Churches; and that the See of the Bishop should be placed, not in Beyrout, but in Jerusalem. Owing to the unobtrusive and sympathetic character of the Anglican Bishop, Dr. Popham Blyth, the Greek and Syrian Churches have learnt to understand and welcome the English Church; to regard us as, in a manner which no other Church does, sympathizing with their difficulties; and even expect that the richer Church of England may give some substantial help, which they cannot afford themselves.

On St. Luke's Day, 1898, took place an event, unique, since the Schism between East and West, in the annals of the Church, and destined probably to have far-reaching consequences in the history of Christendom; viz. the Consecration of the Anglican Church at Jerusalem, dedicated to St. George the Martyr, the Patron Saint of England, who is supposed to have suffered martyrdom in the Diocletian persecution.

The imposing ceremony of Consecration was, at the request of the Anglican Bishop of Jerusalem, performed by the Bishop of Salisbury, deputed by the Archbishop of Canterbury. Two Archbishops, as delegates of the Orthodox Patriarch, attended; the Governor of Jerusalem was represented by his Secretary; the various Churches in Jerusalem, Orthodox, Armenian, Syrian, Coptic and Abyssinian, sent their representatives; the Church was crowded with people of all nationalities [s]; and the whole Consular body, except the Austrian Consul, who was unavoidably prevented, was present.

The wisdom of the resuscitation, by Archbishop Benson, of the Jerusalem Bishopric can be no longer doubted; and one result was shown by a recent incident, in the British Colony of Victoria. At a time when there was no resident Priest of the Orthodox Greek Church in Melbourne, the Patriarch of Jerusalem authorized the Anglican clergyman to Baptize infants, and even to Communicate members of the Greek Church; and the Bishop of Melbourne gave his consent, providing merely that nothing should be done contrary to the spirit or provisions of the English Prayer-book [t].

The friendly relations, which now exist between the Greek and Anglican Churches, do not mean that they are in Communion, nor even that their union is at present within the area of practical politics; but they do mean that the way has been smoothed, and that the two Churches understand each other better than they did sixty years ago. When the Reverend W. Palmer paid, in 1840—1841, his visit to Russia, Count Pratasov was Chief Procurator, and M. Mouraviev Under-Procurator, of the Holy Synod. The latter said to him; "We know you only as heretics. You separated from the Latin Church three hundred years ago, as the Latins had, before that, fallen away from the Greeks. We think even the Latin Church heretical; but you are an apostasy from an apostasy [u]." This misconception the Head of the Orthodox Church, in his recent Answer to the

---

[s] Reuter's Telegram. [t] Times, October 4, 1897.
[u] Palmer's Visit to the Russian Church, p. 229.

Papal Encyclical, refuted; "Britain," his Holiness said, "by its local Synods, in the time of the Seven Œcumenical Councils, managed its own affairs, the Bishop of Rome having no right to interfere (οὐδὲν ἀναμίξεως δικαίωμα ἔχοντος)."

The visit of Mr. Palmer, Deacon, and Fellow of Magdalen College, Oxford, to the Eastern Church, has become historical, and is instructive. It was a time of great political and Ecclesiastical unrest in England, when the Anglican Church was recovering from a long lethargy, and Mr. Palmer, although acknowledging that the Anglican is a true branch of the Catholic Church, fancied he would find rest and unity, which he failed to find in his own, in one of the two other branches of the Church. He first applied to the Russian Church, and was told that, to become a member of it, he must receive the Sacrament of Unction with Chrism. He next applied to the Church of Constantinople, where he was told that he had never been baptized at all, and must receive Baptism. He then went to Rome, where he was brought into connection with Father Passaglia, "who informed him of an opinion which he had never thought of," that, though he agreed with the Greek, rather than the Roman, Church, he could be received in the latter, by merely suspending his private judgment, and affirming nothing contrary to the known dogmas of the Roman Church. On February 28, 1855, without being conditionally baptized, he was received into the Roman Church; but he confessed in a Letter, written three years afterwards, to Count Tolstoi, the Chief Procurator of the Holy Synod of Russia, that he still continued to hold Greek, rather than Roman, predilections [x].

We have said that the union of the Greek and Anglican Churches is not at present within the area of practical politics. There is much in the Greek Church which an Anglican cannot unreservedly accept; though the Church

---

[x] This account the *Tablet* called "*deliciously Protestant*" But see the Letter itself in Birkbeck's Russia and the English Church, I. 182.

of England, as strongly as the Orthodox Greek Church, upholds the first Six Œcumenical Councils, it can never acknowledge the Second Council of Nice as Œcumenical, nor its doctrine as Catholic. It was merely an Eastern Council; and, though the Pope of Rome accepted its decrees, they were never generally received in the West. With the exception of an unappreciable minority, which likes to imitate the practices which it rejected, the English Church is attached to our Reformation; and there is much in that Reformation which the Greek Church, because it does not understand, condemns. Many Greeks confusing it with the German Reformation, regard the English Reformation as the establishment of a new, instead of a return to the old, religion. If the maxim of St. Vincent of Lerins, "Quod semper, quod ubique, quod ab omnibus," is that of the Greek Church; if she holds that the Eucharist ought to be celebrated in both Kinds; that the marriage of the clergy was sanctioned in the early Church; that Church-services ought to be performed in a vernacular language; if she condemns Purgatory, Pardons, the Immaculate Conception of the Virgin Mary, and the Infallibility of the Pope; if she believes her own separation from the Roman Church justifiable; she cannot but be at one with us as to the principle of our Reformation.

A movement towards a clearer understanding between the Churches was lately made in Russia. "Four young Priests," we were told, "who have completed their studies at the Ecclesiastical College, have left here (Petersburg) for London. They have been instructed by the Holy Synod, to promote an active exchange of information concerning Ecclesiastical matters in England, regarding the principal doctrines of the Greek Orthodox Church y."

If the union of the Anglican with the Greek Church is ever effected, it will probably be through Russia, with which England has so much in common. Whilst Rome fears and abhors National Churches, the Russian and the English are

---

y Reported in a Petersburg Journal of September, 1897.

the two greatest National Churches in the world ; not in the sense that the nation made either Church ; nor merely because they have a majority of the people ; but because they have solved the problem, how the Catholic Church can adapt, and enlist in its services, national characteristics, and lead its members into the truth, of which it is the guardian.

But a bond of union, stronger than Nationality, is that of the Bible. The New Testament, says Le Roy Beaulieu, is in greater demand in Russia, than in any part of Europe, except Protestant countries. Many people, in their condemnation of the Roman, which we are not concerned to defend, combine the Greek, Church, and say that one is as uncatholic as the other. But, in the Greek Church, the Bible is an open Book ; and, as a result of the inculcation of the Bible by the two great Metropolitans of Moscow, in succession, Plato, who was tutor to the Tsar Alexander I., and Philaret, who died as recently as 1867, a strong current of Evangelicalism, in the present day, underlies Russian Orthodoxy. "We are now at length," said Count Pratasov, who received his education in the schools of the Jesuits, "finding, even in the Bible itself, an antidote to the abuse of the Bible [z]."

The history of the Bible Societies is a prominent feature in the religious society of Russia in the present century. Before the time of the Tsar Alexander I., the Bible without comment was as much tabooed in Russia, as in any country under the Pope. The reign of Alexander was the period of "the School of Plato." In 1813, the British and Foreign Bible Society, with the approval of the Tsar, who issued a Ukase in its favour, and enrolled himself amongst its members, was enabled to establish itself in Russia ; and Prince Galitzin, the Minister of Public Worship and Education, and Chief Procurator of the Holy Synod, became its President. Under such auspicious circumstances, having moreover the strenuous support of Plato's successor, Phi-

[z] Palmer's Visit, p. 119.

laret, the Society seemed to be promised a prosperous career.

But the Jesuits had found their way into Russia. In 1773, Pope Clement XIV., by the Bull *Dominus ac Redemptor noster*, had abolished the Order. Amongst other matters, the Bull spoke of the great ruin to souls, caused by their quarrels with local dignitaries, and other religious Orders. In 1774, Pope Clement died, not without suspicion of poison imputed to the Jesuits. Far from submitting to the Pope, the Jesuits, after the Bull was issued, retired to the non-Romanist countries of Prussia and Russia; and Russia became the head-quarters of the Society. Till 1772, the law remained in force, by which the Tsar, Peter the Great, had excluded them from the country. But by the partition of Poland, Russia came into possession of several provinces, in which the Jesuits held an influential position, and possessed several Colleges. Notwithstanding the advice of her counsellors, and the desire of the Russian people, who advised that the possessions of the Jesuits should be confiscated, the Empress Catharine II felt that the carrying out the law of Peter would inflict an injustice on her new subjects. Against the remonstrance of Pius VI., the successor of Clement, she decreed, by a Ukase, that the Bull of a Pope had no force in her country; prohibited its publication, and allowed the Jesuits to appoint a Vicar-General in Russia. Paul, the successor of Catharine, carrying on her policy towards the Jesuits, prevailed with the new Pope, Pius VII., to issue, in 1801, the Brief *De Catholicâ Fide*, so far cancelling the Bull of Clement XIV., as to allow the re-establishment of the Order of the Jesuits in Russia. From 1809 until January, 1814, Pius was kept in captivity by the Emperor Napoleon. In August of the latter year, he went further than before, and by the Bull *Sollicitudo Omnium Ecclesiarum*, revoked the Bull of Clement, vindicated the Jesuits from the charges brought by him against them, and revived the Order with all its former rights, under the immediate protection of the Holy See.

So that, soon after the establishment of the Bible Society, two antagonistic parties, the Jesuits and the Bible Societies, ruffled the usually stagnant surface of Russian Orthodoxy, and both the civil and Ecclesiastical authorities took alarm [a]. But the Russian Government, finding that the Jesuits, not confining themselves to members of the Roman Church, had proselytized a considerable number of ladies of rank in the Greek Church, issued an order forbidding them to teach any but those of their own Church. Matters came to a head by their conversion, in 1815, of a nephew of Prince Galitzin; and the Tsar Alexander, by two Ukases, the first in December, 1816, the second in March, 1820, expelled the Jesuits out of the whole of the Russian monarchy, as well as from Russian Poland; on the ground that, "being entrusted with the education of the young, they had abused the confidence placed in them, by misleading their inexperienced pupils; whilst themselves enjoying toleration, they had practised intolerance against others; they had been guilty of dangerous intrigues, and undermined domestic happiness." Thus the Jesuits were expelled from Russia, and have never since succeeded in obtaining a mitigation of the sentence, or regaining admission into the country.

Nor did the Bible Societies long survive them. They met with the same opposition, and on the same grounds, as the reforms of Nicon before them. Prince Galitzin, the trusted confidant of the Tsar, became odious to the clerical party of re-action; he was accused to Alexander by the Archbishop of Novgorod, of revolutionary proceedings, threatening the throne and Altar; as being the forerunner of Antichrist, and trying to introduce a new religion; he told the Tsar that, twelve years before he had had to contend with a temporal, but now with a spiritual, Napoleon. Though the Tsar's own feelings towards the Bible Society were not altered, his superstitious fears were aroused; Seraphim, the Metropolitan of Petersburg, who had succeeded Prince

[a] Beaulieu, III. 84.

Galitzin as President of the Society, wavered; and the result was that, on Ascension Day, 1824, a Ukase was issued removing Galitzin from all his offices [b]; and one of the first acts of Nicolas I. was to abolish, by a Ukase in 1826, the Bible Society; which was described to him as "a revolutionary association, intended for the overthrow of Thrones and Churches, of law, order, and religion throughout the world, with the view to establish a universal Republic."

The Russian Bible Society at the time of its dissolution numbered two hundred and eighty-nine auxiliary branches; it had printed the Sacred Scriptures in between twenty and thirty languages; and its circulation had amounted to above 861,000 copies [c]. A Protestant Bible Society was, with the sanction of the Tsar, founded in 1831, for supplying Protestants in Russia with the Scriptures, and Prince Lieven became its President; but so strong is the feeling of the Holy Synod and the people of Russia, that nothing appertaining to religion should be undertaken by any but the Parish Popes, that the Society, with its head-quarters at Petersburg, and all its branches, were in its turn suppressed, in 1884, by Alexander III. But the Bible Societies left their mark on Russia; and the Holy Governing Synod now promotes the circulation of the Scriptures, especially of the New Testament, and of the Psalms, which are held in great esteem, from the Old Testament; and although it keeps in its own hands a strict supervision, there is no reason for believing that the Scriptures are either mutilated or distorted.

Rarely, if ever, has any branch of the Christian Church, been presided over by two greater Prelates in succession, than the two Metropolitans of Moscow, for the first three quarters of the present century, Plato and Philaret; who, although their teaching was cramped by the horror of innovation which exists in Russia, by their inculcation of the Scriptures, their attacks on the abuse of the Worship

---

[b] Taylor's Russia before and after the War.
[c] History of the British and Foreign Bible Society, I. 396 n.

of Saints and images, their appeal to the faith of the undivided Church, could not but leave their mark on the Orthodox Church of Russia. The Emperor, Joseph II., being asked on his return to Vienna, what he had seen most remarkable in Russia, replied, "The Metropolitan Plato." Of Philaret, Dean Stanley said: "I saw him on the Feast of the Sleep of the Virgin, in the Cathedral of the Kremlin. Never have I seen such respect shown to any Ecclesiastic. Had he been made of pure gold, and had every touch carried away a portion of him, the enthusiasm of the people could not have been greater.'

Latinism still prevails in the Russian Church, but Plato and Philaret opened the door for the gradual development of purer Orthodoxy. Plato said: "We must hold the Divine Word alone, and rest assured that it only contains the rules by which we ought to please God; and therefore Christ said concerning the Scriptures, that in them is contained Eternal Life." Philaret laid down as a principle for the Greek Church; "The only pure and all-sufficient source of the doctrine of faith is the revealed Word of God. Everything necessary to salvation is stated in the Holy Scripture with such clearness, that every one reading it with a serious desire to be enlightened can understand it." And again; " Every one has not only a right, but it is his bounden duty, to read the Holy Scripture in a language which he can understand [d]."

The peculiarity of the school of Plato, of which Philaret was the most distinguished ornament, with its establishments, in which many thousands of clergy were educated, at Moscow and Petersburg, is the weight which it attaches to preaching, and preaching, and teaching by the clergy, is a sign of the revival from the torpor which long characterized them. The introduction of civil and political matters is said frequently to mar the effect of their sermons; and Russian Prelates still too often fall in their sermons into

[d] Palmer's Visit, p. 518.

the common failure in the Greek Church, undue adulation of the Emperors; so that the Emperor Alexander II. found himself compelled to issue a Ukase forbidding reference to be made to himself in sermons [e].

Everything leads to the conclusion that, in the coming century, the greatest powers in the world will be the Teutonic and Slavic nations. The emancipation of the Eastern Patriarchates from Islam, and the rapid growth of Russia in the Councils of Europe, point to a glorious future for the Orthodox Greek Church, and the mighty destiny which it seems again to be called to fill in the history of Christendom. Whilst Rome is retrogressive; the Slavic and Teutonic races are progressive. The two great crises in Church history, says Dean Farrar in his Bampton Lectures, when faith almost died out, have been in Roman countries; viz., in Italy at this period, and in France during the Eighteenth Century; nations which have for centuries been under Roman Catholic teaching. Whilst the Church of England contended successfully in the last century against the Deists, Rome had no weapons with which to oppose the Encyclopædists; Infallibility is no argument with those who do not believe it. A useful lesson may be learnt from a comparison of the political condition of Romanist and non-Romanist nations, since the Reformation; of Spain with England, Poland with Russia, Austria with Prussia, France with Germany, Portugal and Naples with Holland; and now, within the last months, of Spain with America.

The Tsar of Russia has inaugurated the last year of the Nineteenth Century with a plan for the cessation in the armaments of Europe. Perhaps some good providence may inaugurate the commencement of the Twentieth Century, with the spiritual disarmament of the conflicting Churches of Christendom. Friendly relations between the Anglican and the Russian, the principal member of the Greek, Church, cannot but be of the first importance.

[e] Beaulieu, III. 272.

Autocracy, Orthodoxy, Nationality, were the three watchwords of Nicolas I.; with Russian people the last two are identical; Russians are at heart sincerely attached to the English nation; and the union of the Churches might be the means of composing differences, and effecting friendly relations between the civil governments of the two countries.

ERRATA.

p 101, last line but one, *after* supported *read* him.
pp. 109, 235, *for* Acæmetæ *read* Accemetæ.
p 112, last line, *for* in *read* on.
p 113, line 19, *for* Bishop *read* Bishops
p. 171, line 17, *for* binding *read* besides
p. 178, last line but one, *for* Arianzus *read* Arianza.
p. 197, line 15, *for* charity *read* character.
p 231, line 4, *for* ἥuas *read* ἡuâs.
p. 246, line 30, and p 247, line 8, *for* Haidaseir *read* Hardascir.
p. 255, line 26, *for* Monophytism *read* Monophysitism.
p 275, line 14, *for* 1896 *read* 1895
p. 284, line 7, *for* 635 *read* 535.
p 326, line 7, *for* language *read* religion.
p. 335, summary, line 16, *for* Theodora *read* Theodore.
p 442, summary, line 11, *for* Emir *read* Emperor
,, ,, ,, 23, *for* He *read* Suleiman
p. 471, line 17, *for* confirmed *read* confined.
p. 512, line 4, *for* Roman *read* Romanov
p. 565, line 5, *for* John *read* Ivan.
p. 659, summary, line 6, *for* Greek *read* Great.

INDEX.

Abelpharagius, 257.
Abuna, 269.
Abyssinia, or Ethiopia, 52, 268—271.
Acacius, Bishop of Cæsarea, 141, 142, 153—155, 177, 178
—— Patriarch of Constantinople, 232—235, 238
Acephali, 235, 241.
Achillas, 113.
Accœmetæ, 109, 235.
Acre, taken by Crusaders, 423.
—————— Saracens, 437
—————— combined fleets, 643.
Adeodatus, 198, 199
Adoptionism, heresy of, 355.
Adrian, 583, 584.
Adrianople, Treaty of, 626, 633.
Aer, the, 28, 29
Ælia Capitolina founded, 78.
Ætius, 153, 155.
Agapetus I., Pope, 285.
Agilulf, 346, 347.
Akmet, 517, 518.
Alban, 96
Albania, 627.
Alexander, Bishop of Alexandria, 113, 123.
—————— Patriarch of Antioch, 195, 196.
—————— Bishop of Constantinople, 138.
—————— Nevski, 500—502.
—————— I., Tsar, 687—689.
—————— II 649, 692
—————— III, 690.
—————— VI., Prince of Lithuania, 515, 519
—————— VI , Pope, 478, 515
Alexandria, Church of, founded by St. Mark, 62.
—————— See of, 98.
—————— Fall of, 330.
Alexandrine Bishops, election of, 99, 113, 38j.
Alexis, Metropolitan of Moscow, 505, 506
—————— Tsar, 563 sq., 572
Alexius I., Comnenus, 412, 416.
—————— IV., 428
—————— V , Ducas, 428, 430.
Ali, Caliph, 327.
—— Pasla, 627.

Almeric, 420,
Alp Arslan, 409, 410.
Alypius, 199.
Ambrose, 167, 180, 183, 185, 198, 199.
America and Re-union with Russo-Greek Church, 673.
Amrou, 329, 330.
Anaphora, 26.
Anastasia, Church of, Constantinople, 169, 191.
Anastasia Romanov, 523, 525.
Anastasius, Patriarch of Constantinople, 345.
—————— I., Emperor, 237, 239, 240.
—————— II , Pope, 280.
Anatolius, 218, 220, 230, 343.
Ancyra, Council of, 105.
Andrew, preaching of, 68,
—————— Bobolupski, 492, 493.
—————— Archbishop of Crete, 343.
Andronicus I., 421, 422.
—————— II , 450—455.
—————— III., 455—458.
Anglican Orders, 660, 661.
Angora, Battle of, 463.
Anicetus, 81, 82.
Anna, wife of Vladimir, 404—406.
Anomœans, 153, 156, 179.
Anselm, 414.
Answers of the Patriarch Jeremias, 10.
Anthemius, Patriarch of Constantinople, 284, 285.
Anthimus, Bishop of Nicomedia, 95.
—————————— Tyana, 164.
Anthusa, 185
Antioch, disciples first called Christians at, 53, 54.
—————— school of, 112.
—————— tradition of Peter being Bishop of, 54.
—————— taken by Mahometans, 437.
Antoninus, Metropolitan of Ephesus, 187, 188
Antonius, Archbishop of Finland, 681, 682.
Antony, 107, 108.
Aphthardocetæ, 294.
Apiarius, 146.
Apollinarius, 174.
Apologies, Christian, 77, 78.
Apostolicæ Curæ, Bull, 660—662.
Appanages, 407, 487, 493, 519.

Arcadius, 185—195.
Archimandrites, 8.
Architecture, Church, 295, 296.
Ariadne, 232, 237, 239.
Arians, 118 *sq.*, 133 *sq*, 152 *sq*, 178, 179.
Arius, 112 *sq.*, 132, 138.
Arles, Council of, 103, 150.
Armenian massacres, 654.
Armenians, 242, 271—276.
Arsacius, 193.
Arsenius, 185
────── Meletian Bishop, 134—136.
────── Patriarch of Constantinople, 442, 444.
────── Archbishop of Thebais, 595, 609, 610
Artavasdes, 345.
Articles of the Synod of Bethlehem, 11.
Asceticism, 107.
Ascholius, 168.
Association for the Furtherance of Christianity in Egypt, 267, 656, 657.
────── for Promoting the Unity of Christianity, 673
Athanasius, 117, 122—124, 134 *sq.*, 197.
────── Metropolitan of Moscow, 525.
Atticus, 194, 195, 202, 204
Augsburg Confession, 537, 538, 541
Augustine, 180, 198—203
Authority of General Councils, 604, 608
Avignon, Popes at, 456, 457.
Azyms, 439.

Bajazet I, 461—463.
────── II., 483.
Baldwin, Count of Flanders, 430, 432.
────── I., King of Jerusalem, 416, 419
────── II., Emperor, 438, 446.
Baptism, 19—22, 88, 557, 575.
Barbarossa, Emperor, 422.
Bardas, 365, 379
Bari, Council of, 413.
Barlaam, 457, 458.
Barnabas, 55
Barsumas, Bishop of Nisibis, 246—248.
────── Monophysite monk, 216, 217.
Bartholomew, preaching of, in India, 69
Basil the Great, 108, 159, 162 *sq*, 172.
Basil I, 379, 380.
──── II., 386, 389, 390.
──── V., 519—521.
Basiliscus, 232.

Basle, Council of, 466.
Batory, Stephen, 540.
Belgrade, Peace of, 623.
Belisarius, 288, 289.
Bells in Greek Churches, 17.
Bema, 15, 16.
Benedict XII., Pope, 457.
Benevento, Battle of, 446.
Benson, Archbishop, 251, 657, 660.
Berlin, Treaty of, 654, 655
Bernard of Clairvaux, 419.
Berthold, 494
Bessarion, 468—470, 477.
Bethlehem, Synod of, 574, 575
Bez-Popofsky, the, 617, 618
Bible Societies in Russia, 687, 689, 690
────── Translation of, 371, 372, 539, 544.
Bishops, 51
Bohemia, conversion of, 373.
Boleslav, 373
Boniface I, Pope, 146.
────── IX., Pope, 461.
Bonn, Conference of, 679
Book of the Hundred Chapters, 524.
Boris, Michael, 369, 370
────── Prince, Baptism of, 656.
────── Godonov, 531—534, 540, 546, 547
Bosnia, 650—652, 654.
Boyars, 404, 521, 522, 531.
Bread, Eucharistic, 24, 25, 27, 400, 605, 606
────── leavened and unleavened, 469.
Brzesc, Synod of, 544
Bucharest, Treaty of, 626, 632.
Bulgaria, 368—371, 651, 656
Bulgarians, 359, 379, 385, 389
Burial of Englishmen by the Greek Church, 676, 677.
Byron, Lord, 630, 631.

Cæcilian, 101—104.
Cænobitic life, 107.
Cæsareas, three, 177.
Cæsarini, Julian, 467, 472.
Cairo, 265, 266.
Caliphs, 326, 327.
Candidian, 209, 210.
Canning, George, 630—632.
Cantacuzene, John, 458—460.
Cantoirs, 593
Capodistrias, 632—634.
Carlowitz, Treaty of, 622.
Caroline Books, 354, 355.
Carthage, 102, 331.
Catechisms, Longer and Shorter, 13.
Catharine I, 585, 586.
────── II., 623, 624.

Index. 697

Celestine, 207, 210.
Celestius, 201—203.
Celibacy of the Clergy, 120, 121.
Chalcedon, Council of, 176, 219, 227
Charlemagne, 353—357.
Charles of Anjou, 445—447.
—— I. of England, 560.
Chenouda I., 259.
Cherson, 404
Chorepiscopi, 105.
Chosroes II, 305, 306, 325.
Choudov monastery, 506
Christ's Kingdom, foundation of, 44—50
Christian children, tribute of, 455, 456.
Christianity, the Religion of the Roman Empire, 107
Christians of St. Thomas, 252, 255
Chrysostom, 184—190, 206
Church, foundation of, at Jerusalem, 50
Churches, Greek, ritual of, 13—42.
Circumcellions, 104
Clement I Pope, 75, 82.
—— IV., —— 445—447.
—— VIII. —— 543.
—— XIV. —— 688.
Clementine Forgery, 82.
Clergy, marriage of, 8, 38, 105, 120, 121, 318, 319, 379, 539, 543.
Clermont, Council of, 413
Code, the, of Justinian, 294.
Codex Alexandrinus, 560
Comana, 195, 213
Communion in one or both Kinds, 24, 25, 464.
Conciliabulum at Ephesus, 210.
Concordat, proposals for, by Non-jurors, 596—602.
Confession of Faith, Cyril Lucar's, 556—558, 561, 562, 567, 575, 599
—— of Peter Mogila, 11, 575.
Confirmation, institution of, 52.
Conrad, 419
Constance, Council of, 464.
Constans I, 141, 144, 148, 149.
—— II., 312—314.
Constantine I, the Great, 96, 100, 101, 106, 107 sq., 124 sq., 140.
—— II., 141.
—— Pogonatus, 314.
—— Copronymus, 344—349.
—— Porphyrogenitus, 349, 384.
—— Monomachus, 392, 397—401.
—— Dragases, 473.
—— Prince of Ostrog, 544.
—— Donation of, 140.
Constantinople, Councils at, 137, 138, 155, 285, 361, 447, 448.

Constantinople, 1st Œcumenical Council, 170, 176
—— 2nd —— 291.
—— 3rd —— 315.
—— Iconoclastic —— 346.
—— Synods at, 377, 379, 380, 381
—— Dedication of, 128.
—— Sieges of, 331, 332.
—— taken by Crusaders, 427—429
—— Fall of, 475, 476
—— Church of, omitted in Article XIX, 677.
Constantinopolitan Creed, 173, 176, 223
Constantius Chlorus, 93, 96.
—— II, —— 141 sq., 156.
Coptic Church, 657, 658.
Copts, 257—268.
Cornelius, conversion of, 53.
Cosmas I, Patriarch of Alexandria, 258, 259.
—— Bishop of Mazuma, 342, 343.
Covel, Dr., 577, 578.
Crete, 658
Crimean War, 648, 649.
Crispus, 96, 125.
Cross, Discovery of the, 126, 127.
—— Constantine's Vision of the, 97.
Crowns in Greek marriages, 37, 38.
Crusade, First, 414—419
—— Second, 419, 420.
—— Third, 421—424
—— Fourth, 425
—— Fifth, 435.
—— Sixth, 435.
—— Seventh, 436.
—— Eighth, 437
—— Attempt at Ninth, 477, 478
Crusades, Character of, 410.
Cucusus, 193, 194.
Cyprian, 86—88, 90
Cyprus, Church of, 423
—— ceded to England, 654.
—— Society, 655.
Cyriacus, 305.
Cyril, Patriarch of Alexandria, 204—214
—— Lucar (see under Lucar).
—— of Berrhœa, 558, 561, 562.
—— Bishop of Jerusalem, 150, 171, 177, 178
—— II., Metropolitan of Kiev, 501.
—— X., Coptic Patriarch of Cairo, 264, 265.
—— XI, —— —— 266.
—— the Philosopher, 368, 369.
Czechs, or Bohemians, 373.

Dalmatius, 211.
Damasius, 284.
Damasus I., Pope, 3, 165, 169, 197, 198.
Deacons, appointment of, 51.
——— marriage of, 105.
Decretals, the forged, 140, 366.
Dedication Council at Antioch, 142.
Delegation of the Church of England to the Russian Church (1896), 681.
Demetrius II , 266
Demophilus, 161, 169, 179.
Dianius, 155, 163
Dioceses, jurisdiction of, 175.
Diocletian, 93, 95, 96, 100.
Diodorus, 186, 204
Dionysius the Areopagite, 77
——— Bishop of Alexandria, 88—91.
——— ——— Milan, 150.
——— Exiguus, 296
——— Archimandrite of the Troitsa Monastery, 549
Dioscorus, 214, 221, 228, 255.
Dissent in Russia, 616
Division of Empire, East and West, 184.
Dmitri Donskoi, 506, 507
——— son of Ivan IV., 530, 531.
——— the False, 547, 548.
Domitian, Emperor, 71.
——— Bishop of Ancyra, 285, 286.
Domnus, 213, 215—217
Don, Victory of the, 507.
Donation of Constantine, 140.
Donatists, 102—104, 200
Donatus, Bishop of Casa Nigra, 102.
——— ——— Carthage, 104.
Dositheus, 574, 575.
Druses, 278.
Dushan, Stephen, 625, 652.
Dyophysites, 244.

Easter, observance of, 81, 104, 119, 120.
Eastern Church Association, objects of, 673.
——— Syrians, 245—255.
Ecthesis, the, 312.
Edessa, School of, 246.
Egypt, 260, 263, 267, 656.
Emperors, power over Popes, 302—304, 339.
Empires, the first Four, 43.
Encyclical Letter of Pius IX. and Answer, 663—666.
——— ——— of Leo XIII and Answer, 272, 666, 667.
Enrico Dandolo, 426, 427.
Ephesus, Church of, 60, 454.

Ephesus, Council of, 176, 209—211.
Ephraim, 283, 288.
Epigonation, 18.
Epimanikia, 17.
Epiphanius, 190.
Epitrachelion, 17, 18.
Etchmiadzen, 273, 275.
Eucharist, the, 19, 24, 35.
Eudocia, 208, 229.
Eudoxia, wife of Arcadius, 188, 191—193.
——— ——— Valens III , 236.
——— ——— Peter the Great, 582—585.
Eudoxius, 154—156, 161.
Eugenius IV., Pope, 419.
——— V., ——— 466.
Eunomius, 153.
Euphemius, 232, 238, 239.
Eusebius, Bishop of Cæsarea, 116—118, 135, 141, 163
——— ——— Constantinople, 116—118, 133, 137, 141.
——— ——— Dorylæum, 206, 214, 215, 217.
Eustathius, 116, 117, 133.
Eustathian schism, 134, 195, 196.
Euthymius, 229.
Eutropius, 186.
Eutyches, 214—216, 255.
Eutychianism, 227, 242
Eutychius, Patriarch of Alexandria, 385
——— ——— Constantinople, 291, 294, 297.
Euzoius, 156, 165, 167.
Evagrius, 180.
Exarchs at Ravenna, 289.
Excommunication, 5, 131.
Exorcism, 21.

Fans, use of, by Greek Church, 30.
Fasting, 32
Fasts, 9, 10.
Fatima, 321, 327.
Fausta, 96—125.
Favritta, 238
Felix III , Pope, 235.
——— IV. ——— 283.
——— V. ——— 470.
Feodor I , 530—532, 546.
——— II , 572.
Ferrara, Council of, 467, 468, 508.
Filioque Clause, 369, 370, 382, 397, 414, 543.
Firmilian, 88—92.
Flavian, Bishop of Antioch, 172, 180, 186, 194.
——— Patriarch of Constantinople, 213—217

Florence, Council of, 274, 469.
Formosus, 369, 370, 382.
Frankfort, Council of, 355.
Frederic II, 434, 435
Frumentius, 151, 268.

Galerius, 93, 94, 96.
Galich, 495
Galitzin, 689, 690
Gangra, Council of, 147.
Gates, the, in Greek Churches, 15
Gedymin, 510
Gelasius I., Pope, 238, 239.
Genghis Khan, 248, 496.
Gennadius, 230, 232.
George, King of Greece, 640.
Georgirenes, 578.
Germanus, 338.
Gerontius, 516, 518.
Godfrey de Bouillon, 415—417, 419.
Golden Horde, the, 499, 505, 517
Gordon, 657, 658.
Gratian, 161, 167, 179.
Greek Church, authorities of Faith in, 10.
——— the most ancient of Churches, 2, 3
Greek and Anglican Church, points of difference, 597, 604, 605
——— present relations between, 671, 687.
Greek, Separatist Communities, 8.
——— Fathers, 196.
——— Hymnologists, 230, 231, 343
——— language, diffusion of by Septuagint, 46.
——— original language of the Church, 1, 2
——— Independence, War of, 627—629, 633, 634
——— and Roman Churches, differences between, 40, 42, 670
——————————— relations between, 662—670.
——— College at Oxford, 578.
Gregorios, 629.
Gregory, Apostle of Armenia, 271, 272.
——— Bishop of Alexandria, 143, 148, 151
——— Bishop of Nyssa 162, 168, 171, 174
——— Metropolitan of Kiev, 512, 513.
——— Monophthalmos, 555, 556.
——— Nazianzus, 155, 162—164, 168—171, 178, 197
——— Patriarch of Antioch, 297.
——— VI, Patriarch of Constantinople, 665.

Gregory I. Pope, 3, 227, 298.
——— II. ——— 338.
——— III. ——— 343.
——— VII ——— 411, 412.
——— IX. ——— 435.
——— X. ——— 447
——— Thaumaturgus, 86.
Guy de Lusignan, 420, 423.
Gytha, 489.

Hadrian, Emperor, 77.
——— I, Pope, 350
——— II, ——— 380.
Hegira, the, 325.
Hegumens, 8.
Helena, 93, 96, 125—127.
——— Glinsky, 520, 521.
Hellenic Constitution, 640.
Henoticon, the, 234, 235.
Henry IV., Emperor, 411, 412
Heraclius, 306, 308, 309, 312, 325.
Herzegovina, 650—652, 654.
Hesychasts, 458.
Hetæria, 628, 629.
Hexapla, the, 86.
Hilarion, 487.
Hilary, Pope, 215—217.
Holy Alliance, 629—631.
——— Eucharist, Deacons prohibited from celebrating, 104
——— Governing Synod of Russia, 586—593
——————————— Greece, 637.
——— Orders, 36, 37.
——— Sepulchre, Church of, 125, 484
——————— Disputes about the, 648.
——— Table, 15, 16
Homoousion, 117, 133, 149, 152, 154, 155, 166.
Honorius, Emperor, 185.
——— I., Pope, 309--311.
——— III., ——— 434.
Hormisdas, Pope, 281
Hosius, 115, 117, 118, 144, 150, 152.
Humbert, 396, 397, 398.
Hymns, Greek, 230, 231, 343.
Hypatia, 207

Ibas, 222, 246.
Iconoclastic controversy, 335 *sq.*
Icons, 16, 41, 42, 265
Ignatius, martyrdom of, 76, 77.
——— Patriarch of Constantinople, 364—366, 371, 377, 380.
——— Pociej, 543
Igor, 400, 401
——— II, Prince of Suzdal, 491
Illyricum, 340
Images, 336—338, 347, 351—355, 360—362, 609

Indulgences, 434.
Innocent I, Pope, 202.
—— III, —— 425, 430—432.
Institutes of Justinian, 265
Invocation of Saints and Angels, 40, 605, 609.
Ionian Islands, 628, 641.
Irenæus, 81.
Irene, wife of Leo IV., 349, 350, 356, 358.
Isaac II., Emperor, 422.
Isiaslav I., 487—489.
—— II, 491.
Isidore, 474, 507, 508.
Isidorus Mercator, 366.
Islam, 324.
Ivan I., 503, 504.
—— II, 505, 506, 509.
—— III, 513—516.
—— IV., 521—523.

Jacob Baradai, 255, 256.
Jacobites, 245, 248, 255—257.
Jadwiga, 511.
Jagiello, 511, 512
James the Less, Bishop of Jerusalem, 51, 61.
James I. of England, 560.
Janissaries, 455, 456, 625, 647.
Jassy, Synod of, 562.
Javorski, Stephen, 585—588, 613.
Jeremias, 10, 533, 534, 536—538.
Jerome, 190, 196, 197, 386.
Jerusalem, attempt to rebuild, 158.
———— Council of, 56
———— First Gentile Bishop of, 79
———— Mother Church of Christianity, 51.
———— Pilgrims to, 187, 410.
———— raised to a Patriarchate, 222.
———— taken, 44, 70, 78, 307, 328, 410, 417, 421, 435, 436.
———— foundation of Anglican Bishopric (1841), 672.
———— revival of Anglican Bishopric (1885), 683.
———— Consecration of St. George's Church, 683, 684.
Jesuits, 545, 553 *sq.*
———— in Poland, 539, 540.
———— in Russia, 688, 689.
———— in Sweden, 541.
Jews, reason of their opposition to the Gospel, 48.
Joachim V., 532, 533.
Job, 533—535, 546, 547.
John at Patmos, 72, 73
—— Patriarch of Antioch, 204, 207, 208, 210, 212.
—— the Almoner, 307, 308.

John Damascene, 341, 342.
—— the Faster, 297, 304
—— the Grammarian, 361.
—— à Lasco, 539.
—— II., Patriarch of Constantinople, 280
—— Bishop of Jerusalem, 190, 202.
—— I, Pope, 282
—— VIII, Pope, 371.
—— XXII, —— 456.
—— Scholasticus, 294, 297
—— Zimisces, 387, 388, 389.
—— III, Ducas Vatatces, 439.
—— IV., Emperor, 440, 442.
—— V., —— 458—461.
—— VI., —— 465, 467
Jovian, 160.
Julian the Apostate, 156—160.
—— Cæsarini, 467, 472.
Justin I, 279.
Justin Martyr, 64, 80.
Justina, 161, 167, 180.
Justinian I., 283, 286, 293—295.
—— II., 317
Juvenal, 204, 209, 210, 217, 220, 222, 229.

Kainardji, Treaty of, 624, 631.
Kalka, Battle of, 497.
Kara George, 625, 626.
Kennobin, 277.
Khadijah, 321.
Khans, 498
Khartoum, Christian Churches at, 261.
———— fall and recovery of, 657, 658.
Khazars, 368.
Kiev, 401—407, 487 *sq.*, 492, 581, 582
Knights Hospitallers, 418, 437, 453.
———— of Malta, 484.
———— the Sword, 494.
———— Templars, 417, 437, 453.
Koran, 322—324.
Kossova, Battle of, 461.
Kromieshniks, 526.

Labarum, 98, 110, 156, 160.
Ladislaus, 472, 473.
Lambeth Conferences, 674, 675.
Laodicea, Council of, 2, 147.
———— Church of, 454.
Lapsed, the, 85
Lascaris, Theodore, 429, 438, 439.
Lateran Councils, First, 313.
———————————— Fourth, 433.
Latin Empire of Constantinople, 429 *sq.*
———————————— end of, 441.

Latin Fathers, 196.
—— Patriarchs of Constantinople. 440.
Latrocinium Council, 176, 215—218.
Leo   I., Emperor, 228, 231, 232.
—— III., Emperor, 337, 338.
—— IV , —— 349.
—— V , —— 359
—— VI , —— 382, 384.
—— I., Pope, 215, 216, 218, 224—226
—— II , —— 317
—— III., —— 356
—— IX., —— 394—397
—— XIII , —— 666—668.
Leonidas, 83
Leopold, Prince, 634
Lepanto, Battle of, 484, 621.
Libellatici, the, 85.
Lichoudi, 581
Licinius, 100, 106.
Lithuania, 509—513, 539, 542.
Liturgical Books of the Russian Church, 520
Liturgies, 24—26, 601, 602, 607.
Livonia, Conversion of, 493, 494.
Lombards, 297, 302, 303, 339, 341.
London, Treaty of, 632
Louis IX of France, 435—437.
Lowe, Sir Thomas, 555, 556, 561.
Lublin, Diet of, 539, 541
Lucar, Cyril, 480, 544, 546, 551—559.
Lucian, 99
Lucius, 165, 167, 169
Ludmila, 373.
Luitbrand, 339, 341.
Lutheran Reformers and the Greek Church, 537, 538
Luthero-Calvinists, 586, 599, 600, 608.
Lycurgus, 676, 678.
Lyons, Second Council of, 81.
—— Persecution of Church of, 81.

Macabees, the, 48
Macarius, Patriarch of Antioch, 315—317
—— Bishop of Jerusalem, 116, 125.
—— Metropolitan of Moscow, 522, 523, 525
Macedonians, 172.
Macedonius, 141, 142, 149, 154, 155, 170, 239
Magi, the, 45.
Magnentius, 149, 150.
Magyars or Hungarians, 373.
Mahdi Insurrection, 657.
Mahmoud II , 626, 642.
Mahomet, 321—326.
—— II., 473, 477, 479, 483.

Mahomet Ali, 261, 264, 642, 643.
Mahometanism, 309, 320—328.
Mahometans, 258, 478.
Malek Shah, 410
Manichæans, 178, 198.
Manichæus, 282.
Manuel I., 420, 421.
—— II., 461—466
Manzikert, Battle of, 409, 410.
Maphrian, 256.
Marcellinus, 96.
Marcellus, 137, 138, 143, 144, 146, 147, 174.
Marcian, 219, 222, 228.
Marcus Aurelius, 80.
Mark, Church of Alexandria founded by, 62
—— of Ephesus, 469—471.
Maro, 276.
Maronites, 244, 276—278.
Marriage, Sacrament of, 37, 38
—— of brothers and sisters-in-law, 105
—— of Clergy, 8, 105, 120, 121, 318, 319, 379.
Martel, Charles, 344.
Martin I , Pope, 313.
Martyrius, 230.
Martyrs, era of, 93
Mary, Virgin, little known of, 71.
Mattran, the, 250.
Maurice, 93, 94.
Maxentius, 96, 97.
Maximian, Emperor, 93, 95, 96, 98, 100
—— of Constantinople, 211—213, 218, 220
Maximus, Bishop of Jerusalem, 137, 139
—— Cynic philosopher, 169, 170, 172, 177
—— Emperor, 236.
—— 312—314.
—— of Mount Athos, 520, 521.
Medvedev, Silvester, 581.
Meinhard, 493
Melchiades, 96, 102.
Meletian Schism, 119, 135.
Meletius, 119
—— Patriarch of Alexandria, 551, 552.
—— Bishop of Antioch, 156, 167, 171, 185, 186.
Memnas, 285.
Memnon, 209—211.
Menexis, Alexis de, 254.
Mensurius, 101.
Metaxa, 556.
Methodius, 368, 371, 372.
Metousiosis, 32, 33.

Metrophanes, Bishop of Constantinople, 128
—— Patriarch ———, 471.
—— Critopulus, 560, 561
Michael Cerularius, 392—396, 398, 399.
—— I., Emperor, 359, 364.
—— II , —— 360
—— III , —— 361.
—— IV , —— 392.
—— Palæologus, —— 440, 442—450
—— Romanov, Tsar, 550.
Milan, Council of, 150
—— Edict of, 100
Milosh Obrenovich, 626, 627.
Milvian Bridge, Battle of, 97.
Mindovg, 509, 510.
Mistilav, 492
Modestus, 309, 310.
Mogila, Peter, 545, 562, 563.
Moguls, 496—499, 505.
Moldavia, 649, 650
Monasteries, 497, 498, 593
Monasticism, 107, 108, 487, 490, 491.
Monica, 198.
Monophysite heresy, 174, 227.
Monophysites, 230, 244, 279
Monothelitism, 309, 310, 314, 315.
Montanists, 83, 84.
Montenegro, 482, 651, 652.
Moravia, Conversion of, 371—373.
Moscow, 503, 504, 524, 535, 536, 549, 571, 617, 618.
Murad I., 460.
—— IV , 559.
Mursa, Battle of, 150.
Mysteries, or Sacraments, 18, 19.

Nag's Head Fable, 660, 661.
Narses, 297.
Narthex, 14, 15.
National Assembly of Greece, 639.
Nauplia, Synod of, 636
Navarino, Battle of, 633.
Nave, or Trapeza, 15.
Nazarites, 249
Nectarius, 172, 177, 185, 188.
Neo Cæsarea, Council of, 105.
Nerva, Christianity under, 73
Nestorianism, 242—243, 245, 255.
Nestorius, 204, 213
Nice, First Council of, 116—122.
—— Second —— 350.
—— Greek Empire at, 438.
Nicene Creed, 17, 118, 173, 223, 448
Nicephorus, Patriarch of Constantinople, 358, 360.
—— —— Metropolitan of Kiev, 490.
—— —— I., Emperor, 358.

Nicephorus Phocas, Emperor, 387—389.
Nicetas, Metropolitan of Kiev, 490.
—— Priest of Moscow, 571.
Nicolas I , Pope, 365.
—— V , —— 474—477
—— I., Tsar, 619, 643, 646, 648, 649
Nicomedia, 93, 95.
Nicon, 563—569, 574
Nicopolis, Battle of, 462.
Niphon, 451, 452
Niphont, 491, 492.
Nisibis, School of, 247
Nitria, Monastery of, 191.
Noetus, 90.
Non-jurors, the and the Greek Church, 593 *sq.*
Novatian, 87.
Novatians, 87, 120, 122, 179, 207.
Novatus, 87
Novels, the, 295.
Novgorod, 375, 376.
—— Massacre of, 528
Nubia, 262.
Nymphæum, Council of, 439.
Nziri, the, 249.

Odoacer, 237
Œcumenical, meaning of, 176, 298.
Old and New Rome, 4, 128—130.
Old Catholics, 678, 679.
Olgar, 401—403.
Olgerd, 510.
Omar, Mosque of, 328
Omdurman, 658.
Omophorion, 18
Onesiphorus, 542.
Opreechniks, 526, 527
Orarion, 18.
Ordination, Episcopal, 113.
Orestes, 207
Organs, 17, 569.
Origen, 85, 86, 190.
Origenism, 190, 286.
Orkhan, 455, 456, 459, 460.
Orthodox Confession, 600
Othman, 453, 455
Otto, King of Greece, 635, 638—640.
Ottoman Turks, 452 *sq.*
—— Decline of power of, 621, 622.
Ottos, the, 390.

Pachomius, 107, 108
Paganism, 161, 184, 284.
Pagan Temples, Destruction of, 181, 182
Palæologi, the, 443.
Palæologus, John, 458—461, 465—473.

Index. 703

Palæologus, Michael, 440, 442—450
Palladius, 238
Palmer, Rev W., Visit to the Eastern Church, 685.
Pamphilus, 98.
Pantænus, 69.
Papal Infallibility and Supremacy, 311, 662, 663, 668—670.
—— Power, foundation of, 129.
Parabolani, 207.
Paris, Council of, 355.
—— Treaty of, 649, 650.
Parish Priests, Treatise on Duties of, 13, 480.
Parker, Archbishop, Consecration of, 661
Passarowitz, Peace of, 623.
Patriarchates, number of, 7, 532, 536.
Patriarchs of Constantinople, disadvantages of, 131.
Patrimony of Peter, 347.
Paul, 1st Apostolical Journey, 55—57.
—— 2nd —————————— 57—59
—— 3rd —————————— 59—60
—— Imprisonment of, 61, 66.
—— Martyrdom of, 68.
—— Bishop of Constantinople, 141— 143, 149
—— III , ———————— 318
—— IV , ———————— 349, 350.
—— of Somosata, heresy of, 91.
Paulicians, 362, 363
Paulinus, Bishop of Antioch, 171, 180.
Pechersky Monastery, 506
Pelagianism, 200—202, 205.
Pelagius, 201—203.
———— I., Pope, 286, 293.
Penance, 35, 36.
Penances, 105
Period of Troubles, 547—550
Persecution, 1st, under Nero, 67.
———————— 2nd, —— Domitian, 71
———————— 3rd, —— Trajan, 75
———————— 4th, —— Marcus Aurelius, 80.
———————— 5th, —— Septimius Severus, 83
———————— 6th, —— Maximin, 84.
———————— 7th, —— Decius, 84.
———————— 8th, —— Valerian, 90.
———————— 9th, —— Aurelian, 92.
———————— 10th, —— Diocletian, 92.
Persia, Fall of, 325.
Persians, 305, 309.
Peter, whether Bishop of Antioch, 54.
———— ———————— Rome, 63 *sq.*
—— Martyrdom of, 68.
—— Mission of, 63
—— Bishop of Alexandria, 99, 165, 167, 169.

Peter Fuller, 230—233.
—— the Great, 580, 582 *sq.*
—— the Hermit, 412, 413.
—— Mongus, 233, 234
—— of Sebaste, 162, 171.
—— of Vladimir, 504.
—— II., 585.
Petersburg, foundation of, 584.
Phælonion or Phænolion, 18
Philadelphia, Church of, 454, 455.
Philaret, Patriarch of Moscow, 547, 548, 550
———— Metropolitan ———— 690, 691.
Philip, Deacon, 51
———— of Moscow, 527.
Philipopolis, 145, 578, 579
Phocas, 304, 305
Photinians, 167, 178.
Photius, 365—369, 376—383.
Phthartolatræ, 294
Pilgrims to Jerusalem, 410.
Pipin the Little, 346, 347
Pisa, Council of, 464
Pius II., Pope, 477, 481.
—— IX , —— 663—666
Plato, Metropolitan of Moscow, 690, 691
—— The Orthodox Doctrine of, 12.
Pneumatomachi, 172, 174.
Pociej, 543, 544
Poland, 374, 538—540, 620, 644.
Polotsk, Synod of, 645.
Polycarp, 80, 81
Popes, Parish Priests in Russia styled, 9.
Popofsky, 617, 618
Porphyry, 193—195.
Possevin, 530
Pothinus, 81.
Pratasov, 645.
Prester John, 269
Priests, 51, 105, 106, 119, 121, 122
———— Parish, Treatise on the duties of, 13.
Prisca, 94, 100, 101.
Pro-Anaphora, 26, 28.
Procession of Holy Ghost, 448, 449, 457, 458, 469, 562, 575, 677, 678.
Proclus, 213
Procopia, 359, 364
Procopovich Theophanes, 585—587.
Prosphers, 27, 28, 574.
Proterius, 228, 229
Prothesis, 16, 27, 28.
Pseudo-Synod, 351
Pulcheria, 208, 209, 218, 219, 222, 228.
Purgatory, 469, 557, 576, 604
Pyrrhus, 312, 313

Rabulas, 246.

Ragoza, 542, 543, 545.
Raskol, 583.
Raskolniks, 615—619.
Re-baptism, 104, 122.
Reformation, the English, and the Greek Church, 686.
——— in Poland and Lithuania, 538, 539.
Re-union of Christendom, 119, 122, 456—459, 465—469, 471, 472, 474, 659 sq.
Revolution in Greece, 639.
Ricaut, Sir Paul, 577.
Richard I. of England, 423, 424.
Rimini, Council of, 154.
Robber Council, 176 (*note*), 214, 215.
Roman, 495.
Romans, Emperors of the, 443.
Rome, appeals to, 145, 146
—— fiction of Peter being Bishop of, 63—66.
—— fire of, 67.
—— precedence of Bishop of, 89, 128, 129, 175.
Roumania, Church of, 656.
Rufinus, 190.
———— (Pelagian), 201.
Rule of St. Basil, 162.
Ruric, 375.
Russia, Conversion of, 375.
—— spread of Christianity in, 400—407.
Russian Church, Ninth Centenary of, 680.
—————— and the Non-jurors, 610—613.
—— State of in Patriarchate of Nicon, 565, 566.
—————— on accession of Peter the Great, 583, 584, 585.
—— bond of Union between Anglican and Greek Church, 686, 687.
—— Episcopate, 593.
—— Patriarchate, abolition of, 584, 587, 589.
—— Priests, Visit of to England, 686.

Sabas, 285, 286.
—— Lavra of St , 238, 342, 343.
Sabellianism, 90, 133, 147, 156, 174.
Sabellius, 90, 91.
Sabiniana, 194.
Saccos, 18.
Sacraments of the Greek Church, 18, 19, 557, 603.
Sacristy, 16.
Saladin, 334, 420, 424.
Sallustius, 238.
Saluminus, 150.
Samaria, Conversion of, 52.

San Stephano, Treaty of, 653, 654.
Saracens, 311, 326—334.
Sardica, Council of, 144—146.
Saul, conversion of, 52, 53.
Schism, the great, between the Eastern and Roman Churches, 364 sq.
Seleucia, Synod of, 154.
———— 2nd Synod and School of, 247, 248
Selim I , 483.
—— II , 484.
—— III , 625, 626
Seljuk, 409
———— Turks, 408—413, 452.
Septuagint, 1, 3, 46, 99.
Serapeum, Destruction of, 181, 182.
Serapis, 181, 182.
Sergius, 306, 310, 311.
Servia, 472, 625, 626, 633, 654.
Service-books, Russian, revision of, 566—568, 571, 572.
Services, length of, in Greek Church, 9.
Seven Churches of Asia, Fall of the, 453.
Severa, 161.
Severus, 241.
Shiites, 327.
Sicilian Vespers, massacre, 449.
Siena, Council of, 466.
Sigismund I , 519, 538, 539.
—————— II , 539.
—————— III , 538, 541.
Silverius, Pope, 288—290.
Silvester, 96, 103, 139, 140.
Simeon Stylites, 109.
———— Gordii, 505.
Simon Magus at Rome, 64.
Simplicius, 233.
Siricius, 197.
Sistova, Peace of, 623.
Slavs, 368, 374.
Smolensk, 519.
Smyrna, Church of, 453.
Solomon, the Magnificent, 484.
Sonnites, 327.
Sophia, Church of St., at Constantinople, 128, 295.
—— wife of Ivan III., 513, 514.
—— sister of Peter the Great, 580, 582.
Sophronius, Patriarch of Jerusalem, 307, 309—311, 328, 329.
Sophronicus, Archbishop of Nea-Justiniana, 654
Sorbonne Academy, 613.
Spiridion, 117.
Spiritual Regulations of the Holy Governing Synod, 586, 587, 588.
Stanislaus Hosen, 539.
Starobredski, 572.

Index. 705

Starovíertsi, 615.
Stauropegia, 593.
Stephen, Hymn writer, 343.
—— Proto-Martyr, 52.
—— I., Bishop of Rome, 88—90.
—— IX , Pope, 396.
Sticharion or Stoicharion, 17, 18.
Streltsi, 580, 582, 583
Strigolniks, 518, 519, 521, 548, 571.
Stylites or Pillar monks, 109.
Suleiman, 460
Sutri, Synod of, 394.
Suzdal, 492, 493.
Sviatapolk of Moravia, 373.
—— of Russia, 489
Sviatoslav, 401, 402
Symmachus, 280.
Synod of Bethlehem, 11, 12.
Synodical Tome, 637, 638.

Tall Brothers, the, 191.
Taiasius, 350, 359
Tel-el-Kebir, Battle of, 656.
Terlecki, Cyril, 542, 543.
Ter Sanctus, the, 29.
Tertullian, 83.
Thalaia, John, 233, 234.
Theban Legion, 93, 94
Theodora, wife of the Emperor Justinian, 284, 289, 290.
—— wife of the Emperor Theophilus, 361, 362
Theodore Ascidas, 285—287.
—— of Mopsuestia, 186, 205.
—— Bishop of Tyana, 178.
—— I., Pope, 312, 313.
—— Studita, 360.
Theodoret, 207, 209—214, 220, 222
Theodoric, 237, 280, 283, 284
Theodosius, Bishop of Jerusalem, 229.
—— the Great, 161, 167—169, 178—184.
—— II., 208, 211, 212, 216, 218.
Theodota, 356
Theodotus, 288.
Theognostes, 505, 506.
Theoleptus, 533
Theonas, 118, 119.
Theopaschites, 231.[1]
Theopemptus, 486, 487.
Theophanes, Patriarch of Antioch, 316.
—————————— Jerusalem, 549
Theophano, 386—388.
Theophilus, Patriarch of Alexandria, 179, 181, 186—191, 193—195.
—— Emperor, 361.
Theophylact, 385, 386.
Theotokos, the, 205, 206, 222, 605.
Thessalonica, Massacre at, 180.

Thirty-nine Articles, the, and the Greek Church, 677
Thomas, Apostle of India, 69.
—— Christians of St , 252—255.
Thorn, Massacre at, 619
Three Chapters, Controversy of, 287.
Thurificati, the, 85.
Thyatira, 454
Tiberias, Battle of, 420.
Tilsit, Treaty of, 625, 641.
Timothy Ælurus, 229, 231—233.
—— Salophaciolus, 231, 233
—— Patriarch of Constantinople, 240.
Timour, 248, 463.
Togril Beg, 409
Tours, Battle of, 344.
Tovin, Synod of, 273
Traditors, 102, 104.
Trajan, 75.
Translation of Bishops, 122.
Transubstantiation, 32—34, 576, 581, 608
Trisagion, the, 29, 231
Troitsa Monastery, foundation of, 505.
Trullan Councils, 315, 318, 691
Tsar, the, and the Russian Church, 590, 591
Type, the, 313.
Tyre, Council of, 135, 136.

Ulfilas, 367, 368
Unction with Chrism, 19, 22, 24, 29.
—— Oil, 19, 38, 39.
Unia, the, 543, 546, 552—554, 644
—— return of Uniats to the Greek Church, 643—646.
Union with the Greek Church, requisites for, 671, 679
—————————— how regarded in Russia, 614, sq.
Urban II., Pope, 412, 413.
—— IV , —— 444, 445.
—— V , —— 460.
Ursacius, 136, 145, 149, 150, 152, 154.

Valens, Bishop of Mursa, 136, 145, 149, 150, 152, 154
—— Emperor, 161, 162, 164—166.
Valentinian I , 160, 161, 165
—— II , 161, 167, 180, 182.
—— III , 208, 218, 236.
Valeria, 93, 94, 100, 101.
Valerius, 199
Varna, Battle of, 473.
Veccus, 448—450.
Victor I , 81, 82.
Vienna, Congress of 644.
—— defeat of Turks at, 622.
Vienne, Council of, 453.

Vienne, persecution of Church of, 81.
Vigilius, Pope, 289—291.
Vision of the Cross, 97.
Vitalian, 241
Vitoft, 512, 513.
Vladika, the 652.
Vladimir I , 402, 403, 407
——— II , 489.
——— Metropolitan See at, 493, 503.
——— two cities of the same name, 543
Vratislav, 372, 373.

Wake, Archbishop, 612—614.
Wallachia, 472, 649, 650
Wenzeslaus, 373
Wine, Eucharistic, 27.
World, State of the, at the Coming of Christ, 44.

Yaropolk, 403
Yaroslav I., the Great, 406, 407, 487.
——— II., 499.
Ysevolod, 489.
Yury Dolgorouki, 492.
——— II., 499.
——— III , 503.

Zacharias, Patriarch of Alexandria, 260
——————— Jerusalem, 306.
Zeno, 230, 232, 233, 234, 237.
Zoe, 391, 392
Zoilus, 286, 287.
Zosimus, historian, 125.
——— Metropolitan of Moscow, 518, 519
——— Bishop of Rome, 146, 202, 203